BEN
JONSON

Robert Vaughan's portrait of Jonson

BEN JONSON

Edited by C. H. HERFORD
and PERCY SIMPSON

VOLUME III

A Tale of a Tub
The Case is Altered
Every Man in His Humour
Every Man out of His Humour

OXFORD
At the Clarendon Press

Oxford University Press, Amen House, London E.C.4
GLASGOW NEW YORK TORONTO MELBOURNE WELLINGTON
BOMBAY CALCUTTA MADRAS KARACHI CAPE TOWN IBADAN
Geoffrey Cumberlege, Publisher to the University

FIRST EDITION 1927
REPRINTED LITHOGRAPHICALLY IN GREAT BRITAIN
AT THE UNIVERSITY PRESS, OXFORD
FROM CORRECTED SHEETS OF THE FIRST EDITION
1954

PREFACE

THE present volume is a first instalment of the text, which we hope to complete in four more volumes. A critical introduction to the text as a whole and a commentary will be given in the last three volumes.

The frontispiece, taken from a rare print in the Hope Collection, is reproduced by permission of the Visitors of the Ashmolean Museum.

In editing *The Case is Altered* we gratefully record our obligation to the late Duke of Devonshire for permission to collate the Kemble copy, formerly at Chatsworth.

Our debt to Dr. W. W. Greg is very heavy. The original conclusion of *Every Man out of his Humour* is missing from the only copy of the First Quarto as yet traced in England. Dr. Greg placed at our disposal the rotographs used for the Malone Society's reprint of the play, and gave permission to use the Society's text. He also communicated to us privately the solution of a difficult problem in *The Case is Altered* : he has given a convincing explanation (quoted on pp. 95–6) of the two states of the second title-page of the Quarto, showing that Jonson's name was added to it, and not, as is generally supposed, deleted.

Preface

Some corrections of our earlier volumes and some additional notes are printed at the end of this volume. For a number of these we are indebted to Dr. W. W. Greg, Mr. W. J. Lawrence, Professor H. B. Charlton, Dr. R. F. Patterson, and Mr. T. Harbottle.

For help in the work of collation we are indebted to Mrs. Simpson, and the readers and staff of the Clarendon Press deserve our warm thanks for their skill and patience, especially in coping with the complicated critical apparatus of the last play.

P. S.

Oriel College, Oxford.
12 February 1927.

CONTENTS

	PAGE
THE TEXT: Introductory Notes	ix
A TALE OF A TUB	1
THE CASE IS ALTERED	93
EVERY MAN IN HIS HUMOUR: The Original Version of 1598, from the Quarto of 1601	191
EVERY MAN IN HIS HUMOUR: The Revised Version from the Folio of 1616	291
EVERY MAN OUT OF HIS HUMOUR	405
Appendix X. 1. The Original Conclusion in the Quartos	602
2. The Revised Conclusion in the Quartos	603
Corrections to Volumes I and II	605
Additional Notes to Volumes I and II	607

LIST OF ILLUSTRATIONS AND FACSIMILES

VOLUME III

ROBERT VAUGHAN'S PORTRAIT OF JONSON   *Frontispiece*

This engraving is undated, and three states of the plate are recorded. It was first issued as a separate print. (1) The original state has the underline '*Are to be sould in Popes head alley at the white horse by Geo: Humble*'. A beautiful impression, here reproduced, has been inserted in Henry Holland's *Basiliωlogia. A Booke of Kings* (1618), no. 150 in the Hope Collection at Oxford, a copy made up with many extra prints by its former owner, T. W. Jackson. The date of the print can be fixed approximately. The earliest recorded engravings of Robert Vaughan are in a book entitled *The Pourtraitures of Nine Moderne Worthies*, which was entered on the Stationers' Register to Henry Holland on March 30, 1622. George Humble, bookseller and print-seller, traded at the sign of the White Horse in Pope's Head Alley from 1610 to 1627; in 1627 he changed his address to Pope's Head Palace. The poetaster Abraham Holland, who composed the verses below the portrait, died on February 18, 1626. The engraving was probably issued early in Charles I's reign, and it was certainly not later than 1627. (2) Humble is last heard of in 1632: at a date which we have not traced the engraving was reissued by the print-seller William Peake, who had a shop on Snow Hill near Holborn Conduit. The underline was altered to '*Are to be Sould by William Peake*'. The collector Thomas Grenville inserted one of these prints in his large-paper copy of the Jonson First Folio (1616), now in the British Museum. His note on the copy is preserved in it, and he states: 'I have added to my Copy the head by Vaughan.' (3) The print finally appears as a frontispiece to the small quarto collection, *Ben: Jonson's Execration against Vulcan. With divers Epigrams*, published by John Benson early in 1640, and again as the frontispiece to the first volume of the 1640 Folio. In both these editions the underline has been erased. In the copies examined better impressions of the plate are found in the *Execration* than in the Folio.

An idealized redrawing of this portrait was engraved by William Elder for a frontispiece to the 1692 Folio of Jonson's *Works*. In this the verses are anonymous. The sixth and seventh lines are mispunctuated in all the issues: there should be a comma after 'audax' and a full stop after 'politus'.

A TALE OF A TUB: the title-page in the 1640 Folio .   *page* 7

THE CASE IS ALTERED, 1609:

    The earlier title-page . . . ⎫
    The later title-page . . . ⎬ *between pages* 102, 103

There are two states of the later title-page: the first is anonymous; the second, which is here reproduced, has the author's name inserted, 'Written by BEN IONSON', but the insertion is badly centred and gives a less-balanced page.

EVERY MAN IN HIS HUMOUR:

    The title-page in the Quarto, 1601 . . . . *page* 195
    The title-page in the Folio, 1616 . . . . *page* 297
    The title-page in the Folio, 1640 . . . . *page* 299

EVERY MAN OUT OF HIS HUMOUR:

    The title-page in the First Quarto ⎫
    The title-page in the Second Quarto ⎪
    The title-page in the Third Quarto ⎬ *between pages* 418, 419
    The title-page of the 1616 Folio, with ⎪
      ornamental border ⎭
    The plain title-page in the 1616 Folio . . . *page* 419
    The title-page in the 1640 Folio . . . *page* 420

THE TEXT: INTRODUCTORY NOTES

THE text of this edition is conservative and ignores unnecessary variants. The early texts are generally sound; Jonson wrote a clear hand, and he edited much of his work. All this leaves little scope to the conjecturalist, and the misreadings of an editor have no further significance than to show that he was unfit for his task. To substitute 'affected Courtier' for 'affecting Courtier' in the character of Briske prefixed to *Every Man out of his Humour* is either sheer carelessness in copying or ignorance of Elizabethan English, and nothing is gained by noticing it in a critical edition. On the other hand, the modernizings of the 1692 Folio, which sometimes reflect changing seventeenth-century usage, have an historical value, and variants of spelling and punctuation in the Quartos and Folio often give a clue to Jonson's own practice. Any reading which appears to have this justification will be preserved.

The readings of Peter Whalley, who made the first serious attempt to edit Jonson in 1756, and of William Gifford, whose elaborate edition in 1816 did much for the poet's reputation, are sometimes judicious and often interesting: a selection of these will be given.

No problem arises in editing the first two plays in this volume. They depend on a single text. *A Tale of a Tub* first appeared in the 1640 Folio: a few passages, perhaps marginal additions made by Jonson in the manuscript, are confused, and there are a number of misprints, but the text as a whole is clear. *The Case is Altered* was first printed in a bad Quarto in 1609. Here an editor has to correct many misprints and to adjust the verse, but the pioneer work was done by Whalley and Gifford, and their corrections are usually sound. The present text is more conservative than Gifford's, but accepts most of his readjustments.

The two Humour plays, on the other hand, bring us face to face with two authoritative texts issued in Quarto and in Folio, and with the interesting problem of revision by the author. The original text of *Every Man in his Humour* was printed only in the Quarto of 1601. A few corrections can be made in it from the later Folio text, but they are trivial or obvious, such as the correction of 'friends' to 'fiends' in III. iv. 6. Errors in punctuation and verse-lining are frequent, but the text is substantially sound. The revised Folio version of 1616, in which the play was rewritten,[1] is very carefully printed. The most noteworthy error is the false rhyming of 'fame' and 'come' in V. v. 80–1, and this could be easily cured even if the 1601 Quarto and the 1640 Folio did not read 'some' and 'come'.

In *Every Man out of his Humour* Jonson did not rewrite, he revised his early version. He worked over the Quarto text, submitted it to a close scrutiny, and retouched it in detail. Occasionally he makes a point a little clearer for the actor, but usually he strengthens or improves the phrasing. The underlying spirit of the changes is not so much the attitude of a practical playwright as a distant approach to Pope's standard of correctness.

We regard the 1616 Folio as the final authority for all the works which it contains—the plays up to *Catiline*, the *Epigrams* and the *Forest*, and the masques up to *The Golden Age Restored*. In the textual introduction to *Every Man out of his Humour* we give our reasons for this high estimate of the Folio. We find in it clear traces of Jonson's own proof-correcting, and in the critical introduction that will precede the commentary we shall complete the evidence by a survey of all the plays in this memorable volume, the first collected edition of the works of an Elizabethan playwright.

The 1640 Folio was published three years after Jonson's death, and its complicated history does not concern us at this stage, for the first volume is a reprint of its predecessor, with occasional corrections which may be Jonson's. The second volume is the sole authority for all the later plays except *The New Inn*, for the later masques beginning with *The Masque of Christmas*, the *Underwoods*, and the prose works. The dates of the contents range from 1631, when *Bartholomew Fair*, *The Devil is an Ass*, and *The Staple*

---

[1] See Appendix V in vol. i, pp. 358–70.

of News were first published, to 1641, the date in the imprint of *The Sad Shepherd* and *The Discoveries*.[1]

It remains to explain the symbols and abbreviations used in the critical apparatus and such technical points as the scene arrangements.

A Tale of a Tub

F = the Folio of 1640, the sole authority for the text.
$F3$ = the Folio of 1692.

The Case is Altered

Q = the Quarto of 1609, the sole authority for the text.

Every Man in his Humour

Q = the Quarto of 1601, the sole authority for the original version of the play acted in 1598.
$F1$ = the Folio of 1616, in which the revised version first appeared.
$F2$ = the Folio of 1640, a reprint of the text of 1616.
Ff = readings common to the Folios of 1616 and 1640.
$F3$ = the Folio of 1692.

Every Man out of his Humour

$Q1$ = the original Quarto of 1600, published by William Holme.
$Q2$ = a reissue of this Quarto by William Holme in 1600, set up from the first Quarto.
$Q3$ = the third Quarto, published by Nicholas Ling, set up from the second Quarto, and dated 1600.
Qq = readings in which all three Quartos agree.
$F1$ = the Folio of 1616, set up from the first Quarto.
$F2$ = the Folio of 1640.

---

[1] The Folio of 1640 differs from its predecessor by using ' j ' and ' v ' for ' i ' and ' u '. But by a peculiarity not uncommon when this modern usage began, it keeps the capital ' I ' and ' V ' on title-pages and for proper names. Thus, in *A Tale of a Tub* it prints ' In *Ianuary* ' (I. i. 83), ' *Iohn Clay* ' (I. iv. 30), but ' Justice *Bramble* ' (I. i. 93).

Ff = readings common to the Folios of 1616 and 1640.
$F3$ = the Folio of 1692.

Throughout the volume

W = Whalley's edition of 1756.
G = Gifford's edition of 1816.
om. = an earlier reading omitted from a later text.
not in Q (or Qq) = a new reading first found in the Folio text.

PRINTER'S AND AUTHOR'S CORRECTIONS

These are indicated by the formula ' corr. Q ' or ' corr. F '. Thus, in *The Case is Altered*, I. v. 30, the printer set up ' *Maximllian* of *Vicenzia* '; he corrected it to ' *Maximilian* of *Vicenza* '. The corrected reading is in the text, and the note in the critical apparatus is ' *Maximilian* of *Vicenza* corr. Q : *Maximllian* of *Vicenzia* Q originally '. As an example of an author's correction we may take *Every Man out of his Humour*, IV. viii. 110 : the 1616 Folio at first reproduced a reading found in all the Quartos, ' My selfe shall *manfrede* it for them ' ; Jonson corrected this to ' My selfe shall vndertake for them ', and this is also the reading in the Folio of 1640. The note in the critical apparatus is, ' vndertake *corr. F1, F2* : *manfrede* it *Qq, F1 originally* '.

STAGE DIRECTIONS

In the Folio of 1616 Jonson pruned severely the lavish stage directions given in the Quartos. He liked the look of a clean page in which the text stood out clear. In the Quartos exits and short stage directions are printed at the end of a speech wherever the space allows. Longer stage directions, such as the entrance of several characters, or a detailed notice such as ' *Enter Fallace running, at another doore, and claps it too* ' in *Every Man out of his Humour*, IV. ii. 80, are centred in the text and take up a line. The brief notes appended to a speech are indicated by the formula ' *add Qq* '; the fuller stage directions by ' *Qq in text after* . . .' Thus, in *Every Man out of his Humour*, IV. vi. 140, the First Quarto prints '*Exeunt.*' in a line by itself after the speech; the Second and Third Quartos print '*Exit.*' at the end of the last line of the speech. The critical note is ' After 140 *Exeunt.* Q1 : Qq 2, 3 add *Exit.* to 140 '.

SCENE-NUMBERING AND SCENE-LOCATION

In the Folio of 1616 Jonson adopted the system of scene-division which he found in the early texts of Plautus and Terence. The entrance of a new character marks a new scene, and the names of all the characters taking part in it are given in the heading. To take an extreme example : in Gifford's text the third act of *Sejanus* has only two scenes ; in the Folio there are six. In the two Roman plays, *Sejanus* and *Catiline*, no scene-numberings are given ; only the acts are numbered. But Jonson numbers the scenes in his other plays.

The habit of definitely locating the scene is a modern pedantry. In the revised *Every Man in his Humour* Jonson appended to the list of characters the laconic notice ' *THE SCENE* LONDON '. In *Every Man out of his Humour* he dispensed even with this, but in Elizabethan fashion he incorporated in the text any necessary references when the place of action had to be indicated : ' the *Scene* is the country still, remember ' (I. iii. 198) ; ' we must desire you to presuppose the stage, the middle isle in *Paules* ; and that, the west end of it ' (II. vi. 183–4) ; ' Conceiue him but to be enter'd the Mitre, and 'tis enough ' (V. iii. 92–3).

Gifford's modern renumbering of the scenes and his elaborate locations are cited in the critical apparatus.

A TALE OF A TUB

THE TEXT

Two entries in Herbert's Office Book relate to the performance of this play in 1633:

> R. for allowinge of The Tale of the Tubb, Vitru Hoop's parte wholly strucke out, and the motion of the tubb, by commande from my lorde chamberlin; exceptions being taken against it by Inigo Jones, surveyor of the kings workes, as a personal injury unto him. May 7, 1633,—2*l*. 0. 0.
>
> The Tale of the Tub was acted on tusday night at Court, the 14 Janua. 1633, by the Queenes players, and not likte.
>
> Malone, *Variorum Shakspeare*, 1821, iii, pp. 232, 236.

There is possibly an allusion to this play in the gibe which Chapman penned in his last illness upon the work of his old friend and colleague. After alluding to Ben's fire and the writings lost in it, he continues:

> Some pore thinge wright new; a Riche Caskett Ben
> All of riche Jems t'adorne most learned men
> or a Reclaime of most facete supposes
> To teach full-habited men to blowe their noses
> make the king merrie.
>
> Ashmole MS. 38, p. 17.

A Tale of a Tub, in the form in which it has come down to us, consists therefore of (1) the original play, written about 1596 or 1597, clear traces of which survive in the extant text, (2) the 1633 reissue of this discarded work, in which Jonson inserted his satire on Inigo Jones and—in all probability—recast the original prose passages in verse form, (3) the final touches of revision forced upon him by the Censor. As much as he could save of Vitruvius Hoop was clumsily attached to In-and-In Medlay; and it is possible that the flat and colourless epitome of the play, which now constitutes the 'motion', replaced something more pungent of which Inigo may have had reason to complain.[1]

The sole authority for the text is the Folio of 1640-1, in

---

[1] See vol. i, pp. 275–307.

A Tale of a Tub

which *A Tale of a Tub* is printed on pages 65–113,[1] signatures I–P⁴, Q², of the later group of plays beginning with *The Magnetic Lady*. The following copies have been collated for the present reprint: two copies in the British Museum with press-marks C. 39. k. 9, C. 28. m. 12; the Douce copy in the Bodleian with press-mark Douce I. 303; a copy in the Library of All Souls College, Oxford, and two copies in the possession of the editor. Two copies belonging to Professor W. Bang were collated by Dr. Hans Scherer for his edition of the play in *Materialien zur Kunde des älteren Englischen Dramas*, vol. xxxix, 1913. Dr. Florence M. Snell edited the play for a Yale thesis in 1915 from the Yale Library copy: Mr. George van Santvoord has kindly checked the doubtful readings of this edition.

While the sheets of the Folio were passing through the press a number of corrections were made in the text. To show the nature of these corrections, which are marred occasionally by the blundering of the printer, a full list is appended for *A Tale of a Tub*.

Sig. I 2	ll. 19–21	IONE IOYCE, MADGE PARNEL, KATE,	IONE, IOYCE, MADGE, PARNEL, KATE.
I 3	I. i. 6	keepe,	keepe
	I. i. 11	errand,	errand
	I. i. 12	Squire,	Squire !
	I. i. 20	spirit her sonne	spirither, sonne [2]
	I. i. 28	would	would,
	I. i. 29	*Tripoly.*	*Tripoly* ;
	I. i. 31	morning ;	morning,
	I. i. 33	y-styl'd	y-styl'd,
I 4ᵛ	I. ii. 32	As I may zay, Mr. *Tobias Turfe* ;	As I may zay. Mr. *Tobias Turfe,*
	I. iii. 20	uppi-nions	uppinions
	I. iii. 29	married :	married ?
K 3ᵛ	I. vii. 29	me :	me !
L	II. ii. 75	Hine!	Hine.
L 4ᵛ	II. v. 38	was.—. Well,	was. Well,
	II. v. 41	from me ?	from me.
	II. vi. 6	Sir, speake.	Sir ? speake ? [3]

[1] Pages 70–79 are duplicated.
[2] A miscorrection, inserting the comma at the wrong point and disturbing the type.   [3] A miscorrection: 'speake.' was correct.

The Text

	II. vi. 15	you must obey.	You must obey!
M 4	III. v. 58	for my sonne!	for my sonne.
	III. v. 62	soune	sonne
Oᵛ	IV. ii. 49	weekes,	weekes
	IV. ii. 51	this bold bright blade,	this, bold bright blade?
	IV. ii. 52	shred thee,	shred thee
	IV. ii. 59	heare,	heare;
	IV. ii. 65	not I,	not I;
O 4	IV. vi. 16	yet,	yet
Pᵛ	V. ii. 26	I man *Hilts*	my man *Hilts*
	V. ii. 52	Ladies Mothers	Ladie Mothers
P 4	V. vii. 31	old Lanterne-paper	oild Lanterne-paper
Q 2	V. x. 81	enter!	enter.[1]
			FINIS. is added to the Epilogue.

Three errors or inconsistencies in the use of names remain uncorrected: in II. i. 38 and 56 '*Sc.*' and '*Ite.*' are prefixed to speeches, and in V. x. 95 '*Giles*' is found in place of '*Miles*'. '*Sc.*' may mark a stage cancel of a lost speech of Scriben, and '*Ite.*' be the name of a character in the first draft, overlooked by the editor and the printer, just as '*Old.*' in *2 Henry IV*, I. ii. 138, is a clue to the cancelled name of Oldcastle, the original Falstaff.

The dialect of *A Tale of a Tub* is a curious study. Aubrey in his notes on Jonson (Aubrey MS. 8. 54, of the Bodleian) has this statement: 'He tooke a Catalogue from Mʳ Lacy (the Player) of the Yorkshire Dialect—'twas his Hint for Clownery to his Comœdy called,—The Tale of a Tub. This I had from Mʳ Lacy.' Lacy was a Yorkshireman and one of the King's players; Aubrey repeats the statement in a short notice of his in the same manuscript, fol. 20. But this is evidently a confusion of the present play with *The Sad Shepherd*, which has some northern forms.

Gill's *Logonomia Anglica*, 1621 (second edition), has a perfunctory discussion of dialect in chapter vi. The account of southern dialect is as follows:

Australes vsurpant ü, *pro* ï, *ut* hü, *pro* hï *ille*: v, *pro* f, *vt*, vil, *pro* fil *impleo*: *to* vech *pro* fech *affero*: *& contra* f, *pro* v. *vt* fineger, *pro* vineger *acetum*; ficar, *pro* vicar

---

[1] A miscorrection: there should be no stop.

vicarius. Habent & o. *pro* a. *ut* ronk, *pro* rank *rancidus, aut luxurians, adiect*; *substantivum etiam significat ordines in acie, aut alios.* Pro s. *substituunt* z. *vt* zing *pro* sing *cano*: *& * Ich, *pro* J *ego*: cham, *pro* J am *sum*: chil, *pro* J wil *volo*: chi vör yi, *pro* J warant you, *certum do. in* ai *etiam post diphthongi dialysin, a, odiosè producunt*: *vt, to* päi *solvo,* d̄äi *illi.*

The substitution of *v* and *z* for *f* and *s* was no doubt regularly observed by the actors. A quaint passage in Samuel Rowlands's *The Letting of Humours Blood in the Head-vaine,* 1600 (Satire iv), comments on two contemporary actors :
     What meanes *Singer* then ?
 And *Pope* the Clowne, to speake so Boorish, when
 They counterfaite the Clownes vpon the Stage ?

But oftener than not the printer keeps the normal spelling, or he prints it along with the dialect form : see ' vive feet ' (I. iii. 19), ' Feet, vrom . . . (ib. 20), ' vull of favour ' (III. v. 45), or ' search ' (III. i. 22) and ' zearch'd ' (ib. 23). These inconsistencies have not been interfered with in the reprint : to have adjusted them would have cumbered the critical apparatus with a mass of trivial corrections and obscured important variants.

' Che ' and ' Cham ' are used sparingly, and ' Che vore 'hun ' is found in II. ii. 70. ' Him ' most frequently appears as ' un ' or ' hun '. The old prefix of the past participle is kept in ' y-styl'd ' (I. i. 33), ' yvound ' (III. i. 26). Confusions of the prefix appear in ' praforme ' (I. i. 75, ii. 25), ' parzent ' (I. iv. 18, 53), ' purcepts ' (III. i. 41), ' perportions ' (IV. Scene interloping 46), ' subperiors ' (II. ii. 51), ' survere ' (ib. 53), ' upstantiall ' (II. i. 20), ' disgriev'd ' (IV. i. 33), ' revise ' for ' advise ' (II. ii. 44, v. vii. 28), ' ra'tempt ' (III. i. 80), ' Returney ' (IV. i. 58) ; ' satisfied ' appears as ' sussified ' (II. i. 59, III. viii. 38), and ' suspected ' and ' suspicion ' as ' respected ' (III. i. 17), ' dispected ' (ib. 21) and ' conspition ' (ib. 30) ; and the clipped form ' 'dority ' occurs once (I. iii. 24), though Turfe uses ' authority ' elsewhere (I. iv. 55, II. ii. 38).

A TALE
OF
A TUB.

A COMEDY compoſed

By

Ben: Iohnson.

Catul.—*Inficeto ſt inficetior rure.*

LONDON,
Printed M. DC. XL.

The Persons that act.

CHAN: HVGH,	*Vicar of* Pancrace, *and Captaine* Thums.
SQVIRE TVB,	*Of* Totten-Court, *or Squire* TRIPOLY.
BASKET HILTS,	*His man, and Governour.*
JVST: PREAMBLE,	*Of* Maribone, alias BRAMBLE.
MILES METAPHOR,	*His Clarke.*
LADY TVB,	*Of* Totten, *the Squires Mother.*
POL-MARTEN,	*Her Huisher.*
DIDO WISPE,	*Her Woman.*
TOBIE TVRFE,	*High Constable of* Kentish Towne.
DA: SIBIL TVRFE,	*His Wife.*
Mrs. AWDREY TVRFE,	*Their Daughter the Bride.*
IOHN CLAY,	*Of* Kilborne, *Tile-maker, the appointed Bride-groome.*
IN-AND-IN MEDLAY,	*Of* Islington, *Cooper and Headborough.*
RASI: CLENCH,	*Of* Hamsted, *Farrier, and petty Constable.*
TO-PAN,	*Tinker, or Mettal-man of* Belsise. *Thirdborough.*
D'OGE: SCRIBEN,	*Of* Chalcot, *the great* Writer.
BALL PVPPY,	*The high Constables man.*
FATHER ROSIN,	*The Minstrell, and His 2 Boyes.*
IONE, IOYCE, MADGE, PARNEL, GRISELL, KATE.	} *Maids of the Bridall.*
BLACK IACK,	*The Lady* Tubs *Butler.*
	2 Groomes.

The *Scene*, Finsbury-hundred.

---

1 CHAN:] CHAN *F*: CHAM *F3*.   8 DIDO ... woman. *Added in smaller type to l. 7, as if inserted after the page was set up*   10 TVRFE,] TVRFE *F*   12 Kilborne,] Kilborne *F*   13 IN-AND-IN MEDLAY,] IN-AND-IN. MEDLAY. *F*   16 Chalcot,] Chalcot *F*   19 IONE, *corr. F*: IONE *F originally*   20 MADGE, *corr. F*: MADGE *F originally*   21 KATE. *corr. F*: KATE *F originally*

PROLOGVE.

No State-*affaires*, *nor any politique* Club,
    Pretend wee in our Tale, *here, of a* Tub.
But *acts of* Clownes *and* Constables, *to day*
    Stuffe out the Scenes *of our ridiculous* Play.
5 *A Coopers wit, or some such busie Sparke,*
    Illumining the high Constable, *and his Clarke,*
And all the Neighbour-hood, from old Records,
    Of antick Proverbs, drawne from Whitson-Lord's,
And their Authorities, at Wakes *and* Ales,
10 *With countrey precedents, and old Wives Tales*;
Wee bring you now, to shew what different things
    The Cotes *of* Clownes, *are from the* Courts *of* Kings.

Prologve *precedes* The Persons *F3*   6 *Clarke,*] *Clarke.* F

A TALE
OF
A TUB.

Act I. Scene I.

Sir *Hugh. Tub. Hilts.*

Hug. Now o' my faith, old Bishop *Valentine*,
You' ha' brought us nipping weather:
Februere
Doth cut and sheare; your day, and diocesse
Are very cold. All your Parishioners;
As well your Layicks, as your Quiristers,   5
Had need to keepe to their warme Fether-beds,
If they be sped of loves : this is no season,
To seeke new Makes in; though Sir *Hugh* of *Pancrace*,
Be hither come to *Totten*, on intelligence,
To the young Lord o' the Mannor, Squire *Tripoly*,   10
On such an errand as a Mistris is.
What, Squire! I say? *Tub*, I should call him too :
Sir *Peter Tub* was his father, a Salt-peeter-man ;
Who left his Mother, Lady *Tub* of *Totten-
Court*, here, to revell, and keepe open house in ;   15
With the young Squire her sonne, and's Governour *Basket-
Hilts*, both by sword, and dagger : *Domine,
Armiger Tub,* Squire *Tripoly, Expergiscere.*
I dare not call aloud, lest she should heare me ;
And thinke I conjur'd up the spirit, her sonne,   20

I. i. Scene I.—Totten Court. Before Lady Tub's House, *G*   6 keepe *corr. F*: keepe, *F originally*   11 errand *corr. F*: errand, *F originally*   12 Squire! *corr. F*: Squire, *F originally*   Tub,] Tub. *F*   20 spirit, her] spirither, *F in an attempt to correct to* spirit, her

At the Windor.
He comes downe in his night Gowne.

In Priests-lack-*latine* : O shee is jealous
Of all man-kind for him. *Tub.* Chanon, is't you?
  Hug. The Vicar of *Pancrace*, Squire *Tub*! wa'hoh!
  Tub. I come, I stoop unto the call; Sir *Hugh*!
  Hug. He knowes my lure is from his Love: faire *Awdrey*,
Th'high Constables Daughter of *Kentish* Towne, here, Mr.
Tobias Turfe. *Tub.* What newes of him? *Hug.* He has wak'd me,
An houre before I would, Sir. And my duty,
To the young worship of *Totten-Court*, Squire *Tripoly*;
30 Who hath my heart, as I have his: your Mrs.
Is to be made away from you, this morning,
Saint *Valentines* day: there are a knot of Clownes,
The Counsell of *Finsbury*, so they are y-styl'd,
Met at her Fathers; all the wise o' th'hundred;
35 Old *Rasi' Clench* of *Hamsted*, petty Constable;
In-and-In Medlay, Cooper of *Islington*,
And Headborough; with lowd *To-Pan* the Tinker,
Or Mettall-man of *Belsise*, the Third-borough:
And *D'ogenes Scriben*, the great Writer of *Chalcot*.
40 *Tub.* And why all these? *Hug.* Sir to conclude in Counsell,
A Husband, or a Make for Mrs. *Awdrey*;
Whom they have nam'd, and prick'd downe, *Clay* of *Kilborne*,
A tough young fellow, and a Tile-maker.
  Tub. And what must he doe? *Hugh.* Cover her, they say:
45 And keepe her warme Sir: Mrs. *Awdrey Turfe*
Last night did draw him for her *Valentine*;
Which chance, it hath so taken her Father, and Mother,
(Because themselves drew so, on *Valentine*'s Eve
Was thirty yeare) as they will have her married
50 To day by any meanes; they have sent a Messenger

  1. i. 22 is't] i'st *F*, *F3*   26 here, *F3* : here *F*   28 would, *corr. F*: would *F originally*   29 *Tripoly*; *corr. F*: *Tripoly*. *F originally*   31 morning, *corr. F*: morning; *F originally*   33 y-styl'd, *corr. F*: y-styl'd *F originally*   35 *Rasi'* W: *Basi'* *F*, *F3*   45 *Turfe*] *Turfe*, *F*, *F3*

To *Kilborne*, post, for *Clay*; which when I knew,
I posted with the like to worshipfull *Tripoly*,
The Squire of *Totten* : and my advise to crosse it.
  Tub. What is't Sir *Hugh*?   *Hugh*. Where is your
    Governour *Hilts* ?
Basquet must doe it.   *Tub*. *Basquet* shall be call'd :   55
Hilts, can you see to rise ?   *Hil*. Cham not blind Sir
With too much light.   *Tub*. Open your tother eye,
And view if it be day.   *Hil*. Che can spy that
At's little a hole, as another, through a Milstone.
  Tub. Hee will ha' the last word, though he talke Bilke 60
    for't.
  Hugh. Bilke? what's that?   *Tub*. Why nothing, a word
    signifying
Nothing ; and borrow'd here to expresse nothing.
  Hugh. A fine device!   *Tub*. Yes, till we heare a finer.
What's your device now, Chanon *Hugh* ?   *Hugh*. In
    private.
Lend it your eare; I will not trust the ayre with it;   65
Or scarce my Shirt ; my Cassock sha' not know it ; .
If I thought it did, Ile burne it.   *Tub*. That's the way,
You ha' thought to get a new one, *Hugh* : Is't worth it?
Let's heare it first.   *Hugh*. Then hearken, and receive it. *They*
This 'tis Sir, doe you relish it ?   *Tub*. If *Hilts*   *whisper.*
Be close enough to carry it ; there's all.   *Hilts*
                                                                       enters,
  Hil. It i' no sand ? nor Butter-milke ? If't be,   *and*
Ich' am no zive, or watring pot, to draw   *walkes by,*
Knots i' your 'casions. If you trust me, zo :   *making*
                                                                        himselfe
If not, praforme it your zelves. 'Cham no mans wife,   *ready.*
But resolute *Hilts* : you'll vind me i' the Buttry.
  Tub. A testie Clowne : but a tender Clowne, as wooll :
And melting as the Weather in a Thaw :
Hee'll weepe you, like all *Aprill* : But he'ull roare you
Like middle *March* afore : He will be as mellow,   80
And tipsie too, as *October* : And as grave,
And bound up like a frost (with the new yeare)

       1. i. 77 testie Clowne : but] testy, but G

In *Ianuary*; as rigid, as he is rusticke.
  Hug. You know his nature, and describe it well;
85 Ile leave him to your fashioning.   *Tub.* Stay, Sir *Hugh*;
Take a good Angell with you, for your Guide:
And let this guard you home-ward, as the blessing,
To our devise.   *Hug.* I thanke you Squires-worship,
Most humbly (for the next, for this I am sure of.)

The Squire goes off.

O for a Quire of these voices, now,
To chime in a mans pocket, and cry chinke!
One does not chirpe: it makes no harmony.
Grave Justice *Bramble*, next must contribute;
His charity must offer at this wedding:
95 Ile bid more to the Bason, and the Bride-ale;
Although but one can beare away the Bride.
I smile to thinke how like a Lottery
These Weddings are.   *Clay* hath her in possession;
The Squire he hopes to circumvent the *Tile-Kill*:
100 And now, if Justice *Bramble* doe come off,
'Tis two to one but *Tub* may loose his botome.

Act I.   Scene II.

Clench. Medlay. Scriben. Pan. Puppy.

  Cle. Why, 'tis thirty yeare, eene as this day now:
Zin Valentines day, of all dayes cursin'd, looke you;
And the zame day o' the moneth, as this *Zin Valentine*,
Or I am vowly deceiv'd.   *Med.* That our High Constable,
5 Mr. *Tobias Turfe*, and his Dame were married.
I thinke you are right.   But what was that *Zin Valentine*?
Did you ever know 'un, Good-man *Clench*?   *Cle. Zin Valentine*,
Hee was a deadly *Zin*, and dwelt at *High-gate*,
As I have heard, but 't was avore my time:
10 Hee was a Cooper too, as you are, *Medlay*,

    1. i. 86 with] w i t h *F*   1. ii. Scene II.—Kentish Town.   A Room in
  Turfe's House *G*   7 'un *G*; 'um *F*   10 are, *F3*: are. *F*

An In-an'-In : A woundy, brag young vellow :
As th' port went o' hun, then, and i' those dayes.
  Scri. Did he not write his name, *Sim Valentine* ?
Vor I have met no *Sin* in *Finsbury* bookes ;
And yet I have writ 'hem sixe or seven times over.   15
  Pan. O, you mun looke for the nine deadly *Sims*,
I' the Church bookes, *D'oge* ; not the'high Constables ;
Nor i' the Counties : Zure, that same *Zin Valentine*,
Hee was a stately *Zin* : an' hee were a *Zin*,
And kept brave house.   *Cle.* At the Cock and Hen, in 20
  High-gate.
You ha' 'fresh'd my rememory well in't ! neighbour *Pan* :
He had a place, in last King *Harrie*'s time,
Of sorting all the young couples ; joyning 'hem ;
And putting 'hem together ; which is, yet,
Praform'd, as on his day—*Zin Valentine* ;   25
As being the *Zin* o' the shire, or the whole Countie :
I am old Rivet still, and beare a braine,
The *Clench*, the Varrier, and true Leach of *Hamsted*.
  Pan. You are a shrewd antiquity, neighbour *Clench* !
And a great Guide to all the Parishes !   30
The very Bel-wether of the Hundred, here,
As I may zay.   Mr. *Tobias Turfe*,
High Constable, would not misse you, for a score on us,
When he doe 'scourse of the great Charty to us.
  Pup. What's that, a Horse ?   Can 'scourse nought but 35
  a Horse ?
I neere read o' hun, and that in *Smith-veld* Chartie :
I' the old *Fabians* Chronicles :   nor I thinke
In any new.   He may be a Giant there,
For ought I know.   *Scri.* You should doe well to study
Records, Fellow *Ball*, both Law and Poetry.   40
  Pup. Why, all's but writing, and reading, is it *Scriben* ?

  I. ii. 11 An' In-an In *F*, *F3*   16 O,] O' *F*   *Sims*] Sins *G*   17 *D'oge F3* : Doge' *F*   20 brave *F3* : 'brave *F*   32 zay. *corr. F* : zay, *F originally*   *Turfe*, corr. F : *Turfe* ; F originally   33 a Score *F3* : a' score *F* : Query, a score on's   36 And that in Smithveld. Charty ! I ne'er read o' hun, *G* (*a probable rearrangement*)   39 For ought *F3* : For I ought *F*

An't be any more, it's meere cheating zure.
Vlat cheating: all your Law, and Poets too.
    Pan. Mr. High Constable comes.   *Pup.* Ile zay't avore
        'hun.

Act I.   Scene III.

Turfe. Clench. Medlay. Scriben. Puppy. Pan.

Tur. What's that, makes you'all so merry, and lowd,
    Sirs, ha?
I could ha' heard you to my privie walke.
    Cle. A Contervarsie, 'twixt your two learn'd men here:
Annibal Puppy sayes, that Law and Poetry
5 Are both flat cheating; All's but writing and reading,
He sayes, be't verse or prose.   *Tur.* I thinke in conzience,
He do' zay true? Who is't doe thwart 'un, ha?
    Med. Why my friend *Scriben*, and't please your worship.
    Tur. Who *D'oge*? my *D'ogenes*? a great Writer, marry!
10 Hee'll vace mee down, mee my selfe sometimes,
That verse goes upon veete, as you and I doe:
But I can gi' 'un the hearing; zit me downe;
And laugh at 'un; and to my selfe conclude,
The greatest Clarkes, are not the wisest men
15 Ever. Here they'are both! What Sirs, disputin,
And holdin Arguments of verse, and prose?
And no greene thing afore the Door, that shewes,
Or speakes a wedding?   *Scr.* Those were verses now,
Your worship spake, and run upon vive feet.
20   *Tur.* Feet, vrom my mouth, *D'oge*? Leave your 'zurd
        uppinions:
And get me in some boughes.   *Scr.* Let 'hem ha' leaves first.
There's nothing greene but Bayes, and Rosemary.
    Pup. And they're too good for strewings, your Maids say.
    Tur. You take up 'dority still, to vouch against me.
25 All the twelve smocks i' the house, zur, are your Authors.

    I. iii. 8 and't] an it *G*   15 disputing *F3*   16 holding *F3*
    19 feet *F*: veet *F3*   20 Feet *F*: Veet *F3*   uppinions *corr. F*:
    uppi-nions *F originally*

A Tale of a Tub

Get some fresh hay then, to lay under foot :
Some Holly and Ivie, to make vine the posts :
Is't not Sonne *Valentines* day ? and Mrs. *Awdrey*, ⟨*Puppy goes out.*⟩
Your young Dame to be married ? I wonder *Clay*
Should be so tedious : Hee's to play *Sonne Valentine* ! 30
And the Clowne sluggard's not come fro' *Kilborne* yet ?
   Med. Do you call your Son i' Law Clowne, and't please
      your worship ?
   Tur. Yes, and vor worship too ; my neighbour *Medlay*.
A *Midlesex* Clowne ; and one of *Finsbury* :
They were the first Colon's o' the kingdome here : 35
The Primitory Colon's ; my *D'ogenes* sayes.
Where's *D'ogenes*, my Writer, now ? What were those
You told me, *D'ogenes*, were the first Colon's
O' the Countrey ? that the *Romans* brought in here ?
   Scr. The *Coloni.* Sir, *Colonus* is an Inhabitant : 40
A Clowne originall : as you'ld zay a Farmer,
A Tiller o' th' Earth, ere sin' the *Romans* planted
Their Colonie first, which was in *Midlesex*.
   Tur. Why so, I thanke you heartily, good *D'ogenes*,
You ha' zertified me. I had rather be 45
An ancient Colon, (as they zay) a Clowne of *Midlesex* :
A good rich Farmer, or high Constable.
I'ld play hun 'gaine a Knight, or a good Squire ;
Or Gentleman of any other Countie
I' the Kindome. *Pan.* Out-cept *Kent*, for there they landed
All Gentlemen, and came in with the Conquerour, 51
Mad *Iulius Cæsar* ; who built *Dover*-Castle :
My Ancestor *To-Pan*, beat the first Ketle-drum,
Avore 'hun, here vrom *Dover* on the March :
Which peice of monumentall copper hangs 55
Up, scourd, at *Hammer-smith* yet ; for there they came
Over the *Thames*, at a low water marke ;

   1. iii. 29 married ? *corr. F* : married : *F originally*   37 Writer, *F3* : Writer *F*   40 *Coloni*] Colony F3   41–5 *Verse as in G : wrongly divided in F* A Clowne ... Earth, | Ere sin' ... first, | Which ... *Midlesex*. | *Tur.* ... zertified me. | I had ... *Midlesex* :   56 Up] Vp *F*   there] the re (?) *F*

445·3   C

Vore either *London*, I, or *Kingston* Bridge—
I doubt were kursind.   *Tur.* Zee, who is here: *Iohn Clay*!
60 *Zonne Valentine*, and Bride-groome! ha' you zeene
Your Valentine-Bride yet, sin' you came? *Iohn Clay*?

ACT I.   SCENE IV.

Clay. ⟨*Puppy.*⟩   To them.

   Cla. No wusse. Che lighted, I, but now i' the yard:
Puppy ha' scarce unswadled my legges yet.
   Tur. What? wispes o' your wedding day, zonne? This is right
Originous Clay: and *Clay* o' *Kilborne* too!
5 I would ha' had bootes o' this day, zure, zonne *Iohn*.
   Cla. I did it to save charges: we mun dance,
O' this day, zure: and who can dance in boots?
No, I got on my best straw-colour'd stockins,
And swaddeld 'hem over to zave charges; I.
10   *Tur.* And his new shamois Doublet too with points;
I like that yet: and his long sawsedge-hose,
Like the Commander of foure smoking Tile-kils,
Which he is Captaine of; Captaine of *Kilborne*:
Clay with his hat turn'd up, o' the leere side, too:
15 As if he would leape my Daughter yet ere night,
And spring a new *Turfe* to the old house:
⟨*Enter the Maids of the Bridall.*⟩ Looke, and the wenches ha' not vound un out;
And doe parzent un, with a van of Rosemary,
And Bayes; to vill a Bow-pot, trim the head
20 Of my best vore-horse: wee shall all ha' Bride-laces,
Or points, I zee; my Daughter will be valiant;
And prove a very *Mary Ambry* i' the busines.
   Cle. They zaid, your worship had sur'd her to Squire *Tub*
Of *Totten-Court* here; all the hundred rings on't.
25   *Tur. A Tale of a Tub*, Sir; a meere tale of a Tub.

    I. iv. 7 O' *F3*: O F   8 -colour'd] -coloured *F*   22 *Ambry* W: *Anbry* F, F3

Lend it no eare I pray you : The Squire *Tub*
Is a fine man, but he is too fine a man,
And has a Lady *Tub* too to his Mother :
Ile deale with none o' these vine silken *Tubs*.
Iohn Clay, and Cloath-breech for my money, and Daughter. 30
Here comes another old Boy too, vor his colours
Will stroake downe my wives udder of purses, empty   Enter
Of all her milke money, this Winter Quarter ;   Father
Old Father *Rosin*, the chiefe Minstrell here :   Rosin
Chiefe Minstrell too of *High-gate* : she has hir'd him   35
And all, his two Boyes for a day and a halfe,
And now they come for Ribbanding, and Rosemary ;
Give 'hem enough Girles, gi' 'hem enough, and take it
Out in his tunes anon.   *Cle.* I'll ha' *Tom Tiler*,
For our *Iohn Clay*'s sake, and the Tile kils, zure.   40
  Med. And I the jolly Joyner, for mine owne sake.
  Pan. Ile ha' the joviall *Tinker* for *To-Pans* sake.
  Tur. Wee'll all be jovy this day, vor sonne *Valentine*,
My sweet sonne *Iohn*'s sake.   *Scri.* There's another
    reading now :
My Mr. reades it *Sonne*, and not *Sinne Valentine*.   45
  Pup. Nor *Zim* : And hee is i' the right : He is high
    Constable.
And who should reade above un, or avore 'hun ?
  Tur. Sonne *Iohn* shall bid us welcome all, this day :
Wee'll zerve under his colours : Leade the troop *Iohn*,
And *Puppy*, see the Bels ring. Presse all noises   50
Of *Finsbury*, in our name ; *D'ogenes Scriben*
Shall draw a score of warrants vor the busines.
Do's any wight parzent hir Majesties person,
This Hundred, 'bove the high Constable ?   *All.* No, no.
  Tur. Use our Authority then, to the utmost on't.   55

    1. iv. 32 s. d. *Rosin.*] *Rosin, and his two Boys.* G   35 *High-gate*] *High
gate* F   42 *To-Pans* F3 : *To. Pans* F   43 *Valentine,*] *Valentine.*
F, F3   50 *Puppy,* F3 : *Puppy* ; F   53 parzent] perzent *F3*
55 Use] Vse *F*

Act I. Scene V.

*Hugh. Preamble.
Metaphor.* ⟨To them.⟩

Hugh. So, you are sure Sir to prevent 'hem all;
And throw a block i' the Bride-groomes way, *Iohn Clay*,
That he will hardly leape ore. *Pre.* I conceive you,
Sir *Hugh*; as if your Rhetoricke would say,
5 Whereas the Father of her is a *Turfe*,
A very superficies of the earth;
Hee aimes no higher, then to match in *Clay*;
And there hath pitch'd his rest. *Hug.* Right Justice
    Bramble:
You ha' the winding wit, compassing all.
10   *Pre.* Subtile Sir *Hugh*, you now are i' the wrong,
And erre with the whole Neighbour-hood, I must tell you;
For you mistake my name. Justice *Preamble*
I write my selfe; which with the ignorant Clownes, here,
(Because of my profession of the Law,
15 And place o' the peace) is taken to be *Bramble*.
But all my warrants Sir, doe run *Preamble*:
Richard Preamble. *Hugh.* Sir I thanke you for't.
That your good worship, would not let me run
Longer in error, but would take me up thus—
20   *Pre.* You are my learned, and canonick neighbour:
I would not have you stray; but the incorrigible
Knot-headed beast, the Clownes, or Constables,
Still let them graze; eat Sallads; chew the Cud:
All the Towne-musicke will not move a log.
25   *Hug.* The Beetle and Wedges will, where you will have
    'hem.
  Pre. True, true Sir *Hugh*, here comes *Miles Metaphore*,
My Clarke: Hee is the man shall carry it, Chanon,
By my instructions. *Hug.* Hee will do't *ad unguem*,
Miles Metaphore: Hee is a pretty fellow.

    I. v. Scene III.—Maribone. A Room in Justice Preamble's House. *G*
Hugh ... Metaphor one line in *F*   13 here, *F3* : here *F*

Pre. I love not to keepe shadowes, or halfe-wits, 30
To foile a busines. *Metaphore*! you ha' seene
A King ride forth in state. *Met.* Sir that I have:
King *Edward* our late Leige, and soveraigne Lord:
And have set downe the pompe. *Pre.* Therefore I ask'd
 you.
Ha' you observ'd the Messengers o' the Chamber? 35
What habits they were in? *Met.* Yes; Minor Coats.
Unto the Guard, a Dragon, and a Grey-hound,
For the supporters of the Armes. *Pre.* Well mark'd;
You know not any of 'hem? *Met.* Here's one dwels
In *Maribone*. *Pre.* Ha' you acquaintance with him, 40
To borrow his coat an houre? *Hug.* Or but his badge,
'Twill serve: A little thing he weares on his brest.
 Pre. His coat, I say, is of more authority:
Borrow his coat for an houre. I doe love
To doe all things compleately, Chanon *Hugh*; 45
Borrow his coat, *Miles Metaphore*, or nothing.
 Met. The Taberd of his office, I will call it,
Or the Coat-Armour of his place: and so
Insinuate with him by that Trope—. *Pre.* I know   Metaph.
Your powers of Rhetorick, *Metaphore*. Fetch him off   *goes out.*
In a fine figure for his coat I say. 51
 Hug. Ile take my leave Sir of your worship too:
Bycause I may expect the issue anone.
 Pre. Stay my diviner Counsell, take your fee;
Wee that take fees, allow 'hem to our Counsell; 55
And our prime learned Counsell, double fees:
There are a brace of Angels to support you
I' your foot-walke this frost, for feare of falling;
Or spraying of a point of Matrimony,
When you come at it. *Hug.* I' your worships service; 60
That the exploit is done, and you possest
Of Mrs. *Awdrey Turfe*— *Pre.* I like your project.   *Preamble*
 goes out.

 I. v. 37 Unto] Vnto *F*   40 him, *F3*: him? *F*   49–51 *Verse as
in G: wrongly divided in F* Insinuate ... Trope—. | *Pre.* ... *Metaphore* |
Fetch ...   59 spraying] *Query,* sprayning   60 it.] it, *W*

Hug. And I, of this effect of two to one ;
It worketh in my pocket, 'gainst the Squire,
65 And his halfe bottome here, of halfe a peice :
Which was not worth the stepping ore the stile for :
His Mother has quite marr'd him : Lady *Tub*,
She's such a vessell of *fæces* : all dry'd earth !
Terra damnata, not a drop of salt !
70 Or *Peeter* in her ! All her Nitre is gone.

Act I. Scene VI.

Lady Tub. Pol-Marten.

Lad. Is the Nag ready *Marten* ? call the Squire.
This frosty morning wee will take the aire,
About the fields : for I doe meane to be
Some-bodies *Valentine*, i' my Velvet Gowne,
5 This morning, though it be but a beggar-man.
Why stand you still, and doe not call my sonne ?

Pol. Madam, if he had couched with the Lambe,
He had no doubt beene stirring with the Larke :
But he sat up at Play, and watch'd the Cock,
10 Till his first warning chid him off to rest.
Late Watchers are no early Wakers, Madam ;
But if your Ladiship will have him call'd—.

Lad. Will have him call'd ? Wherefore did I, Sir, bid him
Be call'd, you Weazell, Vermin of an Huisher ?
15 You will returne your wit to your first stile
Of *Marten Polcat*, by these stinking tricks,
If you doe use 'hem : I shall no more call you
Pol-marten, by the title of a Gentleman,

Pol-marten goes out.
If you goe on thus— *Pol.* I am gone. *Lad.* Be quick then,
I' your come off : and make amends you Stote !
Was ever such a Full-mart for an Huisher,
To a great worshipfull Lady, as my selfe ;
Who, when I heard his name first, *Martin Polcat*,
A stinking name, and not to be pronounc'd

I. vi. Scene IV—Totten-Court. Before Lady Tub's House. G

Without a reverence, in any Ladies presence; 25
My very heart eene earn'd, seeing the Fellow
Young, pretty and handsome; being then I say,
A Basket-Carrier, and a man condemn'd
To the Salt-peeter workes; made it my suit
To Mr. *Peeter Tub*, that I might change it; 30
And call him as I doe now, by *Pol-marten*,
To have it sound like a Gentleman in an Office,
And made him mine owne Fore-man, daily waiter,
And he to serve me thus! Ingratitude!
Beyond the Coursenes yet of any Clownage, 35
Shewen to a Lady! what now, is he stirring? *He re-*
 Pol. Stirring betimes out of his bed, and ready. *turnes.*
 Lad. And comes he then? *Pol.* No Madam, he is gone.
 Lad. Gone? whither? aske the Porter: Where's he gone?
 Pol. I met the Porter, and have ask'd him for him; 40
He sayes he let him forth an houre agoe.
 Lad. An houre agoe! what busines could he have,
So early? where is his man, grave *Basket Hilts*?
His Guide, and Governour? *Pol.* Gone with his Master.
 Lad. Is he gone too? O that same surly knave, 45
Is his right hand: and leads my sonne amisse.
He has carried him to some drinking match, or other:
Pol-marten, I will call you so againe;
I'am friends with you now. Goe get your horse, and ride
To all the Townes about here, where his haunts are; 50
And crosse the fields to meet, and bring me word;
He cannot be gone farre, being a foot.
Be curious to inquire him: and bid *Wispe*
My woman come, and waite on me. The love
Wee Mothers beare our Sonnes, we ha' bought with paine, 55
Makes us oft view them, with too carefull eyes,
And over-looke 'hem with a jealous feare,
Out-fitting Mothers.

 I. vi. 25–6 Without a reverence.] *A marginal note in F, which prints*
In any Ladies ... the Fellow *as one line. Text from W*: In any lady's
presence without a reverence G   55 bought] brought *W*

Act I.   Scene VII.

Lady Tub.   Wispe.

Lad. How now *Wispe*? Ha' you
A Valentine yet : I'm taking th' aire to choose one.
Wis. Fate send your Ladiship a fit one then.
Lad. What kind of one is that ?   *Wis.* A proper man,
5 To please your Ladiship.   *Lad.* Out o' that vanity,
That takes the foolish eye : Any poore creature,
Whose want may need my almes, or courtesie ;
I rather wish ; so Bishop *Valentine*,
Left us example to doe deeds of Charity ;
10 To feed the hungry ; cloath the naked ; visit
The weake, and sicke ; to entertaine the poore ;
And give the dead a Christian Funerall ;
These were the workes of piety he did practise,
And bad us imitate ; not looke for Lovers,
15 Or handsome Images to please our senses.
I pray thee *Wispe*, deale freely with me now :
Wee are alone, and may be merry a little :
Tho' art none o' the Court-glories ; nor the wonders
For wit, or beauty i' the Citie : tell me,
20 What man would satisfie thy present phansie ?
Had thy ambition leave to choose a Valentine,
Within the Queenes Dominion, so a subject.
   Wis. Yo' ha' gi' me a large scope, Madam, I confesse,
And I will deale with your Ladiship sincerely :
25 I'll utter my whole heart to you. I would have him,
The bravest, richest, and the properest man
A Taylor could make up ; or all the Poets,
With the Perfumers : I would have him such,
As not another woman, but should spite me !
30 Three Citie Ladies should run mad for him :
And Countri-Madams infinite.   *Lad.* You'ld spare me,

_{I. vii. 10 naked ;] naked, *F*, *F3*   29 me ! *corr. F*: me : *F originally*}

And let me hold my wits? *Wis.* I should with you—
For the young Squire, my Masters sake: dispense
A little; but it should be very little.
Then all the Court-wives I'ld ha' jealous of me;   35
As all their husbands jealous of them:
And not a Lawyers Pusse of any quality,
But lick her lips, for a snatch in the Terme time. *Lad.* Come,
Let's walke: wee'll heare the rest, as we goe on:
You are this morning in a good veine, *Dido*:   40
Would I could be as merry. My sonnes absence
Troubles me not a little: though I seeke
These wayes to put it off; which will not helpe:
Care that is entred, once into the brest,
Will have the whole possession, ere it rest.   45

Act II. Scene I.

Turfe. Clay. Medlay. Clench. To-Pan. Scriben. Puppy.
⟨To them.
D. Turfe. Awdrey. Maids.⟩

Tur. Zonne *Clay*, cheare up, the better leg avore:
This is a veat is once done, and no more.
Cle. And then 'tis done vor ever, as they say.
Med. Right! vor a man ha' his houre, and a dog his day.
Tur. True neighbour *Medlay*, yo' are still *In-and-In*.   5
Med. I would be Mr. Constable, if 'ch could win.
Pan. I zay, *Iohn Clay*, keepe still on his old gate:
Wedding, and hanging, both goe at a rate.
Tur. Well said *To-Pan*: you ha' still the hap to hit
The naile o' the head at a close: I thinke there never   10
Marriage was manag'd with a more avisement,
Then was this mariage, though I say't, that should not;
Especially 'gain' mine owne flesh, and blood;
My wedded Wife. Indeed my Wife would ha' had

---
    1. vii. 36 jealous] jealous too *W*   *Query*, jealous   II. i. Scene I.—
The fields near Pancras. *G*   6 'ch] 'ch' *F*   10 never] ne ver *F*

15 All the young Batchelers and Maids, forsooth,
O' the zixe Parishes hereabout : But I
Cry'd none, sweet *Sybil* : none of that geare, I :
It would lick zalt, I told her, by her leave.
No, three, or voure our wise, choise honest neighbours :
20 Upstantiall persons : men that ha' borne office :
And mine owne Family, would bee inough
To eate our dinner. What ? Deare meate's a theife :
I know it by the Butchers, and the Mercat-volke ;
Hum drum I cry. No halfe-Oxe in a Pie :
25 A man that's bid to Bride-ale, if hee ha' cake,
And drinke enough, hee need not veare his stake.
    Cle. Tis right : he has spoke as true as a Gun ; beleeve it.
    Tur. Come *Sybil*, come : Did not I tell you o' this ?
This pride, and muster of women would marre all ?
30 Sixe women to one Daughter, and a Mother !
The Queene (God save her) ha' no more her selfe.
    D. Tur. Why, if you keepe so many, Mr. *Turfe*,
Why, should not all present our service to her ?
    Tur. Your service ? good ! I thinke you'll write to her shortly,
35 Your very loving and obedient Mother.
    [*Tur.*] Come, send your Maids off, I will have 'hem sent
Home againe wife : I love no traines o' *Kent*,
Or Christendome, as they say. *Sc.* Wee will not back,
And leave our Dame. *Mad.* Why should her worship lack
40 Her taile of Maids, more then you doe of men ?
    Tur. What, mutinin *Madge* ? *Io.* Zend back your C'lons agen.
And wee will vollow. *All.* Else wee'll guard our Dame.
    Tur. I ha' zet the nest of waspes all on a flame.
    D. Tur. Come, you are such another Mr. *Turfe* :
45 A Clod you should be call'd, of a high Constable :
To let no musicke goe afore your child,
To Church, to cheare her heart up this cold morning.

    II. i. 20 Upstantiall] Vpstantiall *F*   35–6 *Perhaps a speech of Dame Turfe has been lost here and a speech of Scriben at* 38   38 *Sc.*] *Joyce. G*

Tur. You are for Father *Rosin*, and his consort
Of fidling Boyes, the great *Feates*, and the lesse :
Bycause you have entertain'd 'hem all from *High-gate*.   50
To shew your pompe, you'ld ha' your Daughter, and Maids
Dance ore the fields like Faies, to Church, this frost ?
Ile ha' no rondels, I, i' the Queenes pathes ;
Let 'un scrape the Gut at home, where they ha' fill'd it
At after-noòne.   *D. Turfe.* Ile ha' 'hem play at dinner.   55
 Ite. She is i' th' right, Sir ; vor your wedding dinner
Is starv'd without the Musicke.   *Med.* If the Pies
Come not in piping hot, you ha' lost that Proverbe.
 Tur. I yield to truth : wife are you sussified ?
 Pan. A right good man ! when he knowes right, he   60
  loves it.
 Scri. And he will know't, and shew't too by his place
Of being high Constable, if no where else.

Act II. Scene II.

To them.

Hilts bearded, booted and spur'd.

 Hil. Well over-taken, *Gentlemen* ! I pray you,
Which is the Queenes High Constable among you ?
 Pup. The tallest man : who should be else, doe you
  thinke ?
 Hil. It is no matter what I thinke, young Clowne :
Your answer savours of the Cart.   *Pup.* How ? Cart ?   5
And Clowne ? Doe you know whose teame you speake to ?
 Hil. No : nor I care not : Whose Jade may you be ?
 Pup. Jade ? Cart ? and Clowne ? O for a lash of whip-
  cord !
Three-knotted coard !   *Hil.* Doe you mutter ? Sir, snorle
  this way ;
That I may heare, and answer what you say,   10
With my schoole-dagger, 'bout your Costard Sir.
Looke to't, young growse : Ile lay it on, and sure ;

<small>   II. i. 52 Faies] Fairies *F3*   Church, *F3* : Church *F*   54 where]
Query, when   56 *Ite.*] *Clench* W   II. ii. 6. And] and *F*</small>

Take't off who's wull. *Cle.* Nay, pray you Gentleman——.
Hil. Goe too : I will not bate him an ace on't.
15 What ? Rowle-powle ? Maple-face ? All fellowes ?
   Pup. Doe you heare friend, I wou'd wish you, vor your
       good,
Tie up your brended Bitch there, your dun rustie
Pannyer-hilt poinard : and not vexe the youth
With shewing the teeth of it. Wee now are going
20 To Church, in way of matrimony, some on us :
Tha' rung all in a'ready. If it had not,
All the horne beasts are grazing i' this close,
Sould not ha' pull' me hence, till this Ash-plant
Had rung noone o' your pate, Mr. Broome-beard.
25 *Hil.* That would I faine zee, quoth the blind *George*
Of *Holloway* : Come Sir. *Awd.* O their naked weapons !
   Pan. For the passion of man, hold Gentleman, and *Puppy*.
   Cla. Murder, O Murder ! *Awd.* O my Father, and
       Mother !
   D. Tur. Husband, what doe you meane ? Sonne *Clay*
       for Gods sake—
30 *Tur.* I charge you in the Queenes name, keepe the peace.
   Hil. Tell me o' no Queene, or *Keysar* : I must have
A legge, or a hanch of him, ere I goe. *Med.* But zir,
You must obey the Queenes high Officers.
   Hil. Why must I, Good-man *Must* ? *Med.* You must,
       an' you wull.
35 *Tur.* Gentleman, I'am here for fault, high Constable—
   Hil. Are you zo ? what then ? *Tur.* I pray you Sir put up
Your weapons ; doe, at my request : For him,
On my authority, he shall lie by the heeles,
Verbatim continente, an' I live.
40 *D. Tur.* Out on him for a knave, what a dead fright
He has put me into ? Come *Awdrey*, doe not shake.
   Awd. But is not *Puppy* hurt ? nor the tother man ?
   Cla. No Bun ; but had not I cri'd Murder, I wusse—
   Pup. Sweet Good-man *Clench*, I pray you revise my Mr.

II. ii. 13 who's] who G

I may not zit i' the stocks, till the wedding be past. 45
Dame, Mrs. *Awdrey*: I shall breake the Bride-cake else.
  Cle. Zomething must be, to save authority, *Puppy*.
  D. Tur. Husband— *Cle.* And Gossip— *Awd.* Father—
   Tur. 'Treat mee not.
It is i' vaine. If he lye not by the heeles,
Ile lie there for 'hun. Ile teach the Hine, 50
To carry a tongue in his head, to his subperiors.
  Hil. This 's a wise Constable! where keepes he schoole?
  Cle. In *Kentish Towne*, a very survere man.
  Hil. But as survere as he is; Let me Sir tell him,
He sha' not lay his man by the heeles for this. 55
This was my quarrell: And by his office leave,
If't carry 'hun for this, it shall carry double;
Vor he shall carry me too. *Tur.* Breath of man!
Hee is my chattell, mine owne hired goods:
An' if you doe abet 'un in this matter, 60
Ile clap you both by the heeles, ankle to ankle.
  Hilt. You'll clap a dog of waxe as soone, old *Blurt*?
Come, spare not me, Sir; I am no mans wife:
I care not, I, Sir, not three skips of a Lowse for you,
And you were ten tall Constables, not I. 65
  Tur. Nay, pray you Sir, be not angry; but content:
My man shall make you, what amends you'll aske 'hun.
  Hil. Let 'hun mend his manners then, and know his
   betters:
It's all I aske 'hun: and 'twill be his owne;
And's Masters too, another day. Che vore 'hun. 70
  Med. As right as a Club, still. Zure this angry man
Speakes very neere the marke, when he is pleas'd.
  Pup. I thanke you Sir, an' I meet you at *Kentish Towne*,
I ha' the courtesie o' ⟨the⟩ hundred for you.
  Hil. Gramercy, good high Constables Hine. But hear you? 75
Mass: Constable, I have other manner o' matter,
To bring you about, then this. And so it is,

II. ii. 45 past.] past, *F3*: past *F*   46 Dame, *F3*: Dame. *F*   51 sub-
periors] Superiours *F3*   74 the *G*   75 Hine. *corr. F*: Hine! *F originally*

I doe belong to one o' the Queenes Captaines ;
A Gent'man o' the Field, one Captaine *Thum's* :
80 I know not, whether you know 'hun, or no : It may be
You doe, and't may be you doe not againe.

    Tur. No, I assure you on my Constable-ship,
I doe not know 'hun.   *Hil.* (Nor I neither i' faith.)
It skils not much ; my Captaine, and my selfe,
85 Having occasion to come riding by, here,
This morning, at the corner of Saint *Iohn*'s wood,
Some mile o' this Towne, ⟨we⟩ were set upon
By a sort of countrey fellowes : that not onely
Beat us, but rob'd us, most sufficiently ;
90 And bound us to our behaviour, hand and foot ;
And so they left us. Now, *Don Constable*,
I am to charge you in her Majesties name,
As you will answer it at your apperill,
That forth-with you raise Hue and Cry i' the Hundred,
95 For all such persons as you can dispect,
By the length and bredth, o' your office : vor I tell you,
The losse is of some value, therefore looke to't.

    Tur. As Fortune mend me, now, or any office
Of a thousand pound, if I know what to zay,
100 Would I were dead ; or vaire hang'd up at *Tiburne*,
If I doe know what course to take ; or how
To turne my selfe ; just at this time too, now,
My Daughter is to be married : Ile but goe
To *Pancridge* Church, hard by, and returne instantly,
105 And all my Neighbour-hood shall goe about it.

    Hil. Tut, *Pancridge* me no *Pancridge*, if you let it
Slip, you will answer it, and your Cap be of wooll ;
Therefore take heed, you'll feele the smart else, Constable.

    Tur. Nay, good Sir stay. Neighbours ! what thinke you
      o' this ?
110   *D. Tur.* Faith, Man—.   ⟨*Tur.*⟩ Odd pretious woman,
      hold your tongue ;

    II. ii. 83 *Aside not marked in* F   87 mile] mile west *G*   we *W*
    110 *Tur.* W

And mind your pigs o' the spit at home ; you must
Have Ore in every thing. Pray you Sir, what kind
Of fellowes were they?   *Hil.* Theev's kind, I ha' told you.
   Tur. I meane, what kind of men ?   *Hil.* Men of our make.
   Tur. Nay, but with patience, Sir, we that are Officers   115
Must 'quire the speciall markes, and all the tokens
Of the despected parties, or perhaps—else,
Be nere the nere of our purpose in 'prehending 'hem.
Can you tell, what 'parrell any of them wore ?
   Hil. Troth no : there were so many o' hun, all like   120
So one another : Now I remember me,
There was one busie fellow, was their Leader ;
A blunt squat swad, but lower then your selfe,
He' had on a Lether Doublet, with long points.
And a paire of pin'd-up breech's, like pudding bags :   125
With yellow stockings, and his hat turn'd up
With a silver Claspe, on his leere side.   *D. Tur.* By these
Markes it should be *Iohn Clay*, now blesse the man !
   Tur. Peace, and be nought : I thinke the woman be
     phrensick.
   Hil. Iohn Clay? what's he, good Mistris ?   *Awd.* He   130
     that shall be
My husband—   *Hil.* How ! your husband, pretty one ?
   Awd. Yes, I shall anone be married : That's he.
   Tur. Passion o' me, undone !   *Pup.* Blesse Masters sonne !
   Hil. O you are well 'prehended : know you me Sir ?
   Clay. No's my record : I never zaw you avore.   135
   Hil. You did not ? where were your eyes then ? out at
     washing ?
   Tur. What should a man zay ? who should he trust
In these dayes ? Harke you *Iohn Clay*, if you have
Done any such thing, tell troth, and shame the Divell.
   Cle. Vaith doe : my Gossip *Turfe* zaies well to you *Iohn.*   140
   Med. Speake man, but doe not convesse, nor be avraid.
   Pan. A man is a man, and a beast's a beast, looke to't.
   D. Tur. I' the name of men, or beasts ! what doe you
     doe ?

Hare the poore fellow out on his five wits,
145 And seven senses? Doe not weepe *Iohn Clay*.
I sweare the poore wretch is as guilty from it,
As the Child was, was borne this very morning.
  Cla. No, as I am a kyrsin soule, would I were hang'd
If ever I—alasse I! would I were out
150 Of my life, so I would I were, and in againe—
  Pup. Nay, Mrs. *Awdrey* will say nay to that.
No In-and-out? an' you were out o' your life,
How should she doe for a husband? who should fall
Aboord o' her then? (*Ball?* He's a *Puppy?*
155 No; *Hanniball* has no breeding: well! I say little;
But hitherto all goes well, pray it prove no better.)
  Awd. Come Father; I would wee were married: I am a cold.
  Hil. Well, Mr. Constable, this your fine Groome here,
Bride-groome, or what Groome else, soere he be,
160 I charge him with the felonie; and charge you
To carry him back forthwith to *Paddington*,
Unto my Captaine, who staies my returne there:
I am to goe to the next Justice of peace,
To get a warrant to raise *Huy* and *Cry*,
165 And bring him, and his fellowes all afore 'hun.
Fare you well Sir, and looke to 'hun I charge you,
As yo'll answer it. Take heed; the busines
If you deferre, may prejudiciall you
Hilts goes out. More then you thinke-for, zay I told you so.
  Tur. Here's a Bride-ale indeed! Ah zonne *Iohn*, zonne *Clay!*
171 I little thought you would ha' prov'd a peece
Of such false mettall. *Cla.* Father, will you beleeve me?
Would I might never stirre i' my new shoes,
If ever I would doe so voule a fact.
175 *Tur.* Well Neighbours, I doe charge you to assist me
With 'hun to *Paddington*. Be he a true man, so:
The better for 'hun. I will doe mine office,

II. ii. 152 No] No, F   154 then?] then, F   154–6 *Aside not marked in F*   162 Unto] Vnto F   169 s. d. *out.*] out F

An' he were my owne begotten a thousand times.
 D. Tur. Why, doe you heare man? Husband? Mr. 179
  Turfe!
What shall my Daughter doe? *Puppy*, stay here.   *She fol-*
 Awd. Mother, Ile goe with you, and with my Father. *lowes her husb. and neighbours.*

Act II. Scene III.

Puppy. Awdrey.
⟨To them.⟩
Hilts.

 Pup. Nay, stay sweet Mrs. *Awdrey* : here are none
But one friend (as they zay) desires to speake
A word, or two, cold with you : How doe you veele
Your selfe this frosty morning?   *Awd.* What ha' you
To doe to aske, I pray you? I am a cold. 5
 Pup. It seemes you are hot, good Mrs. *Awdrey*.
 Awd. You lie ; I am as cold as Ice is : Feele else.
 Pup. Nay, you ha' coold my courage : I am past it,
I ha' done feeling with you.   *Awd.* Done with me?
I doe defie you. So I doe, to say 10
You ha' done with me : you are a sawcy *Puppy*.
 Pup. O you mistake! I meant not as you meane.
 Awd. Meant you not knavery, *Puppy*? ⟨*Pup.*⟩ No :
  not I.
Clay meant you all the knavery, it seemes,
Who rather, then he would be married to you, 15
Chose to be wedded to the Gallowes first.
 Awd. I thought he was a dissembler ; he would prove
A slippery Merchant i' the frost. Hee might
Have married one first, and have beene hang'd after,
If hee had had a mind to't. But you men, 20
Fie on you.   *Pup.* Mrs. *Awdrey*, can you vind,
I' your heart to fancie *Puppy*? me poore *Ball*?
 Awd. You are dispos'd to jeere one, Mr. *Hanniball*.

II. iii. (Heading) *Puppy* ... *Hilts* one line in F   13 knavery,
Puppy? *Pup.* No:] Knavery? *Puppy.* No, *F3*   22 I' *F3* : I *F*

Enter Hilts.

Pitty o' me! the angry man with the beard!
Hil. Put on thy hat, I looke for no despect.
26 Where's thy Master?   *Pup.* Marry, he is gone
With the picture of despaire, to *Paddington*.
   Hil. Pr'y thee run after 'hun, and tell 'hun he shall
Find out my Captaine, lodg'd at the red-*Lyon*
30 In *Paddington*; that's the Inne. Let 'un aske
Vor Captaine *Thum's*; And take that for thy paines:
He may seeke long enough else. Hie thee againe.
   Pup. Yes, Sir you'll looke to Mrs. Bride the while?
   Hil. That I will: prethee haste.   *Awd.* What *Puppy*?
⟨Puppy goes out.⟩   Puppy?
35 *Hil.* Sweet Mrs. Bride, Hee'll come againe presently.
Here was no subtile device to get a wench.
This Chanon has a brave pate of his owne!
A shaven pate! And a right monger, y' vaith!
This was his plot! I follow Captaine *Thum's*?
40 Wee rob'd in Saint *Iohn's* wood? I' my tother hose!
I laugh, to thinke what a fine fooles finger they have
O' this wise Constable, in pricking out
This Captaine *Thum's* to his neighbours: you shall see
The Tile-man too set fire on his owne *Kill*,
45 And leap into it, to save himselfe from hanging.
You talke of a Bride-ale, here was a Bride-ale broke,
I' the nick. Well: I must yet dispatch this Bride,
To mine owne master, the young Squire, and then
My taske is done. Gen'woman! I 'have in sort
50 Done you some wrong, but now Ile doe you what right
I can: It's true, you are a proper woman;
But to be cast away on such a Clowne-pipe
As *Clay*; me thinkes, your friends are not so wise
As nature might have made 'hem; well, goe too:
55 There's better fortune comming toward you,
An' you doe not deject it. Take a voole's
Counsell, and doe not stand i' your owne light.
It may prove better then you thinke for: Looke you.

II. iii. 42 O' *F3*: O F

Awd. Alas Sir, what is't you would ha' me doe?
I'ld faine doe all for the best, if I knew how.   60
  Hil. Forsake not a good turne, when 'tis offered you;
Faire Mistris *Awdrey*, that's your name, I take it.
  Awd. No Mistris, Sir, my name is *Awdrey*.
  Hil. Well, so it is, there is a bold young Squire,
The blood of *Totten*, *Tub*, and *Tripoly*—.   65
  Awd. Squire *Tub*, you meane? I know him: he knowes
    me too.
  Hil. He is in love with you: and more, he's mad for you.
  Awd. I, so he told me: in his wits, I thinke.
But hee's too fine for me; and has a Lady
Tub to his Mother. Here he comes himselfe!   70

Act II. Scene IV.

Tub. Hilts. Awdrey.

  Tub. O you are a trusty Governour! *Hil.* What ailes
    you?
You doe not know when yo' are well, I thinke:
You'ld ha' the Calfe with the white face, Sir, would you?
I have her for you here; what would you more?
  Tub. Quietnes, *Hilts*, and heare no more of it.   5
  Hil. No more of it, quoth you? I doe not care,
If some on us had not heard so much of't,
I tell you true; A man must carry, and vetch,
Like *Bungy*'s dog for you. *Tub.* What's he? *Hil.* A
    Spaniel.
And scarce be spit i' the mouth for't. A good Dog   10
Deserves, Sir, a good bone, of a free Master:
But, an' your turnes be serv'd, the divell a bit
You care for a man after, ere a Lard of you.
Like will to like, y-faith, quoth the scab'd Squire
To th' mangy Knight, when both met in a dish   15
Of butter'd vish. One bad, there's nere a good;
And not a barrell better Hering among you.

D 2

Tub. Nay *Hilts*! I pray thee grow not fram-pull now.
Turne not the bad Cow, after thy good soape.
20 Our plot hath hitherto tane good effect :
And should it now be troubled, or stop'd up,
'Twould prove the utter ruine of my hopes.
I pray thee haste to *Pancridge*, to the Chanon :
And gi' him notice of our good successe ;
25 Will him that all things be in readinesse.
Faire *Awdrey*, and my selfe, will crosse the fields,
The nearest path. Good *Hilts*, make thou some haste,
And meet us on the way. Come gentle *Awdrey*.

Hil. Vaith, would I had a few more geances on't :
30 An' you say the word, send me to *Iericho*.
Out-cept a man were a Post-horse, I ha' not knowne
The like on't ; yet, an' he had kind words,
'Twould never irke 'hun. But a man may breake
His heart out i' these dayes, and get a flap
35 With a fox-taile, when he has done. And there is all.

Tub. Nay, say not so *Hilts* : hold thee ; there are Crownes—
My love bestowes on thee, for thy reward.
If Gold will please thee, all my land shall drop
In bounty thus, to recompence thy merit.

40 *Hil.* Tut, keepe your land, and your gold too Sir : I
Seeke neither-nother of 'hun. Learne to get
More : you will know to spend that zum you have
Early enough : you are assur'd of me.
I love you too too well, to live o' the spoyle :
45 For your owne sake, were there no worse then I.
All is not Gold that glisters : Ile to *Pancridge*.

Tub. See, how his love doth melt him into Teares !
An honest faithfull servant is a Jewell.
Now th' adventurous Squire hath time, and leisure,
50 To aske his *Awdrey* how she do's, and heare
A gratefull answer from her. Shee not speakes :

II. iv. 32 had] had had *G*   41 neither-nother] neither—nother *F, F3*
45 were there] were there were *F* : would there were *W*   49 adventurous] adventrous *F3*

Hath the proud Tiran, Frost, usurp'd the seate
Of former beauty in my Loves faire cheek;
Staining the roseat tincture of her blood,
With the dull die of blew-congealing cold?   55
No, sure the weather dares not so presume
To hurt an object of her brightnesse. Yet,
The more I view her, shee but lookes so, so.
Ha? gi' me leave to search this mysterie!
O now I have it: Bride, I know your griefe;   60
The last nights cold, hath bred in you such horror
Of the assigned Bride-groomes constitution,
The *Kilborne* Clay-pit; that frost-bitten marle;
That lumpe in courage; melting cake of Ice;
That the conceit thereof hath almost kill'd thee.   65
But I must doe thee good wench, and refresh thee.
   Awd. You are a merry man, Squire *Tub*, of *Totten*!
I have heard much o' your words, but not o' your deeds.
   Tub. Thou sayest true, sweet; I' ha' beene too slack in
     deeds.
   Awd. Yet, I was never so straight-lac'd to you, Squire.   70
   Tub. Why, did you ever love me, gentle *Awdrey*?
   Awd. Love you? I cannot tell: I must hate no body,
My Father sayes.   *Tub.* Yes, *Clay*, and *Kilburne*; *Awdrey*,
You must hate them.   *Awd.* It shall be for your sake then.
   Tub. And for my sake, shall yield you that gratuitie.   75
   Awd. Soft, and faire, Squire, there goe two word's to   *He offers*
     a bargaine.   *to kisse her.*
   Tub. What are those *Awdrey*?   *Awd.* Nay, I cannot   *She puts him back.*
     tell.
My Mother said, zure, if you married me,
You'ld make me a Lady the first weeke: and put me
In, I know not what, the very day.   *Tub.* What was it?   80
Speake gentle *Awdrey*, thou shalt have it yet.
   Awd. A velvet dressing for my head, it is,
They say will make one brave: I will not know
Besse Moale, nor *Margery Turne-up*: I will looke

      II. iv. 64 courage;] courage: *F, F3*

85 Another way upon 'hem, and be proud.
    Tub. Troth I could wish my wench a better wit ;
But what she wanteth there, her face supplies.
There is a pointed lustre in her eye
Hath shot quite through me, and hath hit my heart :
90 And thence it is, I first receiv'd the wound,
That ranckles now, which only shee can cure.
Faine would I worke my selfe, from this conceit ;
But, being flesh, I cannot. I must love her,
The naked truth is : and I will goe on,
95 Were it for nothing, but to crosse my Rivall's.
Come *Awdrey* : I am now resolv'd to ha' thee.

Act II.   Scene V.
Preamble. Metaphore. Tub. Awdrey.

  Pre. Nay, doe it quickly, *Miles* ; why shak'st thou man ?
Speake but his name : Ile second thee my selfe.
    Met. What is his name ?   *Pre.* Squire *Tripoly* or *Tub.*
Any thing—   *Met.* Squire *Tub*, I doe arrest you
5 I' the Queenes Majesties name, and all the Councels.
    Tub. Arrest me, Varlet ?   *Pre.* Keepe the peace I
       charge you.
    Tub. Are you there, Justice *Bramble* ? where's your
       warrant ?
    Pre. The warrant is directed here to me,
From the whole table ; wherefore I would pray you
10 Be patient Squire, and make good the peace.
    Tub. Well, at your pleasure, Iustice.   I am wrong'd :
Sirrah, what are you have arrested me ?
    Pre. He is a Purs'yvant at Armes, Squire *Tub*.
    Met. I am a Purs'yvant, see, by my Coat else.
15   *Tub.* Well Purs'yvant, goe with me : Ile give you baile.
    Pre. Sir he may take no baile.   It is a warránt,
In speciall from the Councell, and commands
Your personall appearance.   Sir, your weapon

II. v. 13 Purs'yvant *F3* : Pursy'vant *F*

I must require : And then deliver you
A Prisoner to this officer. Squire *Tub*, 20
I pray you to conceive of me no other,
Then as your friend, and neighbour. Let my person
Be sever'd from my office in the fact,
And I am cleare. Here Purs'yvant, receive him
Into your hands ; And use him like a Gentleman. 25
   Tub. I thanke you Sir : But whither must I goe now ?
   Pre. Nay, that must not be told you, till you come
Unto the place assign'd by his instructions.
Ile be the Maidens Convoy to her father,
For this time, Squire. *Tub.* I thanke you Mr. *Bramble*. 30
I doubt, or feare, you will make her the ballance
To weigh your Justice in. Pray yee doe me right,
And lead not her, at least out of the way.
Justice is blind, and having a blind Guide,
She may be apt to slip aside. *Pre.* Ile see to her 35
   Tub. I see my wooing will not thrive. Arrested !
As I had set my rest up, for a wife ?
And being so faire for it, as I was. Well, fortune,
Thou art a blind Bawd, and a Beggar too,
To crosse me thus ; and let my onely Rivall, 40
To get her from me. That's the spight of spights.
But most I muse at, is, that I, being none
O' th' Court, am sent for thither by the Councell !
My heart is not so light, as 't was i' the morning.

Act II. Scene VI.

Hilts. Tub. Metaphor.

   Hil. You meane to make a Hoiden, or a Hare
O' me, t' hunt Counter thus, and make these doubles :
And you meane no such thing, as you send about ?
Where's your sweet-heart now, I marle ? *Tub.* Oh *Hilts* !
   Hil. I know you of old ! nere halt afore a Criple. 5

II. v. 20 officer.] officer, *F* : Officer, *F3*   *Tub,*] *Tub. F, F3*   28 Unto] Vnto *F*   38 was. Well *corr. F* : was.—. Well *F originally*   41 me. *corr. F* : me ? *F originally*   II. vi. 2. O' *F3* : O *F*   make *F3* : makes *F*

Will you have a Cawdle ? where's your griefe, Sir ? speake.
    Met. Doe you heare friend ? Doe you serve this
        Gentleman ?
    Hil. How then, Sir ? what if I doe ? peradventure yea :
Peraventure nay, what's that to you Sir ? Say.
10   *Met.* Nay, pray you Sir, I meant no harme in truth :
But this good Gentleman is arrested.   *Hil.* How ?
Say me that againe.   *Tub.* Nay *Basket*, never storme ;
I am arrested here, upon command
From the Queenes Councell ; and I must obey !
15   *Met.* You say Sir very true, you must obey.
An honest Gentleman, in faith !   *Hil.* He must ?
    Tub. But that which most tormenteth me, is this,
That Justice *Bramble* hath got hence my *Awdrey*.
    Hil. How ? how ? stand by a little, sirrah, you
20 With the badge o' your brest. Let's know Sir what you
      are ?
    Met. I am Sir (pray you doe not looke so terribly)
A Purs'yvant.   *Hil.* A Purs'yvant ? your name Sir ?
    Met. My name Sir—   *Hil.* What is't ? speake ?   *Met.*
        Miles Metaphor ;
And Justice *Preambles* Clarke.   *Tub.* What sayes he ?
    Hil. Pray you,
25 Let us alone. You are a Purs'yvant ?
    Met. No faith, Sir, would that I might never stirre from
        you,
I' is made a Purs'yvant against my will.
    Hil. Ha ! and who made you one ? tell true, or my will
Shall make you nothing, instantly.   *Met.* Put up
30 Your frightfull Blade ; and your dead-doing looke,
And I shall tell you all.   *Hil.* Speake then the truth,
And the whole truth, and nothing but the truth.
    Met. My Master, Justice *Bramble*, hearing your Master,
The Squire *Tub*, was comming on this way,
35 With Mrs. *Awdrey*, the high Constables Daughter ;

    II. vi. 6 Sir ? speake.] Sir, speake. *F originally* : Sir ? speake ? *corr.*
F.   15 obey ! *corr. F* : obey. *F originally*

Made me a Purs'yvant : and gave me warrant
To arrest him, so that hee might get the Lady,
With whom he is gone to *Pancridge*, to the Vicar,
Not to her Fathers. This was the device,
Which I beseek you, doe not tell my Master. 40
   Tub. O wonderfull ! well *Basket,* let him rise :
And for my free escape, forge some excuse.
Ile post to *Paddington,* t' acquaint old *Turfe,*
With the whole busines, and so stop the mariage.
   Hil. Well, blesse thee : I doe wish thee grace, to keepe 45
Thy Masters secrets, better, or be hang'd.
   Met. I thanke you, for your gentle admonition.
Pray you, let me call you God-father hereafter.
And as your God-sonne *Metaphore* I promise,
To keepe my Masters privities, seald up 50
I' the vallies o' my trust, lock'd close for ever,
Or let me be truss'd up at *Tiburne* shortly.
   Hil. Thine owne wish, save, or choake thee ; Come away.

Act III. Scene I.

Turfe. Clench. Medlay. To-Pan. Scriben. Clay.

   Tur. Passion of me, was ever man thus cross'd ?
All things run *Arsie-Varsie* ; upside downe.
High Constable ! Now by our Lady o' *Walsingham,*
I had rather be mark'd out *Tom Scavinger* :
And with a shovell make cleane the high wayes, 5
Then have this office of a Constable,
And a high Constable ! The higher charge
It brings more trouble, more vexation with it.
Neighbours, good neighbours, 'vize me what to doe :
How wee shall beare us in this *Huy* and *Cry.* 10
We cannot find the Captaine ; no such man
Lodg'd at the *Lion,* nor came thither hurt.

   II. vi. 40 beseek] beseech *F3*   III. i. Scene I.—Kentish Town *G* 3
Walsingham, F3 : *Walsingham.* F

The morning wee ha' spent in privie search;
And by that meanes the Bride-ale is differr'd;
15 The Bride, shee's left alone in *Puppie's* charge;
The Bride-groome goes under a paire of sureties;
And held of all as a respected person.
How should we bussle forward? Gi' some counsell,
How to bestirre our stumps i' these crosse wayes.
20   *Cle.* Faith Gossip *Turfe*, you have, you say, Remission,
To comprehend all such, as are dispected:
Now, would I make another privie search
Through this Towne, and then you have zearch'd two
    towns.
    Med. Masters, take heed, let's not vind too many:
25 One's enough to stay the Hang-mans stomack.
There is *Iohn Clay*, who is yvound already;
A proper man: A Tile-man by his trade:
A man as one would zay, moulded in clay:
As spruce as any neighbours child among you:
30 And he (you zee) is taken on conspition,
And two, or three (they zay) what call you 'hem?
Zuch as the Justices of *Coram nobis*
Grant— (I forget their names, you ha' many on 'hem,
Mr. High Constable they come to you.)
35 I ha' it at my tongues end—Cunni-borroughes,
To bring him straight avore the zessions house.
    Tur. O you meane warrens, neighbour, doe you not?
    Med. I, I, thick same! you know 'un well enough.
    Tur. Too well, too well; wou'd I had never knowne 'hem.
40 Wee good Vree-holders cannot live in quiet,
But every houre new purcepts, *Huy's* and *Cry's*,
Put us to requisitions night and day:
What shud a man zay, shud we leave the zearch?
I am in danger, to reburse as much
45 As he was rob'd on; I, and pay his hurts.
If I should vollow it, all the good cheare

III. i. 45 hurts.] hurts, *F, F3*

That was provided for the wedding dinner ;
Is spoil'd, and lost. Oh there are two vat pigs,
A zindging by the vier : Now by Saint *Tony*,
Too good to eate, but on a wedding day ;   50
And then, a Goose will bid you all, Come cut me.
Zun *Clay*, zun *Clay* (for I must call thee so)
Be of good comfort ; take my Muckinder ;
And dry thine eyes. If thou beest true, and honest ;
And if thou find'st thy conscience cleare vrom it   55
Pluck up a good heart, wee'll doe well enough.
If not, confesse a truths name. But in faith
I durst be sworne upon all holy bookes,
Iohn Clay would nere commit a Robberie
On his owne head.   *Cla.* No ; Truth is my rightfull Judge : 60
I have kept my hands, here hence, fro' evill speaking,
Lying, and slandering ; and my tongue from stealing.
He doe not live this day can say, *Iohn Clay*
I ha' zeene thee, but in the way of honesty.
   Pan. Faith neighbour *Medlay*, I durst be his burrough, 65
He would not looke a true man in the vace.
   Cla. I take the towne to concord, where I dwell,
All *Kilburne* be my witnesse ; If I were not
Begot in bashfulnesse, brought up in shamefac'tnesse :
Let 'un bring a dog, but to my vace, that can   70
Zay, I ha' beat 'hun, and without a vault ;
Or but a cat, will sweare upon a booke,
I have as much as zet a vier her taile ;
And Ile give him, or her a crowne for 'mends.
But to give out, and zay, I have rob'd a Captaine !   75
Receive me at the latter day, if I
Ere thought of any such matter ; or could mind it—.
   Med. No *Iohn*, you are come of too good personage ;
I thinke my Gossip *Clench*, and Mr. *Turfe*
Both thinke, you would ra'tempt no such voule matter. 80
   Tur. But how unhappily it comes to passe !

   III. i. 47 provided *F3* : provided ; *F*   dinner *F, F3*   49 *Tony* G :
Tomy F, *F3*   80 ra'tempt] *Query*, n'atempt

Just on the wedding day ! I cry me mercy :
I had almost forgot the *Huy* and *Cry* :
Good neighbour *Pan*, you are the Third-burrow,
85 And *D'ogenes Scriben*, you my learned Writer,
Make out a new purcept—Lord, for thy goodnesse,
I had forgot my Daughter, all this while ;
The idle knave hath brought no newes from her.
Here comes the sneaking *Puppy* ; What's the newes ?
90 My heart ! my heart ! I feare all is not well,
Some thing's mishap'd, that he is come without her.

Act III. Scene II.

To them.

Puppy. Da: Turfe.

Pup. Oh, where's my Master ? my Master ? my Master ?
D. Tur. Thy Master ? what would'st with thy Master, man ?
There's thy Mr. *Tur.* What 's the matter *Puppy* ?
Pup. Oh Master ! oh Dame ! oh Dame ! oh Master !
5 *D. Tur.* What sai'st thou to thy Master, or thy Dame ?
Pup. Oh *Iohn Clay* ! *Iohn Clay* ! *Iohn Clay* ! *Tur.* What of *Iohn Clay* ?
Med. Luck grant he bring not newes he shall be hang'd.
Cle. The world forfend, I hope, it is not so well.
Cla. Oh Lord ! oh me ! what shall I doe ? poore *Iohn* !
10 *Pup.* Oh *Iohn Clay* ! *Iohn Clay* ! *Iohn Clay* ! *Cla.* Alas,
That ever I was borne ! I will not stay by't,

⟨Clay goes out.⟩ For all the Tiles in *Kilburne.* *D. Tur.* What of *Clay* ?
Speake *Puppy*, what of him ? *Pup.* He hath lost, he hath lost.
Tur. For luck sake speake, *Puppy*, what hath he lost ?
15 *Pup.* Oh *Awdrey, Awdrey, Awdrey* ! *D. Tur.* What of my daughter *Awdrey* ?

III. i. 91 thing's] things *F, F3*

Pup. I tell you *Awdrey*—doe you understand me?
Awdrey, sweet Master! *Awdrey*, my dear Dame—
   Tur. Where is she? what's become of her, I pray thee?
   Pup. Oh the serving-man! the serving-man! the serving-man!
   Tur. What talk'st thou of the serving-man? where's 20
   Awdrey?
   Pup. Gone with the serving-man, gone with the serving-man.
   D. Tur. Good *Puppy*, whither is she gone with him?
   Pup. I cannot tell, he bad me bring you word,
The Captaine lay at the *Lion*, and before
I came againe, *Awdrey* was gone with the serving-man;   25
I tell you, *Awdrey*'s run away with the serving-man.
   Tur. 'Od 'socks! my woman, what shall we doe now?
   D. Tur. Now, so you helpe not, man, I know not, I.
   Tur. This was your pompe of Maids. I told you on't.
Sixe Maids to vollow you, and not leave one   30
To wait upo' your Daughter: I zaid, Pride
Would be paid one day, her old vi'pence, wife.
   Med. What of *Iohn Clay, Ball Puppy*?   *Pup.* He hath lost—
   Med. His life for velonie?   *Pup.* No, his wife by villanie.
   Tur. Now, villaines both! oh that same *Huy* and *Cry*! 35
Oh neighbours! oh that cursed serving-man!
O maids! O wife! But *Iohn Clay*, where's he?   Clay's
How! fled for veare, zay yee? will he slip us now?   *first mist.*
Wee that are sureties, must require 'hun out.
How shall wee doe to find the serving-man?   40
Cocks bodikins! wee must not lose *Iohn Clay*:
Awdrey, my daughter *Awdrey* too! let us zend
To all the townes, and zeeke her; but alas,
The *Huy* and *Cry*, that must be look'd unto.

Act III. Scene III.

To them.
Tub.

Tub. What, in a passion *Turfe*? *Tur.* I good Squire
Tub.
Were never honest Varmers thus perplext.
Tub. *Turfe*, I am privie to thy deepe unrest:
The ground of which, springs from an idle plot,
5 Cast by a Suitor, to your daughter *Awdrey*—
And thus much, *Turfe*, let me advertise you;
Your daughter *Awdrey*, met I on the way,
With Justice *Bramble* in her company:
Who meanes to marry her at *Pancridge* Church.
10 And there is Chanon *Hugh*, to meet them ready:
Which to prevent, you must not trust delay;
But winged speed must crosse their slie intent:
Then hie thee, *Turfe*, haste to forbid the Banes.
  Tur. Hath Justice *Bramble* got my daughter *Awdrey*?
15 A little while, shall he enjoy her, zure.
But O the *Huy* and *Cry*! that hinders me:
I must pursue that, or neglect my journey:
Ile ene leave all: and with the patient Asse,
The over-laden Asse, throw off my burden,
20 And cast mine office; pluck in my large eares
Betimes, lest some dis-judge 'hem to be hornes:
I'll leave to beat it on the broken hoofe,
And ease my pasternes. Ile no more High Constables.
  Tub. I cannot choose, but smile, to see thee troubled
25 With such a bald, halfe-hatched circumstance!
The Captaine was not rob'd, as is reported;
That trick the Justice craftily deviz'd,
To breake the mariage with the Tile-man *Clay*.
The *Huy*, and *Cry*, was meerely counterfeit:
30 The rather may you judge it to be such,
Because the Bride-groome, was describ'd to be

III. iii. 17 pursue] prusue *F*

A Tale of a Tub

One of the theeves, first i' the velonie.
Which, how farre 'tis from him, your selves may guesse :
'Twas Justice *Bramble*'s vetch, to get the wench.
   Tur. And is this true Squire *Tub* ?   *Tub.* Beleeve me 35
      Turfe,
As I am a Squire : or lesse, a Gentleman.
   Tur. I take my office back : and my authority,
Upon your worships words. Neighbours, I am
High Constable againe : where's my zonne *Clay* ?
He shall be zonne, yet, wife, your meat by leasure :   40
Draw back the spits.   *D. Tur.* That's done already man.
   Tur. Ile breake this mariage off : and afterward,
She shall be given to her first betroth'd.
Looke to the meate, wife : looke well to the rost.
   Tub. Ile follow him aloofe, to see the event.   45
   Pup. Dame, Mistris, though I doe not turne the spit ;
I hope yet the Pigs-head.   *D. Tur.* Come up, Jack-sauce :
It shall be serv'd in to you.   *Pup.* No, no service,
But a reward for service.   *D. Tur.* I still tooke you
For an unmannerly *Puppy* : will you come,   50
And vetch more wood to the vier, Mr. *Ball* ?
   Pup. I wood to the vier ? I shall pisse it out first :
You thinke to make me ene your oxe, or asse ;
Or any thing. Though I cannot right my selfe
On you ; Ile sure revenge me on your meat.   55

ACT III. SCENE IV.

La: Tub. Pol-Marten. Wispe.
                      ⟨To them.⟩
        Puppy.

   Pol. Madam, to *Kentish* Towne, wee are got at length ;
But, by the way wee cannot meet the Squire :
Nor by inquiry can we heare of him.
Here is *Turfe*'s house, the father of the Maid.

   III. iii. 38 Upon] Vpon *F*   III. iv. Scene II.—The Same [i. e. Kentish Town] before Turfe's House. *G*   *La: Tub. ... Puppy* one line in F

Lad. *Pol-Marten*, see, the streets are strew'd with herbes,
And here hath beene a wedding, *Wispe*, it seemes !
Pray heaven, this Bridall be not for my sonne !
Good *Marten*, knock : knock quickly : Aske for *Turfe*.
My thoughts misgive me, I am in such a doubt——
   Pol. Who keepes the house here ?   *Pup.* Why the
      doore, and wals
Doe keepe the house.   *Pol.* I aske then, who's within ?
   Pup. Not you that are without.   *Pol.* Looke forth, and
      speake
Into the street, here.   Come before my Lady.
   Pup. Before my Lady ?   Lord have mercy upon me :
If I doe come before her, shee will see
The hand-som'st man in all the Towne, pardee !
Now stand I vore her, what zaith velvet she ?
   Lad. Sirrah, whose man are you ?   *Pup.* Madam, my
      Masters.
   Lad. And who's thy Master ?   *Pup.* What you tread
      on, Madam.
   Lad. I tread on an old Turfe.   *Pup.* That *Turfe*'s my
      Master.
   Lad. A merry fellow ! what's thy name ?   *Pup.* Ball
      Puppy
They call me at home : abroad, *Hanniball Puppy*.
   Lad. Come hither, I must kisse thee, Valentine *Puppy*.
Wispe ! ha' you got you a Valentine ?   *Wis.* None,
      Madam ;
He's the first stranger that I saw.   *Lad.* To me
Hee is so, and such.   Let's share him equally.
   Pup. Helpe, helpe good Dame.   A reskue, and in time.
In stead of Bils, with Colstaves come ; in stead of Speares,
      with Spits ;
Your slices serve for slicing swords, to save me, and my wits :
A Lady, and her woman here, their Huisher eke by side,
   (But he stands mute) have plotted how your *Puppy* to
      divide.

Act III. Scene V.

To them.

D. Turfe. Maids.

D. Turfe. How now? what noise is this with you, *Ball Puppy*?

Pup. Oh Dame! And fellowes o' the Kitchin! Arme,
Arme, for my safety; if you love your *Ball*:
Here is a strange thing, call'd a Lady, a Mad-dame:
And a device of hers, yclept her woman; 5
Have plotted on me, in the Kings high-way,
To steale me from my selfe, and cut me in halfes,
To make one *Valentine* to serve 'hem both;
This for my right-side, that my left-hand love.

D. Tur. So sawcy, *Puppy*? to use no more reverence 10
Unto my Lady, and her velvet Gowne?

Lad. Turfe's wife, rebuke him not: Your man doth please me
With his conceit. Hold: there are ten old nobles,
To make thee merrier yet, halfe-*Valentine*.

Pup. I thanke you right-side: could my left as much, 15
'Twould make me a man of marke: young *Hanniball*!

Lad. Dido shall make that good; or I will for her.
Here *Dido Wispe*, there's for your *Hanniball*:
He is your Countrey-man, as well as *Valentine*.

Wis. Here Mr. *Hanniball*: my Ladies bounty 20
For her poore woman, *Wispe*. *Pup.* Brave *Carthage Queene*!
And such was *Dido*: I will ever be
Champion to her, who *Iuno* is to thee.

D. Tur. Your Ladiship is very welcome here.
Please you, good Madam, to goe nere the house. 25

Lad. Turfe's wife, I come thus farre to seeke thy husband,
Having some busines to impart unto him.
Is he at home? *D. Tur.* O no, and't shall please you:

III. v. 9 love] loves *F3*   11 Unto] Vnto *F*   17 Dido] Dido, *F, F3*

He is posted hence to *Pancridge* with a witnesse.
30 Young Justice *Bramble* has kept levell coyle
Here in our Quarters, stole away our Daughter,
And Mr. *Turfe*'s run after, as he can,
To stop the marriage, if it will be stop'd.
    Pol. Madam, these tydings are not much amisse!
35 For if the Justice have the Maid in keepe,
You need not feare the mariage of your sonne.
    Lad. That somewhat easeth my suspitious brest.
Tell me, *Turfe*'s wife, when was my sonne with *Awdrey*?
How long is't, since you saw him at your house?
40 *Pup.* Dame, let me take this rump out of your mouth.
    D. Tur. What meane you by that Sir?   *Pup.* Rumpe,
   and taile's all one.
But I would use a reverence for my Lady:
I would not zay surreverence, the tale
Out o' your mouth, but rather take the rumpe.
45 *D. Tur.* A well bred youth! and vull of favour you are.
   Pup. What might they zay, when I were gone, if I
Not weigh'd my wordz? This *Puppy* is a voole!
Great *Hanniball*'s an Asse; he had no breeding:
No Lady gay, you shall not zay,
50 That your *Val. Puppy*, was so unlucky,
In speech to faile, as t' name a taile,
Be as be may be, 'vore a faire Lady.
   Lad. Leave jesting, tell us, when you saw our sonne.
   Pup. Marry, it is two houres agoe.   *Lad.* Sin' you saw
   him?
55 *Pup.* You might have seene him too, if you had look'd up.
For it shind, as bright as day.   *Lad.* ⟨I⟩ meane my sonne.
   Pup. Your sunne, and our sunne are they not all one?
   Lad. Foole, thou mistak'st; I ask'd thee, for my sonne.
   Pup. I had thought there had beene no more sunnes, then
   one.
60 I know not what you Ladies have, or may have.
   Pol. Did'st thou nere heare, my Lady had a sonne?

    III. v. 56 I *W*   58 sonne. *corr. F*: sonne! *F originally*

Pup. She may have twenty ; but for a sonne, unlesse
She meane precisely, Squire *Tub*, her zonne,
He was here now ; and brought my Mr. word
That Justice *Bramble* had got Mrs. *Awdrey*. 65
But whither he be gone, here's none can tell.
 Lad. Marten, I wonder at this strange discourse :
The foole it seemes tels true ; my sonne the Squire
Was doubtlesse here this morning. For the match,
Ile smother what I thinke, and staying here, 70
Attend the sequell of this strange beginning.
Turfe's wife ; my people, and I will trouble thee :
Untill we heare some tidings of thy husband.
The rather, for my partie *Valentine.*

Act III.   Scene VI.

*Turfe. Awdrey. Clench. Medlay.
Pan. Scriben.*

 Tur. Well, I have carried it, and will triumph
Over this Justice, as becomes a Constable ;
And a high Constable : next our Saint *George,*
Who rescued the Kings Daughter, I will ride ;
Above Prince *Arthur.*   *Cle.* Or our *Shore-ditch* Duke. 5
 Med. Or *Pancridge* Earle.   *Pan.* Or *Bevis,* or Sir *Guy,*
Who were high Constables both.   *Cle.* One of *South-
   hampton*—.
 Med. The tother of *Warwick*-Castle.   *Tur.* You shall
   worke it
Into a storie for me, neighbour *Medlay,*
Over my Chimney.   *Scri.* I can give you Sir, 10
A *Roman* storie of a petty-Constable,
That had a Daughter, that was call'd *Virginia,*
Like Mrs. *Awdrey,* and as young as she ;
And how her Father bare him in the busines,

<small>III. v. 62 sonne *corr.* F : soune. F *originally*   71 beginning, *F3* :
beginning, F   73 Untill] Vntill F   III. vi. Scene III.—Pancras. G
(Heading) *Medlay* F3 : *Med-lay* F   6 *Pan.* F3 : *Pan* : F   *Guy,*
F3 : *Guy.* F</small>

15 'Gainst Justice *Appius*, a *Decemvir* in *Rome*,
   And Justice of Assise.   *Tur.* That, that good *D'ogenes*!
   A learned man is a Chronikell!   *Scri.* I can tell you
   A thousand, of great *Pompei'*, *Cæsar*, *Trajan*,
   All the high Constables there.   *Tur.* That was their place:
20 They were no more.   *Scr.* Dictator, and high Constable
   Were both the same.   *Med.* High Constable was more,
      tho'!
   He laid *Dick: Tator* by the heeles.   *Pan. Dick: Toter*!
   H' was one o' the Waights o' the Citie : I ha' read o' hun :
   He was a fellow would be drunke, debauch'd—
25 And he did zet un i' the stocks indeed :
   His name ⟨was⟩ *Vadian*, and a cunning Toter.
      Awd. Was ever silly Maid thus posted off?
   That should have had three husbands in one day ;
   Yet (by bad fortune) am possest of none ?
30 I went to Church to have beene wed to *Clay* ;
   Then Squire *Tub* he seiz'd me on the way,
   And thought to ha' had me : but he mist his aime ;
   And Justice *Bramble* (nearest of the three)
   Was well nigh married to me ; when by chance,
35 In rush'd my Father, and broke off that dance.
      Tur. I, Girle, there's nere a Justice on 'hem all,
   Shall teach the Constable to guard his owne :
   Let's back to *Kentish*-Towne, and there make merry ;
   These newes will be glad tidings to my wife :
40 Thou shalt have *Clay*, my wench. That word shall stand.
   Hee's found by this time, sure, or else hee's drown'd :
   The wedding dinner will be spoil'd : make haste.
      Awd. Husbands, they say, grow thick ; but thin are
      sowne.
   I care not who it be, so I have one.
45   *Tur.* I ? zay you zo ? Perhaps you shall ha' none, for
      that.
      Awd. Now out ⟨up⟩on me ! what shall I doe then ?
      Med. Sleepe Mistris *Awdrey*, dreame on proper men.

III. vi. 26 was *G*   43 sowne. *F3* : sowne, *F*   46 upon *G*

A Tale of a Tub

Act III.   Scene VII.

Hugh. Preamble.
Metaphore.   ⟨To them.⟩

Hugh. O *bone Deus*! have you seene the like?
Here was, *Hodge* hold thine eare, faire, whilst I strike.
Body o' me, how came this geare about?
  Pre. I know not, Chanon, but it fals out crosse.
Nor can I make conjecture by the circumstance   5
Of these events; it was impossible,
Being so close, and politickly carried,
To come so quickly to the eares of *Turfe*.
O Priest, had but thy slow delivery
Beene nimble, and thy lazie *Latine* tongue   10
But run the formes ore, with that swift dispatch,
As had beene requisite, all had beene well!
  Hug. What should have beene, that never lov'd the
     Friar;
But thus you see th'old *Adage* verified,
Multa cadunt inter—you can ghesse the rest.   15
Many things fall betweene the cup, and lip:
And though they touch, you are not sure to drinke.
You lack'd good fortune, wee had done our parts:
Give a man fortune, throw him i' the Sea.
The properer man, the worse luck: Stay a time;   20
Tempus edax—In time the stately Oxe, &c.
Good counsels lightly never come too late.
  Pre. You Sir will run your counsels out of breath.
  Hug. Spurre a free horse, hee'll run himselfe to death.
Sancti Evangelistæ! Here comes *Miles*!   25
  Pre. What newes man, with our new made Purs'yvant?
  Met. A Pursuyvant? would I were, or more pursie,
And had more store of money; or lesse pursie,
And had more store of breath: you call me Pursyvant!
But, I could never vant of any purse   30

  iii. vii. Scene iv.—Another part of the same [i. e. Pancras]. G
Hugh ... Metaphore one line in F   10 tongue] tongue, *F, F3*

I had, sin' yo' were my God-fathers, and God-mothers,
And ga' me that nick-name.   *Pre.* What now's the
    matter?
    Met. Nay, 'tis no matter.   I ha' beene simply beaten.
    Hugh. What is become o' the Squire, and thy Prisoner?
35 *Met.* The lines of blood, run streaming from my head,
Can speake what rule the Squire hath kept with me.
    Pre. I pray thee *Miles* relate the manner, how?
    Met. Be't knowne unto you, by these presents, then,
That I *Miles Metaphore*, your worships Clarke:
40 Have ene beene beaten, to an Allegory,
By multitude of hands.   Had they beene but
Some five or sixe, I' had whip'd 'hem all, like tops
In *Lent*, and hurl'd 'hem into *Hoblers*-hole;
Or the next ditch: I had crack'd all their costards,
45 As nimbly as a Squirrell will crack nuts:
And flourish'd like to *Hercules*, the Porter,
Among the Pages.   But, when they came on
Like Bees about a Hive, Crowes about carrion,
Flies about sweet meats; nay, like water-men
50 About a Fare: then was poore *Metaphore*
Glad to give up the honour of the day,
To quit his charge to them, and run away
To save his life, onely to tell this newes.
    Hug. How indirectly all things have falne out!
55 I cannot choose but wonder what they were
Reskued your rivall from the keepe of *Miles*:
But most of all I cannot well digest,
The manner how our purpose came to *Turfe*.
    Pre. Miles, I will see that all thy hurts be drest.
60 As for the Squires escape, it matters not:
Wee have by this meanes disappointed him;
And that was all the maine I aimed at.
But Chanon *Hugh*, now muster up thy wits,
And call thy thoughts into the Consistory.

  III. vii. 32 What *F3*: What, *F*   35 run *W*: ran *F*   46 flourish'd]
flourished *F*   Porter, *F3*: Porter *F*

A Tale of a Tub

Search all the secret corners of thy cap, 65
To find another queint devised drift,
To disappoint her mariage with this *Clay*;
Doe that, and Ile reward thee jovially.
  Hug. Well said *Magister* Justice. If I fit you not
With such a new, and well-laid stratagem, 70
As never yet your eares did heare a finer,
Call me, with Lilly, *Bos, Fur, Sus, atq; Sacerdos.*
  Pre. I heare, there's comfort in thy words yet, Chanon.
Ile trust thy regulars, and say no more.
  Met. Ile follow too. And if the dapper Priest 75
Be but as cunning, point in his devise,
As I was in my lie : my Master *Preamble*
Will stalke, as led by the nose with these new promises,
And fatted with supposes of fine hopes.

Act III. Scene VIII.

Turfe. D. Turfe. L. Tub. Pol-mart⟨en⟩. Awd⟨rey⟩.
Pup⟨py⟩.

  Tur. Well Madam, I may thanke the Squire your sonne :
For, but for him, I had beene over-reach'd.
  D. Tur. Now heavens blessing light upon his heart :
Wee are beholden to him, indeed, Madam.
  Lad. But can you not resolve me where he is ? 5
Nor about what his purposes were bent ?
  Tur. Madam, they no whit were concerning me :
And therefore was I lesse inquisitive.
  Lad. Faire maid, in faith, speake truth, and not dissemble :
Do's hee not often come, and visit you ? 10
  Awd. His worship now, and then, please you, takes paines
To see my Father, and Mother : But for me,
I know my selfe too meane for his high thoughts
To stoop at, more then asking a light question,

III. viii. Scene v.—Kentish Town. Before Turfe's House. *G* 4
indeed, *F3* : indeed *F*

15 To make him merry, or to passe his time.
    Lad. A sober Maid ! call for my woman *Marten.*
    Pol. The maids, and her halfe-*Valentine* have pli'd her
With court'sie of the Bride-Cake, and the Bowle,
As she is laid awhile.   *Lad.* O let her rest !
20 We will crosse ore to *Can*[*ter*]*bury*, in the interim ;
And so make home.   Farewell good *Turfe*, and thy wife.
I wish your daughter joy.   *Tur.* Thankes to your Ladiship,
Where is *Iohn Clay* now ?   have you seene him yet ?
    D. Tur. No, he has hid himselfe out of the way,
25 For feare o' the *Huy* and *Cry*.   *Tur.* What, walkes that shadow
Avore 'un still ? *Puppy* goe seeke 'un out,
Search all the corners that he haunts unto,
And call 'un forth. Wee'll once more to the Church,
And try our vortunes. Luck, sonne *Valentine* :
30 Where are the wise-men all of *Finzbury* ?
    Pup. Where wise-men should be ; at the Ale, and Bride-cake.
I would this couple had their destinie,
Or to be hang'd, or married out o' the way :

Enter the neigh-bours to Turfe. Man cannot get the mount'nance of an Egge-shell,
To stay his stomack. Vaith, vor mine owne part,
I have zup'd up so much broth, as would have cover'd
A legge o'Beefe, ore head and eares, i' the porredge pot :
And yet I cannot sussifie wild nature.
Would they were once dispatch'd, we might to dinner.
40 I am with child of a huge stomack, and long ;
Till by some honest Midwife-peice of Beefe,
I be deliver'd of it : I must goe now,
And hunt out for this *Kilburne* Calfe, *Iohn Clay* :
Whom where to find, I know not, nor which way.

        III. viii. 20 *Canbury* G

Act III. Scene IX.

To them.
Chanon *Hugh*, like Captaine *Thumbs*.

Hug. (Thus as a begger in a Kings disguise,
Or an old Crosse well sided with a May-pole,
Comes Chanon *Hugh*, accoutred as you see
Disguis'd *Soldado* like : marke his devise :
The Chanon, is that Captaine *Thum's*, was rob'd : 5
These bloody scars upon my face are wounds ;
This scarfe upon mine arme shewes my late hurts :
And thus am I to gull the Constable.
Now have among you, for a man at armes :)
Friends by your leave, which of you is one *Turfe* ? 10
  Tur. Sir, I am *Turfe*, if you would speake with me.
  Hug. With thee *Turfe*, if thou beest High Constable.
  Tur. I am both *Turfe*, Sir, and High Constable.
  Hug. Then *Turfe*, or *Scurfe*, high, or low Constable :
Know, I was once a Captaine at Saint *Quintins*, 15
And passing crosse the wayes over the countrey,
This morning betwixt this and *Hamsted*-Heath,
Was by a crue of Clownes rob'd, bob'd, and hurt.
No sooner had I got my wounds bound up,
But with much paine, I went to the next Justice, 20
One Mr. *Bramble* here, at *Maribone* :
And here a warrant is, which he hath directed
For you one *Turfe* ; if your name be *Tobie Turfe* ;
Who have let fall (they say) the *Huy*, and *Cry* :
And you shall answer it afore the Justice. 25
  Tur. Heaven, and Hell, Dogges, Divels, what is this ?
Neighbours, was ever Constable thus cross'd ?
What shall we doe ?   *Med.* Faith, all goe hang our selves :
I know no other way to scape the Law.
  Pup. Newes, newes, O newes—   *Tur.* What, hast thou 30
    found out *Clay* ?

III. ix. 1–9 *Aside not marked in* F   2 May-pole, *F3* : May-pole *F*

Pup. No Sir, the newes is that I cannot find him.
　　Hug. Why doe you dally, you dam'd russet coat,
　You Peasant, nay you Clowne, you Constable ;
　See that you bring forth the suspected partie,
35 Or by mine honour (which I won in field)
　Ile make you pay for it, afore the Justice.
　　Tur. Fie, fie ; O wife, I'am now in a fine pickle.
　He that was most suspected is not found ;
　And which now makes me thinke, he did the deed,
40 He thus absents him, and dares not be seene.
　Captaine, my innocence will plead for me.
　Wife, I must goe, needs, whom the Divell drives :
　Pray for me wife, and daughter ; pray for me.
　　Hug. Ile lead the way : (Thus is the match put off,
45 And if my plot succeed, as I have laid it,
　My Captaine-ship shall cost him many a crowne.)

They goe out.　　*D. Tur.* So, wee have brought our egges to a faire Market.
　Out on that villaine *Clay* : would he doe a robbery ?
　Ile nere trust smooth'fac'd Tile-man for his sake.

They goe out.　　*Awd.* Mother, the still Sow eates up all the draffe.
　　Pup. Thus is my Master, *Toby Turfe*, the patterne
　Of all the painefull a'ventures, now in print.
　I never could hope better of this match :
　This Bride-ale : For the night before to day,
55 (Which is within mans memory, I take it)
　At the report of it, an Oxe did speake ;
　Who dy'd soone after : A Cow lost her Calfe :
　The Belwether was flead for't : A fat Hog
　Was sing'd, and wash'd, and shaven all over ; to
60 Looke ugly 'gainst this day : The Ducks they quak'd ;
　The Hens too cackled : at the noise whereof,
　A Drake was seene to dance a headlesse round :
　The Goose was cut i' the head, to heare it too :
　Brave *Chant-it-cleare,* his noble heart was done ;
65 His combe was cut : And two or three o' his wives,
　Or fairest Concubines, had their necks broke,

　　　　III. ix. 44–6 *Aside not marked in* F

Ere they would zee this day : To marke the verven
Heart of a beast, the very Pig, the Pig,
This very mornin, as hee was a rosting,
Cry'd out his eyes, and made a show as hee would   70
Ha' bit in two the spit, as he would say ;
There shall no rost-meat be this dismall day.
And zure, I thinke, if I had not got his tongue
Betweene my teeth, and eate it, he had spoke it.
Well, I will in, and cry too ; never leave   75
Crying, untill our maids may drive a Buck
With my salt teares at the next washing day.

ACT IV. SCENE I.

Preamble. Hugh. Turfe. Metaphor.

Pre. KEepe out those fellowes ; Ile ha' none come in,
But the High Constable, the man of peace,
And the Queenes Captaine, the brave man of warre.
Now neighbour *Turfe*, the cause why you are call'd,
Before me by my warrant, but unspecified,   5
Is this ; and pray you marke it thoroughly !
Here is a Gentleman, and as it seemes,
Both of good birth, faire speech, and peaceable,
Who was this morning rob'd here in the wood :
You for your part a man of good report,   10
Of credit, landed, and of faire demeanes,
And by authority, high Constable ;
Are notwithstanding touch'd in this complaint,
Of being carelesse in the *Huy* and *Cry*.
I cannot choose but grieve a Soldiers losse :   15
And I am sory too for your neglect,
Being my neighbour ; this is all I object.

Hug. This is not all ; I can alledge far more,
And almost urge him for an accessorie.
Good Mr. Justice gi' me leave to speake,   20

    III. ix. 69 rosting,] roasting, *F3* : rosting *F*   73 if] If *F*   IV. i.
Maribone. A Room in Justice Preamble's House. *G*

For I am Plaintife. Let not neighbour-hood
Make him secure, or stand on priviledge.
   Pre. Sir, I dare use no partiality :
Object then what you please, so it be truth.
25   *Hug.* This more : and which is more, then he can answer,
Beside his letting fall the *Huy*, and *Cry*,
He doth protect the man, charg'd with the felonie,
And keepes him hid I heare, within his house,
Because he is affied unto his Daughter.
30   *Tur.* I doe defie 'hun, so shall shee doe too.
I pray your worships favour, le' me have hearing.
I doe convesse, 'twas told me such a velonie,
And't not disgriev'd me a little when 'twas told me,
Vor I was going to Church, to marry *Awdrey* :
35 And who should marry her, but this very *Clay*,
Who was charg'd to be the chiefe theife o' hun all.
Now I (the halter stick me, if I tell
Your worships any leazins) did fore-thinke 'un
The truest man, till he waz run away.
40 I thought, I had had 'un as zure as in a zaw-pit,
Or i' mine Oven. Nay, i' the Towne-pound.
I was zo sure o' hun : I'ld ha' gi'n my life for 'un,
Till he did start. But now, I zee 'un guilty,
Az var as I can looke at 'un. Would you ha' more ?
45   *Hug.* Yes, I will have Sir what the Law will give me.
You gave your word to see him safe, forth comming ;
I challenge that : But, that is forfeited ;
Beside, your carelesnesse in the pursuit,
Argues your slacknesse, and neglect of dutie,
50 Which ought be punish'd with severity.
   Pre. He speakes but reason *Turfe*. Bring forth the man,
And you are quit : But otherwise, your word
Binds you to make amends for all his losse,
And thinke your selfe befriended, if he take it
55 Without a farder suit, or going to law.

    IV. i. 26 *Cry*, *F3* : *Cry F*   37 tell *F3* : tell, *F*   38 leazins)]
Leazins] *F3* : leazins *F*   42 zo *G* : za *F*, *F3*

Come to a composition with him, *Turfe* :
The Law is costly, and will draw on charge.
 Tur. Yes, I doe know, I vurst mun vee a Returney,
And then make legges to my great man o' Law,
To be o' my counsell, and take trouble-vees,   60
And yet zay nothing vor me, but devise
All district meanes, to ransackle me o' my money.
A Pest'lence prick the throats o' hun. I doe know hun
As well az I waz i' their bellies, and brought up there.
What would you ha' me doe ? what would you aske of me ? 65
 Hug. I aske the restitution of my money ;
And will not bate one penny o' the summe :
Foure score, and five pound. I aske, besides,
Amendment for my hurts ; my paine, and suffering
Are losse enough for me, Sir, to sit downe with ;   70
Ile put it to your worship ; what you award me,
Ile take ; and gi' him a generall release.
 Pre. And what say you now, neighbour *Turfe* ?   *Tur.*
  I put it
Ene to your worships bitterment, hab, nab.
I shall have a chance o'the dice for't, I hope, let 'hem ene 75
  run : And—
 Pre. Faith then Ile pray you, 'cause he is my neighbour,
To take a hundred pound, and give him day.
 Hug. Saint *Valentines* day, I will, this very day,
Before Sunne set : my bond is forfeit else.
 Tur. Where will you ha'it paid ? *Hug.* Faith, I am a 80
  stranger
Here i' the countrey : Know you Chanon *Hugh*,
The Vicar of *Pancrace* ? *Tur.* Yes, wee—who not him ?
 Hug. Ile make him my Attorney to receive it,
And give you a discharge. *Tur.* Whom shall I send for't ?
 Pre. Why, if you please, send *Metaphore* my Clarke. 85
And *Turfe*, I much commend thy willingnesse ;
It's argument of thy integrity.

 IV. i. 68 I] And I *G*   82 wee—who not] wee who not *F* : who knows not *W*

Tur. But, my integrity shall be my zelfe still :
Good Mr. *Metaphore,* give my wife this key ;
90 And doe but whisper it into her hand :
(She knowes it well inow) bid her, by that
Deliver you the two zeal'd bags o' silver,
That lie i' the corner o' the cup-bord, stands
At my bed-side, they'are viftie pound a peece ;
95 And bring 'hem to your Master.   *Met.* If I prove not
As just a Carrier as my friend *Tom Long* was,
Then call me his curtall, change my name of *Miles,*
To *Guile's, Wile's, Pile's, Bile's,* or the foulest name
You can devise, to crambe with, for ale.
100   *Hug.* Come hither *Miles,* bring by that token, too,
Faire *Awdrey* ; say her father sent for her :
Say *Clay* is found, and waits at *Pancrace* Church,
Where I attend to marry them in haste.
For (by this meanes) *Miles* I may say't to thee,
105 Thy Master must to *Awdrey* married be.
But not a word but mum : goe get thee gone ;
Be warie of thy charge, and keepe it close.
    Met. O super-dainty Chanon ! Vicar in cóney,
Make no delay, *Miles,* but away.
110 And bring the wench, and money.
    Hug. Now Sir, I see you meant but honestly ;
And, but that busines cals me hence away,
I would not leave you, till the sunne were lower.
But Mr. Justice, one word, Sir, with you.
115 By the same token, is your Mistris sent for
By *Metaphore* your Clarke, as from her Father.
Who when she comes, Ile marry her to you,
Vnwitting to this *Turfe,* who shall attend
Me at the parsonage. This was my plot :
120 Which I must now make good ; turne Chanon, againe,
In my square cap. I humbly take my leave.
    Pre. Adieu, good Captaine. Trust me, neighbour *Turfe,*
He seemes to be a sober Gentleman :

        IV. i. 99 crambe] crambo *W*   108 in cóney] incony *G*

But this distresse hath somewhat stir'd his patience.
And men, you know, in such extremities,   125
Apt not themselves to points of courtesie ;
I' am glad you ha' made this end.   *Tur.* You stood my
   friend :
I thanke your Justice-worship ; pray you be
Prezent anone, at tendring o' the money,
And zee me have a discharge : Vor I ha' no craft   130
I' your Law quiblins.   *Pre.* Ile secure you, neighbour.

The *Scene* interloping.

Medlay. Clench. Pan. Scriben.

Med. Indeed, there is a woundy luck in names, Sirs,
And a maine mysterie, an' a man knew where
To vind it. My God-sires name, Ile tell you,
Was *In-and-In Shittle*, and a Weaver he was,
And it did fit his craft : for so his Shittle   5
Went in, and in, still : this way, and then that way.
And he nam'd me, *In-and-In Medlay* : which serves
A Joyners craft, bycause that wee doe lay
Things in and in, in our worke. But, I am truly
Architectonicus professor, rather :   10
That is (as one would zay) an Architect.
   Cle. As I am a Varrier, and a Visicarie :
Horse-smith of *Hamsted*, and the whole Towne Leach—.
   Med. Yes, you ha' done woundy cures, Gossip *Clench*.
   Cle. An' I can zee the stale once, through a Urine-hole, 15
Ile give a shrew'd ghesse, be it man, or beast.
I cur'd an Ale-wife once, that had the staggers
Worse then five horses, without rowelling.
My God-phere was a *Rabian*, or a *Iew*,
(You can tell *D'oge* !) They call'd un Doctor *Rasi*.   20
   Scr. One *Rasis* was a great *Arabick* Doctor.
   Cle. Hee was King *Harry*'s Doctor, and my God-phere.
   Pan. Mine was a merry *Greeke, To-Pan*, of *Twyford* :

The Scene interloping] Scene ii.—The Country near Maribone. *G*
15 Urine] Vrine *F*

A joviall Tinker, and a stopper of holes;
25 Who left me mettall-man of *Belsise*, his heire.
    Med. But what was yours *D'oge*?   *Scr.* Vaith, I cannot tell
If mine were kyrsind, or no. But, zure hee had
A kyrsin name, that he left me, *Diogenes*.
A mighty learned man, but pest'lence poore.
30 Vor, h' had no house, save an old *Tub*, to dwell in,
(I vind that in records) and still he turn'd it
I' the winds teeth, as't blew on his back-side,
And there they would lie rowting one at other,
A weeke, sometimes.   *Med.* Thence came *A Tale of a Tub*;
35 And the virst *Tale of a Tub*, old *D'ogenes Tub*.
    Scr. That was avore Sir *Peter Tub*, or his Lady.
    Pan. I, or the Squire their sonne, *Tripoli Tub*.
    Cle. The Squire is a fine Gentleman!   *Med.* He is more:
A Gentleman and a halfe; almost a Knight;
40 Within zixe inches: That's his true measure.
    Cle. Zure, you can gage 'hun.   *Med.* To a streake, or lesse:
I know his d'ameters, and circumference:
A Knight is sixe diameters; and a Squire
Is vive, and zomewhat more: I know't by compasse,
45 And skale of man. I have upo' my rule here,
The just perportions of a Knight, a Squire;
With a tame Justice, or an Officer, rampant,
Upo' the bench, from the high Constable
Downe to the Head-borough, or Tithing-man;
50 Or meanest Minister o' the peace, God save 'un.
    Pan. Why, you can tell us by the Squire, Neighbour,
Whence he is call'd a Constable, and whaffore.
    Med. No, that's a booke-case: *Scriben* can doe that.
That's writing and reading, and records.   *Scr.* Two words,
55 *Cyning* and *Staple*, make a Constable:
As wee'd say, A hold, or stay for the King.
    Cle. All Constables are truly *Iohn's* for the King,

        48 Upo'] Vpo' F

What ere their names are ; be they *Tony*, or *Roger*.
   Med. And all are sworne, as vingars o' one hand,
To hold together 'gainst the breach o' the peace ;   60
The High Constable is the Thumbe, as one would zay,
The hold-fast o' the rest.   *Pan.* Pray luck he speed
Well i' the busines, beweene Captaine *Thums*,
And him.   *Med.* Ile warrant 'un for a groat :
I have his measures here in Rithmetique.   65
How he should beare un selfe in all the lines
Of's place, and office : Let's zeeke 'un out.

Act IIII.   Scene II.

Tub. Hilts.
   ⟨To them.⟩
Metaphor.

   Tub. Hilts, how do'st thou like o' this our good dayes
     worke ?
   Hil. As good ene nere a whit, as nere the better.
   Tub. Shall we to *Pancridge*, or to *Kentish-Towne, Hilts* ?
   Hil. Let *Kentish-Towne*, or *Pancridge* come to us,
If either will : I will goe home againe.   5
   Tub. Faith *Basket*, our successe hath beene but bad,
And nothing prospers, that wee undertake ;
For we can neither meet with *Clay*, nor *Awdrey*,
The Chanon *Hugh*, nor *Turfe* the Constable :
We are like men that wander in strange woods,   10
And loose our selves in search of them wee seeke.
   Hil. This was because wee rose on the wrong side :
But as I am now here, just in the mid-way,
Ile zet my sword on the pommell, and that line
The point valles too, wee'll take : whether it be   15
To *Kentish-Towne*, the Church, or home againe.
   Tub. Stay, stay thy hand : here's Justice *Brambles* Enter
     Clarke,   Metaphor.

---

iv. ii. Scene iii.—The Country near Kentish Town. G   Tub . . .
Metaphor one line in F   4 *Hil.* F 3 : *Hit.* F

The unlucky Hare hath crost us all this day.
Ile stand aside whilst thou pump'st out of him
20 His busines, *Hilts*; and how hee's now employ'd.
    Hil. Let mee alone, Ile use him in his kind.
    Met. Oh for a Pad-horse, Pack-horse, or a Post-horse,
To beare me on his neck, his back, or his croupe!
I am as weary with running, as a Mil-horse
25 That hath led the Mill once, twice, thrice about,
After the breath hath beene out of his body.
I could get up upon a pannier, a pannell,
Or, to say truth, a very Pack-sadle,
Till all my honey were turn'd into gall,
30 And I could sit in the seat no longer:
Oh ⟨for⟩ the legs of a lackey now, or a foot-man,
Who is the Surbater of a Clarke currant,
And the confounder of his treslesse dormant.
But who have we here, just in the nick?
35   *Hil.* I am neither nick, nor in the nick: therefore
You lie Sir *Metaphor*.   *Met.* Lye? how?   *Hil.* Lye so Sir.

He strikes up his heeles.
    Met. I lye not yet i' my throat.   *Hil.* Thou ly'st o' the ground.
Do'st thou know me?   *Met.* Yes, I did know you too late.
    Hil. What is my name then?   *Met. Basket. Hil. Basket?* what?
40   *Met. Basket*, the Great—   *Hil.* The Great? what?   *Met.* Lubber—
I should say Lover, of the Squire his Master.
    Hil. Great is my patience, to forbeare thee thus,
Thou Scrape-hill Skoundrell, and thou skum of man;
Uncivill, orenge-tawny-coated Clarke:
45 Thou cam'st but halfe a thing into the world,
And wast made up of patches, parings, shreds:
Thou, that when last thou wert put out of service,
Travaild'st to *Hamsted* Heath, on a *Ash-we'nsday*,
Where thou didst stand sixe weekes the *Iack* of *Lent*,

iv. ii. 20 employ'd] employed *F*   29 Gall, *F3*: gall; *F*   30 longer: *F3*: longer, *F*   31 for *G*   43 scrape-hill *G*: Scrape-hill, *F, F3*
44 Uncivill] Vncivill *F*   49 weekes *corr. F*: weekes, *F originally*

For boyes to hoorle, three throwes a penny, at thee, 50
To make thee a purse : Seest thou this, bold bright blade ?
This sword shall shred thee as small unto the grave,
As minc'd meat for a pie. Ile set thee in earth
All save thy head, and thy right arme at liberty,
To keepe thy hat off, while I question thee, 55
What ? why ? and whether thou wert going now
With a face, ready to breake out with busines ?
And tell me truly, lest I dash't in peeces.
 Met. Then *Basket* put thy smiter up, and heare ;
I dare not tell the truth to a drawne sword. 60
 Hil. 'Tis sheath'd, stand up, speake without feare, or wit.
 Met. I know not what they meane ; but Constable *Turfe*
Sends here his key ; for monies in his cubbard,
Which he must pay the Captaine, that was rob'd
This morning. Smell you nothing ? *Hil.* No, not I ; 65
Thy breeches yet are honest. *Met.* As my mouth.
Doe you not smell a rat ? I tell you truth,
I thinke all's knavery : For the Chanon whisper'd
Me in the eare, when *Turfe* had gi'n me his key,
By the same token to bring Mrs. *Awdrey*, 70
As sent for thither ; and to say *Iohn Clay*
Is found, which is indeed to get the wench
Forth for my Master, who is to be married,
When she comes there : The Chanon has his rules
Ready, and all there to dispatch the matter. 75
 Tub. Now on my life, this is the Chanon's plot !
Miles, I have heard all thy discourse to *Basket*.
Wilt thou be true, and Ile reward thee well,
To make me happy, in my Mistris *Awdrey* ?
 Met. Your worship shall dispose of *Metaphore*, 80
Through all his parts, ene from the sole o' the head,
To the crowne o' the foot, to manage of your service.
 Tub. Then doe thy message to the Mistris *Turfe*,

 iv. ii. 51 this, *corr. F*: this *F originally* blade ? *corr. F*: blade, *F
originally* 52 thee *corr. F*: thee, *F originally* 59 heare; *corr. F*:
heare, *F originally* 63 cubbard,] Cubbard, *F3* : cubbard *F* 65 I;
corr. F: I, *F originally*

Tell her thy token, bring the money hither,
85 And likewise take young *Awdrey* to thy charge :
Which done, here, *Metaphore*, wee will attend,
And intercept thee. And for thy reward,
You two shall share the money ; I the Maid :
If any take offence, Ile make all good.
90   *Met.* But shall I have halfe the money Sir, in faith ?
    Tub. I on my Squire-ship, shalt thou : and my land.
    Met. Then, if I make not, Sir, the cleanliest scuse
To get her hither, and be then as carefull
To keepe her for you, as't were for my selfe :
95 Downe o' your knees, and pray that honest *Miles*
May breake his neck ere he get ore two stiles.

Act IV. Scene III.

Tub. Hilts.

  Tub. Make haste then : we will wait here thy returne.
This luck unlook'd for, hath reviv'd my hopes,
Which were opprest with a darke melancholly.
In happy time, we linger'd on the way,
5 To meet these summons of a better sound,
Which are the essence of my soules content.
  Hil. This heartlesse fellow ; shame to serving-men ;
Staine of all livories ; what feare makes him doe !
How sordid, wretched, and unworthy things ;
10 Betray his Masters secrets, ope the closet
Of his devises, force the foolish Justice,
Make way for your Love, plotting of his owne :
Like him that digs a trap, to catch another,
And falls into't himselfe !   *Tub.* So wou'd I have it.
15 And hope 'twill prove a jest to twit the Justice with.
  Hil. But that this poore white-liver'd Rogue should do't ?
And meerely out of feare ?   *Tub.* And hope of money, *Hilts*.
A valiant man will nible at that bait.
  Hil. Who, but a foole, will refuse money proffer'd ?
20   *Tub.* And sent by so good chance. Pray heaven he speed.

Hil. If he come empty-handed, let him count
To goe back empty-headed ; Ile not leave him
So much of braine in's pate, with pepper and vinegar,
To be serv'd in for sawce, to a Calves head.
 Tub. Thou serv'st him rightly, *Hilts.* *Hil.* Ile scale az 25
  much
With my hand, as I dare say now with my tongue ;
But if you get the Lasse from *Dargison,*
What will you doe with her ? *Tub.* Wee'll thinke o' that
When once wee have her in possession, Governour.

Act IV.   Scene IV.

 Puppy.   Metaphore.   Awdrey.
 Pup. You see wee trust you, Mr. *Metaphore,*
With Mrs. *Awdrey* : pray you use her well,
As a Gentle-woman should be us'd. For my part,
I doe incline a little to the serving-man ;
Wee have been of a coat—I had one like yours :   5
Till it did play me such a sleevelesse errand,
As I had nothing where to put mine armes in,
And then I threw it off. Pray you goe before her,
Serving-man-like : and see that your nose drop not.
As for example : you shall see me : marke,   10
How I goe afore her. So doe you : sweet *Miles.*
She for her owne part, is a woman cares not
What man can doe unto her, in the way
Of honesty, and good manners. So farewell
Faire Mrs. *Awdrey* : Farewell Mr. *Miles.*   15
I ha' brought you thus farre, onward o' your way :
I must goe back now to make cleane the roomes,
Where my good Lady has beene. Pray you commend mee
To Bride-groome *Clay* ; and bid him beare up stiffe.
 Met. Thanke you good *Hanniball Puppy* ; I shall fit 20

 iv. iii. 21 empty-handed *F3* : empty-headed *F*   iv. iv. Another
part of the same [i. e. the Country near Kentish Town]. *G*   11 *Miles.*]
Miles, F

The leg of your commands, with the straight buskins
Of dispatch presently.   *Pup.* Farewell fine *Metaphore.*
   Met. Come gentle Mistris, will you please to walke?
   Awd. I love not to be led : I'd goe alone.
25   *Met.* Let not the mouse of my good meaning, Lady,
Be snap'd up in the trap of your suspition,
To loose the taile there, either of her truth,
Or swallow'd by the Cat of misconstruction.
   Awd. You are too finicall for me ; speake plaine Sir.

Act IV.   Scene V.

Tub.   Awdrey.   Hilts.   Metaphore.
To them.
Lady.   Pol-marten.

   Tub. Welcome againe my *Awdrey* : welcome Love :
You shall with me ; in faith deny me not.
I cannot brook the second hazzard Mistris.
   Awd. Forbeare Squire *Tub,* as mine owne mother sayes,
5 I am not for your mowing.   Youle be flowne
Ere I be fledge.   *Hil.* Hast thou the money *Miles* ?
   Met. Here are two bags, there's fiftie pound in each.
   Tub. Nay *Awdrey,* I possesse you for this time :
Sirs ; Take that coyne betweene you, and divide it.
10 My pretty sweeting give me now the leave
To challenge love, and marriage at your hands.
   Awd. Now, out upon you, are you not asham'd ?
What will my Lady say ?   In faith I thinke
She was at our house :   And I thinke shee ask'd for you :
15 And I thinke she hit me i' th' teeth with you,
I thanke her Ladiship, and I thinke she meanes
Not to goe hence, till she has found you.   How say you ?
   Tub. Was then my Lady Mother at your house ?
Let's have a word aside.   *Awd.* Yes, twenty words.
20   *Lad.* 'Tis strange, a motion, but I know not what,
Comes in my mind, to leave the way to *Totten,*

IV. v. 17, 18 How say you ? *Tub.*] *Tub.* How say you ? *W*

And turne to *Kentish-Towne*, againe, my journey:
And see my sonne *Pol-marten* with his *Awdrey*:
Erewhile we left her at her fathers house:
And hath he thence remov'd her in such haste!   25
What shall I doe? shall I speake faire, or chide?
  Pol. Madam, your worthy sonne, with dutious care,
Can governe his affections: Rather then
Breake off their conference some other way,
Pretending ignorance of what you know.   30
  Tub. And this ⟨is⟩ all, faire *Awdrey*: I am thine.
  Lad. Mine you were once, though scarcely now your own.
  Hil. 'Slid my Lady! my Lady! *Met.* Is this my Lady
    bright?
  Tub. Madam, you tooke me now a little tardie.
  Lad. At prayers, I thinke you were: what, so devout   35
Of late, that you will shrive you to all Confessors
You meet by chance? Come, goe with me, good Squire,
And leave your linnen: I have now a busines,
And of importance, to impart unto you.
  Tub. Madam, I pray you, spare me but an houre;   40
Please you to walke before, I follow you.
  Lad. It must be now, my busines lies this way.
  Tub. Will not an houre hence, Madam, excuse me?
  Lad. Squire, these excuses argue more your guilt.
You have some new device now, to project,   45
Which the poore Tile-man scarce will thanke you for.
What? will you goe? *Tub.* I ha' tane a charge upon me,
To see this Maid conducted to her Father,
Who, with the Chanon *Hugh*, staies her at *Pancrace*,
To see her married to the same *Iohn Clay*.   50
  Lad. Tis very well; but Squire take you no care.
Ile send *Pol-marten* with her, for that office:
You shall along with me; it is decreed.
  Tub. I have a little busines, with a friend Madam.
  Lad. That friend shall stay for you, or you for him.   55

  IV. v. 22 againe,] againe *F*, *F3*   28 then] than *F3*   29 con-
ference] Conference, *F3*   31 is] be *W*

Pol-marten ; Take the Maiden to your care ;
Commend me to her Father.   *Tub.* I will follow you.
   Lad. Tut, tell not me of following.   *Tub.* Ile but speake
A word.   *Lad.* No whispering : you forget your selfe,
60 And make your love too palpable : A Squire ?
And thinke so meanely ? fall upon a Cow-shard ?
You know my mind. Come, Ile to *Turfe*'s house,
And see for *Dido*, and our *Valentine*.

<small>They all goe out but Pol-marten and Awdrey.</small>   *Pol-marten*, looke to your charge ; Ile looke to mine.
   Pol. (I smile to thinke after so many proffers
This Maid hath had, she now should fall to me :
That I should have her in my custody :
Twere but a mad trick to make the essay,
And jumpe a match with her immediately :
70 She's faire, and handsome : and shee's rich enough :
Both time, and place minister faire occasion :
Have at it then :) Faire Lady, can you love ?
   Awd. No Sir, what's that ? *Pol.* A toy, which women
use.
   Awd. If't be a toy, it's good to play withall.
75 *Pol.* Wee will not stand discoursing o' the toy :
The way is short, please you to prov't Mistris ?
   Awd. If you doe meane to stand so long upon it ;
I pray you let me give it a short cut, Sir.
   Pol. It's thus, faire Maid : Are you dispos'd to marry ?
80 *Awd.* You are dispos'd to aske. *Pol.* Are you to grant ?
   Awd. Nay, now I see you are dispos'd indeed.
   Pol. (I see the wench wants but a little wit ;
And that defect her wealth may well supply :)
In plaine termes, tell me, Will you have me *Awdrey* ?
85 *Awd.* In as plaine termes, I tell you who would ha' me.
Iohn Clay would ha' me; but he hath too hard hands ;
I like not him : besides, hee is a thiefe.
And Justice *Bramble*, he would faine ha' catch'd me :
But the young Squire, hee, rather then his life,
90 Would ha' me yet ; and make me a Lady, hee sayes,

<small>IV. v. 65–72, 82–3, *Asides not marked in* F   83 defect] Defect, *F3*</small>

A Tale of a Tub

And be my Knight; to doe me true Knights service,
Before his Lady Mother. Can you make me
A Lady, would I ha' you? *Pol.* I can gi' you
A silken Gowne, and a rich Petticoat:
And a french Hood. (All fooles love to be brave: 95
I find her humour, and I will pursue it.)

Act IIII. Scene VI.

Lady. D. Turfe. Squire Tub. Hilts.
⟨To them.⟩
Puppy. Clay.

Lad. And as I told thee, shee was intercepted
By the Squire here, my sonne: and this bold Ruffin
His man, who safely would have carried her
Unto her Father; and the Chanon *Hugh*;
But for more care of the security, 5
My Huisher hath her now, in his grave charge.
 D. Tur. Now on my faith, and holy-dom, we are
Beholden to your worship. She's a Girle,
A foolish Girle, and soone may tempted be:
But if this day passe well once ore her head, 10
Ile wish her trust to her selfe. For I have beene
A very mother to her, though I say it.
 Tub. Madam, 'tis late, and *Pancridge* is i' your way:
I thinke your Ladiship forgets your selfe.
 Lad. Your mind runs much on *Pancridge*. Well, young 15
   Squire,
The black Oxe never trod yet o' your foot:
These idle Phant'sies will forsake you one day.
Come Mrs. *Turfe*, will you goe take a walke
Over the fields to *Pancridge*, to your husband?
 D. Tur. Madam, I had beene there an houre agoe: 20
But that I waited on my man *Ball Puppy*.
What *Ball* I say? I thinke the idle slouch
Be falne asleepe i' the barne, he stayes so long.

iv. v. 95–6 *Aside not marked in* F   iv. vi. Scene v.—Kentish Town.
G   4 Unto] Vnto F   16 yet *corr.* F: yet, F *originally*   o' F3: O F

  Pup. Sattin, i' the name of velvet-*Sattin*, Dame!
25 The Divell! O the Divell is in the barne:
Helpe, helpe, a legion—Spirit Legion,
Is in the barne! in every straw a Divell.
  ⟨*D.*⟩ *Tur.* Why do'st thou bawle so *Puppy*? Speake, what ailes thee?
  Pup. My name's *Ball Puppy*, I ha' seene the Divell
30 Among the straw: O for a Crosse! a Collop
Of Friar *Bacon*, or a conjuring stick
Of Doctor *Faustus*! Spirits are in the barne.
  Tub. How! Spirits in the barne? *Basket*, goe see.
  Hil. Sir, an' you were my Master ten times over,
35 And Squire to boot; I know, and you shall pardon me:
Send me 'mong Divels? I zee you love me not:
Hell be at their game: Ile not trouble them.
  Tub. Goe see; I warrant thee there's no such matter.
  Hil. An' they were Giants, 't were another matter.
40 But Divells! No, if I be torne in peeces,
What is your warrant worth? Ile see the Feind
Set fire o' the barne, ere I come there.
  D. Tur. Now all Zaints blesse us, and if he be there,
He is an ugly spright, I warrant. *Pup.* As ever
45 Held flesh-hooke, Dame, or handled fire-forke rather:
They have put me in a sweet pickle, Dame:
But that my Lady-*Valentine* smels of muske,
I should be asham'd to presse into this presence.
  Lad. Basket, I pray thee see what is the miracle!
50 *Tub.* Come, goe with me: Ile lead. Why stand'st thou man?
  Hil. Cocks pretious Master, you are not mad indeed?
You will not goe to hell before your time?
  Tub. Why art thou thus afraid? *Hil.* No, not afraid:
But by your leave, Ile come no neare the barne.
55 ⟨*D.*⟩ *Tur. Puppy*! wilt thou goe with me? *Pup.* How? goe with you?

  IV. vi. 26 a legion—Spirit Legion *F 3*: a legion—Spirit legion *F*: a legion of spirits, a legion *G*

Whither, into the Barne? To whom, the Divell?
Or to doe what there? to be torne 'mongst 'hum?
Stay for my Master, the High Constable,
Or *In-and-In*, the Head-borough; let them goe,
Into the Barne with warrant; seize the Feind;   60
And set him in the stocks for his ill rule:
'Tis not for me that am but flesh and blood,
To medle with 'un. Vor I cannot, nor I wu' not.
   Lad. I pray thee *Tripoly*, looke, what is the matter?
   Tub. That shall I Madam.   *Hil.* Heaven protect my 65
    Master.
I tremble every joynt till he be back.
   Pup. Now, now, even now they are tearing him in peeces:
Now are they tossing of his legs, and armes,
Like Loggets at a Peare-tree: Ile to the hole,
Peepe in, and looke whether he lives or dies.   70
   Hil. I would not be i' my Masters coat for thousands.
   Pup. Then pluck it off, and turne thy selfe away.
O the Divell! the Divell! the Divell!   *Hil.* Where
   man? where?
   D. Tur. Alas that ever wee were borne. So neere too?
   Pup. The Squire hath him in his hand, and leads him 75
Out by the Collar.   *D. Tur.* O this is *Iohn Clay*.
   Lad. Iohn Clay at *Pancrace*, is there to be married.
   Tub. This was the spirit reveld i' the Barne.
   Pup. The Divell hee was: was this he was crawling
Among the Wheat-straw? Had it beene the Barley,   80
I should ha' tane him for the Divell in drinke;
The Spirit of the Bride-ale: But poore *Iohn*,
Tame *Iohn* of *Clay*, that sticks about the bung-hole—
   Hil. If this be all your Divell, I would take
In hand to conjure him: But hell take me   85
If ere I come in a right Divels walke,
If I can keepe me out on't.   *Tub.* Well meant *Hilts*.
   Lad. But how came *Clay* thus hid here i' the straw,
When newes was brought, to you all, hee was at *Pancridge*;

        IV. vi. 89 all, *F3* : all *F*

90 And you beleev'd it ?   *D. Tur.* Justice *Brambles* man
   Told me so, Madam : And by that same token,
   And other things, he had away my Daughter,
   And two seal'd bags of money.   *Lad.* Where's the Squire ?
   Is hee gone hence ?   *Tub.* H' was here Madam, but now.
95 *Clay.* Is the *Huy* and *Cry* past by ?   *Pup.* I, I, *Iohn Clay.*
   Clay. And am I out of danger to be hang'd ?
   Pup. Hang'd *Iohn* ? yes sure ; unlesse, as with the Proverbe,
   You meane to make the choice of your own gallowes.
   Cla. Nay, then all's well, hearing your newes *Ball Pupy,*
100 You ha' brought from *Paddington,* I ene stole home here,
   And thought to hide me, in the Barne ere since.
   Pup. O wonderfull ! and newes was brought us here,
   You were at *Pancridge,* ready to be married.
   Cla. No faith, I nere was furder then the Barne.
105 *D. Tur.* Haste *Puppy.* Call forth Mistris *Dido Wispe,*
   My Ladies Gentle-woman, to her Lady ;
   And call your selfe forth, and a couple of maids,
   To waite upon me : we are all undone !
   My Lady is undone ! her fine young sonne,
110 The Squire is got away.   *Lad.* Haste, haste, good *Valentine.*
   D. Tur. And you *Iohn Clay* ; you are undone too ! All !
   My husband is undone, by a true key,
   But a false token : And my selfe's undone,
   By parting with my Daughter, who'll be married
115 To some body, that she should not, if wee haste not.

IV. vi. 104 furder] further *F3*

ACT V. SCENE I.

Tub. Pol-marten.

Tub. I Pray thee good *Pol-marten,* shew thy diligence,
And faith in both : Get her, but so disguis'd,
The Chanon may not know her, and leave me
To plot the rest : I will expect thee here.
   Pol. You shall Squire. Ile performe it with all care,   5
If all my Ladies Ward-robe will disguise her.
Come Mistris *Awdrey.*   *Awd.* Is the Squire gone ?
   Pol. Hee'll meet us by and by, where he appointed :
You shall be brave anone, as none shall know you.

ACT V. SCENE II.

Clench. Medlay. Pan. Scriben.
                                         To them.
        Tub. Hilts.

Cle. I wonder, where the Queenes High Constable is !
I veare, they ha' made 'hun away.   *Med.* No zure ; The
    Justice
Dare not conzent to that. Hee'll zee'un forth comming.
   Pan. He must, vor wee can all take corpulent oath,
Wee zaw 'un goe in there.   *Scr.* I, upon record !   5
The Clock dropt twelve at *Maribone.*   *Med.* You are
    right, *D'oge* !
Zet downe to a minute, now 'tis a'most vowre.
   Cle. Here comes Squire *Tub.*   *Scr.* And's Governour,
    Mr. *Basket*
Hilts, doe you know 'hun, a valiant wise vellow !
Az tall a man on his hands, as goes on veet.   10
Blesse you Mass' *Basket.*   *Hil.* Thanke you good *D'oge.*
   Tub. Who's that ?

    v. i. The Fields near Kentish Town. *G*   v. ii. Scene II.—Kentish
Town. *G*   (Heading) *Tub.*] *Tub* F : *Tub,* F3   8 *Basket* F3 :
Basket. F   11 Who's *F3* : who's *F*

    Hil. D'oge Scriben, the great Writer Sir of *Chalcot*.
    Tub. And, who the rest?   *Hil.* The wisest heads o' the
      hundred.
Medlay the *Ioyner*, Head-borough of *Islington*,
15 *Pan* of *Belsize*, and *Clench* the Leach of *Hamsted*.
The High Constables Counsell, here of *Finsbury*.
    Tub. Prezent me to 'hem, *Hilts*, Squire *Tub* of *Totten*.
    Hil. Wise men of *Finsbury* : make place for a Squire,
I bring to your acquaintance, *Tub of Totten*.
20 Squire *Tub*, my Master, loves all men of vertue.
And longs (az one would zay) till he be one on you.
    Cle. His worship's wel'cun to our company :
Would 't were wiser for 'hun.   *Pan.* Here be some on us,
Are call'd the witty men, over a hundred ;
25   *Scr.* And zome a thousand, when the Muster day comes.
    Tub. I long (as my man *Hilts* said, and my Governour)
To be adopt in your society.
Can any man make a Masque here i' this company?
    Pan. A Masque, what's that?   *Scr.* A mumming, or
      a shew.
30 With vizards, and fine clothes.   *Cle.* A disguise, neighbour,
Is the true word : There stands the man, can do't Sir.
Medlay the Joyner, *In-and-In* of *Islington*,
The onely man at a disguize in *Midlesex*.
    Tub. But who shall write it?   *Hil. Scriben*, the great
      Writer.
35   *Scr.* Hee'll do't alone Sir, He will joyne with no man,
Though he be a Joyner, in designe he cals it,
He must be sole Inventer : *In-and-In*
Drawes with no other in's project, hee'll tell you,
It cannot else be feazeable, or conduce :
40 Those are his ruling words?   Pleaze you to heare 'hun?
    Tub. Yes Mr. *In-and-In*, I have heard of you ;
    Med. I can doe nothing, I.   *Cle.* Hee can doe all Sir.

    v. ii. 26 my man *corr. F* : I man *F originally*   29 shew.] Shew, *F3*
35 man,] man : *F, F3*   36 Joyner :] Joyner, *F, F3*   it, *F3* : it. *F*
37 *In-and-In F3* : *In-and-In. F*

 Med. They'll tell you so. *Tub.* I'ld have a toy presented,
A Tale of a Tub, a storie of my selfe,
You can expresse a Tub. *Med.* If it conduce   45
To the designe, what ere is feazeable :
I can expresse a Wash-house (if need be)
With a whole pedigree of Tubs. *Tub.* No, one
Will be enough to note our name, and family :
Squire *Tub* of *Totten*, and to shew my adventures   50
This very day. I'ld have it in *Tubs*-Hall,
At *Totten-Court*, my Ladie Mothers house,
My house indeed, for I am heire to it.
 Med. If I might see the place, and had survey'd it,
I could say more : For all Invention, Sir,   55
Comes by degrees, and on the view of nature ;
A world of things, concurre to the designe,
Which make it feazible, if Art conduce.
 Tub. You say well, witty Mr. *In-and-In*.
How long ha' you studied Ingine ? *Med.* Since I first   60
Joyn'd, or did in-lay in wit, some vorty yeare.
 Tub. A pretty time ! *Basket*, goe you and waite
On Master *In-and-In* to *Totten-Court*,
And all the other wise Masters ; shew 'hem the Hall :
And taste the language of the buttery to 'hem ;   65
Let 'hem see all the Tubs about the house,
That can raise matter, till I come—which shall be
Within an houre at least. *Cle.* It will be glorious,
If *In-and-In* will undertake it, Sir :
He has a monstrous medlay wit o' his owne.   70
 Tub. Spare for no cost, either in boords, or hoops,
To architect your Tub : Ha' you nere a Cooper
At *London* call'd *Vitruvius* ? send for him ;
Or old *Iohn Haywood*, call him to you, to helpe.
 Scr. He scornes the motion, trust to him alone.   75

 v. ii. 47 if *F3* : If *F*   52 Ladie *corr. F* : Ladies *F originally*   61
Joyn'd] Ioyn'd *F*   68 houre] houre, *F3*   70 owne] ow ne *F*

Act V. Scene III.

Lady ⟨Tub⟩. Tub. D. Tur⟨fe⟩. Clay. Puppy. Wispe.
⟨To them⟩
Preamble. Turfe.

Lad. O, here's the Squire! you slip'd us finely sonne!
These manners to your Mother, will commend you;
But in an other age, not this: well *Tripoly*,
Your Father, good Sir *Peter* (rest his bones)
5 Would not ha' done this: where's my Huisher *Martin*?
And your faire Mrs. *Awdrey*? *Tub.* I not see 'hem,
No creature, but the foure wise Masters here,
Of *Finsbury* Hundred, came to cry their Constable,
Who they doe say is lost. *D. Tur.* My husband lost?
10 And my fond Daughter lost, I feare mee too.
Where is your Gentleman, Madam? Poore *Iohn Clay*,
Thou hast lost thy *Awdrey*. *Cla.* I ha' lost my wits,
My little wits, good Mother; I am distracted.
  Pup. And I have lost my Mistris *Dido Wispe*,
15 Who frownes upon her *Puppy, Hanniball.*
Losse! losse on every side! a publike losse!
Losse o' my Master! losse of his Daughter! losse
Of Favour, Friends, my Mistris! losse of all!
  Pre. What Cry is this? *Tur.* My man speakes of some
  losse.
20 *Pup.* My Master is found: Good luck, and't be thy will,
Light on us all. *D. Tur.* O husband, are you alive?
They said you were lost. *Tur.* Where's Justice *Brambles*
  Clarke?
Had he the money that I sent for? *D. Tur.* Yes,
Two houres agoe; two fifty pounds in silver,
25 And *Awdrey* too. *Tur.* Why *Awdrey*? who sent for her?
  D. Tur. You Master *Turfe*, the fellow said. *Tur.* Hee
  lyed.
I am cozen'd, rob'd, undone: your man's a Thiefe,

v. iii. 10. lost,] lost? F ,F3

And run away with my Daughter, Mr. *Bramble*,
And with my money. *Lad.* Neighbour *Turfe* have
 patience,
I can assure you that your Daughter is safe, 30
But for the monies I know nothing of.
 Tur. My money is my Daughter ; and my Daughter
She is my money, Madam. *Pre.* I doe wonder
Your Ladiship comes to know any thing
In these affaires. *Lad.* Yes, Justice *Preamble* 35
I met the maiden i' the fields by chance,
I' the Squires company my sonne : How hee
Lighted upon her, himselfe best can tell.
 Tub. I intercepted her, as comming hither,
To her Father, who sent for her, by *Miles Metaphore*, 40
Justice *Preambles* Clarke. And had your Ladiship
Not hindred it, I had paid fine Mr. Justice
For his young warrant, and new Purs'yvant,
He serv'd it by this morning. *Pre.* Know you that Sir ?
 Lad. You told me, Squire, a quite other tale, 45
But I beleev'd you not, which made me send
Awdrey another way, by my *Pol-marten* :
And take my journey back to *Kentish-Towne*,
Where we found *Iohn Clay* hidden i' the barne,
To scape the *Huy* and *Cry* ; and here he is. 50
 Tur. Iohn Clay age'n ! nay, then—set Cock a hoope :
I ha' lost no Daughter, nor no money, Justice.
Iohn Clay shall pay. Ile looke to you now *John*.
Vaith out it must, as good at night, as morning.
I am ene as vull as a Pipers bag with joy, 55
Or a great Gun upon carnation day !
I could weepe Lions teares to see you *Iohn*.
'Tis but two viftie pounds I ha' ventur'd for you :
But now I ha' you, you shall pay whole hundred.
Run from your Burroughs, sonne : faith ene be hang'd. 60
An' you once earth your selfe, *Iohn*, i' the barne,

 v. iii. 35 Preamble *G* : *Bramble* F. F3   42 Justice] Justice, *F3*
55 bag] Bag, *F3*

I ha' no Daughter vor you : Who did verret 'hun ?
  D. Tur. My Ladies sonne, the Squire here, vetch'd 'hun
    out.
Puppy had put us all in such a vright,
65 We thought the Devill was i' the barne ; and no body
Durst venture o' hun.   *Tur.* I am now resolv'd,
Who shall ha' my Daughter.   *D. Tur.* Who ?   *Tur.* He
    best deserves her.
Here comes the Vicar.   Chanon *Hugh*, we ha' vound
Iohn Clay agen ! the matter's all come round.

Act V.   Scene IV.

To them.

Chanon Hugh.

  Hugh. Is *Metaphore* return'd yet ?   *Pre.* All is turn'd
Here to confusion : we ha' lost our plot ;
I feare my man is run away with the money,
And *Clay* is found, in whom old *Turfe* is sure
5 To save his stake.   *Hug.* What shall wee doe then Justice ?
  Pre. The Bride was met i' the young Squires hands.
  Hug. And what's become of her ?   *Pre.* None here
    can tell.
  Tub. Was not my Mothers man, *Pol-marten*, with you ?
And a strange Gentlewoman in his company,
10 Of late here, Chanon ?   *Hug.* Yes, and I dispatch'd 'hem.
  Tub. Dispatch'd 'hem ! how doe you meane ?   *Hug.*
Why married 'hem.
As they desir'd ; But now.   *Tub.* And doe you know
What you ha' done, Sir *Hugh* ?   *Hug.* No harme, I hope.
  Tub. You have ended all the Quarrell.   *Awdrey* is
    married.
15   *Lad.* Married ! to whom ?   *Tur.* My Daughter *Awdrey*
    married,

    v. iii. 62 'hun ?] 'hun. *F* : 'un ? *F3*   v. iv. (Heading) them. *F3* :
them *F*

And she not know of it!   D. *Tur.* Nor her Father, or
   Mother!
   Lad. Whom hath she married?   *Tub.* Your *Pol-marten*,
   Madam.
A Groome was never dreamt of.   *Tur.* Is he a man?
   Lad. That he is *Turfe*, and a Gentleman, I ha' made him.
   D. Tur. Nay, an' he be a Gentleman, let her shift.   20
   Hug. She was so brave, I knew her not, I sweare;
And yet I married her by her owne name.
But she was so disguis'd, so Lady-like;
I thinke she did not know her selfe the while!
I married 'hem as a meere paire of strangers: 25
And they gave out themselves for such.   *Lad.* I wish 'hem
Much joy, as they have given me hearts ease.
   Tub. Then Madam, Ile intreat you now remit
Your jealousie of me; and please to take
All this good company home with you, to supper: 30
Wee'll have a merry night of it, and laugh.
   Lad. A right good motion, Squire; which I yeeld to:
And thanke them to accept it.   Neighbour *Turfe*,
Ile have you merry, and your wife: And you,
Sir *Hugh*, be pardon'd this your happy error,   35
By Justice *Preamble*, your friend and patron.
   Pre. If the young Squire can pardon it, I doe.

Act V.   Scene V.

Puppy. Dido. Hugh.   tarry be-
                         hind.
   Pup. Stay my deare *Dido*, and good Vicar *Hugh*,
We have a busines with you: In short, this.
If you dare knit another paire of strangers,
Dido of *Carthage*, and her Countrey-man,
Stout *Hanniball* stands to't.   I have ask'd consent,   5
And she hath granted.   *Hug.* But saith *Dido* so?

   v. iv. 35 error,] error. *F*: Error. *F3*   v. v. 2 this.] this *F*: this, *F3*

Did. From what *Ball-Hanny* hath said, I dare not goe.
Hug. Come in then, Ile dispatch you.   A good supper
Would not be lost, good company, good discourse;
10 But above all where wit hath any source.

Act V.   Scene VI.

Pol-marten.   Awdrey.   Tub.   Lady ⟨Tub⟩.
⟨To them.⟩
Preamble.   Turfe.   D. Turfe.   Clay.

Pol. After the hoping of your pardon, Madam,
For many faults committed.   Here my wife,
And I doe stand, expecting your mild doome.
  Lad. I wish thee joy *Pol-marten*;   and thy wife:
5 As much, Mrs. *Pol-marten.*   Thou hast trick'd her
Up very fine, me thinkes.   *Pol.* For that I made
Bold with your Ladiships Wardrobe, but have trespass'd
Within the limits of your leave—I hope.
  Lad. I give her what she weares.   I know all women
10 Love to be fine.   Thou hast deserv'd it of me:
I am extreamely pleas'd with thy good fortune.
Welcome good Justice *Preamble*;   And *Turfe*,
Looke merrily on your Daughter: She has married
A Gentleman.   *Tur.* So me thinkes.   I dare not touch her,
15 She is so fine: yet I will say, God blesse her.
  D. Tur. And I too, my fine Daughter.   I could love her
Now, twice as well, as if *Clay* had her.
  Tub. Come, come, my Mother is pleas'd.   I pardon all,
Pol-marten in, and waite upon my Lady.
20 Welcome good Ghests: see supper be serv'd in,
With all the plenty of the house, and worship.
I must conferre with Mr. *In-and-In*,
About some alterations in my Masque;

v. v. 10 all] all, *F3*   v. vi. Scene iii.—Totten-Court.   Before the
House. G   (Heading) *Pol-marten* . . . *Preamble* one line in F   1 *Pol.*
F3 : *Lad.* F   4 wife :] Wife *F3*   6 Up] Vp *F*   that] that, *F3*
14 her, *F3* : her *F*

A Tale of a Tub

Send *Hilts* out to me : Bid him bring the Councell
Of *Finsbury* hither. Ile have such a night
Shall make the name of *Totten-Court* immortall :
And be recorded to posterity.

Act V.   Scene VII.

Tub. Medlay. Clench. Pan. Scriben. Hilts.

Tub. O Mr. *In-and-In,* what ha' you done ?
  Med. Survey'd the place Sir, and design'd the ground,
Or stand-still of the worke : And this it is.
First, I have fixed in the earth, a *Tub* ;
And an old *Tub,* like a Salt-Peeter Tub,
Preluding by your Fathers name Sir *Peeter,*
And the antiquity of your house, and family,
Originall from Salt-Peeter.   *Tub.* Good yfaith,
You ha' shewne reading, and antiquity here, Sir.
  Med. I have a little knowledge in designe,
Which I can varie Sir to *Infinito.*
  Tub. Ad Infinitum Sir you meane.   *Med.* I doe.
I stand not on my Latine, Ile invent,
But I must be alone then, joyn'd with no man.
This we doe call the Stand-still of our worke.
  Tub. Who are those wee, you now joyn'd to your selfe ?
  Med. I meane my selfe still, in the plurall number,
And out of this wee raise our *Tale of a Tub.*
  Tub. No, Mr. *In-and-In,* my *Tale of a Tub.*
By your leave, I am *Tub,* the Tale's of me,
And my adventures ! I am Squire *Tub,*
Subjectum Fabulæ.   *Med.* But I the Author.
  Tub. The Worke-man Sir ! the Artificer ! I grant you.
So *Skelton*-Lawreat ; was of *Elinour Rumming* :
But she the subject of the Rout, and Tunning.
  Cle. He has put you to it, Neighbour *In-and-In.*
  Pan. Doe not dispute with him, he still will win,

v. vii. 3 stand-still] stand still *F*   16 wee,] wee ? *F*   selfe ?]
selfe. *F*   24 *Rumming* W : *Bumming* F, F3   27 win,] win. *F*

That paies for all.   *Scr.* Are you revis'd o' that?
A man may have wit, and yet put off his hat.
30   *Med.* Now, Sir this Tub, I will have capt with paper:
A fine oild Lanterne-paper, that we use.
    Pan. Yes every Barber, every Cutler has it.
    Med. Which in it doth containe the light to the busines.
And shall with the very vapour of the Candle,
35 Drive all the motions of our matter about:
As we present 'hem. For example, first
The worshipfull Lady *Tub*.   *Tub.* Right worshipfull,
I pray you, I am worshipfull my selfe.
    Med. Your Squire-ships Mother, passeth by (her Huisher,
40 Mr. *Pol-marten* bareheaded before her)
In her velvet Gowne.   *Tub.* But how shall the Spectators,
As it might be, I, or *Hilts*, know 'tis my Mother?
Or that *Pol-marten* there that walkes before her?
    Med. O wee doe nothing, if we cleare not that.
45   *Cle.* You ha' seene none of his workes Sir?   *Pan.* All
    the postures
Of the train'd bands o' the Countrey.   *Scr.* All their
    colours.
    Pan. And all their Captaines.   *Cle.* All the Cries o' the
    Citie:
And all the trades i' their habits.   *Scr.* He has his whistle
Of command: Seat of authority!
50 And virge to' interpret, tip'd with silver! Sir,
You know not him.   *Tub.* Well, I will leave all to him.
    Med. Give me the briefe o' your subject. Leave the
    whole
State of the thing to me.   *Hil.* Supper is ready, Sir.
My Lady cals for you.   *Tub.* Ile send it you in writing.
55   *Med.* Sir, I will render feazible, and facile,
What you expect.   *Tub.* *Hilts*, be't your care,
To see the Wise of *Finsbury* made welcome:

v. vii. 31 oild *corr. F.*: old *F. originally*   41 Spectators, *F3*:
Spectators? *F*   43 *Pol-marten* there] *Pol-martin*, there, *F3*   her?]
her. *F, F3*   48, 49 He has | His whistle of *G*   50 silver!] silver, *F*:
Silver, *F3*   Sir, *F3*: Sir *F*

Let 'hem want nothing. Iz old *Rosin* sent for? *The*
   Hil. Hee's come within.   *Scri.* Lord! what a world of *Squire*
    busines *goes out.*
The Squire dispatches!   *Med.* Hee is a learned man: 60
I thinke there are but vew o' the Innes o' Court,
Or the Innes o' Chancery like him.   *Cle.* Care to fit 'un *The rest*
    then. *follow.*

Act V. Scene VIII.

Iack. Hilts.

   Iac. Yonder's another wedding, Master *Basket,*
Brought in by Vicar *Hugh.*   *Hil.* What are they, *Iack?*
   Iac. The High Constables Man, *Ball Hanny*; and Mrs.
    Wispes,
Our Ladies woman.   *Hil.* And are the Table merry?
   Iac. There's a young Tile-maker makes all laugh;   5
He will not eate his meat, but cryes at th' boord,
He shall be hang'd.   *Hil.* He has lost his wench already:
As good be hang'd.   *Iac.* Was she that is *Pol-marten,*
Our fellowes Mistris, wench to that sneake-*Iohn?*
   Hil. I faith, *Black Iack,* he should have beene her Bride- 10
    groome:
But I must goe to waite o' my wise Masters.
Iack, you shall waite on me, and see the Maske anone:
I am halfe Lord Chamberlin, i' my Masters absence.
   Iac. Shall wee have a Masque? Who makes it?   *Hil.*
    In-and-In,
The Maker of *Islington*: Come goe with me   15
To the sage sentences of *Finsbury.*

    v. vii. 58 (stage-dir.) *out*] ou t F   v. viii. Scene iv.—The same
[i. e. Totten-Court].   A Room in the House *G*   2 What *F3*: what *F*
3 *Wispes*] Wispe *G*   14 *In-and-In,*] *In-and-In.* F, F3   15 Maker]
Master *F3*

Act V. Scene IX.

2 Groomes.

Gro. 1. Come, give us in the great Chaire, for my Lady;
And set it there: and this for Justice *Bramble*.
Gro. 2. This for the Squire my Master, on the right hand.
Gro. 1. And this for the High Constable.   *Gro.* 2. This
his wife.
5 *Gro.* 1. Then for the Bride, and Bride-groome, here,
Pol-marten.
Gro. 2. And she *Pol-marten*, at my Ladies feet.
Gro. 1. Right.   *Gro.* 2. And beside them Mr. *Hanniball
Puppy*.
Gro. 1. And his shee *Puppy*, Mrs. *Wispe* that was:
Here's all are in the note.   *Gro.* 2. No, Mr. Vicar:
10 The petty Chanon *Hugh*..   *Gro.* 1. And Cast-by *Clay*:
There they are all.   *Tub*. Then cry a Hall, a Hall!
'Tis merry in *Tottenham* Hall, when beards wag all.
Come Father *Rozin* with your Fidle now,
Loud musicke. And two tall-toters: Flourish to the Masque.

Act V. Scene X.

Lady. Preamble before her.   *Tub. Turfe. D. Turfe.
Pol-marten. Awdrey. Puppy. Wispe. Hugh. Clay.*
All take their Seats.   *Hilts* waits on the by.

Lad. Neighbours, all welcome: Now doth *Totten-Hall*
Shew like a Court: and hence shall first be call'd so.
Your witty short confession Mr. Vicar,
Within hath beene the *Prologue*, and hath open'd
5 Much to my sonnes device, his *Tale of a Tub*.
Tub. Let my Masque shew it selfe: And *In-and-In*,

v. ix.] Scene v.—Another Room in the same, with a curtain drawn
across it *G*   5 Bride-groome, here,] Bride-groome, here *F* : Bride-
groom here, *F3*   v. x. (Heading) *Lady*.] *Lady* F, *F3*   *Pol-marten.*]
Pol-marten, F : *Pol-martin, F3*   4 Within] Within, *F3*

A Tale of a Tub

The Architect, appeare : I heare the whistle.　　　　*Hil.*
　Med. Thus rise I first, in my light linnen breeches,　*Peace.*
　　To run the meaning over in short speeches.　　　*Medlay*
　　Here is a *Tub* ; A *Tub* of *Totten-Court* :　　　*appeares*
　　An ancient *Tub*, hath call'd you to this sport :　　*above the*
　　　　　　　　　　　　　　　　　　　　　　　　Curtain.
　　His Father was a Knight, the rich Sir *Peeter* ;
　　Who got his wealth by a *Tub*, and by Salt-Peeter :
　　And left all to his Lady *Tub* ; the mother
　　Of this bold Squire *Tub*, and to no other.　　　　15
　　Now of this *Tub*, and's deeds, not done in ale,　　He
　　Observe, and you shall see the very *Tale*.　　　　drawes
　　　　　　　　　　　　　　　　　　　　　　　　the
　　　　　　　　　　　　　　　　　　　　　　　　Curtain,
　　　　　　　　　　　　　　　　　　　　　　　　and
　　　　　The first Motion.　　　　　　　　　　　discovers
　　　　　　　　　　　　　　　　　　　　　　　　the top of
　　　　　　　　　　　　　　　　　　　　　　　　the *Tub.*
　　　　　　　　　　　　　　　　　　　　　　　　Hil. Ha'
Med. Here Chanon *Hugh*, first brings to *Totten-Hall*　Peace.
　　The high Constables councell, tels the Squire all ;　Loud Mu-
　　Which, though discover'd (give the Divell his due :) 20 sick.
　　The wise of *Finsbury* doe still pursue.
　　Then with the Justice, doth he counterplot,
　　And his Clarke *Metaphore*, to cut that knot :
　　Whilst Lady *Tub*, in her sad velvet Gowne,
　　Missing her sonne, doth seeke him up and downe. 25
Tub. With her *Pol-marten* bare before her.　*Med.* Yes,
I have exprest it here in figure, and Mis-
tris *Wispe* her woman, holding up her traine.
　Tub. I' the next page, report your second straine.

　　　　　　　　　　　　　　　　　　　　　　　　Hil. Ha'
　　　　　　　　　　　　　　　　　　　　　　　　Peace.
　　　　The second Motion.　　　　　　　　　　Loud Mu-
　　　　　　　　　　　　　　　　　　　　　　　　sick.

Med. Here the high Constable, and Sages walke　　30
　　To Church, the Dame, the Daughter, Bride-maids
　　　　talke,
　　Of wedding busines ; till a fellow in comes,
　　Relates the robbery of one Captaine *Thum's* :
　　Chargeth the Bride-groome with it : Troubles all,

35　　　And gets the Bride; who in the hands doth fall
　　　Of the bold Squire, but thence soone is tane
　　　By the sly Justice, and his Clarke profane
　　　In shape of Pursuyvant; which he not long
　　　Holds, but betrayes all with his trembling tongue:
40　　　As truth will breake out, and shew, &c.

Tub. O thou hast made him kneele there in a corner,
I see now: there is simple honour for you *Hilts*!
　Hil. Did I not make him to confesse all to you?
　Tub. True; *In-and-In* hath done you right, you see.
45 Thy third I pray thee, witty *In-and-In*.
　Cle. The Squire commends 'un. He doth like all well.
　Pan. Hee cannot choose. This is geare made to sell.

Hil. Ha'
peace.
Loud
musick.

The third Motion.

　Med. The carefull Constable, here drooping comes,
　　In his deluded search, of Captain *Thum's*.
50　*Puppy* brings word, his Daughter's run away
　　With the tall Serving-man. He frights Groome *Clay*,
　　Out of his wits. Returneth then the Squire,
　　Mocks all their paines, and gives Fame out a Lyar:
　　For falsely charging *Clay*, when 'twas the plot,
55　Of subtile *Bramble*, who had *Awdrey* got,
　　Into his hand, by this winding device.
　　The Father makes a reskue in a trice:
　　And with his Daughter, like Saint *George* on foot,
　　Comes home triumphing, to his deare Hart root,
60　And tell's the Lady *Tub*, whom he meets there,
　　Of her sonnes courtesies, the Batchelor.
　　Whose words had made 'hem fall the *Huy* and *Cry*.
　　When Captaine *Thum's* comming to aske him, why
　　He had so done? he cannot yeeld him cause:
65　But so he runs his neck into the Lawes.

　　v. x. 47–8 s. d. musick.] musick *F*　　56 this] his *F3*　　59 root,]
　　root. *F, F3*　　64 he cannot] He cannot *F, F3*

The fourth Motion.

Med. The Lawes, who have a noose to crack his neck,
    As Iustice *Bramble* tels him, who doth peck
    A hundreth pound out of his purse, that comes
    Like his teeth from him, unto Captaine *Thum's.*
    Thum's is the Vicar in a false disguise: 70
    And employes *Metaphore*, to fetch this prize.
    Who tels the secret unto *Basket-Hilts,*
    For feare of beating. This the Squire quilts
    Within his Cap; and bids him but purloine
    The wench for him: they two shall share the coine. 75
    Which the sage Lady in her 'foresaid Gowne
    Breaks off, returning unto *Kentish-Towne,*
    To seeke her *Wispe*; taking the Squire along,
    Who finds *Clay Iohn,* as hidden in straw throng.
Hil. O, how am I beholden to the Inventer,   80
That would not, on record against me enter
My slacknesse here, to enter in the barne,
Well *In-and-In*, I see thou canst discerne!
Tub. On with your last, and come to a Conclusion.

Hil. Ha' peace. Loud Musick.

The fift Motion.

Med. The last is knowne, and needs but small infusion 85
    Into your memories, by leaving in
    These Figures as you sit. I, *In-and-In,*
    Present you with the show: First of a Lady
    Tub, and her sonne, of whom this Masque here,
        made I.
    Then Bride-groome *Pol,* and Mistris *Pol* the Bride: 90
    With the sub-couple, who sit them beside.
Tub. That onely verse, I alter'd for the better, ἐυφονία
    gratiâ.

Hil. Ha' peace. Loud Musicke.

v. x. 81 enter] enter! F originally: *miscorrected to* enter.   92 ἐυφονία] *Grammar requires* εὐφωνίας

Med. Then Justice *Bramble*, with Sir *Hugh* the Chanon:
And the Bride's Parents, which I will not stan'on,
Or the lost *Clay*, with the recovered *Giles*:
Who thus unto his Master, him 'conciles,
On the Squires word, to pay old *Turfe* his Club,
And so doth end our *Tale*, here, of a *Tub*.

The end.

EPILOGVE

Squire T V B.

THis Tale of mee, the Tub of Totten-Court,
  A Poet, *first invented for your sport.*
Wherein the fortune of most empty Tubs
  Rowling in love, are shewne ; and with what rubs,
W'are commonly encountred : when the wit
  Of the whole Hundred *so opposeth it.*
Our petty Chanon's *forked plot in chiefe,*
  Slie Iustice arts, with the High Constables briefe,
And brag Commands ; my Lady Mothers care ;
  And her Pol-martens *fortune ; with the rare*
Fate of poore Iohn, *thus tumbled in the Caske ;*
  Got In-and-In, *to gi't you in a* Masque :
That you be pleas'd, who come to see a Play,
  With those that heare, and marke not what wee say.
Wherein the Poets *fortune is, I feare,*
  Still to be early up, but nere the neare.

FINIS.

v. x. 95 *Giles* :] Miles, W   Epilogue 5 *when*] When F, F3   8 *briefe*]
Briefe F : *Brief* F3   17 FINIS *added in some copies*

THE CASE IS ALTERED

THE TEXT

THE play was twice entered on the Stationers' Register in 1609:

26to Januarij

Henry Walleys Richard Bonion vide ad 20 Julij 1609.
Entred for their Copye vnder thandes of master Segar deputy to Sir George Bucke and of thwardens a booke called, The case is altered   vj^d

Arber, *Transcript* III, 400.

20 Julij

Henry Walley Richard Bonyon Bartholomew Sutton.
Entred for their copie by direction of master Waterson warden. a booke called the case is altered whiche was Entred for H. Walley and Richard Bonyon the 26 of January Last.   vj^d

Ibid., 416.

Bonian and Walley were in partnership from 1608 to 1610. They published *Troilus and Cressida* and *The Masque of Queens* early in 1609 (the latter was entered on the Register on February 22), and *The Faithful Shepherdess* either in 1609 or 1610.

Sutton went into partnership with Barrenger in 1609. On March 3 they published Barnaby Rich's *Short Survey of the Realm of Ireland*. *The Case is Altered* was the second book published by the partners.

The play was issued in quarto with two distinct title-pages:

(1) Ben: Ionson, His Case is Altered. As it hath beene sundry times Acted by the Children of the Blacke-friers. [Device.] At London Printed for Bartholomew Sutton, dwelling in Paules Church-yard neere the great north doore of S. Paules Church. 1609.

(2) A Pleasant Comedy, called: The Case is Alterd. As it hath beene sundry times acted by the children of the Black-friers. Written by Ben. Ionson. [Device.] London, Printed for Bartholomew Sutton, and William Barrenger, and are to be sold at the great North-doore of Saint Paules Church. 1609.

Collation: A–K in fours, with the title on A and the text beginning at A2.

The first title-page is in the British Museum copy with press-mark 644. b. 54; the second is the commoner form and corresponds with the running title *A pleasant Comedy, called The Case is Alterd*. The other Museum Copy originally contained both titles, but the earlier has been stolen from it in recent years.

The Kemble copy, formerly in Chatsworth Library, presents a striking variant of the second title-page; it omits the words 'Written by Ben. Ionson,' though in all other respects there is exact correspondence; e.g. in the turned 'r' of 'sundry' and in the broken lines above and below the printer's device. What is the history of this change of title?

Early in 1609 Jonson had published with Bonian and Walley *The Masque of Queens*; the text of this masque, encumbered with a series of scholarly notes, shows an accuracy which could have been ensured only by Jonson's presence at the printing-house when the work was being set up in type. Bonian and Walley no doubt hoped to publish something more of Jonson's, but *The Case is Altered* is the only work which they managed to secure, and even this Sutton took over from them. The printing of this is so vile that it is certain that Jonson did not see it through the press.

In our critical introduction to the play[1] we noted the absence of Jonson's name from the second title-page in the Kemble copy, and we assumed that Jonson had intervened to force this omission upon the printer. Dr. W. W. Greg has sent us a very valuable correction. The words 'Written by Ben. Ionson' were added, not deleted. The spacing of the page is more regular without the author's name, and this particular line is badly centred. The original title 'Ben: Ionson, his Case is Alterd' was cancelled because Barrenger, who is not mentioned in the entries in the Stationers' Register, had taken a share in the venture and his name had to appear in the imprint. In the cancel a more normal wording of the title was

See vol. i, p. 305.

adopted, but the printer, having removed Ben's name from the beginning, forgot to put it in at the end. After a few copies had been struck off—only one is recorded—the error was discovered in the printing-office, and the name was unskilfully inserted.

The printer has not been traced. The device of a fleur-de-lis set in a frame, with the motto 'In Domino confido', appears in a variety of forms recorded in Dr. R. B. McKerrow's *Printers' & Publishers' Devices*, nos. 263 to 272. The pattern here employed is no. 269, with the broad bud of the flower actually touching the leaf on the left and with the F of 'CONFIDO' so badly cut that it looks like a T. John Wolfe had used the device, but it is not known into whose hands it passed after his death in 1601. Dr. McKerrow traces it again in *The Tragedy of Thierry and Theodoret*, printed for T Walkley in 1621.

The Case is Altered is a rare example of a Jonson text which may be described as thoroughly bad. The following copies have been collated for the text of the present edition:

British Museum copy, with press-mark 644. b. 54, wanting sig. K (= A in the list below).
British Museum copy, T. 492 (9), wanting all leaves after sig. H 4 (= B).
Bodleian Copy, Malone 225 (= C).
Dyce copy with inlaid title-page (= D).
Dyce copy with T. Jolley's book-plate (= E).
Dyce copy loosely bound with MS. verses at end, badly cropped and with torn title-page (= F).
The Kemble copy, formerly at Chatsworth, now in the Henry E. Huntington Library (= G).

The sheets of the Quarto were much corrected in passing through the press. The following is a list of the corrections:

Sig.			
A 4ᵛ	I. v. 11	dost *C, D, F*	doo's *A, B, E, G*
B.	I. v. 30	*Maximllian of Vicenzia D.*	*Maximlian of Vicenza* the rest.
	I. v. 36	valient, *D.*	valient. *the rest.*
	I. v. 40	well *D.*	Well *the rest*

Sig. B	I. v. 40 s. d.	*Inniper* D.	*Iuniper* the rest.
	I. v. 43	*Capricioi* D.	*Capriceio* the rest.
	I. vi. 3	*Angelio.* D.	*Angelio,* the rest.
	I. vi. 4	him *om.* D.	(*Inserted in the rest.*)
		means. D.	meanes, *the rest.*
	I. vi. 13	scence D.	sence *the rest.*
	I. vi. 16	weakes D.	weaknes *the rest.*
	I. vi. 17	concepted D.	conceited *the rest.*
	I. vi. 18 s. d.	*Angelio* D.	*Angelo* the rest.
	I. vi. 71	No ? *A.*	No. *the rest.*
B 2ᵛ	I. vi. 90	*Angello* D.	*Angelo* the rest.
	I. vii heading	*Sebast,* D.	*Sebast.* the rest.
	I. vii. 4 s. d.	*Matino* D.	*Martino* the rest.
	I. vii. 6	nought D.	nought, *the rest.*
	I. vii. 17	crost D.	crost, *the rest.*
B 3	I. vii. 25	*your* D.	*his* the rest.
B 4ᵛ	I. ix. 33	prauer *D*	deprauer *the rest.*
	I. ix. 37	presently : *D*	presently. *the rest.*
	I. ix. 40	Maddame. *D*	Maddame, *the rest.*
	I. ix. 56	my *D*	mine *the rest.*
	I. ix. 57	sound. *D, G*	sound, *the rest.*
Cᵛ	I. ix. 98	ranged *A, E*	rang'd *the rest.*
	I. x. 4	*Pau* ! *A*, E, and (?) F	*Pau.* the rest.
		well, *A, C, E*	well. *the rest.*
	I. x. 15	returned *A, E*	return'd *the rest.*
	I. x. 16	heauily *A, E*	heauily, *the rest.*
	I. x. 17	want nothing *A, E*	want nothing. *the rest.*
	I. x. 18	all *A, E*	all : *the rest.*
	I. x. 19	sweet *A, E*	sweet, *the rest.*
	I. x. 25	soule, *B, C, D, F*	soule. *A, E*
	I. x. 26	Rsceiue hi *A, E*	Receiue him *the rest.*
		loue *A, E*	loue, *the rest.*
		deffects, *A, E*	deffects *the rest.*
C 2	I. x. 27	a bsence *A, E*	absence *the rest.*
	I. x. 30	you, *A, E*	you. *the rest.*
	I. x. 31	Faiᴣh *A, E*	Faith *the rest.*
	I. x. 36	meꝫne *A, E*	meane *the rest.*
	I. x. 37	good *A, E*	good, *the rest.*
	I. x. 45	*Satrapas.* A, E	*Satrapas* the rest.
	I. x. 47	no *A, E*	not *the rest.*
	I. x. 48	go : *A, E*	go. *the rest.*
C 3	II. i. 66	Tho *G*	The *the rest.*
C 4	II. ii. 49	I *om. A, E*	(*Inserted in the rest.*)
C 4	II. ii. 53	Though *A, E*	Thought *the rest.*
Dᵛ	II. iv. 46	cerimon y *B, C, E*	cerimony *the rest.*
	II. iv. 58	Iealous. *A, D, F, G*	Iealous : *B, C, E.*

445·3   H

Sig. D 2ᵛ	II. vi. 19	it- *A, D, F*	it- - *the rest.*
E 4	III. v. 27	wi thin, *B, C, D, E* : w i thin *F*	within *A.*
F	IV. i. 67	Chamount, *B, C, D, E, F, G*	Chamount *A*
F 3	IV. iii. 31	signior *A*	signior. *the rest.*
	IV. iii. 42	abroad, *A*	abroad. *the rest.*
	IV. iii. 43	Mounsieur : *A*	Mounsieur. *the rest.*
F 4ᵛ	IV. v. 41	Onion A	Onion, the rest.
	IV. v. 45	para-| hrase *A*	para-| phrase *the rest.*
G	IV. v. 50	heauy *C, D*	heauy, *the rest.*
	IV. v. 53	speakefor *C, D*	speake for *the rest.*
		will *C, D*	wil *the rest*
		being ratitude *A, B, E, F, G*	be ingratitude *C, D.*
	IV. v. 54	ould *C, D*	old *the rest.*
		all, *C, D*	all. *the rest.*
	IV. v. 58	circumference *C, D*	circumference, *the rest.*
	IV. vi heading	*Rachel*, C, D	*Rachel.* the rest.
	IV. vi. 1	thee, *A, C, D*	thee ; *the rest.*
	IV. vi. 4	ye'are *C, D*	y'are *the rest.*
	IV. vi. 5	e lection *A, B, E, F, G*	election, *C, D*
Gᵛ	IV. vi. 19	I that *C, D*	I, that *the rest.*
	IV. vi. 20	practise, *C, D*	practise. *the rest.*
	IV. vi. 23	leau *C, D*	leaue *the rest.*
	IV. vi. 29	n ow *C, D*	now *the rest.*
G 2ᵛ	IV. viii. 10	kinsman *A, B*	kinsman, *the rest.*
	IV. viii. 17	dur, tno-| *D* : dur, tno | *C*	durt, no | *the rest.*
	IV. viii. 39	firsbush : *C*	firsbush. *the rest.*
	IV. viii. 40	teare, *C, D*	teare *the rest.*
		m y *G*	my *the rest.*
		haire *C, D*	haire, *the rest.*
		reloulue *C, D*	reluolue *the rest.*
G 3	IV. viii. 57	ground, *C, D*	ground. *the rest.*
	IV. viii. 70	sences ; *C, G*	sences, *the rest.*
G 3ᵛ	IV. viii. 78	wit h *C, D*	with *the rest.*
G 4	IV. ix. 41	gupgeon *C, D*	gudgeon *the. rest.*
G 4ᵛ	IV. x. 15	Counȝ *C, D*	Count the rest.
	IV. x. 17	spaeke *C, D*	speake *the rest.*
	IV. x. 18	sim ple *B*	simple *the rest.*
	IV. x. 26	prtext *C, D*	pretext *the rest.*
	IV. x. 27	ccanno *C, D*	canno *the rest.*
	IV. x. 28	Lord, *C, D*	Lord. *the rest.*
	IV. x. 39	lotah *C, D*	loath *the rest.*
	IV. x. 42	willy ou *C, D.*	will you *the rest.*

Sig. G 4ᵛ	IV. xi. 1	substance : *C. D.*	substance, *the rest.*
		Chamont, C, D.	*Chamont* : the rest.
	IV. xi. 4	secreet *C, D.*	secret *the rest.*
H 2	IV. xi. 79	giuet rue *G.*	giue true *the rest.*
H 3ᵛ	V. vi. 7	rapi er *C, D.*	rapier *the rest.*

In the critical apparatus of the text these corrections are indicated thus : ' doo's *corr. Q*: dost, *Q originally.*' But it is necessary to tabulate them here lest they should be lost sight of in the mass of minor corrections required to adjust the wrong punctuation, the jumbled sentences, and the dislocated verse in which the Quarto abounds. Even after his efforts to revise, the printer left in the text ' Capriceio ' (I. v. 43) and ' reluolue ' (IV. viii. 40). Perhaps his commonest error is to interchange two stops in the same sentence : thus at IV. xi. 1 he printed originally

Come on false substance : shadow to *Chamont,*
Had you none else to worke vpon but me, . . .

Seeing his error, he corrected the first line to

Come on false substance, shadow to *Chamont* :

but he seldom adjusted errors of this kind. Minor proofs of his incompetence, such as turned letters and the use of wrong founts, are frequent ; these are ignored in this edition except where the original printer himself corrected them. So are inconsistencies in the catchwords ; only the errors of these are noted.

Mr. W. C. Hazlitt wrongly stated, both in his *Manual for the Collector and Amateur of Old English Plays* and in his *Bibliographical Collections, Second Series*, p. 320, that *The Case is Altered* was reprinted in the Folio of 1692. Mr. H. C. Hart (*The Works of Ben Jonson*, I, p. xxviii) even added that the reprint was careless. The play was not reprinted till 1756, when Whalley included it in his edition. He modernized the text and made a few perfunctory corrections. Gifford was the first to attempt a critical recension. Accusing Whalley of negligence and of ' even adding to the blunders of the original '—a charge wholly unjustified—

he concluded complacently, ' In revenge, I have given a double portion of attention to it '. Gifford's most marked improvement of the text was to distribute the verse correctly: in this he has been followed by all later editors; the passages are indicated in the critical apparatus of the present text by the formula ' Prose in Q '. In addition he carried through the numbering of acts and scenes, localized the latter, inserted stage directions freely, and tinkered the false French of Pacue. He interfered with the text far less than might be expected from his ominous statement that he had paid special attention to it. He expands colloquial forms like ' let's ', ' 'hem ', ' ha' '; he generally substitutes ' O lord ' and ' 'Odso ' for ' O God ' and ' Godso '; but it is only occasionally that he alters a word, e. g. in v. i. 7 ' wooing trickes ' appears as ' coying tricks ', and in IV. iii. 45 he inserts a ' voila ' to touch up the French.

The play has been four times reprinted in recent years—separately as an acting copy for the students of the University of Chicago, who performed this comedy on May 17, 1902, and also by Mr. H. C. Hart, who lived to complete only two volumes of his projected edition for Methuen's *Standard Library*, and by Professor F. Schelling, who has edited the plays for the *Everyman Library*. All three editions are based on the Quarto, but frequently accept Gifford's corrections. In 1917 Dr. W. E. Selin issued a careful reprint of the Quarto from the copy in the collection of Mr. W. A. White, of New York (' Yale Studies in English ', no. lvi). With this text he collated the Bodleian and British Museum copies, and the Kemble copy, then at Chatsworth; he records many of the printer's variants. The present edition is a revised text, as conservative as it is possible to make it. It is a reissue of the Quarto with just that minimum of correction which is required to give effect to the printer's good intentions; unfortunately, from the condition of the text, the minimum looks persistently like a maximum. *The Case is Altered* is thus in glaring contrast to all Jonson's other works except *The English Grammar* published after his death in the Folio of 1640, the technical form of which baffled the printer.

The Quarto marks the acts and scenes inaccurately as far as the opening of the fourth act. Sometimes it prefixes a list of the characters taking part in the scene: this is the method in the manuscripts of Plautus and Terence, and Jonson adopted it in the plays which he himself sent to press. But the Quarto also heads scenes in the usual way (e. g. I. vi); sometimes it follows up the enumeration of characters by marking entrances and exits afterwards (e. g. I. i, where '*Iuniper, Onion, Antony Baladino*' probably come from Jonson's own manuscript, while the stage direction at ll. 2, 3, '*Enter Onion in hast*', is a playhouse annotation); sometimes the printer makes nonsense by prefixing '*Enter*' to the list of characters (e. g. I. v, '*Enter Iuniper, Antonio, Sebastian, Vincentio, Balthasar and Christophero*', where Juniper, Antonio, and Valentine, who is ignored, are on the stage already; Sebastian, Martino, Vincentio, and Balthasar actually enter; and Christophero enters later at l. 8).

Jonson's own method was to mark a new scene in nearly every case where a new character enters. The Quarto shows sufficient traces of this method to suggest that it was in the manuscript, but it has been disturbed, perhaps by stage requirements. Thus, in Act I, if scenes iv and v are to be retained, as marked in the Quarto, they must be preceded by ii and iii, which are not marked. It has been decided to adopt this system in the reprint and so bring *The Case is Altered* into harmony with Jonson's other plays.

In one important point the Quarto has been wrongly altered by most modern editions. The fourth act is correctly marked. Gifford carried on the third act to the end of IV. ii. But Maximilian's return opens a new phase of the plot and is an excellent starting-point for the new act. Modern editors seem disposed to shrink from a short act as an anomaly; hence even in *Hamlet* they are content to start the fourth act ' at a time when ', as Johnson puts it,

' there is more continuity of action than in almost any other of the scenes '.

Mr. Crawford noted[1] that the following lines from this play were quoted in *Bel-vedére or the Garden of the Muses*, compiled by A. M. and published in 1600, nine years before the play was printed :

On page 128 ' *Of Couetousnes, Auarice* '.
Gold, that makes all men false, is true it selfe. (= II. i. 31)
The more we spare, the more we hope to haue. (= II. i. 66)
To haue gold, and to haue it safe, is all. (= III. v. 28).

On page 67 ' *Of Nobilitie* '.
He is not noble, but most basely bred,
That ransacks tombes, and doth deface the dead. (= II. i. 45–6).

A. M. adapted his quotations freely, to make them even five-feet lines.

---

[1] *Notes and Queries*, 10th Series, xi, pp. 41–2.

BEN: IONSON,

HIS

CASE IS ALTERD.

As it hath beene sundry times Acted by the Children of the Blacke-friers.

AT LONDON
Printed for *Bartholomew Sutton,* dwelling in Paules Church-yard neere the great north doore of S. Paules Church. 1609.

The earlier title-page

A Pleasant Comedy,

CALLED:

The Case is Alterd.

As it hath beene sundry times acted by the
children of the Black-friers.

Written by BEN. IONSON.

LONDON,
Printed for *Bartholomew Sutton*, and *William Barrenger*,
and are to be sold at the great North-doore
of Saint Paules Church. 1609.

The later title-page

⟨The Persons of the Play.

COVNT FERNEZE.
LORD PAVLO FERNEZE, *his son.*
AVRELIA ⎫
PHŒNIXELLA ⎭ *his daughters.*
CAMILLO FERNEZE, *supposed Gasper.*
MAXIMILIAN, *general of the Milanese.*
CHAMONT, *a soldier of France, friend to Gasper.*
ANGELO, *friend to Paulo.*
FRANCISCO COLONNIA.
IAQVES DE PRIE, *supposed a beggar* (MELVN, *steward to Chamont's father*).
RACHEL DE PRIE, *supposed his daughter* (ISABEL, *sister to Chamont*).
ANTONIO BALLADINO, *pageant poet to the City of Milan.*
PETER ONION, *groom of the hall to Count Ferneze.*
IVNIPER, *a cobbler.*
CHRISTOPHERO, *steward to Count Ferneze.*
SEBASTIAN ⎫
MARTINO ⎪
VINCENTIO ⎬ *his seruants.*
BALTHASAR ⎭
VALENTINE, *seruant to Colonnia.*
NVNCIO.
PACVE, *page to Gasper.*
FINIO, *page to Camillo.*
Page to Paulo.
Sewer.
Seruingmen.
Soldiers.

THE SCENE
MILAN.⟩

A list of characters was first given by Whalley 9 COLONNIA G :
Colonia W : Colomia, Colomea, *or* Coloma *in* Q

A pleasant Comedy called, the
Case is Alterd.

Actus primi, Scæna prima.

Sound : after a flourish, Iuniper *a Cobler is discouered, sitting at worke in his shoppe and singing.*

Iuniper, Onion, [Antony Baladino].

Y OV *wofull wights giue eare a while,*
  And marke the tenor of my stile,
Which shall such trembling hearts vnfold
As seldome hath to fore bene told.
Such chances rare and dolefull newes
  peace a Gods name.
As may attempt your wits to muse.
  man. A pox a God on you.
And cause such trickling teares to passe,
Except your hearts be flint or brasse :
To heare the newes which I shall tell,
That in Castella *once befell.*
Sbloud, where didst thou learne to corrupt a man in the midst of a verse, ha ?

Enter Onion in hast.

Oni. Fellow *Iuniper* 5

Oni. Gods so, heere

Oni. Iuniper, Iuniper. 10

  Onion. Gods lid man, seruice is ready to go vp man, you 15 must slip on your coate and come in, we lacke waiters pittyfully.
  Iunip. A pittifull hearing, for now must I of a merry Cobler become ⟨a⟩ mourning creature.
  Onion. Well youle come. 20
  Iunip. Presto. Go to, a word to the wise, away, flie, vanish :   *Exit Onion.*
  Lye there the weedes that I disdaine to weare.

<sub>1. i. stage dir. *Sound* : . . . *flourish*,] *Sound* ? . . . *flourish* : Q   *Antony*]
Antouy Q   5 Fellow] fellow Q   6 peace] Peace Q   19 a G
21 flie,] flie ? Q   22 Stage dir. at 19 *in* Q</sub>

⟨Scæne 2.

Enter Antonio Balladino.⟩

Anto. God saue you Maister *Iuniper.*

Iuni. What *Signior Antonio Balladino,* welcome sweet *Ingle.*

Anto. And how do you sir?

5 *Iuni.* Faith you see, put to my shifts here as poore retainers be oftentimes. Sirrah *Antony* ther's one of my fellowes mightely enamored of thee, and I faith you slaue, now you're come I'le bring you together, it's *Peter Onion,* the groome of the hal, do you know him?

10 *Anto.* No not yet, I assure you.

Iuni. O he is one as right of thy humour as may be, a plaine simple Rascal, a true dunce, marry he hath bene a notable vilaine in his time: he is in loue, sirrah, with a wench, & I haue preferd thee to him, thou shalt make
15 him some prety *Paradox* or some *Aligory,* how does my coate sit? well?

Anto. I very well.   *Enter Onion.*

Oni. Na⟨y⟩ Gods so, fellow *Iuniper,* come away.

Iun. Art thou there mad slaue, I come with a powder.
20 Sirrah fellow *Onion,* I must haue you peruse this Gentleman well, and doe him good offices of respect and kindnesse, as instance shall be giuen.   ⟨*Exit.*⟩

Anto. Nay good maister *Onion* what do you meane, I pray you sir, you are to respectiue in good faith.

25 *Onion.* I would not you should thinke so sir, for though I haue no learning, yet I honour a scholer in any ground of the earth sir. Shall I request your name sir?

Anto. My name is *Antonio Balladino.*

Oni. Balladino? you are not *Pageant* Poet to the City
30 of *Millaine* sir, are you?

<small>1. ii.] *Enter Antonio Balladino.* G   6 oftentimes. Sirrah] oftentimes, sirrah *Q*   8 you're] your *Q*   it's] i'ts *Q*   9 him?] him *Q*   13 a notable] anotable *Q*   14 a wench] awench *Q*   16 well?] well. *Q*   19 powder.] powder ?. *Q*   20 Sirrah *begins a new line in Q*   Onion,] Onion. *Q*   22 *Exit.* G   24 sir,] sir *Q*   respectiue] respectue *Q*   27 earth sir.] earth sir, *Q*   Shall *begins a new line in Q*   29 *Oni.*] *Oni, Q*   30 you?] you. *Q*</small>

The Case is Alterd 107

Anto. I supply the place sir: when a worse cannot be had sir.

Oni. I crie you mercy sir, I loue you the better for that sir, by Iesu you must pardon me, I knew you not, but I'ld pray to be better acquainted with you sir, I haue seene 35 of your works.

Anto. I am at your seruice good Maister *Onion,* but concerning this maiden that you loue sir? what is she?

Onion. O did my fellow *Iuniper* tell you? marry sir, she is as one may say, but a poore mans child indeede, and 40 for mine owne part I am no Gentleman borne I must confesse, but *my mind to me a kingdome is* truly.

Anto. Truly a very good saying.

Onion. 'Tis somewhat stale, but that's no matter.

Anto. O 'tis the better, such things euer are like bread, 45 which the staler it is, the more holesome.

Onion. This is but a hungry comparison in my iudgement.

Anto. Why, I'le tell you, *M. Onion,* I do vse as much stale stuffe, though I say it my selfe, as any man does in that kind I am sure. Did you see the last *Pageant,* I set forth? 50

Onion. No faith sir, but there goes a huge report on't.

Anto. Why, you shal be one of my *Mæcen-asses,* I'le giue you one of the bookes, O you'le like it admirably.

Oni. Nay that 's certaine, I'le get my fellow *Iuniper* to read it. 55

Anto. Reade it sir, I'le reade it to you.

Onion. Tut then I shall not chuse but like it.

Anto. Why looke you sir, I write so plaine, and keepe that old *Decorum,* that you must of necessitie like it; mary you shall haue some now (as for example, in plaies) 60 that will haue euery day new trickes, and write you nothing but humours: indeede this pleases the Gentlemen: but the common sort they care not for't, they know not what to make on't, they looke for good matter, they, and are not edified with such toyes. 65

1. ii. 31 a worse] aworse *Q*   34 I'ld] Il'd *Q*   38 she?] she, *Q*
42 truly *om. G*   44 'Tis] T'is *Q*   45 'tis] t'is *Q*

Onion. You are in the right, I'le not give a halfepeny to see a thousand on 'hem. I was at one the last Tearme, but & euer I see a more roguish thing, I am a peece of cheese, & no *onion*, nothing but kings & princes in it, the foole came not out a iot.

Anto. True sir, they would haue me make such plaies, but as I tell hem, and they'le giue me twenty pound a play, I'le not raise my vaine.

Onion. No, it were a vaine thing, and you should sir.

Anto. Tut giue me the penny, giue me the peny, I care not for the Gentlemen I, let me haue a good ground, no matter for the pen, the plot shall carry it.

Onion. Indeed that's right, you are in print already for the best plotter.

Anto. I, I might as well ha bene put in for a dumb shew too.

Oni. I marry sir, I marle you were not, stand aside sir a while : ⟨*Exit Antonio.*⟩

⟨Scæne 3.⟩

Enter an armd Sewer : some halfe-dozen in mourning coates following, and passe by with seruice.

Enter Valentine.

Onion. How now friend, what are you there? be vncouered. Would you speake with any man here?

Valen. I, or else I must ha' returnd you no answer.

Oni. Friend, you are somewhat to peremptory, let's craue your absence : nay neuer scorne it, I am a little your better in this place.

Valen. I do acknowledge it.

Onion. Do you acknowledge it? nay then you shall go forth, Ile teach you how ⟨you⟩ shall acknowledge it another time ; go to, void, I must haue the hall purg'd, no setting vp of a rest here, packe, begone.

1. ii. 83 *Exit Antonio.* G 1. iii. (Heading) *following,*] *following* Q
2 vncouered.] vncouered, Q   Would *begins a new line in* Q 7 *ranged*
with 6 *in* Q   9 you *W*

Valen. I pray you sir is not your name *Onion*?
Oni. Your friend as you may vse him, and *M. Onion*, say on.
Valen. M. Onion with a murraine, come come put off this Lyons hide, your eares haue discouered you, why *Peter*! do not I know you *Peter*?
Onion. Gods so, *Valentine*!
Valen. O can you take knowledge of me now sir?
Oni. Good Lord, sirra, how thou art altred with thy trauell?
Valen. Nothing so much as thou art with thine office, but sirra *Onion*, is the *Count Ferneze* at home?
                                              [*Exit Anthony.*]
Oni. I *Bully*, he is aboue; and the Lord *Paulo Ferneze*, his son, and Maddam *Aurelia*, & maddam *Phœnixella*, his daughters, But O *Valentine*?
Valen. How now man, how dost thou?
Oni. Faith sad, heauy, as a man of my coate ought to be.
Valen. Why man, thou wert merry inough euen now.
Oni. True, but thou knowest
  All creatures here soiorning, vpon this wretched earth,
  Sometimes haue a fit of mourning, as well as a fit of mirth.
O *Valentine*, mine old Lady is dead, man.
Valen. Dead!
Oni. I faith.
Valen. When dyed she?
Onion. Mary, to morrow shall be three months, she was seene going to heauen they say, about some fiue weekes agone! how now? trickling teares, ha?
Valen. Faith thou hast made me weepe with this newes.
Onion. Why I have done but the parte of an *Onion*, you must pardon me.

          1. iii. 23 sirra *Onion*,] sirra, *Onion* Q

Scæne 4.

Enter the Sewer, passe by with seruice againe, the seruing-men take knowledge of Valentine *as they goe.* Iuniper *salutes him.*

Iuni. What *Valentine*? fellow *Onion*, take my dish I prithee. You rogue sirrah, tell me, how thou dost, sweet *Ingle.* *Exit Oni.*

Valen. Faith, *Iuniper*, the better to see thee thus frolicke.

5 *Iuni.* Nay, slid I am no changling, I am *Iuniper* still, I keepe the pristinate ha, you mad *Hierogliphick*, when shal we swagger?

Valen. Hieroglyphick, what meanest thou by that?

Iuni. Meane? Gods so, ist not a good word man? what?
10 stand vpon meaning with your freinds? Puh, *Absconde.*

Valen. Why, but stay, stay, how long has this sprightly humor haunted thee?

Iuni. Foe humour, a foolish naturall gift we haue in the *Æquinoctiall.*

15 *Valen.* Naturall, slid it may be supernaturall, this?

Iuni. Valentine, I prithee ruminate thy selfe welcome. What *fortuna de la Guerra*?

(*Valen.* O how pittifully are these words forc't. As though they were pumpt out on's belly.)

20 *Iuni.* Sirrah *Ingle*, I thinke thou hast seene all the strange countries in Christendome since thou wentst?

Valen. I haue seene some *Iuniper.*

Iuni. You haue seene *Constantinople*?

Valen. I, that I haue.

25 *Iuni.* And *Ierusalem*, and the *Indies*, and *Goodwine Sands*, and the tower of *Babylon*, and *Venice* and all.

---

1. iv. Scæne 4.] Scæne. 2. *Q*   Stage dir. *Sewer*] sewer Q   1 *Valentine*] *Valentiue* Q   2 prithee. You] prithee you *Q*   3 *Stage dir. inserted in Q after* still *in l.* 5   5 still,] still. *Q*   6 I keepe *a new line in Q* pristinate *W* : pristmate *Q*   7 swagger ?] swagger. *Q*.   8 that ?] that. *Q*   10 freinds ? Puh] freinds. *Puh* Q   17 *Guerra* ?] *Guerra*. Q   18-19, 27-28 *Asides not marked in Q* : *Jonson's use of brackets for this purpose has been adopted in the text*   18 As *begins a new line in Q*

Valen. I all ; (no marle and he haue a nimble tong, if he practise to vault thus from one side of the world to another.)

Iuni. O it's a most heauenly thing to trauel, & see countries, especially at sea, and a man had a pattent not to be sicke.

Valen. O sea sicke Iest, and full of the scuruie.

Scæne 5.

Enter [Iuniper, Antonio,] Sebastian, Martino, Vincentio, Balthasar [and Christophero].

Seba. Valentine ? welcome I faith, how dost sirra ?
Mart. How do you good *Valentine*?
Vincen. Troth, *Valentine*, I am glad to see you.
Balth. Welcome sweet rogue.
Sebast. Before God he neuer lookt better in his life.
Balth. And how ist man ? what, *Alla Coragio.*
Valen. Neuer better gentlemen I faith.
Iuni. S'will here comes the steward.

⟨*Enter Christophero.*⟩

Christ. Why how now fellowes, all here ? and nobody to waight aboue now they are ready to rise ? looke vp one or two. *Signior Francesco Colonnia's* man how doo's your good maister ? *Exeunt Iuniper, Martino, Vincentio.*

Valen. In health sir, he will be here anon.
Christo. Is he come home, then ?
Valen. I sir, he is not past sixe miles hence, he sent me before to learne if *Count Ferneze* were here and returne him word.

Christo. Yes, my Lord is here ; and you may tel your maister he shal come very happily to take his leaue of Lord *Paulo Ferneze* : who is now instantly to depart with other noble gentlemen, vpon speciall seruice.

1. v. Scæne 5] Scæne 3 *Q*   1 faith,] faith *Q*   2 *Valentine* ?] *Valentine*. *Q*   6 *Alla*] *Allo* G   8 *Enter Christophero*. G   9 fellowes,] fellowes *Q*   11 two.] two *Q*   *Colonnia's* G : *Colomia's* Q : *Colonia's* W   doo's *corr*. *Q* : dost *Q originally*   12 maister ?] maister *Q*   13, 15 sir,] sir *Q*

Valen. I will tell him sir.
Christo. I pray you doe, fellowes make him drinke.
⟨*Exit.*⟩
Valen. Sirs, what seruice ist they are imployed in?
25 *Sebast.* Why against the *French*, they meane to haue a fling at *Millaine* againe they say.
Valen. Who leades our forces, can you tell?
Sebast. Marry that do's Signior *Maximilian*; he is aboue, now.
30 *Valen.* Who, *Maximilian* of *Vicenza*?
Balt. I he; do you know him?
Valen. Know him? O yes he's an excellent braue soldier.
Balt. I so they say, but one of the most vaineglorious
35 men in *Europe*.
Valen. He is indeed, marry exceeding valient.
Sebast. And that is rare.
Balt. What?
Sebast. Why to see a vaineglorious man valient.
40 *Valen.* Well he is so I assure you.   Enter *Iuniper.*
Iuni. What no further yet, come on you precious rascall, sir *Valentine*, Ile giue you a health I faith; for the heauens you mad *Capriccio*, hold hooke and line.   ⟨*Exeunt.*⟩

Scæne 6.

Enter Lord *Paulo Ferneze*, his boy following him.

Pau. Boy.
Boy. My Lord.
Pau. Sirrah go vp to Signior *Angelo*,
And pray him (if he can) deuise some meanes,

I. v. 25 *French*,] *French* Q   28 *Maximilian* ;] *Maximilian* ? Q
30 *Maximilian* of *Vicenza* corr. Q: *Maximllian* of *Vicenzia* Q originally
31 he ;] he ? Q   34 vaineglorious] vaine glorious Q   36 valient.
corr. Q: valient, Q *originally*   38 What ?] What. Q   40 Well *corr.*
Q: well Q *originally*   Stage dir. *Iuniper* corr. Q: *Inniper* Q originally
43 *Capriccio*] *Capriceio* corr. Q: *Capricioi* Q originally: *Capricio* W
Exeunt. G   I. vi. Scæne 6] Scæne 4 Q: SCENE II. A Room in Count
Ferneze's House. G   3 *Angelo*, W: *Angelio*, corr. Q: *Angelio*.
Q originally   4 him *om. originally in* Q   meanes, *corr.* Q: means.
Q *originally*

The Case is Alterd

To leaue my father, and come speake with me.
  Boy. I will my Lord. ⟨*Exit.*⟩
  Pau. Well, heauen be auspicious in the euent ;
For I do this against my *Genius*,
And yet my thoughts cannot propose a reason,
Why I should feare, or faint thus in my hopes,
Of one so much endeered to my loue.
Some sparke it is, kindled within the soule :
Whose light yet breaks not to the outward sence,
That propagates this tymerous suspect ;
His actions neuer carried any face
Of change, or weaknes : then I iniury him,
In being thus cold conceited of his faith,
O here he comes.   *Enter Angelo* ⟨*with the boy.*⟩
  Ang. How now sweet Lord, whats the matter ?
  Pau. Good faith his presence makes me halfe ashamd
Of my straid thoughts. Boy, bestow your selfe. *Exit Boy.*
Where is my father, Signior *Angelo* ?
  Ang. Marry in the galery, where your Lordship left him.
  Pau. Thats well. Then *Angelo* I will be briefe,
Since time forbids the vse of circumstance.
How well you are receiu'd in my affection,
Let it appeare by this one instance, onely,
That now I will deliuer to your trust,
The deerest secrets, treasurd in my bosome.
Deare *Angelo*, you are not euery man,
But one, whome my election hath design'd,
As the true proper obiect of my soule :
I vrge not this t'insinuate my desert,
Or supple your tri'd temper, with soft phrases ;

   1. vi. 6 *Boy.*] *Boy* Q   *Stage dir. supplied by* G   7 Well, heauen] Well heauen, Q   13 sence *corr.* Q : scence Q *originally*   16 weaknes *corr.* Q : weakes Q *originally*   him,] him ? Q   17 conceited *corr.* Q : concepted Q *originally*   18 stage dir. *Enter Angelo.*] *Re-enter Page with Angelo.* G   *Angelo* corr. Q : *Angelio originally*   20 ashamd] ashamd. Q   21 Boy, bestow] *Boy.* Bestow Q   22 *Angelo* ?] Angelo ? W : *Angelio.* Q   24 *Angelo*] Angelo W : *Angelio* Q   briefe,] briefe. Q   25 circumstance.] circumstance, Q   26 receiu'd] receiued Q   27 onely,] onely Q   29 bosome.] bosome, Q   30 *Angelo,* you] Angelo, you W : *Angelio.* You Q

35 True frendship lothes such oyly complement :
But from th'aboundance of that loue, that flowes
Through all my spirits, is my speech enforc'd.
    Ang. Before your Lordship do proceed too far,
Let me be bould to intimate thus much ;
40 That what so ere your wisedome hath t'expose,
Be it the waightiest and most rich affaire,
That euer was included in your breast,
My faith shall poise it, if not—
    Pau.   O no more,
Those words haue rapt me with their sweet affects,
45 So freely breath'd, and so responsible
To that which I endeuour'd to extract,
Arguing a happy mixture of our soules.
    Ange. Why were there no such *sympathy* sweete Lord,
Yet the impressure of those ample fauours,
50 I haue deriu'd from your vnmatched spirit,
Would bind my faith to all obseruances.
    Pau. How! fauours *Angelo*, ô speake not of them,
They are meere paintings, and import no merit.
Lookes my loue well? thereon my hopes are plac't :
55 Faith, that is bought with fauours, cannot last. *Enters Boy.*
    Boy. My Lord.
    Pau. How now?
    Boy. You are sought for all about the house, within,
The *Count* your father cals for you.
60   *Pau.* God, what crosse euents do meet my purposes?
Now will he violently fret and grieue
That I am absent. Boy, say I come presently : *Exit Boy.*
Sweet *Angelo*, I cannot now insist
Vpon particulars, I must serue the time.
65 The maine of all this is, I am in loue.
    Ange. Why starts your Lordship?
    Pau.   I thought I heard

    1. vi. 44 affects] effects *Q*   45 responsible] responsible, *Q*   46 endeuour'd] endeauoured *Q*   48 Lord,] Lord? *Q*   52, 63 *Angelo*] An-gelo *W* : *Angello Q*   53 merit.] merit *Q*   64 time.] time *Q*   66–70 Prose in *Q*

My father comming hitherward, list, ha ?
  Ange. I heare not any thing,
It was but your imagination sure.   70
  Pau. No.
  Ange. No, I assure your Lordship.
  Pau. I would worke safely.
  Ange. Why, has he no knowledge of it then ?
  Pau. O no, no creature yet pertakes it but your selfe 75
In a third person, and beleeue me friend,
The world containes not now another spirit,
To whom I would reueile it. Harke, harke,
         Seruants { *Signior Paulo* / *Lord Ferneze.* } *within.*   80
  Ange. A pox vpon those brazen throated slaues,
What are they mad, trow ?
  Pau.   Alas, blame not them,
Their seruices are (clock-like) to be set,
Backward and forward, at their Lords command.
You know my father's wayward, and his humour   85
Must not receiue a check, for then all obiects,
Feede both his griefe and his impatience,
And those affections in him, are like powder,
Apt to enflame with euery little sparke,
And blow vp reason, therefore *Angelo,* peace.   90
within. { *Count.* Why this is rare, is he not in the garden ? / *Christ.* I know not my Lord. / *Count.* See, call him ! }
  Pau. He is comming this way, let's withdraw a little,
                                                          Exeunt.
within. { *Seruants.* Signior *Paulo,* Lord *Ferneze,* Lord *Paulo.* } 95

I. vi. 71 No. *corr. Q* : No ? *Q originally*   80 *Seruants*] Seruants. Q
84 command.] command, *Q*   90 *Angelo* corr. Q : *Angello* Q *originally*
93 him !] him ? *Q*

Scæne 7.

Enter Count Ferneze, Maximilian, Aurelia, Phœnixella, Sebast⟨ian,⟩ Balthasar.

Count. Where should he be, trow? did you looke in the armory?
Sebast. No my Lord.
Count. No, why there? ô who would keepe such drones?
Exeunt Sebast. and Baltha.
How now, ha ye found him?   *Enter Martino.*
Mart.   No my Lord.
Count.   No my Lord,
5 I shall haue shortly all my family
Speake nought, but no my Lord. Where is *Christophero?*
Enter Christophero.
Looke how he stands, you sleepy knaue,   *Exit Martino.*
What is he not in the Garden?
Christo.   No my good Lord.
Count. Your good Lord, ô how this smels of fennell.
Enter Sebast. Baltha.
10 You have bene in the garden it appeares, well, well.
Balth. We cannot find him my Lord.
Sebast. He is not in the armory.
Count. He is not, he is no where, is he?
Maxi. Count *Ferneze.*
15 *Count.* Signior.
Maxi. Preserue your patience honorable *Count.*
Count. Patience? a Saint would loose his patience to be crost,
As I am with a sort of motly braines,
See, see, how like a nest of Rookes they stand, *Enter Onion.*
20 Gaping on one another! Now *Diligence,*
What news bring you?
Oni. Ant please your honour.

1. vii. Scæne 7] Scæne 5 Q   *Sebast.* corr. Q : *Sebast,* Q originally   4 Stage dir. *Martino* corr. Q : *Matino* Q originally   4–5 *Count's speech two lines in Q, divided after* family   6 nought, *corr.* Q: nought Q *originally* Lord. Where] Lord, where Q   *Christophero?*] *Christophero,* Q   17 crost, *corr.* Q.: crost Q *originally*   20 Now] now Q   21 *Ranged with* 20 *in* Q

Count. Tut, tut, leaue pleasing of my honour *Diligence*, You double with me, come.
Oni. How : does he find fault with *Please his Honour* ? 25 S'wounds it has begun a seruingmans speech, euer since I belongd to the blew order : I know not how it may shew, now I am in blacke, but - - -
Count. Whats that, you mutter sir ? will you proceed ?
Oni. Ant like your good Lordship. 30
Count. Yet more, Gods precious.
Oni. What, do not this like him neither ?
Count. What say you sir knaue ?
Oni. Mary I say your Lordship were best to set me to schoole againe, to learne how to deliuer a message. 35
Count. What do you take exception at me then ?
Oni. Exception ? I take no exceptions, but by Gods so your humours - - - -
Count. Go to, you are a Raskall, hold your tongue.
Oni. Your Lordships poore seruant, I. 40
Count. Tempt not my patience.
Oni. Why I hope I am no spirit, am I ?
Maxi. My Lord, command your Steward to correct the slaue.
Oni. Correct him ? S'bloud come you and correct him 45 and you have a minde to it. Correct him, that's a good iest I faith, the Steward and you both, come and correct him.
Count. Nay see, away with him, pull his cloth ouer his eares.
Oni. Cloth ? tell me of your cloth, here's your cloth, nay 50 and I mourne a minute longer, I am the rottenest *Onion* that euer spake with a tongue. *They thrust him out.*
Maxi. What call ⟨you⟩ your hind's ⟨name⟩ count *Ferneze* ?
Count. His name is *Onion* Signior. 55

I. vii. 23–4 *Prose in* Q   24 me *W* : we *Q*   25 *his* corr. Q: *your* Q originally   Honour ?] Honour. Q   36 then ?] then. Q   36 exception] exceptions Q   37 Exception ?] Exceptions ! G   39 to,] to Q
45 him ?] him, Q   46 it. Correct] it, correct Q   53 you *W*   hind's] hind *W*   name *G*   55 Signior.] Signior, Q

Maxi. I thought him some such sawcy companion.
Count. Signior *Maximillian.*
Maxi. Sweet Lord.
Count. Let me intreat you, you would not regard
60 Any contempt flowing from such a spirit,
So rude, so barbarous.
    Maxi.   · Most noble *Count*
Vnder your fauour · · ·
    Coun.   Why Ile tell you Signior,
Heele bandy with me word for word, nay more,
Put me to silence, strike me perfect dumb ;
65 And so amaze me, that oft[en]times I know not,
Whether to check or cherish his presumption :
Therefore good Signior.
    Maxi. Sweet Lord satisfie your selfe, I am not now to
learn how to manage my affections, I haue obseru'd, and
70 know the difference betweene a base wretch and a true
man, I can distinguish them ; the property of the wretch
is, he would hurt and cannot, of the man, he can hurt, and
will not.   ⟨*Aurelia smiles.*⟩
    Coun. Go to, my merry daughter, ô these lookes,
75 Agree well with your habit, do they not ?

⟨Scæne 8.⟩

Enter Iuniper.

    Iunip. Tut, let me alone. By your fauour, this is the
Gentleman I thinke. Sir, you appeare to be an honorable
Gentleman, I vnderstand, and could wish (for mine owne
part) that things were conden't otherwise then they are :
5 but (the world knowes) a foolish fellow, somewhat procliue,
and hasty, he did it in a preiudicate humour ; mary now
vpon better computation, he wanes ; he melts ; his poore
eyes are in a cold sweat. Right noble *Signior*, you can have

---

    I. vii. 61–2 Most ... fauour ... *one line in Q.*   71 them ;] them, *Q*
73 *Stage dir. supplied by* G   I. viii. *Stage dir. added to* vii. 75 *in Q.*
Enter Juniper in his cobler's dress. G   2 thinke.] thinke, *Q*

but compunction, I loue the man, tender your compassion.
  Maxi. Doth any man here vnderstand this fellow? 10
  Iunip. O God sir, I may say *frustra* to the comprehension of your intellection.
  Maxi. Before the Lord, he speakes all riddle, I thinke. I must haue a comment ere I can conceiue him.
  Count. Why he sues to have his fellow *Onion* pardon'd, 15 And you must grant it Signior.
  Maxi. O with all my soule my Lord, is that his motion?
  Iunip. I sir, and we shall retort these kind fauours with all allacrity of spirit, we can sir, as may be most expedient, as well for the quality as the cause, till when in spight of 20 this complement: I rest a poore Cobler, seruant to my honorable Lord here your friend, and *Iuniper.*   *Exit.*
  Maxi. How, *Iuniper?*
  Count. I Signior.
  Maxi. He is a sweete youth, his tongue has a happy 25 turne when he sleepes.
  Count. I, for then it rests.

⟨Scæne 9.⟩

Enter Paulo Ferneze, Francisco Colonnea, Angelo, Valentine.

            O Sir you're welcome,
Why God be thanked you are found at last:
Signior *Colonnia* truly you are welcome,
I am glad to see you sir so well return'd.
  Fran. I gladly thanke your honour, yet indeed 5
I am sory for such cause of heauinesse,
As hath possest your Lordship in my absence.
  Count. O *Francisco*, you knew her what she was!
  Fran. She was a wise and honorable Lady.
  Count. I was she not! well, weepe not she is gone. 10

  I. viii. 13–14 *Two lines in Q, divided at* thinke   22 here] here, *Q*
friend,] friend *Q*   23 How,] How *Q*   27 Begins ix. 1. *in Q*   rests.]
rests, *Q*   I. ix. Stage dir. Colonnea] Colomea *Q*: Colonia W:
Colonnia G   1 you're] your *Q*   3 Colonnia G: Coloma *Q*: Colonia
W   4 return'd] returned *Q*   8 Francisco,] Francisco' *Q*   10 well,]
well *Q*

120 *The Case is Alterd*

Pass⟨i⟩ons duld eye can make two grieues of one,
Whom death marke⟨s⟩ out, vertue, nor bloud can saue.
Princes, as beggers, all must feed the graue.
    Max. Are your horse ready Lord *Paulo* ?
15   *Pau.* I signior, the⟨y⟩ stay for vs at the gate.
    Max. Well tis good. Ladies I will take my leaue of you, be your fortunes as your selues, faire. Come let vs to horse. Count *Ferneze* I beare a spirit full of thanks for all your honorable courtesies.
20   *Count.* Sir I could wish the number and value of them more in respect of your deseruings. But Signior *Maximillian*, I p⟨r⟩ay you a word in priuate.
    Aur. I faith brother, you are fitted for a generall yonder. Beshrow my heart (if I had *Fortunatus* hat here) and
25 I would not wish my selfe a man and go with you, only t'enioy his presence.
    Pau. Why, do you love him so well sister?
    Aur. No by my troth, but I haue such an odde prety apprehension of his humour me thinks: that I am eene
30 tickled with the conceite of it. O he is a fine man.
    Ang. And me thinks another may be as fine as he.
    Aur. O *Angelo*, do you thinke I do vrge any comparison against you? no, I am not so ill bred, as to be a deprauer of your worthines: beleeue me, if I had not some hope of
35 your abiding with vs, I should neuer desire to go out of black whilst I liued: but learne to speake i' the nose, and turne puritan presently.
    Ang. I thanke you Lady: I know you can flout.
    Aur. Come doe you take it so? I faith you wrong me.
40   *Fran.* I, but Maddame,

1. ix. 12 markes] marks *W*   bloud] bluod *Q*   14 *Paulo* ?] *Paulo*, *Q*   15 signior,] signior *Q*   they *W*   16–18 *Divided in Q at* you *and* horse   17 be] Be *Q*   selues,] selues ? *Q*   horse.] horse, *Q*   21 *Maximillian*,] *Maximillian*. *Q*   22 pray *W*   I pay *begins a new line in Q. They walk aside.* add *G*   23 faith brother,] Faith brother *Q*   yonder.] yonder, *Q*   24 Beshrow *begins a new line in Q*   if] If *Q*   *Fortunatus*] Fortnnatus *Q*   27 Why,] Why *Q*   sister ?] sister. *Q*   30 O he] Ohe *Q, beginning a new line*   32 *Angelo*] Angelo *W* : *Angelio* Q   do vrge] urge *G*   any] my *W*   33 deprauer *corr. Q :* prauer *Q originally*   37 presently. *corr. Q :* presently : *Q originally*   40 Maddame, *corr. Q :* Maddame. *Q. originally*

Thus to disclaime in all the affects of pleasure,
May make your sadnesse seeme to much affected,
And then the proper grace of it is lost.
   Phœnix. Indeed sir, if I did put on this sadnesse
Onely abroad, and in Society,   45
And were in priuate merry ; and quick humor'd ;
Then might it seeme affected and abhord :
But as my lookes appeare, such is my spirit,
Drown'd vp with confluence of griefe, and melancholy,
That like to riuers run through all my vaines,   50
Quenching the pride and feruour of my bloud.
   Max. My honorable Lord ? no more :
There is the honour of my bloud ingag'd,
For your sonnes safety.
   Count.   Signior, blame me not,
For tending his security so much,   55
He is mine onely sonne, and that word onely,
Hath with his strong, and repercussiue sound,
Stroke my heart cold, and giuen it a deepe wound.
   Max. Why but stay, I beseech you, had your Lordship
euer any more sonnes then this ?   60
   Count. Why, haue you not knowen it *Maximilian* ?
   Max. Let my Sword faile me then.
   Count. I had one other yonger borne then this,
By twise so many howers as would fill
The circle of a yeare, his name *Camillo*,   65
Whome in that blacke, and fearfull night I lost,
(Tis now a nineteene yeares agone at least,
And yet the memory of it sits as fresh
Within my braine as twere but yesterday)
It was that night wherein the great *Chamont*,   70
The generall for *France*, surpris'd *Vicenza*.
Me thinks the horrour of that clamorous shout

    1. ix. 41 affects *C. H. Herford*: effects *Q*   44 *Phœnix*.] *Phœnix Q*
56 mine *corr. Q*: my *Q originally*   57 repercussiue] reprecussiue *Q*
sound, *corr. Q*: sound. *Q originally*   60 this ?] this. *Q*   61 Why,]
Why *Q*   64 howers] how ers *Q*   71 *France*, surpris'd *Vicenza*.]
France surprised *Vicenza*, *Q*

His souldiers gaue, when they attaind the wall,
Yet tingles in mine eare, me thinkes I see
75 With what amazed lookes, distracted thoughts,
And minds confus'd, we, that were citizens,
Confronted one another : euery street
Was fild with bitter selfe tormenting cries,
And happy was that foote, that first could presse
80 The flowry champaigne, bordering on *Verona*.
Heere I (imploy'd about my dear wiues safety,
Whose soule is now in peace) lost my *Camillo*.
Who sure was murdered by the barbarous Souldiers,
Or else I should haue heard—my heart is great.
85 *Sorrow is faint ; and passion makes me sweat.*
  Max. Grieue not sweet *Count*, comfort your spir⟨i⟩ts :
you haue a sonne a noble gentleman, he stands in the face
of honour : For his safety, let that be no question. I am
maister of my fortune, and he shall share with me. Fare-
90 well my honorable Lord. Ladies once more adiew : for your
selfe maddam, you are a most rare creature, I tell you so,
be not proud of it, I loue you : come Lord *Paulo* to horse.
  Pau. Adieu good Signior *Francesco* : farewell sister.
     Sound a tucket, and as they passe euery one seuerally de-
        part, Maximilian, Paulo Ferneze, and Angelo remaine.
  Ang. How shall we rid him hence ?
95 *Pau.* Why well inough : sweet *Signior Maximilian*,
I haue some small occasion to stay :
If it may please you but take horse afore,
Ile ouer take you, ere your troopes be rang'd.
  Max. Your motion doth tast well : Lord *Ferneze* I go.
                                           Exit Max.

<small> 1. ix. 73 gaue, when] gaue' when *Q*   74 eare] ears *W*   79 presse]
presse, *Q*   81 safety,] safety) *Q*   85 faint ;] faint ? *Q*   86
Max.] *Max Q*   *Count*,] Count: *Q*   spirits :] spirits, *Q*   88 safety,]
safety *Q*   90 once more adiew :] onc emore adiew, *Q*   91 maddam,]
maddam *Q*   93 sister] sisters *G*   After 93 SCENE III. The street
before Jaques de Prie's house. | *Enter Paulo Ferneze ; and Angelo,*
followed by Maximilian. G   94 hence ?] hence. *Q*   After 94 c.w.
Pan. Q   95 inough :] inough ? *Q*   97 afore,] afore *Q*   98 rang'd
corr. Q : ranged *Q originally*   99 doth *W* : hath *Q*</small>

⟨Scæne 10.⟩

Pau. Now if my loue, faire *Rachel*, were so happy,
But to looke forth. See fortune doth me grace,
Enter Rachel.
Before I can demaund. How now ⟨my⟩ loue?
Where is your father?
   Rach.   Gone abroad my Lord.
   Pau.   Thats well.
   Rach. I but I feare heele presently returne.   5
Are you now going my most honor'd Lord?
   Pau. I my sweet *Rachel*.
   (*Ang.* Before God, she is a sweet wench.)
   Pau. Rachel I hope I shall not need to vrge,
The sacred purity of our affects,   10
As if it hung in triall or suspence :
Since in our hearts, and by our mutuall vowes,
It is confirmd and seald in sight of heauen.
Nay doe not weepe, why starte you? feare not, Loue,
Your father cannot be return'd so soone,   15
I prithee doe not looke so heauily,
Thou shalt want nothing.
   Rach.   No? is your presence nothing?
I shall want that, and wanting that, want all :
For that is all to me.
   Pau.   Content thee sweet,
I haue made choise here of a constant friend,   20
This gentleman ; one, ⟨on⟩ whose zealous loue
I doe repose more, then on all the world,

---

1. x. 1 loue,] loue *Q*   2 grace,] grace. *Q*   *Stage dir. centred in Q*
3 demaund.] demaund? *Q*   loue?] loue. *Q*   4 Lord.] Lord : *Q*   Pau.
corr. *Q* : *Pau* : *Q* originally   well. *corr. Q* : well, *Q originally*   5 returne.] returne, *Q*   6 honor'd] honored *Q*   8 *Aside not marked in Q*
10 affects *W* : effects *Q*   14 Loue,] *Loue. Q*   15 return'd *corr.
Q* : returned *Q originally*   16 heauily, *corr. Q* : heauily *Q originally*
17 want nothing. *corr. Q* : want nothing *Q originally*   No?] No *Q*
18 all: *corr. Q* : all *Q originally*   19 sweet, *corr. Q* : sweet *Q originally*   20 made] Made *Q*   friend,] friend *Q*   21 gentleman ;]
gentleman? *Q*   one, on *G* : one *Q* : on *W*

Thy beauteous selfe excepted : and to him,
Haue I committed my deere care of thee,
25 As to my genius, or my other soule.
Receiue him gentle loue, and what deffects
My absence proues, his presence shall supply.
The time is enuious of our longer stay.
Farewell deere *Rachel.*
    Rach.   Most deere Lord, adew,
30 Heauen and honour crowne your deeds, and you.
                                            Exit Rachel.
    Pau. Faith tell me *Angelo*, how dost thou like her?
    Ang. Troth well my Lord, but shall I speake my mind?
    Pau. I prithee doe.
    Ang. She is deriud too meanely to be wife
35 To such a noble person, in my iudgement.
    Pau. Nay then thy iudgement is to meane, I see :
Didst thou neare read in difference of good,
Tis more to shine in vertue then in bloud?   *Enter Iaques.*
    Ang. Come you are so sententious my Lord.
40   *Pau.* Here comes her father. How dost thou good
       Iaques?
    Ang. God saue thee *Iaques.*
    Iaq. What should this meane?   *Rachel* open the dore.
                                            Exit Iaques.
    Ang. Sbloud how the poore slaue lookes, as though
He had bene haunted by the spirit *Lar,*
45 Or seene the ghost of some great *Satrapas*
In an vnsauory sheet.
    Pau. I muse he spake not, belike he was amazd
Comming so suddenly and vnprepard?   Well lets go.
                                                Exeunt.

    I. x. 25 soule. *corr.* Q: soule, Q *originally*   26 Receiue him...
loue,...deffects *corr.* Q: Rsceiue hi...loue...deffects, Q *originally*
27 absence *corr.* Q: a bscence Q *originally*   29 *Rach.*] *Rach*: Q   30
Stage dir. centred in Q   31 Faith *corr.* Q: Faiṭh Q *originally*   *Angelo,*]
Angelo W: *Angelio* Q   32 mind?] mind. Q   36 meane *corr.* Q:
meene Q *originally*   37 good, *corr.* Q: good Q *originally*   38
bloud?] bloud. Q   43 lookes] looks aghast G   45 *Satrapas* corr.
Q: *Satrapas.* Q originally   47 not *corr.* Q: no Q *originally*   48
go. *corr.* Q: go : Q *originally*

Actus secundi Scæna prima.

Enter Iaques solus.

So now inough my heart, beat now no more ;
At least for this afright. What a could sweat
Flow'd on my browes, and ouer all my bosome !
Had I not reason ? to behold my dore
Beset with vnthrifts, and my selfe abroad ?   5
Why *Iaques* ? was there nothing in the house
Worth a continuall eye, a vigelent thought,
Whose head should neuer nod, nor eyes once wincke ?
Looke on my coate, my thoughts ; worne quite thred bare,
That time could neuer couer with a nappe,   10
And by it learne, neuer with nappes of sleepe,
To smother your conceipts of that you keepe.
But yet, I maruell, why these gallant youths
Spoke me so faire, and I esteemd a beggar ?
The end of flattery, is gaine, or lechery :   15
If they seeke gaine of me, they thinke me rich,
But that they do not : For their other obiect :
Tis in my handsome daughter, if it be.
And by your leaue, her handsomnesse may tell them
My beggery counterfeits, and, that her neatnesse,   20
Flowes from some store of wealth, that breakes my coffers,
With this same engine, loue to mine owne breed.
But this is answered : *Beggers will keepe fine,*
Their daughters, being faire, though themselues pine.
Well then, it is for her, I, 'tis sure for her,   25
And I make her so briske for some of them,
That I might liue alone once with my gold.
O 'tis a sweet companion ! kind and true !
A man may trust it when his father cheats him ;
Brother, or friend, or wife ! ô wondrous pelfe,   30
,, *That which makes all men false, is true it selfe.*

II. i. Actus ... prima.] SCENE I. The Court-yard at the back of Jaques'
House. G   1 more ;] more.; *Q*   2 afright. What] afright, what *Q*
6 there] their *Q*   17 For] for *Q*   25, 28 'tis] t'is *Q*   28 true !]
true, *Q*   30 wife !] wife, *Q*

But now this maid, is but suppos'd my daughter:
For I being Steward to a Lord of France,
Of great estate, and wealth, call'd Lord *Chammount*,
35 He gone into the warres, I stole his treasure;
(But heare not, any thing) I stole his treasure,
And this his daughter, being but two yeares old,
Because it lou'd me so, that it would leaue
The nurse her selfe, to come into mine armes,
40 And had I left it, it would sure haue dyed.
Now herein I was kinde, and had a conscience;
And since her Lady mother that did dye
In child-bed of her, lou'd me passing well,
It may be nature fashiond this affection,
45 Both in the child and her: but hees ill bred,
That ransackes tombes, and doth deface the dead.
I'le therefore say no more: suppose the rest,
Here haue I chang'd my forme, my name and hers,
And liue obs⟨c⟩urely, to enioy more safe
50 My deerest treasure. But I must abroad.
    Rachel.   *Enter Rachel.*
       Rach. What is your pleasure sir?
       Iaq. *Rachel* I must abroad.
    Lock thy selfe in, but yet take out the key,
55 That whosoeuer peepes in at the key-hole,
    May yet imagine there is none at home.
       Rach. I will sir.
       Iaq. But harke thee *Rachel*: say a theefe should come,
    And misse the key, he would resolue indeede
60 None were at home, and so breake in the rather:
    Ope the doore *Rachel*, set it open daughter;
    But sit in it thy selfe: and talke alowd,
    As if there were some more in house with thee:
    Put out the fire, kill the chimnies hart,
65 That it may breath no more then a dead man.
    The more we spare my child, the more we gaine. *Exeunt.*

II. i. 34 call'd] called *Q*   43 lou'd] loued *Q*   50-1 abroad, *Rachel Q* (*in one line*)   *Stage dir. in Q at* 49   Enter] Ent er *Q*   59 resolue] resoule *Q*   63 thee:] thee.: *Q*   65 man.] man, *Q*   66 The *corr. Q*: Tho *Q originally*

Scæne 2.

Enter Christophero, Iuniper and Onion.

Christ. Why sayes my fellow *Onion*? come on.

Oni. All of a house sir, but no fellowes, you are my Lords Steward, but I pray you what thinke you of loue, sir?

Christ. Of loue *Onion*? Why it's a very honourable humor.   5

Oni. Nay if it be but worshipfull I care not.

Iunip. Go to, it's honorable, checke not at the conceit of the Gentleman.

Oni. But in truth sir, you shall do well to think well of loue: for it thinkes well of you, in me, I assure you.   10

Chris. Gramercy fellow *Onion*: I do thinke well, thou art in loue, art thou?

Oni. Partly sir, but I am asham'd to say wholy.

Chris. Well, I will further it in thee to any honest woman, or maiden, the best I can.   15

Iunip. Why now you come neere him sir, he doth vaile, he doth remunerate, he doth chaw the cud in the kindnesse of an honest imperfection to your worship.

Chris. But who is it thou louest fellow *Onion*?

Oni. Mary a poore mans daughter, but none of the   20 honestest, I hope.

Chris. Why, wouldst thou not haue her honest?

Oni. O no, for then I am sure she would not haue me. 'Tis *Rachel de Prie*.

Chris. Why, she hath the name of a very vertuous   25 mayden.

Iunip. So shee is sir, but the fellow talkes in quiddits, he.

Chris. What wouldst thou haue me do in the matter?

Oni. Do nothing sir, I pray you, but speake for me.

Chris. In what maner?   30

II. ii. Scæne 2.] SCENE II. A Room in Count Ferneze's House. G
10 for] For *Q, beginning a new line*   17 He doth remunerate *begins a new line in Q.*   18 Of *begins a new line in Q.*   19 Chris.] Chris Q
21 honestest] ho nestest Q   24 'Tis] T'is Q

Oni. My fellow *Iuniper* can tell you sir.
Iunip. Why as thus sir. Your worship may commend him for a fellow fit for consanguinity, and that he shaketh with desire of procreation, or so.
35 *Chris.* That were not so good, me thinkes.
Iunip. No sir, why so sir? what if you should say to her, corroborate thy selfe sweete soule, let me distinguish thy pappes with my fingers, diuine Mumps, prety *Pastorella*? lookest thou so sweet and bounteous? comfort my friend
40 here.
Chris. Well I perceiue you wish, I should say something may do him grace, and further his desires, and that be sure I will.
Oni. I thanke you sir, God saue your life, I pray God sir.
45 *Iunip.* Your worship is too good to liue long: youle contaminate me no seruice?
Chris. Command thou wouldest say, no good *Iuniper*.
Iunip. Health and wealth sir. *Exeunt Onion and Iuniper.*
Chris. This wench wil I solicite for my selfe,
50 Making my Lord and maister priuy to it;
And if he second me with his consent,
I will proceede, as hauing long ere this,
Thought her a worthy choyce to make my wife. *Exit.*

Scæne 3.

Enter Aurelia, Phœnixella.

Vre. Roome for a case of matrons colour'd blacke,
How motherly my mothers death hath made vs?
I would I had some girles now to bring vp;
O I could make a wench so vertuous,
5 She should say grace to euery bit of meate,
And gape no wider then a wafers thicknesse:
And she should make French cursies, so most low,

<small>II. ii. 37 corroborate] correbate *Q*   46 seruice?] seruice. *Q*   49 I *corr. Q*: om. *originally*   53 Thought *corr. Q*: Though *Q originally*
II. iii. Scæne 3.] SCENE III. Another Room in the Same. *G*   1 colour'd] coloured *Q*</small>

The Case is Alterd

That euery touch should turne her ouer backward.
 Phœni. Sister, these words become not your attire,
Nor your estate : our vertuous mothers death   10
Should print more deep effects of sorrow in vs,
Then may be worne out in so little time.
 Aure. Sister, ⟨i'⟩ faith you take too much Tobacco,
It makes you blacke within, as y'are without.
What true-stich sister ? both your sides alike ?   15
Be of a sleighter worke : for of my word,
You shall be sold as deere, or rather deerer.
Will you be bound to *customes* and to *rites* ?
Shed profitable teares, weepe for aduantage ;
Or else, do all things, as you are enclynd.   20
Eate when your stomacke serues (saith the *Physitian*)
Not at *eleuen* and *sixe*. So if your humour
Be now affected with this heauinesse,
Giue me the reines and spare not, as I do,
In this my pleasurable appetite.   25
It is *Præcisianisme* to alter that
With austere iudgement, that is giuen by nature.
I wept you saw too, when my mother dyed :
For then I found it easier to do so,
And fitter with my moode, then not to weepe.   30
But now tis otherwise, another time
Perhaps I shall haue such deepe thoughts of her,
That I shall weepe a fresh, some tweluemonth hence,
And I will weepe, if I be so dispos'd,
And put on blacke, as grimly then, as now ;   35
Let the minde go still with the bodies stature,
Iudgement is fit for Iudges, giue me nature.

 II. iii. 13 i' *W*   17 deere,] deere *Q*   deerer.] deerer ? *Q*   21 Eate]
Eat *W* : Hate *Q*   23 heauinesse,] heauinesse. *Q*   24 me] it *W*
25 appetite.] appetite, *Q*

445·3   K

Scæne 4.

[Enter] *Aurelia, Phœnixella, Francisco, Angelo.*

Fran. See Signior *Angelo* here are the Ladies,
Go you and comfort one, Ile to the other.
  Ange. Therefore I come sir, I'le to the eldest.
God saue you Ladies, these sad moodes of yours,
5 That make you choose these solitary walkes,
Are hurtfull for your beauties.
  Aure.   If we had them.
  Ange. Come, that condition might be for your hearts,
When you protest faith, since we cannot see them.
But this same heart of beauty, your sweet face,
10 Is in mine eye still.
  Aure.   O you cut my heart
With your sharpe eye.
  Ange.   Nay Lady, thats not so,
Your heart's to hard.
  Aure.   My beauties hart?
  Ange.   O no.
I meane that regent of affection, *Maddam*,
That tramples on al loue with such contempt
15 ⟨I⟩n this faire breast.
  Aur.   No more, your drift is sauour'd,
I had rather seeme hard hearted
  Ang.   Then hard fauour'd,
Is that your meaning, Lady?
  Aur.   Go too sir.
Your wits are fresh I know, they need no spur.
  Ang. And therefore you wil ride them.
  Aur.   Say I doe,
20 They will not tire I hope?
  Ang.   No, not with you,
Hark you sweet Lady.   ⟨*They walk aside.*⟩

II. iv. 3 I'le] I will *G*   9 face,] face *Q*   11 With] with *Q*   11, 12 Nay ... hard. *one line in Q*   19 doe,] doe. *Q*   20, 21 No ... Lady. *one line in Q*   21 Stage dir. *They walk aside.*] *Walks aside with Aur. G*

Fran.   Tis much pitty Maddam,
You should haue any reason to retaine
This signe of griefe, much lesse the thing disignde.
  Phœ. Griefes are more fit for Ladies then their pleasures.
  Fran. That is for such as follow nought but pleasures.   25
But you that temper them so wel with vertues,
Vsing your griefes so, it would prooue them pleasures.
And you would seeme in cause of griefes & pleasures
Equally pleasant.
  Phœ.   Sir so I do now.
It is the excesse of either that I striue   30
So much to shun in all my proou'd endeauours.
Although perhaps vnto a generall eye,
I may appeare most wedded to my griefes,
Yet doth my mind forsake no tast of pleasure,
I meane that happy pleasure of the soule,   35
Deuine and sacred contemplation
Of that eternall, and most glorious blisse,
Proposed as the crowne vnto our soules.
  Fran. I will be silent, yet that I may serue
But as a *Decade* in the art of memory   40
To put you stil in mind of your owne vertues
(When your too serious thoughts make you too sad)
Accept me for your seruant honor'd Lady.
  Phœn. Those cerimonies are too common signior *Francis*,
For your vncommon grauitie, and iudgement,   45
And fits them onely, that are nought but cerimony.
               ⟨*Angelo and Aurelia come forward.*⟩
  Ang. Come, I will not sue, stal⟨e⟩ly to be your seruant,
But a new tearme, will you be my refuge?
  Aur. Your refuge, why sir?
  Ange. That I might fly to you, when all else faile me.   50
  Aur. And you be good at flying, be my Plouer.

<small>II. iv. 21 Maddam,] Maddam. *Q*   27 so,] so *Q*   28–9 And you . . . pleasant. *one line in Q*   31 endeauours.] endeauours, *Q*   42 (When] When *Q*   43 honor'd] honored *Q*.   *Phœu* c.w. in *Q*   46 fits] fit *G*   nought but] noughtbut *Q*   cerimony *corr. Q*: cerimon y *Q originally*   Stage dir. *Angelo . . . forward.*] *Comes forward with Aur. G*   47 stalely *W*   49 sir?] sir. *Q*</small>

Ang. Nay take away the P.
Aur.   Tut, then you cannot fly.
Ang. Ile warrant you. Ile borrow *Cupids* wings.
Aur. Masse then I feare me youle do strange things :
55 I pray you blame me not, if I suspect you,
Your owne confession simply doth detect you.
Nay and you be so great in *Cupids* bookes,
'Twill make me Iealous : you can with your lookes
(I warrant you) enflame a womans heart,
60 And at your pleasure take loues golden dart,
And wound the brest of any vert⟨u⟩ous maide.
Would I were hence : good faith I am affraid,
You can constraine one ere they be aware,
To run mad for your loue !
Ang.   O this is rare.

Scæne 5.

Aurelia, Phœnixella, Francisco, Angelo, Count.

Count. Close with my daughters gentlemen ? wel done,
Tis like your selues : nay lusty *Angelo,*
Let not my presence make you bauke your sport,
I will not breake a minute of discourse
5 Twixt you and one of your faire Mistresses.
Ang. One of my mistresses ? why, thinks your Lordship
I haue so many ?
Count.   Many, no *Angelo.*
I do not thinke th'ast many some fourteene
I here thou hast, euen of our worthiest dames,
10 Of any note, in *Millaine.*
Ang. Nay good my Lord fourteene : it is not so.
Count. By'th [the] Masse that ist, here are their names
to shew,

II. iv. 52 fly.] fly : *Q*   54 youle] you will *W*   56 you.] you, *Q*
58 'Twill] T'will *Q*   Iealous : *corr. Q* : Iealous. *Q originally*   62
faith] Faith *Q*   64 loue !] loue ? *Q*   rare *W* : rate *Q*   II. v
Scæne 5] Scæne 6 *Q*   *Aurelia* W : *Aurelio Q*   6 why,] why *Q*
7 many ?] many *Q*   10 *Millaine.*] *Millaine* : *Q*   12 shew,] shew *Q*

Fourteene, or fifteene t'one. Good *Angelo*,
You need not be ashamd of any of them,
They are gallants all.
    Ang.   Sbloud you are such a Lord.   *Exit Ang.* 15
    Count. Nay stay sweet *Angelo*, I am dispos'd
A little to be pleasant past my coustome,
He's gone, he's gone? I haue disgrast him shrewdly.
Daughters take heede of him, he's a wild youth,
Looke what he sayes to you beleeue him not,   20
He will sweare loue to euery one he sees.
Francisco, giue them councell, good *Francisco*,
I dare trust thee with both, but him with neither.
    Fran. Your Lordship yet may trust both them with him.
    Count. Well goe your waies, away.   25
        Ex⟨e⟩unt ⟨Aurelia, Phœnixella, Francisco⟩.

Scæne 6.

    Count. Christopher⟨o⟩.

    Count. How now *Christopher⟨o⟩*, what newes with you?
    Christ. I haue an humble suit to your good Lordship.
    Count. A suit *Christopher⟨o⟩*? what suit I prithee?
    Christ. I would craue pardon at your Lordships hands,
If it seeme vaine or simple in your sight.   5
    Count. Ile pardon all simplicity, *Christopher⟨o⟩*,
What is thy suit?
    Christ. Perhaps being now so old a batchelor,
I shall seeme halfe vnwise, to bend my selfe
In strict affection to a poore yong maide.   10
    Count. What? is it touching loue *Christopher⟨o⟩*?
Art thou dispost to marry, why tis well.
    Christo. I, but your Lordship may imagine now

    II. v. 13 Good *Angelo*,] Good *Angelo*. Q   15 st. d. *Ang*.] *Ang*: Q at l. 16
16 dispos'd] disposed *Q*   18 He's gone,] He's gone? *Q*   gone? I] g one,
I *Q*   shrewdly.] shrewdly, *Q*   25 *Begins sc. vi in Q*   away.] away,
Q   II. vi. Scæne 6] Scæne 7 *Q*   *Christophero*. W *(and so in ll.* 1-18):
Christopher, Q   1 How] how *Q*   What *begins a new line in Q*

That I being steward of your honours house,
15 If I be maried once, will more regard
The maintenance of my wife and of my charge,
Then the due discharge of my place and office.
    Count. No, no, *Christopher⟨o⟩*, I know thee honest.
    Christo. Good faith my Lord, your honour may suspect it,
20 But——
    Count. Then I should wrong thee, thou hast euer been
Honest and true, and wilt be still I knowe.
    Chris. I but this marriage alters many men :
And you may feare, it will do me my Lord,
25 But ere it do so, I will vndergoe
Ten thousand seuerall deaths.
    Count.   I know it man.
Who wouldst thou haue I prithee ?
    Chris.   *Rachel de prie,*
If your good Lordship, graunt me your consent.
    Count. Rachel de prie ? what the poore beggers daughter ?
30 Shees a right handsome maide, how poore soeuer,
And thou hast my consent, with all my hart.
    Chris. I humbly thanke your honour. Ile now aske her
father.
    Count. Do so *Christofero*, thou shalt do well.
                               Exit ⟨Christophero⟩.
35 Tis strange (she being so poore) he should affect her,
But this is more strange that my selfe should loue her.
I spide her, lately, at her fathers doore,
And if I did not see in her sweet face
Gentry and noblenesse, nere trust me more :
40 But this perswasion, fancie wrought in me,
That fancie being created with her lookes,
For where loue is he thinke⟨s⟩ his basest obiect
Gentle and noble : I am farre in loue,
And shall be forc'd to wrong my honest steward,

    II. vi. 14 house,] house. *Q*   17 office.] office : *Q*   19 your] yout *Q*   it,] it- *corr. Q* : it -- *Q originally*   20 But] but *Q*   22 wilt] will *Q*   25 so,] so ? *Q*   33 *Christofero,*] *Christofero Q*   *Exit* at line 32 in *Q*   42 thinkes] thinks *W*

For I must sue, and seeke her for my selfe ; 45
How much my duetie to my late dead wife,
And my owne deere renowne, so ere it swaies.
Ile to her father straight. *Loue hates delays.*   *Exit.*

Scæne 7.

Enter Onion, Iuniper, Valentine, Sebastian, Balthasar, Martino.

ONion. Come on Ifaith, lets to some exercise or other my hearts: fetch the hilts. Fellow *Iuniper*, wilt thou play?
                                Exit Martino.
 Iun. I cannót resolue you : tis as I am fitted with the ingenuity, quantity, or quality of the cudgell.
 Valen. How dost thou bastinado the poore cudgell with 5 tearmes?
 Iuni. O *Ingle*, I haue the phrases man, and the *Anagrams* and the *Epitaphs,* fitting the mistery of the noble science.
 Oni. Ile be hangd & he were not misbegotten of some fencer. 10
 Sebast. Sirrah *Valentine,* you can resolue me now, haue they their maisters of defence in other countries as we haue here in *Italy* ?
 Valen. O Lord, I, especially they in *Vtopia,* there they performe their prizes and chalenges, with as great cerimony 15 as the *Italian* or any nation else.
 Balt. Indeed? how is the manner of it (for gods loue) good *Valentine* ?
 Iuni. Ingle, I prithee make recourse vnto vs, wee are thy friends and familiars : sweet *Ingle.* 20
 Valen. Why thus sir.
 Oni. God a mercy good *Valentine,* nay go on.
 Iuni. Silentium bonus socius Onionus, good fellow *Onion*

 II. vi. 47 renowne,] renowne *Q*   swaies.] swaies, *Q*   II. vii. Scæne 7]
Scæne 8 *Q* :   SCENE IV. A Hall in the Same. *G*   2 Fetch *begins a new
line in Q*   hilts. Fellow] hilts fellow *Q*   play ?] play : *Q*   3 you:]
you ? *Q*   17 *Balt.] Balt Q*   18 *Valentine] Valeniine Q*   19 *Ingle,*]
Ingle ? *Q*

be not so ingenious, and turbulent : so sir ? and how ? how sweete *Ingle* ?

Valen. Marry, first they are brought to the publicke *Theater* :

Iuni. What ? ha' they *Theater⟨s⟩* there ?

Valen. Theaters ? I and plaies to : both tragidy and comedy, & set foorth with as much state as can be imagined !

Iuni. By Gods so ; a man is nobody, till he has trauelled.

Sebast. And how are their plaies ? as ours are ? extemporall ?

Valen. O no ! all premeditated things, and some of them very good I faith, my maister vsed to visite them often when he was there.

Balth. Why how, are they in a place where any man may see them ?

Valen. I, in the common *Theaters*, I tell you. But the sport is at a new play to obserue the sway and variety of oppinion that passeth it. A man⹀shall haue such a con‐fus'd mixture of iudgement, powr'd out in the throng there, as ridiculous, as laughter it selfe : one saies he likes not the writing, another likes not the plot, another not the playing. And sometimes a fellow that comes not there past once in fiue yeare at a *Parliament* time or so, will be as deepe myr'd in censuring as the best, and sweare by Gods foote he would neuer stirre his foote to see a hundred such as that is.

Oni. I must trauell to see these things, I shall nere think well of my selfe else.

Iunip. Fellow *Onion*, Ile beare thy charges and thou wilt but pilgrimize it along with me, to the land of *Vtopia*.

Sebast. Why but me thinkes such rookes as these should be asham'd to iudge.

Valen. Not a whit ! the rankest stinkard of them all, will take vpon him as peremptory, as if he had writ himselfe *in artibus magister.*

II. vii. 28 ha'] ha ? *Q*   Theaters *W*   30 comedy,] comedy *Q*
31 imagined !] imagined ? *Q*   35 no !] no ? *Q*   38 how,] how *Q*
56 whit !] whit ? *Q*

The Case is Alterd 137

Sebast. And do they stand to a popular censure for any thing they present? 60

Valen. I euer, euer, and the people generally are very acceptiue and apt to applaud any meritable worke, but there are two sorts of persons that most commonly are infectious to a whole auditory.

Balth. What be they? 65

Iunip. I come lets know them.

Oni. It were good they were noted.

Valen. Marry; one is the rude barbarous crue, a people that haue no braines, and yet grounded iudgements, these will hisse any thing that mounts aboue their grounded 70 capacities. But the other are worth the obseruation, I faith.

Omnes. What be they? what be they?

Valen. Faith a few *Caprichious* gallants.

Iunip. Caprichious? stay, that word's for me. 75

Valen. And they haue taken such a habit of dislike in all things, that they will approue nothing, be it neuer so conceited or elaborate, but sit disperst, making faces, and spitting, wagging their vpright eares, and cry filthy, filthy. Simply vttering their owne condition, and vsing their wryed 80 countenances in stead of a vice, to turne the good aspects of all that shall sit neere them, from what they behold.

Enter Martino with cudgels.

Oni. O that's well sayd, lay them downe, come sirs, who plaies? fellow *Iuniper, Sebastian, Balthasar*: Some body take them vp, come. 85

Iunip. Ingle Valentine?

Valen. Not I sir, I professe it not.

Iunip. Sebastian.

Sebast. Balthasar.

Balth. Who? I? 90

Oni. Come, but one bout, Ile giue hem thee, I faith.

Balth. Why, heres *Martino.*

_{II. vii. 60 present?] present. *Q* 68 Marry;] Marry? *Q* 79 eares,] eares *Q* 83 sirs,] sirs. *Q* who] Who *Q, beginning a new line* 84 plaies?] plaies, *Q* Some *begins a new line in Q*}

Oni. Foe he, alas he cannot play a whit, man.
Iunip. That's all one: no more could you *in statu quo
95 prius*. *Martino*, play with him, euery man has his beginning
and conduction.
Mart. Will you not hurt me fellow *Onion*?
Oni. Hurt thee, no? and I do, put me among pot-hearbs,
and chop me to peeces, come on?
100 *Iunip.* By your fauor sweet bullies giue them roome,
back, so. *Martino*, do not looke so thin vpon the matter.
⟨*They play a bout.*⟩
Oni. Ha, well plaid, fall ouer to my legge now! so, to
your guard againe, excellent, to my head now, make home
your blow: spare not me, make it home, good, good againe.
⟨*Martino breaks his head.*⟩
105 *Sebast.* Why how now *Peter*?
Valen. Gods so, *Onion* has caught a bruise.
Iunip. Couragio! be not *caprichious*! what?
Oni. Caprichious? not I, I scorn to be *caprichious* for
a scrach, *Martino* must haue another bout, come.
110 *Val. Seb. Balth.* No, no, play no more, play no more.
Oni. Foe, tis nothing, a philip, a deuise, fellow *Iuniper*
prithee get mee a Plantan, I had rather play with one that
had skil by halfe.
Mart. By my troth, fellow *Onion*, twas against my will.
115 *Oni.* Nay that's not so, twas against my head. But
come, weele ha one bout more.
Iunip. Not a bout, not a stroke.
Omnes. No more, no more. ⟨*Exit Martino.*⟩
Iunip. Why Ile giue you demonstration, how it came.
120 Thou openest the dagger to falsifie ouer with the back sword
trick, and he interrupted, before he could fall to the close.

II. vii. 94 *statu* W : *stata* Q   *prius.*] *prius,* Q   *Martino* begins a new line in Q   99 and] And Q, *beginning a new line*   101 so.] so, Q   Stage dir. *They . . . bout.*] Mart. *and* Onion *play a bout at cudgels.* G   102 now!] now? Q   104 *Stage dir. supplied by* G   107 Couragio!] Couragio? Q   *caprichious*!] *caprichious*? Q   109 *Martino* must] Martino, I must G   115 head.] head, Q   But *begins a new line in* Q   118 *Stage dir.* G   119 came.] came, Q   120 Thou *begins a new line in* Q   openest] openedst W   121 trick] frick Q   he could] *Query* you could

Oni. No, no, I know best how it was, better then any man here, I felt his play presently : for looke you, I gathered vpon him thus, thus do you see ? for the double locke, and tooke it single on the head. 125

Valen. He sayes very true, he tooke it single on the head.
Sebast. Come lets go.   *Enter Martino with a cob-web.*
Mar. Here fellow *Onion,* heres a cob-web.
Oni. How ? a cob-web *Martino,* I will haue another bout with you ! S'wounds do you first breake my head, and then 130 giue me a plaister in scorne ? come, to it, I will haue a bout.
Mart. God's my witnesse.
Oni. Tut ! your witnesse cannot serue.
Iunip. S'bloud ! why what, thou art not lunatike, art thou ? and thou bee'st, auoide *Mephistophiles.* Say the 135 signe shoud be in *Aries* now : or it may be for all vs, where were your life ? Answere me that.
Sebast. Hee sayes well, *Onion.*
Valen. I indeed doo's he.
Iunip. Come, come, you are a foolish *Naturalist,* go, get 140 a white [a] of an egge, and a little flax, and close the breach of the head, it is the most conducible thing that can be. *Martino,* do not insinuate vpon your good fortune, but play an honest part and beare away the bucklers.   *Exeunt.*

Act 3.   Scæne 1.

Enter Angelo solus.

A Nge. My yong and simple friend, *Paulo Ferneze,*
Bound me with mighty solemne coniurations,
To be true to him, in his loue to *Rachel,*
And to solicite his remembrance still,
In his enforced absence, much, I faith. 5
True to my friend in cases of affection ?

<small>II. vii. 122 was,] was *Q*   130 you !] you ? *Q*   131 come,] come *Q*
134 S'bloud !] S'bloud ? *Q*   135 bee'st,] bee'st *Q*   137 that.]
that ? *Q*   III. i. Scæne 1] SCENE I. The Street before Jaques de Prie's
House. G   3 loue] loue, *Q*</small>

In womens cases ? what a iest it is ?
How silly he is, that imagines it !
He is an asse that will keepe promise stricktly
10 In any thing that checkes his priuate pleasure ;
Chiefly in loue. S'bloud am not I a man ?
Haue I not eyes that are as free to looke ?
And bloud to be enflam'd as well as his ?
And when it is so, shall I not pursue
15 Mine owne loues longings, but preferre my friends ?
I tis a good foole, do so, hang me then.
Because I swore ? alas, who doo's not know,
That louers periuries are ridiculous ?
Haue at thee *Rachel* : Ile go court her sure :
20 For now I know her father is abroad.   *Enter Iaques.*
S'bloud see, he is here, ô what damn'd lucke is this ?
This labour's lost, I must by no meanes see him.
Tau, dery, dery.   *Exit.*

Scæne 2.

Iaques, Christophero.

Aq. Mischiefe and hell, what is this man a spirit ?
Haunts he my houses ghost, still at my doore ?
He has beene at my doore, he has beene in,
In my deere doore : pray God my gold be safe.
  Enter Christophero.
5 Gods pitty, heres another. *Rachel*, ho *Rachel*.
  Chris. God saue you honest father.
  Iaq. Rachel, Gods light, come to me, *Rachel, Rachel*!
  Exit.
  Chris. Now in Gods name what ayles he ? this is strange !
He loues his daughter so, Ile lay my life,
10 That hee's afraid, hauing beene now abroad,
I come to seeke her loue vnlawfully.   *Enter Iaques.*

   III. i. 16 then.] then Q   17 swore ?] swore, Q   23 *tau . . . dery,*
in Q as part of the stage dir.   *Exit.*] *Exit singing.* G   III. ii. 1 man]
man ? G   spirit ?] spirit, Q   2 ghost,] ghost ? Q

The Case is Alterd 141

(*Iaq.* Tis safe, tis safe, they haue not rob'd my treasure.)
Chris. Let it not seeme offensiue to you sir.
(*Iaq.* Sir, Gods my life, sir, sir, call me sir?)
Chris. Good father here me.
    Iaq.   You are most welcome sir,   15
(I meant almost) and would your worship speake?
Would you abase your selfe to speake to me?
    Chris. Tis no abasing father : my intent
Is to do further honour to you sir
Then onely speake : which is to be your sonne.   20
    Iaq. (My gold is in his nostrels, he has smelt it,
Breake breast, breake heart, fall on the earth my entrailes,
With this same bursting admiration!
He knowes my gold, he knowes of all my treasure,)
How do you know sir? whereby do you guesse?   25
    Chris. At what sir? what is ⟨i⟩t you meane?
    Iaq.   I aske,
An't please your Gentle worship, how you know?
I meane, how I should make your worship know
That I haue nothing—
To giue with my poore daughter? I haue nothing: 30
The very aire, bounteous to euery man,
Is scant to me, sir.
    Chris.   I do thinke good father,
You are but poore.
    (*Iaq.*   He thinkes so, harke, but thinke⟨s⟩ so :
He thinkes not so, he knowes of all my treasure.)   *Exit.*
    Chris. Poor man he is so ouerioy'd to heare   35
His daughter may be past his hopes bestow'd,
That betwixt feare and hope (if I meane simply)
He is thus passionate.   *Enter Iaques.*
    Iaq. Yet all is safe within, is none without?
No body breake⟨s⟩ my walles?   40

III. ii. 12, 14, 16, 21-4, 33-4 *Asides not marked in* Q   14 sir?]
sir. Q   16 almost] almost ; Q   26-7 I aske ... know? *one line in* Q
26 is it G : ist Q   32-33 I do ... poore. *one line in* Q   33 but
thinkes] but thinks W   34 *Christ.* c.w. in Q   35 ouerioy'd] ouerioyed Q
36 bestow'd] bestowed Q   40 walles?] wall *Chicago Acting Edition*

Chris. What say you father, shall I haue your daughter?
Iaq. I haue no dowry to bestow vpon her.
Chris. I do expect none father.
Iaq. That is well,
Then I beseech your worship make no question
45 Of that you wish, tis too much fauour to me.
Chris. Ile leaue him now to giue his passions breath,
Which being setled, I will fetch his daughter :
I shall but moue too much, to speake now to him.
Exit Christophero.
Iaq. So, hee's gone, would all were dead and gone,
50 That I might liue with my deere gold alone.

Scæne 3.

Iaques, Count.

Count. Here is the poore old man.
(*Iaq.* Out o' my soule another, comes he hither?)
Count. Be not dismaid old man, I come to cheere you.
Iaq. (To me my heauen,
5 Turne ribs to brasse, turne voice into a trumpet,
To rattle out the battels of my thoughts,
One comes to hold me talke, while th'other robbes me.) *Exit.*
Count. He has forgot me sure : what should this meane?
He feares authority, and my want of wife
10 Will take his daughter from him to defame her :
He that hath naught on earth but one poor daughter,
May take this extasie of care to keepe her.   *Enter Iaques.*
Iaq. (And yet tis safe : they meane not to vse force,
But fawning cunning. I shall easly know
15 By his next question, if he thinke me rich.)
Whom see I? my good Lord?
Count. Stand vp good father,
I call thee not ⟨good⟩ father for thy age,

<small>III. iii. 2, 4-7, 13-15, 20-2 *Asides not marked in Q*   2 o' *G* : of *Q*
14 cunning *G* : comming *Q*   15 rich.] rich, *Q*   16-17 Stand ...
age, *one line in Q*   17 good *W*</small>

The Case is Alterd

But that I gladly wish to be thy sonne,
In honour'd marriage with thy beauteous daughter.
   Iaq. (O, so, so, so, so, so, this is for gold,   20
Now it is sure, this is my daughters neatnesse,
Makes them beleeue me rich.) No, my good Lord,
Ile tell you all; how my poore haplesse daughter
Got that attire she weares from top to toe.
   Count. Why father, this is nothing.   25
   Iag. O yes, good my Lord.
   Count. Indeed it is not.
   Iaq. Nay sweet Lord pardon me; do not dissemble,
Heare your poore beads-man speake; tis requisite
That I (so huge a beggar) make account   30
Of things that passe my calling : she was borne
To enioy nothing vnderneath the sonne :
But that, if she had more then other beggars,
She should be enuied : I will tell you then
How she had all she weares, her warme shooes (God wot)   35
A kind maide gaue her, seeing her go barefoot
In a cold frosty morning ; God requite her ;
Her homely stockings
   Count. Father, Ile heare no more, thou mou'st too much
With thy too curious answere for thy daughter,   40
That doth deserue a thousand times as much.
Ile be thy Sonne in law, and she shall weare
Th'attire of Countesses.
   Iaq.   O good my Lord,
Mocke not the poore, remembers not your Lordship,
That pouerty is the precious gift of God,   45
As well as riches? tread vpon me, rather
Then mocke my poorenes.
   Count.   Rise I say :
When I mocke poorenes, then heauens make me poore.
                   Enter Nuntius.

III. iii. 19 honour'd] honoured *Q*   28 me ;] me ? *Q*   32 To enioy] T'enioy *Q*   33 beggars,] beggars *Q*   41 much.] much, *Q*   45 God,] God. *Q*   46 riches?] riches, *Q*   *Kneels.* added in G

Scæne 4.

Nuncio, Count.

Nun. See heres the *Count Ferneze*, I will tell him
    The haplesse accident of his braue sonne,
That hee may seeke the sooner to redeeme him.
God saue your Lordship.   *Exit Iaques.*
    Count.   You are right welcome sir.
5   *Nun.* I would I brought such newes as might deserue it.
    Count. What, bring you me ill newes?
    Nun.   Tis ill my Lord,
Yet such as vsuall chance of warre affoords,
And for which all men are prepar'd that vse it,
And those that vse it not, but in their friends,
Or in their children.
10 *Count.*   Ill newes of my sonne,
My deere and onely sonne, Ile lay my soule.
Ay me accurs'd, thought of his death doth wound me,
And the report of it will kill me quite.
    Nun. Tis not so ill my Lord.
15 *Count.* How then?
    Nun. Hee's taken prisoner, and that ⟨i⟩s all.
    Count. That ⟨i⟩s enough, enough.
I set my thoughts on loue, on seruile loue,
Forget my vertuous wife, feele not the dangers,
20 The bands and wounds of mine owne flesh and bloud,
And therein am a mad man: therein plagu'd,
With the most iust affliction vnder heauen.
Is *Maximilian* taken prisoner to?
    Nun. Nay good my Lord, he is return'd with prisoners.
25 *Count.* Ist possible, can *Maximilian*
Returne, and view my face without my sonne,
For whom he swore such care as for himselfe?

III. iv. Scæne 4] Scæne 7 *Q*   3 him.] him, *Q*   4 stage dir. *Iaques.*]
Iaques: *Q*   10 sonne,] sonne? *Q*   11 soule.] soule, *Q*   16 is *G*
17 is *G*   enough.] enough, *Q*   24 Nay] My *Q*: No *W*   25
Maximilian] *Maximilian*? *Q*

The Case is Alterd 145

Nun. My Lord no care can change the euents of war.
Count. O! in what tempests do my fortunes saile,
Still wrackt with winds more foule and contrary, 30
Then any northe⟨r⟩n gust, or Southerne flawe,
That euer yet inforc't the sea to gape,
And swallow the poore Marchants traffique vp?
First in *Vicenza,* lost I my first sonne;
Next here in *Millaine* my most deere lou'd Lady: 35
And now my *Paulo,* prisoner to the *French,*
Which last being printed with my other griefes,
Doth make so huge a volume, that my brest
Cannot containe them. But this is my loue:
I must make loue to *Rachel!* Heauen hath throwne 40
This vengeance on me most deseruedly:
Were it for nought but wronging of my steward.
  Nun. My Lord since onely mony may redresse
The worst of this misfortune, be not grieud,
Prepare his ransome, and your noble sonne 45
Shall greet your cheered eyes, with the more honour.
  Count. I will prepare his ransome: gratious heauen
Grant his imprisonment may be his worst,
Honor'd and souldier-like imprisonment,
And that he be not manacled and made 50
A drudge to his proude foe. And here I vow,
Neuer to dreame of seeme-les amorous toyes,
Nor aime at ⟨any⟩ other ioy on earth,
But the fruition of my onely sonne. *Ex⟨e⟩unt.*

   III. iv. 31 gust *W*: guest *Q*   flawe,] flawe? *Q*   34 *Vicenza,*]
Vieenza Q   39 loue:] *The colon is doubtful in Q*   40 *Rachel* !
Heauen] *Rachel,* heauen *Q*   throwne] throwue, *Q*   44 grieud,]
griued *Q*   45 ransome,] ransome *Q*   49 Honor'd] Honored *Q*
53 any *G*   54 *Exeunt.*] *Exunt* Q

445·3   L

Scæne 5.

Enter Iaques with his gold and a scuttle full of horse-dung.

Iaq. He's gone : I knew it ; this is our hot louer !
I will beleeue them ! I ! they may come in
Like simple woers, and be arrant theeues,
And I not know them ! tis not to be told,
5 What seruile villanies, men will do for gold.
O it began to haue a huge strong smell,
With lying so long together in a place ;
Ile giue it vent, it shall ha shift inough,
And if the diuell, that enuies all goodnesse,
10 Haue told them of my gold, and where I kept it,
Ile set his burning nose once more a worke,
To smell where I remou'd it, here it is :
Ile hide and couer it with this horse-dung :
Who will suppose that such a precious nest
15 Is crownd with such a dunghill excrement ?
In, my deere life, sleepe sweetly my deere child.
,, Scarce lawfully begotten, but yet gotten,
,, And thats enough. Rot all hands that come neere thee,
Except mine owne. Burne out all eyes that see thee,
20 Except mine owne. All thoughts of thee be poyson
To their enamor'd harts, except mine owne.
Ile take no leaue, sweet Prince, great Emperour,
But see thee euery minute. King of Kings,
Ile not be rude to thee, and turne my backe,
25 In going from thee, but go backward out,
With my face toward thee, with humble curtesies.
None is within. None ouerlookes my wall.
To haue gold, and to haue it safe, is all.   *Exit.*

III. v. Scæne 5] SCENE II. A Court-yard, at the back of Jaques' House.
G   1 *Iaq.*] *Iaq,* Q   louer !] louer, Q   5 gold.] gold, Q   7 With
W : Which Q   13 *Digs a hole in the ground.* G   16 In,] In Q
18 thee,] thee Q   21 owne.] owne, Q   22 Prince,] Prince Q   23
minute.] minute, Q   25 out,] out : Q   26 curtesies.] curtesies, Q
27 within *corr.* Q : wi thin *and* w i thin Q *originally*   28 gold,] g old Q

Act 4. Scæne 1.

Enter Maximilian, with souldiers, Chamount, Camillo Ferneze, Pacue.
⟨*Maximilian turns to Camillo.*⟩

Max. Lord *Chamount* and your valient friend there, I cannot say welcome to *Millaine* : your thoughts and that word are not musicall, but I can say you are come to *Millaine*.
Pac. Mort diew. 5
Cha. Garsoone.
Max. Gentlemen (I would cal an Emperour so) you are now my prisoners, I am sorry ; marry this, spit in the face of your fortunes, for your vsage shall be honorable.
Cam. Wee know it signior *Maximilian*, 10
The fame of al your actions sounds nought else,
But perfect honour from her swelling cheeks.
Max. It shall do so still I assure you, and I will giue you reason : there is in this last action (you know) a noble gentleman of our party, & a right valient, semblably 15 prisoner to your general, as your honor'd selfe's to me ; for whose safety, this tongue hath giuen warrant to his honorable father, the *Count Ferneze*. You conceiue me?
Cam. I signior.
Max. Well ; then I must tell you your ransomes be to 20 redeeme him, what thinke you ? your answer ?
C⟨h⟩am. Marry with my Lord's leaue here I say signior, This free & ample offer you haue made, Agrees well with your honour, but not ours :
For I thinke not but *Chamount* [is] aswell borne 25
As is *Ferneze* ; then if I mistake not,

iv. i. Act 4] Actus 3 *Q*   Scæne i.] SCENE iii. A Gallery in count Ferneze's House. *G (continuing Act III)*   Stage dir. *souldiers,] souldiers Q   Camillo Ferneze] Camilla, Ferneze Q*   2 *Millaine*]Millaine *Q*   3 musicall] mu sicall *Q*   4 *Millaine.] Millaine : Q*   6 Garsoone.] Gar soone *Q*   8 sorry ;] sorry, *Q*   14 reason :] reason, *Q*   15 valient,] valient ; *Q*   16 selfe's] selves *G*   me ;] me *Q*   18 me ?] me. *Q*   19 *Ranged with* 18 *in Q*   20 Well ;] Well ; *Q*   21 answer ?] answer. *Q*   22 *Cham.*] *Cam. Q* (and all editors)   here] he re *Q*   26 *Ferneze ;] Ferneze, Q*

He scornes to haue his worth so vnderprised,
That it should neede an adiunct, in exchange
Of any equall fortune. Noble Signior,
30 I am a souldier, and I loue *Chamount*;
Ere I would bruse his estimation,
With the least ruine of mine owne respect,
In this vild kind, these legs should rot with irons,
This body pine in prison, till the flesh
35 Dropt from my bones in flakes, like withered leaues,
In heart of *Autumne*, from a stubborne Oke.
    Maxi. Mounsieur *Gasper* (I take it so is your name)
misprise me not, I wil trample on the hart, on the soule of
him that shall say, I will wrong you : what I purpose, you
40 cannot now know ; but you shall know, and doubt not to
your contentment. Lord *Chamount*, I will leaue you,
whilest I go in and present my selfe to the honorable *Count* ;
till my regression so please you, your noble feete may
measure this priuate, pleasant and most princely walke.
45 Souldiers regard them and respect them.   ⟨*Exit.*⟩
    Pac. O ver bon: excellenta gull, he tak'a my Lord
Chamount for Mounsieur *Gaspra*, & Mounsieur *Gaspra* for
my Lord *Chamont*, ô dis be braue for mak'a me laugh'a,
ha, ha, ha, ô my heart tickla.
50 *Cam.* I but your Lordship knowes not what hard fate
Might haue pursued vs, therefore howsoere
The changing of our names was necessary,
And we must now be carefull to maintaine
This error strongly, which our owne deuise
55 Hath thrust into their ignorant conceits,
For should we (on the taste of this good fortune)
Appeare our selues, 'twould both create in them
A kind of iealousie, and perchaunce inuert
Those honourable courses they intend.

   IV. i. 28 exchange] exchange, Q   29 Signior,] *Signior*? Q   30
Chamount ;] *Chamount*, Q   42 *Count* ;] *Count*, Q   44 walke.]
walke, Q   45 *Exit.* G   46 *ver*] *Ver* Q   48 mak'a] make a Q
52 necessary,] necessary Q   54 deuise] deuise, Q   57 'twould]
t'would Q

The Case is Alterd

Cha. True my deere *Gasper* : but this hangby here, 60
Will (at one time or other) on my soule
Discouer vs : A secret in his mouth
Is like a wild bird put into a cage,
Whose door no sooner opens, but tis out.
But sirra ⟨*Pacue*⟩, if I may but know 65
Thou vtterst it
    Pac. Vttera vat Mounsieur ?
    Cha. That he is *Gasper*, and I true *Chamont*.
    Pac. O *pardone moy*, fore my tongue shall put out de
secreta, shall breede *de cankra* in my mouth.
    Cha. Speake not so loud *Pacue*. 70
    Pac. Foe, you shall not heare foole, for all your long eare.
Reguard Mounsieur : you be [*de*] *Chamont*, *Chamont* be
Gaspra.

              Enter Count *Ferneze*, *Maximilian*, *Francesco*,
                    Aurelia, *Phœnixella*, *Finio*.

    Cha. Peace, here comes *Maximilian*.
    Cam. O belike
That is the *Count Ferneze*, that old man. 75
    Cha. Are those his daughters, trow ?
    Cam. I sure, I thinke they are.
    Cha. Fore God the taller is a gallant Lady.
    Cam. So are they both beleeue me.

⟨Scæne 2.⟩

    Max. True my honorable Lord, that *Chamont* was the
father of this man.
    Count. O that may be, for when I lost my sonne,
This was but yong it seemes.
    Fran. Faith had *Camillo* liu'd,
He had beene much about his yeares, my Lord. 5

  IV. i. 66 Vttera] Uttera G : Vtteria ? *Q*   67 *Chamont* corr. Q :
Chamount Q originally   68–9 de secreta, shall] *Query, read* de
secreta, de secreta shall   Shall *begins a new line in Q*   70 Cha.]
Count. Q : Cam. G   71 eare.] eare, *Q*   72 de *om. G, who reads*
de fool *in* 71.   74–5 O . . . man *one line in Q*   75 That is *G* :
that's *Q*   IV. ii. 4 liu'd,] liu'd *Q*

Count. He had indeed, well, speake no more of him.

Max. Signior perceiue you the errour? twas no good office in vs to stretch the remembrance of so deere a losse. *Count Ferneze,* let sommer sit in your eye, looke cheerefully
10 sweete *Count,* will you do me the honour to confine this noble spirit within the circle of your armes?

Count. Honor'd *Chamont* reach me your valiant hand,
I could haue wisht some happier accident
Had made the way vnto this mutuall knowledge,
15 Which either of vs now must take of other,
But sure it is the pleasure of our fates,
That we should thus be wrack't on Fortunes wheele,
Let vs prepare with steeled patience
To tread on torment, and with mindes confirm'd
20 Welcome the worst of enuy.

Max. Noble Lord, tis thus. I haue here (in mine honour) set this gentleman free, without ransome, he is now himselfe, his valour hath deseru'd it, in the eye of my iudgement. Mounsieur *Gasper* you are deere to me : *fortuna non mutat*
25 *genus.* But to the maine ; if it may square with your Lordships liking, and his loue, I could desire that he were now instantly imployed to your noble Generall in the exchange of *Ferneze* for your selfe, it is the businesse that requires the tender hand of a friend.

30 *Count.* I, and it would be with more speed effected, If he would vndertake it.

Max. True my Lord. Mounsieur *Gasper,* how stand you affected to this motion?

Cha. My duty must attend his Lordships will.

35 *Max.* What says the Lord *Chamont*?

Cam. My will doth then appr[r]oue what these haue vrg'd.

Max. Why there is good harmony, good musicke in this : Mounsieur *Gasper,* you shall protract no time, onely I will
40 giue you a bowle of rich wine to the health of your Generall,

    iv. ii. 16 sure] since *G*   24 *mutat* W : *mutuat Q*   25 maine ;] maine, *Q*   36 doth then] doththen *Q*

another to the successe of your iourney, and a third to the
loue of my sword. *Passe.*
       Exeunt all but Aurelia and Phœnixella.
 Aure. Why how now sister, in a motley muse?
Go to, thers somewhat in the wind, I see.
Faith this browne study suites not with your blacke,   45
Your habit and your thoughts are of two colours.
 Phœn. Good faith me thinkes that this young Lord
  Chamont
Fauours my mother, sister, does he not?
 Aure. A motherly conceite, ô blind excuse,
Blinder then Loue himselfe. Well sister, well.   50
Cupid hath tane his stand in both your eyes,
The case is alterd.
 Phœn. And what of that?
 Aure.   Nay nothing. But a Saint,
Another *Bridget,* one that for a face
Would put downe *Vesta,* in whose lookes doth swim   55
The very sweetest creame of modesty,
You to turne tippet? fie, fie, will you giue
A packing penny to Virginity?
I thought you'ld dwell so long in *Cypres* Ile,
You'd worship *Maddam Venus* at the length;   60
But come, the strongest fall, and why not you?
Nay, do not frowne.
 Phœn.   Go, go, you foole. Adiew. *Exit.*
 Aure. Well I may iest, or so: but *Cupid* knowes
My taking is as bad, or worse then hers.
O Mounsieur *Gasper*! if thou bee'st a man,   65
Be not affraid to court me, do but speake,
Challenge thy right and weare it: for I sweare
Till thou arriud'st, nere came affection here.   *Exit.*

  IV. ii. 43 *Aure.*] *Anre. Q*   sister,] sister *Q.*   47–8 *Prose in Q*
48 he not] henot *Q*   49 motherly] mothelry *Q*   50 Loue] loue *Q*
51–2 *One line in Q*   53 nothing. But] nothing but *Q*   Saint,]
Saint. *Q*   55 swim] swim, *Q*   56 modesty,] modesty. *Q*   58
Virginity?] Virginity. *Q*   65 *Gasper*!] *Gasper? Q*

⟨Scæne 3.⟩

Enter Pacue, Finio.

Fin. Come on my sweet finicall *Pacue*, the very prime of Pages, heres an excellent place for vs to practise in, no body sees vs here, come lets to it.   *Enter Onion.*

Pac. Contenta : Reguarde, vou le Premier.

5 *Oni.* Sirra *Finio* ?

Pac. Mort dieu le pesant.

Oni. Didst thou see *Valentine* ?

Finio. Valentine ? no.

Oni. No ?

10 *Fini.* No. Sirrah *Onion*, whither goest ?

Oni. O I am vext, he that would trust any of these lying trauellers.

Finio. I prithee stay good *Onion*.

Pac. Mounsieur *Onion*, vene ca, come hidera, Ie vou
15 prey. By gar me ha see two, tree, foure hundra towsand of your Cousan hang. Lend me your hand, shall prey for know you bettra.

Oni. I thanke you good signior *Parla vou*. (O that I were in an other world, in the *Ingies*, or some where, that I might
20 haue roome to laugh.)

Pac. A we fort boon : stand ! you be deere now, me come, Boon iour Mounsieur.   *Vnder the arme.*

Fin. God morrow good signior.

Pac. By gar, be mush glad for see you.

25 *Fin.* I returne you most kind thanks sir.

Oni. How ? how ? Sbloud this is rare !

Pac. Nay, shall make you say rare by and by, reguard. Mounsieur *Finio*.   *The shoulder.*

IV. iii. Scæne 3.] ACT IV. SCENE I. A Room in count Ferneze's House. G   1–3 *As verse in Q, divided at* Of *and* No   4 Premier] Preimer Q   6 dieu] deiu Q   18 *vou.*] vou ? Q   18–20 *Aside not marked in Q*   20 laugh.] laugh : *Q apparently, but the colon is doubtful*   21 we] oui G   stand !] stand ? Q   21–2 stand . . . come,] stand you dere—now me come, G (cf. 56)   22 Boon *begins a new line in Q*   24 *Pac.*] Pac Q   be] me be G (*but cf.* 49)   25 *Fin.*] Fin Q   26 rare !] rare ? Q   27–8 reguard. Mounsieur *Finio*.] Reguard Mounsieur *Finio*, Q   28 Stage dir. *The shoulder.*] Theshoulder Q

The Case is Alterd   153

Fin. Signior *Pacue.*
Pac. Dieu vou gard Mounsieur.   30
Fin. God saue you sweet signior.
Pac. Mounsieur *Onion* ? is not fort bein ?
Oni. Beane, quoth he ? would I were in debt of a pottle of beanes I could do as much.
Fin. Welcome signior, whats next ?   35
Pac. O here, Voi[d] de grand admiration, as should meet perchance Mounsieur *Finio.*
Fin. Mounsieur *Pacue.*
Pac. Iesu ? by Gar who thinke wee shall meete here ?
Fin. By this hand I am not a little proud of it, sir.   40
Oni. This trick is onely for the [the] chamber, it cannot be cleanly done abroad.
Pac. Well what say you for dis den ?   Mounsieur.
Fin. Nay pray, sir.
Pac. Par ma foy vou bein encounters !   45
Fin. What doe you meane sir, let your gloue alone.
Pac. Comen se porte la sante ?
Fin. Faith exceeding well sir.
Pac. Trot, be mush ioy for heire.
Fin. And how ist with you sweet signior *Pacue* ?   50
Pac. Fat comme vou voyer.
Oni. Yong gentlemen, spirits of bloud, if euer youle tast of a sweet peece of mutton, do *Onion* a good turne now.
Pac. Que que, parla Mounseir, what ist ?
Oni. Faith teach me one of these tricks.   55
Pac. O me shall doe presently, stand you deere, you signior deere, my selfe is here : so fort bein, now I parle to Mounseir *Onion, Onion* pratla to you, you speaka to me, so, and as you parle chang the bonet, Mounseir *Onion.*

iv. iii. 29 *Pacue*] *Pache* Q   31 sweet] s weet *Q*   signior. *corr. Q* : signior *Q originally*   32 bein ?] bien ? *G* : boon. *Q*   33 Beane,] Beane ? *Q*   he ?] he, *Q*   40 sir.] sir *Q*   41 *Oni.*] *Oni* : *Q*   42 abroad. *corr. Q* : abroad, *Q originally*   43 Mounsieur. *corr. Q* : Mounsieur : *Q originally*   45 vou] *vous voilà* G   encounters !] encounters ? *Q*   46 *Fin.*] *Fin* Q   47 Comen] Comen ? *Q*   sante ?] sante. *Q*   49 *Pac.*] *Pac,* Q   50 *Pacue* ?] *Pache.* Q   51 Fat] Fait, *G*   52 gentlemen,] gentlemen ? *Q*   54 ist ?] ist. *Q*

154 The Case is Alterd

60 *Oni.* Mounsieur *Finio.*
    Fin. Mouns⟨i⟩eur *Pacue.*
    Pac. Pray be couera.
    Oni. Nay I beseech you sir.
    Fin. What do you meane?
65 *Pac.* Pardon moy, shall be so.
    Oni. O God sir.
    Fin. Not I in good faith sir.
    Pac. By gar you must.
    Oni. It shall be yours.
70 *Fin.* Nay then you wrong me.
    Oni. Well and euer I come to be great.
    Pac. You be big enough for de *Onion* already.
    Oni. I meane a great man.
    Fin. Then thou'dst be a monster.
75 *Oni.* Well God knowes not what fortune may doe, commaund me, vse me from the soule to the crowne, and the crowne to the soule: meaning not onely from the crowne of the head, and the sole of the foot, but also the foote of the mind and the crownes of the purse, I cannot stay now yong
80 gentlemen but—time was, time is, and time shall be.
                                                    Exeunt.

⟨Scæne 4.⟩

Enter Chamount, Camillo.

Cha. Sweet *Iasper* I am sorry we must part,
But strong necessity enforceth it.
Let not the time seeme long vnto my friend,
Till my returne, for by our loue I sweare
5 (The sacred spheare wherein our soules are knit)
I will endeauour to affect this busines
With all industrious care and happy speed.
    Cam. My Lord these circumstances would come well,
To one less capable of your desert

IV. iii. 60 Mounsieur] Mounseiur *Q*   64 meane?] meane. *Q*   65 so.] so, *Q*   66 *Oni.*] *Oni Q*   69 *Oni.*] *Oni:* Q   70 me.] me, *Q*   71 great.] great: *Q* (*but colon doubtful*)   72 already.] already, *Q*   IV. iv. Scæne 4.] SCENE II. Another Room in the Same. *G*   4 returne,] returne *Q*.

Then I : in whom your merrit is confirm'd 10
With such authenticall and grounded proues.
  Cha. Well I will vse no more. *Gasper* adiew.
  Cam. Farewell my honor'd Lord.
  Cha. Commend me to the Lady, my good *Gasper*.
  Cam. I had remembred that, had not you vrgd it. 15
  Cha. Once more adiew sweet *Gasper*.
  Cam.   My good Lord.
                                   Exit Camillo.
  Cha. Thy vertues are more precious then thy name,
Kind gentleman I would not sell thy loue,
For all the earthly obiects that mine eyes
Haue euer tasted. Sure thou art nobly borne, 20
How euer fortune hath obscurd thy birth :
For natiue honour sparkles in thine eyes.
How may I blesse the time wherein *Chamont*
My honor'd father did surprise *Vicenza*,
Where this my friend (knowen by no name) was found, 25
Being then a child and scarce of power to speake,
To whom my father gaue this name of *Gasper*,
And as his owne respected him to death,
Since when wee two haue shard our mutuall fortunes,
With equall spirits, and but deathes rude hand, 30
No violence shall dissolue this sacred band.   *Exit.*

⟨Scæne 5.⟩

Enter Iuniper in his shop singing : to him Onion.

  Oni. Fellow *Iuniper*, no more of thy songs and sonets, sweet *Iuniper*, no more of thy hymnes and madrigals, thou sing'st, but I sigh.
  Iuni. Whats the matter *Peter* ha ? what, in an Academy still, still in sable, and costly black array ? ha ? 5

iv. iv. 10 merrit] mirrit Q   confirm'd] confirmed Q   13, 24 honor'd] honored Q   14 *Gasper.*] *Gasper* : Q   15 that,] that Q   19 eyes] eyes, Q   20 tasted. Sure] tasted, sure Q   22 eyes.] eyes, Q   23 *Chamont*] *Chomont* Q (but reading doubtful)   24 *Vicenza,*] vicenza Q
iv. v. Scæne 5.] SCENE III. G   Stage dir. *Enter Iuniper*] *Juniper is discovered* G   4 what,] what Q

The Case is Alterd

Oni. Prithee rise, mount, mount sweet *Iuniper*, for I goe downe the wind, and yet I puffe : for I am vext.

Iuni. Ha Bully ? vext ? what intoxicate ? is thy braine in a quintescence ? an Idea ? a metamorphosis ? an
10 Apology ? ha rogue ? Come this loue feeds vpon thee, I see by thy cheekes, and drinkes healthes of vermilion teares, I see by thine eyes.

Oni. I confesse *Cupids* carouse, he plaies super negulum with my liquor of life.

15 *Iuni.* Tut, thou art a goose to be *Cupids* gull, go to, no more of this contemplations, & calculations, mourne not, for *Rachels* thine owne.

Oni. For that, let the higher powers worke : but sweet *Iuniper*, I am not sad for her, and yet for her in a second
20 person, or if not so, yet in a third.

Iuni. How second person ? away, away, in the crotchets already, Longitude and Latitude ? what second ? what person ? ha ?

Oni. Iuniper, Ile bewray my selfe before thee, for thy
25 company is sweet vnto me, but I must entreat thy helping hand in the case.

Iuni. Tut ? no more of this surquedry ; I am thine owne, ad vnguem, vpsie freeze, pell mell : come, what case ? what case ?

30 *Oni.* For the case it may be any mans case, aswell as mine, *Rachel* I meane, but Ile medle with her anon ; in the meane time, *Valentine* is the man hath wrongd me.

Iuni. How ? my *Ingle* wrong thee, ist possible ?

Oni. Your *Ingle*, hang him infidell, well and if I be not
35 reuengd on[e] him, let *Peter Onion* (by the infernall Gods) be turned to a leeke or a scalion ! I spake to him for a ditty for this handkerchier.

Iuni. Why, has he not done it ?

  IV. v. 6 rise,] rise *Q*   9 quentescence *c.w. in Q*   10 Come] come *Q*
11–12 vermilion teares,] vermilion, teares *Q*   14 life.] life *Q*   16
this] this, *H. C. Hart* : these *G*   not,] *The comma is ill printed in some copies*   17 owne.] owne *Q*   22 already,] already *Q*   27
owne,] owne ? *Q*   28 vnguem,] vnguem *Q*   freeze,] freeze : *Q*   mell :]
mell, *Q*   31 anon ;] anon, *Q*   35 him,] him *Q*   36 scalion !] scalion, *Q*

Oni. Done it, not a verse by this hand.

Iuni. O in diebus illis, O preposterous, wel come be blith, 40
the best inditer of them al is somtimes dul, fellow *Onion*,
pardon mine *Ingle* : he is a man, has impe⟨r⟩fections and
declinations, as other men haue, his muse somtimes cannot
curuet nor prognosticat and come of, as it should ; no
matter, Ile hammer out a paraphrase for thee my selfe. 45

Oni. No sweet *Iuniper*, no, danger doth breed delay,
loue makes me chollericke, I can beare no longer.

Iuni. Not beare what my mad Meridian slaue ? not
beare what ?

Oni. Cupids burden, tis to heauy, to tollerable : and as 50
for the handkerchire and the posie, I will not trouble thee :
but if thou wilt goe with me into her fathers backside, old
Iaques backside, and speake for me to *Rachel*, I will not be
ingratitude, the old man is abroad and all.

Iuni. Art thou sure on't ? 55
Oni. As sure as an obligation.
Iuni. Lets away then, come we spend time in a vaine
circumference, trade I cashire thee til to morrow, fellow
Onion for thy sake I finish this workiday.

Oni. God a mercy, and for thy sake Ile at any time make 60
a holiday.   *Ex⟨e⟩unt.*

IV. v. 41 *Onion,* corr. *Q* : *Onion Q* originally   43 muse *W* : masse *Q*
44 curuet *W* : caruet *Q*   should ;] should, *Q*   45 para-|phrase
corr. Q : para-| hrase *Q originally*   46 no, danger] no danger *Q*
48 Not beare] Not beare ? *Q*   48–9 not beare] not beare ? *Q*   50
burden,] burden : *Q*   heauy, *corr. Q* : heauy *Q originally*   tollerable :]
tollerable, *Q*   51 posie,] posie : *Q*   53 speake for *corr. Q* : speake-
for *Q originally*   wil *corr. Q* : will *Q originally*   53–4 be ingratitude
corr. Q : being ratitude *Q originally*   54 old *corr. Q* : ould *Q originally*
all. *corr. Q* : all, *Q originally*   55 on't ?] on't. *Q*   58 circumference, *corr. Q* : circumference *Q originally*

⟨Scæne 6.⟩

Enter Angel[i]o, Rachel.

Ang. Nay I prithee *Rachel*, I come to comfort thee;
Be not so sad.
    Rach.   O signior *Angelo*,
No comfort but his presence can remoue
This sadnesse from my heart.
    Ang.   Nay then y'are fond,
5 And want that strength of iudgement and election,
That should be attendent on your yeares and forme.
Will you, because your Lord is taken prisoner,
Blubber and weepe and keepe a peeuish stirre,
As though you would turne turtle with the newes?
10 Come, come, be wise. Sblood say your Lord should die:
And you goe marre your face as you begin,
What would you doe trow? who would care for you?
But this it is, when nature will bestow
Her gifts on such as know not how to vse them.
15 You shall haue some that had they but one quarter
Of your faire beauty, they would make it shew
A little otherwise then you do this,
Or they would see the painter twice an hower,
And I commend them I, that can vse art,
20 With such iudiciall practise.
    Rach.   You talk i[e]dly,
If this be your best comfort keepe it still,
My sences cannot feede on such sower cates.
    Ang. And why sweet heart?
    Rach.   Nay leaue good signior.
    Ang. Come I haue sweeter vyands yet in store.

iv. vi. Scæne 6.] SCENE IV. The Court-yard at the back of Jaques'
House *G.* Stage dir. *Rachel.* corr. *Q*: *Rachel, Q* originally   1 thee;
corr. Q: thee, *Q originally*   3 remoue] remoue, *Q*   4 y'are *corr.*
Q: ye'are *Q originally*   5 election *corr. Q*: e lection *Q originally*
6 forme.] forme, *Q*   9 newes?] newes, *Q*   12 for you?] for you;
Q   16 beauty,] beauty? *Q*   them.] them, *Q*   19 I, that *corr. Q*:
I that *Q originally*   20 practise. *corr. Q*: practise, *Q originally*   23
heart?] heart. *Q*   leaue *corr. Q*: leau *Q originally*

The Case is Alterd

Iuni. I in any case. Mistres *Rachel.* ⟨*Within.*⟩ 25
Ang. Rachel?
Rach. Gods pitty signior *Angelo*, I here my father, away for Gods sake.
Ang. S'bloud, I am bewitcht, I thinke, this is twice now, I haue been serued thus. *Exit.* 30
Rach. Pray God he meet him not.

⟨Scæne 7.⟩

Enter Onion and Iuniper.

Oni. O braue! she's yonder, O terrible! shee's gone.
Exit Rachel.

Iuni. Yea? so nimble in your *Dilemma's*, and your *Hiperbole's*? Hay my loue, O my loue, at the first sight? By the masse:

Oni. O how she skudded, O sweet scud, how she tripped, 5 O delicate trip and goe.

Iuni. Come thou art enamored with the influence of her profundity, but sirrah harke a little.

Oni. O rare, what? what? passing Ifaith, what ist? what ist? 10

Iuni. What wilt thou say now, if *Rachel* stand now, and play hity tity through the keyhole, to behold the equipage of thy person?

Oni. O sweet equipage, try good *Iuniper*, tickle her, talke, talke, O rare! 15

Iuni. Mistris *Rachel* (watch then if her father come) *Rachel? Madona? Rachel?* No.

Oni. Say I am here, *Onion* or *Peter* or so.

Iuni. No, Ile knock, weele not stand vpon Horizons, and tricks, but fall roundly to the matter. 20

IV. vi. 25 case. Mistres] case mistres *Q*   *Within.* G   26–9 Apparently defective verse   29 *Ang.*] *Ang: Q*   bewitcht *W*: betwixt *Q*   now corr. *Q* : n ow *Q* originally   30 *Exit.*] *Exit Q*
IV. vii. Stage dir. *Enter . . . Iuniper* in Q at vi. 25   1 braue!] braue? *Q* terrible!] terrible *Q*   *Exit Rachel.*] *Exit Rechel.* Q (at vi. 31)
3 *Hiperbole's?*] *Hiperbole's* Q   loue, O] loue? O *Q*   sight?] sight: *Q*   13 person?] person: *Q*   14 *Oni.*] *Oni:* Q   15 O rare!] O? rare *Q*   16 *A new line after* come *in Q.*

160   *The Case is Alterd*

    Oni. Well said sweet *Iuniper* : Horizons ? hang hem ! knock, knock.   ⟨*Iuniper knocks.*⟩
    Rach. Who's there ? father ?   ⟨*Within.*⟩
    Iuni. Father no ; and yet a father, if you please to be
25 a mother.
    Oni. Well said *Iuniper*, to her againe, a smack or two more of the mother.
    Iuni. Do you here ? sweet soule, sweet *Radamant*, sweet *Machauell* ? one word *Melpomine*, are you at leasure ?
30   *Rach.* At leasure ? what to doe ?   ⟨*Within.*⟩
    Iuni. To doe what, to doe nothing, but to be liable to the extasie of true loues exigent, or so, you smell my meaning ?
    Oni. Smell, filthy, fellow *Iuniper* filthy ? smell ? O most
35 odious.
    Iuni. How filthy ?
    Oni. Filthy, by this finger ! smell ? smell a rat, smel a pudding, away, these tricks are for truls, a plaine wench loues plaine dealing, ile vpon ⟨her⟩ my selfe, smel to ⟨a⟩
40 march paine wench ?
    Iuni. With all my heart, Ile be legitimate and silent as an apple-squire, Ile see nothing, and say nothing.
    Oni. Sweet hart, sweet hart ?
    Iuni. And bag pudding, ha, ha, ha ?
45   *Iaq.* What *Rachel* my girle, what *Rachel* ?   *Within.*
    Oni. Gods lid ?
    Iaq. What *Rachel* ? ⎫
    Rach. Here I am.   ⎬ *Within.*
    Oni. What rakehell cals *Rachel* : O treason to my loue.
50   *Iuni.* Its her father on my life, how shall wee entrench and edifie our selues from him ?
    Oni. O conni-catching *Cupid.*

    IV. vii. 21 hem !] hem ? *Q*   22 *Iuniper knocks.* G   23 Who's] Whose *Q*   father ?] father. *Q*   23, 30 *Within.* G   24 no ;] no ? *Q*   27 mother.] mother *Q*   28 *Radamant*,] radamant ? *Q*   29 *Machauell* ?] mathauell *Q* : Machavel G   *Melpomine*,] *Melpomine* ? *Q*   leasure ?] leasure. *Q*   33 meaning ?] meaning. *Q*   36 filthy ?] filthy. *Q*   37 finger !] finger ? *Q*   38 away,] away *Q*   39 her *W*   a *G*   40 wench ?] wench. *Q*   42 an apple-] anapple- *Q*   45 girle,] girle *Q*   *Rachel* ?] *Rachel* ; *Q*   46 lid ?] lid ⸫ *Q*   47 *Rachel* ?] *Rachel*, *Q*   48 am.] am *Q*

Scæne 8.

Enter Iaques.

Iaq. How, in my back side? where? what come they for? *Onion gets vp into a tree.*
Where are they, *Rachel*? theeues, theeues!
⟨*He seizes Iuniper.*⟩
Stay villaine slaue: *Rachel*? vntye my dog.
Nay theife thou canst not scape.
   Iuni. I pray you sir.   5
   (*Oni.* A⟨h⟩ pitifull *Onion*, that thou hadst a rope.)
   Iaq. Why *Rachel*: when I say? let loose my dog, Garlique my mastiue, let him loose I say.
   Iuni. For Gods sake here me speake, keepe vp your cur.
   (*Oni.* I feare not Garlique, heele not bit *Onion* his kins- 10 man, pray God he come out, and then theile not smell me.)
   Iaq. Well then deliuer, come deliuer slaue!
   Iuni. What should I deliuer?
   Iaq. O thou wouldst haue me tell thee, wouldst thou? shew me thy hands, what hast thou in thy hands?   15
   Iuni. Here be my hands.
   Iaq. Stay, are not thy fingers ends begrimd with durt? no, thou hast wipt them.
   Iuni. Wipt them?
   Iaq. I thou villaine, thou art a subtile knaue! put off 20 thy shewes, come I will see them, giue me a knife here *Rachel*, Ile rip the soles.
   (*Oni.* No matter, he's a cobler, he can mend them.)
   Iuni. What are you mad, are you detestable, would you make an Anatomy of me, thinke you I am not true 25 Ortographie?

   IV. viii. 1 How,] How *Q*   3 they,] they? *Q*   theeues!] theeues? *Q*   Stage dir. *Seizes Jun. as he is running.* G   5 *Iuni.*] Inni *Q* 6, 10–11, 23 *Asides not marked in Q*   6 *Oni.*] Oni *Q*   Ah *W* 7 say?] say : *Q*   dog,] dog? *Q*   8, 10 Garlique] garlique *Q*   10 kinsman, *corr.* *Q* : kinsman *Q originally*   12 Well] well *Q*   slaue!] slaue? *Q*   14 thee,] thee? *Q*   thou?] thou *Q*   17 Stay,] Stay *Q*   17–18 durt? no,] durt, no *corr.* *Q* : dur, tno- *and* dur, tno *Q originally*   20 villaine,] villaine? *Q*   knaue!] knaue, *Q*   23 matter,] matter *Q*   24 mad,] mad? *Q*

445·3   M

Iaq. Ortographie, Anatomy?

Iuni. For Gods sake be not so inuiolable, I am no ambuscado, what predicament call you this, why do you intimate so much?

Iaq. I can feele nothing.

(*Oni.* Bir Lady but *Onion* feeles something.)

Iaq. Soft sir, you are not yet gon, shake your legs, come, and your armes, be briefe, stay let me see these drums, these kilderkins, these bombard slops, what is it crams hem so?

Iuni. Nothing but haire.

Iaq. Thats true, I had almost forgot this rug, this hedghogs nest, this haymowe, this beares skin, this heath, this firsbush.

Iuni. O let me goe, you teare my haire, you reuolue my braines and understanding.

Iaq. (Heart, thou art somewhat eas'd; halfe of my feare
Hath tane his leaue of me, the other halfe
Still keepes possession in dispight of hope,
Vntill these amorous eyes, court my faire gold:
Deare I come to thee :) Fiend, why art not gone?
Auoid my soules vexation, Sathan hence!
Why doest thou stare on me, why doest thou stay?
Why por'st thou on the ground with theeuish eyes?
What see'st thou there, thou curre? what gap'st thou at?
Hence from my house! *Rachel*, send Garlick forth.

Iunip. I am gone sir, I am gone, for Gods sake stay.

Exit Iuniper.

Iaq. Packe, and thanke God thou scap'st so well away.

(*Oni.* If I scape this tree, destinies, I defie you.)

Iaq. I cannot see by any Characters
Writ on this earth, that any fellon foote
Hath tane acquaintance of this hallow'd ground.

IV. viii. 30 much?] much. *Q*   32, 42–6, 54 *Asides not marked in Q*
35 so?] so. *Q*   39 firsbush. *corr. Q*: firsbush: *Q originally*   40 teare
corr. Q: teare, *Q originally*   my *corr. Q*: m y *Q originally*   haire, *corr. Q*:
haire *Q originally*   reuolue] reluolue *corr. Q*: reluolue *Q originally*   42
eas'd;] eas'd? *Q*   43 me *W*: my *Q*   46 Fiend *G*: friend *Q*   47 hence!]
hence? *Q*   51 house!] house, *Q*   Garlick] garlick *Q*   53 Packe]
' e ' *visible in the Bodleian copy of Q*; *in other copies the space of a dropped
letter*   57 hallow'd] hallowed *Q*   ground. *corr. Q*: ground, *Q originally*

The Case is Alterd 163

None sees me : knees do homage to your Lord.
⟨*He kneels and vncouers the treasure.*⟩
Tis safe, tis safe, it lyes and sleepes so soundly,
Twould do one good to looke on't. If this blisse 60
Be giuen to any man that hath much gold,
Iustly to say tis safe, I say tis safe.
O what a heauenly round these two words dance
Within me and without me : First I thinke hem,
And then I speake hem, then I watch their sound, 65
And drinke it greedily with both mine eares,
Then thinke, then speake, then drinke their sound againe,
And racket round about this bodies court
These two sweet words : *tis safe* : stay I will feed
My other sences, ô how sweet it smels. 70
 (*Oni.* I mar'le he smels not *Onion*, being so neere it.)
 Iaq. Downe to thy graue againe, thou beauteous Ghost,
Angels men say, are spirits : Spirits be
Inuisible, bright angels are you so ?
Be you inuisible to euery eye, 75
Saue onely these : Sleepe, Ile not breake your rest,
Though you breake mine : Deare Saints adiew, adiew :
⟨*He rises.*⟩
My feete part from you, but my soule dwels with you. *Exit.*
 Oni. Is he gone ? ô Fortune my friend, and not fortune
  my foe,
I come downe to embrace thee, and kisse thy great toe. 80

Scæne 9.

 Enter Iuniper ⟨*as Onion comes down from the tree.*⟩
 Iunip. Fellow *Onion* ? *Peter* ?
 Oni. Fellow *Iuniper.*
 ⟨*Iunip.*⟩ What's the old panurgo gone ? departed ? cosmografied, ha ?

<small>IV. viii. 58 Stage dir. *Kneels and removes the dung from the treasure.* G
68 court] court. *Q*   70 sences, *corr. Q:* sences; *Q originally*   71 *Aside not marked in Q*   75 eye,] eye. *Q*   78 with *corr. Q:* with *Q originally*
Exit.] *Rises and Exit.* G   81 Stage dir. *Comes down from the tree.* G
IV. ix. 1 *Peter* ?] *Peter. Q*   3 *Iunip.* W   departed ?] departed, *Q*</small>

M 2

5 *Oni.* O I, and harke sirrah. Shall I tell him? no.

Iunip. Nay, be briefe and declare, stand not vpon conondrums now, thou knowest what contagious speeches I haue sufferd for thy sake: and he should come againe and inuent me here——

10 *Oni.* He saies true, it was for my sake, I will tell him. Sirra *Iuniper*? and yet I will not.

Iunip. What sayest thou sweete *Onion*?

Oni. And thou hadst smelt the sent of me when I was in the tree, thou wouldest not haue said so: but sirra, *The 15 case is alterd* with me, my heart has giuen loue a box of the eare, made him kicke vp the heeles I faith.

Iunip. Sayest thou me so, mad Greeke? how haps it? how chances it?

Oni. I cannot hold it, *Iuniper*, haue an eye, looke, haue 20 an eye to the doore. The old prouerb's true, I see: gold is but mucke. Nay Gods so *Iuniper*, to the doore, an eye to the maine chance, here you slaue, haue an eye.

⟨*He remoues the dung, and shows him the gold.*⟩

Iunip. O inexorable! ô infallible! ô intricate, deuine, and superficiall fortune!

25 *Oni.* Nay, it will be sufficient anon, here, looke heere.

Iunip. O insolent good lucke! How didst thou produce th'intelligence of the gold mynerals?

Oni. Ile tell you that anon, heere, make shift, conuey, cramme. Ile teach you how you shall call for Garlike 30 againe I faith.

Iunip. S'bloud what shall we do with all this? we shall **nere** bring it to a consumption.

Oni. Consumption? why weele bee most sumptuously attir'd, man.

35 *Iunip.* By this gold, I will haue three or foure most stigmaticall suites presently.

    IV. ix. 5 sirrah.] Sirrah *Q*   8 sake:] sake *Q*   9 here—] here. *Q*
11 Sirra *begins a new line in Q*   14 sirra] Sirra *Q*   18 chances it?] chances it. *Q*   20 doore. The] doore, the *Q*   21 *Iuniper*,] *Iuniper Q*   22 *Stage dir. supplied by G*   23 intricate,] infricate *Q*
24 fortune!] fortune. *Q*   27 gold mynerals?] gold' mynerals. *Q*
29 Ile teach *begins a new line in Q*   Garlike] garlike *Q*

Oni. Ile go in my foot-cloth, Ile turne Gentleman.
Iunip. So will I.
Oni. But what badge shall we giue, what cullison?
Iunip. As for that lets vse the infidelity and commisera- 40
tion of some harrot of armes, he shall giue vs a gudgeon.
Oni. A gudgeon? a scut⟨c⟩heon thou wouldst say, man.
Iunip. A scutcheon or a gudgeon, all is one.
Oni. Well, our armes be good inough, lets looke to our
legges. 45
Iunip. Content, weele be iogging.
Oni. Rachel, we retire: Garlike God boy ye.
Iunip. Farewell sweete *Iaques*.
Oni. Farewell sweete *Rachel*, sweet dogge adiew. *Exeunt.*

⟨Scæne 10.⟩

*Enter Maximilian, Count Ferneze, Aurelia, Phœnixella,
Pacue.*

Max. Nay but sweet *Count*.
Count.   Away, Ile heare no more,
Neuer was man so palpably abusd,
My sonne so basely marted; and my selfe
Am made the subiect of your mirth and scorne.
Max. Count *Ferneze* you tread to hard vpon my patience, 5
do not persist I aduise your Lordship.
Count. I will persist, and vnto thee I speake.
Thou *Maximilian* thou hast iniur'd me.
Max. Before the Lord:
Aur. Sweet signior.
Phœ. O my father. 10
Max. Lady let your father thank your beauty.
Pac. By gar me shall be hang for tella dis same, me tella
madamoyselle, she tell her fadera.

iv. ix. 42 gudgeon *corr.* Q: gupgeon Q *originally.*   47 *Rachel,*]
Rachel? Q   Garlike] garlike Q   iv. x. Scæne 10.] Scene v. A
Room in count Ferneze's House. G.   Enter] Fnter Q   Pacue] Pache Q
6 Do not *begins a new line in* Q   12 *Max.*] Mvx. Q   c.w. Pacue Q
13 Me tella *begins a new line in* Q

15 *Count.* The true *Chamount* set free, and one left here
Of no descent, clad barely in his name.
Sirrah boy come hither, and be sure, you speake
The simple truth :
    Pac.   O pardone moy mounsieur,
    Count. Come leaue your pardons, and directly say,
20 What villaine is the same, that hath vsurpt
The honor'd name and person of *Chamount* ?
    Pac. O Mounsieur, no point villaine, braue Cheualier,
Mounsieur *Gasper.*
    Count. Mounsieur *Gasper,*
25 On what occasion did they change their names,
What was their policy, or their pretext ?
    Pac. Me canno tell, par ma foy Mounsieur.
    Max. My honorable Lord.
    Count. Tut tut, be silent.
30   *Max.* Silent ? *Count Ferneze,* I tell thee if *Amurath* the
great Turke were here I would speake, and he should here me :
    Count. So will not I.
    Max. By my fathers hand, but thou shalt *Count,* I say
till this instant, I was neuer touch't in my reputation : here
35 me, you shall knowe that you haue wrongd me, and I wil
make you acknowledge it, if I cannot my sword shall.
    Count. By heauen I will not, I will stop mine eares,
My sences loath the sauour of thy breath,
Tis poyson to me, I say I will not heare.
40 What shall I know ? tis you haue iniurd me.
What will you make ? make me acknowledge it ?
Fetch forth that *Gasper,* that lewd counterfeit. ⟨*Exit Pacue.*⟩
Ile make him to your face approue your wrongs.

       iv. x. 15 Count *corr. Q* : Coun₃ *Q originally*   17–18 Sirrah . . . truth *one line in Q*   17 speake *corr. Q* : spaeke *Q originally*   18 simple *corr. Q* : sim ple *Q originally*   19 *Count.*] *Count* Q   say,] *The comma is blurred in some copies*   20 same,] same *Q*   vsurpt] vsurpt, *Q*   21 *Chamount* ?] *Chamount* : Q   24–6 *Prose in Q*   24 Mounsieur] Monusieur *Q*   26 pretext. *corr. Q* : prtext. *Q originally*   27 canno *corr. Q* : ccanno *Q originally*   28 Lord. *corr. Q* : Lord, *Q originally*   34–5 here me,] here me *Q*   38 loath *corr. Q* : lotah *Q originally*   sauour] savour *W* : Sauiour *Q*   breath,] breath. *Q*   40 know ?] know, *Q* me.] me, *Q*   41 will you *corr. Q* : willy ou *Q originally*   it ?] it. *Q*

⟨Scæne 11.⟩

Enter seruing⟨men⟩ with Camillo.

⟨*Count.*⟩ Come on false substance, shadow to *Chamont* :
Had you none else to worke vpon but me,
Was I your fittest proiect ? well confesse,
What you intended by this secret plot,
And by whose policy it was contriu'd.   5
Speake truth, and be intreated courteously,
But double with me, and resolue to proue
The extremest rigor that I can inflict.
   Cam. My honor'd Lord, heare me with patience.
Nor hope of fauour, nor the feare of torment,   10
Shall sway my tongue, from vttring of a truth.
   Count. Tis well, proceed then.
   Cam. The morne before this battell did begin,
Wherein my Lord *Chamount* and I were tane,
We vow'd one mutuall fortune, good or bad,   15
That day should be imbraced of vs both,
And vrging that might worst succeede our vow,
We there concluded to exchange our names.
   Count. Then *Maximilian* tooke you for *Chamount* ?
   Cam. True noble Lord.
   Count.   Tis false, ignoble wretch,   20
Twas but a complot to betray my sonne.
   Max. Count, thou lyest in thy bosome, *Count* :
   Count. Lye ?
   Cam. Nay I beseech you honor'd gentlemen,
Let not the vntimely ruine of your loue   25
Follow these sleight occur⟨r⟩ents ; be assur'd
Chamounts returne will heale these wounds againe,
And breake the points of your too piercing thoughts.

IV. xi. *Stage dir. in* Q *after* x. 42   1 substance, *corr.* Q : substance :
Q *originally*   Chamont : corr. Q : *Chamont,* Q *originally*   4 secret
corr. Q : secreet Q *originally*   plot,] plot. Q   duy *c.w. in* Q   5
contriu'd.] contriu'd, Q   9 patience.] patience, Q   17 worst]
worse W   19 Chamount ?] Chamount. Q   20, 23 Count.] Count : Q
25 loue] loue, Q   26 assur'd] assured Q

Count. Returne? I when? when will *Chamount* returne?
30 Heele come to fetch you, will he? I tis like,
You'ld haue me thinke so, that's your policy.
No, no, yong gallant, your deuice is stale,
You cannot feed me with so vaine a hope.
  Cam. My Lord, I feede you not with a vaine hope,
35 I know assuredly he will returne,
And bring your noble sonne along with him.
  Max. I, I dare pawne my soule he will returne.
  Count. O impudent dirision? open scorne?
Intollerable wrong? is't not inough,
40 That you haue plaid vpon me all this while;
But still to mocke me, still to iest at me?
Fellowes, away with him: Thou ill-bred slaue,
That sets no difference twixt a noble spirit,
And thy owne slauish humour, do not thinke
45 But ile take worthy vengeance on thee, wretch!
  Cam. Alas, these threats are idle, like the wind,
And breed no terror in a guiltlesse mind.
  Count. Nay, thou shalt want no torture, so resolue,
Bring him away.   ⟨*Exit.*⟩
50 *Cam.* Welcome the worst, I suffer for a friend,
Your tortures will, my loue shall neuer end.   *Exeunt.*
      Manent Maximillian, Aurelia, Phœnixella, [*Pacue.*]
  Phœn. Alas poore gentleman, my fathers rage
Is too extreame, too sterne and violent!
O that I knew with all my strongest powers,
55 How to remoue it from thy patient breast,
But that I cannot, yet my willing heart
Shall minister in spight of tyranny
To thy misfortune. Something there is in him,
That doth enforce this strange affection,
60 With more then common rapture in my breast:
For being but *Gasper,* he is still as deare

    iv. xi. 39 inough,] inough? *Q*   42 him: Thou] him, thou *Q*   45 wretch!] wretch? *Q*   48–9 *One line in Q*   56 heart] heart, *Q*
58 misfortune. Something] misfortune, something *Q*

The Case is Alterd

To me, as when he did *Chamount* appeare. *Exit Phœnixella.*
  Aure. But in good sadnesse Signior, do you thinke *Chamount* will returne ?
  Max. Do I see your face, Lady ?
  Aure. I sure, if loue haue not blinded you.
  Max. That is a question, but I will assure you no, I can see, and yet loue is in mine eye : well, the *Count* your father simply hath dishonor'd me : and this steele shall engraue it on his burgonet.
  Aure. Nay, sweet Signior.
  Max. Lady, I do preferre my reputation to my life, but you shall rule me, come let 's march. *Exit Maximillian.*
  Aure. Ile follow Signior, ô sweet Queene of loue,
Soueraigne of all my thoughts, and thou faire Fortune,
Who (more to honour my affections)
Hast thus translated *Gasper* to *Chamount* !
Let both your flames now burne in one bright speare,
And giue true light to my aspiring hopes ;
Hasten *Chamounts* returne, let him affect me,
Though father, friends, and all the world reiect me. *Exit.*

⟨Act 5. Scæne 1.⟩

Enter Angelo, Christopher⟨o⟩.

  Ange. Sigh for a woman, would I fould mine armes,
Raue in my sleepe, talke idly being awake,
Pine and looke pale, make loue-walkes in the night,
To steale cold comfort from a day-starres eyes ?
Kit, thou art a foole, wilt thou be wise ? then lad
Renounce this boy-gods nice idolatry,
Stand not on complement, and wooing trickes,
Thou louest old *Iaques* daughter, doest thou ?

iv. xi. 64 returne] e'er return *W*   72 But *begins a new line in Q*
74 loue,] loue ! *Q*   75 Fortune] fortune *Q*   77 Chamount !] *Cha-mount.* *Q*   78 speare,] speare ; *Q*   79 giue true *corr.* *Q* : giuet rue *Q originally*   hopes ;] hopes, *Q*   v. i. Scæne 1.] Scene i. The Court at the back of Jaques' House. *G.*   Stage dir. *Christophero* W   4 eyes ?] eyes. *Q*   5 thou art] thou'rt *W*   7 wooing] coying *G*

  Chris.   Loue her?
10 *Ange.* Come, come, I know't, be rul'd and shee's thine
   owne.
 Thou'⟨l⟩t say her father *Iaques*, the old begger,
 Hath pawnd his word to thee, that none but thou,
 Shalt be his sonne in law.
  Chris.   He has.
  Ange.   He has?
 Wilt thou beleeue him, and be made a Rooke,
15 To waite on such an antique wethercocke?
 Why he is more inconstant then the sea,
 His thoughts, *Cameleon*-like, change euery minute:
 No *Kit*, worke soundly, steale the wench away,
 Wed her, and bed her, and when that is done,
20 Then say to *Iaques*, shall I be your sonne?
 But come, to our deuice, where is this gold?
  Chris. Heere Signior *Angelo*.
  Ange. Bestow it, bid thy hands shed golden drops,
 Let these bald french crownes be vncouered,
25 In open sight, to do obeysance
 To *Iaques* staring eyes when he steps forth,
 The needy begger will be glad of gold.
 So, now keepe thou aloofe, and as he treades
 This guilded path, stretch out his ambling hopes,
30 With scattring more & more, & as thou go'st,
 Cry *Iaques, Iaques.*
  Chris.   Tush, let me alone.
  Ang. ⟨And⟩ first ile play the ghost, Ile cal him out,
 Kit keep aloofe.
  Chris.   But Signior *Angelo*,
 Where wil your selfe and *Rachel* stay for me,
35 After the iest is ended?
  Ange.   Masse, that's true,

  v. i. 10 owne.] owne, Q   13–14 *Ange.* He . . . Rooke, *one line in* Q
  14 Wilt] wilt Q   Rooke] kooke Q : cook *W* : cokes *G*   15 wethercocke?] wethercocke; Q   21 come,] come Q   30–1 With . . .
Iaques one line in Q   32–3 First . . . aloofe *one line in* Q   32
first] First Q   33–6 *Prose in* Q   33 *Angelo*,] *Angelo*. Q

At the old Priory behinde S. *Foyes.*
  Chris. Agreed, no better place, ile meete you there.
⟨*He retires, dropping the gold.*⟩
Ange. Do good foole, do, but ile not meet you there.
Now to this geere, *Iaques, Iaques,* what *Iaques*?
{within} *Iaq.* Who cals? who's there?   40
Ange. Iaques.
{within} *Iaq.* Who cals?
Ange. Steward, he comes, he comes. *Iaques.*

⟨Scæne 2.⟩

Enter Iaques.

Iaq. What voice is this?
No body here, was I not cald? I was.
And one cride *Iaques* with a hollow voyce,
I was deceiu'd, no I was not deceiu'd,
See see, it was an Angell cald me forth,   5
Gold, gold, man-making gold, another starre,
Drop they from heauen? no, no, my house I hope
Is haunted with a Fairy. My deere Lar,
My houshold God, my Fairy, on my knees.
  Christ. Iaques.   *Exit Christophero.*
  Iaq.   My Lar doth call me, ô sweet voyce, 10
Musicall as the spheares, see, see, more gold.
{within} *Chris. Iaques.*
  Iaq.   What *Rachel, Rachel,* lock my doore,
Enter Rachel.
Looke to my house.
{within} *Chris. Iaques.*
  Iaq.   Shut fast my doore,
A golden crowne, *Iaques* shall be a king.   *Exit.*
  Ange. To a fooles paradice that path will bring 15
Thee and thy houshold Lar.

    v. i. 37 Stage dir. supplied by G   40 who's] whose *Q*   41 *Ranged with* 40 *in Q*   43 comes. *Iaques*] comes *Iaques Q*   v. ii. 1–2 *One line in Q*   7 heauen?] heauen, *Q*   9 my Fairy,] My Fairy *Q*
11 see, more] see more *Q*   12–13 What... doore, *prose in Q.*   12 *Stage dir. precedes Iaques' speech in Q*   13–14 Shut... king. *prose in Q*

⟨Scæne 3.⟩

Rach. What means my father?
I wonder what strange humor.
    Ange. Come sweete'soule,
Leaue wondring, start not, twas I laid this plot
To get thy father forth.
    Rach. O *Angelo.*
5   *Ange.* O me no oo's, but heare, my Lord your loue,
Paulo Ferneze, is returnd from warre,
Lingers at *Pont Valerio,* and from thence
By post at midnight last, I was coniur'd
To man you thither, stand not on replies,
10 A horse is sadled for you, will you go,
And I am for you, if you will stay, why so.
    Rach. O *Angelo,* each minute is a day
Till my *Ferneze* come; come, weele away [sir]. ⟨*Exit.*⟩
    Ange. Sweete soule I guesse thy meaning by thy lookes,
15 At *Pont Valerio* thou thy loue shalt see,
But not *Ferneze.* Steward fare you well.
You wait for Rachel to, when can you tell? *Exit.*

⟨Scæne 4.⟩

Enter Iaques.

    Iaq. O in what golden circle haue I dans't?
Millaine these od'rous and enfloured fields
Are none of thine, no heres *Elizium,*
Heere blessed Ghosts do walke, this is the Court
5 And glorious palace where the God of gold
Shines like the sonne, of sparkling maiesty;
O ⟨my⟩ faire fethered, my red-brested birds,

    v. iii. 1–4 *Prose in Q.*   1 father?] father, Q   6 *Ferneze,*]
Ferneze Q   7 *Valerio* W: *Valeria* Q   12, 13 *Prose in Q.*
13 come; come] come, come Q   sir *om* G   *Exit.* G   15 *Pont*] pont
Q   16 *Ferneze.*] *Ferneze,* Q   17 *Exit*] *Exeunt* Q: *Exit hastily* G
v. iv. 2 *Millaine*] Millaine Q   7 my W

Come flye with me, ile bring you to a quier,
Whose consort being sweetned with your sound,
The musique will be fuller, and each hower   10
These eares shall banquet with your harmony, ô, ô, ô.
⟨*He counts ouer the gold, and goes slowly to the hiding-place
of his treasure.*⟩

⟨Scæne 5.⟩

Enter Christ⟨ophero⟩.

Chris. At the old priorie, behind Saint Foyes,
That was the place of our appointment sure :
I hope he will not make me loose my gold,
And mock me to. Perhaps they are within : Ile knock.
  Iaq. O God, the case is alterd.   5
  Christ. Rachel ? Angelo ? Signior *Angelo* ?
  Iaq. Angels ? I where ? mine *Angels* ? wher's my gold ?
Why *Rachel* ? O thou theeuish *Canibal*,
Thou eat'st my flesh in stealing of my gold.
  Chris. What gold ?
  Iaq.   What gold ? *Rachel* call help, come forth, 10
Ile rip thine entrailes, but ile haue my gold :
Rachel why comes thou not ? I am vndone,
Ay me she speakes not, thou hast slaine my child. *Exit.*
  Chris. What is the man possest trow ? this is strange,
Rachel I see is gone with *Angelo* :   15
Well, ⟨well,⟩ ile once againe vnto the priory,
And see if I can meete them.   *Exit Christopher⟨o⟩.*
  Iaq.   Tis too true,   *Enter Iaques.*
Th'hast made away my child, thou hast my gold :
O what *Hienna* cald me out of dores ?
The thiefe is gone : my gold's gone, *Rachel*'s gone,   20
Al's gone ! saue I that spend my cries in vaine,
But ile hence too, and die or end this paine.   *Exit.*

v. iv. 9 sound,] sound : *Q*   v. v. 4 to. Perhaps] to, perhaps *Q*
9 eatest] eat'st *Q*   *Exit.*] *Exit Q*   16 Well ile *Q*.: Well, I will *W*
17 Stage dir. *Christophero W*   18 thou *W* : how *Q*   19 dores ?]
dores, *Q*   20 *Rachel*'s] *Rachels Q*   21 gone !] gone ? *Q*

⟨Scæne 6.⟩

Enter Iuniper, Onion, ⟨in rich Suits, Iuniper drunk,⟩
Finio, Valentine.

Iuni. Swo⟨u⟩nds, let me goe, hay catso, catch him aliue, I call, I call, boy, I come, I come sweet heart :

Oni. Page hold my rapier, while I hold my freind here.

Valen. O heer's a sweet metamorphosis, a cupple of 5 buzzards turn'd to a paire of peacocks.

Iuni. Signior *Onion*, lend me thy boy to vnhang my rapier.

On. Signior *Iuniper* for once or so, but troth is, you must inueigle, as I have done, my Lords page here, a poor folower 10 of mine.

Iuni. Hei ho, your page then sha'not be super intendent vpon me? he shall not be addicted? he shall not be incident? he shall not be incident? he shall not be incident, shall he?   *He foynes.*

15 *Fin.* O sweet signior *Iuniper*.

Iuni. Sbloud stand away princocks! do not aggrauate my ioy.

Valen. Nay good Maister *Onion*.

Oni. Nay and he haue the heart to draw my bloud, let 20 him come.

Iuni. Ile slice you *Onion*, Ile slice you.

Oni. Ile cleave you *Iuniper*.

Valen. Why hold, hold, hough? what do you meane?

Iuni. Let him come *Ingle*, stand by boy, his allebaster 25 blad cannot feare me.

Fin. Why heare you sweet signior, let not there be any

v. vi. Scæne 6] SCENE II. The street before count Ferneze's House. G Enter . . . Valentine.] Enter Juniper and Onion, richly dressed and drunk, followed by Finio and Valentine. G   1 Q begins a new line after aliue   2 boy,] boy. Q   7 rapier corr. Q: rapi er (perhaps rapier :) Q originally   9 here,] here Q   14 Stage dir. in Q at 15. foynes.] foynes Q   16 Iuni.] Iuni Q   princocks!] princocks? Q   18 Maister] Maister. Q   21 you.] you? Q

contention, betweene my Maister & you, about me ; if you want a page sir, I can helpe you to a proper stripling.

Iuni. Canst thou ? what parentage ? what ancestry ? what genealogy is he ? 30

Fin. A french boy sir.

Iuni. Has he his French linguist ? has he ?

Fin. I, sir.

Iuni. Then transport him : her's a crusado for thee.

Oni. You will not imbecell my seruant with your beneuo- 35 lence, will you ? hold boy, there's a portmantu for thee.

Fin. Lord sir.

On. Do take it boy, its three pounds ten shill⟨ings,⟩ a portmantu.

Fin. I thanke your Lordship. *Exit Finio.* 40

Iuni. Sirrah *Ningle* : thou art a traueller, and I honour thee. I prithee discourse ! cherish thy muse ! discourse !

Valen. Of what sir ?

Iuni. Of what thou wilt. Sbloud ! hang sorrow !

Oni. Prithy *Valentine* assoile me one thing. 45

Valen. Tis pitty to soile you sir, your new apparell.

On. Masse thou saist true, aparel makes a man forget himselfe.

Tun. Begin, find your tongue *Ningle*.

Val. (Now will ⟨I⟩ gull these ganders rarely :) Gentle- 50 men hauing in my peregrination through Mesopotamia.

Iun. Speake legibly, this gam 's gone, without the great mercy of God, heres a fine tragedy indeed. Thers a Keisars royall. By Gods bid, nor King nor Keisar shall ?

---

v. vi. 27 me :] me, *Q*   33 *Ranged with* 32 *in Q*   35 not] not, *Q*
beneuolence,] beneuolence *Q*   36 you ?] you, *Q*   boy, there's]
boy their 's *Q*   38 shill. *Q*   42 discourse !] discourse ? *Q*
muse !] muse ? *Q*   discourse !] discourse ? *Q*   44 Sbloud !]
Sbloud ? *Q*   sorrow !] sorrow ? *Q*   50 *Aside not marked in Q*
I *W*   50 Gentlemen *begins a new line in Q*   53 here's] Heres *Q*,
beginning a new line   Keisars] keisar *W*   54 By Gods *begins a new line in Q*

Scæne 7.

Enter Finio, Pacue, Balt⟨hasar,⟩ Martino.

Balt. Where? where? *Finio,* where be they?
Iun. Go to, ile be with you anon.
Oni. O her's the page signior *Iuniper.*
Iun. What sayth monsier *Onion,* boy?
Fin. What say you sir?
Iuni. Tread out boy.
Fin. Take vp, you meane sir.
Iun. Tread out I say, so, I thanke you, is this the boy?
Pac. We mounsieur.
Iuni. Who gaue you that name?
Pac. Gaue me de name, vat name?
Oni. He thought your name had been we, yong gentleman, you must do more then his legges can do for him, beare with him sir.
Iuni. Sirrah giue me instance of your cariage; youle serue my turne, will you?
Pac. What turne? vpon the toe?
Fin. O signior no.
Iuni. Page will you follow me, ile giue you good exhibition.
Pac. By gar, shal not alone follow you, but shal leade you to.
Oni. Plaguie boy, he sooths his humour; these french villaines ha pockie wits.
Iuni. Here! disarme me! take my semitary.
Valen. O rare, this would be a rare man, and he had a little trauell. *Balthasar, Martino,* put off your shooes, and bid him coble them.

v. vii. Stage dir. *Balt.* Q   1 they?] they: *Q*   3 *Iuniper.*]
Iuniper: Q   4, 8 boy?] boy. *Q*   5, 7 *Fin.*] *Fin*: Q   5 sir?]
sir. *Q*   6 *Ranged with* 5 *in Q*   9 We] Aue *Q* : Oui *G*   10 *Ranged
with* 9 *in Q*   name?] name. *Q*   11 name?] name : *Q*   12 been
we,] been, we *Q* : been Oui *G*   gentleman *W* : gentlemen *Q*   15
cariage;] cariage? *Q*   17 *Ranged with* 16 *in Q*   What turne?]
What? turne *Q*   toe?] toe. *Q*   22 humour;] humour? *Q*   24
Here!] Here? *Q*   me!] me? *Q*   26 trauell.] trauell, *Q*

Iuni. Freinds, friends, but pardon me for fellows, no more in occupation, no more in corporation, tis so pardon me, the case is alterd, this is law, but ile stand to nothing. 30
Pac. Fat so me tinke.
Iuni. Well then God saue the dukes Maiesty, is this any harme now? speake, is this any harme now?
Oni. No, nor good neither, sbloud!
Iuni. Do you laugh at me? do you laugh at me? do 35 you laugh at me?
Valen. I sir, we do.
Iunip. You do indeed?
Valen. I indeed sir.
Iuni. Tis sufficient, Page carry my purse, dog me! *Exit.* 40
Oni. Gentlemen leaue him not, you see in what case he is, he is not in aduersity, his purse is full of money, leaue him not! *Exeunt.*

⟨Scæne 8.⟩

Enter Angelo with Rachel.

Ang. Nay gentle *Rachel*?
Rach. Away! forbeare! vngentle *Angelo*,
Touch not my body, with those impious hands,
That like hot Irons seare my trembling heart,
And make it hisse, at your disloyalty. 5
Was this your drift? to vse *Fernezes* name? *Enter Chamount,*
Was he your fittest stale, ô wild dishonor! *Paulo Ferneze.*
(*Pau.* Stay noble sir.)
Ange. Sbloud how like a puppet do you talke now?
Dishonor? what dishonor? come, come, foole, 10
Nay then I see y'are peeuish. S'heart dishonor?
To haue you to a priest and marry you,
And put you in an honorable state?

v. vii. 31 Fat] Fait *G*   33 speake...now?] speake...now *Q*   34 No,] No *Q*   sbloud!] Sbloud? *Q*   37, 39 Ranged with 36 and 38 in *Q*   40 me!] me? *Q*   43 not!] not? *Q*   v. viii. Scæne 8.] SCENE III. The open Country. *G*   2 Away! forbeare!] Away? forbeare? *Q*   6–7 Stage-dir. at 4–5 in *Q*   6 *Q* has the incorrect c.w. '*Ang*' though the next page opens with l. 7   7 wild] vile G : vild Chicago Acting Edition   8 Ranged with 7 in *Q* : the aside is not marked   12 to a priest] a topriest *Q*   13 state?] state. *Q*

445·3   N

Rach. To marry me? ô heauen, can it be,
That men should liue with such vnfeeling soules,
Without or touch of conscience or religion,
Or that their warping appetites should spoile
Those honor'd formes, that the true seale of friendship
Had set vpon their faces?
   Ange.   Do you heare?
What needs all this? say, will you haue me, or no?
   Rach. I'le haue you gone, and leaue me, if you would.
   Ange. Leaue you? I was accurst to bring you hither,
And make so faire an offer to a foole.
A pox vpon you, why should you be coy,
What good thing haue you in you to be proud of?
Are y' any other then a beggars daughter?
Because you haue beauty? O Gods light a blast.
(*Pau.* I *Angelo.*)
   Ange. You scornefull baggage,
I lou'd thee not so much, but now I hate thee.
   Rach. Vpon my knees, you heauenly powers, I thanke you,
That thus haue tam'd his wild affections.
   Ange. (This will not do, I must to her againe.)
Rachel, ô that thou sawst my heart, or didst behold
The place from whence that scalding sigh euented.
Rachel, by Iesu I loue thee as my soule,
Rachel, sweet *Rachel*.
   Rach.   What, againe returnd
Vnto this violent passion?
   Ange.   Do but heare me,
By heauen I loue you *Rachel*.
   Rach.   Pray forbeare,
O that my Lord *Ferneze* were but here.
   Ange. Sbloud and he were, what would he do?

---

v. viii. 14 be,] be? *Q*   16 of conscience or *J. P. Collier*: or conscience of *Q*   19 faces?] faces. *Q*   19–20 Do...no? one line in *Q*.   21 I'le] Il'e *Q*   27 beauty?] beauty. *Q*   28, 33 *Asides not marked in Q*   29–30 One line in *Q*   33 againe.] againe, *Q*   34 behold] behold, *Q*   36–40 As prose in *Q*   38 passion?] passion. *Q*   40 O] ô *Q*   41 do?] do. *Q*

Pau. This would he do base villaine :
⟨*He flings Angelo off.*⟩
Rach. My deere Lord,
Pau. Thou monster, euen the soule of trechery !
O what dishonord title of reproch,
May my tongue spit in thy deserued face ? 45
Me thinkes my very presence should inuert
The steeled organs of those traytrous eyes,
To take into thy heart, and pierce it through :
Turn'st thou them on the ground ? wretch, dig a graue,
With their sharp points, to hide th⟨y⟩ abhorred head ! 50
Sweet loue, thy wrongs haue beene too violent
Since my departure from thee, I perceiue :
But now true comfort shall againe appeare,
And like an armed angell guard thee safe
From all th' assaults of couer'd villany. 55
Come Mounsieur, let vs go, & leaue this wretch
To his despaire.
Ange. My noble ⟨Lord⟩ *Ferneze.*
Pau. What, canst thou speake to me, and not thy tongue,
Forc't with the torment of thy guilty soule,
Breake that infected circle of thy mouth 60
Like the rude clapper of a crazed bell ?
I, ⟨I,⟩ that in thy bosome lodg'd my soule,
With all her traine of secrets, thinking them
To be as safe, and richly entertain'd
As in a Princes court, or tower of strength, 65
And thou to proue a traitor to my trust,
And basely to expose it, ô this world !
Ange. My honorable Lord.
Pau. The very owle,
Whom other birds do stare & wonder at,
Shall hoot at thee, and snakes in euery bush 70

v. viii. 42 Stage dir. *Flings him off.* G   46 inuert] inuert, *Q*   50
thy] th' *Q*   head !] head ; *Q*   55 couer'd] couered *Q*   56–7
Come . . . despaire. *one line in* Q   56 let vs] let us G : let's *Q*   57
Lord G   58 What,] What *Q*   59 soule,] soule *Q*   61 bell ?] bell. *Q*
62 I, I G   64 entertain'd] entertained, *Q*   68–9 The very . .
wonder at, *one line in* Q

N 2

Shall deafe thine eares with their—
 Cha.   Nay good my Lord,
Giue end vnto your passions.
 Ange.   You shall see,
I will redeeme your lost opinion.
 Rach. My Lord beleeue him.
 Cha.   Come, be satisfied,
75 Sweet Lord you know our haste, let vs to horse,
The time for my engag'd returne is past ;
Be friends againe, take him along with you.
 Pau. Come signior *Angelo,* hereafter proue more true.
              Exeunt.

⟨Scæne 9.⟩

 Enter Count Ferneze, Maximillian, Francesco.
 Count. Tut *Maximillian,* for your honor'd selfe,
I am perswaded, but no words shall turne
The edge of purposd vengeance on that wretch,
Come, bring him forth to execution.

    Enter Camillo bound, with Seruants.
5 Ile hang him for my sonne, he shall not scape,
Had he an hundred liues : Tell me vile slaue,
Think'st thou I loue my sonne ? is he my flesh ?
Is he my bloud, my life ? and shall all these
Be torturd for thy sake, and not reueng'd ?
10 Trusse vp the villaine.
 Max. My Lord, there is no law to confirme this action.
Tis dishonorable.
 Count. Dishonorable ? *Maximillian ?*
It is dishonorable in *Chamount,*
15 The day of his prefixt returne is past,

<small> v. viii. 71–3 Nay . . . opinion *as prose in* Q   74–6 *Verse wrongly divided in* Q *at* haste *and* past   76 engag'd] engaged Q   78 signior *om.* G   v. ix. Scæne 9.] Scene iv. A room in count Ferneze's House. G   4 *Enter.* c.w. in Q. Stage dir. *with Seruants.*] withseruants. Q   7 Think'st *W* : Thinkest *Q*   8–10 *Prose in* Q   12–13 Tis . . . Maximillian ? *one line in* Q.   13–16 *The Count's speech as prose in* Q, *but* My Lord, my Lord *ranged with the final words*.</small>

And he shall pay for it.
    Cam.   My Lord, my Lord,
Vse your extreamest vengeance, ile be glad
To suffer ten times more, for such a friend.
    Count. O resolute and peremptory wretch!
    Fran. My honor'd Lord, let vs intreat a word.   20
    Count. Ile heare no more, I say he shall not liue,
My selfe will do it. Stay, what forme is this
Stands betwixt him and me, and holds my hand?
What miracle is this? tis my owne fancy,
Carues this impression in me, my soft nature,   25
That euer hath retaind such foolish pitty,
Of the most abiect creatures misery,
That it abhorres it. What a child am I
To haue a child? Ay me, my son, my son.

⟨Scæne 10.⟩

Enter Christophero.

    Chris. O my deere loue, what is become of thee?
What vniust absence layest thou on my brest,
Like waights of lead, when swords are at my backe,
That run me th⟨o⟩rough with thy vnkind flight?
My gentle disposition waxeth wild,   5
I shall run frantike, ô my loue, my loue.

⟨Scæne 11.⟩

Enter Iaques.

    Iaq. My gold, my gold, my life, my soule, my heauen,
What is become of thee? see, ile impart
My miserable losse to my good Lord,
Let me haue search my Lord, my gold is gone.
    Count. My sonne, *Christophero,* thinkst ⟨thou⟩ it possible,

---

  v. ix. 16 for it *G*: fort *Q*   20 honor'd] honored *Q*   word] wor d
Q   23 hand?] hand. *Q*   28 it. What] it, what *Q*   v. x. 4
thorough *W*   flight?] flight, *Q*   v. xi. 5 thou *W*

I euer shall behold his face againe?
    Chris. O father wher's my loue, were you so carelesse
To let an vnthrift steale away your child?
    Iaq. I know your Lordship may find out my gold,
10 For Gods sake pitty me, iustice, sweet Lord.
    Count. Now they haue yong *Chamount, Christophoro,*
Surely they neuer will restore my sonne?
    Chris. Who would haue thought you could haue beene so carelesse
To loose your onely daughter?
    Iaq.   Who would thinke,
15 That looking to my gold with such hares eyes,
That euer open, I euen when th⟨e⟩y sleepe,
I thus should loose my gold? My noble Lord,
What saies your Lordship?
    Count.   O my sonne, my sonne.
    Chris. My deerest *Rachel.*
    Iaq.   My most hony gold.
20 *Count.* Heare me *Christophoro.*
    Chris.   Nay heare me *Iaques.*
    Iaq. Heare me most honor'd Lord.
    Max.   What rule is here?
    Count. O God that we should let *Chamount* escape.
    Chris. I and that *Rachel,* such a vertuous mayd,
Should be thus stolne away.
    Iaq.   And that my gold,
25 Being so hid in earth, should bee found out.
    Max. O confusion of languages, & yet no tower of *Babel*!
                                   Enter *Aurelia, Phœnixella.*
    Fran. Ladies, beshrew me, if you come not fit
To make a iangling consort, will you laugh
To see three constant passions?

    v. xi. 6 againe?] againe. *Q*   8 child?] child. *Q*   11 *Chamount, Christophoro,*] *Chamount? Christophoro? Q*   12 sonne?] sonne. *Q*   13–14 *Christophero's speech as prose in Q*   14 daughter?] daughter. *Q*   16 they *W*   17–18 I thus ... Lordship *as prose in Q*   17 gold? *Q* My] gold, my *Q*   19 *Rachel.*] *Rachel? Q*   23–5, 27–9, 37–8 *Prose in Q*   26 *Stage dir. after* 22 *in Q*   29 passions?] passions. *Q*

Max. Stand by, I will vrge them : sweet *Count*, will you 30
be comforted ?
Count. It cannot be
But he is handled the most cruelly,
That euer any noble prisoner was.
Max. Steward, go cheere my Lord.
Chris. Well, if *Rachel* tooke her flight willingly ? 35
Max. Sirrah, speake you touching your daughters flight.
Iaq. O that I could so soone forget to know
The thiefe againe, that had my gold, my gold.
Max. Is not this pure ?
Count. O thou base wretch, ile drag thee through the 40
streets,
And as a monster, make thee wondred at,
How now ?   *Enter Balthasar, and whispers with him.*
Phœn. Sweet Gentleman, how too vnworthily
Art thou thus tortured ? braue *Maximillian,*
Pitty the poore youth, and appease my father. 45
Count. How, my sonne returnd ? O *Maximillian,*
Francisco, daughters ? bid him enter here.
Dost thou not mocke me ?

⟨Scæne 12.⟩

Enter Chamount, ⟨Paulo⟩ Ferneze, Rachel, Angelo.
⟨*Count*⟩. O my deere *Paulo* welcome.
Max.   My Lord *Chamount* ?
Cha. My *Gasper.*
Chris.   *Rachel.*
Iaq.   My gold *Rachel* ? my gold ?
Count. Some body bid the beggar cease his noise.
Chris. O signior *Angelo*, would you deceiue
Your honest friend, that simply trusted you ? 5

v. xi. 30 them :] them, *Q*   comforted ?] comforted. *Q*   31–2 *One
line in Q*   34 Lord.] Lord, *Q*   36 flight.] flight ? *Q*   39 *Ranged
with* 38 *in Q*   pure ?] pure : *Q*   42 *Ranged with* 41 *in Q*   How now ?]
how now. *Q*   *Stage dir. after* 40 *in Q*   43 Gentleman,] Gentleman ? *Q*
44 tortured ?] tortured, *Q*   45 father.] father, *Q*   48 *With* xii. 1 *in
Q*   v. xii. 1–2 *Divided in Q after* welcome, *Gasper,* gold

Well *Rachel* : I am glad tho'art here againe.
  Ang. I faith she is not for you steward.
  Iaq. I ⟨do⟩ beseech you maddam vrge your father.
  Phœ. I will anon ; good *Iaques* be content.
10 *Aur.* Now God a mercy, Fortune, and sweet Venus,
Let *Cupid* do his part, and all is well.
  Phœ. Me thinks my heart's in heauen with this comfort.
  Cha. Is this the true *Italian* courtesie,
Ferneze were you torturd thus in France ?
15 By my soules safety.
  Count.   My most noble Lord ?
I do beseech your Lordship.
              ⟨*He kneels, Chamont raises him.*⟩
  Cham.   Honor'd *Count*,
Wrong not your age with flexure of a knee,
I do impute it to those cares and griefes,
That did torment you in your absent sonne.
20 *Count.* O worthy gentlemen, I am ashamd
That my extreame affection to my sonne,
Should giue my honour so vncur'd a maime,
But my first sonne, being in *Vicenza* lost.
  Cha. How in *Vicenza* ? lost you a sonne there ?
About what time my Lord ?
25 *Count.*   O the same night,
Wherein your noble father tooke the towne.
  Cha. How long's that since my Lord ? can you remember ?
  Count. Tis now well nie vpon the twentith yeare.
  Cha. And how old was he then ?
  Count.   I cannot tel,
30 Betweene the yeares of three and foure, I take it.
  Cha. Had he no speciall note in his attire,
Or otherwise, that you can call to mind ?

v. xii. 9 anon ;] anon ? *Q*   10 mercy, Fortune,] mercy fortune *Q*
13 courtesie,] courtesie. *Q*   14–15 *Ferneze* ... safety *one line in Q*   15
By] by *Q*   15–16 My ... Lordship *one line in Q*   15 Stage dir. *Kneels*. G
16–17 Honor'd ... knee *one line in Q*   16 Honor'd] Honored *Q*   Stage
dir. *Raises him*. G   22 maime] maim *W* : maine *Q*   25–6 O...town
as prose in Q   25 O] O' *Chicago Acting Edition*   27 remember ?] remember. *Q*   29–30 I cannot ... it *as prose in Q*   32 mind ?] mind. *Q*

Count. I cannot well remember his attire,
But I haue often heard his mother say :
He had about his necke a tablet,   35
Giuen to him by the Emperour *Sigismund*,
His Godfather, with this inscription,
Vnder the figure of a siluer Globe :
In minimo, mundus.
    Cha.   How did you call
Your sonne my Lord ?
    Count.   *Camillo* Lord *Chamount.*   40
    Cha. Then ⟨now⟩ no more my *Gasper*, but *Camillo*,
Take notice of your father : gentlemen,
Stand not amazd ; here is a tablet,
With that inscription, found about his necke
That night, and in *Vicenza* by my father,   45
(Who being ignorant, what name he had,
Christned him *Gasper*) nor did I reueale
This secret till this hower to any man.
    Count. O happy reuelation ! ô blest hower !
O my *Camillo* !
    Phœ.   O strange my brother !
    Fran.   *Maximilian* !   50
Behold how the aboundance of his ioy
Drownds him in teares of gladnesse.
    Count.   O my boy !
Forgiue thy fathers late austerity.
    Max. My Lord, I deliuered as much before, but your
honour would not be perswaded. I will hereafter giue more 55
obseruance to my visions, I drempt of this.

   v. xii. 36 *Sigismund,*] *Sigismund.* Q   38–9 Vnder . . . *mundus* one line in Q   39 *In* W : *En* Q   39–40 How . . . Lord *one line in* Q   40 *Count.*] *Count* Q   41 *Gasper,*] *Gasper* ? Q   42 father : gentlemen,] father, gentlemen : Q   43 amazd ;] amazd ? Q   44 inscription,] inscription ? Q   46 had,] had) Q   47 *Gasper*)] *Gasper,* Q   reueale] reueale, Q   49–50 O . . . *Camillo* one line in Q   49 reuelation !] reuelation ? Q   hower !] hower ? Q   50 O my] ô my Q   brother !] brother. Q   *Maximilian* !] *Maximilion* ? Q   50–1 *Maximilian* . . . ioy *one line in* Q   52–3 O . . . austerity *one line in* Q   boy !] boy ? Q   53 austerity.] austerity : Q   54 Lord,] Lord ? Q   55 perswaded.] perswaded, Q   56 visions,] visions ? Q

Iaq. I can be still no longer, my good Lord,
Do a poore man some grace mongst all your ioyes.
   Count. Why whats the matter *Iaques* ?
   Iaq.   I am robd,
60 I am vndone my Lord, robd and vndone :
A heape of thirty thousand golden crownes,
Stolne from me in one minute, and I feare :
By her confedracy, that cals me father,
But she is none of mine : therefore sweet Lord,
65 Let her be tortur'd to confesse the truth.
   Max. More wonders yet.
   Count. How *Iaques*, is not *Rachel* then thy daughter ?
   Iaq. No, I disclaime in her, I spit at her,
She is a harlot, and her customers,
70 Your sonne, this gallant, and your steward here,
Haue all been partners with her in my spoile ;
No lesse then thirty thousand.
   Count.   *Iaques, Iaques,*
This is impossible, how shouldst thou come
To the possession of so huge a heape :
75 Being always a knowen begger ?
   Iaq.   Out alas,
I haue betraid my selfe with my owne tongue,
The case is alterd.
   Count.   ⟨Some⟩ one stay him there.
   Max. What, meanes he to depart ? *Count Ferneze*, vpon my soule [this begger,] this begger is a counterfait : vrge
80 him. Didst thou loose gold ?
   Iaq. O no I lost no gold.
   Max. Said I not true ?

---

     v. xii. 59 *Iaques* ?] *Iaques.* Q   59–60 I . . . and vndone *one line in Q*
64 she is *G* : she's *Q*   mine :] mine, *Q*   Lord,] Lord : *Q*   65 tortur'd]
tortured *Q*   67 *Iaques*,] *Iaques Q*   daughter ?] daughter. *Q*   70 sonne,]
sonne *Q*   71–2 Haue . . . thousand *prose in Q*   71 spoile ;]
spoile ? *Q*   72–4 *Iaques* . . . heape *as prose in Q*   73 impossible]
impossiole *Q*   come] come ? *Q*   75 begger ?] begger. *Q*   75–6
Out . . . tongue *one line in Q*   77 Some *W*   78 What,] What *Q*
depart ?] depart, *Q*   80 him. Didst] him ? didst *Q*   81 *Ranged
with* 80 *in Q*   82 true ?] true. *Q*

The Case is Alterd

Count. How? didst thou first loose thirty thousand
  crowns,
And now no gold? was *Rachel* first thy child,
And is shee now no daughter? sirra *Iaques*, 85
You know how farre our *Millaine* lawes extend,
For punishment of liars.
  Iaq.   I my Lord!
(What shall I doe? I haue no starting hols!)
Mounsieur *Chamount* stand you my honor'd Lord.
  Cha. For what old man?
  Iaq.   Ill gotten goods ne'er thriue, 90
I plaid the thiefe, and now am robd my selfe:
I am not as I seeme, *Iaques de prie*,
Nor was I borne a begger as I am:
But sometime steward to your noble father.
  Cha. What *Melun*, that robd my fathers treasure, stole 95
my sister?
  Iaq. I, I, that treasure is lost, but *Isabell*
Your beautious sister here suruiues in *Rachel*:
And therefore on my knes;
  Max. Stay *Iaques* stay! the case still alters? 100
  Count. Faire *Rachel* sister to the Lord *Chamount*?
  Ang. Steward your cake is dow, as well as mine.
  Pau. I see that honours flames cannot be hid,
No more then lightening in the blackest cloud.
  Max. Then sirra tis true, you haue lost this gold? 105
  Iaq. I worthy signior, thirty thousand crownes.
  Count. Masse who was it told me, that a couple of my
men, were become gallants of late?
  Fran. Marry twas I my Lord, my man told me.

v. xii. 84 child,] child : *Q*   85 daughter?] daughter, *Q*   86–7
You . . . liars *as prose in Q*   87 liars.] liars, *Q*   87–8 I . . . hols! *one
line in Q : aside not marked*   87 *Iaq.*] *Iaq: Q*   Lord!] Lord? *Q*
89 honor'd] honored *Q*   90 ne'er *W* : neuer *Q*   95 *Melun*,] *Melun Q*
97–9 *Prose in Q*   97 treasure is] treasure's *W*   98 suruiues] seruiues
Q   99 knes;] knes? *Q*   100 stay!] stay? *Q*   101 *Chamount* ?]
Chamount. Q   105 true,] true? *Q*   gold?] gold, *Q*   108 men *c.w.
in Q*   late?] late. *Q*   109 Lord,] Lord? *Q*   me.] me? *C*

⟨Scæne 13.⟩

Enter Onion and Iuniper.

Max. How now, what pagent is this?
Iuni. Come signior *Onion*, lets not be ashamd to appeare. Keepe state! looke not ambiguous now!
Oni. Not I while I am in this sute.
5 *Iuni.* Lordings, equiualence to you all.
Oni. We thought good, to be so good, as see you gentlemen.
Max. What? mounsieur *Onion*?
Oni. How dost thou good captaine?
10 *Count.* What, are my hinds turnd gentlemen?
Oni. Hinds sir? Sbloud and that word will beare action, it shall cost vs a thousand pound a peece, but weele be reuenged.
Iuni. Wilt thou sell thy Lordship *Count*?
15 *Count.* What? peasants purchase Lordships?
Iuni. Is that any Nouels sir?
Max. O transmutation of elements, it is certified you had pages.
Iuni. I sir, but it is knowen they proued ridiculus, they
20 did pilfer, they did purloine, they did procrastinate our purses, for the which wasting of our stocke, we haue put them to the stocks.
Count. And thither shall you two ⟨go⟩ presently, These be the villaines, that stole *Iaques* gold,
25 Away with them, and set them with their men.
Max. Onion you will now bee peeld.
Fran. The case is alterd now.
Oni. Good my Lord, good my Lord:

v. xiii. 1 now,] now *Q*   this?] this, *Q*   3 appeare.] appeare, *Q* Keepe state *begins a new line in Q*   now!] now? *Q*   6 gentlemen.] gentlemen *Q*   9 captaine?] captaine. *Q*   10 gentlemen?] gentlemen. *Q*   16 sir?] sir. *Q*   18 pages.] pages: *Q*   24 *Iaques* gold] *Iaques* gold *Q*   27 *Fran.*] *Fran*: *Q*   now.] now *Q*

Iuni. Away scoundrell! dost thou feare a little elocu-
tion? shall we be confiscate now? shal we droope now? 30
shall we be now in helogabolus?
 Oni. Peace, peace, leaue thy gabling!
 Count. Away, away with them; whats this they prate?
     Exeunt ⟨Seruants⟩ with Iuniper and Onion.
Keepe the knaues sure, strickt inquisition
Shall presently be made for *Iaques* gold,   35
To be disposd at pleasure of *Chamount.*
 Cha. She is your owne Lord *Paulo,* if your father
Giue his consent.
 Ang. How now *Christofero*? The case is alterd.
 Chris. With you, as well as me, I am content sir.   40
 Count. With all my heart! and in exchange of her,
(If with your faire acceptance it may stand)
I tender my *Aurelia* to your loue.
 Cha. I take her from your Lordship, with all thanks,
And blesse the hower wherein I was made prisoner: 45
For the fruition of this present fortune,
So full of happy and vnlookt for ioyes.
Melun, I pardon thee, and for the treasure,
Recouer it, and hold it as thine owne:
It is enough for me to see my sister   50
Liue in the circle of *Fernezes* armes,
My friend, the sonne of such a noble father,
And my vnworthy selfe rapt aboue all,
By being the Lord to so diuine a dame.
 Max. Well, I will now sweare the case is alterd. Lady 55
fare you well, I will subdue my affections. Maddam (as for
you) you are a profest virgin, and I will be silent. My
honorable Lord *Ferneze,* it shall become you at this time
not be frugall, but bounteous, and open handed, your

---

v. xiii. 29 scoundrell!] scoundrell? *Q*   30-1 Shall we be confiscate
and Shall we be now *begin new lines in Q*   31 helogabolus?] helogabolus: *Q*   32 gabling!] gabling? *Q*   33 prate?] prate, *Q*   Stage dir.
Servants G   36 Chamount] Chamouut *Q*   41 heart!] heart? *Q*
50 sister] sister: *Q*   56 affections.] affections, *Q*   57 silent.
My] silent, my *Q*

60 fortune hath been so to you. Lord *Chamount,* you are now no stranger, you must be welcome, you haue a faire, amiable and splendi⟨dio⟩us Lady: but signior *Paulo,* signior *Camillo,* I know you valiant; be louing. Lady I must be better knowne to you. Signiors for you, I passe you not:
65 though I let you passe; for in truth I passe not of you. Louers to your nuptials, Lordings to your dances. March faire al, for a faire March, is worth a kings ransome.

Exeunt.

The end.

v. xiii. 60 to you. Lord *Chamount,*] to you Lord *Chamount.* Q   You are *begins a new paragraph in Q*   61 faire,] faire Q   62 splendidious *H. C. Hart*   63 valiant;] valiant ? Q   louing.] louing : Q   64 you. Signiors] you, signiors Q   65 you. Louers] you, louers Q   66 dances.] dances, Q   68 *Exeunt.*] *Exeunt* Q

EVERY MAN IN HIS HUMOUR

The Original Version of 1598,
from the Quarto of 1601

THE TEXT

THIS play is extant in two forms—the original version issued in Quarto in 1601, and the revised version of the 1616 Folio. Two entries relating to the Quarto are found in the Stationers' Register in 1600. On August 4, 'Euery man in his humour / a booke' is entered along with *As You Like It*, *King Henry the Fifth*, and *Much Ado about Nothing* as one of 'My lord chamberlens mens plaies', the publication of which was 'to be staied'. The company was responsible for this entry, probably, as Mr. A. W. Pollard suggests,[1] in order to secure the copyright and checkmate a possible pirate. Ten days later it was entered for Cuthbert Burby and Walter Burre.

14. Augusti.

Master Burby.   Entred for yeir copie vnder the handes of
Walter Burre.   master PASVILL (=Pasfield) and ye Wardens. a booke called *Euery man in his humour.* vjd

(Arber's *Transcript*, III. 169)

The play appeared next year with Burre's imprint.

Collation: A², B–L⁴, M², with the title on A, 'The number and names of *the Actors*' on A2, and the text beginning on B.

The copies in the British Museum, the Bodleian, and the Dyce Library have been collated in preparing the present text. Three printers' variants have been noted:

III. iii. 56	abruptly	B.M. C. 34. c. 59, Bodl. Malone 229, 213, Dyce copies.
	abruptly?	B.M. 162. c. 70.
IV. iii. 109	the.	B.M. C. 34. c. 59.
	thee.	other copies.
V. iii. 12	messago	B.M. copies.
	message	Bodleian & Dyce copies.

Purely typographical errors, such as turned letters and the use of a wrong fount, have been silently corrected. A few textual corrections have been introduced from the Folio version (marked 'F' in the critical notes).

[1] See *Shakespeare's Fight with the Pirates*, pp. 45–6.

There have been three reprints of the Quarto. The first, which is not very accurate, was issued by Dr. Carl Grabau in the *Shakespeare-Jahrbuch*, 1902, vol. xxxviii, and was made from the two Museum copies. Dr. W. W. Greg edited a sound text in Bang's *Materialien zur Kunde des älteren englischen Dramas*, 1905, vol. x, from the Bodleian copy, checked with one copy in the British Museum. Dr. H. Holland Carter edited the Quarto and Folio texts in parallel columns for the Yale Studies in English, 1921, no. lii. His text of the Quarto was taken from a copy belonging to Mr. William Augustus White, and checked with a second copy in the same collection. He records three variants which are not found in the five copies collated for the present edition: ' *stockada* ' for ' *stockado* ' in I. iii. 219; ' Phœbus ' in roman, instead of italic, ibid. 229; and ' wound ' not followed by a comma in III. ii. 79. In this last example Dr. Carter notes that the paper of one copy is worn; by a curious coincidence this defect is found also in one of the Dyce copies.

EVERY MAN IN
his Humor.

As it hath beene sundry times *publickly acted by the right* Honorable the Lord Chamberlaine his seruants.

Written by BEN. IOHNSON.

Quod non dant proceres, dabit Histrio.

Haud tamen inuidias vati, quem pulpita pascunt.

Imprinted at London for *Walter Burre*, and are to be sould at his shoppe in Paules Church-yarde.
1601.

The number and names of the Actors.

Lorenzo senior.	*Giulliano.*
Prospero.	*Lorenzo iunior.*
Thorello.	*Biancha.*
Stephano.	*Hesperida.*
Doctor Clement.	*Peto.*
Bobadilla.	*Matheo.*
Musco.	*Pizo.*
Cob.	*Tib.*

EVERY MAN

in his Humor.

ACTVS PRIMVS, SCENA PRIMA.

Enter Lorenzo di Pazzi Senior, Musco.

NOw trust me, here's a goodly day toward. *Musco,*
　Call vp my sonne *Lorenzo* : bid him rise :
Tell him, I haue some businesse to imploy him in.
　Mus. I will, sir, presently.
　Lore.se. But heare you, sirrah ;　　　　　　　　　　5
If he be at study, disturbe him not.
　Mus. Very good, sir.　　　　　　*Exit Musco.*
　Lore.se. How happy would I estimate my selfe,
Could I (by any meane) retyre my sonne,
From one vayne course of study he affects ?　　　　10
He is a scholler (if a man may trust
The lib'rall voyce of double-toung'd report)
Of deare account, in all our *Academies.*
Yet this position must not breede in me
A fast opinion, that he cannot erre.　　　　　　　　15
My selfe was once a *student,* and indeede
Fed with the selfe-same humor he is now,
Dreaming on nought but idle *Poetrie* :
But since, Experience hath awakt my sprit's, *Enter Stephano.*
And reason taught them, how to comprehend　　20
The soueraigne vse of study.　What, cousin *Stephano* ?
What newes with you, that you are here so earely ?
　Steph. Nothing : but eene come to see how you doe, vncle.
　Lore.se. That's kindly done, you are welcome, cousin.

　　　　　　I. i. 1–3 *Prose in Q*

25   *Steph.* I, I know that sir, I would not haue come else: how doeth my cousin, vncle?

    Lore.se. Oh well, well, goe in and see; I doubt hee's scarce stirring yet.

    Steph. Vncle, afore I goe in, can you tell me, and he haue
30 e're a booke of the sciences of hawking and hunting? I would fayne borrow it.

    Lor. Why I hope you will not a hawking now, will you?

    Step. No wusse; but ile practise against next yeare: I haue bought me a hawke, and bels and all; I lacke no-
35 thing but a booke to keepe it by.

    Lor. Oh most ridiculous.

    Step. Nay looke you now, you are angrie vncle, why you know, and a man haue not skill in hawking and hunting now a daies, ile not giue a rush for him; hee is for no gentlemans
40 company, and (by Gods will) I scorne it I, so I doe, to bee a consort for euerie *hum-drum*; hang them *scroiles*, ther's nothing in them in the world, what doe you talke on it? a gentleman must shew himselfe like a gentleman, vncle I pray you be not angrie, I know what I haue to do I trow,
45 I am no nouice.

    Lor. Go to, you are a prodigal, and selfe-wild foole,
Nay neuer looke at me, it's I that speake,
Take't as you will, ile not flatter you.
What? haue you not meanes inow to wast
50 That which your friends haue left you, but you must
Go cast away your money on a *Buzzard*,
And know not how to keepe it when you haue done?
Oh it's braue, this will make you a gentleman,
Well Cosen well, I see you are e'ene past hope
55 Of all reclaime; I so, now you are told on it,
You looke another way.

    Step. What would you haue me do trow?

    Lor. What would I haue you do? mary
Learne to be wise, and practise how to thriue,
60 That I would haue you do, and not to spend

1. i. 55–6 *Prose in Q*

Your crownes on euerie one that humors you :
I would not haue you to intrude your selfe
In euerie gentlemans societie,
Till their affections or your owne desert,
Do worthily inuite you to the place. 65
For he thats so respectlesse in his course,
Oft sels his reputation vile and cheape.
Let not your cariage, and behauiour taste
Of affectation, lest while you pretend
To make a blaze of gentrie to the world 70
A little puffe of scorne extinguish it,
And you be left like an vnsauorie snuffe,
Whose propertie is onely to offend.
Cosen, lay by such superficiall formes,
And entertaine a perfect reall substance, 75
Stand not so much on your gentility,
      Enter a seruingman.
But moderate your expences (now at first)
As you may keepe the same proportion still.
Beare a low saile : soft who's this comes here.
 Ser. Gentlemen, God saue you. 80
 Step. Welcome good friend, we doe not stand much vpon our gentilitie ; yet I can assure you mine vncle is a man of a thousand pounde land a yeare ; hee hath but one sonne in the world ; I am his next heire, as simple as I stand here, if my cosen die : I haue a faire liuing of mine owne too beside. 85
 Ser. In good time sir.
 Step. In good time sir ? you do not flout, do you ?
 Ser. Not I sir.
 Step. And you should, here be them can perceiue it, and 90 that quickly too : Go too, and they can giue it againe soundly, and need be.
 Ser. Why sir let this satisfie you. Good faith I had no such intent.
 Step. By God, and I thought you had sir, I would talke 95 with you.
 Ser. So you may sir, and at your pleasure.

Step. And so I would sir, and you were out of mine vncles ground, I can tell you.

Lor. Why how now cosen, will this nere be left?

Step. Horson base fellow, by Gods lid, and't were not for shame, I would.

Lor.se. What would you do? you peremptorie Asse, And yowle not be quiet, get you hence. You see, the gentleman contaynes himselfe In modest limits, giuing no reply To your vnseason'd rude comparatiues; Yet yowle demeane your selfe, without respect Eyther of duty, or humanity. Goe get you in: fore God I am asham'd   *Exit Steph.* Thou hast a kinsmans interest in me.

Ser. I pray you, sir, is this *Pazzi* house?

Lor.se. Yes mary is it, sir.

Ser. I should enquire for a gentleman here, one *Signior Lorenzo di Pazzi*; doe you know any such, sir, I pray you?

Lore.se. Yes, sir: or else I should forget my selfe.

Ser. I crye you mercy, sir, I was requested by a gentleman of Florence (hauing some occasion to ride this way) to deliuer you this letter.

Lor.se. To me, sir? What doe you meane? I pray you remember your curt'sy.

To his deare and most elected friend, Signior Lorenzo di Pazzi. What might the gentlemans name be, sir, that sent it? Nay, pray you be couer'd.

Ser. Signior *Prospero*.

Lore.se. Signior *Prospero*? A young gentleman of the family of *Strozzi*, is he not?

Ser. I, sir, the same: Signior *Thorello*, the rich Florentine merchant, married his sister.

Lore.se. You say very true.   *Musco.*   *Enter Musco.*

Mus. Sir.

Lore.se. Make this Gentleman drinke, here.

I. i. 130 merchant,] merchant *Q*   131 Stage dir. in *Q* at 130

I pray you goe in, sir, and't please you. *Exeunt.*
Now (without doubt) this letter's to my sonne.   135
Well : all is one : Ile be so bold as reade it,
Be it but for the *styles* sake, and the *phrase* ;
Both which (I doe presume) are excellent,
And greatly varied from the vulgar forme,
If *Prospero's* inuention gaue them life.   140
How now ? what stuffe is here ?

 Sirha Lorenzo, *I muse we cannot see thee at* Florence :
S'blood, I doubt, Apollo *hath got thee to be his* Ingle, *that thou
commest not abroad, to visit thine old friends : well, take heede
of him ; hee may doe somewhat for his houshold seruants, or* 145
*so ; But for his Retayners, I am sure, I haue knowne some of
them, that haue followed him, three, foure, fiue yeere together,
scorning the world with their bare heeles, & at length bene glad
for a shift, (though no cleane shift) to lye a whole winter, in
halfe a sheete, cursing* Charles wayne, *and the rest of the*   150
starres intolerably. But (quis contra diuos ?) *well ; Sirha,
sweete villayne, come and see me ; but spend one minute in my
company, and 'tis inough : I thinke I haue a world of good
Iests for thee : oh sirha, I can shew thee two of the most perfect,
rare, & absolute true* Gulls, *that euer thou saw'st, if thou wilt* 155
*come. S'blood, inuent some famous memorable lye, or other,
to flap thy father in the mouth withall : thou hast bene father
of a thousand, in thy dayes, thou could'st be no* Poet *else : any
sciruy roguish excuse will serue ; say thou com'st but to fetch
wooll for thine Inke-horne. And then too, thy Father will say* 160
*thy wits are a wooll-gathering. But it's no matter ; the worse,
the better. Any thing is good inough for the old man. Sirha,
how if thy Father should see this now ? what would he thinke
of me ? Well, (how euer I write to thee) I reuerence him in my
soule, for the generall good all* Florence *deliuers of him.*   165
Lorenzo, *I coniure thee (by what, let me see) by the depth of our
loue, by all the strange sights we haue seene in our dayes, (I or
nights eyther) to come to me to* Florence *this day. Go to, you
shall come, and let your* Muses *goe spinne for once. If thou
wilt not, s'hart, what's your gods name ?* Apollo ? *I ;* Apollo. 170

If this melancholy rogue (Lorenzo *here*) *doe not come, graunt, that he doe turne Foole presently, and neuer hereafter, be able to make a good Iest, or a blanke verse, but liue in more penurie of wit and Inuention, then eyther the* Hall-Beadle, *or* Poet
175 Nuntius.

    Well, it is the strangest letter that euer I read.
Is this the man, my sonne (so oft) hath prays'd
To be the happiest, and most pretious wit
That euer was familiar with Art?
180 Now (by our Ladies blessed sonne) I sweare,
I rather thinke him most infortunate,
In the possession of such holy giftes,
Being the master of so loose a spirit.
Why what vnhallow'd ruffian would haue writ,
185 With so prophane a pen, vnto his friend?
The modest paper eene lookes pale for griefe
To feele her virgin-cheeke defilde and staind
With such a blacke and criminall *inscription*.
Well, I had thought my son could not haue straied,
190 So farre from iudgement, as to mart himselfe
Thus cheaply, (in the open trade of scorne)
To geering *follie*, and fantastique *humour*.
But now I see *opinion* is a foole,
And hath abusde my sences. *Musco.*   *Enter Musco.*
195   *Mus.* Sir.
  Lor.se. What is the fellow gone that brought this letter?
  Mus. Yes sir, a prettie while since.
  Lor.se. And wher's *Lorenzo*?
  Mus. In his chamber sir.
200   *Lor.se.* He spake not with the fellow, did he?
  Mus. No sir, he saw him not.
  Lor.se. Then *Musco* take this letter, and deliuer it
Vnto *Lorenzo* : but sirra, (on your life)
Take you no knowledge I haue open'd it.
205   *Mus.* O Lord sir, that were a iest indeed.   *Exit Mus.*
  Lor.se. I am resolu'd I will not crosse his iourney.

    1. i. 184 vnhallow'd] vnhallowed *Q*   202–4 *Prose* in *Q*

Nor will I practise any violent meane,
To stay the hot and lustie course of youth.
For youth restrained straight growes impatient,
And (in condition) like an eager dogge, 210
Who (ne're so little from his game withheld)
Turnes head and leapes vp at his masters throat.
Therefore ile studie (by some milder drift)
To call my sonne vnto a happier shrift. *Exit.*

SCENA SECVNDA.

Enter Lorenzo iunior, with Musco.

Mus. Yes sir, (on my word) he opend it, & read the contents.

Lor.iu. It scarse contents me that he did so. But *Musco* didst thou obserue his countenance in the reading of it, whether hee were angrie or pleasde? 5

Mus. Why sir I saw him not reade it.

Lo.iu. No? how knowest thou then that he opend it?

Mus. Marry sir because he charg'd mee (on my life) to tell no body that he opend it, which (vnlesse he had done) he wold neuer feare to haue it reueald. 10

Lo.iu. Thats true: well *Musco* hie thee in againe,
Least thy protracted absence do lend light,

Enter Stephan⟨o⟩.

To darke suspition: *Musco* be assurde
Ile not forget this thy respectiue loue.

Step. Oh *Musco*, didst thou not see a fellow here in a 15 what-sha-callum doublet; he brought mine vncle a letter euen now?

Mus. Yes sir, what of him?

Step. Where is he, canst thou tell?

Mus. Why he is gone. 20

Step. Gone? which way? when went he? how long since?

Mus. Its almost halfe an houre ago since he rid hence.

Step. Horson Scanderbag rogue, oh that I had a horse; by Gods lidde i'de fetch him backe againe, with heaue and ho.

Mus. Why you may haue my masters bay gelding, and you will.

Step. But I haue no boots, thats the spite on it.

Mus. Then its no boot to follow him. Let him go and hang sir.

Step. I by my troth ; *Musco*, I pray thee help to trusse me a little ; nothing angers mee, but I haue waited such a while for him all vnlac'd and vntrust yonder, and now to see hee is gone the other way.

Mus. Nay I pray you stand still sir.

Step. I will, I will : oh how it vexes me.

Mus. Tut, neuer vexe your selfe with the thought of such a base fellow as he.

Step. Nay to see, he stood vpon poynts with me too.

Mus. Like inough so ; that was, because he saw you had so fewe at your hose.

Step. What ? Hast thou done ? Godamercy, good *Musco*.

Mus. I marle, sir, you weare such ill-fauourd course stockings, hauing so good a legge as you haue.

Step. Fo, the stockings be good inough for this time of the yeere ; but Ile haue a payre of silke, e're it be long : I thinke, my legge would shewe well in a silke hose.

Mus. I afore God would it rarely well.

Step. In sadnesse I thinke it would : I haue a reasonable good legge.

Mus. You haue an excellent good legge, sir : I pray you pardon me, I haue a little haste in, sir.

Step. A thousand thankes, good Musco. *Exit* ⟨*Musco*⟩. What, I hope he laughs not at me ; and he doe——

Lo.iun. Here is a *style* indeed, for a mans sences to leape ouer, e're they come at it : why, it is able to breake the shinnes of any old mans patience in the world. My father reade this with patience ? Then will I be made an *Eunuch*, and learne to sing Ballads. I doe not deny, but my father may haue as much patience as any other man ; for hee vses to take phisicke, and oft taking phisicke, makes a man a

I. ii. 32 little] liltle *Q*

very patient creature. But, Signior *Prospero*, had your swaggering *Epistle* here, arriued in my fathers hands, at such an houre of his patience, (I meane, when hee had tane phisicke) it is to bee doubted, whether I should haue read *sweete villayne* here. But, what? My wise cousin; Nay then, Ile furnish our feast with one Gull more toward a messe; hee writes to mee of two, and here's one, that's three, Ifayth. Oh for a fourth: now, *Fortune*, or neuer *Fortune*.

Step. Oh, now I see who he laught at: hee laught at some body in that letter. By this good light, and he had laught at me, I would haue told mine vncle.

Lo.iun. Cousin Stephano: good morrow, good cousin, how fare you?

Step. The better for your asking, I will assure you. I haue beene all about to seeke you; since I came I saw mine vncle; & ifaith how haue you done this great while? Good Lord, by my troth I am glad you are well cousin.

Lor.iu. And I am as glad of your comming, I protest to you, for I am sent for by a priuate gentleman, my most speciall deare friend, to come to him to *Florence* this morning, and you shall go with me cousin, if it please you, not els, I will enioyne you no further then stands with your owne consent, and the condition of a friend.

Step. Why cousin you shall command me and't were twise so farre as *Florence* to do you good; what doe you thinke I will not go with you? I protest.

Lo.iu. Nay, nay, you shall not protest.

Step. By God, but I will sir, by your leaue ile protest more to my friend then ile speake of at this time.

Lo.iu. You speake very well sir.

Step. Nay not so neither, but I speake to serue my turne.

Lo.iu. Your turne? why cousin, a gentleman of so faire sort as you are, of so true cariage, so speciall good parts; of so deare and choice estimation; one whose lowest condition beares the stampe of a great spirit; nay more,

I. ii. 66 here] *here* Q

a man so grac'd, guilded, or rather (to vse a more fit *Metaphor*) tinfoyld by nature, (not that you haue a leaden constitution, couze, although perhaps a little inclining to that temper, & so the more apt to melt with pittie, when you fall into the fire of rage) but for your lustre onely, which reflects as bright to the world as an old Ale-wiues pewter againe a good time ; and will you now (with nice modestie) hide such reall ornaments as these, and shadow their glorie as a Millaners wife doth her wrought stomacher, with a smoakie lawne or a blacke cipresse ? Come, come, for shame doe not wrong the qualitie of your desert in so poore a kind : but let the *Idea* of what you are, be portraied in your aspect, that men may reade in your lookes ; *Here within this place is to be seene, the most admirable rare & accomplisht worke of nature* ; Cousin what think you of this ?

Step. Marry I do thinke of it, and I will be more melancholie, and gentlemanlike then I haue beene, I doe ensure you.

Lo.iu. Why this is well : now if I can but hold vp this humor in him, as it is begun, *Catso* for *Florence*, match him & she can ; Come cousin.

Step. Ile follow you.

Lo.iu. Follow me ? you must go before.

Step. Must I ? nay then I pray you shew me good cousin.

Exeunt.

SCENA TERTIA.

Enter Signior Matheo, to him Cob.

Mat. I thinke this be the house : what howgh ?

Cob. Who's there ? oh Signior *Matheo*. God giue you good morrow sir.

Mat. What ? *Cob* ? how doest thou good *Cob* ? doest thou inhabite here *Cob* ?

Cob. I sir, I and my lineage haue kept a poore house in our daies.

1. ii. 119–20 *One line in* Q

Mat. Thy lineage *monsieur Cob* ? what lineage, what lineage ?
Cob. Why sir, an ancient lineage, and a princely : mine ancetrie came from a kings loynes, no worse man ; and yet no man neither, but *Herring* the king of fish, one of the monarches of the world I assure you. I doe fetch my pedegree and name from the first redde herring that was eaten in *Adam,* & *Eues* kitchin : his *Cob* was my great, great, mighty great grandfather.
Mat. Why mightie ? why mightie ?
Cob. Oh its a mightie while agoe sir, and it was a mightie great *Cob.*
Mat. How knowest thou that ?
Cob. How know I ? why his ghost comes to me euery night.
Mat. Oh vnsauorie iest : the ghost of a herring *Cob.*
Cob. I, why not the ghost of a herring *Cob,* as well as the ghost of *Rashero Baccono,* they were both broild on the coales : you are a scholler, vpsolue me that now.
Mat. Oh rude ignorance. *Cob* canst thou shew me, of a gentleman, one Signior *Bobadilla,* where his lodging is ?
Cob. Oh my guest sir, you meane ?
Mat. Thy guest, alas ? ha, ha.
Cob. Why do you laugh sir ? do you not meane signior *Bobadilla* ?
Mat. Cob I pray thee aduise thy selfe well : do not wrong the gentleman, and thy selfe too. I dare be sworne hee scornes thy house hee. He lodge in such a base obscure place as thy house ? Tut, I know his disposition so well, he would not lie in thy bed if thould'st giue it him.
Cob. I will not giue it him. Masse I thought (somewhat was in it) we could not get him to bed all night. Well sir, though he lie not on my bed, he lies on my bench : and't please you to go vp sir, you shall find him with two cushions vnder his head, and his cloake wrapt about him, as though

1. iii. 39 *Cob.*] Cob, Q   41 bench :] bench, Q

he had neither won nor lost, and yet I warrant hee ne're
cast better in his life then hee hath done to night.
  Mat. Why, was he drunke?
  Cob. Drunk sir? you heare not me say so; perhaps he
swallow'd a tauerne token, or some such deuise sir; I haue
nothing to doe withal: I deale with water and not with
wine. Giue me my tankard there, ho. God be with you sir,
its sixe a clocke: I should haue caried two turnes by this,
what ho? my stopple, come.
  Mat. Lie in a waterbearers house, a gentleman of his
note? well ile tell him my mind.   *Exit.*
  Cob. What *Tib*, shew this gentleman vp to Signior
Bobadilla: oh and my house were the Brazen head now,
faith it would eene crie moe fooles yet: you should haue
some now, would take him to be a gentleman at the least;
alas God helpe the simple, his father's an honest man,
a good fishmonger, and so forth: and now doth he creep
and wriggle into acquaintance with all the braue gallants
about the towne, such as my guest is, (oh my guest is a fine
man) and they flout him inuinciblie. He vseth euery day
to a Marchants house (where I serue water) one M. *Thorellos*;
and here's the iest, he is in loue with my masters sister,
and cals her mistres: and there he sits a whole afternoone
sometimes, reading of these same abhominable, vile,
(a poxe on them, I cannot abide them) rascally verses,
Poetrie, poetrie, and speaking of *Enterludes,* 't will make
a man burst to heare him: and the wenches, they doe so
geere and tihe at him; well, should they do as much to me,
Ild forsweare them all, by the life of Pharaoh, there's an
oath: how many waterbearers shall you heare sweare such
an oath? oh I haue a guest (he teacheth me) he doth sweare
the best of any man christned: By Phœbus, By the life
of Pharaoh, By the body of me, As I am ⟨a⟩ gentleman, and
a soldier: such daintie oathes; & withall he doth take this
same filthie roaguish Tabacco the finest, and cleanliest; it
wold do a man good to see the fume come forth at his

1. iii. 46 Why,] Why *Q*   52 stopple,] stopple *Q*   69 't will!] t'will *Q*

nostrils : well, he owes me fortie shillings (my wife lent him out of her purse ; by sixpence a time) besides his lodging ; I would I had it : I shall haue it he saith next *Action*. *Helter skelter*, hang sorrow, care will kill a cat, vptailes all, and a poxe on the hangman. *Exit.*

Bobadilla discouers himselfe : on a bench ; to him Tib.

Bob. Hostesse, hostesse.
Tib. What say you sir ?
Bob. A cup of your small beere sweet hostesse.
Tib. Sir, ther's a gentleman below would speake with you.
Bob. A gentleman, (Gods so) I am not within.
Tib. My husband told him you were sir.
Bob. What ha plague ? what meant he ?
Mat. Signior Bobadilla.   *Matheo within.*
Bob. Who's there ? (take away the bason good hostesse) come vp sir.
Tib. He would desire you to come vp sir ; you come into a cleanly house here.
Mat. God saue you sir, God saue you.   *Enter Matheo.*
Bob. Signior Matheo, is't you sir ? please you sit downe.
Mat. I thanke you good Signior, you may see, I am somewhat audacious.
Bob. Not so Signior, I was requested to supper yester-night by a sort of gallants where you were wisht for, and drunke to I assure you.
Mat. Vouchsafe me by whom good Signior.
Bob. Marrie by Signior *Prospero*, and others, why hostesse, a stoole here for this gentleman.
Mat. No haste sir, it is very well.
Bob. Bodie of me, it was so late ere we parted last night, I can scarse open mine eyes yet ; I was but new risen as you came : how passes the day abroad sir ? you can tell.
Mat. Faith some halfe houre to seuen : now trust me you haue an exceeding fine lodging here, very neat, and priuate.
Bob. I sir, sit downe I pray you : Signior *Matheo* (in any

115 case) possesse no gentlemen of your acquaintance with notice of my lodging.

Mat. Who I sir? no.

Bob. Not that I neede to care who know it, but in regard I would not be so popular and generall, as some be.

120 *Mat.* True Signior, I conceiue you.

Bob. For do you see sir, by the hart of my selfe (except it be to some peculiar and choice spirits, to whom I am extraordinarily ingag'd, as your selfe, or so) I would not extend thus farre.

125 *Mat.* O Lord sir I resolue so.

Bob. What new booke haue you there? what? *Go by Hieronimo.*

Mat. I, did you euer see it acted? is't not well pend?

Bob. Well pend: I would faine see all the Poets of our 130 time pen such another play as that was; they'l prate and swagger, and keepe a stirre of arte and deuises, when (by Gods so) they are the most shallow pittifull fellowes that liue vpon the face of the earth againe.

Mat. Indeede, here are a number of fine speeches in this 135 booke: *Oh eyes, no eyes but fountaines fraught with teares;* there's a conceit: Fountaines fraught with teares. *Oh life, no life, but liuely forme of death:* is't not excellent? *Oh world, no world, but masse of publique wrongs; O Gods mee: confusde and fild with murther and misdeeds.* Is't not 140 simply the best that euer you heard? Ha, how do you like it?

Bob. Tis good.

Mat. *To thee the purest obiect to my sence,*
The most refined essence heauen couers,
145 *Send I these lines, wherein I do commence*
The happie state of true deseruing louers.
If they proue rough, vnpolish't, harsh and rude,
Haste made that waste; thus mildly I conclude.

Bob. Nay proceed, proceed, where's this? where's this?

150 *Mat.* This sir, a toy of mine owne in my nonage: but

I. iii. 139–41 Three lines in Q: *misdeeds.* | Is't ... heard? | Ha,

when will you come and see my studie? good faith I can shew you some verie good thinges I haue done of late: that boote becomes your legge passing well sir, me thinks.

Bob. So, so, it's a fashion gentlemen vse.

Mat. Masse sir, and now you speake of the fashion, Signior *Prosperos* elder brother and I are fallen out exceedingly: this other day I hapned to enter into some discourse of a hanger, which I assure you, both for fashion & workmanship was most beautifull and gentlemanlike; yet hee condemned it for the most pide and ridiculous that euer he saw.

Bob. Signior *Giuliano*, was it not? the elder brother?

Mat. I sir, he.

Bob. Hang him Rooke, he? why he has no more iudgement then a malt horse. By S. *George*, I hold him the most peremptorie absurd clowne (one a them) in Christendome: I protest to you (as I am a gentleman and a soldier) I ne're talk't with the like of him: he ha's not so much as a good word in his bellie, all iron, iron, a good commoditie for a smith to make hobnailes on.

Mat. I, and he thinkes to carrie it away with his manhood still where he comes: he brags he will giue mee the bastinado, as I heare.

Bob. How, the bastinado? how came he by that word trow?

Mat. Nay indeed he said cudgill me; I tearmd it so for the more grace.

Bob. That may bee, for I was sure it was none of his word: but when, when said he so?

Mat. Faith yesterday they say, a young gallant a friend of mine told me so.

Bob. By the life of Pharaoh, and't were my case nowe, I should send him a challenge presently: the bastinado? come hither, you shall challenge him; ile shew you a tricke or two, you shall kill him at pleasure, the first *stockado* if you will, by this ayre.

1. iii. 164 Rooke,] Rooke *Q*

Mat. Indeed you haue absolute knowledge in the mistery, I haue heard sir.

Bob. Of whom ? of whom I pray ?

Mat. Faith I haue heard it spoken of diuers, that you haue verie rare skill sir.

Bob. By heauen, no, not I, no skill in the earth : some small science, know my time, distance, or so, I haue profest it more for noblemen and gentlemens use, then mine owne practise I assure you. Hostesse, lend vs another bedstaffe here quickly : looke you sir, exalt not your point aboue this state at any hand, and let your poyneard maintaine your defence thus : giue it the gentleman. So sir, come on, oh twine your bodie more about, that you may come to a more sweet comely gentlemanlike guard ; so, indifferent. Hollow your bodie more sir, thus : now stand fast on your left leg, note your distance, keep your due proportion of time : oh you disorder your point most vilely.

Mat. How is the bearing of it now sir ?

Bob. Oh out of measure ill, a well experienced man would passe vpon you at pleasure.

Mat. How meane you passe vpon me ?

Bob. Why thus sir ; make a thrust at me ; come in vpon my time ; controll your point, and make a full carriere at the bodie : the best practis'd gentlemen of the time terme it the *passado*, a most desperate thrust, beleeue it.

Mat. Well, come sir.

Bob. Why you do not manage your weapons with that facilitie and grace that you should doe, I haue no spirit to play with you, your dearth of iudgement makes you seeme tedious.

Mat. But one veny sir.

Bob. Fie veney, most grosse denomination, as euer I heard : oh the *stockado* while you liue Signior, note that. Come put on your cloake, and weele go to some priuate place where you are acquainted, some tauerne or so, & weele send for one of these fencers, where he shall breath you at

 1. iii. 200 so,] so *Q*   208 sir ;] sir ? *Q*

my direction, and then ile teach you that tricke, you shall
kill him with it at the first if you please : why ile learne
you by the true iudgement of the eye, hand and foot, to 225
controll any mans point in the world ; Should your
aduersary confront you with a pistoll, 'twere nothing, you
should (by the same rule) controll the bullet, most certaine
by *Phœbus* : vnles it were haile-shot : what mony haue
you about you sir ?   230

   Mat. Faith I haue not past two shillings, or so.

   Bob. Tis somewhat with the least, but come, when we
haue done, weele call vp Signior *Prospero* ; perhaps we shal
meet with *Coridon* his brother there.   *Exeunt.*

SCENA QVARTA.

Enter *Thorello, Giuliano, Piso.*

   Tho. Piso, come hither : there lies a note within vpon
my deske ; here take my key : it's no matter neither,
where's the boy ?

   Piso. Within sir, in the warehouse.

   Thor. Let him tell ouer that Spanish gold, and weigh it, 5
and do you see the deliuerie of those wares to Signior
Bentiuole : ile be there my selfe at the receipt of the
money anon.

   Piso. Verie good sir.   *Exit Piso.*

   Tho. Brother, did you see that same fellow there ?   10

   Giu. I, what of him ?

   Tho. He is e'ene the honestest faithfull seruant, that is
this day in *Florence* ; (I speake a proud word now) and
one that I durst trust my life into his hands, I haue so
strong opinion of his loue, if need were.   15

   Giu. God send me neuer such need : but you said you
had somewhat to tell me, what is't ?

   Tho. Faith brother, I am loath to vtter it,
As fearing to abuse your patience,
But that I know your iudgement more direct,   20
Able to sway the nearest of affection.

       I. iii. 227 'twere] t'were *Q*

Giu. Come, come, what needs this circumstance?
   Tho. I will not say what honor I ascribe
Vnto your friendship, nor in what deare state
25 I hold your loue; let my continued zeale,
   The constant and religious regard,
   That I haue euer caried to your name,
   My cariage with your sister, all contest,
   How much I stand affected to your house.
30 *Giu.* You are too tedious, come to the matter, come to the matter.
   Tho. Then (without further ceremony) thus.
   My brother *Prospero* (I know not how)
   Of late is much declin'd from what he was,
35 And greatly alterd in his disposition.
   When he came first to lodge here in my house,
   Ne're trust me, if I was not proud of him:
   Me thought he bare himselfe with such obseruance,
   So true election and so faire a forme:
40 And (what was chiefe) it shewd not borrow'd in him,
   But all he did became him as his owne,
   And seemd as perfect, proper, and innate,
   Vnto the mind, as collor to the blood,
   But now, his course is so irregular,
45 So loose affected, and depriu'd of grace,
   And he himselfe withall so farre falne off
   From his first place, that scarse no note remaines,
   To tell mens iudgements where he lately stood;
   Hee's growne a stranger to all due respect,
50 Forgetfull of his friends, and not content
   To stale himselfe in all societies,
   He makes my house as common as a *Mart*,
   A *Theater*, a publike receptacle
   For giddie humor, and diseased riot,
55 And there, (as in a Tauerne, or a stewes,)
   He, and his wilde associates, spend their houres,
   In repetition of lasciuious iests,

I. iv. 40 borrow'd] borrowed *Q*

Sweare, leape, and dance, and reuell night by night,
Controll my seruants: and indeed what not?
   Giu. Faith I know not what I should say to him: so
God saue mee, I am eene at my wits end, I haue tolde him
inough, one would thinke, if that would serue: well, he
knowes what to trust to for me: let him spend, and spend,
and domineere till his hart ake: & he get a peny more of
me, Ile giue him this eare.
   Tho. Nay good Brother haue patience.
   Giu. S'blood, he mads me, I could eate my very flesh
for anger: I marle you will not tell him of it, how he
disquiets your house.
   Tho. O there are diuers reasons to disswade me,
But would your selfe vouchsafe to trauaile in it,
(Though but with plaine, and easie circumstance,)
It would, both come much better to his sence,
And sauor lesse of griefe and discontent.
You are his elder brother, and that title
Confirmes and warrants your authoritie:
Which (seconded by your aspect) will breed
A kinde of duty in him, and regard.
Whereas, if I should intimate the least,
It would but adde contempt, to his neglect,
Heape worse on ill, reare a huge pile of hate,
That in the building, would come tottring downe,
And in the ruines, bury all our loue.
Nay more then this brother; (if I should speake)
He would be ready in the heate of passion,
To fill the eares of his familiars,
With oft reporting to them, what disgrace
And grosse disparagement, I had propos'd him.
And then would they straight back him, in opinion,
Make some loose comment vpon euery word,
And out of their distracted phantasies;
Contriue some slander, that should dwell with me.
And what would that be thinke you? mary this,
          I. iv. 83 the *F* : her *Q*

They would giue out, (because my wife is fayre,
95 My selfe but lately married, and my sister
Heere soiourning a virgin in my house)
That I were iealous : nay, as sure as death,
Thus they would say : and how that I had wrongd
My brother purposely, thereby to finde
100 An apt pretext to banish them my house.
    Giu. Masse perhaps so.
    Tho. Brother they would, beleeue it : so should I
(Like one of these penurious quack-saluers,)
But trie experiments vpon my selfe,
105 Open the gates vnto mine owne disgrace,
Lend bare-ribd enuie, oportunitie,
To stab my reputation, and good name.

       Enter Boba⟨dilla⟩ and Matheo.
    Mat. I will speake to him.
    Bob. Speake to him ? away, by the life of *Pharoah* you
110 shall not, you shall not do him that grace : the time of daye
to you Gentleman : is Signior *Prospero* stirring ?
    Giu. How then ? what should he doe ?
    Bob. Signior *Thorello*, is he within sir ?
    Tho. He came not to his lodging to night sir, I assure you.
115   *Giu.* Why do you heare ? you.
    Bob. This gentleman hath satisfied me, Ile talke to no Scauenger.
    Giu. How Scauenger ? stay sir stay.   *Exeunt.*
    Tho. Nay Brother *Giuliano*.
120   *Giu.* S'blood stand you away, and you loue me.
    Tho. You shall not follow him now I pray you,
Good faith you shall not.
    Giu. Ha ? Scauenger ? well goe to, I say little, but, by
this good day (God forgiue me I should sweare) if I put it
125 vp so, say I am the rankest —— that. euer pist. S'blood
and I swallowe this, Ile neere drawe my sworde in the sight

    1. iv. 102 would,] would *Q*   103 quack-saluers] quack-slaluers *Q*
    106 oportunitie,] oportunitie. *Q*

of man againe while I liue; Ile sit in a Barne with Madge-
owlet first. Scauenger? 'Hart and Ile goe neere to fill that
huge tumbrell slop of yours with somewhat and I haue
good lucke, your *Garagantua* breech cannot carry it away so. 130
  Tho. Oh do not fret your selfe thus, neuer thinke on't.
  Giu. These are my brothers consorts these, these are his
Cumrades, his walking mates, hees a gallant, a *Caueliero*
too, right hangman cut. God let me not liue, and I could
not finde in my hart to swinge the whole nest of them, one 135
after another, and begin with him first. I am grieu'd it
should be said he is my brother, and take these courses, well
he shall heare on't, and that tightly too, and I liue Ifaith.
  Tho. But brother, let your apprehension (then)
Runne in an easie current, not transported 140
With heady rashnes, or deuouring choller,
And rather carry a perswading spirit,
Whose powers will pearce more gently; and allure
Th'imperfect thoughts you labour to reclaime,
To a more sodaine and resolu'd assent. 145
  Gui. I, I, let me alone for that I warrant you. *Bell rings.*
  Tho. How now? oh the bell rings to breakefast.
Brother *Giuliano,* I pray you go in and beare my wife
company: Ile but giue order to my seruants for the
dispatche of some busines and come to you presently. 150
                        Exit Guil⟨iano⟩.

              Enter Cob.

What *Cob?* our maides will haue you by the back (Ifaith)
for comming so late this morning.
  Cob. Perhaps so sir, take heede some body haue not them
by the belly for walking so late in the euening. *Exit.*
  Tho. Now (in good faith) my minde is somewhat easd, 155
Though not reposd in that securitie,
As I could wish; well, I must be content.

  1. iv. 128 first.] first, *Q*   129 tumbrell *in the catchword of sig.* D 2,
timbrell *in text of sig.* D 2 verso   136 first.] first, *Q*   143 allure]
allure, *Q*   150 Stage dir. *Guiliano*] Guil. *Q*   151-2 *As verse in Q,
divided at* For   157 content. *F* : content, *Q*

How e're I set a face on't to the world,
Would I had lost this finger at a vente⟨r⟩,
160 So *Prospero* had ne're lodg'd in my house,
Why't cannot be, where there is such resort
Of wanton gallants, and young reuellers,
That any woman should be honest long.
Is't like, that factious beauty will preserue
165 The soueraigne state of chastitie vnscard,
When such strong motiues muster, and make head
Against her single peace? no, no: beware
When mutuall pleasure swayes the appetite,
And spirits of one kinde and qualitie,
170 Do meete to parlee in the pride of blood.
Well (to be plaine) if I but thought, the time
Had answer'd their affections: all the world
Should not perswade me, but I were a cuckold:
Mary I hope they haue not got that start.
175 For opportunity hath balkt them yet,
And shall do still, while I haue eyes and eares
To attend the imposition of my hart,
My presence shall be as an Iron Barre,
Twixt the conspiring motions of desire,
180 Yea euery looke or glaunce mine eye obiects,
Shall checke occasion, as one doth his slaue,
When he forgets the limits of prescription.

Enter Biancha, with Hesperida.

Bia. Sister *Hesperida*, I pray you fetch downe the Rose water aboue in the closet: Sweete hart will you come in to
185 breakfast?   *Exit Hesperida.*

Tho. And she haue ouer-heard me now?

Bia. I pray thee (good *Musse*) we stay for you.

Tho. By Christ I would not for a thousand crownes.

Bia. What ayle you sweete hart, are you not well, speake
190 good *Musse.*

Tho. Troth my head akes extreamely on a suddaine.

I. iv. 164 Is't] I'st *Q*   185 breakfast?] breakfast. *Q*

Bia. Oh Iesu!
Tho. How now? what?
Bia. Good Lord how it burnes? *Musse* keepe you
warme, good truth it is this new disease, there's a number 195
are troubled withall: for Gods sake sweete heart, come in
out of the ayre.
Tho. How simple, and how subtill are her answeres?
A new disease, and many troubled with it.
Why true, she heard me, all the world to nothing. 200
Bia. I pray thee good sweet heart come in; the ayre
will do you harme in troth.
Tho. Ile come to you presently, it will away I hope.
Bia. Pray God it do. *Exit.*
Tho. A new disease? I know not, new or old, 205
But it may well be call'd poore mortals Plague;
For like a pestilence it doth infect
The houses of the braine: first it begins
Solely to worke vpon the fantasie,
Filling her seat with such pestiferous aire, 210
As soone corrupts the iudgement, and from thence,
Sends like contagion to the memorie,
Still each of other catching the infection,
Which as a searching vapor spreads it selfe
Confusedly through euery sensiue part, 215
Till not a thought or motion in the mind
Be free from the blacke poison of suspect.
Ah, but what error is it to know this,
And want the free election of the soule
In such extreames? Well, I will once more striue, 220
(Euen in despight of hell) my selfe to be,
And shake this feauer off that thus shakes me.
Exit.

I. iv. 200 me,] me Q   205–17 *Quoted in* England's Parnassus,
1600, p. 143, *with these variants*: (206) term'd, poore mortall plaine.
(207) the pestilence. (213) taking like infection. (217) Be farre. 220
Well] well Q

ACTVS SECVNDVS,
SCENA PRIMA.

Enter Musco disguised like a soldier.

Musco. S'blood, I cannot chuse but laugh to see my selfe translated thus, from a poore creature to a creator; for now must I create an intolerable sort of lies, or else my profession looses his grace, and yet the lie to a man of my coat, is as ominous as the *Fico* : oh sir, it holds for good policie to haue that outwardly in vilest estimation, that inwardly is most deare to vs : So much for my borrowed shape. Well, the troth is, my maister intends to follow his sonne drie-foot to Florence, this morning : now I knowing of this conspiracie, and the rather to insinuate with my young master, (for so must wee that are blew waiters, or men of seruice doe, or else perhaps wee may weare motley at the yeares end, and who weares motley you know :) I haue got me afore in this disguise, determining here to lie in ambuscado, & intercept him in the midway : if I can but get his cloake, his purse, his hat, nay any thing so I can stay his iourney, *Rex Regum*, I am made for euer ifaith : well, now must I practise to get the true garbe of one of these *Launce-knights* : my arme here, and my : Gods so, young master and his cousin.

Enter Lo⟨renzo⟩ iu⟨nior⟩ and Step⟨hano⟩.

Lo.iu. So sir, and how then?

Step. Gods foot, I haue lost my purse, I thinke.

Lo.iu. How? lost your purse? where? when had you it?

Step. I cannot tell, stay.

Mus. S'lid I am afeard they will know me, would I could get by them.

Lo.iu. What? haue you it?

Step. No, I thinke I was bewitcht, I.

II. i. 5 *Fico* :] *Fico*, Q

Lo.iu. Nay do not weep, a poxe on it, hang it let it go.

Step. Oh it's here; nay and it had beene lost, I had not car'd but for a iet ring *Marina* sent me.

Lo.iu. A iet ring? oh the poesie, the poesie?

Step. Fine ifaith: *Though fancie sleepe, my loue is deepe:* meaning that though I did not fancie her, yet shee loued mee dearely.

Lo.iu. Most excellent.

Step. And then I sent her another, and my poesie was; *The deeper the sweeter, Ile be iudg'd by Saint Peter.*

Lo.iu. How, by S. *Peter*? I do not conceiue that.

Step. Marrie, S. *Peter* to make vp the meeter.

Lo.iu. Well, you are beholding to that Saint, he help't you at your need; thanke him, thanke him.

Mus. I will venture, come what will: Gentlemen, please you chaunge a few crownes for a verie excellent good blade here; I am a poore gentleman, a soldier, one that (in the better state of my fortunes) scornd so meane a refuge, but now its the humour of necessitie to haue it so: you seeme to be gentlemen well affected to martiall men, els I should rather die with silence, then liue with shame: how e're, vouchsafe to remember it is my want speakes, not my selfe: this condition agrees not with my spirit.

Lo.iu. Where hast thou seru'd?

Mus. May it please you Signior, in all the prouinces of *Bohemia, Hungaria, Dalmatia, Poland*, where not? I haue beene a poore seruitor by sea and land, any time this xiiij. yeares, and follow'd the fortunes of the best Commaunders in Christendome. I was twise shot at the taking of *Aleppo*, once at the reliefe of *Vienna*; I haue beene at *America* in the galleyes thrise, where I was most dangerously shot in the head, through both the thighes, and yet being thus maim'd I am voide of maintenance, nothing left me but my scarres, the noted markes of my resolution.

Step. How will you sell this Rapier friend?

II. i. 65 *Step.*] *Step,* Q

Mus. Faith Signior, I referre it to your owne iudgement; you are a gentleman, giue me what you please.

Step. True, I am a gentleman, I know that; but what though? I pray you say, what would you aske?

Mus. I assure you the blade may become the side of the best prince in *Europe*.

Lo.iu. I, with a veluet scabberd.

Step. Nay and't be mine it shall haue a veluet scabberd, that is flat, i'de not weare it as 'tis and you would giue me an angell.

Mus. At your pleasure Signior, nay it's a most pure *Toledo*.

Step. I had rather it were a *Spaniard*: but tell me, what shal I giue you for it? and it had a siluer hilt—

Lo.iu. Come, come, you shall not buy it; holde there's a shilling friend, take thy Rapier.

Step. Why but I will buy it now, because you say so: what shall I go without a rapier?

Lo.iu. You may buy one in the citie.

Step. Tut, ile buy this, so I will; tell me your lowest price.

Lo.iu. You shall not I say.

Step. By Gods lid, but I will, though I giue more then 'tis worth.

Lo.iu. Come away, you are a foole.

Step. Friend, ile haue it for that word: follow me.

Mus. At your seruice Signior. *Exeunt.*

SCENA SECVNDA.

Enter Lorenzo senior.

Lore. My labouring spirit being late opprest
With my sonnes follie, can embrace no rest,
Till it hath plotted by aduise and skill,
How to reduce him from affected will
To reasons manage; which while I intend,

II. i. 69 though?] though, *Q*

My troubled soule beginnes to apprehend
A farther secret, and to meditate
Vpon the difference of mans estate :
Where is deciphered to true iudgements eye
A deep, conceald, and precious misterie.   10
Yet can I not but worthily admire
At natures art : who (when she did inspire
This heat of life) plac'd Reason (as a king)
Here in the head, to haue the marshalling
Of our affections : and with soueraigntie   15
To sway the state of our weake emperie.
But as in diuers commonwealthes we see,
The forme of gouernment to disagree :
Euen so in man who searcheth soone shal find
As much or more varietie of mind.   20
Some mens affections like a sullen wife,
Is with her husband reason still at strife.
Others (like proud Arch-traitors that rebell
Against their soueraigne) practise to expell
Their liege Lord Reason, and not shame to tread   25
Vpon his holy and annointed head.
But as that land or nation best doth thriue,
Which to smooth-fronted peace is most procliue,
So doth that mind, whose faire affections rang'd
By reasons rules, stand constant and vnchang'd,   30
Els, if the power of reason be not such,
Why do we attribute to him so much ?
Or why are we obsequious to his law,
If he want spirit our affects to awe ?
Oh no, I argue weakly, he is strong,   *Enter Musco.*   35
Albeit my sonne haue done him too much wrong.

  Mus. My master : nay faith haue at you : I am flesht now I haue sped so well : Gentleman, I beseech you respect the estate of a poor soldier ; I am asham'd of this base course of life (God's my comfort) but extremitie prouokes 40 me to't, what remedie ?

  Loren. I haue not for you now.

Mus. By the faith I beare vnto God, gentleman, it is no ordinarie custome, but onely to preserue manhood. I protest to you, a man I haue bin, a man I may be, by your sweet bountie.

Lor. I pray thee good friend be satisfied.

Mus. Good Signior : by Iesu you may do the part of a kind gentleman, in lending a poore soldier the price of two cans of beere, a matter of small value, the King of heauen shall pay you, and I shall rest thankfull : sweet Signior.

Loren. Nay and you be so importunate——

Mus. Oh Lord sir, need wil haue his course : I was not made to this vile vse ; well, the edge of the enemie could not haue abated me so much : it's hard when a man hath serued in his Princes cause and be thus. Signior, let me deriue a small peece of siluer from you, it shall not be giuen in the course of time. By this good ground, I was faine to pawne my rapier last night for a poore supper, I am a Pagan els : sweet Signior.

Loren. Beleeue me I am rapte with admiration,
To thinke a man of thy exterior presence,
Should (in the constitution of the mind)
Be so degenerate, infirme, and base.
Art thou a man ? and sham'st thou not to beg ?
To practise such a seruile kinde of life ?
Why were thy education ne're so meane,
Hauing thy limbes : a thousand fairer courses
Offer themselues to thy election.
Nay there the warres might still supply thy wants,
Or seruice of some vertuous Gentleman,
Or honest labour ; nay what can I name,
But would become thee better then to beg ?
But men of your condition feede on sloth,
As doth the *Scarabe* on the dung she breeds in,
Not caring how the temper of your spirits
Is eaten with the rust of idlenesse.
Now afore God, what e're he be, that should

II. ii. 58 time. By] time, by *Q*

Releeue a person of thy qualitie,
While you insist in this loose desperate course,   80
I would esteeme the sinne not thine, but his.
  Mus. Faith signior, I would gladly finde some other course if so.
  Loren. I, you'ld gladly finde it, but you will not seeke it.
  Mus. Alasse sir, where should a man seeke? in the 85
warres, there's no assent by desart in these dayes, but:
and for seruice would it were as soone purchast as wisht for
(Gods my comfort) I know what I would say.
  Loren. Whats thy name?
  Mus. Please you: *Portensio.*   90
  Loren. Portensio?
Say that a man should entertaine thee now,
Would thou be honest, humble, iust and true?
  Mus. Signior: by the place and honor of a souldier.
  Loren. Nay, nay, I like not these affected othes;   95
Speake plainly man: what thinkst thou of my words?
  Mus. Nothing signior, but wish my fortunes were as
happy as my seruice should be honest.
  Loren. Well follow me, ile prooue thee, if thy deedes
Will cary a proportion to thy words.   *Exit Lor.*   100
  Mus. Yes sir straight, ile but garter my hose; oh that
my bellie were hoopt now, for I am readie to burst with
laughing. S'lid, was there euer seene a foxe in yeares to
betray himselfe thus? now shall I be possest of all his
determinations, and consequently [and] my young master. 105
Well, hee is resolu'd to proue my honestie: faith and I am
resolued to proue his patience: oh I shall abuse him
intollerablie: this small peece of seruice will bring him
cleane out of loue with the soldier for euer. It's no matter,
let the world thinke me a bad counterfeit, if I cannot giue 110
him the slip at an instant: why this is better then to haue
staid his iourney by halfe. Well, ile follow him: oh how
I long to be imployed.   *Exit.*

  II. ii. 81 thine,] thine *Q*   89 name?] name *Q.*   93 true?] true
Q   105–6 master. Well,] master well *Q*   112 halfe. Well,] halfe, well *Q*

SCENA TERTIA.

Enter Prospero, Bobadilla, and Matheo.

Mat. Yes faith sir, we were at your lodging to seeke you too.
 Pros. Oh I came not there to night.
 Bob. Your brother deliuered vs as much.
5 *Pros.* Who, *Giuliano* ?
 Bob. Giuliano ? Signior *Prospero*, I know not in what kinde you value me, but let me tell you this : as sure as God I do hold it so much out of mine honor & reputation, if I should but cast the least regard vpon such a dunghill of 10 flesh ; I protest to you (as I haue a soule to bee saued) I ne're saw any gentlemanlike part in him : and there were no more men liuing vpon the face of the earth, I should not fancie him by *Phœbus*.
 Mat. Troth nor I, he is of a rusticall cut, I know not 15 how : he doth not carrie himselfe like a gentleman.
 Pros. Oh Signior Matheo, that's a grace peculiar but to a few ; *quos æquus amauit Iupiter.*
 Mat. I vnderstand you sir.

Enter Lorenzo iunior, and Step⟨hano⟩.

 Pros. No question you do sir : Lorenzo ; now on my 20 soule welcome ; how doest thou sweet raskall ? my Genius ? S'blood I shal loue *Apollo*, & the mad Thespian girles the better while I liue for this ; my deare villaine, now I see there's some spirit in thee : Sirra these be the[y] two I writ to thee of, nay what a drowsie humor is this 25 now ? why doest thou not speake ?
 Lo.Iu. Oh you are a fine gallant, you sent me a rare letter.
 Pros. Why, was't not rare ?
 Lo.Iu. Yes ile be sworne I was ne're guiltie of reading 30 the like, match it in all *Plinies* familiar Epistles, and ile

II. iii. 5 Who,] Who *Q*   28 Why,] Why *Q*

The Quarto of 1601

haue my iudgement burnd in the eare for a rogue, make much of thy vaine, for it is inimitable. But I marle what Camell it was, that had the cariage of it? for doubtlesse he was no ordinarie beast that brought it.

Pros. Why? 35

Lo.Iu. Why sayest thou? why doest thou thinke that any reasonable creature, especially in the morning, (the sober time of the day too) would haue taine my father for me?

Pros. S'blood you iest I hope? 40

Lo.Iu. Indeed the best vse we can turne it to[o], is to make a iest on't now: but ile assure you, my father had the prouing of your copy, some howre before I saw it.

Pros. What a dull slaue was this? But sirrah what sayd he to it yfaith? 45

Lo.Iu. Nay I know not what he said. But I haue a shrewd gesse what he thought.

Pro. What? what?

Lo.Iu. Mary that thou art a damn'd dissolute villaine, and I some graine or two better, in keeping thee company. 50

Pros. Tut that thought is like the Moone in the last quarter, twill change shortly: but sirrha, I pray thee be acquainted with my two *Zanies* heere, thou wilt take exceeding pleasure in them if thou hearst them once, but what strange peece of silence is this? the signe of the 55 dumbe man?

Lo.Iu. Oh sir a kinsman of mine, one that may make our Musique the fuller and he please, he hath his humor sir.

Pros. Oh what ist? what ist?

Lo.Iu. Nay: ile neyther do thy iudgement, nor his folly 60 that wrong, as to prepare thy apprehension: ile leaue him to the mercy of the time, if you can take him: so.

Pros. Well signior *Bobadilla*: signior *Matheo*: I pray you know this Gentleman here, he is a friend of mine, & one hat will wel deserue your affection. I know not your name 65

II. iii. 50 and] And *Q* (*a new line as if verse*)   65 affection.] affec-ion, *Q*

signior, but I shalbe glad of any good occasion, to be more familiar with you.

Step. My name is signior *Stephano*, sir, I am this Gentlemans cousin, sir his father is mine vnckle; sir I am somewhat melancholie, but you shall commaund me sir, in whatsoeuer is incident to a Gentleman.

Bob. Signior, I must tell you this, I am no generall man, embrace it as a most high fauour, for (by the host of Egypt) but that I conceiue you, to be a Gentleman of some parts. I loue few words: you haue wit: imagine.

Step. I truely sir, I am mightily giuen to melancholy.

Mat. Oh Lord sir, it's your only best humor sir, your true melancholy, breedes your perfect fine wit sir: I am melancholie my selfe diuers times sir, and then do I no more but take your pen and paper presently, and write you your halfe score or your dozen of sonnets at a sitting.

Lo.iu. Masse then he vtters them by the grosse.

Step. Truely sir, and I loue such things out of measure.

Lo.iu. I faith, as well as in measure.

Mat. Why I pray you signior, make vse of my studie, it's at your seruice.

Step. I thanke you sir, I shalbe bolde I warrant you, haue you a close stoole there?

Mat. Faith sir, I haue some papers there, toyes of mine owne doing at idle houres, that you'le say there's some sparkes of wit in them, when you shall see them.

Prosp. Would they were kindled once, and a good fire made, I might see selfe loue burnd for her heresie.

Step. Cousin, is it well? am I melancholie inough?

Lo.iu. Oh I, excellent.

Prosp. Signior *Bobadilla*? why muse you so?

Lo.iu. He is melancholy too.

Bob. Faith sir, I was thinking of a most honorable piece of seruice was perform'd to morow; being S. *Marks* day: shalbe some ten years.

Lo.iu. In what place was that seruice, I pray you sir?

II. iii. 74 parts.] parts, *Q*   83 sir,] sir *Q*

Bob. Why at the beleagring of *Ghibelletto*, where, in lesse then two houres, seuen hundred resolute gentlemen, as any were in *Europe*, lost their liues vpon the breach : ile tell you gentlemen, it was the first, but the best league that euer I beheld with these eyes, except the taking in of *Tortosa* last yeer by the *Genowayes*, but that (of all other) was the most fatall & dangerous exploit, that euer I was rang'd in, since I first bore armes before the face of the enemy, as I am a gentleman and a souldier.

Step. So, I had as liefe as an angell I could sweare as well as that gentleman.

Lo.iu. Then you were a seruitor at both it seemes.

Bob. Oh Lord sir : by *Phaeton* I was the first man that entred the breach, and had I not effected it with resolution, I had bene slaine if I had had a million of liues.

Lo.iu. Indeed sir ?

Step. Nay & you heard him discourse you would say so : how like you him ?

Bob. I assure you (vpon my saluation) 'tis true, and your selfe shall confesse.

Prosp. You must bring him to the racke first.

Bob. Obserue me iudicially sweet signior : they had planted me a demy culuering, iust in the mouth of the breach ; now sir (as we were to ascend) their master gunner (a man of no meane skill and courage, you must thinke) confronts me with his Linstock ready to giue fire ; I spying his intendement, discharg'd my Petrinell in his bosome, and with this instrument my poore Rapier, ran violently vpon the *Moores* that guarded the ordinance, and put them pell-mell to the sword.

Pros. To the sword ? to the Rapier signior.

Lo.iu. Oh it was a good figure obseru'd sir : but did you all this signior without hurting your blade ?

Bob. Without any impeach on the earth : you shall perceiue sir, it is the most fortunate weapon, that euer rid on a poore gentlemans thigh : shall I tell you sir, you

II. iii. 105 leagure] leaugre *Q*   134 blade ?] blade *Q*

talke of *Morglay, Excaliber, Durindana*, or so : tut, I lend no credit to that is reported of them, I know the vertue of mine owne, and therefore I dare the boldlier maintaine it.
   Step. I marle whether it be a *Toledo* or no ?
   Bob. A most perfect *Toledo*, I assure you signior.
   Step. I haue a countriman of his here.
   Mat. Pray you let's see sir : yes faith it is.
   Bob. This a *Toledo* ? pish.
   Step. Why do you pish signior ?
   Bob. A Fleming by *Phœbus*, ile buy them for a guilder a peece and ile haue a thousand of them.
   Lo.iu. How say you cousin, I told you thus much.
   Pros. Where bought you it signior ?
   Step. Of a scuruy rogue Souldier, a pox of God on him, he swore it was a *Toledo*.
   Bob. A prouant Rapier, no better.
   Mat. Masse I thinke it be indeed.
   Lo.iu. Tut now it's too late to looke on it, put it vp, put it vp.
   Step. Well I will not put it vp, but by Gods foote, and ere I meete him——
   Pros. Oh it is past remedie now sir, you must haue patience.
   Step. Horson conny-catching Raskall ; oh I could eate the very hilts for anger.
   Lo.iu. A signe you haue a good Ostrich stomack Cousin.
   Step. A stomack ? would I had him here, you should see and I had a stomacke.
   Pros. It's better as 'tis : come gentlemen shall we goe ?

Enter Musco.

   Lo.iu. A miracle cousin, looke here, looke here.
   Step. Oh, Gods lid, by your leaue, do you know me sir ?
   Mus. I sir, I know you by sight.
   Step. You sold me a Rapier, did you not ?
   Mus. Yes marry did I sir.

II. iii. 168 sir ?] sir *Q*

Step. You said it was a *Toledo* ha?
Mus. True I did so.
Step. But it is none.
Mus. No sir, I confesse it, it is none. 175
Step. Gentlemen beare witnesse, he has confest it. By Gods lid, and you had not confest it———
Lo.iu. Oh cousin, forbeare, forbeare.
Step. Nay I haue done cousin.
Pros. Why you haue done like a Gentleman, he ha's 180 confest it, what would you more?
Lo.iu. Sirra how doost thou like him?
Pros. Oh its a pretious good foole, make much on him: I can compare him to nothing more happely, then a Barbers virginals; for euery one may play vpon him. 185
Mus. Gentleman, shall I intreat a word with you?
Lo.iu. With all my heart sir, you haue not another *Toledo* to sell, haue yee?
Mus. You are pleasant, your name is signior *Lorenzo* as I take it. 190
Lo.iu. You are in the right: S'bloud he meanes to catechize me I thinke.
Mus. No sir, I leaue that to the Curate, I am none of that coate.
Lo.iu. And yet of as bare a coate; well, say sir. 195
Mus. Faith signior, I am but seruant to God *Mars* extraordinarie, and indeed (this brasse varnish being washt off, and three or foure other tricks sublated) I appeare yours in reuersion, after the decease of your good father, *Musco.* 200
Lo.iu. *Musco*, s'bloud what winde hath blowne thee hither in this shape?
Mus. Your Easterly winde sir, the same that blew your father hither.
Lo.iu. My father? 205
Mus. Nay neuer start, it's true, he is come to towne of purpose to seeke you.

    II. iii. 182 him?] him. *Q*   202 shape?] shape. *Q*

Lo.iu. Sirra *Prospero* : what shall we do sirra, my father is come to the city.

210 *Pros.* Thy father : where is he ?

Mus. At a Gentlemans house yonder by Saint *Anthonies,* where he but stayes my returne ; and then——

Pros. Who's this ? *Musco* ?

Mus. The same sir.

215 *Pros.* Why how comst thou trans-muted thus ?

Mus. Faith a deuise, a deuise, nay for the loue of God, stand not here Gentlemen, house your selues and ile tell you all.

Lo.iu. But art thou sure he will stay thy returne ?

220 *Mus.* Do I liue sir ? what a question is that ?

Pros. Well wee'le prorogue his expectation a little : *Musco* thou shalt go with vs : Come on Gentlemen : nay I pray thee (good raskall) droope not, s'hart and our wits be so gowty, that one old plodding braine can out-strip vs all,

225 Lord I beseech thee, may they lie and starue in some miserable spittle, where they may neuer see the face of any true spirit againe, but bee perpetually haunted with some *church-yard Hobgoblin in secula seculorum.*

Mus. Amen, Amen. *Exeunt.*

ACTVS TERTIVS.
SCENA PRIMA.

Enter Thorello, and Piso.

Pis. He will expect you sir within this halfe houre.

Tho. Why what's a clocke ?

Pis. New striken ten.

Tho. Hath he the money ready, can you tell ?

5 *Pis.* Yes sir, *Baptista* brought it yesternight.

Tho. Oh that's well : fetch me my cloake. *Exit Piso.*
Stay, let me see ; an hower to goe and come,

<small>II. iii. 228 *in secula*] in *seculo* Q</small>

I that will be the least : and then 'twill be
An houre, before I can dispatch with him ;
Or very neare : well, I will say two houres ;   10
Two houres ? ha ? things neuer drempt of yet
May be contriu'd, I and effected too,
In two houres absence : well I will not go.
Two houres ; no fleering opportunity
I will not giue your trecherie that scope.   15
Who will not iudge him worthy to be robd,
That sets his doores wide open to a theefe,
And shewes the felon, where his treasure lyes ?
Againe, what earthy spirit but will attempt
To taste the fruite of beauties golden tree,   20
When leaden sleepe seales vp the dragons eyes ?
Oh beauty is a *Proiect* of some power,
Chiefely when oportunitie attends her :
She will infuse true motion in a stone,
Put glowing fire in an Icie soule,   25
Stuffe peasants bosoms with proud *Cæsars* spleene,
Powre rich deuice into an empty braine :
Bring youth to follies gate : there traine him in,
And after all, extenuate his sinne.
Well, I will not go, I am resolu'd for that.   30
Goe cary it againe, yet stay : yet do too,   *Enter Piso.*
I will deferre it till some other time.

   Piso. Sir, signior *Platano* wil meet you there with the bond.

   Tho. That's true : by Iesu I had cleane forgot it.   35
I must goe, what's a clocke ?

   Pis. Past ten sir.

   Tho. 'Hart, then will *Prospero* presently be here too,
With one or other of his loose consorts.
I am a Iew, if I know what to say,   40
What course to take, or which way to resolue.
My braine (me thinkes) is like an hower-glasse,
And my imaginations like the sands,

      III. i. 31 *Stage dir. after* 32 *in Q*

Runne dribling foorth to fill the mouth of time,
45 Still chaung'd with turning in the ventricle.
What were I best to doe ? it shalbe so.
Nay I dare build vpon his secrecie.
Piso.
    Piso. Sir.
50   *Tho.* Yet now I haue bethought me to, I wil not.
Is *Cob* within ?
    Pis. I thinke he be sir.
    Tho. But hee'le prate too, there's no talke of him.
No, there were no course vpon the earth to this,
55 If I durst trust him ; tut I were secure,
But there's the question now, if he should prooue,
Rimarum plenus, then, s'blood I were *Rookt.*
The state that he hath stood in till this present,
Doth promise no such change : what should I feare then ?
60 Well, come what will, ile tempt my fortune once.
Piso, thou mayest deceiue mee, but I thinke
Thou louest mee *Piso.*
    Piso. Sir, if a seruants zeale and humble duetie
May bee term'd loue, you are possest of it.
65   *Tho.* I haue a matter to impart to thee,
But thou must be secret, *Piso.*
    Pis. Sir for that——
    Tho. Nay heare me man ; thinke I esteeme thee well,
To let thee in thus to my priuate thoughts ;
70 *Piso*, it is a thing, sits neerer to my crest,
Then thou art ware of : if thou shouldst reueale it——
    Pis. Reueale it sir ?
    Tho. Nay, I [do] not think thou wouldst,
But if thou shouldst :
75   *Pis.* Sir, then I were a villaine :
Disclaime in me for euer if I do.
    Tho. He will not sweare : he has some meaning sure,
Else (being vrg'd so much) how should he choose,

    III. i. 47–8 *One line in* Q   47 secrecie.] secrecie ? Q   61–7 *Prose in* Q   73–4 Nay . . . shouldst : *prose in* Q

But lend an oath to all this protestation?
He is no puritane, that I am certaine of.   80
What should I thinke of it? vrge him againe,
And in some other forme: I will do so.
Well *Piso*, thou hast sworne not to disclose;
I you did sweare?
   Pis. Not yet sir, but I will,   85
So please you.
   Tho. Nay I dare take thy word.
But if thou wilt sweare; do as you thinke good,
I am resolu'd without such circumstance.
   Pis. By my soules safetie sir I here protest,   90
My tongue shall ne're take knowledge of a word
Deliuer'd me in compasse of your trust.
   Tho. Enough, enough, these ceremonies need not,
I know thy faith to be as firme as brasse.
Piso come hither: nay we must be close   95
In managing these actions: So it is,
(Now he ha's sworne I dare the safelier speake;)
I haue of late by diuers obseruations——
But, whether his oath be lawfull, yea, or no, ha?
I will aske counsel ere I do proceed: 100
Piso, it will be now too long to stay,
Wee'le spie some fitter time soone, or to morrow.
   Pis. At your pleasure sir.
   Tho. I pray you search the bookes gainst I returne
For the receipts twixt me and *Platano*.   105
   Pis. I will sir.
   Tho. And heare you: if my brother *Prospero*
Chance to bring hither any gentlemen
Ere I come backe: let one straight bring me word.
   Pis. Very well sir.   110
   Tho. Forget it not, nor be not [you] out of the way.
   Pis. I will not sir.
   Tho. Or whether he come or no, if any other,

   III. i. 83–7 *Divided in Q* Well ... sweare | Not ... please you   Nay
99 lawfull.] lawfull *Q*   111 **you** *om. F*

Stranger or els ? faile not to send me word.
115   *Pis.* Yes sir.
      Tho. Haue care I pray you and remember it.
      Pis. I warrant you sir.
      Tho. But *Piso,* this is not the secret I told thee of.
      Pis. No sir, I suppose so.
120   *Tho.* Nay beleeue me it is not.
      Pis. I do beleeue you sir.
      Tho. By heauen it is not, that's enough.
      Marrie, I would not thou shouldst vtter it
      To any creature liuing, yet I care not.
125 Well, I must hence : *Piso* conceiue thus much,
    No ordinarie person could haue drawne
    So deepe a secret from me ; I meane not this,
    But that I haue to tell thee : this is nothing, this.
    Piso, remember, silence, buried here :
130 No greater hell then to be slaue to feare.   *Exit Tho.*
      Piso. Piso, remember, silence, buried here :
    Whence should this flow of passion (trow) take head ? ha ?
    Faith ile dreame no longer of this running humor,
    For feare I sinke, the violence of the streame
135 Alreadie hath transported me so farre,
    That I can feele no ground at all : but soft,   *Enter Cob.*
    Oh it's our waterbearer : somewhat ha's crost him now.
      Cob. Fasting dayes : what tell you me of your fasting
    dayes ? would they were all on a light fire for mee : they
140 say the world shall be consum'd with fire and brimstone in
    the latter day : but I would we had these ember weekes, and
    these villanous fridaies burnt in the meane time, and
    then——
      Pis. Why how now *Cob,* what moues thee to this choller ?
145 ha ?
      Cob. Coller sir ? swounds I scorne your coller, I sir, ⟨I⟩
    am no colliers horse sir, neuer ride me with your coller, and
    you doe, ile shew you a iades tricke.

<small>III. i. 123–4 *Divided in* Q Marrie, I . . . liuing, | Yet   146 I sir,
I am *F* : I sir am *Q*</small>

The Quarto of 1601 237

Pis. Oh you'le slip your head out of the coller : why *Cob* you mistake me. 150

Cob. Nay I haue my rewme, and I be angrie, as well as another, sir.

Pis. Thy rewme ; thy humor man, thou mistakest.

Cob. Humor ? macke, I thinke it bee so indeed : what is this humor ? it's some rare thing I warrant. 155

Piso. Marrie ile tell thee what it is (as tis generally receiued in these daies) it is a monster bred in a man by selfe loue, and affectation, and fed by folly.

Cob. How ? must it be fed ?

Pis. Oh I, humor is nothing if it be not fed, why, didst 160 thou neuer heare of that ? it's a common phrase, *Feed my humor.*

Cob. Ile none on it : humor, auaunt, I know you not, be gon. Let who will make hungry meales for you, it shall not bee I : Feed you quoth he ? s'blood I haue much adoe to 165 feed my self, especially on these leane rascall daies too, and't had beene any other day but a fasting day : a plague on them all for mee : by this light one might haue done God good seruice and haue drown'd them al in the floud two or three hundred thousand yeares ago, oh I do stomacke them 170 hugely : I haue a mawe now, and't were for sir Beuisses horse.

Pis. Nay, but I pray thee *Cob,* what makes thee so out of loue with fasting daies ?

Cob. Marrie that, that will make any man out of loue with 175 them, I thinke : their bad conditions and you wil needs know : First, they are of a Flemmish breed I am sure on't, for they rauen vp more butter then all the daies of the weeke beside : Next, they stinke of fish miserably : Thirdly, they'le keep a man deuoutly hungry all day, & at night send 180 him supperlesse to bed.

Pis. Indeed these are faults *Cob.*

Cob. Nay and this were all, 'twere something, but they are the onely knowne enemies to my generation. A fasting

III. i. 151 angrie,] angrie *Q*   179 Next] next *Q*

185 day no sooner comes, but my lineage goes to racke, poore
Cobbes they smoake for it, they melt in passion, and your
maides too know this, and yet would haue me turne
Pul's out Hannibal, and eat my owne fish & blood : * my princely
a red
Herring. couze, feare nothing ; I haue not the heart to deuoure you,
190 and I might bee made as rich as Golias : oh that I had
roome for my teares, I could weep salt water enough now
to preserue the liues of ten thousand of my kin : but I may
curse none but these filthy Almanacks, for and't were not
for them, these daies of persecution would ne're bee knowne.
195 Ile be hang'd and some Fishmongers sonne doe not make
on 'hem, and puts in more fasting daies then hee should
doe, because he would vtter his fathers dried stockfish.

    Pis. 'Soule peace, thou'lt be beaten *Enter Matheo, Pro-*
like a stockfish else: here is Signior *Ma-* *spero, Lo⟨renzo⟩ iunior,*
                                                        Bobadilla, Stephano,
200 *theo.* Now must I looke out for a mes- *Musco.*
senger to my Master.   *Exeunt Cob & Piso.*

SCENA SECVNDA.

  Pros. Beshrew me, but it was an absolute good iest, and
exccedingly well caried.

  Lo.iu. I and our ignorance maintained it as well, did it
not ?

5 *Pros.* Yes faith, but was't possible thou should'st not
know him ?

  Lo.iu. Fore God not I, and I might haue beene ioind patten with one of the nine worthies for knowing him. S'blood
man, he had so writhen himselfe into the habit of one of
10 your poore *Disparuiew's* here, your decaied, ruinous,
worme-eaten gentlemen of the round : such as haue vowed
to sit on the skirts of the city, let your Prouost & his half
dozen of halberders do what they can ; and haue translated
begging out of the olde hackney pace, to a fine easy amble,
15 and made it runne as smooth of the toung, as a shoue-groat

    III. i. 196 on'hem,] on 'them *Q*   198 'Soule] S'oule *Q* shilling. Into the likenes of one of these leane *Pirgo's*, had hee moulded himselfe so perfectly, obseruing euerie tricke of their action, as varying the accent: swearing with an *Emphasis*. Indeed all with so speciall and exquisite a grace, that (hadst thou seene him) thou wouldst haue sworne he might haue beene the Tamberlaine, or the Agamemnon of the rout.

Pros. Why Musco: who would haue thought thou hadst beene such a gallant?

Lo.iu. I cannot tell, but (vnles a man had iuggled begging all his life time, and beene a weauer of phrases from his infancie, for the apparrelling of it) I thinke the world cannot produce his Riuall.

Pros. Where got'st thou this coat I mar'le?

Mus. Faith sir, I had it of one of the deuils neere kinsmen, a Broker.

Pros. That cannot be, if the prouerbe hold, a craftie knaue needs no broker.

Mus. True sir, but I need a broker, *Ergo* no crafty knaue.

Pros. Well put off, well put off.

Lo.iu. Tut, he ha's more of these shifts.

Mus. And yet where I haue one, the broker ha's ten sir.

Enter Piso.

Piso. Francisco: Martino: ne're a one to bee found now, what a spite's this?

Pros. How now *Piso*? is my brother within?

Pis. No sir, my master went forth e'ene now: but Signior *Giuliano* is within. *Cob*, what *Cob*: is he gone too?

Pros. Whither went thy master? *Piso* canst thou tell?

Piso. I know not, to Doctor *Clements*, I thinke sir. *Cob.*

Exit Piso.

Lo.iu. Doctor *Clement*, what's he? I haue heard much speech of him.

Pros. Why, doest thou not know him? he is the *Gonfa-*

III. ii. 16 shilling. Into] shilling, into *Q*   22 of] on *Q*   29 mar'le?] marl'e *Q*   47 Gonfaloniere] Gonfalionere *Q*

loniere of the state here, an excellent rare ciuilian, and a great scholler, but the onely mad merry olde fellow in Europe : I shewed him you the other day.

    Lo.iu. Oh I remember him now ; Good faith, and he hath a very strange presence me thinkes, it shewes as if he stoode out of the ranke from other men. I haue heard many of his iests in Padua : they say he will commit a man for taking the wall of his horse.

    Pros. I or wearing his cloake of one shoulder, or any thing indeede, if it come in the way of his humor.

    Pis. Gasper, Martino, Cob : S'hart, where should they be trow ?

Enter Piso.

    Bob. Signior *Thorello's* man, I pray thee vouchsafe vs the lighting of this match.

    Pis. A pox on your match, no time but now to vouchsafe? *Francisco, Cob.*   *Exit.*

    Bob. Body of me : here's the remainder of seuen pound, since yesterday was seuennight. It's your right *Trinidado* : did you neuer take any, signior ?

    Step. No truly sir ; but i'le learne to take it now, since you commend it so.

    Bob. Signior beleeue me, (vpon my relation) for what I tel you, the world shall not improue. I haue been in the Indies (where this herbe growes) where neither my selfe, nor a dozen Gentlemen more (of my knowledge) haue recciued the taste of any other nutriment, in the world, for the space of one and twentie weekes, but Tabacco onely. Therefore it cannot be but 'tis most diuine. Further, take it in the nature, in the true kinde so, it makes an Antidote, that (had you taken the most deadly poysonous simple in all Florence) it should expell it, and clarifie you, with as much ease, as I speake. And for your greene wound, your *Balsamum*, and your —— are all meere gulleries, and trash to it, especially your *Trinidado* : your *Newcotian* is good too : I could say what

---

    III. ii. 67 sir ;] sir ? *Q*   77 Florence) it] Florence, it *Q*   79 wound one Dyce copy owing to a defect in the paper   81 *Newcotian*] *Nicotian* F

I know of the vertue of it, for the exposing of rewmes, raw humors, crudities, obstructions, with a thousand of this kind ; but I professe my selfe no quack-saluer : only thus much : by *Hercules* I doe holde it, and will affirme it (before 85 any Prince in Europe) to be the most soueraigne, and pretious herbe, that euer the earth tendred to the vse of man.

Lo.iu. Oh this speech would haue done rare in a pothecaries mouth. 90

Enter Piso and Cob.

Pis. I : close by Saint *Anthonies* : Doctor *Clements*.
Cob. Oh, Oh.
Bob. Where's the match I gaue thee ?
Pis. S'blood would his match, and he, and pipe, and all were at Sancto Domingo. *Exit.* 95

Cob. By gods deynes : I marle what pleasure or felicitie they haue in taking this rogish Tabacco : it's good for nothing but to choake a man, and fill him full of smoake, and imbers : there were foure died out of one house last weeke with taking of it, and two more the bell went for 100 yester-night, one of them (they say) will ne're scape it, he voyded a bushell of soote yester-day, vpward and downeward. By the stockes ; and there were no wiser men then I, I'ld haue it present death, man or woman, that should but deale with a Tabacco pipe ; why, it will stifle them all in 105 th'end as many as vse it ; it's little better then rats bane.

Enter Piso.

All. Oh good signior ; hold, hold.
Bob. You base cullion, you.
Pis. Sir, here's your match ; come, thou must needes be talking too. 110
Cob. Nay he wil not meddle with his match I warrant you : well it shall be a deere beating, and I liue.
Bob. Doe you prate ?
Lo.iu. Nay good signior, will you regard the humor of a foole ? away knaue. 115

III. ii. 90 *Enter ... Cob.* after 91 in Q.   105–6 in th'end] in the'nd Q
445·3   R

Pros. *Piso* get him away.   *Exit Piso, and Cob.*
Bob. A horson filthy slaue, a turd, an excrement. Body of *Cesar*, but that I scorne to let forth so meane a spirit, i'ld haue stab'd him to the earth.
120 *Pros.* Mary God forbid sir.
Bob. By this faire heauen I would haue done it.
Step. Oh he sweares admirably : (by this faire heauen :) (Body of *Cesar* :) I shall neuer doe it, sure (vpon my saluation) no I haue not the right grace.
125 *Mat.* Signior will you any ? By this ayre the most diuine Tabacco as euer I drunke.
Lo.iu. I thanke you sir.
Step. Oh this Gentleman doth it rarely too, but nothing like the other. By this ayre, as I am a Gentleman : by
130 *Phœbus.*   *Exit Bob. and Mat.*
Mus. Master glaunce, glaunce : Signior *Prospero.*
Step. As I haue a soule to be saued, I doe protest ;
Pros. That you are a foole.
Lo.iu. Cousin will you any Tabacco ?
135 *Step.* I sir : vpon my saluation.
Lo.iu. How now cousin ?
Step. I protest, as I am a Gentleman, but no souldier indeede.
Pros. No signior, as I remember you seru'd on a great
140 horse, last generall muster.
Step. I sir that's true : cousin may I sweare as I am a souldier, by that ?
Lo.iu. Oh yes, that you may.
Step. Then as I am a Gentleman, and a souldier, it is
145 diuine Tabacco.
Pros. But soft, where's signior *Matheo* ? gone ?
Mus. No sir, they went in here.
Pros. Oh let's follow them : signior *Matheo* is gone to salute his mistresse, sirra now thou shalt heare some of his
150 verses, for he neuer comes hither without some shreds of poetrie : Come signior *Stephano*, *Musco.*

III. ii. 123 (Body of *Cesar* :)] Body of *Cesar* : Q

Step. *Musco*? where? is this *Musco*?
Lo.iu. I, but peace cousin, no words of it at any hand.
Step. Not I by this faire heauen, as I haue a soule to be saued, by *Phœbus*. 155
Pros. Oh rare! your cousins discourse is simply suted, all in oathes.
Lo.iu. I, he lacks no thing but a little light stuffe, to draw them out withall, and he were rarely fitted to the time.
Exeunt.

ACTVS TERTIVS, SCENA TERTIA.

Enter Thorello with Cob.

Tho. Ha, how many are there, sayest thou?
Cob. Marry sir, your brother, Signior *Prospero*.
Tho. Tut, beside him: what strangers are there man?
Cob. Strangers? let me see, one, two; masse I know not well, there's so many. 5
Tho. How? so many?
Cob. I, there's some fiue or sixe of them at the most.
Tho. A swarme, a swarme,
Spight of the Deuill, how they sting my heart!
How long hast thou beene comming hither *Cob*? 10
Cob. But a little while sir.
Tho. Didst thou come running?
Cob. No sir.
Tho. Tut, then I am familiar with thy haste.
Bane to my fortunes: what meant I to marrie? 15
I that before was rankt in such content,
My mind attir'd in smoothe silken peace,
Being free master of mine owne free thoughts,
And now become a slaue? what, neuer sigh,
Be of good cheare man: for thou art a cuckold, 20
'Tis done, 'tis done: nay when such flowing store,
Plentie it selfe fals in my wiues lappe,
The *Cornu-copiæ* will be mine I know. But *Cob*,

III. iii. 5 well,] well Q

What entertainment had they? I am sure
25 My sister and my wife would bid them welcome, ha?
   Cob. Like ynough: yet I heard not a word of welcome.
   Tho. No, their lips were seal'd with kisses, and the voice
Drown'd in a flood of ioy at their arriuall,
Had lost her motion, state and facultie.
30 *Cob*, which of them was't that first kist my wife?
(My sister I should say) my wife, alas,
I feare not her: ha? who was it sayst thou?
   Cob. By my troth sir, will you haue the truth of it?
   Tho. Oh I good *Cob*: I pray thee.
35 *Cob.* God's my iudge, I saw no body to be kist, vnlesse
they would haue kist the post, in the middle of the ware-
house; for there I left them all, at their Tabacco with a poxe.
   Tho. How? were they not gone in then e're thou cam'st?
   Cob. Oh no sir.
40 *Tho.* Spite of the Deuill, what do I stay here then?
Cob, follow me.   *Exit Tho.*
   Cob. Nay, soft and faire, I haue egges on the spit; I
cannot go yet sir: now am I for some diuers reasons hammering, hammering reuenge: oh for three or foure gallons
45 of vineger, to sharpen my wits: Reuenge, vineger reuenge,
russet reuenge; nay, and hee had not lyne in my house,
'twould neuer haue greeu'd me; but being ny guest, one
that ile bee sworne, my wife ha's lent him her smocke off
her backe, while his owne shirt ha beene at washing:
50 pawnd her neckerchers for cleane bands for him: sold
almost all my platters to buy him Tabacco; and yet to see
an ingratitude wretch: strike his host; well I hope to
raise vp an host of furies for't: here comes M. Doctor.

Enter Doctor Clement, Lorenzo sen⟨ior,⟩ Peto.

   Clem. What's Signior *Thorello* gone?
55 *Pet.* I sir.
   Clem. Hart of me, what made him leaue vs so abruptly?

III. iii. 41 Stage dir. *Exit*] *Exit.* Q   46 russet] mustard *F*   48
'twould] t'would *Q*   56 abruptly? *corr. Q*: abruptly *Q originally*

How now sirra; what make you here? what wold you haue, ha?

Cob. And't please your worship, I am a poore neighbour of your worships. 60

Clem. A neighbour of mine, knaue?

Cob. I sir, at the signe of the water-tankerd, hard by the greene lattice: I haue paide scot and lotte there any time this eighteene yeares.

Clem. What, at the greene lattice? 65

Cob. No sir: to the parish: mary I haue seldome scap't scot-free at the lattice.

Clem. So: but what busines hath my neighbour?

Cob. And't like your worship, I am come to craue the peace of your worship. 70

Clem. Of me, knaue? peace of me, knaue? did I e're hurt thee? did I euer threaten thee? or wrong thee? ha?

Cob. No god's my comfort, I meane your worships warrant, for one that hath wrong'd me sir: his armes are at too much libertie, I would faine haue them bound to a 75 treatie of peace, and I could by any meanes compasse it.

Loren. Why, doest thou goe in danger of thy life for him?

Cob. No sir; but I goe in danger of my death euery houre by his meanes; and I die within a twelue-moneth and a day, I may sweare, by the lawes of the land, that he kil'd me. 80

Clem. How? how knaue? sweare he kil'd thee? what pretext? what colour hast thou for that?

Cob. Mary sir: both blacke and blew, colour ynough, I warrant you I haue it here to shew your worship.

Clem. What is he, that gaue you this sirra? 85

Cob. A Gentleman in the citie sir.

Clem. A Gentleman? what call you him?

Cob. Signior *Bobadilla.*

Clem. Good: But wherefore did he beate you sirra? how began the quarrel twixt you? ha: speake truly knaue, I 90 aduise you.

Cob. Marry sir, because I spake against their vagrant Tabacco, as I came by them: for nothing else.

Clem. Ha, you speake against Tabacco ? *Peto*, his name.
Pet. What's your name sirra ?
Cob. *Oliuer Cob*, sir, set *Oliuer Cob*, sir.
Clem. Tell *Oliuer Cob* he shall goe to the iayle.
Pet. Oliuer Cob, master Doctor sayes you shall go to the iayle.
Cob. Oh I beseech your worship for gods loue, deare master Doctor.
Clem. Nay gods pretious : and such drunken knaues as you are come to dispute of Tabacco once ; I haue done : away with him.
Cob. Oh good master Doctor, sweete Gentleman.
Lore. Sweete *Oliuer*, would I could doe thee any good ; master Doctor let me intreat sir.
Clem. What ? a tankard-bearer, a thread-bare rascall, a begger, a slaue that neuer drunke out of better then pispot mettle in his life, and he to depraue, and abuse the vertue of an herbe, so generally receyu'd in the courts of princes, the chambers of nobles, the bowers of sweete Ladies, the cabbins of souldiers : *Peto* away with him, by gods passion, I say, goe too.
Cob. Deare master Doctor.
Loren. Alasse poore *Oliuer*.
Clem. Peto : I : and make him a warrant, he shall not goe, I but feare the knaue.
Cob. O diuine Doctor, thankes noble Doctor, most dainty Doctor, delicious Doctor.   *Exeunt Peto with Cob.*
Clem. Signior *Lorenzo* : Gods pitty man, be merry, be merry, leaue these dumpes.
Loren. Troth would I could sir : but enforced mirth
(In my weake iudgement) ha's no happy birth.
The minde, being once a prisoner vnto cares,
The more it dreames on ioy, the worse it fares.
A smyling looke is to a heauie soule,
As a guilt bias, to a leaden bowle,
Which (in it selfe) appeares most vile, being spent

III. iii. 96 sir, set] sir set *Q*   121 man, be] man, | Be *Q* (as *verse*).
124 ha's] h'as *Q*

To no true vse ; but onely for ostent. 130

   Clem. Nay but good Signior : heare me a word, heare me a word, your cares are nothing ; they are like my cap, soone put on, and as soone put off. What ? your sonne is old inough, to gouerne himselfe ; let him runne his course, it's the onely way to make him a stay'd man : if he were an 135 vnthrift, a ruffian, a drunkard or a licentious liuer, then you had reason : you had reason to take care : but being none of these, Gods passion, and I had twise so many cares, as you haue, I'ld drowne them all in a cup of sacke : come, come, I muse your parcell of a souldier returnes not all this 140 while.   *Exeunt.*

SCENA QVARTA.

Enter Giuliano, with Biancha.

   Giul. Well sister, I tell you true : and you'le finde it so in the ende.

   Bia. Alasse brother, what would you haue me to doe ? I cannot helpe it ; you see, my brother *Prospero* he brings them in here, they are his friends. 5

   Giu. His friends ? his f[r]iends. s'blood they do nothing but haunt him vp and downe like a sorte of vnlucky Sprites, and tempt him to all maner of villany, that can be thought of ; well, by this light, a little thing would make me play the deuill with some of them ; and't were not 10 more for your husbands sake, then any thing else, I'ld make the house too hot for them ; they should say and sweare, Hell were broken loose, e're they went : But by gods bread, 'tis no bodies fault but yours : for and you had done as you might haue done, they should haue beene damn'd e're they 15 should haue come in, e're a one of them.

   Bia. God's my life ; did you euer heare the like ? what a strange man is this ? could I keepe out all them thinke you ? I should put my selfe against halfe a dozen men ? should I ? Good faith you'ld mad the patient'st body in the world, to 20 heare you talke so, without any sense or reason.

          III. iv. 6 fiends. *F* : friends ? *Q*

*Enter Matheo with Hesperida, Bobadilla, Stephano,
Lorenzo iu⟨nior,⟩ Prospero, Musco.*

Hesp. Seruant (in troth) you are too prodigall
Of your wits treasure; thus to powre it foorth
Vpon so meane a subiect, as my worth?
25 *Mat.* You say well, you say well.
Giu. Hoyday, heare is stuffe.
Lo.iu. Oh now stand close: pray God she can get him to reade it.
Pros. Tut, feare not: I warrant thee, he will do it of
30 himselfe with much impudencie.
Hes. Seruant, what is that same I pray you?
Mat. Mary an *Elegie*, an *Elegie*, an odde toy.
Gui. I to mocke an Ape with all, Oh Iesu.
Bia. Sister, I pray you lets heare it.
35 *Mat.* Mistresse Ile reade it if you please.
Hes. I pray you doe *seruant*.
Gui. Oh heares no foppery, sblood it freates me to the galle to thinke on it. *Exit.*
Pros. Oh I, it is his condition, peace: we are farely ridde
40 of him.
Mat. Fayth I did it in an humor: I know not how it is, but please you come neare signior: this gentleman hath iudgement, he knowes how to censure of a——I pray you sir, you can iudge.
45 *Step.* Not I sir: *as I haue a soule to be saued, as I am a gentleman.*
Lo.iu. Nay its well; so long as he doth not forsweare himselfe.
Bob. Signior you abuse the excellencie of your mistresse,
50 and her fayre sister. Fye while you liue auoyd this prolixity.
Mat. I shall sir: well, *Incipere dulce.*
Lo.iu. How, *Insipere dulce?* a sweete thing to be a Foole indeede.

III. iv. 22–4, *Prose in Q*   33 Iesu] Icsu *Q*   37 sblood] Sblood *Q*
43 censure of a] censnre of a. *Q*   49 Bob.] Bob, *Q*   53 *Insipere*] *Incipere* Q

Pros. What, do you take *Incipere* in that sence? 55
Lo.iu. You do not you? Sblood this was your villanie to gull him with a motte.
Pros. Oh the Benchers phrase: *Pauca verba, Pauca verba.*
Mat. Rare creature let me speake without offence, 60
Would God my rude woords had the influence
To rule thy thoughts, as thy fayre lookes do mine,
Then shouldst thou be his prisoner, who is thine.
Lo.iu. S'hart, this is in *Hero and Leander?*
Pros. Oh I: peace, we shall haue more of this. 65
Mat. Be not vnkinde and fayre, mishapen stuffe
Is of behauiour boysterous and rough:
⟨*Pros.*⟩ How like you that signior? Sblood he shakes his head like a bottle, to feele and there be any brayne in it. 70
Mat. But obserue the *Catastrophe* now,
And I in dutie will exceede all other,
As you in bewtie do excell loues mother.
Lo.iu. Well ile haue him free of the brokers, for he vtters no thing but stolne remnants. 75
Pros. Nay good *Critique* forbeare.
Lo.iu. A pox on him, hang him filching rogue, steale from the deade? its worse then sacriledge.
Pros. Sister what haue you heare? *verses*? I pray you lets see. 80
Bia. Do you let them go so lightly sister?
Hes. Yes fayth when they come lightly.
Bia. I but if your *seruant* should heare you, he would take it heauely.
Hes. No matter, he is able to beare. 85
Bia. So are *Asses.*
Hes. So is hee.
Pros. Signior *Matheo*, who made these verses? they are excellent good.

<small>III. iv. 61 *influence*] influence : *Q*   64 *and*] and *Q*   66 *fayre,*] fayre *Q*   *stuffe*] stuffe, *Q*   68 signior? Sblood] signior, sblood *Q*   81 sister?] sister. *Q*   85 matter,] matter *Q*   87 So] so *Q*</small>

90   *Mat.* Oh God sir, its your pleasure to say so sir. Fayth I made them *extempore* this morning.
    Pros. How *extempore*?
    Mat. I would I might be damnd els: aske signior *Bobadilla*. He sawe me write them, at the: (poxe on it)
95 the *Miter* yonder.
    Mus. Well, and the Pope knew hee curst the *Miter*, it were enough to haue him excommunicated all the Tauerns in the towne.
    Step. Cosen how do you like this gentlemans verses?
100   *Lo.iu.* Oh admirable, the best that euer I heard.
    Step. By this fayre heauen[s], they are admirable, The best that euer I heard.

                    Enter Giuliano.

    Giu. I am vext, I can hold neuer a bone of me still, sblood I think they meane to build a *Tabernacle* heare, well?
105 *Pros.* Sister you haue a simple seruant heare, that crownes your bewtie with such *Encomions* and *Deuises*, you may see what it is to be the mistresse of a wit, that can make your perfections so transeparent, that euery bleare eye may looke thorough them, and see him drowned ouer
110 head and eares, in the deepe well of desire. Sister *Biancha* I meruaile you get you not a seruant that can rime and do *trickes* too.
    Giu. Oh monster? impudence it selfe; *trickes*?
    Bia. Trickes, brother? what *trickes*?
115 *Hes.* Nay, speake I pray you, what *trickes*?
    Bia. I, neuer spare any body heare: but say, what *trickes*?
    Hes. Passion of my heart? do *trickes*?
    Pros. Sblood heares a *tricke* vied, and reuied: why you
120 monkies you? what a catterwaling do you keepe? has he not giuen you *rymes*, and *verses*, and *trickes*.
    Giu. Oh see the Diuell?
    Pros. Nay, you lampe of virginitie, that take it in snuffe

III. iv. 90 Fayth *a new line in* Q   96 *Miter,*] *Miter* Q   99 verses?]
verses. Q   103 vext,] vext Q   sblood] Sblood *a new line in* Q

so : come and cherish this tame poetical fury in your *seruant*, youle be begd else shortly for a concealement : go to, rewarde his muse, you cannot giue him lesse then a shilling in conscience, for the booke he had it out of cost him a teston at the least, how now gallants, *Lorenzo*, signior *Bobadilla* ? what all sonnes of scilence ? no spirite ?

Giu. Come you might practise your Ruffian trickes somewhere else, and not heare I wisse : this is no Tauerne, nor no place for such exploites.

Pros. Shart how now ?

Giu. Nay boy, neuer looke askaunce at me for the matter ; ile tell you of it by Gods bread, I, and you and your companions mend your selues when I haue done.

Pros. My companions.

Gui. I your companions sir, so I say ! Sblood I am not affrayed of you nor them neyther, you must haue your Poets, & your caueleeres, & your fooles follow you vp and downe the citie, and heare they must come to domineere and swagger ? sirha, you *Ballad singer*, and *Slops* your fellow there, get you out ; get you out : or (by the will of God) Ile cut of your eares, goe to.

Pros. Sblood stay, lets see what he dare do : cut of his eares, you are an asse, touch any man heare, and by the Lord ile run my rapier to the hilts in thee.

Gui. Yea, that would I fayne see, boy.
Bia. Oh Iesu *Piso*, *Matheo* murder.
Hes. Helpe, helpe, *Piso*.
Lo.iu. Gentlemen, *Prospero*, forbeare I pray you.

They all draw, enter Piso and some more of the house to part them, the women make a great crie.

Bob. Well sirrah, you *Holofernes* : by my hand I will pinck thy flesh full of holes with my rapier for this, I will by this good heauen : nay let him come, let him come, gentlemen by the body of S. *George* ile not kill him.

The⟨y⟩ offer to fight againe and are parted.

<small>III. iv. 129 signior] siignior *Q*   spirite ?] spirite. *Q*   133 now ?] now. *Q*   135 bread,] bread ? *Q*   138 sir] fir *Q*   say !] say ? *Q*
144 eares,] eares *Q*   153 *Holofernes*] *Hollofernus Q*</small>

Piso. Hold, hold, forbeare :
Gui. You whorson bragging coystryll.   *Enter Thorello.*
160 *Tho.* Why, how now? whats the matter? what stirre
is heare,
Whence springs this quarrell, *Pizo* where is he?
Put vp your weapons, and put of this rage.
My wife and sister they are cause of this,
What, *Pizo*? where is this knaue?
165 *Pizo.* Heare sir.
Pros. Come, lets goe : this is one of my brothers auncient humors, this!
Steph. I am glad no body was hurt by this auncient humor.

Exeunt Prospero, Lorenzo iu⟨nior,⟩ Musco, Stephano, Bobadilla, Matheo.

170 *Tho.* Why how now brother, who enforst this braule?
Gui. A sorte of lewd rakehelles, that care neither for God nor the Diuell. And they must come heare to read *Ballads* and *Rogery*, and *Trash*, Ile marre the knot of them ere I sleepe perhaps : especially signior *Pithagoras*, he thats
175 al manner of shapes : and *Songs and sonnets*, his fellow there.
Hes. Brother indeede you are to violent,
To sudden in your courses, and you know
My brother *Prosperos* temper will not beare
180 Any reproofe, chiefely in such a presence,
Where euery slight disgrace he should receiue,
Would wound him in opinion and respect.
Gu. Respect? what talke you of respect mongst such as ha' neyther sparke of manhood nor good manners, by
185 God I am ashamed to heare you : respect?   *Exit.*
Hes. Yes there was one a ciuill gentleman,

III. iv. 158 hold, forbeare] hold forbeare Q   164 knaue?] knaue. Q
167 humors, this!] humors this? Q   168 auncient] auncienr Q   169
Stage dir. *Exeunt] Exit* Q   *Lorenzoiunior*,] *Lorenzoiu.* Q   *Bobadilla, Matheo*.] *Bobadillo, Matheo*, Q   170 braule?] braule. Q   172 Diuell.]
Diuell, Q   173 *Rogery*,] *Rogery'* Q   174 *Pithagoras*] *Pithagorus* Q
179 *Prosperos*] *Prosperus* Q   181 receiue,] receiue. Q   183–5
Verse in Q, divided at As ha', By God   184 ha' F : had Q

And very worthely demeand himselfe.
   Tho. Oh that was some loue of yours, sister.
   Hes. A loue of mine ? in fayth I would he were
No others loue but mine.   190
   Bia. Indeede he seemd to be a gentleman of an exceeding fayre disposition, and of very excellent good partes.
                          Exeunt Hesperida, Biancha.
   Tho. Her loue, by Iesu : my wifes minion,
Fayre disposition ? excellent good partes ?   195
S'hart, these phrases are intollerable,
Good partes ? how should she know his partes ? well,
   well :
It is too playne, too cleare : *Pizo,* come hether.
What are they gone ?
   Pi. I sir they went in.
   Tho. Are any of the gallants within ?   200
   Pi. No sir they are all gone.
   Tho. Art thou sure of it ?
   Pi. I sir I can assure you.
   Tho. Pizo what gentleman was that they prays'd so ?
   Pizo. One they call him signior *Lorenzo,* a fayre young 205 gentleman sir.
   Tho. I, I thought so : my minde gaue me as much :
Sblood ile be hangd if they haue not hid him in the house,
Some where, ile goe search, *Pizo* go with me,
Be true to me and thou shalt finde me bountifull. *Exeunt.* 210

SCENA QVINTA.

         Enter Cob, *to him* Tib.

   Cob. What *Tib, Tib,* I say.
   Tib. How now, what cuckold is that knockes so hard ?
Oh husband ist you, whats the newes ?
   Cob. Nay you haue stonnd me I fayth ; you h⟨a⟩ue

  III. iv. 189 in fayth] infayth *Q*   192 Stage dir. *Exeunt*] *Exit Q*
196 well, well :] well : well, *Q*   III. v. 2, 3 *As verse in Q, divided at*
hard ? | Oh   4 fayth ;] fayth ? *Q*

giuen me a knocke on the forehead, will sticke by me: cuckold? Swoundes cuckolde?

   Tib. Away you foole, did I know it was you that knockt? Come, come, you may call me as bad when you list.

   Cob. May I? swoundes *Tib* you are a whore:

   Tib. S'hart you lie in your throte.

   Cob. How the lye? and in my throte too? do you long to be stabd, ha?

   Tib. Why you are no souldier?

   Cob. Masse thats true, when was *Bobadilla* heare? that *Rogue*, that *Slaue*, that fencing *Burgullian*? ile tickle him I faith.

   Tib. Why what's the matter?

   Cob. Oh he hath basted me rarely, sumptiously: but I haue it heare will sause him, oh the *doctor*, the honestest old *Troian* in all *Italy*, I do honour the very flea of his dog: a plague on him, he put me once in a villanous filthy feare: marry it vanisht away like the smooke of *Tobacco*: but I was smookt soundly first, I thanke the Diuell, and his good *Angell* my guest: well wife: or *Tib* (which you will) get you in, and locke the doore I charge you, let no body in to you: not *Bob[b]adilla* himselfe; nor the diuell in his likenesse; you are a woman; you haue flesh and blood enough in you; therefore be not tempted; keepe the doore shut vpon all cummers.

   Tib. I warrant you there shall no body enter heare without my consent.

   Cob. Nor with your consent sweete *Tib*, and so I leaue you.

   Tib. Its more then you know, whether you leaue me so.

   Cob. How?

   Tib. Why sweete.

   Cob. Tut sweete, or soure, thou art a flower, Keepe close thy doore, I aske no more.   *Exeunt.*

   III. v. 7 foole,] foole *Q*   knockt?] knockt, *Q*   21 him,] him *Q* 26 in to] into *Q*   32 *Tib*,] *Tib* Q   35–6 *One line in Q*

SCENA SEXTA.

Enter Lorenzo iu⟨nior⟩ Prospero, Stephano, Musco.

Lo.iu. Well *Musco* performe this businesse happily, and thou makest a conquest of my loue foreuer.

Pros. I fayth now let thy spirites put on their best habit, but at any hand remember thy message to my brother: for theres no other meanes to start him.   5

Mus. I warrant you sir, feare nothing, I haue a nimble soule that hath wakt all my imaginatiue forces by this time, and put them in true motion : what you haue possest me withall, Ile discharge it amply sir. Make no question.
                                        Exit Musco.

Pros. Thats well sayd *Musco* : fayth sirha how dost   10 thou aproue my wit in this deuise ?

Lo.iu. Troth well, howsoeuer ; but excellent if it take.

Pros. Take man : why it cannot chuse but take, if the circumstances miscarry not, but tell me zealously : dost thou affect my sister *Hesperida* as thou pretendest ?   15

Lo.iu. Prospero by Iesu.

Pros. Come do not protest, I beleeue thee : I fayth she is a virgine of good ornament, and much modestie, vnlesse I conceiud very worthely of her, thou shouldest not haue her.   20

Lo.iu. Nay I thinke it a question whether I shall haue her for all that.

Pros. Sblood thou shal⟨t⟩ haue her, by this light thou shalt !

Lo.iu. Nay do not sweare.   25

Pros. By *S. Marke* thou shalt haue her : ile go fetch her presently, poynt but where to meete, and by this hand ile bring her.

III. vi. 1–5 *As verse in Q, divided* happily, | And ... foreuer, | I fayth ... habit, | But ... brother. | For   5 him.] him ? *Q*   6 nothing,] nothing *Q*   9 withall,] withall ? *Q*   11 thou] thou, *Q*   12 howsoeuer ;] howsoeuer ? *Q*   17 protest,] protest *Q*   24 shalt !] shalt ? *Q*   28 her.] her ? *Q*

Lo.iu. Hold, hold, what all pollicie dead? no preuention
30 of mischiefes stirring?

Pros. Why, by what shall I sweare by? thou shalt haue her by my soule.

Lo.iu. I pray the⟨e⟩ haue patience, I am satisfied: *Prospero* omit no offered occasion, that may make my
35 desires compleate, I beseech thee.

Pros. I warrant thee. *Exeunt.*

ACTVS QVARTVS, SCENA PRIMA.

Enter Lorenzo senior, Peto, meeting Musco.

Peto. Was your man a souldier sir?
Lo. I a knaue, I tooke him vp begging vpon the way,
This morning as I was cumming to the citie,
Oh? heare he is; come on, you make fayre speede:
5 Why? where on Gods name haue you beene so long?
Mus. Mary (Gods my comfort) where I thought I should haue had little comfort of your worships seruice:
Lo. How so?
Mus. Oh God sir; your cumming to the cittie, & your
10 entertaynement of me[n], and your sending me to watch; indeede, all the circumstances are as open to your sonne as to your selfe.
Lo. How should that be? vnlesse that villaine *Musco* Haue told him of the letter, and discouered
15 All that I strictly chargd him to conceale? tis soe.
Mus. I fayth you haue hit it: tis so indeede.
Lo. But how should he know thee to be my man?
Mus. Nay sir, I cannot tell; vnlesse it were by the blacke arte? is not your sonne a scholler sir?
20 *Lo.* Yes; but I hope his soule is not allied
To such a diuelish practise: if it were,
I had iust cause to weepe my part in him,

III. vi. 30 stirring?] stirring *Q*   33 patience,] patience *Q*   35 compleate,] compleate *Q*   IV. i. 1 sir?] sir *Q*   2 knaue,] knaue *Q*
5 where on] whereon *Q*   9 sir;] sir? *Q*   10 me *F*: men *Q*   13
Musco] *Museo Q*   17 man?] man. *Q*

The Quarto of 1601

And curse the time of his creation.
But where didst thou finde them *Portensio* ?

Mus. Nay sir, rather you should aske where the⟨y⟩ found me ? for ile be sworne I was going along in the streete, thinking nothing, when (of a suddayne) one calles, *Signior Lorenzos man* : another, he cries, *souldier* : and thus halfe a dosen of them, till they had got me within doores, where I no sooner came, but out flies their rapiers and all bent agaynst my brest, they swore some two or three hundreth oathes, and all to tell me I was but a dead man, if I did not confesse where you were, and how I was imployed, and about what, which when they could not get out of me : (as Gods my iudge, they should haue kild me first) they lockt me vp into a roome in the toppe of a house, where by great miracle (hauing a light hart) I slidde downe by a bottome of packthread into the streete, and so scapt : but maister, thus much I can assure you, for I heard it while I was lockt vp : there were a great many merchants and rich citizens wiues with them at a banquet, and your sonne *Signior Lorenzo*, has poynted one of them to meete anone at one *Cobs* house, a waterbearers, that dwelles by the wall : now there you shall be sure to take him : for fayle he will not.

Lo. Nor will I fayle to breake this match, I doubt not ;
Well : go thou along with maister doctors man,
And stay there for me ; at one *Cobs* house sayst thou ?
                                                    Exit.

Mus. I sir, there you shall haue him : when, can you tell ? Much wench, or much sonne : sblood when he has stayd there three or foure houres, trauelling with the expectation of somewhat ; and at the length be deliuered of nothing : oh the sport that I should then take to look on him if I durst, but now I meane to appeare no more afore him in this shape : I haue another tricke to act yet ; oh

_{IV. i. 43 waterbearers,] waterbearers ? *Q*   48 me ;] me ? *Q*   thou ?] thou *Q*   49 when,] when *Q*   50 Much] much *Q*   54 durst,] durst *Q*   55 yet ;] yet ? *Q*}

that I were so happy, as to light vpon an ounce now of this doctors clarke : God saue you sir.

Peto. I thanke you good sir.

Mus. I haue made you stay somewhat long sir.

60 *Peto.* Not a whit sir, I pray you what sir do you meane? you haue beene lately in the warres sir, it seemes.

Mus. I marry haue I sir.

Peto. Troth sir, I would be glad to bestow a pottle of wine of you if it please you to accept it.

65 *Mus.* Oh Lord sir.

Peto. But to heare the manner of you⟨r⟩ seruises, and your deuises in the warres, they say they be very strange, and not like those a man reades in the Romane histories.

Mus. Oh God no sir, why at any time when it please you, 70 I shall be ready to descourse to you what I know : and more to somewhat.

Peto. No better time then now sir, weele goe to the *Meeremaide*, there we shall haue a cuppe of neate wine, I pray you sir let me request you.

75 *Mus.* Ile follow you sir, he is mine owne I fayth. *Exeunt.*

⟨SCENA SECVNDA.⟩

Enter Bobadilla, Lorenzo iu⟨nior,⟩ Matheo, Stephano.

Mat. Signior did you euer see the like cloune of him, where we were to day : signior *Prosperos* brother ? I thinke the whole earth cannot shew his like by Iesu.

Lo. We were now speaking of him, signior *Bobadilla* 5 telles me he is fallen foule of you two.

Mat. Oh I sir, he threatned me with the bastinado.

Bo. I but I think I taught you a trick this morning for that. You shall kill him without all question : if you be so minded.

10 *Mat.* Indeede it is a most excellent tricke.

IV. i. 57 sir.] sir, *Q*   60 meane ?] meane : *Q*   61 sir,] sir *Q*   62 marry] Marry *Q*   73 *Meeremaide*,] *Meeremaide Q*   IV. ii. stage dir. *Bobadilla*] *Babadillo Q*   1 *Mat.*] *Mat Q*   4 *Bobadilla*] *Bobadillo Q*   5 two] too *F*

Bo. Oh you do not giue spirit enough to your motion, you are too dull, too tardie: oh it must be done like lightning, hay?

Mat. Oh rare.

Bob. Tut tis nothing and't be not done in a——

Lo.iu. Signior did you neuer play with any of our maisters here?

Mat. Oh good sir.

Bob. Nay for a more instance of their preposterous humor, there came three or foure of them to me, at a gentlemans house, where it was my chance to bee resident at that time, to intreate my presence at their scholes, and withall so much importund me, that (I protest to you as I am a gentleman) I was ashamd of their rude demeanor out of all measure: well, I tolde them that to come to a publique schoole they should pardon me, it was opposite to my humor, but if so they would attend me at my lodging, I protested to do them what right or fauour I could, as I was a gentleman, &c.

Lo.iu. So sir, then you tried their skill.

Bob. Alasse soone tried: you shall heare sir, within two or three dayes after, they came, and by Iesu good signior beleeue me, I grac't them exceedingly, shewd them some two or three trickes of preuention, hath got them since admirable credit, they cannot denie this; and yet now they hate me, and why? because I am excellent, and for no other reason on the earth.

Lo.iu. This is strange and vile as euer I heard.

Bob. I will tell you sir, vpon my first comming to the citie, they assaulted me some three, foure, fiue, six, of them together as I haue walkt alone, in diuers places of the citie; as vpon the exchange, at my lodging, and at my ordinarie: where I haue driuen them afore me the whole length of a streete, in the open view of all our gallants, pittying to hurt them beleeue me; yet all this lenety will not depresse

iv. ii. 17 here?] here. *Q*   29 gentleman,] gentleman. *Q*   34 hath] haue *F*   39 sir,] sir *Q*

their spleane : they will be doing with the Pismier, raysing a hill, a man may spurne abroade with his foote at pleasure : by my soule I could haue slayne them all, but I delight not in murder : I am loth to beare any other but a bastinado
50 for them, and yet I hould it good pollicie not to goe disarmd, for though I be skilfull, I may be suppressd with multitudes.

Lo.iu. I by Iesu may you sir, and (in my conceite) our whole nation should sustayne the losse by it, if it were so.

Bob. Alasse no : whats a peculiar man, to a nation ?
55 not seene.

Lo.iu. I but your skill sir.

Bob. Indeede that might be some losse, but who respects it ? I will tel you Signior (in priuate) I am a gentleman, and liue here obscure, and to my selfe : but were I known
60 to the Duke (obserue me) I would vndertake (vpon my heade and life) for the publique benefit of the state, not onely to spare the intire liues of his subiects in generall, but to saue the one halfe : nay three partes of his yeerely charges, in houlding warres generally agaynst all his enemies ; and
65 how will I do it thinke you ?

Lo.iu. Nay I know not, nor can I conceiue.

Bo. Marry thus, I would select 19 more to my selfe, throughout the land, gentlemen they should be of good spirit, strong & able constitution ; I would chuse them by
70 an instinct, a trick that I haue : & I would teach these 19. the special tricks, as your *Punto,* your *Reuerso,* your *Stoccato,* your *Imbroccato,* your *Passado,* your *Montaunto,* till they could all play very neare or altogether as well as my selfe. This done ; say the enemie were forty thousand
75 strong : we twenty wold come into the field the tenth of *March,* or therabouts ; & would challendge twenty of the enemie ; they could not in their honor refuse the combat : wel, we would kil them : challenge twentie more, kill them ;

iv. ii. 52 sir,] sir *Q*   62 in generall] ingenerall *Q*   63 three *F* : there *Q*   64 enemies ;] enemies ? *Q*   67 more to] moreto *Q* 69 spirit,] spirit ; *Q*   constitution ;] constitutiō, *Q*   73 well as] wellas *Q*   74 This] this *Q*   76 therabouts] ther abouts *Q*   77 enemie ;] enemie ? *Q*   their] there *Q*

twentie more, kill them ; twentie more, kill them too ; and
thus would we kill euery man, his twentie a day, thats 80
twentie score ; twentie score, thats two hundreth ; two
hundreth a day, fiue dayes a thousand : fortie thousand ;
fortie times fiue, fiue times fortie, two hundreth dayes killes
them all, by computation, and this will I venture my life
to performe : prouided there be no treason practised 85
vpon vs.

   Lo.iu. Why are you so sure of your hand at all times ?
   Bob. Tut, neuer miss thrust vpon my soule.
   Lo.iu. Masse I would not stand in signior *Giuliano⟨s⟩*
state, then, and you meete him, for the wealth of *Florence*. 90
   Bob. Why signior, by Iesu if hee were heare now : I
would not draw my weapon on him, let this gentleman doe
his mind, but I wil bastinado him (by heauen) & euer
I meete him.
   Mat. Fayth and ile haue a fling at him.   95

        Enter Giuliano *and goes out agayne.*

   Lo.iu. Looke yonder he goes I thinke.
   Gui. Sblood what lucke haue I, I cannot meete with these
bragging rascalls.
   Bob. Its not he : is it ?
   Lo.iu. Yes fayth it is he.   100
   Mat. Ile be hangd then if that were he.
   Lo.iu. Before God it was he : you make me sweare.
   Step. Vpon my saluation it was hee.
   Bob. Well had I thought it had beene he : he could not
haue gone so, but I cannot be induc'd to beleeue it was 105
he yet.

            Enter Giulliano.

   Giu. Oh gallant haue I found you ? draw, to your tooles,
draw, or by Gods will ile thresh you.
   Bob. Signior heare me !
   Gui. Draw your weapons then :   110

---

iv. ii. 88 misse thrust *F* : mistrust *Q*   90 then, and] then ; | And *Q*
100 he.] he ? *Q*   107 draw,] draw *Q*   109 me !] me ? *Q*

Bob. Signior, I neuer thought ⟨on⟩ it till now : body of S. *George*, I haue a warrant of the peace serued on me euen now, as I came along, by a waterbearer, this gentleman saw it, signior *Matheo*.   *Matheo runnes away.*

Giu. The peace? Sblood, you will not draw ?
                    He beates him and desarmes him.

Lo.iu. Hold signior hold, vnder thy fauour forbeare.

Giu. Prate agayne as you like this you whoreson cowardly rascall, youle controule the poynt you ? your consort hee is gone ? had he stayd he had shard with yow infayth.
                            Exit Giulliano.

Bob. Well gentlemen beare witnesse I was bound to the peace, by Iesu.

Lo.iu. Why and though you were sir, the lawe alowes you to defend your selfe ; thats but a poore excuse.

Bob. I cannot tell ; I neuer sustayned the like disgrace (by heauen) sure I was strooke with a Plannet then, for I had no power to touch my weapon.   *Exit.*

Lo.iu. I like inough, I haue heard of many that haue beene beaten vnder a plannet ; goe get you to the Surgions, sblood and these be your tricks, your passados, & your Mountauntos, ile none of them : oh God that this age should bring foorth such creatures ? come cosen.

Step. Masse ile haue this cloke.

Lo.iu. Gods will : its *Giullianos*.

Step. Nay but tis mine now, another might haue tane it vp aswell as I, ile weare it, so I will.

Lo.iu. How and he see it, heele challenge it, assure your selfe.

Step. I but he shall not haue it ; ile say I bought it.

Lo.iu. Aduise you cosen, take heede he giue not you as much.   *Exeunt.*

IV. ii. 113 along,] along *Q*   114 *Stage dir. in Q at 115*   124 *Bob.*] *Boh. Q*   127 inough,] inough *Q*   130 Mountauntos,] Mountauntos *Q*   ile none] ilenone *Q*   131 such] snch *Q*   135 it, so] it so *Q*   136 challenge it,] challenge it *Q*

⟨SCENA TERTIA.⟩

Enter Thorello, Prospero, Biancha, Hesperida.

  Tho. Now trust me *Prospero* you were much to blame,
T'incense your brother, and disturbe the peace
Of my poore house, for there be sentinelles,
That euery minute watch to giue alarmes
Of ciuill warre, without adiection   5
Of your assistance and occasion.
  Pros. No harme done brother I warrant you : since
there is no harme done, anger costs a man nothing : and
a tall man is neuer his owne man til he be angry : to keep
his valure in obscuritie, is to keepe himselfe as it were in 10
a cloke-bag : whats a musition vnlesse he play ? whats a
tall man vnlesse he fight ? for indeede all this my brother
stands vpon absolutely, and that made me fall in with him
so resolutely.
  Bia. I but what harme might haue come of it ?   15
  Pros. Might ? so might the good warme cloathes your
husband weares be poysond for any thing he knowes, or the
wholesome wine he drunke euen now at the table.
  Tho. Now God forbid : O me ? now I remember,
My wife drunke to me last ; and changd the cuppe,   20
And bad me ware this cursed sute to day.
See, if God suffer murder vndiscouered ?
I feele me ill ; giue me some Mithredate,
Some Mithredate and oyle ; good sister fetch me,
O, I am sicke at hart : I burne, I burne ;   25
If you will saue my life goe fetch it mee.
  Pros. Oh strange humor, my very breath hath poysond
him.
  Hes. Good brother be content, what do you meane ?
The strength of these extreame conceites will kill you.   30

   IV. iii. 2 brother,] brother *Q*   peace] peace, *Q*   4 alarmes]
alarames, *Q*   5 adiection] adiection, *Q*   9 angry :] angry, *Q*
10 obscuritie,] obscuritie : *Q*   21 day.] day, *Q*   27 humor,]
humor *Q*   29 meane ?] meane, *Q*   30 you.] you ? *Q*

Bia. Beshrew your hart blood, brother *Prospero*,
For putting such a toy into his head.
　Pros. Is a fit similie, a toy? will he be poysond with
a similie? Brother *Thorello*, what a strange and vaine
35 imagination is this? For shame be wiser, of my soule
theres no such matter.
　Tho. Am I not sicke? how am I then not poysond?
Am I not poysond? how am I then so sicke?
　Bia. If you be sicke, your owne thoughts make you
40 sicke.
　Pros. His iealoucie is the poyson he hath taken.

　　　　　Enter Musco *like the doctors man.*

　Mus. Signior *Thorello* my maister doctor *Clement* salutes
you, and desires to speake with you, with all speede possible.
　Tho. No time but now? well, ile waite vpon his worship.
45 *Pizo, Cob,* ile seeke them out, and set them sentinelles till
I returne. *Pizo, Cob, Pizo.*　　　　　　　　　*Exit.*
　Pros. Musco, this is rare, but how gotst thou this apparel
of the doctors man?
　Mus. Marry sir. My youth would needes bestow the
50 wine of me to heare some martiall discourse; where I so
marshald him, that I made him monstrous drunke, &
because too much heate was the cause of his distemper,
I stript him starke naked as he lay along a sleepe, and
borrowed his sewt to deliuer this counterfeit message in,
55 leauing a rustie armoure, and an olde browne bill to watch
him, till my returne: which shall be when I haue paund
his apparrell, and spent the monie perhappes.
　Pros. Well thou art a madde knaue *Musco*, his absence
will be a good subiect for more mirth: I pray the⟨e⟩
60 returne to thy young maister *Lorenzo*, and will him to
meete me and *Hesperida* at the Friery presently: for here
tell him the house is so storde with iealousie, that there is
no roome for loue to stand vpright in: but ile vse such

　　　IV. iii. 44 worship.] worship, *Q*　　48 man?] man. *Q*　　56 him,]
him; *Q*　　62 storde] stor'd *F* : sturde *Q*

meanes she shall come thether, and that I thinke will meete
best with his desires : Hye thee good *Musco*. 65
    Mus. I goe sir.   *Exit.*

        Enter Thorello, *to him* Pizo.

    Tho. Ho *Pizo, Cob*, where are these villaines troe ?
Oh, art thou there ? *Pizo* harke thee here :
Marke what I say to thee, I must goe foorth ;
Be carefull of thy promise, keepe good watch, 70
Note euery gallant and obserue him well,
That enters in my absence to thy mistrisse ;
If she would shew him roomes, the ieast is stale,
Follow them *Pizo* or els hang on him,
And let him not go after, marke their lookes ; 75
Note if she offer but to see his band,
Or any other amorous toy about him,
But prayse his legge, or foote, or if she say,
The day is hotte, and bid him feele her hand,
How hot it is, oh thats a monstrous thing : 80
Note me all this, sweete *Pizo* ; marke their sighes,
And if they do but whisper breake them off,
Ile beare thee out in it : wilt thou do this ?
Wilt thou be true sweete *Pizo* ?
    Pi. Most true sir. 85
    Tho. Thankes gentle *Pizo* : where is *Cob* now ? *Cob* ?
                                              Exit Thorello.
    Bia. Hees euer calling for *Cob*, I wonder how hee imployes *Cob* soe.
    Pros. Indeede sister to aske how he imployes *Cob*, is
a necessary question for you that are his wife, and a thing 90
not very easie for you to be satisfied in : but this ile assure
you, *Cobs* wife is an excellent baud indeede : and oftentimes
your husband hauntes her house, marry to what end
I cannot altogether accuse him, imagine you what you

    IV. iii. *stage dir.* Thorello,] Thorello *Q*   75 lookes ;] lookes ? *Q*
77 other] otber *Q*   82 whisper] wisper *Q*   86 *Cob* now ?] *Cob* ?
now : *Q*   92 you,] you *Q*

95 thinke conuenient : but I haue knowne fayre hides haue foule hartes eare now, I can tell you.

Bia. Neuer sayd you truer then that brother ! *Pizo* fetch your cloke, and goe with me, ile after him presently : I would to Christ I could take him there I fayth.

Exeunt Pizo *and* Biancha.

100 *Pros.* So let them goe : this may make sport anone. Now my fayre sister *Hesperida* : ah that you knew how happy a thing it were to be fayre and bewtifull ?

Hes. That toucheth not me brother.

Pros. Thats true : thats euen the fault of it, for indeede 105 bewtie stands a woman in no stead, vnles it procure her touching : but sister whether it touch you or noe, it touches your bewties, and I am sure they will abide the touch, and they doe not a plague of al ceruse say I, and it touches me to in part, though not in thee. Well, theres a deare and 110 respected friend of mine sister, stands very strongly affected towardes you, and hath vowed to inflame whole bonefires of zeale in his hart, in honor of your perfections, I haue already engaged my promise to bring you where you shal heare him conferme much more then I am able 115 to lay downe for him : Signior *Lorenzo* is the man : what say you sister, shall I intreate so much fauour of you for my friend, as to[o] direct and attend you to his meeting ? Vpon my soule he loues you extreamely, approue it sweete *Hesperida* will you ?

120 *Hes.* Fayth I had very little confidence in mine owne constancie if I durst not meete a man : but brother *Prospero* this motion of yours sauours of an olde knight aduenturers seruant, me thinkes.

Pros. Whats that sister ?

125 *Hes.* Marry of the squire.

Pros. No matter *Hesperida* if it did, I would be such an one for my friend, but say, will you goe ?

IV. iii. 97 brother !] brother ? *Q* 100 anone. Now] anone, now *Q*
109 in part,] inpart. *Q* thee] the *some copies of Q* 116 sister,] sister *Q* 117 as] is *Q* 118 Vpon] vpon *Q* 124 sister ?] sister. *Q*

Hes. Brother I will, and blesse my happy starres.
                        Enter Clement *and* Thorello.
  Clem. Why what villanie is this? my man gone on a false message, and runne away when he has done, why what trick is there in it trow? 1.2.3.4. and 5.
  Tho. How: is my wife gone foorth, where is she sister?
  Hes. Shees gone abrode with *Pizo.*
  Tho. Abrode with *Pizo*? oh that villaine dors me,
He hath discouered all vnto my wife,
Beast that I was to trust him: whither went she?
  Hes. I know not sir.
  Pros. Ile tell you brother whither I suspect shees gone.
  Tho. Whither for Gods sake?
  Pros. To *Cobs* house I beleeue: but keepe my counsayle.
  Tho. I will, I will, to *Cobs* house? doth she haunt *Cobs*?
Shees gone a purpose now to cuckold me,
With that lewd rascall, who to winne her fauour,
Hath told her all. *Exit.*
  Clem. But did you mistresse see my man bring him a message?
  Pros. That we did maister doctor.
  Clem. And whither went the knaue?
  Pros. To the Tauerne I thinke sir.
  Clem. What did *Thorello* giue him any thing to spend for the message he brought him? if he did I should commend my mans wit exceedingly if he would make himselfe drunke, with the ioy of it. Farewell Lady: keepe good rule you two, I beseech you now: by Gods marry my man makes mee laugh. *Exit.*
  Pros. What a madde Doctor is this? come sister lets away. *Exeunt.*

    IV iii. 141 haunt *Cobs* ?] haunt *Cobs*, Q   146 message ?] message Q
    153 it. Farewell Lady :] it, farewell Lady, Q   154 two,] two : Q

⟨SCENA QVARTA.⟩

Enter Matheo *and* Bobadilla.

Mat. I wonder signior what they will say of my going away : ha?

Bob. Why, what should they say? but as of a discreet gentleman, quick, wary, respectfull of natures fayre
5 liniamentes, and thats all.

Mat. Why so, but what can they say of your beating?

Bob. A rude part, a touch with soft wood, a kinde of grosse batterie vsed, layd on strongly : borne most paciently, and thats all.

10 *Mat.* I but would any man haue offered it in *Venice*?

Bob. Tut I assure you no : you shall haue there your *Nobilis*, your *Gentelezza*, come in brauely vpon your reuerse, stand you close, stand you ferme, stand you fayre, saue your retricato with his left legge, come to the assaulto with
15 the right, thrust with braue steele, defie your base wood. But wherefore do I awake this remembrance? I was bewitcht by Iesu : but I will be reuengd.

Mat. Do you heare, ist not best to get a warrant and haue him arested, and brought before doctor *Clement*?

20 *Bob.* It were not amisse, would we had it.

Enter Musco.

Mat. Why here comes his man, lets speake to him.
Bob. Agreed, do you speake.
Mat. God saue you sir.
Mus. With all my hart sir!
25 *Mat.* Sir there is one *Giulliano* hath abusd this gentleman and me, and we determine to make our amendes by law, now if you would do vs the fauour to procure vs a warrant for his arest of your maister, you shall be well considered I assure ⟨you⟩, I fayth sir.

<small>IV. iv. *stage dir.* Bobadilla] Bobadillo *Q*   4 *Divided in Q* gentle-man. | Quick, . . . natures, | Fayre   18 heare,] heare *Q*   19 *Clement* ?] *Clement*. *Q*   20 amisse,] amisse *Q*   24 sir !] sir ? *Q*</small>

Mus. Sir you know my seruice is my liuing, such fauours as these gotten of my maister is his onely preferment, and therefore you must consider me, as I may make benefit of my place.

Mat. How is that?

Mus. Fayth sir, the thing is extraordinarie, and the gentleman may be of great accompt : yet be what he will, if you will lay me downe fiue crownes in my hand, you shall haue it, otherwise not.

Mat. How shall we do signior? you haue no monie?

Bob. Not a crosse by Iesu.

Mat. Nor I before God but two pence, left of my two shillings in the morning for wine and cakes : let's giue him some pawne.

Bob. Pawne? we haue none to the value of his demaunde.

Mat. Oh Lord man, ile pawne this iewell in my eare, and you may pawne your silke stockins, and pull vp your bootes, they will neare be mist.

Bob. Well and there be no remedie : ile step aside and put them of.

Mat. Doe you heare sir, we haue no store of monie at this time, but you shall haue good pawnes, looke you sir, this Iewell, and this gentlemans silke stockins, because we would haue it dispatcht ere we went to our chambers.

Mus. I am content sir, I will get you the warrant presently, whats his name say you (*Giulliano.*)

Mat. I, I, *Giulliano.*

Mus. What manner of man is he?

Mat. A tall bigge man sir, he goes in a cloake most commonly of silke russet : layd about with russet lace.

Mus. Tis very good sir.

Mat. Here sir, heres my iewell.

Bob. And heare are stockins.

Mus. Well gentlemen ile procure this wa[a]rrant presently, and appoynt you a varlet of the citie to serue it, if

IV. iv. 39 monie?] monie. Q   41 pence,] pence : Q   42 cakes :] cakes, Q   55 presently,] presently Q   61 iewell.] iewell ? Q

65 youle be vpon the Realto anone, the varlet shall meete you there.

Mat. Very good sir, I wish no better.

Exeunt Bobadilla *and* Matheo.

Mus. This is rare, now will I goe pawne this cloake of the doctors mans at the brokers for a varlets sute, and be the 70 varlet my selfe, and get eyther more pawnes, or more money of *Giulliano* for my arrest. *Exit.*

ACTVS QVINTVS. SCENA PRIMA.

Enter Lorenzo *senior.*

Lo.se. Oh heare it is, I am glad I haue found it now, Ho? who is within heare? *Enter* Tib.

Tib. I am within sir, whats your pleasure?

Lo.se. To know who is within besides your selfe.

5 *Tib.* Why sir, you are no constable I hope?

Lo.se. O feare you the constable? then I doubt not, You haue some guests within deserue that feare, Ile fetch him straight.

Tib. A Gods name sir.

10 *Lo.se.* Go to, tell me is not the young *Lorenzo* here?

Tib. Young *Lorenzo*, I saw none such sir, of mine honestie.

Lo.se. Go to, your honestie flies too lightly from you: Theres no way but fetch the constable.

15 *Tib.* The constable, the man is mad I think.

Claps to the doore.

Enter Pizo, *and* Biancha.

Pizo. Ho, who keepes house here?

Lo.se. Oh, this is the female copes-mate of my sonne. Now shall I meete him straight.

Bia. Knocke *Pizo* pray thee.

20 *Pi.* Ho good wife.

Tib. Why whats the matter with you? *Enter* Tib.

IV. iv 67 sir,] sir *Q*   v. i. 21 you?] you. *Q*

Bia. Why woman, grieues it you to ope your doore?
Belike you get something to keepe it shut.
　Tib. What meane these questions pray ye?
　Bia. So strange you make it? is not *Thorello* my tryed 25
husband here.
　Lo.se. Her husband?
　Tib. I hope he needes not to be tryed here.
　Bia. No dame: he doth it not for neede but pleasure.
　Tib. Neyther for neede nor pleasure is he here. 30
　Lo.se. This is but a deuise to balke me with al; Soft
whoes this? 　　　　　　　　　　　　*Enter* Thorello.
　Bia. Oh sir, haue I fore-stald your honest market?
Found your close walkes? you stand amazd now, do you?
I fayth (I am glad) I haue smokt you yet at last; 35
Whats your iewell trow? In: come lets see her;
Fetch foorth your huswife, dame; if she be fayrer
In any honest iudgement then my selfe,
Ile be content with it: but she is chaunge,
She feedes you fat; she soothes your appetite, 40
And you are well: your wife an honest woman,
Is meate twise sod to you sir; A⟨h⟩ you trecher.
　Lo.se. She cannot counterfeit thus palpably.
　Tho. Out on thy more then strumpets impudencie,
Stealst thou thus to thy hauntes? and haue I taken, 45
Thy baud, and thee, and thy companion,
This hoary headed letcher, this olde goate,
Close at your villanie, and wouldst thou scuse it,
With this stale harlots iest, accusing me?
O ould incontinent, dost thou not shame, 50
When all thy powers inchastitie is spent,
To haue a minde so hot? and to entise
And feede the intisements of a lustfull woman?
　Bia. Out I defie thee I, desembling wretch:
　Tho. Defie me strumpet? aske thy paunder here, 55
Can he denie it? or that wicked elder?

　　v. i. 29 doth] hoth *Q*　　　43 thus *F*: this *Q*　　44 thy *F*:
thee *Q*　　46 companion,] companion? *Q*　　47 goate,] goate *Q*
56 elder?] elder. *Q*

Lo.sen. Why heare you signior.
Tho. Tut, tut, neuer speake,
Thy guiltie conscience will discouer thee :
60 *Lo.se.* What lunacie is this that haunts this man ?

     Enter Giulliano.

Giu. Oh sister did you see my cloake ?
Bia. Not I, I see none.
Giu. Gods life I haue lost it then, saw you *Hesperida* ?
Tho. Hesperida ? is she not at home ?
65 *Giu.* No she is gone abroade, and no body can tell me of it at home.   *Exit.*
Tho. Oh heauen, abroade ? what light ? a harlot too ?
Why ? why ? harke you, hath she ? hath she not a brother ?
A brothers house to keepe ? to looke vnto ?
70 But she must fling abroade, my wife hath spoyld her,
She takes right after her, she does, she does,
Well you goody baud and ——— *Enter* Cob.
That make your husband such a hoddy dody ;
And you young apple squire, and olde cuckold maker,
75 Ile haue you euery one before the Doctor,
Nay you shall answere it, I chardge you goe.
Lo.se. Marry with all my hart, ile goe willingly : how haue I wrongd my selfe in comming here.
Bi. Go with thee ? ile go with thee to thy shame,
80 I warrant thee.
Cob. Why whats the matter ? whats here to doe ?
Tho. What *Cob* art thou here ? oh I am abusd,
And in thy house, was neuer man so wrongd.
Cob. Slid in my house ? who wrongd you in my house ?
85 *Tho.* Marry young lust in olde, and olde in young here,
Thy wifes their baud, here haue I taken them.
Cob. Doe you here ? did I not charge you *Cob beates*
keepe your dores shut here, and do you let *his wife.*
them lie open for all commers, do you scratch ?

<small>v. i. 57 signior.] signior ? *Q* 64 home ?] home *Q* 67 heauen,] heauen, ? *Q* 76 it,] it *Q* 77 with all] withall (?) *Q* 89 lie open] lieopen *Q*   scratch ?] scratch. *Q*</small>

Lo. se. Friend haue patience, if she haue done wrong in this let her answere it afore the Magistrate.
Cob. I, come, you shall goe afore the Doctor.
Tib. Nay, I will go, ile see and you may be alowd to beate your poore wife thus at euery cuckoldly knaues pleasure, the Diuell and the Pox take you all for me : why doe you not goe now?
Tho. A bitter queane, come weele haue you tamd. *Exeunt.*

⟨SCENA SECVNDA.⟩

Enter Musco *alone.*

Mus. Well of all my disguises yet now am I most like my selfe, beeing in this varlets suit, a man of my present profession neuer counterfeites till he lay holde vpon a debtor, and sayes he rests him, for then he bringes him to al manner of vnrest ; A kinde of little kings we are, bearing the diminitiue of a mace made like a young Hartechocke that alwayes carries Pepper and salte in it selfe, well I know not what danger I vnder go by this exploite, pray God I come well of.

Enter Bobadilla *and* Matheo.

Mat. See I thinke yonder is the varlet.
Bob. Lets go in quest of him.
Mat. God saue you friend, are not you here by the appoyntment of doctor *Clements* man ?
Mus. Yes and please you sir, he told me two gentlemen had wild him to procure an arest vpon one signior *Giulliano* by a warrant from his maister, which I haue about me.
Mat. It is honestly done of you both, and see where hee coms you must arest, vppon him for Gods sake before hee beware.

v. i. 90 patience,] patience *Q*   93 alowd] aloud *Q*   96 now ? now. *Q*   97 come] eome *Q*   *Exeunt.*] *Exeunt Q*   v. ii. 11 in quest] inquest *Q*   13 *Clements* man ?] *Clemants* man *Q*

Enter Stephano.

20   *Bob.* Beare backe *Matheo* !
    Mus. Signior *Giulliano* I arest you sir in the Dukes name.
    Step. Signior *Giulliano* ? am I signior *Giulliano* ? I am one signior *Stephano* I tell you, and you do not well by Gods [s]lid to arest me, I tell you truely ; I am not in your 25 maisters bookes, I would you should well know I : and a plague of God on you for making me afrayd thus.
    Mus. Why, how are you deceiued gentlemen ?
    Bob. He weares such a cloake, and that deceiued vs, but see here a coms, officer, this is he.

Enter Giulliano.

30   *Giu.* Why how now signior gull : are you turnd a flincher of late, come deliuer my cloake.
    Step. Your cloake sir ? I bought it euen now in the market.
    Mus. Signior *Giulliano* I must arest you sir.
35   *Giu.* Arrest me sir, at whose suite ?
    Mus. At these two gentlemens.
    Giu. I obey thee varlet ; but for these villaines——
    Mus. Keepe the peace I charge you sir, in the Dukes name Sir.
40   *Giu.* Whats the matter varlet ?
    Mus. You must goe before maister doctor *Clement* sir, to answere what these gentlemen will obiect agaynst you, harke you sir, I will vse you kindely.
    Mat. Weele be euen with you sir, come signior *Bobadilla*, 45 weele goe before and prepare the doctor : varlet looke to him.
    Bob. The varlet is a tall man by Iesu.

Exeunt Bobadilla *and* Matheo.

    Giu. Away you rascalles, Signior I shall haue my cloake.
    Step. Your cloake : I say once agayne I bought it, and 50 ile keepe it.

    v. ii. 20 *Matheo* !] *Matheo* ? Q   29 but] But *begins a new line in* Q
30 turnd a] a turnd Q   31 flincher] filtcher *F*   37 villaines] villianes Q   47 stage dir. *at* 46 *in* Q   48 Signior *begins a new line in* Q

Giu. You will keepe it?
Step. I, that I will.
Giu. Varlet stay, heres thy fee, arrest him.
Mus. Signior *Stephano* I arrest you.
Step. Arrest me? there take your cloake: ile none of it. 55
Giu. Nay that shall not serue your turne, varlet, bring him away, ile goe with thee now to the doctors, and carry him along.
Step. Why is not here your cloake? what would you haue? 60
Giu. I care not for that.
Mus. I pray you sir.
Giu. Neuer talke of it; I will haue him answere it.
Mus. Well sir then ile leaue you, ile take this gentlemans woorde for his appearance, as I haue done yours. 65
Giu. Tut ile haue no woordes taken, bring him along to answere it.
Mus. Good sir I pitie the gentlemans case, heres your monie agayne.
Giu. Gods bread, tell not me of my monie, bring him 70 away I say.
Mus. I warrant you, he will goe with you of himselfe.
Giu. Yet more adoe?
Mus. I haue made a fayre mashe of it.
Step. Must I goe? *Exeunt.* 75

⟨SCENA TERTIA.⟩

Enter doctor Clement, Thorello, Lorenzo se⟨nior,⟩ Biancha, Pizo, Tib, *a seruant or two of the Doctors.*

Clem. Nay but stay, stay, giue me leaue; my chayre sirha? you signior *Lorenzo* say you went thether to meete your sonne.
Lo.se. I sir.
Clem. But who directed you thether? 5

v. ii. 53 fee,] fee *Q*   v. iii. 1 stay, giue] stay giue *Q*

T 2

Lo.se. That did my man sir.
Clem. Where is hee?
Lo.se. Nay I know not now, I left him with your clarke, and appoynted him to stay here for me.
Clem. About what time was this?
Lo.se. Marry betweene one and two as I take it.
Clem. So, what time came my man with the message to you Signior *Thorello*?
Tho. After two sir.
Clem. Very good, but Lady how that you were at *Cobs*: ha?
Bia. And please you sir, ile tell you: my brother *Prospero* tolde me that *Cobs* house was a suspected place.
Clem. So it appeares me thinkes; but on.
Bia. And that my husband vsed thether dayly;
Clem. No matter, so he vse himselfe well.
Bia. True sir, but you know what growes by such haunts oftentimes.
Clem. I, ranke fruites of a iealous brayne Lady: but did you finde your husband there in that case, as you suspected?
Tho. I found her there sir.
Clem. Did you so? that alters the case; who gaue you knowledge of your wiues beeing there?
Tho. Marry that did my brother *Prospero*.
Clem. How *Prospero*, first tell her, then tell you after? where is *Prospero*?
Tho. Gone with my sister sir, I know not whither.
Clem. Why this is a meare tricke, a deuise; you are gulled in this most grosly: alasse poore wench wert thou beaten for this, how now sirha whats the matter?

Enter one of the Do⟨ctors⟩ men.

Ser. Sir theres a gentleman in the court without desires to speake with your worship.
Clem. A gentleman? whats he?

v. iii. 6 sir.] sir? *Q*   9 and] And *beginning a new line in Q*   12 message *corr. Q*: messago *Q originally*   19 on.] on, *Q*   25 suspected?] suspected. *Q*   31 *Prospero*?] *Prospero*. *Q*

Ser. A Souldier, sir, he sayeth.

Clem. A Souldier? fetch me my armour, my sworde, 40
quickly, a souldier speake with me, why when knaues,——
come on, come on, hold my cap there, so; giue me my
gorget, my sword; stand by, I will end your matters
anone; let the souldier enter, now sir what haue you to
say to me? 45

Enter Bobadilla *and* Matheo.

Bob. By your worships fauour.

Clem. Nay keepe out sir, I know not your pretence, you
send me word sir you are a souldier, why sir you shall bee
answered here, here be them haue beene amongst souldiers.
Sir your pleasure. 50

Bob. Fayth sir so it is: this gentleman and my selfe haue
beene most violently wronged by one signior *Giulliano*,
a gallant of the citie here, and for my owne part I protest,
beeing a man in no sorte giuen to this filthy humor of
quarreling, he hath asaulted me in the way of my peace: 55
dispoyld me of mine honor, disarmd me of my weapons,
and beaten me in the open streetes: when I not so much
as once offered to resist him.

Clem. Oh Gods precious is this the souldier? here take
my armour quickly, twill make him swoone I feare; he is 60
not fit to look on't, that will put vp a blow.

Enter Seruant.

Mat. Andt please your worship he was bound to the
peace.

Clem. Why, and he were sir, his hands were not bound,
were they? 65

Ser. There is one of the varlets of the citie, has brought
two gentlemen here vpon arest sir.

Clem. Bid him come in, set by the picture: *Enter* Mus.
now sir, what? signior *Giulliano*? ist you that *with* Giu. *and*
are arested at signior freshwaters suit here. Stephano. 70

    v. iii. 41 quickly,] quickly *Q*   43 sword;] sword *Q*   by,] by *Q*
45 *stage dir.* Bobadilla] Bobadillo] *Q*   52 *Giulliano,*] *Giulliano* : *Q*
53 *The comma after* here *doubtful or missing in some copies*

Giu. Ifayth maister Doctor, and heres another brought at my suite.

Clem. What are yo⟨u⟩ sir?

Step. A gentleman sir, oh vncle?

75 *Clem.* Vncle? who, *Lorenzo*?

Lo.se. I Sir.

Step. Gods my witnesse [my] vncle, I am wrongd here monstrously, he chargeth me with stealing of his cloake, & would I might neuer stir, if I did not finde it in the street 80 by chance.

Giu. Oh did you finde it now? you saide you bought it ere while.

Step. And you sayd I stole it, nay now my vnckle is here I care not.

85 *Clem.* Well let this breath a while; you that haue cause to complaine there, stand foorth; had you a warrant for this arrest?

Bob. I andt please your worship.

Clem. Nay do not speake in passion so, where had you it?

90 *Bob.* Of your clarke sir.

Clem. Thats well and my clarke can make warrants, and my hand not at them; where is the warrant? varlet haue you it?

Mus. No sir your worshippes man bid me doe it for 95 these gentlemen; and he would be my discharge.

Clem. Why signior *Giulliano*, are you such a nouice to be arrested and neuer see the warrant?

Giu. Why sir, he did not arrest me.

Clem. No? how then?

100 *Giu.* Marry sir he came to me and sayd he must arrest me, and he would vse me kindely, and so foorth.

Clem. Oh Gods pittie, was it so sir, he must arrest you: giue me my long sworde there: helpe me of; so, come on sir varlet, I must cut of your legges sirha; nay stand vp, 105 ile vse you kindly; I must cut of your legges I say.

v. iii. 73 sir?] sir. *Q*　　74 sir,] sir? *Q*　　82 while.] while? *Q*
87 arrest?] arrest. *Q*　　94 it] it; *Q*　　95 gentlemen;] gentlemen *Q*
104 vp,] vp *Q*

Mus. Oh good sir I beseech you, nay good maister doctor, oh good sir.

Clem. I must do it; there is no remedie; ·
I must cut of your legges sirha.
I must cut of your eares, you rascall I must do it; 110
I must cut of your nose, I must cut of your head.

Mus. Oh for God sake good Maister Doctor.

Clem. Well rise, how doest thou now? doest thou feele thy selfe well? hast thou no harme?

Mus. No I thanke God sir and your good wor- 115 shippe.

Clem. Why so, I sayd I must cut of thy legges, and I must cut of thy armes, and I must cut of thy head: but I did not do it: so you sayd you must arrest this gentleman, but you did not arrest him you knaue, you slaue, you rogue, do you 120 say you must arrest? sirha away with him to the iayle, ile teach you a tricke for your must.

Mus. Good M. Doctor I beseech you be good to me.

Clem. Marry a God: away with him I say.

Mus. Nay sblood before I goe to prison, ile put on my 125 olde brasen face, and disclaime in my vocation: Ile discouer, thats flat, and I be committed, it shall be for the committing of more villainies then this, hang me, and I loose the least graine of my fame.

Clem. Why? when knaue? by Gods marry, ile clappe 130 thee by the heeles to.

Mus. Hold, hold, I pray you.

Clem. Whats the matter? stay there.

Mus. Fayth sir afore I goe to this house of bondage, I haue a case to vnfolde to your worshippe: which (that it 135 may appeare more playne vnto your worshippes view) I do thus first of all vncase, & appeare in mine owne proper nature, seruant to this gentleman: and knowne by the name of *Musco*.

Lo.se. Ha? *Musco*. 140

v. iii. 107 oh] Oh *Q*   113 rise,] rise *Q*   117 so,] so *Q*   121 arrest?
sirha] arrest sirha : *Q*   127 discouer,] discouer *Q*

280   *Euery man in his Humor*

Step. Oh vncle, *Musco* has beene with my cosen and I all this day.

Clem. Did not I tell you there was some deuise?

Mus. Nay good M. Doctor since I haue layd my selfe
145 thus open to your worship: now stand strong for me, till the progresse of my tale be ended, and then if my wit do not deserue your countenance: Slight throw it on a dogge, and let me goe hang my selfe.

Cle. Body of me a merry knaue, giue me a boule of Sack.
150 Signior *Lorenzo*, I bespeak your patience in perticuler, marry your eares in generall. Here knaue, Doctor *Clement* drinkes to thee.

Mus. I pledge M. Doctor and't were a sea to the bottome.

Cle. Fill his boule for that, fil his boule: so, now speak
155 freely.

Mus. Indeede this is it will make a man speake freely. But to the poynt, know then that I *Musco* (beeing somewhat more trusted of my maister then reason required, and knowing his intent to *Florence*) did assume the habit of
160 a poore souldier in wants, and minding by some meanes to intercept his iorney in the mid way, twixt the grandg and the city, I encountred him, where begging of him in the most accomplisht and true garbe (as they tearme it) contrarie to al expectation, he reclaimd me from that bad course
165 of life; entertayned me into his seruice, imployed me in his busines, possest me with his secrets, which I no sooner had receiued, but (seeking my young maister, and finding him at this gentlemans house) I reuealed all most amply: this done, by the deuise of signior *Prospero*, and him together,
170 I returnd (as the Rauen did to the Arke) to mine olde maister againe, told him he should finde his sonne in what maner he knows, at one *Cobs* house, where indeede he neuer ment to come: now my maister he to maintayne the iest, went thether, and left me with your worships clarke: who
175 being of a most fine supple disposition (as most of your

v. iii. 143 deuise?] deuise. *Q*   144 haue] hane *Q*   149–50 Sack. Signior] Sack, signior *Q*   150 your] yonr *Q*   151 in generall. Here] ingenerall, here *Q*   173 come:] come, *Q*   174 left] ieft *Q*

The Quarto of 1601

clarkes are) proffers me the wine, which I had the grace to accept very easily, and to the tauerne we went : there after much ceremonie, I made him drunke in kindenesse, stript him to his shurt, and leauing him in that coole vayne, departed, frolicke, courtier like, hauing obtayned a suit : which suit fitting me exceedingly well, I put on, and vsurping your mans phrase & action, caried a message to Signior *Thorello* in your name : which message was meerely deuised but to procure his absence, while signior *Prospero* might make a conueiance of *Hesperida* to my maister.

Clem. Stay, fill me the boule agayne, here ; twere pittie of his life would not cherish such a spirite : I drinke to thee, fill him wine, why now do you perceiue the tricke of it ?

Tho. I, I perceiue well we were all abusd.

Lo.se. Well what remedie ?

Clem. Where is *Lorenzo*, and *Prospero*, canst thou tell ?

Mus. I sir, they are at supper at the *Meeremaid*, where I left your man.

Clem. Sirha goe warne them hether presently before me : and if the hower of your fellowes resurrection be come, bring him to. But forwarde, forwarde, when thou hadst beene at *Thor[r]ellos.*   *Exit seruant.*

Mus. Marry sir (comming along the streete) these two gentlemen meet me, and very strongly supposing me to be your worships scribe, entreated me to procure them a warrant, for the arrest of signior *Giulliano*, I promist them vpon some paire of silke stockins or a iewell, or so, to do it, and to get a varlet of the citie to serue it, which varlet I appoynted should meete them vpon the Realto at such an houre : they no sooner gone, but I in a meere hope of more gaine by signior *Giulliano*, went to one of *Satans* old Ingles a broker, & there paund your mans liuerie for a varlets suite, which here with my selfe, I offer vnto your worships consideration.

v. iii. 188 it ?] it. *Q*   189 I, I] I, I, *Q*   abusd.] abusd- *Q*   191 *Prospero*,] *Prospero* Q   195 be come,] become *Q*   203 which varlet] which vatlet *Q*   205 houre :] houre, *Q*

210 *Clem.* Well giue me thy hand: *Proh superi ingenium magnum quis nosset Homerum, Il[l]ias æternum si latuisset, opus?* I admire thee, I honor thee, and if thy maister, or any man here be angry with thee, I shall suspect his wit while I know him for it, doe you heare Signior *Thorello,*
215 Signior *Lorenzo,* and the rest of my good friendes, I pray you let me haue peace when they come, I haue sent for the two gallants and *Hesperida,* Gods marry I must haue you friendes, how now? what noyse is there?

Enter seruant, then Peto.

Ser. Sir it is *Peto* is come home.
220 *Cle. Peto,* bring him hether, bring him hether, what how now signior drunckard, in armes against me, ha? your reason, your reason for this?

Pe. I beseech your worship to pardon me.

Clem. Well, sirha tell him I do pardon him.
225 *Pe.* Truly sir I did happen into bad companie by chance, and they cast me in a sleepe and stript me of all my cloathes.

Clem. Tut this is not to the purpose, touching your armour, what might your armour signifie?

Pe. Marry sir it hung in the roome where they stript me,
230 and I borrowed it of on of the drawers, now in the euening to come home in, because I was loth to come through the street in my shurt.

Enter Lorenzo *iunior,* Prospero, Hesperida.

Clem. Well disarme him, but its no matter, let him stand by, who be these? oh young gallants; welcome, welcome,
235 and you Lady, nay neuer scatter such amazed lookes amongst vs, *Qui nil potest sperare desperet nihil.*

Pros. Faith M. Doctor thats euen I, my hopes are smal, and my dispaire shal be as little. Brother, sister, brother, what cloudy, cloudy? *and will noe sunshine on these lookes*

v. iii. 210 *Proh*] *Proh.* Q 211 *nosset*] *noscit* Q *Homerum,*] *Homerum.* Q 212 thee, I] thee I Q 217 must] musi Q 220 Peto,] Peto Q 222 reason, your] reason your Q this?] this. Q 225 chance,] chance Q 227 purpose,] purpose Q 228 signifie?] signifie. Q 233 matter,] matter Q 238–9 brother, what] brother what Q

appeare? well since there is such a tempest towarde, ile be 240
the porpuis, ile daunce : wench be of good cheare, thou
hast a cloake for the rayne yet, where is he? S'hart how
now, the picture of the prodigal, go to, ile haue the calfe
drest for you at my charges.

Lo.se. Well sonne *Lorenzo*, this dayes worke of yours hath 245
much deceiued my hopes, troubled my peace, and stretcht
my patience further then became the spirite of dutie.

Cle. Nay Gods pitie signior *Lorenzo* you shal vrge it no
more, come since you are here, ile haue the disposing of all,
but first signior *Giulliano* at my request take your cloake 250
agayne.

Giu. Well sir I am content.

Cle. Stay now let me see, oh signior Snow-liuer, I had
almost forgotten him, and your *Genius* there, what doth he
suffer for a good conscience to? doth he beare his crosse 255
with patience?

Mu. Nay they haue scarse one cros between them both
to beare.

Clem. Why doest thou know him, what is he? what
is he? 260

Mus. Marry search his pocket⟨s⟩ sir, and the⟨i⟩le shew
you he is an Author Sir.

Cle. Dic mihi musa virum : are you an Author sir, giue
me leaue a little, come on sir, ile make verses with you now
in honor of the Gods, and the Goddesses for what you dare 265
extempore ; and now I beginne.

    Mount the⟨e⟩ *my Phlegon muse, and testifie,*
      How Saturne *sitting in an Ebon cloud,*
      Disrobd his podex, white as iuorie,
      And through the welkin thundred all aloud. 270
Theres for you sir.

Pros. Oh he writes not in that height of stile.

Clem. No : weele come a steppe or two lower then.

  v. iii. 240 *appeare* ?] *appeare,* Q   243 go to,] go to Q   249 more,]
more Q   253 Snow-liuer,] Snow-liuer Q   256 patience ?] patience.
Q   267 Phlegon muse] *Pblegonmuse* Q   270–1 *One line in* Q   271
Theres] theres Q

From Cataduba and the bankes of Nile,
Where onely breedes your monstrous Crocodile :
Now are we purposd for to fetch our stile.
Pros. Oh too farre fetcht for him still maister Doctor.
Clem. I, say you so ? lets intreat a sight of his vaine then.
Pros. Signior, maister Doctor desires to see a sight of your vaine, nay you must not denie him.
Cle. What, al this verse ? body of me he carries a whole realme ; a common wealth of paper in his hose, lets see some of his subiects.
Vnto the boundlesse ocean of thy bewtie,
Runnes this poor riuer, chargd with streames of zeale,
Returning thee the tribute of my dutie :
Which here my youth, my plaints, my loue reueale.
Good ! is this your owne inuention ?
Mat. No sir, I translated that out of a booke, called *Delia.*
C. Oh but I wold see some of your owne, some of your owne.
Mat. Sir ; heres the beginning of a sonnet I made to my mistresse.
Clem. That that : who ? to *Maddona Hesperida*, is she your mistresse ?
Pros. It pleaseth him to call her so, sir.
Clem. In Sommer time when Phœbus *golden rayes.*
You translated this too ? did you not ?
Pros. No this is inuention ; he found it in a ballad.
Mat. Fayth sir, I had most of the conceite of it out of a ballad indeede.
Clem. Conceite, fetch me a couple of torches, sirha, I may see the conceite : quickly ! its very darke !
Giu. Call you this poetry ?
Lo.iu. Poetry ? nay then call blasphemie, religion ;
Call Diuels, Angels ; and Sinne, pietie :

v. v. 277 Doctor.] Doctor : *Q*   278 so ?] so, *Q*   then.] then ? *Q*
281 What,] what ; *Q*   verse ?] verse, *Q*   288 Good !] Good ? *Q*   294
Hesperida,] *Hesperida* Q   295 mistresse ?] mistresse. *Q*   297
Phœbus] Phæbus *Q*   302–3 *As verse, divided at* sirha, | I *in Q.*   303
quickly !] quickly ? *Q*   darke !] darke ? *Q*

Let all things be preposterously transchangd.
  Lo.se. Why how now sonne? what? are you startled
    now?
Hath the brize prickt you? ha? go to; you see,
How abiectly your Poetry is ranckt,   310
In generall opinion.
  Lo.iu. Opinion, O God let grosse opinion
Sinck & be damnd as deepe as *Barathrum.*
If it may stand with your most wisht content,
I can refell opinion, and approue   315
The state of poesie, such as it is,
Blessed, æternall, and most true deuine:
Indeede if you will looke on Poesie,
As she appeares in many, poore and lame,
Patcht vp in remnants and olde worne ragges,   320
Halfe starud for want of her peculiar foode,
Sacred inuention, then I must conferme,
Both your conceite and censure of her merrite.
But view her in her glorious ornaments,
Attired in the maiestie of arte,   325
Set high in spirite with the precious taste
Of sweete philosophie, and which is most,
Crownd with the rich traditions of a soule,
That hates to haue her dignitie prophand,
With any relish of an earthly thought: 330
Oh then how proud a presence doth she beare.
Then is she like her selfe, fit to be seene
Of none but graue and consecrated eyes:
Nor is it any blemish to her fame,
That such leane, ignorant, and blasted wits,   335
Such brainlesse guls, should vtter their stolne wares
With such aplauses in our vulgar eares:
Or that their slubberd lines haue currant passe,

    v. v. 310–13 *Divided in Q* How ... generall opinion.| Opinion, ...
damnd | As ... *Barathrum,*   315 opinion,] opinion *Q*   approue]
approue, *Q*   320 worne] worn-out *G*   321 foode,] foode: *Q*   323
merrite.] merrite, *Q*   326 taste] taste, *Q*   332 selfe,] selfe *Q*   seene]
seene, *Q*   335 leane,] leane. *Q*

From the fat iudgements of the multitude,
340 But that this barren and infected age,
Should set no difference twixt these empty spirits,
And a true Poet : then which reuerend name,
Nothing can more adorne humanitie. *Enter with torches.*
   Clem. I *Lorenzo*, but election is now gouernd altogether
345 by the influence of humor, which insteed of those holy
flames that should direct and light the soule to eternitie,
hurles foorth nothing but smooke and congested vapours,
that stifle her vp, & bereaue her of al sight & motion. But
she must haue store of *Ellebore* giuen her to purge these
350 grosse obstructions : oh thats well sayd, giue me thy torch,
come lay this stuffe together. So, giue fire ? there, see, see,
how our Poets glory shines brighter, and brighter, still, still
it increaseth, oh now its at the highest, and now it declines
as fast : you may see gallants, *Sic transit gloria mundi.*
355 Well now my two Signior Out-sides, stand foorth, and lend
me your large eares, to a sentence, to a sentence : first you
signior shall this night to the cage, and so shall you sir,
from thence to morrow morning, you signior shall be
carried to the market crosse, and be there bound : and so
360 shall you sir, in a large motlie coate, with a rodde at your
girdle ; and you in an olde suite of sackcloth, and the ashes
of your papers (saue the ashes sirha) shall mourne all day,
and at night both together sing some ballad of repentance
very pitteously, which you shall make to the tune of *Who
365 list to leade and a souldiers life.* Sirha bilman, imbrace you
this torch, and light the gentlemen to their lodgings, and
because we tender their safetie, you shall watch them to
night, you are prouided for the purpose, away and looke
to your charge with an open eye sirha.
370 *Bob.* Well I am armd in soule agaynst the worst of
fortune.
   Mat. Fayth so should I be, and I had slept on it.
   Pe. I am armd too, but I am not like to sleepe on it.

v. v. 349 *Ellebore*] *Ellebore,* Q   355 Out-sides] out sides *Q*   365 bilman] bil man *Q*

Mus. Oh how this pleaseth me.
                    Exeunt ⟨Bobadilla, Matheo, and Piso⟩.
Clem. Now Signior *Thorello, Giulliano, Prospero, Biancha.* 375
Step. And not me sir.
Clem. Yes and you sir : I had lost a sheepe and he had
not bleated. I must haue you all friends : but first a worde
with you young gallant, and you Lady.
Giu. Wel brother *Prospero* by this good light that shines 380
here I am loth to kindle fresh coles, but and you had come in
my walke within these two houres I had giuen you that you
should not haue clawne of agayne in hast, by Iesus I had
done it, I am the arren⟨t⟩st rogue that euer breathd else,
but now beshrew my hart if I beare you any malice in the 385
earth.
Pros. Fayth I did it but to hould vp a iest : and helpe
my sister to a husband. But brother *Thorello,* and sister,
you haue a spice of the yealous yet both of you, (in your
hose I meane,) come do not dwell vpon your anger so much, 390
lets all be smoth foreheaded once agayne.
Tho. He playes vpon my forehead, brother *Giulliano,*
I pray you tell me one thing I shall aske you : is my fore-
heade any thing rougher then it was wont to be ?
Giu. Rougher ? your forehead is smoth enough man.   395
Tho. Why should he then say be smoth foreheaded,
Vnlesse he iested at the smothnesse of it ?
And that may be ; for horne is very smoth ;
So are my browes ? by Iesu, smoth as horne ?
Bia. Brother had he no haunt thether in good fayth ? 400
Pros. No vpon my soule.
Bia. Nay then sweet hart : nay I pray the⟨e⟩ be not
angry, good faith ile neuer suspect thee any more, nay kisse
me sweet musse.
Tho. Tell me *Biancha,* do not you play the woman with 405
me ?

v. v. 375 *Biancha*] *Biancba.* Q   378 bleated.] bleated, Q   388 But]
but Q   391 foreheaded] fore headed Q   392 forehead] fore head Q
394 be ?] be. Q   396 say] say ? Q   404 me sweet] mesweet Q
406 me ?] me. Q

Bia. Whats that sweete hart?
Tho. Dissemble?
Bia. Dissemble?
410 *Tho.* Nay doe not turne away: but say I fayth was it not a match appoynted twixt this old gentleman and you?
Bia. A match?
Tho. Nay if it were not, I do not care: do not weepe I pray thee sweete *Biancha*, nay so now; by Iesus I am not
415 iealous, but resolued I haue the faythfulst wife in *Italie*.
For this I finde where iealousie is fed,
  Hornes in the minde, are worse then on the head.
See what a droue of hornes flie in the ayre,
  Wingd with my cleansed, and my credulous breath:
420 Watch them suspicious eyes, watch where they fall,
  See see, on heades that thinke they haue none at all.
Oh what a plentuous world of this will come,
  When ayre raynes hornes, all men be sure of some.
Clem. Why thats well, come then: what say you, are all
425 agreed? doth none stand out?
Pros. None but this gentleman: to whom in my owne person I owe all dutie and affection: but most seriously intreate pardon, for whatsoeuer hath past in these occurrants, that might be contrarie to his most desired content.
430 *Lo.* Fayth sir it is a vertue that persues
Any saue rude and vncomposed spirites,
To make a fayre construction, and indeede
Not to stand of, when such respectiue meanes
Inuite a generall content in all.
435 *Clem.* Well then I coniure you all here to put of all discontentment, first you Signior *Lorenzo* your cares; you, and you, your iealousie: you your anger, and you your wit sir: and for a peace offering, heres one willing to be sacrifised vppon this aulter: say do you approue my motion?

v. v. 407 hart?] hart. Q   412 match?] match. Q   414 now;] now? Q   416–17 where ... head, quoted in *England's Parnassus*, 1600, p. 145, with the variants '*iealousie is bred*', '*worse then hornes in the head*'   423 be sure] besure Q.   424 you,] you Q   425 out?] out. Q   430 persues] persues, Q   432 construction,] construction Q   433 meanes] meanes, Q

The Quarto of 1601   289

Pros. We doe, ile be mouth for all.   440

Clem. Why then I wish them all ioy, and now to make our euening happinesse more full : this night you shall be all my guestes : where weele inioy the very spirite of mirth, and carouse to the health of this *Heroick* spirite, whom to honor the more I do inuest in my owne robes, desiring you 445 two *Giulliano*, and *Prospero*, to be his supporters ; the trayne to follow, my selfe will leade, vsherd by my page here with this honorable verse. *Claudite iam riuos pueri, sat prata biberunt.*

FINIS.

v. v. 440 doe,] doe Q   446 supporters ;] supporters, Q   448
pueri,] pueri Q

EVERY MAN IN HIS HUMOUR.

The Revised Version
from the Folio of 1616.

THE TEXT

A MINUTE collation of the Folio text of *Every Man in his Humour* shows that it was set up from a copy of the 1601 Quarto which Jonson had worked over with manuscript corrections to prepare it for the press. The evidence is microscopic, but it is cumulative. In estimating it, it should be remembered that the Folio of 1616 was printed with scrupulous care, especially in the matter of punctuation, which Jonson rather elaborated. The following peculiarities are common to the two texts. As a rule, the Folio prints a question with the note of interrogation, but in a few passages it follows the Quarto in using a full stop :

Sweete hart will you come in to breakfast.
(Quarto, sig. D 3. Cf. II. iii. 35–6.)
... but did you all this signior without hurting your blade.
(Sig. E 4. Cf. III. i. 150–1.)
Musco, s'bloud what winde hath blowne thee hither in this shape. (Sig. F. Cf. III. ii. 40–1.)
... are you not here by the appoyntment of doctor *Clemants* man. (Sig. K 4. Cf. IV. xi. 12–13.)

In the following passages the Quarto wrongly inserts a note of interrogation, and is copied by the Folio :

Step. No truly sir ? (Sig. G. Cf. III. v. 74.)
Mat. Here sir, heres my iewell ? (Sig. K 2. Cf. IV. ix. 64.)
Step. A gentleman sir ? (Sig. L 2. Cf. v. iii. 3.)

In III. v. 84–5, ' that (had you taken the most deadly poysonous simple in all Florence, it should expell it ', the Quarto omitted the second bracket ; the Folio revised the passage, but also omitted the bracket.

In three prose passages the Quarto wrongly prints a

semblance of metrical form, which the Folio reproduces :

> What *Cob* ? our maides will haue you by the back (Ifaith)
> For comming so late this morning.
> (Sig. D 2 verso. Cf. II. iii. 1–2.)

> Well *Musco* performe this businesse happily,
> And thou makest a conquest of my loue foreuer,
> (Sigg. H 3 verso, H 4. Cf. IV. v. 1–3.)

> Nay I know not how, I left him with your clarke,
> And appoynted him to stay here for me.
> (Sig. L. Cf. v. i. 8–9.)

Slight though these clues are, they seem to prove that the printer of the Folio had before him a printed copy of the 1601 text interlined with corrections in Jonson's handwriting, and not a new manuscript.

The text of 1640 is substantially a reprint of the earlier Folio. Occasionally it makes a correction, as in v. v. 81 '*all may be sure of some*', where the 1616 Folio misprinted '*fame*'. At III. ii. 52 'At Iustice CLEMENTS house here, in *Colman*-street' the word 'here' is inconsistent with the stage arrangement presupposing that the first two scenes are laid at the Windmill Tavern, and the 1640 text omits it : but such a discrepancy counts for little on the Elizabethan stage, where a change of locality is often indicated in this way. But 'here' may simply mean 'The Old Jewry' as in III. iii. 119, where the 1640 Folio makes no alteration. Other changes are the superlative 'he sweares most admirably !' in III. v. 132, where the 1616 text has 'sweares admirably'; and 'how chance that you were . . .' in v. i. 15–16 for 'how that you were'. The punctuation is corrected from time to time : all deliberate changes in it are recorded in the critical apparatus, and a few have been adopted in the text. The errors of the 1640 in this respect have not been recorded ; they are chiefly errors of omission. But it may be noted that the 1640 editor or press-corrector had carefully studied Jonson's own method, and attempted to harmonize a number of passages which he thought inconsistent with it. In this he did not always succeed; he was apt to misread a lightly stopped sentence, which the actor was meant to deliver 'trippingly on the tongue'. For instance the 1616 Folio uses such natural pointing as this: 'What aile you sweet heart, are you not well, speake good Mvsse' (II. iii. 40–1). The 1640 Folio spoils the effect by making one sentence into three: 'What aile you Sweet-heart? are you not well? speake good Musse.'

Other examples are III. iii. 133–5:
when I meant
So deepe a secret to you, I meane not this,
But that I haue to tell you, this is nothing, this.

Kitely is in a breathless hurry; but he marks time with an emphatic pause in the text of 1640:

But that I have to tell you; this is nothing, this.

Or when Down-right at last catches Bobadill (IV. vii. 120–1), the 1616 Folio prints 'haue I found you? Come, draw, to your tooles: draw, gipsie, or Ile thresh you'. He pauses after 'tooles' to give Bobadill time to draw; but the methodical 'draw, gipsie;' of the 1640 text leaves Downright as limp and dilatory as his victim. There is too a very interesting punctuation of Jonson's which the 1640 Folio frequently misses both in this and other plays—his use of the apostrophe to mark a sequence of two lightly pronounced syllables.[1] The following examples from the 1616 text illustrate this practice:

If he be'at his booke, disturbe him not.—Well sir. (I. i. 5.)
Ah, but what miserie' is it, to know this? (II. iii. 70.)
Nay, rather then 't shall learne
No bawdie song, the mother'her selfe will teach it!
(II. v. 23–4.)
Carry' in my cloke againe. Yet, stay. Yet, doe too.
(III. iii. 40.)
Wherein, my 'imaginations runne, like sands (ib. 50.)

[1] See vol. ii, pp. 430–1.

In the first, third, or fourth of these examples the 1640 Folio omits the apostrophe; in the second and fifth it attempts a press-correction, ' what mis'rie is it ', and ' my 'maginations '.

To decry the 1640 text, as Gifford did, shows a lack of critical insight; but we may be thankful that one-half of Jonson's work was printed in the earlier authoritative Folio.

The 1616 recension of this play has been reproduced four times: by Professor W. Bang in his excellent reprint of the Folio, of which the first part, containing the plays, from *Every Man in his Humour* to *Cynthia's Revels*, appeared at Louvain in 1905; by Dr. G. A. Smithson in Gayley's *Representative English Comedies*, vol. ii, 1913—a text with modernizing touches and some misprints (e. g. 'pinc*h* your flesh, full of holes ' in iv. ii. 132); by Percy Simpson in a critical edition of the play published by the Clarendon Press in 1919; and by Dr. H. Holland Carter in the parallel text of Quarto and Folio already noticed.[1]

[1] See page 194.

Euery
MAN IN
HIS
HVMOVR.

A Comœdie.

Acted in the yeere 1598. By the then
Lord Chamberlaine his
Seruants.

The Author B. I.

IUVEN.
Haud tamen inuideas vati, quem pulpita pascunt.

LONDON,
Printed by WILLIAM STANSBY.

M. DC. XVI.

EVERY MAN
IN HIS
HUMOUR.

A Comedy.

Acted in the yeere 1598. By the then
Lord CHAMBERLAINE
his Servants.

The Author B. I.

JUVEN.
Haud tamen invideas vati, quem pulpita pascunt.

LONDON,
Printed by RICHARD BISHOP.

M. DC. XL.

TO THE MOST
LEARNED, AND
MY HONOR'D
FRIEND,

M^r. Cambden, Clarentiavx.

SIR,

THere are, no doubt, a supercilious race in the world, who will esteeme all office, done you in this kind, an iniurie ; so solemne a vice it is with them to vse the authoritie of their ignorance, to the crying downe of Poetry, or the Professors : 5 But, my gratitude must not leaue to correct their error ; since I am none of those, that can suffer the benefits confer'd vpon my youth, to perish with my age. It is a fraile memorie, that remembers but present things : And, had the fauour of the times so conspir'd with my disposition, as it could haue brought 10 forth other, or better, you had had the same proportion, & number of the fruits, the first. Now, I pray you, to accept this, such, wherein neither the confession of my manners shall make you blush ; nor of my studies, repent you to haue beene the instructer : And, for the profession of my thanke-fulnesse, 15 I am sure, it will, with good men, find either praise, or excuse.

Your true louer,

BEN. IONSON.

CLARENTIAVX *not in* F1 *originally*   5 Poëtry F2   6 *error*]
errour F2   18 IONSON] IOHNSON F2

The Persons of the Play.

Kno'well, *An old Gentleman.*

Ed. Kno'well, *His Sonne.*

Brayne-worme, *The Fathers man.*

M^r. Stephen, *A countrey Gull.*

Downe-right, *A plaine Squier.*

Well-bred, *His halfe Brother.*

Ivst. Clement, *An old merry Magistrat.*

Roger Formall, *His Clarke.*

Kitely, *A Merchant.*

Dame Kitely, *His wife.*

M^{rs}. Bridget, *His Sister.*

M^r. Matthew, *The towne-gull.*

Cash, *Kitelies Man.*

Cob, *A Water-bearer.*

Tib, *His Wife.*

Cap. Bobadill, *A Paules-man.*

THE SCENE

LONDON.

6–7 *countrey Gull*] country-Gull F2   25 *Servants &c.* added by G
After The Scene F2 *inserts the Actor-list and the note on the first performance given in* F1 *at the end of the play*

EVERY MAN IN HIS HVMOVR.

PROLOGVE.

THough neede make many *Poets*, and some such
   As art, and nature haue not betterd much ;
Yet ours, for want, hath not so lou'd the stage,
As he dare serue th'ill customes of the age :
Or purchase your delight at such a rate,   5
As, for it, he himselfe must iustly hate.
To make a child, now swadled, to proceede
Man, and then shoote vp, in one beard, and weede,
Past threescore yeeres : or, with three rustie swords,
And helpe of some few foot-and-halfe-foote words,   10
Fight ouer *Yorke*, and *Lancasters* long iarres :
And in the tyring-house bring wounds, to scarres.
He rather prayes, you will be pleas'd to see
One such, to day, as other playes should be.
Where neither *Chorus* wafts you ore the seas ;   15
Nor creaking throne comes downe, the boyes to please ;
Nor nimble squibbe is seene, to make afear'd
The gentlewomen ; nor roul'd bullet heard
To say, it thunders ; nor tempestuous drumme
Rumbles, to tell you when the storme doth come ;   20
But deedes, and language, such as men doe vse :
And persons, such as *Comœdie* would chuse,
When she would shew an Image of the times,
And sport with humane follies, not with crimes.
Except, we make 'hem such by louing still   25
Our popular errors, when we know th'are ill.
I meane such errors, as you'll all confesse
By laughing at them, they deserue no lesse :
Which when you heartily doe, there's hope left, then,
You, that haue so grac'd monsters, may like men.   30

      3 stage,] stage *originally in F1*

Act 1. Scene 1.

Kno'well, Brayne-Worme, M^r. Stephen.

A Goodly day toward! and a fresh morning! Brayne-
Worme,
Call vp your yong master: bid him rise, sir.
Tell him, I haue some businesse to employ him.
    Bra. I will sir, presently. Kno. But heare you, sirah,
5 If he be'at his booke, disturbe him not. Bra. Well sir.
    Kno. How happie, yet, should I esteeme my selfe
Could I (by any practise) weane the boy
From one vaine course of studie, he affects.
He is a scholler, if a man may trust
10 The liberall voice of fame, in her report
Of good accompt, in both our *vniuersities*,
Either of which hath fauour'd him with graces:
But their indulgence, must not spring in me
A fond opinion, that he cannot erre.
15 My selfe was once a student; and, indeed,
Fed with the selfe-same humour, he is now,
Dreaming on nought but idle *poetrie*,
That fruitlesse, and vnprofitable art,
Good vnto none, but least to the professors,
20 Which, then, I thought the mistresse of all knowledge:
But since, time, and the truth haue wak'd my iudgement,
And reason taught me better to distinguish,
The vaine, from th'vsefull learnings. Cossin Stephen!
What newes with you, that you are here so early?
25   Ste. Nothing, but eene come to see how you doe, vncle.
    Kno. That's kindly done, you are wel-come, cousse.
    Ste. I, I know that sir, I would not ha' come else.
How doe my cousin Edward, vncle?
    Kno. O, well cousse, goe in and see: I doubt he be
30 scarse stirring yet.

    1. i.] A Street. Enter Knowell at the door of his House. *G*   5 be'at]
be at *F2*   23 Cossin] Coussin *F2*   28 doe] does *F2*

S t e. Vncle, afore I goe in, can you tell me, an' he haue ere a booke of the sciences of hawking, and hunting? I would faine borrow it.

K n o. Why, I hope you will not a hawking now, will you?

S t e p. No wusse; but I'll practise against next yeere vncle: I haue bought me a hawke, and a hood, and bells, and all; I lacke nothing but a booke to keepe it by.

K n o. O, most ridiculous.

S t e p. Nay, looke you now, you are angrie, vncle: why you know, an' a man haue not skill in the hawking, and hunting-languages now a dayes, I'll not giue a rush for him. They are more studied then the *Greeke*, or the *Latine*. He is for no gallants companie without 'hem. And by gads lid I scorne it, I, so I doe, to be a consort for euery *hum-drum*, hang 'hem scroyles, there's nothing in 'hem, i' the world. What doe you talke on it? Because I dwell at *Hogsden*, I shall keepe companie with none but the archers of *Finsburie*? or the citizens, that come a ducking to *Islington* ponds? A fine iest ifaith! Slid a gentleman mun show himselfe like a gentleman. Vncle, I pray you be not angrie, I know what I haue to doe, I trow, I am no nouice.

K n o. You are a prodigall absurd cocks-combe: Goe to. Nay neuer looke at me, it's I that speake.
Tak't as you will sir, I'll not flatter you.
Ha' you not yet found meanes enow, to wast
That, which your friends haue left you, but you must
Goe cast away your money on a kite,
And know not how to keepe it, when you ha' done?
O it's comely! this will make you a gentleman!
Well cosen, well! I see you are eene past hope
Of all reclaime. I, so, now you are told on it,
You looke another way.   S t e p. What would you ha' me
   doe?

   I. I. 43 then] than *F2*   49 a ducking] aducking *F2*   62 cosen]
cousen *F2*

65   K N o. What would I haue you doe? I'll tell you kinsman,
Learne to be wise, and practise how to thriue,
That would I haue you doe: and not to spend
Your coyne on euery bable, that you phansie,
Or euery foolish braine, that humors you.
70 I would not haue you to inuade each place,
Nor thrust your selfe on all societies,
Till mens affections, or your owne desert,
Should worthily inuite you to your ranke.
He, that is so respectlesse in his courses,
75 Oft sells his reputation, at cheape market.
Nor would I, you should melt away your selfe
In flashing brauerie, least while you affect
To make a blaze of gentrie to the world,
A little puffe of scorne extinguish it,
80 And you be left, like an vnsauorie snuffe,
Whose propertie is onely to offend.
I'ld ha' you sober, and containe your selfe;
Not, that your sayle be bigger then your boat:
But moderate your expences now (at first)
85 As you may keepe the same proportion still.
Nor, stand so much on your gentilitie,
Which is an aërie, and meere borrow'd thing,
From dead mens dust, and bones: and none of yours
Except you make, or hold it. Who comes here?

Act 1. Scene 11.

SERVANT, M^r. STEPHEN, KNO'WELL, BRAYNE-WORME.

SAue you, gentlemen.
  STEP. Nay, we do' not stand much on our gentilitie, friend; yet, you are wel-come, and I assure you, mine vncle here is a man of a thousand a yeare, *Middlesex* land:

<small>1. i. 77 brauerie] brav'rie *F2*   80 vnsauorie] unsav'ry *F2*   83 then] than *F2*   87 aërie] ayrie *F2*   1 ii. 4 here] here, *some copies of F1*</small>

hee has but one sonne in all the world, I am his next heire
(at the common law) master S T E P H E N, as simple as I
stand here, if my cossen die (as there's hope he will) I haue
a prettie liuing o' mine owne too, beside, hard-by here.

S E R V. In good time, sir.

S T E P. In good time, sir? why! and in very good time,
sir. You doe not flout, friend, doe you?

S E R V. Not I, sir.

S T E P. Not you, sir? you were not best, sir; an' you
should, here bee them can perceiue it, and that quickly
to : goe to. And they can giue it againe soundly to, and
neede be.

S E R V. Why, sir, let this satisfie you : good faith, I had
no such intent.

S T E P. Sir, an' I thought you had, I would talke with
you, and that presently.

S E R V. Good master S T E P H E N, so you may, sir, at
your pleasure.

S T E P. And so I would sir, good my saucie companion!
an' you were out o' mine vncles ground, I can tell you;
though I doe not stand vpon my gentilitie neither in't.

K N O. Cossen! cossen! will this nere be left?

S T E P. Whorson base fellow! a mechanicall seruingman! By this cudgell, and't were not for shame, 1
would——

K N O. What would you doe, you peremptorie gull?
If you can not be quiet, get you hence.
You see, the honest man demeanes himselfe
Modestly to'ards you, giuing no replie
To your vnseason'd, quarrelling, rude fashion :
And, still you huffe it, with a kind of cariage,
As voide of wit, as of humanitie.
Goe, get you in ; fore heauen, I am asham'd
Thou hast a kinsmans interest in me.

1. ii. 7 cossen] cousen *F2*   will)] will.) *F2*   10 very] a very *some
copies of F1*   15 and] an' *F2*   26 Cossen ! cossen !] Cousin !
cousin ! *F2*   37 fore] 'fore *F2*

X 2

308 *Euery Man in his Humour*

S E R V. I pray you, sir. Is this master K N O'W E L L'S
40 house?
  K N O. Yes, marie, is it sir.
  S E R V. I should enquire for a gentleman, here, one
master E D W A R D K N O'W E L L : doe you know any
such, sir, I pray you?
45 K N O. I should forget my selfe else, sir.
  S E R V. Are you the gentleman? crie you mercie sir : I
was requir'd by a gentleman i' the citie, as I rode out at this
end o' the towne, to deliuer you this letter, sir.
  K N O. To me, sir! What doe you meane? pray you
50 remember your court'sie. (*To his most selected friend, master*
E D W A R D K N O'W E L L.) What might the gentlemans
name be, sir, that sent it? nay, pray you be couer'd.
  S E R V. One master W E L L-B R E D, sir.
  K N O. Master W E L L-B R E D! A yong gentleman?
55 is he not?
  S E R V. The same sir, master K I T E L Y married his
sister : the rich merchant i' the old *Iewrie*.
  K N O. You say very true. B R A I N E-W O R M E,
  B R A Y. Sir.
60 K N O. Make this honest friend drinke here : pray you
    goe in.
This letter is directed to my sonne :
Yet, I am E D W A R D K N O'W E L L too, and may
With the safe conscience of good manners, vse
The fellowes error to my satisfaction.
65 Well, I will breake it ope (old men are curious)
Be it but for the stiles sake, and the phrase,
To see, if both doe answere my sonnes praises,
Who is, almost, growne the idolater
Of this yong W E L L-B R E D : what haue we here? what's
    this?

The 70 *Why,* N E D, *I beseech thee ; hast thou for-sworne all thy*
letter.   *friends i' the old* Iewrie? *or dost thou think vs all* Iewes *that*

 1. ii. 39 you *om. F2*   54, 69 yong] young *F2*   64 error]
errour *F2*

*inhabit there, yet? If thou dost, come ouer, and but see our
fripperie: change an olde shirt, for a whole smocke, with vs.
Doe not conceiue that antipathy betweene vs, and* Hogs-den;
as was betweene Iewes, *and hogs-flesh. Leaue thy vigilant* 75
*father, alone, to number ouer his greene apricots, euening, and
morning, o' the north-west wall: An' J had beene his sonne, I
had sau'd him the labor, long since; if, taking in all the yong
wenches, that passe by, at the back-dore, and codd'ling euery
kernell of the fruit for 'hem, would ha' seru'd. But, pr'y thee,* 80
*come ouer to me, quickly, this morning: I haue such a present
for thee (our* Turkie *companie neuer sent the like to the* Grand-
Signior.) *One is a Rimer sir, o' your owne batch, your
owne leuin;. but doth think himselfe* Poet-maior, *o' the towne:
willing to be showne, and worthy to be seene. The other——I* 85
*will not venter his description with you, till you come, because
I would ha' you make hether with an appetite. If the worst of
'hem be not worth your iorney, draw your bill of charges, as
vnconscionable, as any Guild-hall verdict will giue it you,
and you shall be allow'd your viaticum.* 90
     From the wind-mill.
From the *Burdello,* it might come as well;
The *Spittle*: or *Pict-hatch.* Is this the man,
My sonne hath sung so, for the happiest wit,
The choysest braine, the times hath sent vs forth? 95
I know not what he may be, in the arts;
Nor what in schooles: but surely, for his manners,
I iudge him a prophane, and dissolute wretch:
Worse, by possession of such great good guifts,
Being the master of so loose a spirit. 100
Why, what vnhallow'd ruffian would haue writ,
In such a scurrilous manner, to a friend!
Why should he thinke, I tell my Apri-cotes?
Or play th' *Hesperian* Dragon, with my fruit,
To watch it? Well, my sonne, I'had thought 105
Y' had had more iudgement, t'haue made election

 1. ii. 72 *there, yet? If*] *there. Yet if* F3 78 *labor*] *labour* F2 83 *owne*] *owue* F1 87 *hether*] *hither* F2 95 hath] have F3 99 guifts] gifts F2 105 I'had] I had F3

Of your companions, then t'haue tane on trust,
Such petulant, geering gamsters, that can spare
No argument, or subiect from their iest.
110 But I perceiue, affection makes a foole
Of any man, too much the father. BRAYNE-WORME,
BRAY. Sir.
KNO. Is the fellow gone that brought this letter?
BRA. Yes, sir, a pretie while since.
115 KNO. And, where's your yong master?
BRA. In his chamber sir.
KNO. He spake not with the fellow! did he?
BRA. No sir, he saw him not.
KNO. Take you this letter, and deliuer it my sonne,
120 But with no notice, that I haue open'd it, on your life.
BRA. O lord, sir, that were a iest, indeed!
KNO. I am resolu'd, I will not stop his iourney;
Nor practise any violent meane, to stay
The vnbridled course of youth in him: for that,
125 Restrain'd, growes more impatient; and, in kind,
Like to the eager, but the generous grey-hound,
Who ne're so little from his game with-held,
Turnes head, and leapes vp at his holders throat.
There is a way of winning, more by loue,
130 And vrging of the modestie, then feare:
Force workes on seruile natures, not the free.
He, that's compell'd to goodnesse, may be good;
But 'tis but for that fit: where others drawne
By softnesse, and example, get a habit.
135 Then, if they stray, but warne 'hem: and, the same
They should for vertu' haue done, they'll doe for shame.

I. ii. 107 then *not originally in F1*: than *F2*   108 geering] jeering *F2*   111 BRAYNE-WORME,] BRAYN-WORM. *F2 (but cf.* 58).   119 sonne,] sonne *F1*: sonne ; *F2*   123 meane] means *F3*   125 in kind] in-kind *originally in F1*   130 then] than *F2*

Act 1. Scene III.

EDW. KNO'WELL, BRAYNE-WORME, Mr. STEPHEN.

Did he open it, sayest thou?
 BRAY. Yes, o' my word sir, and read the contents.
 E. KN. That scarse contents me. What countenance (pr'y thee) made he, i' the reading of it? was he angrie, or pleas'd? 5
 BRAY. Nay sir, I saw him not reade it, nor open it, I assure your worship.
 E. KN. No? how know'st thou, then, that he did either?
 BRAY. Marie sir, because he charg'd me, on my life, to tell nobodie, that he open'd it: which, vnlesse hee had done, 10 hee would neuer feare to haue it reueal'd.
 E. KN. That's true: well I thanke thee, BRAYNE-WORME.
 STEP. O, BRAYNE-WORME, did'st thou not see a fellow here in a what-sha'-call-him doublet! he brought 15 mine vncle a letter e'en now.
 BRAY. Yes, master STEPHEN, what of him?
 STEP. O, I ha' such a minde to beate him—— Where is hee? canst thou tell?
 BRAY. Faith, he is not of that mind: he is gone, master 20 STEPHEN.
 STEP. Gone? which way? when went he? how long since?
 BRAY. He is rid hence. He tooke horse, at the streete dore. 25
 STEP. And, I staid i' the fields! horson *scander-bag* rogue! ô that I had but a horse to fetch him backe againe.
 BRAY. Why, you may ha' my m^{rs}. gelding, to saue your longing, sir.

I. iii.] *Misnumbered* Scene II *in F1*   Scene II.—A Room in Knowell's House. *G.*   12 BRAYNE-WORME] BLAYNE-WORME *F1*   16 letter] lettler *some copies of F1*   22 he?] he! *Ff*

30   S T E P. But, I ha' no bootes, that's the spight on't.

B R A Y. Why, a fine wispe of hay, rould hard, master S T E P H E N.

S T E P. No faith, it's no boote to follow him, now : let him eene goe, and hang. 'Pray thee, helpe to trusse me,
35 a little. He dos so vexe me——

B R A Y. You'll be worse vex'd, when you are truss'd, master S T E P H E N. Best, keepe vn-brac'd ; and walke your selfe, till you be cold : your choller may foundre you else.

40   S T E P. By my faith, and so I will, now thou tell'st me on't : How dost thou like my legge, B R A Y N E-W O R M E ?

B R A Y. A very good leg ! master S T E P H E N ! but the woollen stocking do's not commend it so well.

S T E P. Foh, the stockings be good inough, now summer
45 is comming on, for the dust : Ile haue a paire of silke, again' winter, that I goe to dwell i' the towne. I thinke my legge would shew in a silke-hose.

B R A Y. Beleeue me, master S T E P H E N, rarely well.

S T E P. In sadnesse, I thinke it would : I haue a reason-
50 able good legge.

B R A Y. You haue an excellent good legge, master S T E P H E N, but I cannot stay, to praise it longer now, and I am very sorie for't.

S T E P. Another time wil serue, B R A Y N E-W O R M E.
55 Gramercie for this.

Kno'well laughes hauing read the letter.

E. K N. Ha, ha, ha !

S T E P. Slid, I hope, he laughes not at me, and he doe——

E. K N. Here was a letter, indeede, to be intercepted by a mans father, and doe him good with him ! Hee cannot but
60 thinke most vertuously, both of me, and the sender, sure ; that make the carefull Costar'-monger of him in our *familiar Epistles.* Well, if he read this with patience, Ile be gelt, and troll ballads for M^r. I O H N T R V N D L E, yonder, the rest of my

---

    I. iii. 34 'Pray thee] Pr'y thee *F2*   47 silke-hose.] silke-hose—— *F2*
    48 B R A Y.] B R A P. *F1*   well.] well, *Ff*   56 stage dir. *Kno'well F2* : *Knowell F1*   laughes] *laught F3*   '62 be gelt *F2* : be-gelt *F1*

mortalítie. It is true, and likely, my father may haue as much patience as another man; for he takes much physicke: 65 and, oft taking physicke makes a man very patient. But would your packet, master W E L-B R E D, had arriu'd at him, in such a minute of his patience ; then, we had knowne the end of it, which now is doubtfull, and threatens—— What! my wise cossen! Nay, then, Ile furnish our feast 70 with one gull more to'ard the messe. He writes to me of a brace, and here's one, that's three : O, for a fourth; Fortune, if euer thou'lt vse thine eyes, I intreate thee——

S T E P. O, now I see, who hee laught at. Hee laught at 75 some-body in that letter. By this good light, and he had laught at me——

E. K N. How now, coussen S T E P H E N, melancholy'?

S T E P. Yes, a little. I thought, you had laught at me, cossen. 80

E. K N. Why, what an' I had cousse, what would you ha' done?

S T E P. By this light, I would ha' told mine vncle.

E. K N. Nay, if you wold ha' told your vncle, I did laugh at you, cousse. 85

S T E P. Did you, indeede?

E. K N. Yes, indeede.

S T E P. Why, then——

E. K N. What then?

S T E P. I am satisfied, it is sufficient. 90

E. K N. Why, bee so gentle cousse. And, I pray you let me intreate a courtesie of you. I am sent for, this morning, by a friend i' the old *Iewrie* to come to him ; It's but crossing ouer the fields to *More-gate*: Will you beare me companie? I protest, it is not to draw you into bond, or any 95 plot against the state, cousse.

S T E P. Sir, that's all one, and 't were : you shall com-

1. iii. 70 cossen] cousen *F2*   Ile furnish] Ilefurnish *F1*   76 and] an' *F2*   78 melancholy'] melancholy *F2* (cf. III. i. 100).   81 cousse,] cousse ? *F2*   83, 86 STEP. *F2* : SERV. *F1*   91 so] so, *F2* 93 *Iewrie*] *Iewrie,* F2   94 *More-gate*] *Moore-gate* F2

mand me, twise so farre as *More-gate* to doe you good, in such a matter. Doe you thinke I would leaue you ? I pro-
100 test——

E. K N. No, no, you shall not protest, cousse.

S T E P. By my fackins, but I will, by your leaue ; Ile protest more to my friend, then Ile speake off, at this time.

E. K N. You speake very well, cousse.

105 S T E P. Nay, not so neither, you shall pardon me : but I speake, to serue my turne.

E. K N. Your turne, couss ? Doe you know, what you say ? A gentleman of your sort, parts, carriage, and estimation, to talke o' your turne i' this companie, and to me,
110 alone, like a tankard-bearer, at a conduit ! Fie. A wight, that (hetherto) his euery step hath left the stampe of a great foot behind him, as euery word the sauour of a strong spirit ! and he ! this man ! so grac'd, guilded, or (to vse a more fit *metaphore*) so tin-foild by nature, as not ten house-wiues
115 pewter (again' a good time) shew's more bright to the world then he ! and he (as I said last, so I say againe, and still shall say it) this man ! to conceale such reall ornaments as these, and shaddow their glorie, as a Millaners wife do's her wrought stomacher, with a smokie lawne, or a black
120 cypresse ? O couss ! It cannot be answer'd, goe not about it. D R A K E S old ship, at *Detford*, may sooner circle the world againe. Come, wrong not the qualitie of your desert, with looking downeward, couz ; but hold vp your head, so : and let the *Idea* of what you are, be pourtray'd i' your face,
125 that men may reade i' your physnomie, (*Here, within this place, is to be seene the true, rare, and accomplish'd monster, or miracle of nature,* which is all one.) What thinke you of this, couss ?

S T E P. Why, I doe thinke of it ; and I will be more
130 prowd, and melancholy, and gentleman-like, then I haue beene : I'le ensure you.

E. K N. Why, that's resolute master S T E P H E N ! Now,

<small>1. iii. 98 *More-gate*] Moore-gate F2   103 then] than F2   111 hetherto] hitherto F2   130 then] than F2   131 beene :] been ; F2</small>

if I can but hold him vp to his height, as it is happily begunne, it will doe well for a suburbe-humor : we may hap haue a match with the citie, and play him for fortie pound. 135 Come, couss.

   S T E P. I'le follow you.

   E. K N. Follow me ? you must goe before.

   S T E P. Nay, an' I must, I will. Pray you, shew me, good cousin.   140

Act 1. Scene 1111.

M*r*. M A T T H E W, C O B.

I Thinke, this be the house : what, hough ?

   C O B. Who's there ? O, master M A T T H E W! gi' your worship good morrow.

   M A T. What! C O B! how do'st thou, good C O B? do'st thou inhabite here, C O B ?   5

   C O B. I, sir, I and my linage ha' kept a poore house, here, in our dayes.

   M A T. Thy linage, *Monsieur* C O B, what linage ? what linage ?

   C O B. Why sir, an ancient linage, and a princely. Mine 10 ance'trie came from a Kings belly, no worse man : and yet no man neither (by your worships leaue, I did lie in that) but *Herring* the King of fish (from his belly, I proceed) one o' the Monarchs o' the world, I assure you. The first red herring, that was broil'd in A D A M, and E V E 's kitchin, 15 doe I fetch my pedigree from, by the Harrots bookes. His C O B, was my great-great-mighty-great Grand-father.

   M A T. Why mightie ? why mightie ? I pray thee.

   C O B. O, it was a mightie while agoe, sir, and a mightie great C O B.   20

   M A T. How know'st thou that ?

   C O B. How know I ? why, I smell his ghost, euer and anon.

   1. iii. 134 suburbe-humor] Suburb-humour *F2*   1. iv.] Scene III.— The Lane before Cob's House. *G*

M A T. Smell a ghost? ô vnsauoury iest! and the
ghost of a herring C o b!

C o b. I sir, with fauour of your worships nose, M^r.
M a t h e w, why not the ghost of a herring-cob, as well
as the ghost of rasher-bacon?

M a t. R o g e r B a c o n, thou wouldst say?

C o b. I say rasher-bacon. They were both broyl'd o' the
coles? and a man may smell broyld-meate, I hope? you
are a scholler, vpsolue me that, now.

M a t. O raw ignorance! C o b, canst thou shew me
of a gentleman, one Captayne B o b a d i l l, where his
lodging is?

C o b. O, my guest, sir! you meane.

M a t. Thy guest! Alas! ha, ha.

C o b. Why doe you laugh, sir? Doe you not meane
Captayne B o b a d i l l?

M a t. C o b, 'pray thee, aduise thyselfe well: doe not
wrong the gentleman, and thy selfe too. I dare bee sworne,
hee scornes thy house: hee! He lodge in such a base,
obscure place, as thy house! Tut, I know his disposition
so well, he would not lye in thy bed, if tho'uldst gi'it
him.

C o b. I will not giue it him, though, sir. Masse, I thought
somewhat was in't, we could not get him to bed, all night!
Well, sir, though he lye not o' my bed, he lies o' my bench:
an't please you to goe vp, sir, you shall find him with two
cushions vnder his head, and his cloke wrapt about him,
as though he had neither wun nor lost, and yet (I warrant)
he ne're cast better in his life, then he has done, to night.

M a t. Why? was he drunke?

C o b. Drunke, sir? you heare not me say so. Perhaps,
hee swallow'd a tauerne-token, or some such deuice, sir:
I haue nothing to doe withall. I deale with water, and not
with wine. Gi'me my tankard there, hough. God b'w'you,
sir. It's sixe a clocke: I should ha' carried two turnes, by
this. What hough? my stopple? come.

    I. iv. 31 coles?] coles; *F2*   52 then] than *F2*

MAT. Lye in a water-bearers house! A gentleman of his
hauings! Well, I'le tell him my mind.
   COB. What TIB, shew this gentleman vp to the
Captayne. O, an' my house were the *Brasen-head* now!
faith, it would eene speake, *Mo fooles yet*. You should ha'
some now would take this M^r. MATTHEW to be a gentleman, at the least. His father's an honest man, a worshipfull fish-monger, and so forth; and now dos he creepe, and
wriggle into acquaintance with all the braue gallants about
the towne, such as my guest is: (ô, my guest is a fine man).
and they flout him invincibly. Hee vseth euery day to
a Merchants house (where I serue water) one master
KITELY'S, i' the *old Iewry*; and here's the iest, he is
in loue with my masters sister, (mistris BRIDGET)
and calls her mistris: and there hee will sit you a whole
after-noone some-times, reading o' these same abominable,
vile, (a poxe on 'hem, I cannot abide them) rascally verses,
poyetrie, poyetrie, and speaking of *enterludes*, 'twill make a
man burst to heare him. And the wenches, they doe so
geere, and ti-he at him—well, should they do so much to me,
Ild for-sweare them all, by the foot of PHARAOH.
There's an oath! How many water-bearers shall you heare
sweare such an oath? ô, I haue a guest (he teaches me) he
dos sweare the legiblest, of any man christned: By S^t.
GEORGE, the foot of PHARAOH, the body of me, as
I am ⟨a⟩ gentleman, and a souldier: such daintie oathes!
and withall, he dos take this same filthy roguish *tobacco*,
the finest, and cleanliest! it would doe a man good to see
the fume come forth at's tonnells! Well, he owes mee fortie
shillings (my wife lent him out of her purse, by sixe-pence
a time) besides his lodging: I would I had it. I shall ha'it,
he saies, the next *Action*. *Helter skelter*, hang sorrow, care 'll
kill a cat, vp-tailes all, and a louse for the hang-man.

Act 1. Scene v.

BOBADILL, TIB, MATTHEW.

Bobad. is discouered lying on his bench.

Bob. Hostesse, hostesse.

Tib. What say you, sir?

Bob. A cup o' thy small beere, sweet hostesse.

Tib. Sir, there's a gentleman, below, would speake with you.

Bob. A gentleman! 'ods so, I am not within.

Tib. My husband told him you were, sir.

Bob. What a plague——what meant he?

Mat. Captaine BOBADILL?

Bob. Who's there? (take away the bason, good hostesse) come vp, sir.

Tib. He would desire you to come vp, sir. You come into a cleanly house, here.

Mat. 'Saue you, sir. 'Saue you, Captayne.

Bob. Gentle master MATTHEW! Is it you, sir? Please you sit downe.

Mat. Thanke you, good Captaine, you may see, I am some-what audacious.

Bob. Not so, sir. I was requested to supper, last night, by a sort of gallants, where you were wish'd for, and drunke to, I assure you.

Mat. Vouchsafe me, by whom, good Captaine.

Bob. Mary, by yong WELL-BRED, and others: Why, hostesse, a stoole here, for this gentleman.

Mat. No haste, sir, 'tis very well.

Bob. Body of me! It was so late ere we parted last night, I can scarse open my eyes, yet; I was but new risen, as you came: how passes the day abroad, sir? you can tell.

Mat. Faith, some halfe houre to seuen: now trust mee, you haue an exceeding fine lodging here, very neat, and priuate!

---

1 v.] Scene iv.—A Room in Cob's House. *G.*   16. sit] to sit *F2*
downe.] down? *F2*   17 MAT.] MAR. *F1*

Bob. I, sir: sit downe, I pray you. Master MAT-
THEW (in any case) possesse no gentlemen of our acquaintance, with notice of my lodging.

Mat. Who? I sir? no.

Bob. Not that I need to care who know it, for the
Cabbin is conuenient, but in regard I would not be too popular, and generally visited, as some are.

Mat. True, Captaine, I conceiue you.

Bob. For, doe you see, sir, by the heart of valour, in
me, (except it be to some peculiar and choice spirits, to
whom I am extraordinarily ingag'd, as your selfe, or so) I
could not extend thus farre.

Mat. O Lord, sir, I resolue so.

Bob. I confesse, I loue a cleanely and quiet priuacy,
aboue all the tumult, and roare of fortune. What new
booke ha' you there? What! *Goe by,* HIERONYMO!

Mat. I, did you euer see it acted? is't not well
pend?

Bob. Well pend? I would faine see all the *Poets,* of
these times, pen such another play as that was! they'll
prate and swagger, and keepe a stir of arte and deuices, when
(as I am a gentleman) reade 'hem, they are the most shallow,
pittifull, barren fellowes, that liue vpon the face of the earth,
againe!

Mat. Indeed, here are a number of fine speeches in this
booke! *O eyes, no eyes, but fountaynes fraught with teares!*
There's a conceit! fountaines fraught with teares! *O life,
no life, but liuely forme of death!* Another! *O world, no
world, but masse of publique wrongs!* A third! *Confus'd and
fil'd with murder, and misdeeds!* A fourth! O, the *Muses!*
Is't not excellent? Is't not simply the best that euer you
heard, Captayne? Ha? How doe you like it?

Bob. 'Tis good.

Mat. *To thee, the purest obiect to my sense,
The most refined essence heauen couers,
Send I these lines, wherein I doe commence
The happy state of turtle-billing louers.*

If they proue rough, vn-polish't, harsh, and rude,
Hast made the wast. Thus, mildly, I conclude.

Bobadill is making him ready all this while.

B o b. Nay, proceed, proceed. Where's this?

M a t. This, sir? a toy o' mine owne, in my nonage: the infancy of my *Muses*! But, when will you come and see my studie? good faith, I can shew you some very good things, I haue done of late——That boot becomes your legge, passing well, Captayne, me thinkes!

B o b. So, so, It's the fashion, gentlemen now vse.

M a t. Troth, Captayne, an' now you speake o' the fashion, master W e l l-b r e d 's elder brother, and I, are fall'n out exceedingly: this other day, I hapned to enter into some discourse of a hanger, which I assure you, both for fashion, and worke-man-ship, was most peremptory-beautifull, and gentlemanlike! Yet, he condemn'd, and cry'd it downe, for the most pyed, and ridiculous that euer he saw.

B o b. Squire D o w n e-r i g h t? the halfe brother? was't not?

M a t. I sir, he.

B o b. Hang him, rooke, he! why, he has no more iudgement then a malt-horse. By S. G e o r g e, I wonder you'ld loose a thought vpon such an animal: the most peremptory absurd clowne of *christendome*, this day, he is holden. I protest to you, as I am a gentleman, and a souldier, I ne're chang'd wordes, with his like. By his discourse, he should eate nothing but hay. He was borne for the manger, pannier, or pack-saddle! He ha's not so much as a good phrase in his belly, but all old iron, and rustie prouerbes! a good commoditie for some smith, to make hob-nailes of.

M a t. I, and he thinks to carry it away with his manhood still, where he comes. He brags he will gi' me the *bastinado*, as I heare.

B o b. How! He the *bastinado*! how came he by that word, trow?

1. v. 78 an'] and *F2*   88 has] ha's *F2*   89 then] than *F2*
90 you'ld] you'l'd *F1*   loose] lose *F2*   95 ha's] has *F2*

MAT. Nay, indeed, he said cudgell me; I term'd it so, for my more grace.

BOB. That may bee: For I was sure, it was none of his word. But, when? when said he so?

MAT. Faith, yesterday, they say: a young gallant, a friend of mine told me so.

BOB. By the foot of PHARAOH, and't were my case now, I should send him a *chartel*, presently. The *bastinado*! A most proper, and sufficient *dependance*, warranted by the great CARANZA. Come hither. You shall *chartel* him. I'll shew you a trick, or two, you shall kill him with, at pleasure: the first *stoccata*, if you will, by this ayre.

MAT. Indeed, you haue absolute knowledge i' the mysterie, I haue heard, sir.

BOB. Of whom? Of whom ha' you heard it, I beseech you?

MAT. Troth, I haue heard it spoken of diuers, that you haue very rare, and vn-in-one-breath-vtter-able skill, sir.

BOB. By heauen, no, not I; no skill i' the earth: some small rudiments i' the science, as to know my time, distance, or so. I haue profest it more for noblemen, and gentlemens vse, then mine owne practise, I assure you. Hostesse, accommodate vs with another bed-staffe here, quickly: Lend vs another bed-staffe. The woman do's not vnderstand the wordes of *Action*. Looke you, sir. Exalt not your point aboue this state, at any hand, and let your poynard maintayne your defence, thus: (giue it the gentleman, and leaue vs) so, sir. Come on: O, twine your body more about, that you may fall to a more sweet comely gentleman-like guard. So, indifferent. Hollow your body more sir, thus. Now, stand fast o' your left leg, note your distance, keepe your due proportion of time——Oh, you disorder your point, most irregularly!

MAT. How is the bearing of it, now, sir?

BOB. O, out of measure ill! A well-experienc'd hand would passe vpon you, at pleasure.

I. v. 125 then] than *F2*   132 sweet comely] sweet, comely, *F2*

140 M a t. How meane you, sir, passe vpon me?
   B o b. Why, thus sir (make a thrust at me) come in, vpon the answere, controll your point, and make a full carreere, at the body. The best-practis'd gallants of the time, name it the *passada* : a most desperate thrust, beleeue it!
145 M a t. Well, come, sir.
   B o b. Why, you doe not manage your weapon with any facilitie, or grace to inuite mee : I haue no spirit to play with you. Your dearth of iudgement renders you tedious.
   M a t. But one *venue*, sir.
150 B o b. *Venue!* Fie. Most grosse denomination, as euer I heard. O, the *stoccata*, while you liue, sir. Note that. Come, put on your cloke, and wee'll goe to some priuate place, where you are acquainted, some tauerne, or so—— and haue a bit——Ile send for one of these Fencers, and hee
155 shall breath you, by my direction ; and, then, I will teach you your tricke. You shall kill him with it, at the first, if you please. Why, I will learne you, by the true iudgement of the eye, hand, and foot, to controll any enemies point i the world. Should your aduersarie confront you with
160 a pistoll, 'twere nothing, by this hand, you should, by the same rule, controll his bullet, in a line : except it were hayle-shot, and spred. What money ha' you about you M^r. M a t t h e w?
   M a t. Faith, I ha' not past a two shillings, or so.
165 B o b. 'Tis somewhat with the least: but, come. W will haue a bunch of redish, and salt, to tast our wine and a pipe of *tobacco*, to close the orifice of the stomach and then, wee'll call vpon yong W e l-b r e d. Perhap wee shall meet the C o r i d o n, his brother, there : an
170 put him to the question.

    i. v. 160 hand,] hand ; *F2*   166 redish] radish *F2*

Act II. Scene I.

Kitely, Cash, Downe-right.

Thomas, Come hither,
There lyes a note, within vpon my deske,
Here, take my key: It is no matter, neither.
Where is the Boy? Cas. Within, sir, i' the ware-house.
    Kit. Let him tell ouer, straight, that *Spanish* gold,   5
And weigh it, with th' pieces of eight. Doe you
See the deliuery of those siluer stuffes,
To Mr. Lvcar. Tell him, if he will,
He shall ha' the grogran's, at the rate I told him,
And I will meet him, on the *Exchange*, anon.   10
    Cas. Good, sir.
    Kit. Doe you see that fellow, brother Downe-right?
    Dow. I, what of him?
    Kit. He is a iewell, brother.   15
I tooke him of a child, vp, at my dore,
And christned him, gaue him mine owne name, Thomas,
Since bred him at the Hospitall; where prouing
A toward impe, I call'd him home, and taught him
So much, as I haue made him my Cashier,   20
And giu'n him, who had none, a surname, Cash:
And find him, in his place so full of faith,
That, I durst trust my life into his hands.
    Dow. So, would not I in any bastards, brother,
As, it is like, he is: although I knew   25
My selfe his father. But you said yo' had somewhat
To tell me, gentle brother, what is't? what is't?
    Kit. Faith, I am very loath, to vtter it,
As fearing, it may hurt your patience:

II. i. *Misnumbered* Scene II *in most copies of F2* Scene I.—The Old Jewry. A Hall in Kiteley's House. *G*   1 hither,] hither. *F2*   4 i' the] i'th *F3*   ware-house.] ware-house, *F2*   6 th'] the *F2* (cf. III. iii. 42)   17 owne] one *F2*

30 But, that I know, your iudgement is of strength,
   Against the neerenesse of affection——
      D o w. What need this circumstance ? pray you be
   direct.
      K i t. I will not say, how much I doe ascribe
35 Vnto your friendship ; nor, in what regard
   I hold your loue : but, let my past behauiour,
   And vsage of your sister, but confirme
   How well I'aue beene affected to your——
      D o w. You are too tedious, come to the matter, the
40 matter.
      K i t. Then (without further ceremonie) thus.
   My brother W e l l-b r e d, sir, (I know not how)
   Of late, is much declin'd in what he was,
   And greatly alter'd in his disposition.
45 When he came first to lodge here in my house,
   Ne're trust me, if I were not proud of him :
   Me thought he bare himselfe in such a fashion,
   So full of man, and sweetnesse in his carriage,
   And (what was chiefe) it shew'd not borrowed in him,
50 But all he did, became him as his owne,
   And seem'd as perfect, proper, and possest
   As breath, with life, or colour, with the bloud.
   But, now, his course is so irregular,
   So loose, affected, and depriu'd of grace,
55 And he himselfe withall so farre falne off
   From that first place, as scarse no note remaines,
   To tell mens iudgements where he lately stood.
   Hee's growne a stranger to all due respect,
   Forgetfull of his friends, and not content
60 To stale himselfe in all societies,
   He makes my house here common, as a *Mart*,
   A *Theater*, a publike receptacle
   For giddie humour, and diseased riot ;
   And here (as in a tauerne, or a stewes)

   II. i. 37 but] both *G*   49 borrowed *Ff*. *Read perhaps* borrow'd
   52 life,] life; *F2*

He, and his wild associates, spend their houres, 65
In repetition of lasciuious iests,
Sweare, leape, drinke, dance, and reuell night by night,
Controll my seruants : and indeed what not ?

  D o w. 'Sdeynes, I know not what I should say to him,
i' the whole world ! He values me, at a crackt three- 70
farthings, for ought I see : It will neuer out o' the flesh
that's bred i' the bone ! I haue told him inough, one would
thinke, if that would serue : But, counsell to him, is as good,
as a shoulder of mutton to a sicke horse. Well ! he knowes
what to trust to, for G E O R G E. Let him spend, and spend, 75
and domineere, till his heart ake ; an' hee thinke to bee
relieu'd by me, when he is got into one o' your citie pounds,
the Counters, he has the wrong sow by the eare, ifaith : and
claps his dish at the wrong mans dore. I'le lay my hand
o' my halfe-peny, e're I part with 't, to fetch him out, I'le 80
assure him.

  K I T. Nay, good brother, let it not trouble you, thus.

  D o w. 'Sdeath, he mads me, I could eate my very spur-
lethers, for anger ! But, why are you so tame ? Why doe
you not speake to him, and tell him how he disquiets your 85
house ?

  K I T. O, there are diuers reasons to disswade, brother.
But, would your selfe vouchsafe to trauaile in it,
Though but with plaine, and easie circumstance)
It would, both come much better to his sense, 90
And sauour lesse of stomack, or of passion.
You are his elder brother, and that title
Both giues, and warrants you authoritie ;
Which (by your presence seconded) must breed
A kinde of dutie in him, and regard : 95
Whereas, if I should intimate the least,
It would but adde contempt, to his neglect,
Heape worse on ill, make vp a pile of hatred
That, in the rearing, would come tottring downe,

  II. i. 77 citie pounds] City-pounds *F2*   87 brother] me *G (from Q)*
  8 trauaile] travell *F2*   93 you] your *F2*

100 And, in the ruine, burie all our loue.
   Nay, more then this, brother, if I should speake
   He would be readie from his heate of humor,
   And ouer-flowing of the vapour, in him,
   To blow the eares of his familiars,
105 With the false breath, of telling, what disgraces,
   And low disparadgments, I had put vpon him.
   Whilst they, sir, to relieue him, in the fable,
   Make their loose comments, vpon euery word,
   Gesture, or looke, I vse ; mocke me all ouer,
110 From my flat cap, vnto my shining shooes :
   And, out of their impetuous rioting phant'sies,
   Beget some slander, that shall dwell with me.
   And what would that be, thinke you ? mary, this.
   They would giue out (because my wife is faire,
115 My selfe but lately married, and my sister
   Here soiourning a virgin in my house)
   That I were iealous ! nay, as sure as death,
   That they would say. And how that I had quarrell'd
   My brother purposely, thereby to finde
120 An apt pretext, to banish them my house.
       D o w. Masse perhaps so : They'are like inough to doe it.
       K i t. Brother, they would, beleeue it : so should I
   (Like one of these penurious quack-saluers)
   But set the bills vp, to mine owne disgrace,
125 And trie experiments vpon my selfe :
   Lend scorne and enuie, oportunitie,
   To stab my reputation, and good name——

  II. i. 101 then] than *F2* speake] speake, *F2* 102 humor] humour *F2* 113 this.] this : *F2* 121 They'are] They're *F2* 126 oportunitie] opportunitie *F2*

Act II. Scene II.

MATTHEW, BOBADIL, DOWNE-RIGHT, KITELY.

I Will speake to him——
    B O B. Speake to him ? away, by the foot of PHARAOH, you shall not, you shall not doe him that grace. The time of day, to you, Gentleman o' the house. Is M^r. WELL-BRED stirring ?   5
    D o w. How then ? what should he doe ?
    B O B. Gentleman of the house, it is to you : is he within, sir ?
    K I T. He came not to his lodging to night sir, I assure you.
    D o w. Why, doe you heare ? you.   10
    B O B. The gentleman-citizen hath satisfied mee, Ile talke to no scauenger.
    D o w. How, scauenger ? stay sir, stay ?
    K I T. Nay, brother DOWNE-RIGHT.
    D o w. 'Heart ! stand you away, and you loue me.   15
    K I T. You shall not follow him now, I pray you, brother, Good faith you shall not : I will ouer-rule you.
    D o w. Ha ? scauenger ? well, goe to, I say little : but, by this good day (god forgiue me I should sweare) if I put it vp so, say, I am the rankest cow, that euer pist. 'Sdeynes, 20 and I swallow this, Ile ne're draw my sword in the sight of *Fleet-street* againe, while I liue ; Ile sit in a barne, with Madge-howlet, and catch mice first. Scauenger ? 'Heart, and Ile goe neere to fill that huge tumbrell-slop of yours, with somewhat, and I haue good lucke : your GARA- 25 GANTVA breech cannot carry it away so.
    K I T. Oh doe not fret your selfe thus, neuer thinke on't.
    D o w. These are my brothers consorts, these ! these are his *Cam'rades*, his walking mates ! hee's a gallant, a *Caualiero* too, right hang-man cut ! Let me not liue, and I could 30

II. ii. 13 Sir, stay ?] Sir, stay. *F2*   19 god] God *F2*   21, 25, 30 and] an *corrected copies of F2*

not finde in my heart to swinge the whole ging of' hem, one
after another, and begin with him first. I am grieu'd, it
should be said he is my brother, and take these courses.
Wel, as he brewes, so he shall drinke, for G E O R G E, againe.
35 Yet, he shall heare on't, and that tightly too, and I liue,
Ifaith.
  K I T. But, brother, let your reprehension (then)
Runne in an easie current, not ore-high
Carried with rashnesse, or deuouring choller ;
40 But rather vse the soft perswading way,
Whose powers will worke more gently, and compose
Th'imperfect thoughts you labour to reclaime :
More winning, then enforcing the consent.
  D O W. I, I, let me alone for that, I warrant you.

Bell rings. K I T. How now ? oh, the bell rings to breakefast.
46 Brother, I pray you goe in, and beare my wife
Companie, till I come ; Ile but giue order
For some dispatch of businesse, to my seruants———

Act II. *Scene* III.

[*To them.*] K I T E L Y, C O B, D A M E K I T E L Y.

  WHat, C O B ? our maides will haue you by the back
   (Ifaith) for comming so late this morning.
  C O B. Perhaps so, sir, take heed some body haue not them
He passes by the belly, for walking so late in the euening.
by with
his K I T. Well, yet my troubled spirit's somewhat eas'd,
tankard. Though not repos'd in that securitie,
As I could wish : But, I must be content.
How e're I set a face on't to the world,
Would I had lost this finger, at a venter,
10 So W E L L-B R E D had ne're lodg'd within my house.

  II. ii. 31 ging] gang *F3* 34 he brewes] hee brews *corrected copies of*
F2 so he shall *F1* : so shall he *F2* 43 then] than *F2* II. iii.
BRIDGET *is added by Dr. G. A. Smithson, but she need not enter at* 34.
2 Ifaith] ifaith *F2* for] For *Ff, beginning a new line* 7 content.]
content, *G* 8 world,] world. *G* 9 venter] venture *F3*

Why't cannot be, where there is such resort
Of wanton gallants, and yong reuellers,
That any woman should be honest long.
Is't like, that factious beautie will preserue
The publike weale of chastitie, vn-shaken,   15
When such strong motiues muster, and make head
Against her single peace ? no, no. Beware,
When mutuall appetite doth meet to treat,
And spirits of one kinde, and qualitie,
Come once to parlee, in the pride of bloud :   20
It is no slow conspiracie, that followes.
Well (to be plaine) if I but thought, the time
Had answer'd their affections : all the world
Should not perswade me, but I were a cuckold.
Mary, I hope, they ha'not got that start :   25
For oportunitie hath balkt 'hem yet,
And shall doe still, while I haue eyes, and eares
To attend the impositions of my heart.
My presence shall be as an iron barre,
'Twixt the conspiring motions of desire :   30
Yea, euery looke, or glance, mine eye eiects,
Shall checke occasion, as one doth his slaue,
When he forgets the limits of prescription.

    D A M E. Sister B R I D G E T, pray you fetch downe the rose-water aboue in the closet. Sweet heart, will you come 35 in, to breakefast ?

    K I T E. An' shee haue ouer-heard me now ?

    D A M E. I pray thee (good M v s s e) we stay for you.

    K I T E. By heauen I would not for a thousand angells.

    D A M E. What aile you sweet heart, are you not well, 40 speake good M v s s E.

    K I T E. Troth my head akes extremely, on a sudden.

    D A M E. Oh, the lord !

    K I T E. How now ? what ?

    II. iii. 12 yong] young *F2*   14 Is't *F2* : I st *F1*   20 bloud *F2* : bluod *F1*   26 oportunitie] opportunitie *F2*   36 breakefast ?] breakefast. *F1* : break-fast. *F2*   40 sweet heart,] Sweet-heart ? *F2* well,] well ? *F2*   43 lord] Lord *F2*

DAME. Alas, how it burnes? MVSSE, keepe you warme, good truth it is this new disease! there's a number are troubled withall! for loues sake, sweet heart, come in, out of the aire.

KITE. How simple, and how subtill are her answeres? A new disease, and many troubled with it! Why, true: shee heard me, all the world to nothing.

DAME. I pray thee, good sweet heart, come in; the aire will doe you harme, in troth.

KITE. The aire! shee has me i' the wind! sweet heart! Ile come to you presently: 't will away, I hope.

DAME. Pray heauen it doe.

KITE. A new disease? I know not, new, or old,
But it may well be call'd poore mortalls plague:
For, like a pestilence, it doth infect
The houses of the braine. First, it begins
Solely to worke vpon the phantasie,
Filling her seat with such pestiferous aire,
As soone corrupts the iudgement; and from thence
Sends like contagion to the memorie:
Still each to other giuing the infection.
Which, as a subtle vapor, spreads it selfe,
Confusedly, through euery sensiue part,
Till not a thought, or motion, in the mind,
Be free from the blacke poyson of suspect.
Ah, but what miserie' is it, to know this?
Or, knowing it, to want the mindes erection,
In such extremes? Well, I will once more striue,
(In spight of this black cloud) my selfe to be,
And shake the feauer off, that thus shakes me.

II. iii. 53 harme, in *F2*: harme in, *F1*   56 DAME. *F2*: Dow. *F1*
66 vapor] vapour *F2*   70 miserie' is] mis'rie is *F2*

Act II. Scene IIII.

BRAYNE-WORME, ED. KNO'WELL,
Mr. STEPHEN.

'Lid, I cannot choose but laugh, to see my selfe translated thus, from a poore creature to a creator; for now must I create an intolerable sort of lyes, or my present profession looses the grace: and yet the lye to a man of my coat, is as ominous a fruit, as the *Fico*. O sir, it holds for 5 good politie euer, to haue that outwardly in vilest estimation, that inwardly is most deare to vs. So much, for my borrowed shape. Well, the troth is, my old master intends to follow my yong, drie foot, ouer *More-fields*, to *London*, this morning: now I, knowing, of this hunting-match, or 10 rather conspiracie, and to insinuate with my yong master (for so must we that are blew-waiters, and men of hope and seruice doe, or perhaps wee may weare motley at the yeeres end, and who weares motley, you know) haue got me afore, in this disguise, determining here to lye in 15 *ambuscado*, and intercept him, in the mid-way. If I can but get his cloke, his purse, his hat, nay, any thing, to cut him off, that is, to stay his iourney, *Veni, vidi, vici*, I may say with Captayne CAESAR, I am made for euer, ifaith. Well, now must I practice to get the true garb of one of 20 these *Lance-knights*, my arme here, and my—yong master! and his cousin, Mr. STEPHEN, as I am true counterfeit man of warre, and no souldier!

E. KN. So sir, and how then, couss?

STEP. 'Sfoot, I haue lost my purse, I thinke. 25

E. KN. How? lost your purse? where? when had you it?

STEP. I cannot tell, stay.

BRAY. 'Slid, I am afeard, they will know mee, would I could get by them, 30

II. iv.] Scene II.—Moorfields. G.   4 looses] loses *F2*   9, 11 yong] young *F2*   9 *More-fields*] Moore Fields, *F2*   10 knowing,] knowing *F2*   18 vici,] vici; *F2*   21 my - - yong *F1* : my - - young *F2*

E. K N. What ? ha' you it ?

S T E P. No, I thinke I was bewitcht, I———

E. K N. Nay, doe not weepe the losse, hang it, let it goe.

S T E P. Oh, it's here : no, and it had beene lost, I had not car'd, but for a iet ring mistris M A R Y sent me.

E. K N. A iet ring ? oh, the *poesie*, the *poesie* ?

S T E P. Fine, ifaith ! *Though fancie sleep, my loue is deepe.* Meaning that though I did not fancie her, yet shee loued me dearely.

E. K N. Most excellent !

STEP. And then, I sent her another, and my *poesie* was : *The deeper, the sweeter, Ile be iudg'd by* S^t. P E T E R.

E. K N. How, by S^t. P E T E R ? I doe not conceiue that !

S T E P. Mary, S^t. P E T E R, to make vp the meeter.

E. K N. Well, there the Saint was your good patron, hee help't you at your need : thanke him, thanke him.

He is come back.   B R A Y. I cannot take leaue on 'hem, so : I will venture, come what will. Gentlemen, please you change a few crownes, for a very excellent good blade, here ? I am a poore gentleman, a souldier, one that (in the better state of my fortunes) scorn'd so meane a refuge, but now it is the humour of necessitie, to haue it so. You seeme to be gentlemen, well affected to martiall men, else I should rather die with silence, then liue with shame : how euer, vouchsafe to remember, it is my want speakes, not my selfe. This condition agrees not with my spirit———

E. K N. Where hast thou seru'd ?

B R A Y. May it please you, sir, in all the late warres of *Bohemia, Hungaria, Dalmatia, Poland,* where not, sir ? I haue beene a poore seruitor, by sea and land, any time this fourteene yeeres, and follow'd the fortunes of the best Commanders in *christendome*. I was twice shot at the taking of *Alepo,* once at the reliefe of *Vienna* ; I haue beene at *Marseilles, Naples,* and the *Adriatique* gulfe, a gentleman-slaue in the galleys, thrice, where I was most dangerously

II. iv. 47 st. dir. *at l.* 46 *in* F1   53 I should F1 : should I F2
54 then] than F2

shot in the head, through both the thighs, and yet, being thus maym'd, I am void of maintenance, nothing left me but my scarres, the noted markes of my resolution.

S t e p. How will you sell this rapier, friend?

B r a y. Generous sir, I referre it to your owne iudgement; you are a gentleman, giue me what you please.

S t e p. True, I am a gentleman, I know that friend: but what though? I pray you say, what would you aske?

B r a y. I assure you, the blade may become the side, or thigh of the best prince, in *Europe*.

E. K n. I, with a veluet scabberd, I thinke.

S t e p. Nay, and't be mine, it shall haue a veluet scabberd, Couss, that's flat: I'de not weare it as 'tis, and you would giue me an angell.

B r a y. At your worships pleasure, sir; nay, 'tis a most pure *Toledo*.

S t e p. I had rather it were a *Spaniard*! but tell me, what shall I giue you for it? An' it had a siluer hilt———

E. K n. Come, come, you shall not buy it; hold, there's a shilling fellow, take thy rapier.

S t e p. Why, but I will buy it now, because you say so, and there's another shilling, fellow. I scorne to be out-bidden. What, shall I walke with a cudgell, like *Higgin-Bottom*? and may haue a rapier, for money?

E. K n. You may buy one in the citie.

S t e p. Tut, Ile buy this i' the field, so I will, I haue a mind to't, because 'tis a field rapier. Tell me your lowest price.

E. K n. You shall not buy it, I say.

S t e p. By this money, but I will, though I giue more then 'tis worth.

E. K n. Come away, you are a foole.

S t e p. Friend, I am a foole, that's granted: but Ile haue it, for that words sake. Follow me, for your money.

B r a y. At your seruice, sir.

II. iv. 77 and't] an't *F2*

Act II. *Scene* v.

KNO'WELL, BRAYNE-WORME.

I Cannot loose the thought, yet, of this letter,
Sent to my sonne : nor leaue t'admire the change
Of manners, and the breeding of our youth,
Within the kingdome, since my selfe was one.
5 When I was yong, he liu'd not in the stewes,
Durst haue conceiu'd a scorne, and vtter'd it,
On a grey head ; age was authoritie
Against a buffon : and a man had, then,
A certaine reuerence pai'd vnto his yeeres,
10 That had none due vnto his life. So much
The sanctitie of some preuail'd, for others.
But, now, we all are fall'n ; youth, from their feare :
And age, from that, which bred it, good example.
Nay, would our selues were not the first, euen parents,
15 That did destroy the hopes, in our owne children :
Or they not learn'd our vices, in their cradles,
And suck'd in our ill customes, with their milke.
Ere all their teeth be borne, or they can speake,
We make their palats cunning ! The first wordes,
20 We forme their tongues with, are licentious iests !
Can it call, whore ? crie, bastard ? ô, then, kisse it,
A wittie childe ! Can't sweare ? The fathers dearling !
Giue it two plums. Nay, rather then 't shall learne
No bawdie song, the mother'her selfe will teach it !
25 But, this is in the infancie ; the dayes
Of the long coate : when it puts on the breeches,
It will put off all this. I, it is like :
When it is gone into the bone alreadie.
No, no : This die goes deeper then the coate,
30 Or shirt, or skin. It staines, vnto the liuer,
And heart, in some. And, rather, then it should not,

II. v.] Scene III. Another Part of Moorfields. *G.*   1 loose] lose *F2*
5 yong] young *F2*   8 buffon :] buffon, *F2*   22 dearling] darling
F2   24 mother'her] mother her *F2*   29, 31, then] than *F2*

Note, what we fathers doe ! Looke, how we liue !
What mistresses we keepe ! at what expense,
In our sonnes eyes ! where they may handle our gifts,
Heare our lasciuious courtships, see our dalliance,   35
Tast of the same prouoking meates, with vs,
To ruine of our states ! Nay, when our owne
Portion is fled, to prey on their remainder,
We call them into fellowship of vice !
Baite 'hem with the yong chamber-maid, to seale !   40
And teach 'hem all bad wayes, to buy affliction !
This is one path ! but there are millions more,
In which we spoile our owne, with leading them.
Well, I thanke heauen, I neuer yet was he,
That trauail'd with my sonne, before sixteene,   45
To shew him, the *Venetian cortezans.*
Nor read the grammar of cheating, I had made
To my sharpe boy, at twelue : repeating still
The rule, *Get money* ; still, *Get money, Boy* ;
No matter, by what meanes ; *Money will doe*   50
More, Boy, then my Lords letter. Neither haue I
Drest snailes, or mushromes curiously before him,
Perfum'd my sauces, and taught him to make 'hem ;
Preceding still, with my grey gluttonie,
At all the ordinaries : and only fear'd   55
His palate should degenerate, not his manners.
These are the trade of fathers, now ! how euer
My sonne, I hope, hath met within my threshold,
None of these houshold precedents ; which are strong,
And swift, to rape youth, to their precipice.   60
But, let the house at home be nere so cleane-
Swept, or kept sweet from filth ; nay, dust, and cob-webs :
If he will liue, abroad, with his companions,
In dung, and leystalls ; it is worth a feare.
Nor is the danger of conuersing lesse,   65
Then all that I haue mention'd of example.

    II. v. 37 states] state *F2*   41 affliction *G* : affiction *F1* : affection
F2   46 cortezans.] *Courtizans* ; F2   49 still] *still* Ff   51 *then*]
than F2   53 sauces] sauce *F2*

BRAY. My master? nay, faith haue at you: I am flesht now, I haue sped so well. Worshipfull sir, I beseech you, respect the estate of a poore souldier; I am asham'd
70 of this base course of life (god's my comfort) but extremitie prouokes me to't, what remedie?

KNO. I haue not for you, now.

BRAY. By the faith I beare vnto truth, gentleman, it is no ordinarie custome in me, but only to preserue manhood.
75 I protest to you, a man I haue beene, a man I may be, by your sweet bountie.

KNO. 'Pray thee, good friend, be satisfied.

BRAY. Good sir, by that hand, you may doe the part of a kind gentleman, in lending a poore souldier the price
80 of two cannes of beere (a matter of small value) the king of heauen shall pay you, and I shall rest thankfull: sweet worship——

KNO. Nay, and you be so importunate——

BRAY. Oh, tender sir, need will haue his course: I was
85 not made to this vile vse! well, the edge of the enemie could not haue abated mee so much: It's hard when a man hath seru'd in his Princes cause, and be thus—Honorable worship, let me deriue a small piece of siluer from you, it shall not bee giuen in the course of time, by this good
90 ground, I was faine to pawne my rapier last night for a poore supper, I had suck'd the hilts long before, I am a pagan else: sweet honor.

Hee weepes.

KNO. Beleeue me, I am taken with some wonder, To thinke, a fellow of thy outward presence
95 Should (in the frame, and fashion of his mind) Be so degenerate, and sordid-base! Art thou a man? and sham'st thou not to beg? To practise such a seruile kind of life? Why, were thy education ne're so meane,
100 Hauing thy limbs, a thousand fairer courses Offer themselues, to thy election.

II. v 70 god's] God's *F2*   86 hard] hard, *F2*   89 time,] time *F2*   92 honor] Honour *F2*   94 presence] presence, *F2*

Either the warres might still supply thy wants,
Or seruice of some vertuous gentleman,
Or honest labour : nay, what can I name,
But would become thee better then to beg ? 105
But men of thy condition feed on sloth,
As doth the beetle, on the dung shee breeds in,
Not caring how the mettall of your minds
Is eaten with the rust of idlenesse.
Now, afore me, what e're he be, that should 110
Relieue a person of thy qualitie,
While thou insist's in this loose desperate course,
I would esteeme the sinne, not thine, but his.

B R A Y. Faith sir, I would gladly finde some other course,
if so—— 115

K N O. I, you'ld gladly finde it, but you will not seeke it.

B R A Y. Alas sir, where should a man seeke ? in the
warres, there's no ascent by desert in these dayes, but——
and for seruice, would it were as soone purchast, as wisht
for (the ayre's my comfort) I know, what I would say—— 120

K N O. What's thy name ?

B R A Y. Please you, F I T Z-S W O R D, sir.

K N O. F I T Z-S W O R D ?
Say, that a man should entertayne thee now,
Would'st thou be honest, humble, iust, and true ? 125

B R A Y. Sir, by the place, and honor of a souldier——

K N O. Nay, nay, I like not those affected othes ;
Speake plainely man : what think'st thou of my wordes ?

B R A Y. Nothing, sir, but wish my fortunes were as
happy, as my seruice should be honest. 130

K N O. Well, follow me, Ile proue thee, if thy deedes
Will carry a proportion to thy words.

B R A Y. Yes sir, straight, Ile but garter my hose. O that
my belly were hoopt now, for I am readie to burst with
laughing ! neuer was bottle, or bag-pipe fuller. S'lid, was 135
there euer seene a foxe in yeeres to betray himselfe thus ?

II. v. 105 then] than *F2*   118 dayes,] dayes ; *F2*   126 honor] honour *F2*

445·3   Z

now shall I be possest of all his counsells : and, by that
conduit, my yong master. Well, hee is resolu'd to proue my
honestie ; faith, and I am resolu'd to proue his patience : oh
140 I shall abuse him intollerably. This small piece of seruice,
will bring him cleane out of loue with the souldier, for euer.
He will neuer come within the signe of it, the sight of
a cassock, or a musket-rest againe. Hee will hate the
musters at Mile-end for it, to his dying day. It's no matter,
145 let the world thinke me a bad counterfeit, if I cannot giue
him the slip, at an instant : why, this is better then to haue
staid his iourney ! well, Ile follow him : oh, how I long to
bee imployed.

Act III. Scene I.

MATTHEW, WELL-BRED, BOBADILL, ED.
KNO'WELL, STEPHEN.

Yes faith, sir, we were at your lodging to seeke you, too.
  W E L. Oh, I came not there to night.
B O B. Your brother deliuered vs as much.
W E L. Who ? my brother DOWNE-RIGHT ?
5   B O B. He. M^r. WELL-BRED, I know not in what
kind you hold me, but let me say to you this : as sure as
honor, I esteeme it so much out of the sunne-shine of
reputation, to through the least beame of reguard, vpon
such a———
10   W E L. Sir, I must heare no ill wordes of my brother.
  B O B. I, protest to you, as I haue a thing to be sau'd
about me, I neuer saw any gentleman-like part———
  W E L. Good Captayne, *faces about*, to some other
discourse.
15   B O B. With your leaue, sir, and there were no more men
liuing vpon the face of the earth, I should not fancie him,
by S. GEORGE.

II. v. 138 yong] young *F3* 146 then] than *F2* 148 imployed.]
imployed ! *F2* III. i.] Scene 1.—The Old Jewry. A Room in
the Windmill Tavern. G (*but at* III. ii. 52, iii. 129 *the action takes
place in the street*) 8 through] throw *F3* 11 I, protest] I
protest *F2*

MAT. Troth, nor I, he is of a rusticall cut, I know not how: he doth not carry himselfe like a gentleman of fashion——

WEL. Oh, M^r. MATTHEW, that's a grace peculiar but to a few; *quos æquus amauit* IVPITER.

MAT. I vnderstand you sir.

WEL. No question, you doe, or you doe not, sir. NED KNO'WELL! by my soule welcome; how doest thou sweet spirit, my *Genius*? S'lid I shall loue APOLLO, and the mad *Thespian* girles the better, while I liue, for this; my deare *furie*: now, I see there's some loue in thee! Sirra, these bee the two I writ to thee of (nay, what a drowsie humour is this now? why doest thou not speake?) *Yong Kno'well enters.*

E. KN. Oh, you are a fine gallant, you sent me a rare letter!

WEL. Why, was't not rare?

E. KN. Yes, Ile bee sworne, I was ne're guiltie of reading the like; match it in all PLINIE, or SYMMACHVS epistles, and Ile haue my iudgement burn'd in the eare for a rogue: make much of thy vaine, for it is inimitable. But I marle what camell it was, that had the carriage of it? for doubtlesse, he was no ordinarie beast, that brought it!

WEL. Why?

E. KN. Why, saiest thou? why doest thou thinke that any reasonable creature, especially in the morning (the sober time of the day too) could haue mis-tane my father for me?

WEL. S'lid, you iest, I hope?

E. KN. Indeed, the best vse wee can turne it to[o], is to make a iest on't, now: but Ile assure you, my father had the full view o' your flourishing stile, some houre before I saw it.

WEL. What a dull slaue was this? But, sirrah, what said hee to it, Ifaith?

E. KN. Nay, I know not what he said: but I haue a shrewd gesse what hee thought.

WEL. What? what?

55 E. KN. Mary, that thou art some strange dissolute yong fellow, and I a graine or two better, for keeping thee companie.

WEL. Tut, that thought is like the moone in her last quarter, 'twill change shortly: but, sirrha, I pray thee be 60 acquainted with my two hang-by's, here; thou wilt take exceeding pleasure in 'hem if thou hear'st 'hem once goe: my wind-instruments. Ile wind 'hem vp——but what strange piece of silence is this? the signe of the dumbe man?

E. KN. Oh, sir, a kinsman of mine, one that may make 65 your musique the fuller, and he please, he has his humour, sir.

WEL. Oh, what ist? what ist?

E. KN. Nay, Ile neither doe your iudgement, nor his folly that wrong, as to prepare your apprehension: Ile leaue 70 him to the mercy o' your search, if you can take him, so.

WEL. Well, Captaine BOBADILL, M^r. MATTHEW, pray you know this gentleman here, he is a friend of mine, *To Master Stephen.* and one that will deserue your affection. I know not your name sir, but I shall be glad of any occasion, to render me 75 more familiar to you.

STEP. My name is M^r. STEPHEN, sir, I am this gentlemans owne cousin, sir, his father is mine vnckle, sir, I am somewhat melancholy, but you shall command me, sir, in whatsoeuer is incident to a gentleman.

To Kno'-well. BOB. Sir, I must tell you this, I am no generall man, but for M^r. WELBRED's sake (you may embrace it, at what height of fauour you please) I doe communicate with you: and conceiue you, to bee a gentleman of some parts, I loue few wordes.

85 E. KN. And I fewer, sir. I haue scarce inow, to thanke you.

To Master Stephen. MAT. But are you indeed, sir? so giuen to it?

STEP. I, truely, sir, I am mightily giuen to melancholy.

III. i. 72 pray] 'pray *F2*   75 you. *F2*: you *F1*   77 vnckle, sir,] uncle, sir; *F2*   87 indeed, sir? *F2*: indeed. Sir? *F1*   88 melancholy. *F2*; melancholy, *F1*

M A T. Oh, it's your only fine humour, sir, your true melancholy breeds your perfect fine wit, sir : I am melan- choly my selfe diuers times, sir, and then doe I no more but take pen, and paper presently, and ouerflow you halfe a score, or a dozen of sonnets, at a sitting.

(E. K N. Sure, he vtters them then, by the grosse.)

S T E P. Truely sir, and I loue such things, out of measure.

E. K N. I faith, better then in measure, Ile vnder-take.

M A T. Why, I pray you, sir, make vse of my studie, it's at your seruice.

S T E P. I thanke you sir, I shall bee bold, I warrant you ; haue you a stoole there, to be melancholy' vpon ?

M A T. That I haue, sir, and some papers there of mine owne doing, at idle houres, that you'le say there's some sparkes of wit in 'hem, when you see them.

W E L. Would the sparkes would kindle once, and become a fire amongst 'hem, I might see selfe-loue burn't for her heresie.

S T E P. Cousin, is it well ? am I melancholy inough ?

E. K N. Oh I, excellent !

W E L. Captaine B O B A D I L L : why muse you so ?

E. K N. He is melancholy, too.

B O B. Faith, sir, I was thinking of a most honorable piece of seruice, was perform'd to morrow, being S^t. M A R K E S day : shall bee some ten yeeres, now ?

E. K N. In what place, Captaine ?

B O B. Why, at the beleag'ring of *Strigonium*, where, in lesse then two houres, seuen hundred resolute gentlemen, as any were in *Europe*, lost their liues vpon the breach. Ile tell you, gentlemen, it was the first, but the best leagure, that euer I beheld, with these eies, except the taking in of ——what doe you call it, last yeere, by the *Genowayes*, but that (of all other) was the most fatall, and dangerous exploit, that euer I was rang'd in, since I first bore armes

III. i. 89–90 true melancholy *F2* : true melancholy, *F1*   91 selfe] selfe, *F2*   96, 116 then] than *F2*   100 melancholy'] melancholy *F2*   105 might] migh *F2*   111 honorable] honourable *F2*   113 day :] day, *F2*   now ?] now. *F2*   118 leagure] Leaguer *F3*

before the face of the enemie, as I am a gentleman, & souldier.

125 STEP. 'So, I had as liefe, as an angell, I could sweare as well as that gentleman!

E. KN. Then, you were a seruitor, at both it seemes! at *Strigonium*? and what doe you call't?

BOB. Oh lord, sir? by S. GEORGE, I was the first 130 man, that entred the breach: and, had I not effected it with resolution, I had beene slaine, if I had had a million of liues.

E. KN. 'Twas pittie, you had not ten; a cats, and your owne, ifaith. But, was it possible?

135 (MAT. 'Pray you, marke this discourse, sir.
STEP. So, I doe.)

BOB. I assure you (vpon my reputation) 'tis true, and your selfe shall confesse.

E. KN. You must bring me to the racke, first.

140 BOB. Obserue me iudicially, sweet sir, they had planted mee three demi-culuerings, iust in the mouth of the breach; now, sir (as we were to giue on) their master gunner (a man of no meane skill, and marke, you must thinke) confronts me with his linstock, readie to giue fire; I spying his 145 intendment, discharg'd my petronel in his bosome, and with these single armes, my poore rapier, ranne violently, vpon the *Moores*, that guarded the ordinance, and put 'hem pell-mell to the sword.

WEL. To the sword? to the rapier, Captaine?

150 E. KN. Oh, it was a good figure obseru'd, sir! but did you all this, Captaine, without hurting your blade?

BOB. Without any impeach, o' the earth: you shall perceiue sir. It is the most fortunate weapon, that euer rid on poore gentlemans thigh: shal I tell you, sir? you 155 talke of *Morglay, Excalibur, Durindana,* or so? tut, I lend no credit to that is fabled of 'hem, I know the vertue

---

III. i. 124 souldier.] a Soldier *F3*   129 lord, sir?] Lord, sir, *F2*
131 slaine,] slain *F2*   142 gunner] gunner, *F2*   147 ordinance] ordnance *F2*   151 blade?] *F2*; blade. *F1*

The Folio of 1616

of mine owne, and therefore I dare, the boldlier, maintaine it.

S T E P. I mar'le whether it be a *Toledo*, or no?

B O B. A most perfect *Toledo*, I assure you, sir. 160

S T E P. I haue a countriman of his, here.

M A T. Pray you, let's see, sir : yes faith, it is!

B O B. This a *Toledo*? pish.

S T E P. Why doe you pish, Captaine?

B O B. A *Fleming*, by heauen, Ile buy them for a guilder, 165
a piece, an' I would haue a thousand of them.

E. K N. How say you, cousin? I told you thus much?

W E L. Where bought you it, M^r. S T E P H E N.?

S T E P. Of a scuruie rogue souldier (a hundred of lice goe
with him) he swore it was a *Toledo*. 170

B O B. A poore prouant rapier, no better.

M A T. Masse, I thinke it be, indeed! now I looke on't, better.

E. K N. Nay, the longer you looke on't, the worse. Put
it vp, put it vp. 175

S T E P. Well, I will put it vp, but by——(I ha' forgot the
Captaynes oath, I thought to ha' sworne by it) an' ere
I meet him——

W E L. O, it is past helpe now, sir, you must haue
patience. 180

S T E P. Horson connie-catching raskall! I could eate
the very hilts for anger!

E. K N. A signe of good digestion! you haue an ostrich
stomack, cousin.

S T E P. A stomack? would I had him here, you should 185
see, an' I had a stomack.

W E L. It's better as 'tis : come, gentlemen, shall we goe?

III. i. 157 owne,] owne. *F2*   165 heauen,] heauen. *F2*   176 vp,]
up; *F2*   181 connie-catching] cunny-catching *F2*   183–4 ostrich
stomack] ostrich-stomack *F2*

Act III. Scene II.

E. KNO'WELL, BRAYNE-WORME, STEPHEN,
WELL-BRED, BOBADILL, MATTHEW.

A Miracle, cousin, looke here! looke here!
S T E P. Oh, gods lid, by your leaue, doe you know me, sir?
B R A Y. I sir, I know you, by sight.
5 S T E P. You sold me a rapier, did you not?
B R A Y. Yes, marie, did I sir.
S T E P. You said, it was a *Toledo*, ha?
B R A Y. True, I did so.
S T E P. But, it is none?
10 B R A Y. No sir, I confesse it, it is none.
S T E P. Doe you confesse it? gentlemen, beare witnesse, he has confest it. By gods will, and you had not confest it———
E. K N. Oh cousin, forbeare, forbeare.
15 S T E P. Nay, I haue done, cousin.
W E L. Why you haue done like a gentleman, he ha's confest it, what would you more?
S T E P. Yet, by his leaue, he is a raskall, vnder his fauour, doe you see?
20 E. K N. I, by his leaue, he is, and vnder fauour: a prettie piece of ciuilitie! Sirra, how doest thou like him?
W E L. Oh, it's a most pretious foole, make much on him: I can compare him to nothing more happily, then a drumme; for euery one may play vpon him.
25 E. K N. No, no, a childes whistle were farre the fitter.
B R A Y. Sir, shall I intreat a word with you?
E. K N. With me, sir? you haue not another *Toledo* to sell, ha' you?
B R A Y. You are conceipted, sir, your name is M^r.
30 K N O'W E L L, as I take it?

III. ii. 6 I] I, *F2*   9 none?] none. *F2*   12 and] an' *F2*   16
Why] Why, *F2*   23 then] than *F2*   29 sir,] sir; *F2*

E. K N. You are i' the right; you meane not to proceede in the catechisme, doe you?

B R A Y. No sir, I am none of that coat.

E. K N. Of as bare a coat, though; well, say sir.

B R A Y. Faith sir, I am but seruant to the drum extra- 35 ordinarie, and indeed (this smokie varnish being washt off, and three or four patches remou'd) I appeare your worships in reuersion, after the decease of your good father, B R A Y N E-W O R M E.

E. K N. B R A Y N E-W O R M E! S'light, what breath of 40 a coniurer, hath blowne thee hither in this shape?

B R A Y. The breath o' your letter, sir, this morning: the same that blew you to the wind-mill, and your father after you.

E. K N. My father? 45

B R A Y. Nay, neuer start, 'tis true, he has follow'd you ouer the field's, by the foot, as you would doe a hare i' the snow.

E. K N. Sirra, W EL-B R E D, what shall we doe, sirra? my father is come ouer, after me. 50

W E L. Thy father? where is he?

B R A Y. At Iustice C L E M E N T s house here, in *Colman*-street, where he but staies my returne; and then———

W E L. Who's this? B R A Y N E-W O R M E?

B R A Y. The same, sir. 55

W E L. Why how, i' the name of wit, com'st thou transmuted, thus?

B R A Y. Faith, a deuise, a deuise: nay, for the loue of reason, gentlemen, and auoiding the danger, stand not here, withdraw, and Ile tell you all. 60

W E L. But, art thou sure, he will stay thy returne?

B R A Y. Doe I liue, sir? what a question is that?

W E L. Wee'le prorogue his expectation then, a little: B R A Y N E-W O R M E, thou thalt goe with vs. Come on,

III. ii. 31 are] are, *F1*   right; *F2*: right? *F1*   34 though; *F2*: though? *F1*   41 shape? *F2*: shape. *F1*   43 wind-mill,] Wind-mill *F2*   47 field's] fields *F2*   52 here *om. F2*   52–3 *Colman*-street] *Coleman*-street *F2*   59 here,] here; *F2*

65 gentlemen, nay, I pray thee, sweet NED, droope not:
'heart, and our wits be so wretchedly dull, that one old
plodding braine can out-strip vs all, would we were eene
prest, to make porters of; and serue out the remnant of
our daies, in *Thames*-street, or at *Custome*-house key, in
70 a ciuill warre, against the car-men.

    BRAY. AMEN, AMEN, AMEN, say I.

Act III.   *Scene* III.

KITELY, CASH.

WHat saies he, THOMAS? Did you speake with him?
    CAS. He will expect you, sir, within this halfe houre.
    KIT. Has he the money readie, can you tell?
    CAS. Yes, sir, the money was brought in, last night.
5   KIT. O, that's well: fetch me my cloke, my cloke.
Stay, let me see, an houre, to goe and come;
I, that will be the least: and then 'twill be
An houre, before I can dispatch with him;
Or very neere: well, I will say two houres.
10 Two houres? ha? things, neuer dreamt of yet,
May be contriu'd, I, and effected too,
In two houres absence: well, I will not goe.
Two houres; no, fleering oportunitie,
I will not giue your subtiltie that scope.
15 Who will not iudge him worthie to be rob'd,
That sets his doores wide open to a thiefe,
And shewes the fellon, where his treasure lies?
Againe, what earthie spirit but will attempt
To taste the fruit of beauties golden tree,
20 When leaden sleepe seales vp the Dragons eyes?
I will not goe. Businesse, goe by, for once.
No beautie, no; you are of too good caract,
To be left so, without a guard, or open!

    III. ii. 65 gentlemen,] gentlemen; *F2*   not:] not; *F2*   66 and]
an' *F2*   III. iii.] Scene II.—The Old Jewry. Kitely's Warehouse. G
1 he,] hee *F2*   13 oportunitie] opportunitie *F2*   17 fellon,]
fellon *F2*   19 taste the *F2*: the taste *F1*

Your lustre too'll enflame, at any distance,
Draw courtship to you, as a iet doth strawes,   25
Put motion in a stone, strike fire from ice,
Nay, make a porter leape you, with his burden!
You must be then kept vp, close, and well-watch'd,
For, giue you oportunitie, no quick-sand
Deuoures, or swallowes swifter! He that lends   30
His wife (if shee be faire) or time, or place;
Compells her to be false. I will not goe.
The dangers are to many. And, then, the dressing
Is a most mayne attractiue! Our great heads,
Within the citie, neuer were in safetie,   35
Since our wiues wore these little caps: Ile change 'hem,
Ile change 'hem, streight, in mine. Mine shall no more
Weare three-pild akornes, to make my hornes ake.
Nor, will I goe. I am resolu'd for that.
Carry' in my cloke againe. Yet, stay. Yet, doe too.   40
I will deferre going, on all occasions.

    CASH. Sir. SNARE, your scriuener, will be there with
        th'bonds.
    KITE. That's true! foole on me! I had cleane forgot it,
I must goe. What's a clocke?   CASH. *Exchange* time,
    sir.
    KITE. 'Heart, then will WELL-BRED presently be   45
        here, too,
With one, or other of his loose consorts.
I am a knaue, if I know what to say,
What course to take, or which way to resolue.
My braine (me thinkes) is like an houre-glasse,
Wherein, my' imaginations runne, like sands,   50
Filling vp time; but then are turn'd, and turn'd:
So, that I know not what to stay upon,

    III. iii. 24 enflame] inflame *F2*   27 you,] you *F2*   29 oportunitie]
opportunitie *F2*   30 Deuoures,] Devoures *F2*   37 'hem,] 'hem
F2   39 Nor,] Nor *F2*   40 Carry' in] Carry in *F2*   42 Sir.]
Sir, *F2* (but cf. 136, 139)   43 it,] it; *F2*   44 *Exchange* time,]
Exchange-time *F2*   46 one,] one *F2*   49 (me thinkes)] me thinks
F2   50 my' imaginations] my 'maginations *F2*   52 So,] So *F2*

And lesse, to put in act. It shall be so.
Nay, I dare build vpon his secrecie,
55 He knowes not to deceiue me. THOMAS? CASH. Sir.
  KITE. Yet now, I haue bethought me, too, I will not.
THOMAS, is COB within? CASH. I thinke he be, sir.
  KITE. But hee'll prate too, there's no speech of him.
No, there were no man o' the earth to THOMAS,
60 If I durst trust him ; there is all the doubt.
But, should he haue a chinke in him, I were gone,
Lost i' my fame for euer : talke for th'Exchange.
The manner he hath stood with, till this present,
Doth promise no such change ! what should I feare then ?
65 Well, come what will, Ile tempt my fortune, once.
  THOMAS——you may deceiue me, but, I hope——
  Your loue, to me, is more—— CAS. Sir, if a seruants
Duetie, with faith, may be call'd loue, you are
More then in hope, you are possess'd of it.
70   KIT. I thanke you, heartily, THOMAS; Gi' me your hand :
With all my heart, good THOMAS. I haue, THOMAS,
A secret to impart, vnto you——but
When once you haue it, I must seale your lips vp :
(So farre, I tell you, THOMAS.) CAS. Sir, for that——
75   KIT. Nay, heare me, out. Thinke,. I esteeme you, THOMAS,
When, I will let you in, thus, to my priuate.
It is a thing sits, neerer, to my crest,
Then thou art ware of, THOMAS. If thou should'st
Reueale it, but—— CAS. How ? I reueale it ? KIT. Nay,
80 I doe not thinke thou would'st ; but if thou should'st :
'Twere a great weakenesse. CAS. A great trecherie.
Giue it no other name. KIT. Thou wilt not do't, then ?
  CAS. Sir, if I doe, mankind disclaime me, euer.
  KIT. He will not sweare, he has some reseruation,

III. iii. 69, 78 then] than *F2*   71 haue,] have *F2*   74 farre,] far *F2*
77 thing sits,] thing, sits *F2*   78 ware] 'ware *F2*   84 has] ha's *F2*

Some conceal'd purpose, and close meaning, sure : 85
Else (being vrg'd so much) how should he choose,
But lend an oath to all this protestation ?
H'is no precisian, that I am certaine of.
Nor rigid *Roman*-catholike. Hee'll play,
At *Fayles*, and *Tick-tack*, I haue heard him sweare. 90
What should I thinke of it ? vrge him againe,
And by some other way ? I will doe so.
Well, T H O M A S, thou hast sworne not to disclose ;
Yes, you did sweare ?   C A S. Not yet, sir, but I will,
Please you——   K I T. No, T H O M A S, I dare take thy 95
   word.
But ; if thou wilt sweare, doe, as thou think'st good ;
I am resolu'd without it ; at thy pleasure.
   C A S. By my soules safetie then, sir, I protest.
My tongue shall ne're take knowledge of a word,
Deliuer'd me in nature of your trust.   100
   K I T. It's too much, these ceremonies need not,
I know thy faith to be as firme as rock.
T H O M A S, come hither, neere : we cannot be
Too priuate, in this businesse. So it is,
(Now, he ha's sworne, I dare the safelier venter) 105
I haue of late, by diuers obseruations————
(But, whether his oath can bind him, yea, or no ;
Being not taken lawfully ? ha ? say you ?
I will aske counsell, ere I doe proceed :)
T H O M A S, it will be now too long to stay, 110
Ile spie some fitter time soone, or to morrow.
   C A S. Sir, at your pleasure ?   K I T. I will thinke.
     And, T H O M A S,
I pray you search the bookes 'gainst my returne,
For the receipts 'twixt me, and T R A P S.   C A S. I will, sir.
   K I T. And, heare you, if your mistris brother, W E L- 115
   B R E D,

   III. iii. 88 precisian] precision *F2*   90 *Tick-tack*] at *Tick-tack F3*
93 Well,] Well *F2*   105 venter)] ventuer *F3*   107 no ; *F2* :
no', *F1*

Chance to bring hither any gentlemen,
Ere I come backe ; let one straight bring me word.
    C A S. Very well, sir.   K I T. To the Exchange ; doe you heare ?
119 Or here in *Colman*-street, to Iustice C L E M E N T S.
Forget it not, nor be not out of the way.
    C A S. I will not, sir.   K I T. I pray you haue a care on't.
Or whether he come, or no, if any other,
Stranger, or else, faile not to send me word.
    C A S. I shall not, sir.   K I T. Be't your speciall businesse
125 Now, to remember it.   C A S. Sir. I warrant you.
    K I T. But, T H O M A S, this is not the secret, T H O M A S,
.I told you of.   C A S. No, sir. I doe suppose it.
    K I T. Beleeue me, it is not.   C A S. Sir. I doe beleeue you.
    K I T. By heauen, it is not, that's enough. But, T H O M A S,
130 I would not, you should vtter it, doe you see ?
To any creature liuing, yet, I care not.
Well, I must hence. T H O M A S, conceiue thus much.
It was a tryall of you, when I meant
So deepe a secret to you, I meane not this,
135 But that I haue to tell you, this is nothing, this.
But, T H O M A S, keepe this from my wife, I charge you,
Lock'd vp in silence, mid-night, buried here.
No greater hell, then to be slaue to feare.
    C A S. Lock'd vp in silence, mid-night, buried here.
140 Whence should this floud of passion (trow) take head ? ha ?
Best, dreame no longer of this running humour,
For feare I sinke ! the violence of the streame
Alreadie hath transported me so farre,
That I can feele no ground at all ! but soft,
145 Oh, 'tis our water-bearer : somewhat ha's crost him, now.

    III. iii. 125, 128 Sir.] Sir, *F2*   129 But,] But *F2*   131 liuing,] living ; *F2*   135 you,] you ; *F2*   136 you,] you. *F2*   138 then] than *F2*

Act III.   Scene IIII.

Cob, Cash.

FAsting dayes? what tell you me of fasting dayes? S'lid, would they were all on a light fire for me: They say, the whole world shall bee consum'd with fire one day, but would I had these ember-weekes, and villanous fridayes burnt, in the meane time, and then——

Cas. Why, how now Cob, what moues thee to this choller? ha?

Cob. Collar, master Thomas? I scorne your collar, I sir, I am none o' your cart-horse, though I carry, and draw water. An' you offer to ride me, with your collar, or halter either, I may hap shew you a jades trick, sir.

Cas. O, you'll slip your head out of the collar? why, goodman Cob, you mistake me.

Cob. Nay, I haue my rewme, & I can be angrie as well as another, sir.

Cas. Thy rewme, Cob? thy humour, thy humour? thou mistak'st.

Cob. Humour? mack, I thinke it be so, indeed: what is that humour? some rare thing, I warrant.

Cas. Mary, Ile tell thee, Cob: It is a gentleman-like monster, bred, in the speciall gallantrie of our time, by affectation; and fed by folly.

Cob. How? must it be fed?

Cas. Oh I, humour is nothing, if it bee not fed. Didst thou neuer heare that? it's a common phrase, *Feed my humour.*

Cob. Ile none on it: Humour, auant, I know you not, be gone. Let who will make hungrie meales for your monster-ship, it shall not bee I. Feed you, quoth he? S'lid, I ha' much adoe, to feed my selfe; especially, on these leane rascally dayes, too; and't had beene any other day, but a fasting-day (a plague on them all for mee) by this

III.] III *F1*   iv. 6 Cob,] Cob? *F2*   18 so,] so *F2*

light, one might haue done the common-wealth good seruice, and haue drown'd them all i' the floud, two or three hundred thousand yeeres agoe. O, I doe stomack them hugely! I haue a maw now, and't were for S^r B E V I S his horse, against 'hem.

C A S. I pray thee, good C O B, what makes thee so out of loue with fasting-dayes?

C O B. Mary that, which will make any man out of loue with 'hem, I thinke: their bad conditions, and you will needs know. First, they are of a *Flemmish* breed, I am sure on't, for they rauen vp more butter, then all the dayes of the weeke, beside; next, they stinke of fish, and leeke-porridge miserably: thirdly, they'le keepe a man deuoutly hungrie, all day, and at night send him supperlesse to bed.

C A S. Indeed, these are faults, C O B.

C O B. Nay, and this were all, 'twere something, but they are the only knowne enemies, to my generation. A fasting-day, no sooner comes, but my lineage goes to racke, poore cobs they smoke for it, they are made martyrs o' the gridiron, they melt in passion: and your maides too know

He pulls out a red herring. this, and yet would haue me turne H A N N I B A L, and eate my owne fish, and bloud: My princely couz, fear nothing; I haue not the hart to deuoure you, & I might be made as rich as King C O P H E T V A. O, that I had roome for my teares, I could weepe salt-water enough, now, to preserue the liues of ten thousand of my kin. But I may curse none but these filthie *Almanacks,* for an't were not for them, these dayes of persecution would ne're be knowne. Ile bee hang'd, an' some Fish-mongers sonne doe not make of 'hem; and puts in more fasting-dayes then he should doe, because hee would vtter his fathers dryed stock-fish, and stinking conger.

C A S. S'light, peace, thou'lt bee beaten like a stock-fish, else: here is M^r. M A T T H E W. Now must I looke out for a messenger to my master.

III. iv. 41 and] an' *F2*   43 then] than *F2*   44 beside;] beside: *F2*   49 enemies,] enemies *F2*   50 lineage] linage *F2* (cf. 1. iv. 6)
51 cobs] cobs, *F2*   54 fish] Flesh *F3*   55 &] an' *F2*   61 'hem *F2*: hem *F1*   62 then] than *F2*   65 here is] here's *F2*

Act III. Scene V.

WELL-BRED, ED. KNO'WELL, BRAYNE-
WORME, BOBADILL, MATTHEW, STEPHEN,
THOMAS, COB.

BEshrew me, but it was an absolute good iest, and exceedingly well carried !

E. KNO. I, and our ignorance maintain'd it as well, did it not ?

WEL. Yes faith, but was't possible thou should'st not know him ? I forgiue M^r. STEPHEN, for he is stupiditie it selfe !

E. KN. 'Fore god, not I, and I might haue been ioyn'd patten with one of the seuen wise masters, for knowing him. He had so writhen himselfe, into the habit of one of your poore *Infanterie*, your decay'd, ruinous, worme-eaten gentlemen of the round : such as haue vowed to sit on the skirts of the citie, let your Prouost, and his halfe-dozen of halberdeirs doe what they can ; and haue translated begging out of the old hackney pace, to a fine easie amble, and made it runne as smooth, of the tongue, as a shoue-groat shilling. Into the likenesse of one of these *Reformado's* had he moulded himselfe so perfectly, obseruing euery tricke of their action, as varying the accent, swearing with an *emphasis*, indeed all, with so speciall, and exquisite a grace, that (hadst thou seene him) thou would'st haue sworne, he might haue beene Serieant-*Maior*, if not Lieutenant-*Coronell* to the regiment.

WEL. Why, BRAYNE-WORME, who would haue thought thou hadst beene such an artificer ?

E. KN. An artificer ! An architect ! except a man had studied begging all his life-time, and beene a weauer of

III. v. BOBADILL] BOBADILI *F2*   5 faith,] faith ; *F2*   8 god] God *F2*   and] an' *F2*   13 let *misprinted* like *F3*   14 halber-deirs] Halberdiers *F2*   16 smooth,] smooth *F2*   of] on *F3*   19 as] as, *F2*   21 would'st] woulst *F2*   22-3 Lieutenant-*Coronell*] Lieu-tenant-*Collonell F2*

language, from his infancie, for the clothing of it! I neuer saw his riuall.

30   W E L. Where got'st thou this coat, I mar'le?

B R A Y. Of a *Hounds-ditch* man, sir. One of the deuil's neere kinsmen, a broker.

W E L. That cannot be, if the prouerbe hold; for, a craftie knaue needs no broker.

35   B R A Y. True sir, but I did need a broker, *Ergo*.

W E L. (Well put off) no craftie knaue, you'll say.

E. K N. Tut, he ha's more of these shifts.

B R A Y. And yet where I haue one, the broker ha's ten, sir.

40   T H O. F R A N C I S, M A R T I N, ne're a one to be found, now? what a spite's this?

W E L. How now, T H O M A S? is my brother K I T E L Y, within?

T H O. No sir, my master went forth eene now: but 45 master D O W N E-R I G H T is within.   C O B, what 'C O B? is he gone too?

W E L. Whither went your master?   T H O M A S, canst thou tell?

T H O. I know not, to Iustice C L E M E N T S, I thinke, 50 sir.   C O B.

E. K N. Iustice C L E M E N T, what's he?

W E L. Why, doest thou not know him? he is a citie-magistrate, a Iustice here, an excellent good Lawyer, and a great scholler: but the onely mad, merrie, old fellow in 55 *Europe!*   I shew'd him you, the other day.

E. K N. Oh, is that he?   I remember him now. Good faith, and he ha's a very strange presence, mee thinkes; it shewes as if hee stood out of the ranke, from other men: I haue heard many of his iests i' ⟨the⟩ *vniuersitie*. They 60 say, he will commit a man, for taking the wall, of his horse.

    III. v. 30 mar'le *F2*: marl'e *F1*   32 kinsmen] kinsman *F2*   37 ha's] has *F2*   39 sir. *F2*: sir, *F1*   49 not,] not; *F2*   55 you,] you *F2*   57 ha's] has *F2*   59 the *F2*

W E L. I, or wearing his cloke of one shoulder, or seruing of god : any thing indeed, if it come in the way of his humour.

C A S. G A S P E R, M A R T I N, C O B : 'heart, where should they be, trow ? *Cash goes in and out calling.*

B O B. Master K I T E L Y's man, 'pray thee vouchsafe vs the lighting of this match.

C A S. Fire on your match, no time but now to vouchsafe? F R A N C I S. C O B. 70

B O B. Bodie of me! here's the remainder of seuen pound, since yesterday was seuen-night. 'Tis your right *Trinidado!* did you neuer take any, master S T E P H E N ?

S T E P. No truely, sir ; but I'le learne to take it now, since you commend it, so. 75

B O B. Sir, beleeue mee (vpon my relation) for what I tell you, the world shal not reproue. I have been in the *Indies* (where this herb growes) where neither my selfe, nor a dozen gentlemen more (of my knowledge) haue receiued the tast of any other nutriment, in the world, for the space 80 of one and twentie weekes, but the fume of this simple onely. Therefore, it cannot be, but 'tis most diuine ! Further, take it in the nature, in the true kind so, it makes an *antidote*, that (had you taken the most deadly poysonous plant in all *Italy*) it should expell it, and clarifie you, with as much ease, 85 as I speake. And, for your greene wound, your *Balsamum*, and your S^t. I O H N's *woort* are all mere gulleries, and trash to it, especially your *Trinidado* : your *Nicotian* is good too. I could say what I know of the vertue of it, for the expulsion of rhewmes, raw humours, crudities, obstructions, with 90 a thousand of this kind ; but I professe my selfe no *quacksaluer*. Only, thus much, by H E R C V L E S, I doe hold it, and will affirme it (before any Prince in *Europe*) to be the most soueraigne, and precious weede, that euer the earth tendred to the vse of man. 95

III. v. 62 of one] on one *F3*   63 god] God *F2*   65 s. d. *out*] out, F2
67 'pray] pray *F2*   70 FRANCIS.] FRANCIS, *F2*   74 sir ; *F2* : sir ? *F1*
84 (had] had *F2*   85 *Italy*)] *Italy*, Ff   86 *Balsamum*,] *Balsamum* F2
87 S^t. IOHN's *woort*] S^t. JOHN's-*woort* F2   88 especially] especially, *F2*

E. KN. This speech would ha' done decently in a *tabacco*-traders mouth!

CAS. At Iustice CLEMENTS, hee is: in the middle of *Colman*-street.

100 COB. O, oh?

BOB. Where's the match I gaue thee? Master KITE-LIES man?

CAS. Would his match, and he, and pipe, and all were at SANCTO DOMINGO! I had forgot it.

105 COB. By gods mee, I marle, what pleasure, or felicitie they haue in taking this roguish *tabacco*! it's good for nothing, but to choke a man, and fill him full of smoke, and embers: there were foure dyed out of one house, last weeke, with taking of it, and two more the bell went for, yester-
110 night; one of them (they say) will ne're scape it: he voided a bushell of soot yester-day, vpward, and downeward. By the stocks, an' there were no wiser men then I, I'ld haue it present whipping, man, or woman, that should but deale with a *tabacco*-pipe; why, it will stifle them all in the end,
115 as many as vse it; it's little better then rats-bane, or rosaker.

Bobadil beates him with a cudgell.

ALL. Oh, good Captayne, hold, hold.

BOB. You base cullion, you.

CAS. Sir, here's your match: come, thou must needs be
120 talking, too, tho'art well inough seru'd.

COB. Nay, he will not meddle with his match, I warrant you: well it shall be a deare beating, and I liue.

BOB. Doe you prate? Doe you murmure?

E. KN. Nay, good Captayne, will you regard the humour
125 of a foole? away, knaue.

WEL. THOMAS, get him away.

BOB. A horson filthie slaue, a dung-worme, an excrement! Body o' CAESAR, but that I scorne to let forth so meane a spirit, I'ld ha' stab'd him, to the earth.

III. v. 99 *Colman*-street] *Coleman*-street F2   105 marle] mar'le F2
107 smoke,] smoke F2   112 then] than F2   115 then] than F2
rats-bane F2: rats bane F1   122 well] well, F2   and] an' F2
129 him,] him F2

W E L. Mary, the law forbid, sir.
B O B. By P H A R O A H S foot, I would haue done it.
S T E P. Oh, he sweares admirably! (by P H A R O A H S foot) (body of C A E S A R) I shall neuer doe it, sure (vpon mine honor, and by Saint G E O R G E) no, I ha' not the right grace.
M A T. Master S T E P H E N, will you any? By this aire, the most diuine *tabacco*, that euer I drunke!
S T E P. None, I thanke you, sir. O, this gentleman do's it, rarely too! but nothing like the other. By this aire, as I am a gentleman: by——
B R A Y. Master, glance, glance! Master W E L L-B R E D! *Master Stephen is practis-*
S T E P. As I haue somewhat to be saued, I protest——— *ing, to the*
W E L. You are a foole: It needes no *affidauit*. *post.*
E. K N. Cousin, will you any *tabacco*?
S T E P. I sir! vpon my reputation——
E. K N. How now, cousin!
S T E P. I protest, as I am a gentleman, but no souldier, indeed———
W E L. No, Master S T E P H E N? as I remember your name is entred in the artillerie garden?
S T E P. I sir, that's true: Cousin, may I swear, as I am a souldier, by that?
E. K N. Oh yes, that you may. It's all you haue for your money.
S T E P. Then, as I am a gentleman, and a souldier, it is diuine *tabacco*!
W E L. But soft, where's M^r. M A T T H E W? gone?
B R A Y. No, sir, they went in here.
W E L. O, let's follow them: master M A T T H E W is gone to salute his mistris, in verse. Wee shall ha' the happinesse, to heare some of his poetrie, now. Hee neuer comes vnfurnish'd. B R A Y N E-W O R M E?
S T E P. B R A Y N E-W O R M E? Where? Is this B R A Y N E-W O R M E?

III. v. 132 admirably] most admirably *F2*   133 of] o' *F2*   134 honor] honour *F2*   149 remember] remember, *F2*

165　E. Kn. I, cousin, no wordes of it, vpon your gentilitie.

　　Step. Not I, body of me, by this aire, S. George, and the foot of Pharoah.

　　Wel. Rare! your cousins discourse is simply drawn out with oathes.

170　E. Kn. 'Tis larded with 'hem. A kind of french dressing, if you loue it.

Act III. Scene VI.

Kitely, Cob.

Ha? how many are there, sayest thou?
　　Cob. Mary sir, your brother, master Well-
bred——
　　Kit. Tut, beside him : what strangers are there, man?
5　Cob. Strangers? let me see, one, two; masse I know not well, there are so many.
　　Kit. How? so many?
　　Cob. I, there's some fiue, or sixe of them, at the most.
　　Kit. A swarme, a swarme,
10 Spight of the deuill, how they sting my head
With forked stings, thus wide, and large! But, Cob,
How long hast thou beene comming hither, Cob?
　　Cob. A little while, sir.
　　Kit. Did'st thou come running?
15　Cob. No, sir.
　　Kit. Nay, then I am familiar with thy haste!
Bane to my fortunes : what meant I to marry?
I, that before was rankt in such content,
My mind at rest too, in so soft a peace,
20 Being free master of mine owne free thoughts,
And now become a slaue? What? neuer sigh,
Be of good cheere, man : for thou art a cuckold,
'Tis done, 'tis done! nay, when such flowing store,
Plentie it selfe, falls in my wiues lap,
25 The *Cornu-copiæ* will be mine, I know. But, Cob,

III. v. 170 french] French *F2*　　III. vi.] Scene III.—Colman Street. A Room in Justice Clement's House. *G.*

What entertaynement had they? I am sure
My sister, and my wife, would bid them welcome! ha?
    C o b. Like inough, sir, yet, I heard not a word of it.
    K i t. No: their lips were seal'd with kisses, and the voyce
Drown'd in a floud of ioy, at their arriuall,   30
Had lost her motion, state, and facultie.
C o b, which of them was't, that first kist my wife?
(My sister, I should say) my wife, alas,
I feare not her: ha? who was it, say'st thou?
    C o b. By my troth, sir, will you haue the truth of it?   35
    K i t. Oh I, good C o b : I pray thee, heartily.
    C o b. Then, I am a vagabond, and fitter for *Bride-well*,
then your worships companie, if I saw any bodie to be kist,
vnlesse they would haue kist the post, in the middle of the
ware-house; for there I left them all, at their *tabacco*, with   40
a poxe.
    K i t. How? were they not gone in, then, e're thou cam'st?
    C o b. Oh no sir.
    K i t. Spite of the deuill! what doe I stay here, then?   45
C o b, follow me.
    C o b. Nay, soft and faire, I haue egges on the spit; I cannot
goe yet, sir.   Now am I for some fiue and fiftie reasons
hammering, hammering reuenge: oh, for three or foure gallons
of vineger, to sharpen my wits. Reuenge: vineger reuenge: 50
vineger, and mustard reuenge : nay, and hee had not lyen
in my house, 't would neuer haue grieu'd me, but being
my guest, one, that Ile be sworne, my wife ha's lent him her
smock off her back, while his one shirt ha's beene at washing;
pawn'd her neckerchers for cleane bands for him; sold   55
almost all my platters, to buy him *tabacco*; and he to turne
monster of ingratitude, and strike his lawfull host! well,
I hope to raise vp an host of furie for't: here comes Iustice
C l e m e n t.

    iii. vi. 35 truth] troth *F2*   36 thee,] thee *F2*   38 then] than
F2   44 Oh] O, *F2*   51 and] an' *F2*   53, 54 h'as] has *F2*   54
one] own *W (from Q)*

Act III. Scene VII.

CLEMENT, KNO'WELL, FORMALL, COB.

WHat's master KITELY gone? ROGER?
FOR. I, sir.
CLEM. 'Hart of me! what made him leaue vs so abruptly! How now, sirra? what make you here? what would you haue, ha?
COB. And't please your worship, I am a poore neighbour of your worships———
CLEM. A poore neighbour of mine? why, speake poore neighbour.
COB. I dwell, sir, at the signe of the water-tankard, hard by the greene lattice: I haue paid scot, and lot there, any time this eighteene yeeres.
CLEM. To the greene lattice?
COB. No, sir, to the parish: mary, I haue seldome scap't scot-free, at the lattice.
CLEM. O, well! what businesse ha's my poore neighbour with me?
COB. And't like your worship, I am come, to craue the peace of your worship.
CLEM. Of mee knaue? peace of mee, knaue? did I e're hurt thee? or threaten thee? or wrong thee? ha?
COB. No, sir, but your worships warrant, for one that ha's wrong'd me, sir: his armes are at too much libertie, I would faine haue them bound to a treatie of peace, an' my credit could compasse it, with your worship.
CLEM. Thou goest farre inough about for't, I'am sure.
KNO. Why, doest thou goe in danger of thy life for him? friend?
COB. No sir; but I goe in danger of my death, euery houre, by his meanes: an' I die, within a twelue-moneth

III. vii. 6, 18 And't] An't *F2*   15 scap't] scap'd *F2*   16, 23 ha's] has *F2*   20 Of mee] Of mee, *F2*   e're] ever *F2*   26 I'am] I am *F2*   29 No] No, *F2*

and a day, I may sweare, by the law of the land, that he kill'd me.

CLEM. How? how knaue? sweare he kill'd thee? and by the law? what pretence? what colour hast thou for that?

COB. Mary, and't please your worship, both black, and blew; colour inough, I warrant you. I haue it here, to shew your worship.

CLEM. What is he, that gaue you this, sirra?

COB. A gentleman, and a souldier, he saies he is, o' the citie here.

CLEM. A souldier o' the citie? What call you him?

COB. Captayne BOBADIL.

CLEM. BOBADIL? And why did he bob, and beate you, sirrah? How began the quarrell betwixt you: ha? speake truely knaue, I aduise you.

COB. Mary, indeed, and please your worship, onely because I spake against their vagrant *tabacco*, as I came by 'hem, when they were taking on't, for nothing else.

CLEM. Ha? you speake against *tabacco*? FORMALL, his name.

FORM. What's your name, sirra?

COB. OLIVER, sir, OLIVER COB, sir.

CLEM. Tell OLIVER COB, he shall goe to the iayle, FORMALL.

FORM. OLIVER COB, my master, Iustice CLEMENT, saies, you shall goe to the iayle.

COB. O, I beseech your worship, for gods sake, deare master Iustice.

CLEM. Nay, gods pretious: and such drunkards, and tankards, as you are, come to dispute of *tabacco* once; I haue done! away with him.

COB. O, good master Iustice, sweet old gentleman.

KNO. Sweet OLIVER, would I could doe thee any good: Iustice CLEMENT, let me intreat you, sir.

CLEM. What? a thred-bare rascall! a begger! a

III. vii. 31 sweare,] swear *F2*   35 and't] an't *F2*   38 he,] he *F2*
44 you: ha? *F2* : you? ha: *F1*   46 and] an't *F2*   48 on't,] on't; *F2*   57 gods] Gods *F2*   59 and such] an' such *F2*   64 good:] good. *F2*

slaue that neuer drunke out of better then pisse-pot mettle in his life! and he to depraue, and abuse the vertue of an herbe, so generally receiu'd in the courts of princes, the chambers of nóbles, the bowers of sweet ladies, the cabbins of souldiers! R o g e r, away with him, by gods pretious ——I say, goe too.

    C o b. Deare master Iustice; Let mee bee beaten againe, I haue deseru'd it: but not the prison, I beseech you.

    K n o. Alas, poore O l i v e r!

    C l e m. R o g e r, make him a warrant (hee shall not goe) I but feare the knaue.

    F o r m. Doe not stinke, sweet O l i v e r, you shall not goe, my master will giue you a warrant.

    C o b. O, the Lord maintayne his worship, his worthy worship.

    C l e m. Away, dispatch him. How now, master K n o'w e l! In dumps? In dumps? Come, this becomes not.

    K n o. Sir, would I could not feele my cares———

    C l e m. Your cares are nothing! they are like my cap, soone put on, and as soone put off. What? your sonne is old inough, to gouerne himselfe: let him runne his course, it's the onely way to make him a stay'd man. If he were an vnthrift, a ruffian, a drunkard, or a licentious liuer, then you had reason; you had reason to take care: but, being none of these, mirth's my witnesse, an' I had twise so many cares, as you haue, I'ld drowne them all in a cup of sacke. Come, come, let's trie it: I muse, your parcell of a souldier returnes not all this while.

    III. vii. 66 then] than *F2*   77 stinke,] stink *F2*

Act IIII. Scene I.

Downe-right, Dame Kitely.

WEll sister, I tell you true : and you'll finde it so, in the end.

Dame. Alas brother, what would you haue mee to doe ? I cannot helpe it : you see, my brother brings 'hem in, here, they are his friends.

Dow. His friends ? his fiends. S'lud, they doe nothing but hant him, vp and downe, like a sort of vnluckie sprites, and tempt him to all manner of villanie, that can be thought of. Well, by this light, a little thing would make me play the deuill with some of 'hem ; and 't were not more for your husbands sake, then any thing else, I'ld make the house too hot for the best on 'hem : they should say, and sweare, hell were broken loose, e're they went hence. But, by gods will, 'tis no bodies fault, but yours : for, an' you had done, as you might haue done, they should haue beene perboyl'd, and bak'd too, euery mothers sonne, e're they should ha' come in, e're a one of 'hem.

Dame. God's my life ! did you euer heare the like ? what a strange man is this ! Could I keepe out all them, thinke you ? I should put my selfe, against halfe a dozen men ? should I ? Good faith, you'ld mad the patient'st body in the world, to heare you talke so, without any sense, or reason !

iv. i.] Scene 1.—A Room in Kiteley's House. *G*   1 so,] so *F2*
5 here,] here ; *F2*   7 hant] haunt *F2*   11 then] than *F2*
12 'hem *F2* : hem *F1*   15 perboyl'd] parboil'd *F3*   17 in,] in *F2*

Act IIII. Scene II.

M*ʳˢ·* Bridget, M*ʳ·* Matthew, Dame Kitely,
Downe-right, Wel-bred, Stephen,
Ed. Kno'well, Bobadil,
Brayne-worme, Cash.

Seruant (in troth) you are too prodigall
Of your wits treasure, thus to powre it forth,
Vpon so meane a subiect, as my worth?
    Mat. You say well, mistris; and I meane, as well.
5   Down. Hoy-day, here is stuffe!
    Well. O, now stand close: pray heauen, shee can get him to reade: He should doe it, of his owne naturall impudencie.
    Brid. Seruant, what is this same, I pray you?
10   Matt. Mary, an *Elegie*, an *Elegie*, an odde toy——
    Down. To mock an ape withall. O, I could sow vp his mouth, now.
    Dame. Sister, I pray you let's heare it.
    Down. Are you rime-giuen, too?
15   Matt. Mistris, Ile reade it, if you please.
    Brid. Pray you doe, seruant.
    Down. O, here's no fopperie! Death, I can endure the stocks, better.
    E. Kn. What ayles thy brother? can he not hold his
20 water, at reading of a ballad?
    Well. O, no: a rime to him, is worse then cheese, or a bag-pipe. But, marke, you loose the protestation.
    Matt. Faith, I did it in an humour; I know not how it is: but, please you come neere, sir. This gentleman ha's
25 iudgement, hee knowes how to censure of a——pray you sir, you can iudge.
    Step. Not I, sir: vpon my reputation, and, by the foot of Pharoah.

    iv. ii. 11 sow] sew *F3*   21 then] than *F2*   22 loose] lose *F2*
    23 an] a *F*

WELL. O, chide your cossen, for swearing.
E. KN. Not I, so long as he do's not forsweare himselfe.
BOB. Master MATTHEW, you abuse the expectation of your deare mistris, and her faire sister: Fie, while you liue, auoid this prolixitie.
MATT. I shall, sir: well, *Incipere dulce.*
E. KN. How! *Insipere dulce?* a sweet thing to be a foole, indeed.
WELL. What, doe you take *Incipere,* in that sense?
E. KN. You doe not? you? This was your villanie, to gull him with a *motte.*
WELL. O, the Benchers phrase: *pauca verba, pauca verba.*
MATT. *Rare creature, let me speake without offence,*
Would god my rude wordes had the influence,
To rule thy thoughts, as thy faire lookes doe mine,
Then should'st thou be his prisoner, who is thine.
E. KN. This is in HERO and LEANDER?
WELL. O, I! peace, we shall haue more of this.
MATT. *Be not vnkinde, and faire, mishapen stuffe*
Is of behauiour boysterous, and rough:
WELL. How like you that, sir?   *Master*
E. KN. S'light, he shakes his head like a bottle, to feele *Stephen answeres*
and there be any braine in it! *with shaking*
MATT. But obserue the *catastrophe,* now, *his head.*
And I in dutie will exceede all other,
As you in beautie doe excell loues mother.
E. KN. Well, Ile haue him free of the wit-brokers, for hee vtters nothing, but stolne remnants.
WEL. O, forgiue it him.
E. KN. A filtching rogue? hang him. And, from the dead? it's worse then sacrilege.
WEL. Sister, what ha' you here? verses? pray you, lets see. Who made these verses? they are excellent good!

IV. ii. 29 cossen] coussen *F2*   37 *Incipere* G: *Insipere* Ff   43 *Would*] The W has got out of position in some copies of *F1* and is printed before MATT. *in* 42   47 I!] I *F2*   48 *faire,*] *faire;* F2
49 *rough:*] rough. F2   60 then] than *F2*

MAT. O, master WEL-BRED, 'tis your disposition to say so, sir. They were good i' the morning, I made 'hem, extempore, this morning.

WEL. How? *extempore?*

MAT. I, would I might bee hang'd else; aske Captayne BOBADILL. He saw me write them, at the——(poxe on it) the starre, yonder.

BRAY. Can he find, in his heart, to curse the starres, so?

E. KN. Faith, his are euen with him: they ha' curst him ynough alreadie.

STEP. Cosen, how doe you like this gentlemans verses?

E. KN. O, admirable! the best that euer I heard, cousse!

STEP. Body o' CAESAR! they are admirable! The best, that euer I heard, as I am a souldier.

DOW. I am vext, I can hold ne're a bone of mee still! Heart, I thinke, they meane to build, and breed here!

WEL. Sister, you haue a simple seruant, here, that crownes your beautie, with such *encomions*, and deuises: you may see, what it is to be the mistris of a wit! that can make your perfections so transparent, that euery bleare eye may looke through them, and see him drown'd ouer head, and eares, in the deepe well of desire. Sister KITELY, I maruaile, you get you not a seruant, that can rime, and doe tricks, too.

DOWN. Oh monster! impudence it selfe! tricks?

DAME. Tricks, brother? what tricks?

BRID. Nay, speake, I pray you, what tricks?

DAME. I, neuer spare any body here: but say, what tricks?

BRID. Passion of my heart! doe tricks?

WEL. S'light, here's a trick vyed, and reuyed! why, you munkies, you? what a catter-waling doe you keepe? ha's hee not giuen you rimes, and verses, and tricks?

IV. ii. 65, 66 *extempore*] *ex tempore* F2   69 starre] Starre F2   70 curse] course F2   81 seruant,] servant F2

Dow. O, the fiend!

Wel. Nay, you, lampe of virginitie, that take it in snuffe so! come, and cherish this tame *poeticall furie*, in your seruant, you'll be begg'd else, shortly, for a concealement: goe to, reward his muse. You cannot giue him lesse then a shilling, in conscience, for the booke, he had it out of, cost him a teston, at least. How now, gallants? M^r. Matthew? Captayne? What? all sonnes of silence? no spirit?

Dow. Come, you might practise your ruffian-tricks somewhere else, and not here, I wusse; this is no tauerne, nor drinking-schole, to vent your exploits in.

Wel. How now! whose cow ha's calu'd?

Dow. Mary, that ha's mine, sir. Nay, Boy, neuer looke askance at me, for the matter; Ile tell you of it, I, sir, you, and your companions, mend your selues, when I ha' done?

Wel. My companions?

Dow. Yes sir, your companions, so I say, I am not afraid of you, nor them neither: your hang-byes here. You must haue your Poets, and your potlings, your *soldado's*, and *foolado's*, to follow you vp and downe the citie, and here they must come to domineere, and swagger. Sirrha, you, ballad-singer, and slops, your fellow there, get you out; get you home: or (by this steele) Ile cut off your eares, and that, presently.

Wel. S'light, stay, let's see what he dare doe: cut off his eares? cut a whetstone. You are an asse, doe you see? touch any man here, and by this hand, Ile runne my rapier to the hilts in you.

Dow. Yea, that would I faine see, boy.

Dame. O Iesu! murder. Thomas, Gaspar!

Brid. Helpe, helpe, Thomas.

E. Kn. Gentlemen, forbeare, I pray you.

Bob. Well, sirrha, you, Holofernes: by my hand, I will pinck your flesh, full of holes, with my rapier for

They all draw, and they of the house make out to part them.

IV. ii. 103 then] than *F2*   115 your] you *F1 originally*   118 fooado's,] foolado's *F2*   122 that,] that *F2*   127 Yea,] Yea *F2*

They offer to fight againe, and are parted. this; I will, by this good heauen: Nay, let him come, let him come, gentlemen, by the body of Saint GEORGE, Ile not kill him.

    CASH. Hold, hold, good gentlemen.

    DOW. You whorson, bragging coystrill!

Act IIII. Scene III.

To them.
                  KITELY.

WHy, how now? what's the matter? what's the stirre here?
Whence springs the quarrell? THOMAS! where is he?
Put vp your weapons, and put off this rage.
5 My wife and sister, they are cause of this,
What, THOMAS? where is this knaue?

    CASH. Here, sir.

    WEL. Come, let's goe: this is one of my brothers ancient humours, this.

10   STEP. I am glad, no body was hurt by his ancient humour.

    KITE. Why, how now, brother, who enforst this brawle?

    DOW. A sort of lewd rake-hells, that care neither for god, nor the deuill! And, they must come here to reade ballads,
15 and rogery, and trash! Ile marre the knot of 'hem ere I sleepe, perhaps: especially BOB, there: he that's all manner of shapes! and *Songs, and sonnets,* his fellow.

    BRID. Brother, indeed, you are too violent,
To sudden, in your humour: and, you know
20 My brother WEL-BREDS temper will not beare
Anie reproofe, chiefly in such a presence,
Where euery slight disgrace, he should receiue,
Might wound him in opinion, and respect.

    DOWN. Respect? what talke you of respect 'mong such,

    IV. iii. 3 rage.] rage, *F2*   13 god] God *F2*   15 trash *some copies of F2*   21 reproofe] repoofe *F2*

As ha' nor sparke of manhood, nor good manners? 25
'Sdeynes I am asham'd, to heare you! respect?
    B R I D. Yes, there was one a ciuill gentleman,
And very worthily demean'd himselfe!
    K I T E. O, that was some loue of yours, sister!
    B R I D. A loue of mine? I would it were no worse, 30
    brother!
You'lld pay my portion sooner, then you thinke for.
    D A M E. Indeed, he seem'd to be a gentleman of an
exceeding faire disposition, and of verie excellent good
parts!
    K I T E. Her loue, by heauen! my wifes minion! 35
Faire disposition? excellent good parts?
Death, these phrases are intollerable!
Good parts? how should shee know his parts?
His parts? Well, well, well, well, well, well!
It is too plaine, too cleere: T H O M A S, come hither. 40
What, are they gone? C A S H. I, sir, they went in.
My mistris, and your sister——
    K I T E. Are any of the gallants within?
    C A S H. No, sir, they are all gone.
    K I T E. Art thou sure of it? 45
    C A S H. I can assure you, sir.
    K I T E. What gentleman was that they prais'd so,
T H O M A S?
    C A S H. One, they call him master K N O'W E L L, a
handsome yong gentleman, sir. 50
    K I T E. I, I thought so: my mind gaue me as much.
Ile die, but they haue hid him i' the house,
Somewhere; Ile goe and search: goe with me, T H O M A S.
Be true to me, and thou shalt find me a master.

    IV. iii. 31 then] than *F2*   35 wifes] Wives *F3*   43 within?] within *Ff*   51 much.] much: *F2*

Act IIII.   Scene IIII.

COB, TIB.

WHat TIB, TIB, I say.
    TIB. How now, what cuckold is that knocks so hard? O, husband, ist you? what's the newes?
    COB. Nay, you haue stonn'd me, Ifaith! you ha' giu'n
5 me a knock o' the forehead, will stick by me! cuckold? 'Slid, cuckold?
    TIB. Away, you foole, did I know it was you, that knockt? Come, come, you may call me as bad, when you list.
10   COB. May I? TIB, you are a whore.
    TIB. You lye in your throte, husband.
    COB. How, the lye? and in my throte too? doe you long to bee stab'd, ha?
    TIB. Why, you are no souldier, I hope?
15   COB. O, must you be stab'd by a souldier? Masse, that's true! when was BOBADILL here? your Captayne? that rogue, that foist, that fencing *Burgullian*? Ile tickle him, ifaith.
    TIB. Why, what's the matter? trow!
20   COB. O, he has basted me, rarely, sumptiously! but I haue it here in black and white; for his black, and blew: shall pay him. O, the Iustice! the honestest old braue *Troian* in *London*! I doe honour the very flea of his dog. A plague on him though, he put me once in a villanous filthy
25 feare; mary, it vanisht away, like the smoke of *tabacco*; but I was smok't soundly first. I thanke the deuill, and his good angell, my guest. Well, wife, or TIB (which you will) get you in, and lock the doore, I charge you, let no body in to you; wife, no body in, to you: those are my wordes.
30 Not Captayne BOB himselfe, nor the fiend, in his likenesse; you are a woman; you haue flesh and bloud enough in you,

iv. iv.] Scene II.—The Lane before Cob's House. G   4 Nay,] Nay F2   5 forehead,] forehead F2   8 Come *begins a new line in Ff*   20 sumptiously] sumptuously F2   22 honestest] honest F3

to be tempted: therefore, keepe the doore, shut, vpon all commers.

TIB. I warrant you, there shall no body enter here, without my consent.

COB. Nor, with your consent, sweet TIB, and so I leaue you.

TIB. It's more, then you know, whether you leaue me so.

COB. How?

TIB. Why, sweet.

COB. Tut, sweet, or sowre, thou art a flowre, Keepe close thy dore, I aske no more.

Act IIII.   Scene v.

ED. KNO'WELL, WELL-BRED, STEPHEN, BRAYNE-WORME.

WEll BRAYNE-WORME, performe this businesse, happily, and thou makest a purchase of my loue, for-euer.

WEL. Ifaith, now let thy spirits vse their best faculties. But, at any hand, remember the message, to my brother: for, there's no other meanes, to start him.

BRAY. I warrant you, sir, feare nothing: I haue a nimble soule ha's wakt all forces of my phant'sie, by this time, and put 'hem in true motion. What you haue possest mee withall, Ile discharge it amply, sir. Make it no question.

WEL. Forth, and prosper, BRAYNE-WORME. Faith, NED, how dost thou approue of my abilities in this deuise?

E. KN. Troth, well, howsoeuer: but, it will come excellent, if it take.

WEL. Take, man? why, it cannot choose but take, if the circumstances miscarrie not: but, tell me, ingenuously, dost thou affect my sister BRIDGET, as thou pretend'st?

E. KN. Friend, am I worth beliefe?

IV. iv. 38 then] than *F2*   IV. v.] Scene III.—A Room in the Windmill Tavern. *G.*   BRAYNE-WORME, *F2*   2 and] And *Ff*, *beginning a new line.*   3 for-euer.] for ever. *F2*: for-euer, *F1*
5 But *F2*: but *F1*   6 meanes,] means *F2*   8 ha's] has *F2*

W E L. Come, doe not protest. In faith, shee is a maid of
20 good ornament, and much modestie: and, except I conceiu'd very worthily of her, thou shouldest not haue her.

E. K N. Nay, that I am afraid will bee a question yet,
whether I shall haue her, or no?

W E L. Slid, thou shalt haue her; by this light, thou shalt.
25 E. K N. Nay, doe not sweare.

W E L. By this hand, thou shalt haue her: Ile goe fetch
her, presently. Point, but where to meet, and as I am an
honest man, I'll bring her.

E. K N. Hold, hold, be temperate.
30 W E L. Why, by——what shall I sweare by? thou shalt
haue her, as I am——

E. K N. 'Pray thee, be at peace, I am satisfied: and doe
beleeue, thou wilt omit no offered occasion, to make my
desires compleat.
35 W E L. Thou shalt see, and know, I will not.

Act IIII. *Scene* VI.

FORMALL, KNO'WELL, BRAYNE-WORME.

WAs your man a souldier, sir?
K N O. I, a knaue, I tooke him begging o' the way,
This morning, as I came ouer *More*-fields!
O, here he is! yo' haue made faire speed, beleeue me:
5 Where, i' the name of sloth, could you be thus——

B R A Y. Mary, peace be my comfort, where I thought
I should haue had little comfort of your worships seruice.

K N O. How so?

B R A Y. O, sir! your comming to the citie, your enter-
10 tainment of me, and your sending me to watch——indeed,
all the circumstances either of your charge, or my imployment, are as open to your sonne, as to your selfe!

    IV. v. 22 that] that, *F2*   afraid] afraid, *F2*   IV. vi.] Scene IV.—
The Old Jewry. *G*: Scene VI.—A Street. *H. B. Wheatley*   3 More-
fields] *Moore*-fields *F2*   5 thus——] thus?——*F2*   6 be] by *F2*
11 imployment,] imployment *F2*

K N O. How should that be! vnlesse that villaine,
 B R A Y N E-W O R M E,
Haue told him of the letter, and discouer'd
All that I strictly charg'd him to conceale? 'tis so!
 B R A Y. I am, partly, o' the faith, 'tis so indeed.
 K N O. But, how should he know thee to be my man?
 B R A Y. Nay, sir, I cannot tell; vnlesse it bee by the
black art! Is not your sonne a scholler, sir?
 K N O. Yes, but I hope his soule is not allied
Vnto such hellish practise: if it were,
I had iust cause to weepe my part in him,
And curse the time of his creation.
But, where didst thou find them, F I T z-S W O R D?
 B R A Y. You should rather aske, where they found me,
sir, for, Ile bee sworne I was going along in the street,
thinking nothing, when (of a suddain) a voice calls, M^r.
K N O-W E L's man; another cries, souldier: and thus, halfe
a dosen of 'hem, till they had cal'd me within a house where
I no sooner came, but they seem'd men, and out flue al their
rapiers at my bosome, with some three or foure score oathes
to accompanie 'hem, & al to tel me, I was but a dead man,
if I did not confesse where you were, and how I was imployed, and about what; which, when they could not get
out of me (as I protest, they must ha' dissected, and made
an *Anatomie* o' me, first, and so I told 'hem) they lockt
mee vp into a roome i' the top of a high house, whence, by
great miracle (hauing a light heart) I slid downe, by a
bottom of pack-thred, into the street, and so scapt. But,
sir, thus much I can assure you, for I heard it, while I was
lockt vp, there were a great many rich merchants, and
braue citizens wiues with 'hem at a feast, and your sonne,
M^r. E D W A R D, with-drew with one of 'hem, and has
pointed to meet her anon, at one C O B S house, a water-
bearer, that dwells by the wall. Now, there, your worship

 IV. vi. 17 am,] am *F2*   27 sir,] sir; *F2*   sworne] sworne, *F2*
 28 calls,] calls *F2*   29 K N O-W E L's] K N O W E L's *F2*   30 house]
house, *F2*   31 they *F2*: thy *F1*   men] mad-men *W. conj.*   flue]
flew *F2*   43 feast,] feast: *F2*   46 there,] there *F2*

shall be sure to take him, for there he preyes, and faile he will not.

K N O. Nor, will I faile, to breake his match, I doubt not. Goe thou, along with Iustice C L E M E N T's man, And stay there for me. At one C O B S house, sai'st thou?

B R A Y. I sir, there you shall haue him. Yes? Inuisible? Much wench, or much sonne! 'Slight, when hee has staid there, three or foure houres, trauelling with the expectation of wonders, and at length be deliuer'd of aire: ô, the sport, that I should then take, to looke on him, if I durst! But, now, I meane to appeare no more afore him in this shape. I haue another trick, to act, yet. O, that I were so happy, as to light on a nupson, now, of this Iustices nouice. Sir, I make you stay somewhat long.

F O R M. Not a whit, sir. 'Pray you, what doe you meane? sir?

B R A Y. I was putting vp some papers——

F O R M. You ha' beene lately in the warres, sir, it seemes.

B R A Y. Mary haue I, sir; to my losse: and expence of all, almost——

F O R M. Troth sir, I would be glad to bestow a pottle of wine o' you, if it please you to accept it——

B R A Y. O, sir——

F O R M. But, to heare the manner of your seruices, and your deuices in the warres, they say they be very strange, and not like those a man reades in the *Romane* histories, or sees, at *Mile-end*.

B R A Y. No, I assure you, sir, why, at any time when it please you, I shall be readie to discourse to you, all I know: and more too, somewhat.

F O R M. No better time, then now, sir; wee'll goe to the wind-mill: there we shall haue a cup of neate grist, wee call it. I pray you, sir, let mee request you, to the wind-mill.

B R A Y. Ile follow you, sir, and make grist o' you, if I haue good lucke.

IV. vi. 47 preyes] presy *F2*   49 KN.] E. KNO. *F2*   56 sport,] sport *F2*
61 'Pray] Pray *F2*   meane?] meane, *F2*   74 sir,] sir; *F2*   77 then] than *F2*   78, 79 wind-mill] Wind-mill *F2*   79 you, to] you to *F2*

Act IIII.   Scene VII.

MATTHEW, ED. KNO'WELL, BOBADILL, STEPHEN,
  DOWNE-RIGHT.   *To them.*

SIr, did your eyes euer tast the like clowne of him, where
we were to day, M`r`. WEL-BRED's halfe brother?
I thinke, the whole earth cannot shew his paralell, by this
day-light.
   E. KN. We were now speaking of him: Captayne 5
BOBADIL tells me, he is fall'n foule o'you, too.
   MAT. O, I, sir, he threatned me, with the bastinado.
   BOB. I, but I thinke, I taught you preuention, this
morning, for that—— You shall kill him, beyond question:
if you be so generously minded.   10
   MAT. Indeed, it is a most excellent trick!
   BOB. O, you doe not giue spirit enough, to your motion, *He prac-*
you are too tardie, too heauie! ô, it must be done like *tises at a post.*
lightning, hay?
   MAT. Rare Captaine!   15
   BOB. Tut, 'tis nothing, and 't be not done in a——*punto*!
   E. KN. Captaine, did you euer proue your selfe, vpon
any of our masters of defence, here?
   MAT. O, good sir! yes, I hope, he has.
   BOB. I will tell you, sir. Vpon my first comming to the 20
citie, after my long trauaile, for knowledge (in that mysterie
only) there came three, or foure of 'hem to me, at a gentlemans house, where it was my chance to be resident, at that
time, to intreat my presence at their scholes, and with-all
so much importun'd me, that (I protest to you as I am a 25
gentleman) I was asham'd of their rude demeanor, out of
all measure: well, I told 'hem, that to come to a publike

IV. vii.] Scene v.—*Moorfields. G*: Scene VI.—*A Street. H. B. Wheat-*
ley.   Ff arrange the characters in two lines, MATTHEW . . . BOBADILL, |
STEPHEN, DOWNE-RIGHT.   *F1 prints ' To them ' parallel with the first*
line, F2 with the second.   16 and 't] an 't *F2*   17 selfe,] selfe *F2*
18 defence,] defence *F2*   19 hope,] hope *F2*   25 you] you, *F2*   26
demeanor] demeanour *F2*   27 that] that, *F2*

schoole, they should pardon me, it was opposite (in *diameter*) to my humour, but, if so they would giue their attendance 30 at my lodging, I protested to doe them what right or fauour I could, as I was a gentleman, and so forth.

E. K N. So, sir, then you tried their skill?

B O B. Alas, soone tried! you shall heare sir. Within two or three daies after, they came; and, by honestie, faire sir, 35 beleeue mee, I grac't them exceedingly, shew'd them some two or three tricks of preuention, haue purchas'd 'hem, since, a credit, to admiration! they cannot denie this: and yet now, they hate mee, and why? because I am excellent, and for no other vile reason on the earth.

40 E. K N. This is strange, and barbarous! as euer I heard!

B O B. Nay, for a more instance of their preposterous natures, but note, sir. They haue assaulted me some three, foure, fiue, sixe of them together, as I haue walkt alone, in diuers skirts i'. the towne, as *Turne-bull*, *White-chappell*, 45 *Shore-ditch*, which were then my quarters, and since vpon the *Exchange*, at my lodging, and at my ordinarie: where I haue driuen them afore me, the whole length of a street, in the open view of all our gallants, pittying to hurt them, beleeue me. Yet, all this lenitie will not ore-come their 50 spleene: they will be doing with a pismier, raysing a hill, a man may spurne abroad, with his foot, at pleasure. By my selfe, I could haue slaine them all, but I delight not in murder. I am loth to beare any other then this bastinado for 'hem: yet, I hold it good politie, not to goe disarm'd, 55 for though I bee skilfull, I may bee oppress'd with multitudes.

E. K N. I, beleeue me, may you sir: and (in my conceit) our whole nation should sustaine the losse by it, if it were so.

B O B. Alas, no: what's a peculiar man, to a nation? not 60 seene.

E. K N. O, but your skill, sir!

    IV. vii. 29 so] so be *F2*   35 grac't] grac'd *F2*   45 quarters,]
    quarters; *F2*   since] since, *F2*   49 Yet,] Yet *F2*   53 then]
    than *F2*   54 yet,] yet *F2*   61 sir!] sir. *F2*

Bob. Indeed, that might be some losse; but, who respects it? I will tell you, sir, by the way of priuate, and vnder seale; I am a gentleman, and liue here obscure, and to my selfe: but, were I knowne to her Maiestie, and the Lords (obserue mee) I would vnder-take (vpon this poore head, and life) for the publique benefit of the state, not only to spare the intire liues of her subiects in generall, but to saue the one halfe, nay, three parts of her yeerely charge, in holding warre, and against what enemie soeuer. And, how would I doe it, thinke you?

E. Kn. Nay, I know not, nor can I conceiue.

Bob. Why thus, sir. I would select nineteene, more, to my selfe, throughout the land; gentlemen they should bee of good spirit, strong, and able constitution, I would choose them by an instinct, a character, that I haue: and I would teach these nineteene, the speciall rules, as your *Punto*, your *Reuerso*, your *Stoccata*, your *Imbroccata*, your *Passada*, your *Montanto*: till they could all play very neare, or altogether as well as my selfe. This done, say the enemie were fortie thousand strong, we twentie would come into the field, the tenth of *March*, or thereabouts; and wee would challenge twentie of the enemie; they could not, in their honour, refuse vs, well, wee would kill them: challenge twentie more, kill them; twentie more, kill them; twentie more, kill them too; and thus, would wee kill, euery man, his twentie a day, that's twentie score; twentie score, that's two hundreth; two hundreth a day, fiue dayes a thousand; fortie thousand; fortie times fiue, fiue times fortie, two hundreth dayes kills them all vp, by computation. And this, will I venture my poore gentleman-like carcasse, to performe (prouided, there bee no treason practis'd vpon vs) by faire, and discreet manhood, that is, ciuilly by the sword.

E. Kn. Why, are you so sure of your hand, Captaine, at all times?

<small>iv. vii. 64 vnder seale] under-seale *F2*   70, 80, 83 enemie] enimy·
F2   84 vs,] us; *F2*</small>

B o b. Tut, neuer misse thrust, vpon my reputation with you.

E. K n. I would not stand in D o w n e-r i g h t s state, then, an' you meet him, for the wealth of any one street in *London*.

B o b. Why, sir, you mistake me! if he were here now, by this welkin, I would not draw my weapon on him! let this gentleman doe his mind: but, I will bastinado him (by the bright sunne) where-euer I meet him.

M a t. Faith, and Ile haue a fling at him, at my distance.

E. K n. Gods so', looke, where he is: yonder he goes.

Downe-right walkes ouer the stage.

D o w. What peeuish luck haue I, I cannot meet with these bragging raskalls?

B o b. It's not he? is it?

E. K n. Yes faith, it is he.

M a t. Ile be hang'd, then, if that were he.

E. K n. Sir, keepe your hanging good, for some greater matter, for I assure you, that was he.

S t e p. Vpon my reputation, it was hee.

B o b. Had I thought it had beene he, he must not haue gone so: but I can hardly be induc'd, to beleeue, it was he, yet.

E. K n. That I thinke, sir. But see, he is come againe!

D o w. O, P h a r o a h s foot, haue I found you? Come, draw, to your tooles: draw, gipsie, or Ile thresh you.

B o b. Gentleman of valour, I doe beleeue in thee, heare me——

D o w. Draw your weapon, then.

B o b. Tall man, I neuer thought on it, till now (body of me) I had a warrant of the peace, serued on me, euen now, as I came along, by a water-bearer; this gentleman saw it, M^r. M a t t h e w.

D o w. 'Sdeath, you will not draw, then?

He beates him, and disarmes him :

B o b. Hold, hold, vnder thy fauour, forbeare.

D o w. Prate againe, as you like this, you whoreson

IV. vii. 107 so'] so, *F2*   110–11 *One line in F2*   111 he.] he? *Ff*
121 gipsie,] gipsie; *F2*

foist, you. You'le controll the point, you? Your consort is *Matthew runnes away.*
gone? had he staid, he had shar'd with you, sir.

B o B. Well, gentlemen, beare witnesse, I was bound to the peace, by this good day. 135

E. K N. No faith, it's an ill day, Captaine, neuer reckon it other: but, say you were bound to the peace, the law allowes you, to defend your selfe: that'll proue but a poore excuse.

B o B. I cannot tell, sir. I desire good construction, in faire sort. I neuer sustain'd the like disgrace (by heauen) 140 sure I was strooke with a plannet thence, for I had no power to touch my weapon.

E. K N. I, like inough, I haue heard of many that haue beene beaten vnder a plannet: goe, get you to a surgean. 'Slid, an' these be your tricks, your *passada's*, and your 145 *mountanto's*, Ile none of them. O, manners! that this age should bring forth such creatures! that Nature should bee at leisure to make 'hem! Come, cousse.

S T E P. Masse, Ile ha' this cloke.

E. K N. Gods will, 'tis D O W N E-R I G H T'S. 150

S T E P. Nay, it's mine now, another might haue tane vp, aswell as I: Ile weare it, so I will.

E. K N. How, an' he see it? hee'll challenge it, assure your selfe.

S T E P. I, but he shall not ha' it; Ile say, I bought it. 155

E. K N. Take heed, you buy it not, too deare, cousse.

Act IIII.   *Scene* VIII.

KITELY, WEL-BRED, DAME KIT. BRIDGET,
BRAYNE-WORME, CASH.

NOw, trust me brother, you were much to blame,
T'incense his anger, and disturbe the peace,
Of my poore house, where there are sentinells
That euery minute watch, to giue alarmes,

IV. vii. 141 strooke] struck *F2*   145 *passada's*] passadaes *F2*
146 *mountanto's,*] mountantoes *F2*   148 'hem *F2* : hem *F1*   151
tane] tane't *F2*   153 an'] an *F2*   IV. viii.] Scene VI.—A Room in
Kitely's House. G

⁵ Of ciuill warre, without adiection
Of your assistance, or occasion.

WELL. No harme done, brother, I warrant you: since there is no harme done. Anger costs a man nothing: and a tall man is neuer his owne man, till he be angrie. To ¹⁰ keepe his valure in obscuritie, is to keepe himselfe, as it were, in a cloke-bag. What's a musitian, vnlesse he play? what's a tall man, vnlesse he fight? For, indeed, all this, my wise brother stands vpon, absolutely: and, that made me fall in with him, so resolutely.

¹⁵ DAME. I, but what harme might haue come of it, brother?

WELL. Might, sister? so, might the good warme clothes, your husband weares, be poyson'd, for any thing he knowes: or the wholesome wine he drunke, euen now, at the table——

²⁰ KITE. Now, god forbid: O me. Now, I remember, My wife drunke to me, last; and chang'd the cup:
And bade me weare this cursed sute to day.
See, if heau'n suffer murder vndiscouer'd!
I feele me ill; giue me some *mithridate*,
²⁵ Some *mithridate* and oile, good sister, fetch me;
O, I am sicke at heart! I burne, I burne.
If you will saue my life, goe, fetch it me.

WELL. O, strange humour! my verie breath ha's poyson'd him.

³⁰ BRID. Good brother, be content, what doe you meane?
The strength of these extreme conceits, will kill you.

DAME. Beshrew your heart-bloud, brother WELL-BRED, now;
For putting such a toy into his head.

WELL. Is a fit *simile*, a toy? will he be poyson'd with ³⁵ a *simile*? Brother KITELY, what a strange, and idle imagination is this? For shame, bee wiser. O' my soule, there's no such matter.

IV. viii. 8 done.] done, *Q, G*   10 valure] valour *F2*   himselfe,] himself; *F2*   12 For,] For *F2*   13 and,] and *F2*   20 god] God *F2*   23 vndiscouer'd] vndiscour'd *F1* : undiscover'd *F2*   32–3 Verse in *Q* : prose in *Ff*.   34 simile,] simile *F2*   36 O'] O *F2*

KITE. Am I not sicke? how am I, then, not poyson'd?
Am I not poyson'd? how am I, then, so sicke?
  DAME. If you be sicke, youre owne thoughts make you sicke.
  WELL. His iealousie is the poyson, he ha's taken.
  BRAY. M^r. KITELY, my master, Iustice CLEMENT, salutes you; and desires to speake with you, with all possible speed. *He comes disguis'd like Justice Clements man.*
  KITE. No time, but now? when, I thinke, I am sicke? very sicke! well, I will wait vpon his worship. THOMAS, COB, I must seeke them out, and set 'hem sentinells, till I returne. THOMAS, COB, THOMAS.
  WELL. This is perfectly rare, BRAYNE-WORME! but how got'st thou this apparell, of the Iustices man?
  BRAY. Mary sir, my proper fine pen-man, would needs bestow the grist o'me, at the wind-mil, to hear some martial discourse; where so I marshal'd him, that I made him drunke, with admiration! &, because, too much heat was the cause of his distemper, I stript him starke naked, as he lay along asleepe, and borrowed his sute, to deliuer this counterfeit message in, leauing a rustie armor, and an old browne bill to watch him, till my returne: which shall be, when I ha' pawn'd his apparell, and spent the better part o' the money, perhaps.
  WELL. Well, thou art a successefull merry knaue, BRAYNE-WORME, his absence will be a good subiect for more mirth. I pray thee, returne to thy yong master, and will him to meet me, and my sister BRIDGET, at the tower instantly: for, here, tell him, the house is so stor'd with iealousie, there is no roome for loue, to stand vpright in. We must get our fortunes committed to some larger prison, say; and, then the tower, I know no better aire: nor where the libertie of the house may doe vs more present seruice. Away.
  KITE. Come hether, THOMAS. Now, my secret's ripe, And thou shalt haue it: lay to both thine eares.

iv. viii. 41 ha's] has *F2*   71 hether] hither *F2*

Harke, what I say to thee. I must goe forth, THOMAS.
Be carefull of thy promise, keepe good watch,
75 Note euery gallant, and obserue him well,
That enters in my absence, to thy mistris:
If shee would shew him roomes, the iest is stale,
Follow 'hem, THOMAS, or else hang on him,
And let him not goe after; marke their lookes;
80 Note, if shee offer but to see his band,
Or any other amorous toy, about him;
But praise his legge; or foot; or if shee say,
The day is hot, and bid him feele her hand,
How hot it is; ô, that's a monstrous thing!
85 Note me all this, good THOMAS, marke their sighes,
And, if they doe but whisper, breake 'hem off:
Ile beare thee out in it. Wilt thou doe this?
Wilt thou be true, my THOMAS? CAS. As truth's selfe, sir.

    KITE. Why, I beleeue thee: where is COB, now? COB?

90   DAME. Hee's euer calling for COB! I wonder, how hee imploies COB, so!

    WELL. Indeed, sister, to aske how hee imploies COB, is a necessarie question for you, that are his wife, and a thing not very easie for you to be satisfied in: but this Ile 95 assure you, COBS wife is an excellent bawd, sister, and, often-times, your husband hants her house, mary, to what end, I cannot altogether accuse him, imagine you what you thinke conuenient. But, I haue knowne, faire hides haue foule hearts, e'er now, sister.

100   DAME. Neuer said you truer then that, brother, so much I can tell you for your learning. THOMAS, fetch your cloke, and goe with me, Ile after him presently: I would to fortune, I could take him there, ifaith. Il'd returne him his owne, I warrant him.

105   WELL. So, let 'hem goe: this may make sport anon.

    IV. viii. 96 house,] house; *F2*   97 end,] end; *F2*   100 then] than *F2*

Now, my faire sister in-law, that you knew, but how happie a thing it were to be faire, and beautifull?

    BRID. That touches not me, brother.

    WELL. That's true; that's euen the fault of it: for, indeede, beautie stands a woman in no stead, vnlesse it procure her touching. But, sister, whether it touch you, or no, it touches your beauties; and, I am sure, they will abide the touch; an' they doe not, a plague of all ceruse, say I: and, it touches mee to in part, though not in the—— Well, there's a deare and respected friend of mine, sister, stands very strongly, and worthily affected toward you, and hath vow'd to inflame whole bone-fires of zeale, at his heart, in honor of your perfections. I haue alreadie engag'd my promise to bring you, where you shall heare him confirme much more. NED KNO'WELL is the man, sister. There's no exception against the partie. You are ripe for a husband; and a minutes losse to such an occasion, is a great trespasse in a wise beautie. What say you, sister? On my soule hee loues you. Will you giue him the meeting?

    BRID. Faith, I had very little confidence in mine owne constancie, brother, if I durst not meet a man: but this motion of yours, sauours of an old knight-aduenturers seruant, a little too much, me thinkes.

    WELL. What's that, sister?

    BRID. Mary, of the squire.

    WELL. No matter if it did, I would be such an one for my friend, but see! who is return'd to hinder vs?

    KITE. What villanie is this? call'd out on a false message? This was some plot! I was not sent for. BRIDGET, Where's your sister? BRID. I thinke shee be gone forth, sir.

    KITE. How! is my wife gone forth? whether for gods sake?

    BRID. Shee's gone abroad with THOMAS.

    IV. viii. 110 for,] for *F2*   112 and,] and *F2*   118 honor] honour *F2*   130-1 *One line in F2*   137 whether] whither *F2*

KITE. Abroad with THOMAS? oh, that villaine dors me.
140 He hath discouer'd all vnto my wife!
Beast that I was, to trust him: whither, I pray you,
Went shee? BRID. I know not, sir. WELL. Ile tell you, brother,
Whither I suspect shee's gone. KITE. Whither, good brother?
WELL. To COBS house, I beleeue: but, keepe my
145 counsaile.
KITE. I will, I will: to COBS house? doth shee hant COBS?
Shee's gone a' purpose, now, to cuckold me,
With that lewd raskall, who, to win her fauour,
Hath told her all. WEL. Come, hee's once more gone.
150 Sister, let's loose no time; th'affaire is worth it.

Act IIII. *Scene* IX.

MATTHEW, BOBADIL, BRAYNE-WORME.
[*To them.*] [DOWNE-RIGHT.]

I Wonder, Captayne, what they will say of my going away? ha?
BOB. Why, what should they say? but as of a discreet gentleman? quick, warie, respectfull of natures faire linea-
5 ments: and that's all?
MAT. Why, so! but what can they say of your beating?
BOB. A rude part, a touch with soft wood, a kind of grosse batterie vs'd, laid on strongly, borne most paciently: and that's all.
10 MAT. I, but, would any man haue offered it in *Venice*? as you say?
BOB. Tut, I assure you, no: you shall haue there your

IV. viii. 141–3 *Whalley's arrangement*: Beast... went shee? | BRID. ...sir. | WELL. Ile... gone. | KITE... brother? *Ff* 145 counsaile.] counsell *F2* 147 a']a *F2* 149 gone.] gone, *F2* 150 loose] lose *F2*
IV. ix.] Scene VII.—A Street. *G* BRAYNE-WORME.] BRAYNE-WORME, *Ff*

Nobilis, your *Gentelezza*, come in brauely vpon your *reuerse*, stand you close, stand you firme, stand you faire, saue your *retricato* with his left legge, come to the *assalto* with the right, thrust with braue steele, defie your base wood! But, wherefore doe I awake this remembrance? I was fascinated, by IVPITER: fascinated: but I will be vn-witch'd, and reueng'd, by law.

MAT. Doe you heare? ist not best to get a warrant, and haue him arrested, and brought before Iustice CLEMENT?

BOB. It were not amisse, would we had it.

MAT. Why, here comes his man, let's speake to him.

BOB. Agreed, doe you speake.

MAT. Saue you, sir.

BRAY. With all my heart, sir.

MAT. Sir, there is one DOWNE-RIGHT, hath abus'd this gentleman, and my selfe, and we determine to make our amends by law; now, if you would doe vs the fauour, to procure a warrant, to bring him afore your master, you shall bee well considered, I assure you, sir.

BRAY. Sir, you know my seruice is my liuing, such fauours as these, gotten of my master, is his only preferment, and therefore, you must consider me, as I may make benefit of my place.

MAT. How is that, sir?

BRAY. Faith sir, the thing is extraordinarie, and the gentleman may be, of great accompt: yet, bee what hee will, if you will lay mee downe a brace of angells, in my hand, you shall haue it, otherwise not.

MAT. How shall we doe, Captayne? he askes a brace of angells, you haue no monie?

BOB. Not a crosse, by fortune.

MAT. Nor I, as I am a gentleman, but two pence, left of my two shillings in the morning for wine, and redish: let's find him some pawne.

iv. ix. 25–6 *One line in F2*   25 Saue] 'Save *F2*   26 sir. *F2*: sir? *F1*   32 liuing,] living; *F2*   33 master,] master *F2*   36 that, sir?] that? sir. *Ff*   45 redish] raddish *F2*

445·3   C C

B o b. Pawne? we haue none to the value of his demand.

M a t. O, yes. I'll pawne this iewell in my eare, and you may pawne your silke stockings, and pull vp your
50 bootes, they will ne're be mist: It must be done, now.

B o b. Well, an' there be no remedie: Ile step aside, and pull 'hem off.

M a t. Doe you heare, sir? wee haue no store of monie at this time, but you shall haue good pawnes: looke you,
55 sir, this iewell, and that gentlemans silke stockings, because we would haue it dispatcht, e're we went to our chambers.

B r a y. I am content, sir; I will get you the warrant presently, what's his name, say you? D o w n e- r i g h t?

M a t. I, I, G e o r g e D o w n e-r i g h t.
60 B r a y. What manner of man is he?

M a t. A tall bigge man, sir; hee goes in a cloke, most commonly, of silke russet, laid about with russet lace.

B r a y. 'Tis very good, sir.

M a t. Here sir, here's my iewell.
65 B o b. And, here, are stockings.

B r a y. Well, gentlemen, Ile procure you this warrant presently, but, who will you haue to serue it?

M a t. That's true, Captaine: that must be consider'd.

B o b. Bodie o'me, I know not! 'tis seruice of danger!
70 B r a y. Why, you were best get one o' the varlets o' the citie, a serieant. Ile appoint you one, if you please.

M a t. Will you, sir? why, we can wish no better.

B o b. Wee'll leaue it to you, sir.

B r a y. This is rare! now, will I goe pawne this cloke
75 of the Iustice's mans, at the brokers, for a varlets sute, and be the varlet my selfe; and get either more pawnes, or more monie of D o w n e-r i g h t, for the arrest.

iv. ix. 49, 55 silke stockings] silke-stockings *F2*   62 silke russet] silke-russet *F2*   64 iewell.] iewell? *Ff*   65 stockings] my stockings *W*   67 presently,] presently; *F2*   69 danger! *F2*: danger? *F1*   71 serieant.] serjeant, *F2*

Act IIII. Scene x.

KNO'WEL, TIB, CASH, DAME KITELY,
KITELY, COB.

OH, here it is, I am glad : I haue found it now.
Ho ? who is within, here ?
  TIB. I am within sir, what's your pleasure ?
  KNO. To know, who is within, besides your selfe.
  TIB. Why, sir, you are no constable, I hope ? 5
  KNO. O ! feare you the constable ? then, I doubt not,
You haue some guests within, deserue that feare,
Ile fetch him straight. TIB. O' gods name, sir.
  KNO. Goe to. Come, tell me, Is not yong KNO'WEL,
    here ?
  TIB. Yong KNO'WEL ? I know none such, sir, o' mine 10
honestie !
  KNO. Your honestie ? dame, it flies too lightly from you :
There is no way, but, fetch the constable.
  TIB. The constable ? the man is mad, I thinke.
  CAS. Ho, who keepes house, here ?
  KNO. O, this is the female copes-mate of my sonne ? 15
Now shall I meet him straight. DAME. Knock,
    THOMAS, hard.
  CAS. Ho, good wife ? TIB. Why, what's the matter
    with you ?
  DAME. Why, woman, grieues it you to ope' your doore ?
Belike, you get something, to keepe it shut.
  TIB. What meane these questions, 'pray yee ?
  DAME. So strange you make it ? is not my husband,
    here ?
  KNO. Her husband ! DAME. My tryed husband,
    master KITELY.
  TIB. I hope, he needes not to be tryed, here.

<small>IV. x.] Scene VIII.—The Lane before Cob's House. G   6 not, Q :
not. Ff   9, 10 yong] young F2   10 KNO'WEL F2 : KNO-WEL F1
18 ope'] ope F2   19 something,] something F2   22 Two lines in Ff</small>

CC 2

DAME. No, dame : he do's it not for need, but pleasure.
25 TIB. Neither for need, nor pleasure, is he here.
    KNO. This is but a deuice, to balke me withall.
    Soft, who is this ? 'Tis not my sonne, disguisd ?

Shee spies her husband come: and runnes to him.

    DAME. O, sir, haue I fore-stald your honest market ?
    Found your close walkes ? you stand amaz'd, now, doe
        you ?
    I faith (I am glad) I have smokt you yet at last !
31 What is your iewell trow ? In : come, lets see her ;
    (Fetch forth your huswife, dame) if shee be fairer,
    In any honest iudgement, then my selfe,
    Ile be content with it : but, shee is change,
35 Shee feedes you fat, shee soothes your appetite,
    And you are well ? your wife, an honest woman,
    Is meat twice sod to you, sir ? O, you trecher !
    KNO. Shee cannot counterfeit thus palpably.
    KITE. Out on thy more then strumpets impudence !
40 Steal'st thou thus to thy haunts ? and, haue I taken
    Thy bawd, and thee, and thy companion,

Pointing to old Kno'well. This horie-headed letcher, this old goat,
    Close at your villanie, and would'st thou 'scuse it,
44 With this stale harlots iest, accusing me ?

To him. O, old incontinent, do'st not thou shame,
    When all thy powers in chastitie is spent,
    To haue a mind so hot ? and to entice,
    And feede th'enticements of a lustfull woman ?
    DAME. Out, I defie thee, I, dissembling wretch.

By Thomas.
50 KITE. Defie me, strumpet ? aske thy pandar, here,
    Can he denie it ? or that wicked elder ?
    KNO. Why, heare you, sir.   KITE. Tut, tut, tut :
        neuer speake.
    Thy guiltie conscience will discouer thee.
    KNO. What lunacie is this, that hants this man ?
55 KITE. Well, good-wife BA'D, COBS wife ; and you,

    IV. x. 28 stage dir. *come :*] *come, F2*   33, 39 then] than *F2*   39
    strumpets] strumpet *F2*   46 is] are *W*   54 hants] haunts *F2*
    55 wife ; and] wife, and *F2*

That make your husband such a hoddie-doddie;
And you, yong apple-squire; and old cuckold-maker;
Ile ha' you euery one before a Iustice:
Nay, you shall answere it, I charge you goe.

    K N O. Marie, with all my heart, sir: I goe willingly.   60
Though I doe tast this as a trick, put on me,
To punish my impertinent search; and iustly:
And halfe forgiue my sonne, for the deuice.

    K I T E. Come, will you goe?   D A M E. Goe? to thy
    shame, beleeue it.

    C O B. Why, what's the matter, here? What's here to doe? 65

    K I T E. O, C O B, art thou come? I haue beene abus'd,
And i' thy house. Neuer was man so, wrong'd!

    C O B. Slid, in my house? my master K I T E L Y? Who
wrongs you in my house?

    K I T E. Marie, yong lust in old; and old in yong, here: 70
Thy wife's their bawd, here haue I taken 'hem.

    C O B. How? bawd? Is my house come to that? Am I *He falls*
prefer'd thether? Did I charge you to keepe your dores shut, *vpon his wife and*
I s'B E L? and doe you let 'hem lie open for all commers? *beates her.*

    K N O. Friend, know some cause, before thou beat'st thy 75
    wife,
This's madnesse, in thee.   C O B. Why? is there no cause?

    K I T E. Yes, Ile shew cause before the Iustice, C O B:
Come, let her goe with me.   C O B. Nay, shee shall goe.

    T I B. Nay, I will goe. Ile see, an' you may bee allow'd to
make a bundle o' hempe, o' your right and lawfull wife thus, 80
at euery cuckoldly knaues pleasure. Why doe you not
goe?

    K I T E. A bitter queane. Come, wee'll ha' you tam'd.

  IV. X. 75, 70, yong] young *F2*   73 thether] thither *F2*   76
madnesse,] madnesse *F2*

Act IIII. Scene XI.

BRAYNE-WORME, MATTHEW, BOBADIL,
STEPHEN, DOWNE-RIGHT.

WEll, of all my disguises, yet, now am I most like my selfe: being in this Serjeants gowne. A man of my present profession, neuer counterfeits, till hee layes hold vpon a debter, and sayes, he rests him, for then hee brings him to all manner of vnrest. A kinde of little kings wee are, bearing the diminutiue of a mace, made like a yong artichocke, that always carries pepper and salt, in it selfe. Well, I know not what danger I vnder-goe, by this exploit, pray heauen, I come well of.

MAT. See, I thinke, yonder is the varlet, by his gowne.

BOB. Let's goe, in quest of him.

MAT. 'Saue you, friend, are not you here, by appointment of Iustice CLEMENTS man?

BRAY. Yes, an't please you, sir: he told me two gentlemen had will'd him to procure a warrant from his master (which I haue about me) to be seru'd on one DOWNE-RIGHT.

MAT. It is honestly done of you both; and see, where the partie comes, you must arrest: serue it vpon him, quickly, afore hee bee aware———

BOB. Beare backe, master MATTHEW.

BRAY. Master DOWNE-RIGHT, I arrest you, i' the queenes name, and must carry you afore a Iustice, by vertue of this warrant.

STEP. Mee, friend? I am no DOWNE-RIGHT, I. I am master STEPHEN, you doe not well, to arrest me, I tell you, truely: I am in nobodies bonds, nor bookes, I, ⟨I⟩ would you should know it. A plague on you heartily, for making mee thus afraid afore my time.

BRAY. Why, now are you deceiued, gentlemen?

IV. xi.] Scene IX.—A Street. *G*   6 yong] young *F2*   12 friend,] friend; *F2*   13 man? *F2*: man. *F1*

BOB. He weares such a cloke, and that deceiued vs: But see, here a comes, indeed! this is he, officer.

DOWN. Why, how now, signior gull! are you turn'd filtcher of late? come, deliuer my cloke.

STEP. Your cloke, sir? I bought it, euen now, in open market.

BRAY. Master DOWNE-RIGHT, I haue a warrant I must serue vpon you, procur'd by these two gentlemen.

DOWN. These gentlemen? these rascals?

BRAY. Keepe the peace, I charge you, in her Maiesties name.

DOWN. I obey thee. What must I doe, officer?

BRAY. Goe before master Iustice CLEMENT, to answere what they can obiect against you, sir. I will vse you kindly, sir.

MATT. Come, let's before, and make the Iustice, Captaine——

BOB. The varlet's a tall man! afore heauen!

DOWN. Gull, you'll gi'me my cloke?

STEP. Sir, I bought it, and Ile keepe it.

DOWN. You will.

STEP. I, that I will.

DOWN. Officer, there's thy fee, arrest him.

BRAY. Master STEPHEN, I must arrest you.

STEP. Arrest mee, I scorne it. There, take your cloke, I'le none on't.

DOWN. Nay, that shall not serue your turne, now, sir. Officer, I'le goe with thee, to the Iustices: bring him along.

STEP. Why, is not here your cloke? what would you haue?

DOWN. I'le ha' you answere it, sir.

BRAY. Sir, Ile take your word; and this gentlemans, too: for his apparance.

DOWN. I'le ha' no words taken. Bring him along.

IV. xi. 32 a comes] acomes, *F2*   40 you,] you *F2*   43 before *F2* : before, *F1*   44 you, sir.] you sir, *some copies of F2*   50 Ile] Ile. *some copies of F2*   51-2 *One line in Ff*   55 mee,] mee ! *F2*   63 apparance] appearance *F2*

BRAY. Sir, I may choose, to doe that: I may take bayle.
DOWN. 'Tis true, you may take baile, and choose; at another time: but you shall not, now, varlet. Bring him along, or I'le swinge you.
BRAY. Sir, I pitty the gentlemans case. Here's your money againe.
DOW. 'Sdeynes, tell not me of my money, bring him away, I say.
BRAY. I warrant you he will goe with you of himselfe, sir.
DOW. Yet more adoe?
BRAY. I haue made a faire mash on't.
STEP. Must I goe?
BRAY. I know no remedie, master STEPHEN.
DOWN. Come along, afore mee, here. I doe not loue your hanging looke behind.
STEP. Why, sir. I hope you cannot hang mee for it. Can hee, fellow?
BRAY. I thinke not, sir. It is but a whipping matter, sure!
STEP. Why, then, let him doe his worst, I am resolute.

Act V.   Scene I.

CLEMENT, KNO'WEL, KITELY, DAME KITELY, TIB, CASH, COB, SERVANTS.

NAy, but stay, stay, giue me leaue: my chaire, sirrha. You, master KNO'WELL, say you went thither to meet your sonne.
KNO. I, sir.
CLEM. But, who directed you, thither?
KNO. That did mine owne man, sir.
CLEM. Where is he?
KNO. Nay, I know not, now; I left him with your clarke: and appointed him, to stay here for me.

v. i.] Colman Street.—A Hall in Justice Clement's House. *G*
And *Ff*: *in F1 beginning a new line, as if verse*

CLEM. My clarke? about what time, was this?
KNO. Mary, betweene one and two, as I take it.
CLEM. And, what time came my man with the false message to you, master KITELY?
KITE. After two, sir.
CLEM. Very good: but, mistris KITELY, how that you were at COBS? ha?
DAME. An' please you, sir, Ile tell you: my brother, WEL-BRED, told me, that COBS house, was a suspected place——
CLEM. So it appeares, me thinkes: but, on.
DAME. And that my husband vs'd thither, daily.
CLEM. No matter, so he vs'd himselfe well, mistris.
DAME. True sir, but you know, what growes, by such hants, often-times.
CLEM. I see, ranke fruits of a iealous braine, mistris KITELY: but, did you find your husband there, in that case, as you suspected?
KITE. I found her there, sir.
CLEM. Did you so? that alters the case. Who gave you knowledge, of your wiues being there?
KITE. Marie, that did my brother WEL-BRED.
CLEM. How? WEL-BRED first tell her? then tell you, after? where is WEL-BRED?
KITE. Gone with my sister, sir, I know not whither.
CLEM. Why, this is a meere trick, a deuice; you are gull'd in this most grosly, all! alas, poore wench, wert thou beaten for this?
TIB. Yes, most pitifully, and't please you.
COB. And worthily, I hope: if it shall proue so.
CLEM. I, that's like, and a piece of a sentence. How now, sir? what's the matter?
SER. Sir, there's a gentleman, i'the court without, desires to speake with your worship.
CLEM. A gentleman? what's he?
SER. A souldier, sir, he saies.

v. i. 15 how] how chance *F2*   18 house,] house. *F2*

C L E M. A souldier? take downe my armor, my sword, quickly: a souldier speake with me! why, when knaues? come on, come on, hold my cap there, so; giue me my gorget, my sword: stand by, I will end your matters, anon——
50 Let the souldier enter, now, sir, what ha' you to say to me?

He armes himselfe.

Act v.   Scene ii.

⟨*To them.*⟩   B O B A D I L L, M A T T H E W.

B Y your worships fauour——
  C L E M. Nay, keepe out, sir, I know not your pretence, you send me word, sir, you are a souldier: why, sir, you shall bee answer'd, here, here be them haue beene amongst
5 souldiers. Sir, your pleasure.

   B O B. Faith, sir, so it is, this gentleman, and my selfe, haue beene most vnciuilly wrong'd, and beaten, by one D O W N E-R I G H T, a course fellow, about the towne, here, and for mine owne part, I protest, being a man, in no sort,
10 giuen to this filthie humour of quarrelling, he hath assaulted mee in the way of my peace; dispoil'd mee of mine honor; dis-arm'd mee of my weapons; and rudely, laid me along, in the open streets: when, I not so much as once offer'd to resist him.
15   C L E M. O, gods precious! is this the souldier? here, take my armour of quickly, 'twill make him swoune, I feare; hee is not fit to looke on't, that will put vp a blow.

   M A T T. An't please your worship, he was bound to the peace.
20   C L E M. Why, and he were, sir, his hands were not bound, were they?

   S E R. There's one of the varlets of the citie, sir, ha's brought two gentlemen, here, one, vpon your worships warrant.

v. i. 46 armor] armuor *F2*   47 with] wirh *F2*   48 s. d. *himselfe.*] *himselfe,* F2   50 enter,] enter; *F2*   v. ii. (margin) *To them.* F2
6 selfe,] selfe *F2*   9 man,] man *F2*   sort,] sort *F2*   11 honor] honour *F2*   16 of] off *F2*   23 here,] here; *F2*

CLEM. My warrant?
SER. Yes, sir. The officer say's, procur'd by these two.
CLEM. Bid him, come in. Set by this picture. What, M^r. DOWNE-RIGHT! are you brought at M^r. FRESH-WATERS suite, here!

Act V. Scene III.

DOWNE-RIGHT, STEPHEN, BRAYNE-WORME. ⟨To them.⟩

I Faith, sir. And here's another brought at my suite.
  CLEM. What are you, sir?
STEP. A gentleman, sir. ô, vncle!
CLEM. Vncle? who? master KNO'WELL?
KNO. I, sir! this is a wise kinsman of mine.
STEP. God's my witnesse, vncle, I am wrong'd here monstrously, hee charges me with stealing of his cloke, and would I might neuer stirre, if I did not find it in the street, by chance.
DOW. O, did you find it, now? you said, you bought it, erewhile.
STEP. And, you said, I stole it; nay, now my vncle is here, I'll doe well inough, with you.
CLEM. Well, let this breath a while; you, that haue cause to complaine, there, stand forth: had you my warrant for this gentlemans apprehension?
BOB. I, an't please your worship.
CLEM. Nay, doe not speake in passion so: where had you it?
BOB. Of your clarke, sir.
CLEM. That's well! an' my clarke can make warrants, and my hand not at'hem! Where is the warrant? Officer, haue you it?
BRAY. No, sir, your worship's man, master FORMAL,

v. ii. 25 warrant!] warrant? *F2*   v. iii. (margin) *To them. F2*   3 sir.] sir? *Ff*   6 here] here, *F2*   10 find it,] find it *F2*   said,] said *F2*   14 a while] awhile *F2*   17 I,] I *F2*   20 sir. *F2* : sir? *F1*

25 bid mee doe it, for these gentlemen, and he would be my discharge.

CLEM. Why, master DOWNE-RIGHT, are you such a nouice, to bee seru'd, and neuer see the warrant?

DOW. Sir. He did not serue it on me.

30 CLEM. No? how then?

DOW. Mary, sir, hee came to mee, and said, hee must serue it, and hee would vse me kindly, and so——

CLEM. O, gods pittie, was it so, sir? he must serue it? 34 giue me my long-sword there, and helpe me of; so. Come on, sir varlet, I must cut off your legs, sirrha: nay, stand vp, Ile vse you kindly; I must cut off your legs, I say.

He flourishes ouer him with his long-sword.

BRAY. O, good sir, I beseech you; nay, good master Iustice.

CLEM. I must doe it; there is no remedie. I must cut 40 off your legs, sirrha, I must cut off your eares, you rascall, I must doe it; I must cut off your nose, I must cut off your head.

BRAY. O, good your worship.

CLEM. Well, rise, how doest thou doe, now? doest thou 45 feele thy selfe well? hast thou no harme?

BRAY. No, I thanke your good worship, sir.

CLEM. Why, so! I said, I must cut off thy legs, and I must cut off thy armes, and I must cut off thy head; but, I did not doe it: so, you said, you must serue this gentleman, 50 with my warrant, but, you did not serue him. You knaue, you slaue, you rogue, doe you say you must? sirrha, away with him, to the **iayle**, Ile teach you a trick, for your *must*, sir.

BRAY. Good sir, I beseech you, be good to me.

55 CLEM. Tell him he shall to the iayle, away with him, I say.

BRAY. Nay, sir, if you will commit mee, it shall bee for committing more then this: I will not loose, by my trauaile, any graine of my fame certaine.

v. iii. 34 long-sword] long sword *F2*   of] off *F2*   35 st. dir. *not in some copies of F2*   long-sword] long sword *F2*   37 beseech] heseech *F1*   53 *must*,] must *F2*   57 then] than *F2*   loose] lose *F2* 58 fame] fame, *F3*

C L E M. How is this!
K N O. My man, B R A Y N E-W O R M E! 60
S T E P. O yes, vncle. B R A Y N E-W O R M E ha's beene with my cossen E D W A R D, and I, all this day.
C L E M. I told you all, there was some deuice!
B R A Y. Nay, excellent Iustice, since I haue laid my selfe thus open to you; now, stand strong for mee: both with 65 your sword, and your ballance.
C L E M. Bodie o' me, a merry knaue! Giue me a bowle of sack: If hee belong to you, master K N O'W E L L, I bespeake your patience.
B R A Y. That is it, I haue most need of. Sir, if you'll 70 pardon me, only; I'll glorie in all the rest, of my exploits.
K N O. Sir, you know, I loue not to haue my fauours come hard, from me. You haue your pardon: though I suspect you shrewdly for being of counsell with my sonne, against me. 75
B R A Y. Yes, faith, I haue, sir; though you retain'd me doubly this morning, for your selfe: first, as B R A Y N E-W O R M E; after, as F I T Z-S W O R D. I was your reform'd souldier, sir. 'Twas I sent you to C O B S, vpon the errand, without end. 80
K N O. Is it possible! or that thou should'st disguise thy language so, as I should not know thee?
B R A Y. O, sir, this ha's beene the day of my *metamorphosis*! It is not that shape alone, that I haue runne through, to day. I brought this gentleman, master 85 K I T E L Y, a message too, in the forme of master Iustices man, here, to draw him out o' the way, as well as your worship: while master W E L L-B R E D might make a conueiance of mistris B R I D G E T, to my yong master.
K I T E. How! my sister stolne away? 90
K N O. My sonne is not married, I hope!
B R A Y. Faith, sir, they are both as sure as loue, a priest, and three thousand pound (which is her portion) can make

v. iii. 59–60 *One line in F2*   62 cossen] coussen *F2*   74 counsell] councell *F2*   79 errand,] errand *F2*   83–4 metamorphosis! *F1 originally ; corrected to italic, and so in F2*

'hem : and by this time are readie to bespeake their wedding
supper at the wind-mill, except some friend, here, preuent
'hem, and inuite 'hem home.

C L E M. Marie, that will I (I thanke thee, for putting me
in mind on't.) Sirrah, goe you, and fetch 'hem hither, vpon
my warrant. Neithers friends haue cause to be sorrie, if
I know the yong couple, aright. Here, I drinke to thee, for
thy good newes. But, I pray thee, what hast thou done
with my man F O R M A L L ?

B R A Y. Faith, sir, after some ceremonie past, as making
him drunke, first with storie, and then with wine (but all in
kindnesse) and stripping him to his shirt : I left him in that
coole vaine, departed, sold your worships warrant to these
two, pawn'd his liuerie for that varlets gowne, to serue it in ;
and thus haue brought my selfe, by my actiuitie, to your
worships consideration.

C L E M. And I will consider thee, in another cup of sack.
Here's to thee, which hauing drunke of, this is my sentence.
Pledge me. Thou hast done, or assisted to nothing, in my
iudgement, but deserues to bee pardon'd for the wit o' the
offence. If thy master, or anie man, here, be angrie with
thee, I shall suspect his ingine, while I know him for't.
How now ? what noise is that !

S E R. Sir, it is R O G E R is come home.

C L E M. Bring him in, bring him in. What ! drunke in
armes, against me ? Your reason, your reason for this.

Act V.   Scene IIII

To them.

FORMALL.

I Beseech your worship to pardon me ; I happen'd into ill
companie by chance, that cast me into a sleepe, and stript
me of all my clothes——

C L E M. Well, tell him, I am Iustice C L E M E N T, and

v. iii. 97 thee,] thee *F2*   102 FORMALL ?] FORMALL. *Ff*   116
now ? now ! *F2*   that !] that ? *F2*

doe pardon him : but, what is this to your armour ! what
may that signifie ?

FORM. And't please you, sir, it hung vp i' the roome, where I was stript ; and I borrow'd it of one o' the drawers, to come home in, because I was loth, to doe penance through the street, i' my shirt.

CLEM. Well, stand by a while. Who be these ? O, the yong companie, welcome, welcome. Gi' you ioy. Nay, mistris BRIDGET, blush not ; you are not so fresh a bride, but the newes of it is come hither afore you. Master Bridegroome, I ha' made your peace, giue mee your hand : so will I for all the rest, ere you forsake my roofe.

Act V. Scene V.

ED. KNO'WEL, WEL-BRED, BRIDGET.   *To them.*

WE are the more bound to your humanitie, sir.

CLEM. Only these two, haue so little of man in 'hem, they are no part of my care.

WELL. Yes, sir, let mee pray you for this gentleman, hee belongs, to my sister, the bride.

CLEM. In what place, sir ?

WELL. Of her delight, sir, below the staires, and in publike : her *poet*, sir.

CLEM. A *poet* ? I will challenge him my selfe, presently, at *extempore*.

    Mount vp thy Phlegon muse, and testifie,
      How SATVRNE, *sitting in an ebon cloud,*
    Disrob'd his podex white as iuorie,
      And, through the welkin, thundred all aloud.

WELL. Hee is not for *extempore*, sir. Hee is all for the pocket-*muse*, please you command a sight of it.

CLEM. Yes, yes, search him for a tast of his veine.

v. iv. 7 And't] An't *F2*   12 yong] young *F2*   v. v. (margin)
them.] Them F2   10, 15 *extempore*] *ex tempore F2*   14 *And,*] *And* F2

WEL. You must not denie the Queenes Iustice, Sir, vnder a writ o' rebellion.

20 CLEM. What! all this verse? Bodie o' me, he carries a whole realme, a common-wealth of paper, in's hose! let's see some of his subiects!

Vnto the boundlesse Ocean of thy face,
Runnes this poore riuer charg'd with streames of eyes.

25 How? this is stolne!

E. KN. A *Parodie*! a *parodie*! with a kind of miraculous gift, to make it absurder then it was.

CLEM. Is all the rest, of this batch? Bring me a torch; lay it together, and giue fire. Clense the aire. Here was 30 enough to haue infected, the whole citie, if it had not beene taken in time! See, see, how our *Poets* glorie shines! brighter, and brighter! still it increases! ô, now, it's at the highest: and, now, it declines as fast. You may see. *Sic transit gloria mundi.*

35 KNO. There's an *embleme* for you, sonne, and your studies!

CLEM. Nay, no speech, or act of mine be drawne against such, as professe it worthily. They are not borne euerie yeere, as an Alderman. There goes more to the making of 40 a good *Poet*, then a Sheriffe, Mʳ. KITELY. You looke vpon me! though, I liue i' the citie here, amongst you, I will doe more reuerence, to him, when I meet him, then I will to the Major, out of his yeere. But, these paper-pedlers! these inke-dablers! They cannot expect reprehension, or 45 reproch. They haue it with the fact.

E. KN. Sir, you haue sau'd me the labour of a defence.

CLEM. It shall be discourse for supper; betweene your father and me, if he dare vnder-take me. But, to dispatch away these, you signe o'the Souldier, and picture o' the 50 *Poet* (but, both so false, I will not ha' you hang'd out at my dore till midnight) while we are at supper, you two shall

v. v. 21 realme,] realme *F2*   27, 40, 42 then] than *F2*   33 and,] & *F2*   35 There's] There's, *F2*   45 reproch] reproach *F2*   49 you] you, *F2* (cf. IV. ii. 99)   Souldier] *Souldier F2*

penitently fast it out in my court, without ; and, if you will, you may pray there, that we may be so merrie within, as to forgiue, or forget you, when we come out. Here's a third, because, we tender your safetie, shall watch you, he is 55 prouided for the purpose. Looke to your charge, sir.

STEP. And what shall I doe?

CLEM. O! I had lost a sheepe, an he had not bleated! Why, sir, you shall giue M^r. DOWNE-RIGHT his cloke: and I will intreat him to take it. A trencher, and a napkin, 60 you shall haue, i' the buttrie, and keepe COB, and his wife companie, here ; whom, I will intreat first to bee reconcil'd : and you to endeuour with your wit, to keepe 'hem so.

STEP. Ile doe my best.

COB. Why, now I see thou art honest, TIB, I receiue 65 thee as my deare, and mortall wife, againe.

TIB. And, I you, as my louing, and obedient husband.

CLEM. Good complement! It will bee their bridale night too. They are married anew. Come, I coniure the rest, to put of all discontent. You, M^r. DOWNE-RIGHT, 70 your anger ; you, master KNO'WELL, your cares ; master KITELY, and his wife, their iealousie. For, I must tell you both, while that is fed, Hornes i' the mind are worse then o' the head.

KITE. Sir, thus they goe from me, kisse me, sweet heart. 75
See, what a droue of hornes flye, in the ayre,
Wing'd with my clensed, and my credulous breath!
Watch 'hem, suspicious eyes, watch, where they fall.
See, see! on heads, that thinke th'haue none at all!
O, what a plenteous world of this, will come! 80
When ayre raynes hornes, all may be sure of some.

I ha' learned so much verse out of a iealous mans part, in a play.

CLEM. 'Tis well, 'tis well! This night wee'll dedicate to friendship, loue, and laughter. Master bride-groome, 85 take your bride, and leade ; euery one, a fellow. Here is my

<small>v. v. 74 then] than *F2*   75 from me,] from me ; *F2*   sweet heart] sweet-heart *F2*   81 *fome* Q, F2 : *fame* F1   86 leade ;] leade : *F2*</small>

445·3   D d

mistris. BRAYNE-WORME! to whom all my addresses of courtship shall haue their reference. Whose aduentures, this day, when our grand-children shall heare to be made a fable, I doubt not, but it shall find both spectators, and applause.

THE END.

This Comoedie was firſt Acted, in the yeere 1598.

By *the then* L. Chamberlayne *his Seruants.*

The principall Comœdians were.

Will. Shakespeare.	Ric. Bvrbadge.
Avg. Philips.	Ioh. Hemings.
Hen. Condel.	Tho. Pope.
Will. Slye.	Chr. Beeston.
Will. Kempe.	Ioh. Dvke.

With the allowance of the Maſter of Revells.

F2 prints this notice on the back of the title-page after 'The Scene London' *in slightly different form:* first, 'The principall Comedians were Will. Shakespeare . . . John Duke'; *then* 'First Acted in the yearè 1598, with allowance of the Master of Revells'; *the reference to the* 'Lord Chamberlayne' *is omitted*

EVERY MAN OUT OF HIS HUMOUR.

THE TEXT.

THE play of *Every Man out of his Humour* was entered in the Stationers' Register by its first publisher, William Holme, on April 8, 1600. The entry is as follows:

                  8 Aprilis.

William holme.   Enterd for his copie vnder the handes of master Harsnet. and master wyndet warden. A Comicall Satyre of euery man out of his humour.   vjd.

             Arber, *Transcript*, III. 159.

The tangled history of this publication has been brilliantly elucidated by Dr. W. W. Greg in an article in *The Library* for December 1920, vol. i, pp. 153–160, and in two supplementary notes in vol. ii, p. 49, and vol. iii, p. 57. He was the first to distinguish between the first and second Quartos.

Holme issued the first Quarto in 1600. The collation, A to R in fours, is in detail—Blank leaf A. Title-page A ij. The names of the actors A ij verso. The Characters A iij to A iv verso. The play B to R iv, with the original conclusion R iij to R iv. 'Strictly speaking', says Dr. Greg, 'only signatures H, P, Q, R are proper quarto, the rest being of that puzzling size (it might be called "bastard quarto") which is commonly folded in fours, and agrees in size and shape with a normal quarto, but according to wire and water marks should be an octavo.'

The printer was probably Adam Islip. Mr. F. S. Ferguson (quoted by Dr. Greg) has pointed out that the headpiece before the Characters and the Induction on signatures A 3 and B 1 was used by Islip near the date of the present play, for instance in Holland's *Pliny* in 1601. The ornament on the title-page, which ought to settle the question, unfortunately is not identified. In the centre is a vase of flowers. Flanking it on either side like heraldic supporters are two satyr-like figures, apparently male and female, with pairs of butterfly wings on each shoulder, amply sprouting tails, and feet that curl into huge tendrils. The whole breathes a hazy suggestion of the *Metamorphoses*.

Three copies are known: one in the British Museum (C. 34. i. 29), wanting the preliminary blank leaf and the two leaves of the original ending; a fine copy wanting only the preliminary leaf in the library of Mr. Henry E. Huntington; and a complete copy with the head-lines cropt in the Public Library of Boston in America. A scholarly reprint by Mr. F. P. Wilson and Dr. Greg was issued by the Malone Society in 1920.

This was the first Humour play which Jonson committed to the press. His new venture in drama was appreciated, for the edition sold out within the year and Holme had the play reprinted at once. The title-page of this second Quarto, verbally reproducing that of its predecessor, has been a snare to bibliographers. When the British Museum acquired its copy of the first Quarto in 1908, the difference between the two texts was not recognized.

The collation of the second Quarto, A to Q in fours, is in detail—Title-page A. The Characters A ij to A iij. The play A iij verso to Q iij ('FINIS'). The original conclusion is on Q iij verso to Q iv verso. The reprint is on the whole very exact, but it shows traces of being set up in a hurry. We may assume that Holme's stock of the first edition was running low or that he had actually sold out. Two compositors, who used slightly different founts of type, worked simultaneously on the reprint, the first setting up sheets A to H, the second sheets I to Q. By dint of various economies, minutely tabulated by Dr. Greg, they saved a sheet. The first compositor set up the title-page on signature A, and thus saved two pages at the start by dropping the preliminary blank leaf of the first edition. He saved another page over the Characters, compressing them into three pages. Up to the end of sheet E he printed thirty-seven lines to a page where the original had thirty-six lines. By saving one line in thirty-six successive pages he had then caught up the original and was two leaves to the good. So he 'followed copy' with thirty-six lines to the end of sheet H. As the last page of the original was blank, the second compositor had only to save three pages. He did it by small economies where the original was lavish over printing headings and stage directions, and by tucking in lines which had been turned over. By the end of M 3 verso he had saved his first page; he saved his second by the end of O 1, and his third by the end of Q 2. The rest of the original he reproduced page for page.

The printer was Peter Short, whose device is on the title-page. It is a book surrounded by beams of light; above it two outspread wings rest on a background of cloud, and at the top is a figure pointing downwards to the book. The motto, taken from Psalm lvi. 11, 'Et vsque ad nubes veritas tua', is on the frame, and below are the initials 'P.S.'[1]

Of this edition two copies have been used: one in the Bodleian (Malone 229), and one in the Dyce collection at South Kensington. An exact reprint by Professor W. Bang and Dr. W. W. Greg was issued in Professor Bang's *Materialien zur Kunde des älteren englischen Dramas*, Band xvi, in 1907.

The third Quarto, also dated 1600, was printed for Nicholas Ling. It follows the second Quarto page for page and line for line, except that by a printer's error sheet N is wrongly imposed, so that two pages of the text of Act v, scene i have changed places.[2] This Quarto is merely a bad reprint of its predecessor. It copies such obvious errors of the earlier text as 'Pastidius' (Characters, 35), 'makes' for 'wakes' (ibid., 54), 'sleeps' for 'steeps' (Induction, 167), 'after' for 'alter' (ibid., 277), 'gard' for 'regard' (II. i. 49), 'world' for 'word' (III. iv. 86), and adds numerous mistakes of its own—'Frenchfield' for 'Frenchefied' (I. iii. 195), 'ratifide' for 'rarefi'd' (II. iii. 84), 'rogue' for 'tongue' (II. iii. 219). It ventures occasionally on a correction, as in deleting the repeated 'one and twentieth'

---
[1] No. 278 in McKerrow's *Printers' and Publishers' Devices.*
[2] See the critical apparatus at v. i. 21.

of I. iii. 50, 51, substituting 'inward' for 'innated' in II. iii. 55, and 'Shotmakers' for 'Shotmarkes' in v. iv. I. The last is ingenious; it assumes that the letter *r* was misplaced, but here the correct reading is 'Shot-sharkes'. None of the special errors here noted are found in the first Quarto.

Ling's device is on the title-page, a ling entwined in the tendrils of a honeysuckle, the whole set in a fancy border. On either side below are the initials 'N. L.'[1]

A reprint by Professor Bang and Dr. Greg was issued in the *Materialien*, Band xvii.

The play next appeared in the Folio of 1616. From this edition in its corrected form the present text is taken. The editor's own copy has been collated with the two copies in the British Museum and the two copies in Bodley. The title-page appears in two forms, one in an ornamental border and one in plain type. The imprint varies in both forms. The fuller imprint is

LONDON,

Printed by WILLIAM STANSBY

for *Iohn Smithwicke*

M. DC. XVI.

But Smethwick's name is not in all copies. Thus, the plain title-page of the Grenville copy in the British Museum and the title-page with ornamental border of the Douce copy in Bodley have simply 'London, Printed by William Stansby, M. DC. XVI.'

The curt imprint of the third Quarto, 'London, Printed for Nicholas Linge, 1600', resembles that of the famous (or infamous) group of Shakespeare Quartos printed in 1619. A normal imprint at this date specifies the printer and the

[1] McKerrow's *Devices*, 301.

publisher, and the publisher's address; or it gives at least the publisher and his address, as in Holme's first Quarto—'Printed for *William Holme*, and are to be sold at his Shop at Sarjeants Inne gate in Fleetstreet. 1600.' Was Ling's Quarto authorized, and was it correctly dated? There is no record in the Stationers' Register of any transfer of copyright by Holme to Ling, and Ling continued in business till 1607, Holme till 1615. The date '1600' on the imprint makes one a little uneasy. It is not impossible in view of the literary importance of the play, but, if Holme had sold out two issues, why did he boggle at a third? There is a gap in the evidence here—*hiatus valde deflendus*. The full imprint of the play in the 1616 Folio states that it was 'Printed by William Stansby for Iohn Smithwicke'. On November 19 1607 Ling's copyrights were transferred to Smethwick. Sixteen books are specified; they include works by Drayton, Lodge, Greene, Shakespeare, Nashe and Munday, but not *Every Man out of his Humour*. In 1638 Smethwick assigned the copyright of the play to Richard Bishop, who published it in the 1640 Folio. The entry runs:

28° Aprilis 1638

Master Bishop. Assigned ouer vnto him by vertue of a note vnder the hand and seale of master Smethw⟨i⟩cke and subscribed by Master Bourne warden all the Right and interest in a play called *Euery man out of his humour* by Ben: Johnson. vjd

Arber, *Transcript*, IV. 417.

The text of the Folio of 1616 was set up from a copy of the carefully printed first Quarto. A few passages are decisive on this point. The Folio follows the first Quarto in reading in III. vi. 89, 90, 'hauing no better a cloke for it, then he has neither'; in IV. vii. 82, 'bee still a fashion behinde with the world'; in V. iv. 1, where Buffone, entering the tavern, calls for the drawers, 'where be these shot-sharkes?' and in V. viii. 49, 50, Fallace's contemptuous question to Macilente, 'Your intents?' why, what may your intents bee, for gods sake?'' In these passages the second and third Quartos[1] read 'hauing no better a cloake than he has for it neither'; 'be still a Fashion behind the world'; 'where be these Shotmarkes?' (Quarto 2), 'where be these Shotmakers?' (Quarto 3); and 'what may your intent be for Gods sake?'

Textually this play is of great importance. It is the first play of which we have parallel texts, Quarto and Folio, and both were scrupulously edited. An exceptionally full collation has therefore been recorded in the critical apparatus, even at the risk of overloading it, to show how minutely Jonson worked over his 'copy' in his anxiety to produce it in a form which satisfied his fastidious judgement. In our reprint of the remaining plays included in the 1616 Folio the critical apparatus will be shortened. But we regard this Folio as authoritative for all the texts contained in it, and the proof that this is so is given once for all.

The most important changes are, of course, the actual alterations of the text. Perhaps the most interesting example occurs in the flattering address to Queen Elizabeth which rounded off the '*Catastrophe* or Conclusion, at the first Playing'. In the Quarto, printed during the last years of the Queen's life, Macilente, who came to the Court 'with a purpos'd resolution . . . to maligne at any thing that should front him', was suddenly, 'against expectation, and all steele of his Malice', struck dumb by the wonder of Elizabeth's presence.

In her Graces
All my malitious Powers haue lost their stings:
Enuie is fled my Soule at sight of her.

Giving a new turn to the old convention of praying for the sovereign at the end of a play, Jonson makes him say on his knees,

I implore,
O *Heauen*: that Shee (whose *Figure* hath effected
This change in me) may neuer suffer Change
In her Admir'd and happie Gouernment.

---

[1] Minute variations of spelling are not noticed here and in later examples. The text is quoted from the earlier Quarto.

Public opinion forced Jonson to cancel this hyperbole, but he printed it characteristically as an appendix. To have retained it in this form in print thirteen years after her death would have been grotesque. In the Folio ' may neuer suffer Change' was softened to 'may suffer most late change', echoing the prayer of Horace to the god on earth, Augustus:

> Serus in caelum redeas diuque
> Laetus intersis populo Quirini.[1]

These textual changes are improvements, with perhaps two exceptions. Puntarvolo says in the Quarto at II. iii. 243-4, 'I doe entend this yeere of *Iubile* to trauaile': the date of performance is 1598, and this periphrasis for ' 1600 ' suits the speaker. The text of 1616, instead of simply cutting out the words ' of *Iubile* ', reads very perversely 'this yeere of *Iubile*, comming on'. One of Fallace's outbursts has the point completely blunted. Originally she said, ' By the Bible of heauen (beast that I am to say it) I haue not one friend i' the world besides my husband ' (IV. i. 19-21). This is attenuated to ' By the faith of a Gentlewoman (beast that I am to say it).' The mincing oaths of ' a comfit-maker's wife ', which was the City standard of good breeding, excited the contempt of Hotspur, who demanded ' good mouth-filling ' terms from Lady Percy.[2] The revision makes Fallace insipid and silly: perhaps, for that very reason, she is true to type. But the context calls for something stronger.

In a few passages the verse is readjusted by filling in incomplete lines. Thus in Act II, scene iv, ll. 17, 18, the Quartos read :

> *Deli.* Dispatch, take heed your mistresse see you not.
> *Fido.* I warrant you sir.   *Exit Fido.*

The Folio completes the second line with ' Ile steale by her softly'. In line 26 'What meanes this Signior *Deliro?*' becomes ' What meanes this, signior DELIRO ? all this

---

[1] *Odes*, I. ii. 45-6.   [2] *Henry IV, Part I*, III. i. 250-60.

censing?' A speech of Fallace in the Quartos (II. iv. 146–50) has an irregular line :

> Alas, you'r simple, you : you cannot change,
> Looke pale at pleasure, and then red with Wonder :
> No, no, not you : I did but cast an amorous eye e'en now
> Vpon a paire of Gloues that somwhat likt me, . . .

The Folio emends :

> No, no, not you ! 'tis pitty o' your naturalls.
> I did but cast an amorous eye, e'en now, . . .

And in II. v. 44 Macilente's 'Good Heauen giue me patience' becomes

> Good heauen, giue me patience, patience, patience.

Corrections such as these might have been made by any careful reviser when they caught his eye on the printed page. But Jonson went much farther. He worked over the entire text with microscopic care, systematically revising spelling, type, and punctuation. He substituted capitals for italic in the names of the characters and of persons mentioned in the text ; he cut down the lavish use of italic for peculiar words, and the still more lavish use of initial capitals. He replaced the light stopping of the Quartos by an elaborate system of punctuation, designed to mark clearly the structure of the sentence. Noteworthy points in it, as compared with the laxer pointing of the Quartos, are the enclosing of adverbial phrases within commas, the use of the interjection (as in IV. i. 29–41) and the hyphen : Jonson affects such spellings as 'out-side', 'vn-did', 'fore-head', 'holy-day', 'in-auspicious'.

Two short passages are added for comparison : Act III, scene v, ll. 8–15, and Act IV, scene viii, ll. 16–25.

Quarto 1	*Folio* 1
Fast. Why do you see sir? they say I am Phantastical : why true, I know it, & I pursue my Humor stil in con-	FAST. Why, doe you see, sir ? they say I am phantasticall : why, true, I know it, and I pursue my humour

tempt of this *censorious* age: S'light & a man should do nothing but what a sort of stale iudgements about this town wil approue in him, he were a sweet Asse, Il'd beg him yfaith: I ne're knew any more find fault with a fashion, then they that knew not how to put themselues into't.

Fasti. O, the most *Celestiall*, and full of wonder and delight that can bee imagin'd Signior, beyond all thought and apprehension of Pleasure. A man liues there in that deuine *Rapture*, that he will thinke himselfe i'the third Heauen for the time, and loose all sence of Mortalitie whatsoeuer; when hee shall behold such glorious (and almost immortall) beauties, heare such Angelicall and Harmonious voices, discourse with such flowing and *Ambrosian* spirits, whose wits as suddaine as Lightning, and humorous as *Nectar*; Oh: it makes a man all *Quintessence* and *Flame*, ...

still, in contempt of this censorious age. S'light, and a man should doe nothing, but what a sort of stale iudgements about this towne will approue in him, he were a sweet asse: Il'd beg him yfaith. I ne're knew any more find fault with a fashion, then they that knew not how to put themselues in to't.

Fast. O, the most celestiall, and full of wonder, and delight, that can be imagin'd, signior, beyond all thought, and apprehension of pleasure! A man liues there, in that diuine rapture, that hee will thinke himselfe i' the ninth heauen for the time, and lose all sense of mortalitie whatsoeuer; when he shall behold such glorious (and almost immortall) beauties, heare such angelicall and harmonious voyces, discourse with such flowing and *ambrosian* spirits, whose wits are as suddaine as lightning, and humorous as *nectar*; Oh: it makes a man al *quintessence*, and *flame*, ...

In the critical apparatus, therefore, typographical peculiarities of the Quarto texts, such as the modern use of 'u' and 'v', 'i' and 'j', are recorded, and most of the variations in spelling and punctuation.

Finishing touches of correction were added while the Folio was passing through the press. They prove beyond question that Jonson supervised the printing. They include all possible forms of correction—punctuation, the use of special type, and changes in the text. The first eight pages of the Induction (ll. 1–292)—a portion of the play which, in Jonson's eyes, would be specially important for its exposition of the doctrine of the humours—yield a number of these final corrections. Thus, in lines 62–4 the printer had set up :

> Let envious Censors with their broadest eyes
> Looke through and through me ; I pursue no fauour.
> Onely vouchsafe me your attentions, . . .

Jonson corrected to 'censors, with their broadest eyes,' and quickened the actor's delivery of the following line by substituting commas after ' me ' and ' fauour '. He adjusted the use of italics, using them for ' *Metaphore* ' and ' *Counters* ' (ibid., 103, 45). He bracketed the parenthetic clause ' (vnderstand you ?) ' in IV. iii. 36. He altered ' howerly ' to ' hourely ' in the Induction, 34, because ' houre ' is there a monosyllable.

One change on pages 82 and 83 of the Folio (containing lines 18–60, 61–102) corrected a printer's error in the setting up of the verse. Jonson liked his lines to be marshalled in even column, and he kept strictly to the verse-arrangement when a speech did not begin the line. Originally the printer set up line 76 :

> Nay doe not turne, but answere.
> M I T. Answere ? what ?

When this was adjusted to a single line, the page was a line short (with 43 lines) and did not balance the opposite page (with 44 lines). To secure uniformity, a stage direction between lines 50 and 51, '*Here hee makes adresse to the People*', was cancelled. Even so a second error remained at line 86 on page 83, and this had to wait for correction till the reprint of 1640.

Jonson also revised a few readings :

> my *soule*
> Was neuer ground into such oyly colours,
> To flatter vice and daube iniquitie :
> (Ind., 13–15)

was improved by reading ' my language ' ; ' you doe me some wrong to make *that* publike, which I imparted to you in priuate ' (IV. vi. 36–8) was changed to ' make occasions publike ' ; and the curious verb ' to manfrede ' was wisely dropped for ' to vndertake ' in IV. viii. 110. In IV. ii. 90–2 the Folio read originally, as the Quartos did, ' and give him warning of my husbands intent ' : Jonson inserted in proof ' malitious ' before ' intent ', and the printer, in order to adjust the spacing, altered ' and tell ' and ' heauens ' to ' & tel ' and ' heuens '. A significant change was made at the end of the dedication to the Court : ' By your true Honorer, BEN. IONSON ' became ' By your Honorer '.

The play was not printed again till the 1640 Folio appeared after Jonson's death. This edition follows the text of 1616, but does not reproduce all its press corrections.[1] This is the clearest evidence we have that there was more than one state of the 1616 proofs. Some minor variants from the earlier text are not without significance. Such a correction as the following must be Jonson's : in II. iv. 33, 34 the 1616 Folio states that no living man

> I doe not say, is not,
> But cannot possibly be worth her kindnesse !

The comma inserted after ' But,' in 1640 to put the emphasis on ' cannot ' is clearly not a printer's correction. The 1616 Folio greatly modified the oaths of the Quartos;[2] the 1640 Folio carries this practice farther by changing ' S'heart ' or ' S'blood ' to a mild ' Why ' or ' What ' or ' Oh ' (as in I. ii. 32, 186, 197) or by omitting them altogether (ibid., 133). The two chief alterations in the text are in the Induction, 114, where the line ' O, 'tis more then most ridiculous ' is given its full ten syllables by reading ' O, it is more ', and in II. iv. 2, 3—

---

[1] Thus, p. 145 of the First Folio, including IV. iv. 110—V. 23, was uncorrected in the copy used.
[2] For example, in the Characters, 29, ' Dam him ' for ' God dam me '.

>   Welcome (good MACILENTE) to my house,
>   To sojourne euen for euer,

where the last line appears in the confused form 'To sojourne at my house for ever'.

For the text of 1640 two copies in the possession of the editor—one a large-paper copy with a few final press-corrections—have been collated with the copies in Bodley and the British Museum.

The Comicall Satyre of
EVERY MAN
OVT OF HIS
HVMOR.

AS IT WAS FIRST COMPOSED
by the AUTHOR B. IOHNSON.

Containing more than hath been Publickely Spoken or Acted.

VVith the seuerall Character of euery Person.

*Non aliena meo pressi pede | * si propius stes
Te capient magis | * & decies repetita placebunt.*

LONDON,
Printed for *William Holme*, and are to be sold at his Shop
at Sarjeants Inne gate in Fleetstreet.
1600.

Title-page in the First Quarto

The Comicall Satyre of
EVERY MAN
OVT OF HIS
HVMOR.

AS IT WAS FIRST COMPOSED
by the Author B. I.

Containing more than hath been publikely Spoken or Acted.

With the seuerall Character of euery Person.

*Non aliena meo pressi pede | * si propius stes
Te capient magis | * & decies repetita placebunt.*

LONDON,
Printed for *William Holme*, and are to be sold at his shoppe
at Sariëants Inne gate in Fleetstreet.
1600.

Title-page in the Second Quarto

The comicall Satyre of
EVERY MAN
OVT OF HIS
HVMOR.

As it was first composed by the Author B. I.

Containing more then hath been publikely spoken or acted.

With the seuerall Character of euery person.

Non aliena meo pressi pede | si propius stes*
Te capient magis| & decies repetita placebunt.*

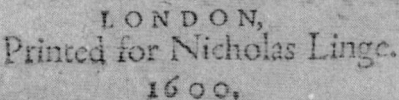

LONDON,
Printed for Nicholas Linge.
1600.

Title-page in the Third Quarto

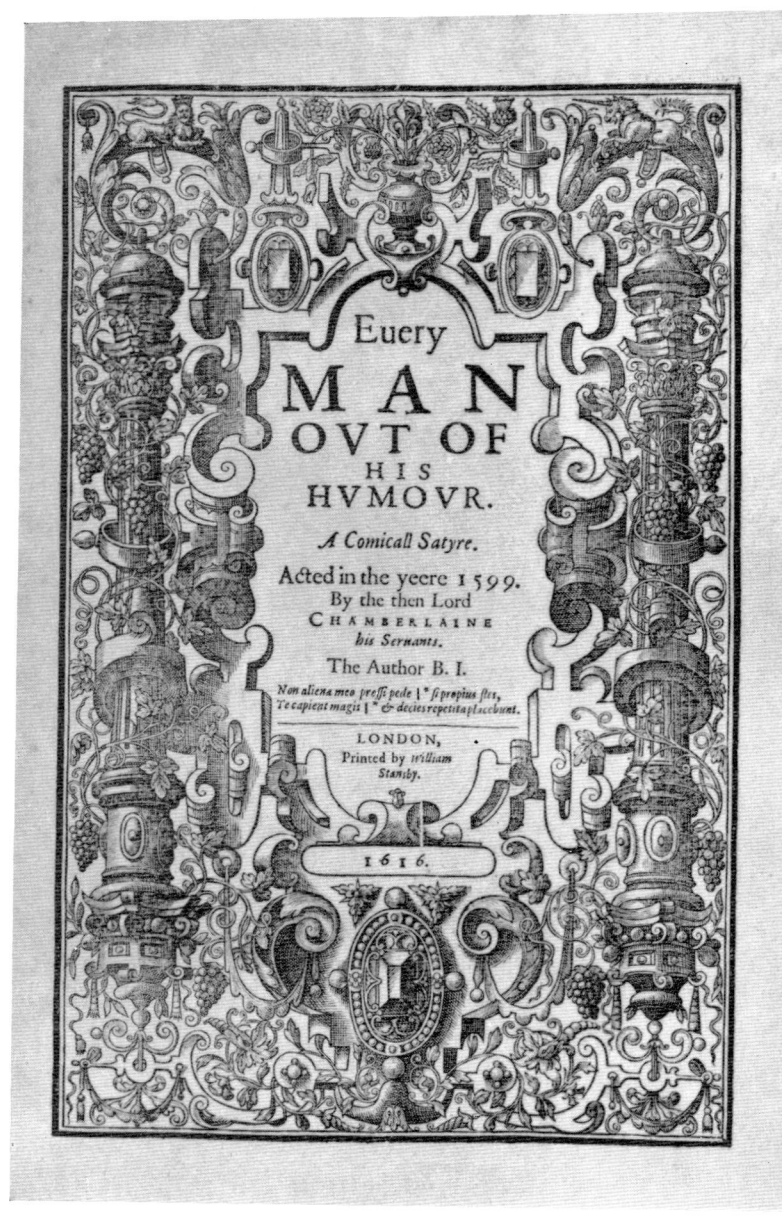

Title-page of the 1616 Folio, with ornamental border

Euery
MAN OVT
OF HIS
HVMOVR.

A Comicall Satyre.

Acted in the yeere 1599. By the then
Lord Chamberlaine his
Seruants.

The Author B. I.

Non aliena meo pressi pede | * *si propius stes,*
Te capient magis | * *& decies repetita placebunt.*

———————————————

LONDON,
Printed by WILLIAM STANSBY
for *Iohn Smithwicke.*

M. DC. XVI.

EVERY MAN
OUT OF HIS
HUMOUR.

A Comicall Satyre.

First Acted in the yeere 1599. By the then Lord CHAMBERLAINE his Servants: With the allowance of the Master of REVELLS.

The Author B. I.

HOR.
Non aliena meo pressi pede | * si propius stes,
Te capient magis | * & decies repetita placebunt.

LONDON,
Printed by RICHARD BISHOP

M. DC. XL.

TO THE NOBLEST NOVRCERIES OF HVMA-NITY, AND LIBERTY, IN THE KINGDOME:

The Innes of Court.

I Vnderstand you, Gentlemen, not your houses: and a worthy succession of you, to all time, as being borne the Iudges of these studies. When *J* wrote this Poeme, *J* had friendship with diuers in your societies; who, as they were great *Names* in learning, so they were no lesse Examples of liuing. Of them, and then (that *J* say no more) it was not despis'd. *Now* that the Printer, by a doubled charge, thinkes it worthy a longer life, then commonly the ayre of such things doth promise; *J* am carefull to put it a seruant to their pleasures, who are the inheriters of the first fauour borne it. Yet, *J* command, it lye not in the way of your more noble, and vse-full studies to the publike. For so I shall suffer for it: But, when the gowne and cap is off, and the Lord of liberty raignes; then, to take it in your hands, perhaps may make some Bencher, tincted with humanity, reade: and not repent him.

By your Honorer,

BEN. IONSON.

DEDICATION. *Not in Qq.*   2 NOVRCERIES] NURSERIES *F3*   6 you] You *F2*   9 Poeme] Poëme *F2*   14 then] than *F2*   24 Honorer, *corr. F1* : true Honorer *Ff*

The Names of the Actors.

ASPER, The Presenter.

MACILENTE.

5 PVNTARVOLO. {
His Lady.
Waiting-Gent.
Huntsman.
Seruingmen, two.
⟨Notary.⟩
Dog and Cat.
}

CARLO BVFFONE.

10 FASTID. BRISKE. {
CINEDO,
his
Page.
}

DELIRO. { FIDO,
15 FALLACE. { their Seruant.
             Musicians.

SAVIOLINA.

SORDIDO. His Hine.

RVSTICI.

FVNGOSO. {
Taylor.
Haber-
dasher.
Shomaker.
} 20

SOGLIARDO.

SHIFT.

CLOVE. {
A Groome.
Drawers. 25
Constable,
and
Officers.
}

ORENGE.

GREX. 30

CORDATVS.   MITIS.

THE NAMES OF THE ACTORS. *In Qq.* ASPER, The Presenter *is followed by* MACILENTE. SAVIOLINA. SORDIDO. His Hind. *in one line; afterwards they differ only in the use of type*   5 PVNTARVOLO, *Large paper F2*, *Qq* : PVNTERVOLO *Ff*   6 Seruingmen, two *corr. F1* : Seruingmen 2. *Ff*, *Qq*   7 Notary *add G*.   10–11 CINEDO, *his* corr. F1 : *Cinedo* his *Ff, Qq*   13 FIDO, *their Seruant* corr. F1 : *Fido* their Seruant *Ff, Qq*   17 Hine *corr. F1* : Hinde *Ff* : Hind *Qq, F3*   18 RVSTICI *corr. F1* : *in Qq, Ff* 'Rustici' *ranged with* SHIFT *at the head of* A Groome *&c.*

ASPER his Character.

HE is of an ingenious and free spirit, eager and constant in reproofe, without feare controuling the worlds abuses. One, whom no seruile hope of gaine, or frosty apprehension of danger, can make to be a Parasite, either to time, place, or opinion.

MACILENTE.

A Man well parted, a sufficient Scholler, and trauail'd; who (wanting that place in the worlds account, which he thinks his merit capable of) falls into such an enuious apoplexie, with which his iudgement is so dazeled, and distasted, that he growes violently impatient of any opposite happinesse in another.

PVNTARVOLO.

A Vaine-glorious Knight, ouer-Englishing his trauels, and wholly consecrated to singularity; the very Iacobs staffe of complement: a Sir, that hath liu'd to see the reuolution of time in most of his apparell. Of presence good ynough, but so palpably affected to his owne praise, that (for want of flatterers) he commends himselfe, to the floutage of his owne family. He deales vpon returnes, and strange performances, resoluing (in despight of publike derision) to sticke to his owne particular fashion, phrase, and gesture.

CARLO BVFFONE.

A Publike, scurrilous, and prophane Iester; that (more swift then Circe) with absurd simile's will transforme any person into deformity. A good Feast-hound, or Banket-

---

1–116 *Headed by W* THE CHARACTER OF THE PERSONS. *In Q3 the body of the type is roman*   2 *ingenious*] ingenuous Q1   *eager*, Q3   3 *feare*, F2   3–4 *abuses. One*] abuses ; One Qq   5 *danger*] Daunger Q1   *either*] iether F2 (*corr. in Large paper*)   10 *enuious*] envious Q1   11 *dazeled*,] dazeled Qq   12 *violently*] voilently Q2   14 PVNTARVOLO] PUNTER-VOLO F2 (*corr. in L. p.*)   17 *Sir*,] Sir Qq   *reuolution*] revolution Q1   18 *ynough*] enough F2, F3   19 *palpably*] palpable F2, F3   20 *him-selfe*, Ff: himself Q1: himselfe Qq 2, 3   24 BVFFONE.] BUFFONE F2   25 *Publike, scurrilous*] Publick, scurrulous Q1, *with the comma ill-pointed: hence* Publik-scurrulous Qq 2, 3   26 *then*] than Qq, F2 (*so in 32, 51*)   *absurd*] obsurd Q3

beagell, that will sent you out a supper some three mile off, and sweare to his Patrons (Dam him) hee came in Oares, when hee was but wafted ouer in a Sculler. A slaue, that hath an extraordinary gift in pleasing his palat, and will swill vp more sacke at a sitting, then would make all the Guard a posset. His religion his rayling, and his discourse ribaldry. They stand highest in his respect, whom he studies most to reproch.

FASTIDIVS BRISKE.

A *Neat, spruce, affecting Courtier, one that weares clothes well, and in fashion; practiseth by his glasse how to salute; speakes good remnants (notwithstanding the Base-violl and Tabacco:) sweares tersely, and with variety; cares not what Ladies fauour he belyes, or great Mans familiarity: a good property to perfume the boot of a coach. Hee will borrow another mans horse to praise, and backs him as his owne. Or, for a neede, on foot can post himselfe into credit with his marchant, only with the gingle of his spurre, and the jerke of his wand.*

DELIRO.

A *Good doting Citizen, who (it is thought) might be of the common Councell for his wealth: a fellow sincerely besotted on his owne wife, and so rapt with a conceit of her perfections, that he simply holds himselfe vnworthy of her. And in that hood-winkt humour, liues more like a suter then a husband; standing in as true dread of her displeasure, as when he first made loue to her. He doth sacrifice two-pence in iuniper to her, euery morning, before shee rises, and wakes her, with villanous-out-of-tune musick, which shee out of her contempt (though not out of her iudgement) is sure to dislike.*

28 *mile*] *miles* F2, F3   29 Dam him *Ff*: God dam me *Qq*   Oares, Ff: Oares, *Q3*: Oars Qq 1, 2   30 *slaue,*] *slaue* Qq   32, 51 *then*] *than* Qq, F2   35 FASTIDIVS] FASTIDIUS *Q1*: PASTIDIVS *Qq* 2, 3; FASTIDIOUS G(*et passim*)   39 *variety;*] *varietie,* Qq   40 *fauour*] *fauor* Qq 1, 2   42 *another*] *an other* Q3   *horse* om. Q3   43 *Or, for a neede,*] *Or for a need (neede* Q2) Qq   44 *marchant* F1: *merchant* F2: *Merchant* Qq, F3   45 *jerke*] *Ierke* Qq 1, 2: *ierke* Q3   48 *common*] *Common* Qq1, 2, F3   51 *humour*] *humor* Q3   *suter*] *sutet* F2   54 *her, euery morning,*] *her euery morning* Qq   *wakes*] *makes* Qq 2, 3   *her,* Ff: *her* Qq 1, 3: *hir* Q2

Fallace.

DEliro's *wife and Idoll: a proud mincing Peat, and as peruerse as he is officious.* Shee dotes as perfectly vpon the Courtier, as her husband doth on her, and only wants the face to be dishonest.

Saviolina.

A *Court Lady, whose weightiest praise is a light wit, admir'd by her selfe, and one more, her seruant* Briske.

Sordido.

A *Wretched hob-nail'd Chuffe, whose recreation, is reading of Almanacks; and felicity, foule weather.* One that neuer pray'd, but for a leane dearth, and euer wept in a fat haruest.

Fvngoso.

THe sonne of Sordido, and a student: one that has reuel'd in his time, and followes the fashion a farre off, like a spie. He makes it the whole bent of his endeuours, to wring sufficient meanes from his wretched father, to put him in the Courtiers cut: at which he earnestly aimes, but so vnluckily, that he still lights short a sute.

Sogliardo.

AN *essentiall Clowne, brother to* Sordido, *yet so enamour'd of the name of a Gentleman, that he will haue it, though he buyes it.* He comes vp euery Terme to learne to take Tabacco, and see new Motions. He is in his kingdome when he can get himselfe into company, where he may be well laught at.

59 *Idoll :*] Idoll, Qq   59 *officious.* Shee] officious, shee Qq   64 *selfe,*] selfe Qq   72 *off.*] off Qq   73 *endeuours,*] endeuours Qq   79 *haue it,*] haue it Qq   80 *Tabacco,*] Tabacco Qq 1, 2

Shift.

A Thred-bare Sharke. One that neuer was Souldier, yet
liues vpon lendings. His profession is skeldring and
odling, his banke Poules, and his ware-house Pict-hatch.
Takes vp single testons vpon othes, till Doomes day. Falls
vnder executions of three shillings, and enters into fiue-groat
bonds. He way-layes the reports of seruices, and connes them
without booke, damming himselfe he came new from them, when
all the while he was taking the dyet in a bawdy house, or lay
pawn'd in his chamber for rent, and victuals. He is of that
admirable and happy memory, that he will salute one for an old
acquaintance, that he neuer saw in his life before. He vsurps
vpon cheats, quarrels, and robberies, which he neuer did, only
to get him a name. His chiefe exercises are, taking the Whiffe,
squiring a Cockatrice, and making priuy searches for Im-
parters.

Clove, and Orange.

An inseparable case of Coxcombs, City-borne; The Gemini
or Twins of foppery: that like a paire of woodden foyles,
are fit for nothing, but to be practis'd vpon. Being well
flatter'd, they'le lend money, and repent when they ha' done.
Their glory is to inuite Plaiers, and make suppers. And in
company of better ranke (to auoide the suspect of insufficiency)
will inforce their ignorance, most desperately, to set vpon the
vnderstanding of any thing. Orange is the more humorous
of the two (whose small portion of iuyce being squeez'd out)
Cloue serues to sticke him, with commendations.

84 Souldier] Soldior Qq 1, 2 : Souldior Q3   86 Poules] Paules F2,
F3   87 othes, Ff: Oths Qq 1, 2: Othes Q3   90 damming] damning
Qq, F3   92 pawn'd] paw'd Q3   rent,] rent Qq   96 are,] are
Qq   99 Clove,] Clove Qq   Orange] Orenge Qq (so in 107)
104 inuite] feast Qq   106 inforce] enforce Qq   ignorance,] Ignorance
Qq   108 being] (being Qq   squeez'd out)] squeez'dout) Q2 : squeez'd
out :) Q3   109 him,] him Qq

CORDATVS. 110

THe Authors friend; A man inly acquainted with the scope and drift of his Plot: Of a discreet, and vnderstanding iudgement; and has the place of a Moderator.

MITIS.

IS a person of no action, and therefore we haue reason to 115 affoord him no Character.

 112 *discreet*,] *discreet* Qq   115 reason] REASON Qq   116 *affoord*] affourd *Qq 1, 2*: afforde *Q3*: *afford* F2   *After* 116 *Qq add* It was not neere his thoughts (*thought* Q3) that hath publisht (published *Qq* 2, 3) this, either to traduce the Authour; or to make vulgar and cheape, any the peculiar and sufficient deserts of the Actors; but rather (whereas many Censures flutter'd about it) to giue all leaue, and leisure, to iudge with Distinction.

EVERY MAN OVT
OF HIS HVMOVR.

After the second Sounding.

GREX.

CORDATVS, ASPER, MITIS.

Nay, my deare ASPER,
  MIT. Stay your mind:
ASP. Away.
Who is so patient of this impious world,
5 That he can checke his spirit, or reine his tongue?
Or who hath such a dead vnfeeling sense,
That heauens horrid thunders cannot wake?
To see the earth, crackt with the weight of sinne,
Hell gaping vnder ·vs, and o're our heads
10 Blacke rau'nous ruine, with her saile-stretcht wings,
Ready to sinke vs downe, and couer vs.
Who can behold such prodigies as these,
And haue his lips seal'd vp? not I: my language
Was neuer ground into such oyly colours,
15 To flatter vice and daube iniquitie:
But (with an armed, and resolued hand)
Ile strip the ragged follies of the time,
Naked, as at their birth: COR. (Be not too bold.

Title] HVMOVR *Ff*: Humor *Qq* (*so in the running title*) Induction.
After ... Sounding] *Inductio, sono secundo* Qq: *The Stage. After ... sounding.* G CORDATVS, ASPER] *Asper, Cordatus* Qq 1 Nay,] *Cord.*
Nay *Qq* 2 mind: *F1*: mind, *Qq*: mind. *F2* 7 heauens] heanens
Q3 10 ruine,] Ruine *Qq* 11 downe,] downe *Qq* 13 language
corr. *F1*: soule *Qq, Ff* 17 time,] time *Qq* 18 Naked,] Naked *Qq*
(Be] Be *Qq* bold.] bold, *Qq 1, 2*

Asp. You trouble me) and with a whip of steele,
Print wounding lashes in their yron ribs.   20
I feare no mood stampt in a priuate brow,
When I am pleas'd t'vnmaske a publicke vice.
I feare no strumpets drugs, nor ruffians stab,
Should I detect their hatefull luxuries :
No brokers, vsurers, or lawyers gripe,   25
Were I dispos'd to say, they're all corrupt.
I feare no courtiers frowne, should I applaud
The easie flexure of his supple hammes.
Tut, these are so innate, and popular,
That drunken custome would not shame to laugh   30
(In scorne) at him, that should but dare to taxe 'hem.
And yet, not one of these but knowes his workes,
Knowes what damnation is, the deuill, and hell,
Yet, hourely they persist, grow ranke in sinne,
Puffing their soules away in perj'rous aire,   35
To cherish their extortion, pride, or lusts.
    Mit. Forbeare, good Asper, be not like your name.
    Asp. O, but to such, whose faces are all zeale,
And (with the words of Hercvles) invade
Such crimes as these ! that will not smell of sinne,   40
But seeme as they were made of sanctitie !
Religion in their garments, and their haire
Cut shorter then their eye-browes ! when the conscience
Is vaster then the ocean, and deuoures
More wretches then the *Counters*. Mit. Gentle Asper, 45
Containe your spirit in more stricter bounds,
And be not thus transported with the violence

  Ind. 19 me)] me, *Qq*   steele,] steele *Qq*   21 priuate] private *Q1*   23 vice.] vice, *Qq 2, 3*   24 luxuries : *corr. F1* : luxuries ; *Qq, Ff*   28 hammes.] hammes : *Qq*   29 innate,] innate *Qq*   31 but] not *F2, F3*   'hem.] 'hem : *Qq* ('em *F3 passim*)   34 Yet,] Yet *Qq* hourely *corr. F1, F2* : howerly *Qq, F1*   35 perj'rous] peri'rous *Qq 2, 3*   37 Forbeare,] Forbeare *Qq*   39 invade] inuade *Qq 2, 3*   40 these !] these ; *Qq*   41 sanctitie ! *corr. F1* : Sanctitie ! *Ff* : Sanctitie ; *Qq*   43, 45 then] than *Qq, Ff (but see* 44)   43 eye-browes ! *Ff* : eie-browes ; *Qq 1, 2* : eie-browes, *Q3*   44 then *corr. F1* : than *Qq, Ff*   ocean *corr. F1* : Ocean *Qq, Ff*   45 *Counters* Qq, corr. F1, F2 : Counters *F1*

430 *Euery Man out of his Humour*

  Of your str*o*ng thoughts. C o R. Vnlesse your breath had
   power
  To melt the world, and mould it new againe,
50 It is in vaine, to spend it in these moods.
   A s P. I not obseru'd this thronged round till now.
  Gracious, and kind spectators, you are welcome,
  A P O L L O, and the M v s E s feast your eyes
  With gracefull obiects, and may our M I N E R V A
55 Answere your hopes, vnto their largest straine.
  Yet here, mistake me not, iudicious friends.
  I doe not this, to begge your patience,
  Or seruilely to fawne on your applause,
  Like some drie braine, despairing in his merit :
60 Let me be censur'd, by th'austerest brow,
  Where I want arte, or iudgement, taxe me freely :
  Let envious censors, with their broadest eyes,
  Looke through and through me, I pursue no fauour,
  Onely vouchsafe me your attentions,.
65 And I will giue you musicke worth your eares.
  O, how I hate the monstrousnesse of time,
  Where euery seruile imitating spirit,
  (Plagu'd with an itching leprosie of wit)
  In a meere halting fury, striues to fling
70 His vlc'rous body in the *Thespian* spring,
  And streight leap's forth a Poet ! but as lame
  As V u L C A N, or the founder of *Cripple-gate*.
   M I T. In faith, this Humour will come ill to some,
  You will be thought to be too peremptorie.

  Ind. 50 vaine,] vaine *Qq* Between 50 and 51 *F1 originally inserted
a stage-direction* 'Here hee makes adresse to the People.', *but it was cancelled : see p.* 416. 51 now.] now : *Qq* 52 Gracious] Gratious *F2*
 54 obiects,] obiects ; *Qq*   MINERVA] *Minerva* Q1 : *Menerua* Q3
 56 not,] not *Qq*   iudicious] judicious *Q1* friends.] friends : *Qq*
 57 this,] this *Qq* 59 merit :] merit. *F2* 61 iudgement] judgement
Q1 62 envious] enuious *Qq 2, 3* censors, *corr. F1, F2* : Censors
F1 : *Critikes* Q*q* eyes, *corr. F1, F2* : eies *Qq* : eyes *F1* 63 me,
corr. F1, F2 : me ; *Qq, F1* fauour, *corr. F1, F2* : fauour. *F1* : fauor :
Qq 66 O,] O *Qq* 67 seruile] servile *Q1* 71 Poet !] Poet ; *Qq*
 72 *Cripple-gate corr.* F1, F2: Cripple-gate *F1* : Criplegate *Qq* 73
faith,] faith *Qq*   Humour] Humor *Qq and so usually, but in* 75 *Q1
prints first* 'Humor' *and then* 'Humour' 74 peremptorie *Qq, corr.
F1, F2* : peremptory *F1*

Asp. This Humour? good; and why this Humour, 75
    Mitis?
Nay, doe not turne, but answere.   Mit. Answere? what?
  Asp. I will not stirre your patience, pardon me,
I vrg'd it for some reasons, and the rather
To giue these ignorant well-spoken dayes,
Some taste of their abuse of this word Humour.   80
    Cord. O, doe not let your purpose fall, good Asper,
It cannot but arriue most acceptable,
Chiefly to such, as haue the happinesse,
Daily to see how the poore innocent word
Is rackt, and tortur'd.   Mit. I, I pray you proceede.   85
  Asp. Ha? what? what is't?   Cor. For the abuse
    of Humour.
  Asp. O, I craue pardon, I had lost my thoughts.
Why, Humour (as 'tis *ens*) we thus define it
To be a quality of aire or water,
And in it selfe holds these two properties,   90
Moisture, and fluxure: As, for demonstration,
Powre water on this floore, 'twill wet and runne:
Likewise the aire (forc't through a horne, or trumpet)
Flowes instantly away, and leaues behind
A kind of dew; and hence we doe conclude,   95
That what soe're hath fluxure, and humiditie,
As wanting power to containe it selfe,
Is Humour. So in euery humane body
The choller, melancholy, flegme, and bloud,
By reason that they flow continually   100
In some one part, and are not continent,

Ind. 76 Nay, *corr. F1, F2*: Nay *Qq, F1*   Mit. . . . what? *So ranged in corr. F1, F2*; *a separate line in F1*   79 dayes,] daies *Qq*   80 Humour] Humor *Qq*   81 O, *corr. F1, F2*: O *Qq, F1*   83 such,] such *Qq*   happinesse,] happinesse *Qq*   85 I, I *Q3, corr. F1, F2*: I; I *Qq 1, 2, F1*   86 Cor. . . . Humour. *So ranged in F2*; *a separate line in F1*   Humour] Humor *Qq*   88 Why, *corr. F1, F2*: Why *Qq, F1*   Humour] Humor *Qq*   it] it, *F2*   89 aire] ayre, *F2*   91 Moisture, *corr. F1, F2*: Moisture *Qq, F1*   As,] As *Qq*   93 horne, *corr. F1, F2*: horne *Qq, F1*   94 leaues] leaves *Q1*   96 fluxure,] fluxure *Qq*   98 Humour. So *corr. F1, F2*: *Humor*: so *Qq*: Humour: so *F1*

Receiue the name of Humours. Now thus farre
It may, by *Metaphore*, apply it selfe
Vnto the generall disposition :
105 As when some one peculiar quality
Doth so possesse a man, that it doth draw
All his affects, his spirits, and his powers,
In their confluctions, all to runne one way,
This may be truly said to be a Humour.
110 But that a rooke, in wearing a pyed feather,
The cable hat-band, or the three-pild ruffe,
A yard of shooetye, or the *Switzers* knot
On his *French* garters, should affect a Humour !
O, 'tis more then most ridiculous.
115   C o r d. He speakes pure truth now, if an Idiot
Haue but an apish, or phantasticke straine,
It is his Humour.   A s p. Well I will scourge those apes ;
And to these courteous eyes oppose a mirrour,
As large as is the stage, whereon we act :
120 Where they shall see the times deformitie
Anatomiz'd in euery nerue, and sinnew,
With constant courage, and contempt of feare.
      M i t. A s p e r, (I vrge it as your friend) take heed,
The dayes are dangerous, full of exception,
125 And men are growne impatient of reproofe.   A s p. Ha, ha:
You might as well haue told me, yond' is heauen,

        Ind. 102 Humours] Humors *Qq*   103 may,] may *Qq*   M e t a p h o r e,
corr. *F1*, *F2* : Metaphore, *F1* : Metaphore *Qq*   104 disposition :]
disposition, *Qq*   107 powers,] powers *Qq*   108 confluctions,] confluctions *Qq*   109 Humour.] Humor, *Qq*   110 rooke, corr. *F1* :
Rooke, *F1* : Rooke *Qq* : rooke *F2*   in] by *F2*, *F3*   112 shooetye corr.
F1 : shoe-tie *Qq 1, 2* : shooe-tie *Q3* : shoo-tye *F2*   113 Humour !]
Humour, *Q1* : Humor, *Qq 2, 3*   114 'tis] it is *F2*, *F3*   then]
than *Qq*, *F2*   115 truth now, corr. *F1*, *F2* : truth : now *Q1*, *F1* :
truth : Now *Q2* : trueth : Now *Q3*   Idiot] Ideot *Qq*   116
Haue] Have *Q1*   apish,] Apish *Qq*   117 Humour] Humor *Qq 2, 3*
Well,] Well *Qq*   apes ; corr. *F1*, *F2* : Apes ; *F1* : apes, *Qq 1, 2* :
Apes, *Q3*   118 mirrour, *Ff* : mirror *Qq 1, 2* ; mirror, *Q3*   119
stage,] stage *Qq*   act :] act, *Qq*   120 deformitie corr. *F1*, *F2* : deformitie, *Q1* : deformity, *Qq 2, 3*, *F1*   121 Anatomiz'd] Anatomiz'd
Qq 2, 3   nerue,] Nerve *Q1* : Nerue *Qq 2, 3*   123 A s p e r, *F2* :
A s p e r. corr. *F1* : A s p e r *F1* originally : *Asper* Qq   vrge] urge *Q1*
125 A s p. Ha, ha: *a separate line in Qq*   126 yond'] yound *F2*

> This earth, these men ; and all had mou'd alike.
> Doe not I know the times condition?
> Yes, M I T I S, and their soules, and who they be,
> That eyther will, or can except against me.   130
> None, but a sort of fooles, so sicke in taste,
> That they contemne all phisicke of the mind,
> And, like gald camels, kicke at euery touch.
> Good men, and vertuous spirits, that lothe their vices,
> Will cherish my free labours, loue my lines,   135
> And with the feruour of their shining grace,
> Make my braine fruitfull to bring forth more obiects,
> Worthy their serious, and intentiue eyes.
> But why enforce I this? as fainting? No.
> If any, here, chance to behold himselfe,   140
> Let him not dare to challenge me of wrong,
> For, if he shame to haue his follies knowne,
> First he should shame to act 'hem : my strict hand
> Was made to ceaze on vice, and with a gripe
> Squeeze out the humour of such spongie natures,   145
> As licke vp euery idle vanitie.
>   CORD. Why this is right *Furor Poeticus!*
> Kind gentlemen, we hope your patience
> Will yet conceiue the best, or entertaine
> This supposition, that a mad-man speakes.   150
>   A s p. What? are you ready there?   M I T I S sit
>   downe :
> And my C O R D A T V S. Sound hough, and begin.

Ind.- 127 men;] men,*F2*   129 Yes, *corr. F1, F2*: Yes *Qq, F1*
MITIS,] *Mitis*; *Qq* 1, 2 : *Mitis, Q3*   be, *corr. F1, F2*: be *Qq, F1*   130
eyther *corr. F1* : either *Qq, Ff*   will,] will *Qq, F2*   against] 'gainst
F2   me.] me : *Qq*   131 None,] None *Qq*   133 And, . . . camels,
corr. F1, F2 : And . . . camels (Camels *Qq*) *Qq, F1*   touch.]
touch *Q1* : touch, *Qq* 2, 3   135 loue] love *Q1*   136 feruour] fervor
Q1 : feruor *Qq* 2, 3   137 obiects,] obiects *Qq*   138 serious,] serious
Qq   139 this ? *corr. F1, F2* : this, *Qq, F1*   No. *corr. F1, F2* : no.
F1: no: *Qq*   140 any, here, *corr. F1, F2* : any here *Qq, F1*   142
For, *corr. F1, F2* : For *Qq, F1*   haue] have *Q1*   144 ceaze]
sieze *F2*   vice,] vice ; *Qq*   145 Squeeze *corr. F1, F2* : Crush
Qq, F1   humour] Humor *Qq*   natures *corr. F1, F2* : soules *Qq,
F1*   147 Why] Why, *F2*   *Poeticus!] Poeticus*: *Qq*   151
downe :] downe ; *Qq*   152 hough] hoe *Qq*   begin.] begin : *Qq*

I leaue you two, as censors, to sit here:
Obserue what I present, and liberally
155 Speake your opinions, vpon euery *Scene*,
As it shall passe the view of these spectators.
Nay, now, y'are tedious Sirs, for shame begin.
And MITIS, note me, if in all this front,
You can espy a gallant of this marke,
160 Who (to be thought one of the iudicious)
Sits with his armes thus wreath'd, his hat pull'd here,
Cryes meaw, and nods, then shakes his empty head,
Will shew more seueral motions in his face,
Then the new *London*, *Rome*, or *Niniueh*,
165 And (now and then) breakes a drie bisquet iest,
Which that it may more easily be chew'd,
He steeps in his owne laughter.   CORD. Why? will that
Make it be sooner swallow'd?   ASP. O, assure you.
Or if it did not, yet as HORACE sings,
170 " *Ieiunus raro stomachus vulgaria temnit,*
" Meane cates are welcome still to hungry guests.
  CORD. 'Tis true, but why should we obserue 'hem,
  ASPER?
  ASP. O I would know 'hem, for in such assemblies,
Th'are more infectious then the pestilence:
175 And therefore I would giue them pills to purge,
And make 'hem fit for faire societies.
How monstrous, and detested is't, to see
A fellow, that has neither arte, nor braine,
Sit like an ARISTARCHVS, or starke-asse,
180 Taking mens lines, with a tabacco face,
In snuffe, still spitting, vsing his wryed lookes

Ind. 153 leaue] leave *Q1*   two, as censors,] two as censors (Censors *Qq*) *Qq*, *F2*   here:] here, *Qq*   156 spectators.] Spectators, *Qq* 157 Nay,] Nay *Qq*   begin.] begin: *Qq*,   158 And] And, *F2* me,] me *Qq*   160 iudicious] judicious *Q1*   163 face,] face *Qq*   164 Then] Than *Qq*, *F2*   165 bisquet iest] bisket jest *Qq*: bisquet-iest *F2* 167 steeps] sleeps *Qq 2, 3*   168 swallow'd] swallowed *F2*   you.] you: *Qq*   169 sings,] sings: *Qq*   172 'hem,] 'hem *Qq*   174 then] than *Qq*, *F2*   pestilence:] Pestilence, *Qq*   177 monstrous, . . is't,] monstrous . . . is't *Qq*   178 fellow, . . . arte,] fellow . . . art *Qq*   179 starke-asse] starke asse *Qq*   180 lines, . . . face,] lines . . . face *Qq*

(In nature of a vice) to wrest, and turne
The good aspect of those that shall sit neere him,
From what they doe behold ! O, 'tis most vile.
   MIT. Nay, ASPER.   185
   ASP. Peace, MITIS, I doe know your thought.
You'le say, your guests here will except at this :
Pish, you are too timorous, and full of doubt.
Then, he, a patient, shall reiect all physicke,
'Cause the physicion tels him, you are sicke :   190
Or, if I say, That he is vicious,
You will not heare of vertue. Come, y'are fond.
Shall I be so extrauagant to thinke,
That happy iudgements, and composed spirits,
Will challenge me for taxing such as these ?   195
I am asham'd.   CORD. Nay, but good pardon vs :
We must not beare this peremptorie saile,
But vse our best endeuours how to please.
   ASP. Why, therein I commend your carefull thoughts,
And I will mixe with you in industrie   200
To please, but whom ? attentiue auditors,
Such as will ioyne their profit with their pleasure,
And come to feed their vnderstanding parts :
For these, Ile prodigally spend my selfe,
And speake away my spirit into ayre ;   205
For these, Ile melt my braine into inuention,
Coine new conceits, and hang my richest words
As polisht jewels in their bounteous eares.
But stay, I loose my selfe, and wrong their patience ;
If I dwell here, they'le not begin, I see :   210

   Ind. 182 wrest,] wrest *Qq*   184 behold ! O,] behold ? O *Qq*   185
Nay,] Nay *Qq*   186 Peace,] Peace *Qq*   thought.] thought : *Qq*
187 guests here] audience *Qq*   this :] this ? *Qq*   188 Pish,] Pish :
Qq 1, 2   doubt.] doubt : *Qq*   189 he,] he *Qq*   physicke,]
Phisicke *Q1* : Physicke *Qq 2, 3*   190 physicion] physitian *Qq 1, 2* :
Physitian *Q3*   him,] him *Qq*   191 say,] say *Qq*   192 vertue. Come,]
vertue : come, *Qq* (Come *F2*)   193 extrauagant] extravagant *Q1*
thinke,] thinke *Qq*   194 iudgements,] judgements *Q1* : iudgements
Qq 2, 3   spirits,] spirits *Qq*   198 endeuours] endevours *Q1*   199
Why,] Why *Qq 1, 2*   201 please,] please ; *Qq*   attentiue] attentive
Q1   202 ioyne] joine *Q1*   206 these,] these *F2*   inuention] in-
vention *Q1*   208 jewels] iewels *Qq 2, 3*

> Friends sit you still, and entertaine this troupe
> With some familiar, and by-conference,
> Ile haste them sound. Now gentlemen, I goe
> To turne an actor, and a Humorist,
> 215 Where (ere I doe resume my present person)
> We hope to make the circles of your eyes
> Flow with distilled laughter: if we faile,
> We must impute it to this onely chance,
> " *Arte* hath an enemy cal'd *Ignorance*.
>
> 220 C o r d. How doe you like his spirit, M i t i s?
>
> M i t. I should like it much better, if he were lesse confident.
>
> C o r d. Why, doe you suspect his merit?
>
> M i t. No, but I feare this will procure him much enuie.
>
> 225 C o r d. O, that sets the stronger seale on his desert, if he had no enemies, I should esteeme his fortunes most wretched at this instant.
>
> M i t. You haue seene his play, C o r d a t v s? pray you, how is't?
>
> 230 C o r d. Faith sir, I must refraine to iudge, only this I can say of it, 'tis strange, and of a particular kind by it selfe, somewhat like *Vetus Comœdia:* a worke that hath bounteously pleased me, how it will answere the generall expectation, I know not.
>
> 235 M i t. Does he obserue all the lawes of *Comedie* in it?
>
> C o r d. What lawes meane you?
>
> M i t. Why, the equall diuision of it into *Acts*, and *Scenes*, according to the *Terentian* manner, his true number of Actors; the furnishing of the *Scene* with G r e x, or
> 240 C h o r v s, and that the whole Argument fall within compasse of a dayes businesse.

Ind. 212 familiar,] familiar *Qq* 213 sound. Now gentlemen,] sound: now gentlemen (Gentlemen *Q3*) *Qq* 219 *Exit.* add Qq: *Exit Asper.* add F2, F3 224 enuie] envie *Q1* 225 desert,] desert; F2 228 haue] have *Q1* play,] play *Qq* pray you,] pray you ; *Qq* 230 iudge] judge *Q1* 231 particular] perticular *Qq* 232 somewhat] some what F2 235 obserue] observe *Q1* 237 Why,] Why *Qq* diuision] deuision *Qq* *Acts*,] Acts *Qq* 239 Grex,] *Grex* Qq 241 businesse] efficiencie *Qq*

CORD. O no, these are too nice obseruations.

MIT. They are such as must be receiued, by your fauour, or it cannot be authentique.

CORD. Troth, I can discerne no such necessity.

MIT. No?

CORD. No, I assure you, Signior. If those lawes you speake of, had beene deliuered vs, *ab initio*, and in their present vertue and perfection, there had beene some reason of obeying their powers: but 'tis extant, that that which we call *Comœdia*, was at first nothing but a simple, and continued *Song*, sung by one only person, till SVSARIO inuented a second, after him EPICHARMVS a third; PHORMVS, and CHIONIDES deuised to haue foure Actors, with a *Prologue* and *Chorus*; to which CRA-TINVS (long after) added a fift, and sixt; EVPOLIS more; ARISTOPHANES more then they: euery man in the dignitie of his spirit and iudgement, supplyed something. And (though that in him this kinde of *Poeme* appeared absolute, and fully perfected) yet how is the face of it chang'd since, in MENANDER, PHILEMON, CECILIVS, PLAVTVS, and the rest; who haue vtterly excluded the *Chorus*, altered the property of the persons, their names, and natures, and augmented it with all liberty, according to the elegancie and disposition of those times, wherein they wrote? I see not then, but we should enioy the same licence, or free power, to illustrate and heighten our inuention as they did; and not bee tyed to those strict and regular formes, which the nicenesse of a few (who are nothing but forme) would thrust vpon vs.

Ind. 242 obseruations] observations *Q1*   243 receiued,] received *Q1*: receiued *Qq 2, 3*   245 Troth,] Troth *Qq*   247 you, Signior.] If] you signior; if *Qq*   248 *initio*,] *Initio*; *Qq*   251 simple,] simple *Qq, F2*   252 *Song*] Satyre *Qq*   253 inuented] invented *Q1*   third;] third, *Qq*   254 deuised] devised *Q1*   254, 262 haue] have *Q1*   256 fift, *Ff*: fift *Qq*: Fifth *F3*   sixt] Sixth *F3*   257 more;] more, *Qq* then] than *Qq 2, 3, F2*   euery] every *Q1*   258 iudgement] judgement *Q1*   258-9 some thing *F1*, *copying the hyphen of Q1, where the word is divided at the end of a line*: somthing *Q3*: *colon in Qq*   259 And] and *Qq*   265 times,] times *Qq*   266 then,] then *Qq*   enioy] enjoy *Q1*   267 licence,] *Licentia* Qq   268 inuention] invention *Q1*   did;] did: *Q3*   bee] to be *Q3*

MIT. Well, we will not dispute of this now : but what's his *Scene* ?

COR. Marry, *Insula Fortunata*, Sir.

MIT. O, the fortunate Iland ? masse, he has bound himselfe to a strict law there.

COR. Why so ?

MIT. He cannot lightly alter the *Scene*, without crossing the seas.

COR. He needs not, hauing a whole Iland to run through, I thinke.

MIT. No ? how comes it then, that in some one Play we see so many seas, countries, and kingdomes, past ouer with such admirable dexteritie ?

COR. O, that but shewes how well the Authors can trauaile in their vocation, and out-run the apprehension of their auditorie. But leauing this, I would they would begin once : this protraction is able to sowre the best-settled patience in the Theatre.

MIT. They haue answered your wish Sir : they sound.

CORD. O, here comes the *Prologue :* Now sir ! if you had staid a little longer, I meant to haue spoke your prologue for you, I faith.

The third sounding.

PROLOGVE.

PROL. Mary, with all my heart, Sir, you shall doe it yet, and I thanke you.

CORD. Nay, nay, stay, stay, heare you ?

PROL. You could not haue studied to ha' done me

Ind. 273 Marry,] Mary *Qq*   274 masse,] masse *Qq*   has] was *Qq* 2, 3   277 alter] after *Qq* 2, 3   Scene,] Scene *Qq*   279 hauing] having *Q1*   282 ouer] over *Q1*   285 trauaile] travaile *Q1* : travel *F3*   apprehension] apprehention *Q3*   286 leauing] leaving *Q1*   287 sowre] sower *Qq*   Between 289 and 290 *Qq*. have '·Sound the third time.| ENTER PROLOGVE'.   290 sir ! *Ff*: sir, *Q1* : sirre, *Qq* 2, 3   After 292] *The third . . . PROLOGVE* not in *Qq*   293 Mary,] Mary *Qq* 1, 3 : Marry *Q2*   heart,] heart *Qq* 1, 2 : hart *Q3*

a greater benefit at the instant, for I protest to you, I am vnperfect, and (had I spoke it) I must of necessity haue beene out.

C o r d. Why, but doe you speake this seriously? 300

P r o l. Seriously! I (wit's my helpe doe I) and esteeme my selfe indebted to your kindnesse for it.

C o r d. For what?

P r o l. Why, for vndertaking the prologue for me.

C o r d. How? did I vndertake it for you? 305

P r o l. Did you! I appeale to all these gentlemen, whether you did or no? Come, it pleases you to cast a strange looke on't now; but 'twill not serue.

C o r d. 'Fore me, but it must serue: and therefore speake your prologue. 310

P r o l. And I doe, let me die poyson'd with some venemous hisse, and neuer liue to looke as high as the two-penny roome againe.

M i t. He has put you to it, sir.

C o r. Sdeath, what a humorous fellow is this? Gentle- 315 men, good faith I can speake no prologue, howsoeuer his weake wit has had the fortune to make this strong vse of me, here before you: but I protest———

C a r l o B v f f o n e.

C a r l. Come, come, leaue these fustian protestations: *He enters* away, come, I cannot abide these gray-headed ceremonies. *with a boy,* Boy, fetch me a glasse, quickly, I may bid these gentlemen 321 welcome; giue 'hem a health here: I mar'le whose wit 'twas to put a prologue in yond' sack-buts mouth: they

Ind. 298 haue] have *Q1*   300, 304 Why,] Why *Qq*   301 wit's] God's *Qq*   helpe] help, *F2*   306 gentlemen, *Ff*: gentlemen *Q1*: Gentlemen *Qq 2, 3*   307 Come,] Come, come, *F2, F3*   309 me,] God *Qq*   313 roome] roome, *Qq 2, 3*   againe.] againe. *Exit. Q1*: in *Q2* 'gaine. Exit.' *as the first line of sig. B iv,* 'a-' *only in the catchword on sig. B iij verso: Q3 omits this line.*   315 Sdeath, *om. F2, F3* 317 me,] me *Q1*: mee *Qq 2, 3*   318 protest———] protest; *Qq*   CARLO BVFFONE.] *Enter Carlo Buffone, with a Boy.* Qq (boy *Q1*)   (*margin*) *Stage direction not in* Qq   319 leaue] leave *Q1*   322 'hem] him *Q3* mar'le] *Qq 2, 3*: marl'e *Q1, Ff*   323 yond'] yon'd *Qq, Ff*

might well thinke hee'd be out of tune, and yet you'ld play vpon him too.

CORD. Hang him, dull blocke.

CARL. O good words, good words, a well-timberd fellow, he would ha' made a good columne, and he had beene thought on, when the house was a building. O, art thou come? well said; giue mee boy, fill, so. Here's a cup of wine sparkles like a diamond. Gentlewomen (I am sworne to put them in first) and Gentlemen, a round, in place of a bad prologue, I drinke this good draught to your health here, *Canarie*, the very *Elixi'r* and spirit of wine. This is that our *Poet* calls *Castalian* liquor, when hee comes abroad (now and then) once in a fortnight, and makes a good meale among Players, where he has *Caninum appetitum*: mary, at home he keepes a good philosophicall diet, beanes and butter milke: an honest pure Rogue, hee will take you off three, foure, fiue of these, one after another, and looke vilanously when he has done, like a one-headed CERBERVS (he do' not heare me I hope) and then (when his belly is well ballac't, and his braine rigg'd a little) he sailes away withall, as though he would worke wonders when he comes home. He has made a Play here, and he calls it, *Euery Man out of his humour*: Sbloud, and he get me out of the humour hee has put mee in, Ile trust none of his Tribe againe, while I liue. Gentles, all I can say for him, is, you are welcome. I could wish my bottle here amongst you: but there's an old rule, *No pledging your owne health.*

Ind. 325 *Exit Boy.* (*boy.* Q1) add Qq   326 him,] him Qq   327 well-timberd] well-timbred F2   328 columne,] columne Qq   and] an' F2, F3   329 on,] on Qq   O,] O Qq   *Enter Boy with a glasse.* (*boy* Q1: *Boie* Q2) inset in Qq after 'O art thou'   330 mee boy] me; boy Qq 1, 2: me, Boy Q3   so. Here's] so: here's Qq   331 Gentlewomen] Gentlewomen, Q1   334 *Elixi'r*] Elixer F2 (large paper) spirit of] (*He drinkes.*) inset in Qq   wine. This] wine: this Qq (Wine Q3)   337 mary,] mary Qq   340 these,] these Qq   342 do' not] do's not F2, F3   344 withall] with all F2, F3   345 home. He] home: he (hee Qq 2, 3) Qq   it,] it; Qq   346 *humour*:] *Humor*: Q1: *humour*. Q2: *Humor.* Q3   Sbloud, and F1: Sbloud and Qq: But an' F2, F3   347 humour] humor Qq 1, 3   trust] ne're trust Qq   348 liue.] liue: Q1   Gentles, all] Gentles all, Q3: Gentles, all F2: Genteels, all F3   350 rule,] rule; Qq   health.] health: Qq

Mary, if any here be thirsty for it, their best way (that I know) is, sit still, seale vp their lips, and drinke so much of the play, in at their eares.   *Exit.*

GREX.

MIT. What may this fellow be, CORDATVS.?

COR. Faith, if the time will suffer his description, Ile 355 giue it you. He is one, the Author calls him CARLO BVFFONE, an impudent common iester, a violent rayler, and an incomprehensible *Epicure* ; one, whose company is desir'd of all men, but belou'd of none ; hee will sooner lose his soule then a iest, and prophane euen the most holy 360 things, to excite laughter : no honorable or reuerend personage whatsoeuer, can come within the reach of his eye, but ís turn'd into all manner of varietie, by his adult'rate *simile's.*

MIT. You paint forth a monster.   365

COR. He will preferre all Countries before his natiue, and thinkes he can neuer sufficiently, or with admiration enough, deliuer his affectionate conceit of forraine Atheisticall policies : but stay—Obserue these, hee'le appeare himselfe anon.   370

MIT. O, this is your enuious man (MACILENTE) I thinke.

COR. The same, sir.

Ind. 351 Mary,] mary *Q1* : marye Q2 : marie *Q3*   thirsty] thristy F2   353 play,] play *Qq*   After 353] *GREX. add Ff*   355 description] discription *Q3*   356 you. He] you : he *Qq*   one,] one ; *Q3*   357 iester] jester *Q1*   358 *Epicure* ;] Epicure : *Qq*   360 lose] loose *Qq*   then] than *Qq,* F2   iest, Q2, *Ff* : jest, *Q1* : iest ; *Q3*   361 honorable] honourable *Qq,* F2   363 into] inro *Q3*   364 *simile's*] *simele's* Q3   368 forraine] forrein *Qq*   369 stay— Obserue] stay, obserue *Qq*   After 370] *Enter Macilente, solus. Qq*

Act 1. Scene 1.

MACILENTE.

Viri est, fortunæ cæcitatem facilè ferre.
Tis true ; but, Stoique, where (in the vast world)
Doth that man breathe, that can so much command
His bloud, and his affection ? well : I see,
5 I striue in vaine to cure my wounded soule ;
For euery cordiall that my thoughts apply,
Turnes to a cor'siue, and doth eate it farder.
There is no taste in this Philosophie,
Tis like a potion that a man should drinke,
10 But turnes his stomacke with the sight of it.
I am no such pild *Cinique*, to beleeue
That beggery is the onely happinesse ;
Or (with a number of these patient fooles)
To sing : *My minde to me a kingdome is,*
15 When the lanke hungrie belly barkes for foode.
I looke into the world, and there I meet
With obiects, that doe strike my bloud-shot eyes
Into my braine : where, when I view my selfe ;
Hauing before obseru'd, this man is great,
20 Mighty, and fear'd : that, lou'd, and highly fauour'd :
A third, thought wise and learned : a fourth, rich,
And therefore honor'd : a fifth, rarely featur'd :
A sixth, admir'd for his nuptiall fortunes :
When I see these (I say) and view my selfe,
25 I wish the organs of my sight were crackt ;

---

1. i.] *Act* . . . MACILENTE.] ACTVS PRIMVS. SCENA PRIMA. *Qq* : ACT I.
SCENE I.—*The Country. Enter* Macilente, *with a book.* G   1 *Viri*]
Mac. Viri Qq   *facilè*] facile Qq   *ferre.*] ferre : Qq   2 Stoique,]
Stoique : *Q1* : Stoique ; *Qq 2, 3*   3 breathe] breath *Qq*   command]
commaund *Q1*   4 bloud,] blood *Q1* : bloud *Qq 2, 3*   6 apply,]
apply *Q1* : applie *Qq 2, 3*   7 farder] farther *F3*   15 foode.]
food : *Q1* : foode : *Qq 2, 3*   18 braine :] braine ; *Qq 2, 3*   selfe ;]
selfe, *Q3*   19 Hauing] Having *Q1*   obseru'd,] obseru'd : *Qq 1, 2*
20 lou'd, *corr. F1, F2* : lou'd *Qq, F1*   22 honor'd] honour'd *Qq, F2*
25 the organs of my sight] my *Optique* instruments *Qq* (*Obtique* Q3)

Every Man out of his Humour

And that the engine of my griefe could cast
Mine eye-balls, like two globes of wild-fire, forth,
To melt this vnproportion'd frame of nature.
Oh, they are thoughts that haue transfixt my heart,
And often (i' the strength of apprehension) 30
Made my cold passion stand vpon my face,
Like drops of dew on a stiffe cake of yce.

GREX

C o r. This alludes well to that of the Poet,
Inuidus suspirat, gemit, incutitq; dentes,
Sudat frigidus, intuens quod odit. 35
M i t. O peace, you breake the *Scene*.

M a c i. Soft, who be these?
I'le lay me downe a while till they be past.

GREX

C o r. Signior, note this gallant, I pray you.
M i t. What is he? 40
C o r. A tame Rooke, youle take him presently : List.

Act I. Scene II.

SOGLIARDO, CARLO BVFFONE,
MACILENTE.

NAy looke you C a r l o : this is my Humour now!
I haue land and money, my friends left me well, and
I will be a Gentleman, whatsoeuer it cost me.
C a r. A most gentleman-like resolution.

I. i. 27 -balls,] -balls *Q1* : -bals *Qq 2, 3* -fire, *corr. F1, F2* : -fire *Qq, F1* forth] foorth *Q3* 32 dew] sweate *Qq* 34 *incutitq;* corr. F1 : *incutitq̄,* F1 : *incutiique* Qq, F2 35 *quod odit*] *quododit* Q2 After 36] *Enter Sogliardo, with Carlo Buffone.* | SCENA SEC. *Qq* 39 gallant,] gallant *Qq 1, 2* I. ii. *Act . . .* MACILENTE. *not in Qq* CARLO] CARLO, F2 1 Nay,] Nay *F2* : Sog. Nay *Qq* you,] you *Qq* now!] now ; *Qq 1, 2* : now : *Q3* 3 Gentleman, *corr. F1* : gentleman *Qq 1, 2* : Gentleman *Q3, F1, F2* whatsoeuer] whatsoever *Q1* 4 CAR. . . . resolution.] *Missing in some copies of F1, in which these words should end page 90.*

S o g. Tut, and I take an humour of a thing once, I am like your taylors needle, I goe through : but, for my name, Signior, how thinke you ? will it not serue for a gentlemans name, when the Signior is put to it ? Ha ?

C a r. Let me heare : how is't ?

S o g. *Signior Insulso Sogliardo* : me thinkes it sounds well.

C a r. O excellent ! tut, and all fitted to your name, you might very well stand for a gentleman : I know many *Sogliardos* gentlemen.

S o g. Why, and for my wealth I might be a Iustice of Peace.

C a r. I, and a Constable for your wit.

S o g. All this is my Lordship you see here, and those Farmes you came by.

C a r. Good steps to gentility too, mary : but S o g l ia r d o, if you affect to be a gentleman indeede, you must obserue all the rare qualities, humours, and complements of a gentleman.

S o g. I know it, Signior, and if you please to instruct, I am not too good to learne, Ile assure you.

C a r. Inough sir : Ile make admirable vse i'the proiection of my medicine vpon this lumpe of copper here. Ile bethinke me, for you sir.

S o g. Signior, I will both pay you, and pray you, and thanke you, and thinke on you.

GREX.

C o r d. Is not this purely good ?

M a c i l. Sbloud, why should such a prick-eard hine as this,

<small>1. ii. 5 humour] humor *Qq 2, 3*   6 name,] name *Qq*   12 excellent ! tut,] excellent : tut *Qq*   15 Why,] Why *Qq*   22 obserue] obserue *Q1* : obserue *Q3*   humours] humors *Qq*   24 it,] it *Qq*   Signior *Qq 2, 3, corr. F1, F2* : signior *Q1, F1*   26 make] maks *F2*   28 me, *Ff* : me *Q1* : mee *Qq 2, 3*   29 pay you,] pay you *Qq*   30 thanke you,] thanke you *Qq 1, 2*   32 Sbloud] Why *F2, F3*   hine] Hind *Qq* this,] this *Qq*</small>

Be rich? Ha? a foole? such a transparent gull
That may be seene through? wherefore should he haue
  land,
Houses, and lordships? O, I could eate my entrailes,   35
And sinke my soule into the earth with sorrow.

  CAR. First (to be an accomplisht gentleman, that is,
a gentleman of the time) you must giue o're house-keeping
in the countrey, and liue altogether in the city amongst
gallants; where, at your first apparance, 'twere good you 40
turn'd foure or fiue hundred acres of your best land into
two or three trunks of apparel (you may doe it without going
to a coniurer) and be sure, you mixe your selfe stil, with such
as flourish in the spring of the fashion, and are least
popular; studie their carriage, and behauiour in all; learne 45
to play at *Primero* and *Passage,* and (euer when you lose)
ha' two or three peculiar othes to sweare by, that no man
else sweares: but aboue all, protest in your play, and
affirme, *Vpon your credit; As you are a true gentleman* (at
euery cast) you may doe it with a safe conscience, I warrant 50
you.

  SOG. O admirable rare! he cannot choose but be
a gentleman, that ha's these excellent gifts: more, more, I
beseech you.

  CAR. You must endeuour to feede cleanly at your 55
Ordinarie, sit melancholy, and picke your teeth when
you cannot speake: and when you come to Playes, be
humorous, looke with a good startch't face, and ruffle your
brow like a new boot; laugh at nothing but your owne
iests, or else as the Noblemen laugh. That's a speciall grace 60
you must obserue.

  I. ii. 35 entrailes] intrailes *F2*   37 gentleman, that] Gentleman;
that *Q3*   40 apparance] appearance *F2*   42 apparel (you] apparell;
you *Qq 1, 2*: apparell, you *Q3*   43 coniurer)] Coniurer: *Qq*   sure,]
sure *Qq*   45 carriage, *Ff*: carriage *Q1*: cariage *Qq 2, 3*   behauiour]
behauior *Qq 1, 2* all; *corr. F1, F2*: all: *Qq, F1*   46 lose] loose
Qq   47 peculiar] peeuliar *Q1*   48 all,] all; *Q2*   49 *true* om.
Qq 2, 3   50 cast)] cast :) *Qq*   52 choose] chuse *Qq, F2*   55 en-
deuour] endevour *Q1*   59 boot ;] boot, *Qq 1, 2, F2*   60 iests] jests
Q1   laugh. That's] laugh; that's *Qq*

S o g. I warrant you, sir.

C a r. I, and sit o'the stage, and flout: prouided, you haue a good suit.

S o g. O, I'le haue a suit only for that, sir.

C a r. You must talke much of your kinred, and allies.

S o g. Lies! no Signior, I shall not neede to doe so, I haue kinred i'the city to talke of: I haue a neece is a marchants wife; and a nephew, my brother S o r d i d o s sonne, of the Innes of Court.

C a r. O, but you must pretend alliance with Courtiers and great persons: and euer when you are to dine or suppe in any strange presence, hire a fellow with a great chaine (though it be copper it's no matter) to bring you letters, feign'd from such a Noble man, or such a Knight, or such a Ladie, *To their worshipfull, right rare, and noble qualified friend or kinsman, Signior Insulso Sogliardo,* giue your selfe stile enough. And there (while you intend circumstances of newes, or enquiry of their health, or so) one of your familiars (whom you must carry about you still) breakes it vp (as 'twere in a iest) and reades it publikely at the table: at which, you must seeme to take as vnpardonable offence, as if he had torne your Mistris colours, or breath'd vpon her picture; and pursue it with that hot grace, as if you would aduance a challenge vpon it presently.

S o g. Stay, I doe not like that humour of challenge, it may be accepted; but I'le tell you what's my humour now: I will doe this. I will take occasion of sending one of my suites to the Taylors to haue the pocket repaired, or so; and there such a letter, as you talke of (broke open and

---

I. ii. 63 flout] floult *Q2*   65 O,] O *Qq*   that,] that *Qq*   66 kinred,] kinred *Q1*: kindred *Qq 2, 3, F2, F3*   68 I haue] Il haue *Q2*: Il'haue *Q3*   kinred *Q1, F1*: kindred *Qq 2, 3, F2, F3*   69 marchants *F1*: marchants *Q1*: Merchants *Qq 2, 3, F2, F3*   71 O,] O *Qq*   Courtiers] Courtiours *Q1*   74 copper] copper, *F2*   76 noble] nobly *F2, F3*   77 Sogliardo,] Sogliardo; *Qq*   79 enquiry] enquire *Q3*   81 iest] jeast *Q1*   83 offence,] offence *Qq*   Mistris] mistresse *Qq 1, 2*: Mistresse *Q3*: Mistresses *F2, F3*   breath'd] breat'd *Q3*   85 aduance] enforce *Qq*   86 humour] humor *Qq 1, 2*: Humor *Q3*   87 accepted ;] accepted: *Qq*   humour] humor *Qq*   88 this.] this, *Qq, F2*   90 letter,] letter *Qq*   of] off *Q3*

all) shall be left : O, the Taylor will presently giue out what I am, vpon the reading of it, worth twentie of your Gallants.

C A R. But then you must put on an extreme face of discontentment at your mans negligence.

S o G. O, so I will, and beat him too : I'le haue a man for the purpose.

M A C I L. You may ; you haue land and crownes : O partiall fate !

C A R L. Masse well remembred, you must keepe your men gallant, at the first, fine pyed liueries, laid with good gold lace, there's no losse in it, they may rip't off and pawne it, when they lacke victuals.

S o G. By'r Ladie, that is chargeable Signior, 'twill bring a man in debt.

C A R. Debt ? why, that's the more for your credit sir : it's an excellent policy to owe much in these daies, if you note it.

S o G. As how good Signior ? I would faine be a Polititian.

C A R. O! looke where you are indebted any great summe, your creditor obserues you with no lesse regard, then if hee were bound to you for some huge benefit, and will quake to giue you the least cause of offence, lest he loose his money. I assure you (in these times) no man has his seruant more obsequious and pliant, then gentlemen their creditors : to whom if (at any time) you pay but a moitie, or a fourth part, it comes more acceptedly, then if you gave 'hem a new-yeares gift.

S o G. I perceiue you, sir : I will take vp, and bring my selfe in credit sure.

C A R. Mary this, alwaies beware you commerce not with

I. ii. 92 am,] am *Qq* it,] it : *Qq 1, 2* 100 liueries,] Liueries *Qq*
103 By'r] Byr *Qq 1, 2* : Bir *Q3* Ladie,] Ladie *Qq 1, 3* : Lady *Q2*
110 O!] O, *Qq* 111 obserues] observes *Q1* 112, 115, 117 then] than *Qq 1, 2, F2* bound] bouud *Q3* 113 lest] least *Qq* 114 loose] lose *F2* money.] money : *Qq 1, 2* 115 seruant] servant *Q1*
116 creditors] creditours *F2* if (at] (if at *Qq, Ff* 117 moitie,] moiety *Qq 1, 2* : moietie *Q3* acceptedly] acceptably *F3* 119 you, sir :] you sir, *Qq* vp] up *Q1* 121 this,] this ; *Qq 1, 2*

bankrupts, or poore needie *Ludgathians* : they are impudent creatures, turbulent spirits, they care not what violent tragedies they stirre, nor how they play fast and loose with a poore gentlemans fortunes, to get their owne. Mary, these rich fellowes (that ha' the world, or the better part of it, sleeping in their counting-houses) they are ten times more placable, they ; either feare, hope, or modestie, restraines them from offering any outrages : but this is nothing to your followers, you shall not run a penny more in arrerage for them, and you list your selfe.

S o G. No ? how should I keepe 'hem then ?

C A R. Keepe 'hem ? Sbloud let them keepe themselues, they are no sheepe, are they ? What ? you shall come in houses, where plate, apparell, iewels, and diuers other pretie commodities lye negligently scattered, and I would ha' those *Mercuries* follow me (I trow) should remember they had not their fingers for nothing.

S o G. That's not so good, me thinkes.

C A R. Why, after you haue kept 'hem a fortnight, or so, and shew'd 'hem ynough to the world, you may turne 'hem away, and keepe no more but a boy, it's ynough.

S o G. Nay, my humour is not for boyes, Ile keepe men, and I keepe any ; and Ile giue coats, that's my humour : but I lacke a cullisen.

C A R. Why, now you ride to the citie, you may buy one, Ile bring you where you shall ha' your choise for money.

S o G. Can you, sir ?

C A R. O, I : you shall haue one take measure of you, and make you a *Coat of armes*, to fit you of what fashion you will.

I. ii. 122 bankrupts] Bankroutes *Q3*   125 fortunes,] fortunes *Qq* owne. Mary,] owne : marry, *Qq*   128 placable] peacable *Q3*   they ;] they : *Qq*   feare,] feare *F2*   131 and] an' *F2, F3*   133 Sbloud *om. F2, F3*   themselues] themselves *Q1*   135 diuers] diverse *Q1*   136 negligently] necligently *Q3*   139 good,] good *Qq* 140, 146 Why,] Why *Qq*   haue] have *Q1*   kept' hem] kept them *Q3* fortnight,] fornight *Q1* : fortnight *Qq 2, 3*   142 ynough] yenough *Q3*   143 Nay,] Nay *Qq*   humour] humor *Qq*   144 that's] rhat's *Q3*   humour] humor *Qq 2, 3*   148 you,] you *Qq, F2*   149 O,] O *Qq*   150 and] an' *F2*   armes,] armes *Qq*

S o G. By word of mouth, I thanke you, Signior; Ile be once a little prodigall in a humour, i'faith, and haue a most prodigious coat.

M A C I. Torment and death! breake head and braine 155
  at once,
To be deliuer'd of your fighting issue.
Who can endure to see blinde *Fortune* dote thus?
To be enamour'd on this dustie turfe?
This clod? a whorson puck-fist? O god, god, god, god, &c.
I could runne wild with griefe now, to behold 160
The ranknesse of her bounties, that doth breed
Such bull-rushes; these mushrompe gentlemen,
That shoot vp in a night to place, and worship.

C A R. Let him alone, some stray, some stray.

S o G. Nay, I will examine him before I goe, sure. 165

C A R. The Lord of the soile ha's al wefts, and straies here? ha's he not?

S o G. Yes, sir.

C A R. Faith, then I pitty the poore fellow, he's falne into a fooles hands. 170

S o G. Sirrah, who gaue you commission to lye in my lordship?

M A C I. Your lordship?

S o G. How? my lordship? doe you know me, sir?

M A C I. I doe know you, sir. 175

C A R. S'heart, he answeres him like an *eccho*.

S o G. Why, who am I, Sir?

M A C I. One of those that fortune fauours.

C A R. The *Periphrasis* of a foole; Ile obserue this better.

S o G. That fortune fauours? how meane you that, 180 friend?

I. ii. 152 mouth,] mouth *Qq*   you,] you *Qq*   153 humour, i'faith] Humor in faith *Qq*   155 death!] death, *Qq*   once,] once *Qq 1, 2*   159 god,...god,] God,...God, *Qq*   160 now,] now *Qq*   163 place,] place *Qq*   165 Nay,] Nay *Qq*   goe,] goe *Qq*   166 wefts,] wefts *Qq*   168 Yes,] Yes *Qq, F2*   169 Faith,] Faith *Qq, F2*   174 me,] me *Qq*   175 you,] you *Qq*   176 S'heart, *om. F2, F3*   177 I,] I *Qq*   178, 180 fauours] fauors *Qq*   180 that,] that *Qq*

MACI. I meane simply. That you are one that liues not by your wits.

SOG. By my wits? No sir, I scorne to liue by my wits, 185 I. I haue better meanes, I tell thee, then to take such base courses, as to liue by my wits. Sbloud, doest thou thinke I liue by my wits?

MACI. Me thinkes, Iester, you should not relish this well.

190 CAR. Ha? does he know me?

MACI. Though yours bee the worst vse a man can put his wit to, of thousands, to prostitute it at euery tauerne and ordinarie; yet (mee thinkes) you should haue turn'd your broad side at this, and haue beene readie with an 195 *Apologie*, able to sinke this hulke of ignorance into the bottome, and depth of his contempt.

CAR. Sbloud 'tis MACILENTE! Signior, you are well encountred, how is't? O, we must not regard what hee saies man, a trout, a shallow foole, he ha's no more braine 200 then a butter-flie, a meere stuft suit, he looks like a mustie bottle, new wickerd, his head's the corke, light, light. I am glad to see you so well return'd, Signior.

MACI. You are? Gramercie, good IANVS.

SOG. Is he one of your acquaintance? I loue him the 205 better for that.

CAR. Gods precious, come away man, what doe you meane? and you knew him as I doe, you'ld shun him, as you'ld doe the plague?

SOG. Why, sir?

210 CAR. O, hee's a black fellow, take heed on him.

SOG. Is he a Scholler, or a Souldier?

CAR. Both, both; a leane mungrell, he lookes as if he

1. ii. 182 simply.] simply; *Qq*   185 I. I] I; I *Qq*   meanes,] meanes *Qq*   then] than *Qq, F2 (So in* 200, 217)   186 Sbloud, *F1*: Sbloud *Qq 1, 2*: Sblood *Q3*: What *F2, F3*   188 thinkes,] thinkes *Qq*   192 to,] too *Qq*   195 hulke] bulk *F3*   197 Sbloud *Q1, F1*: Sboud *Q2*: Sblood *Q3*: Oh *F2, F3*   MACILENTE !] *Macilente* : *Qq*   198 O,] O *Qq*   202 return'd,] return'd *Qq*   203 Gramercie,] Gramercie *Qq*   207 and] an' *F2*   209 Why,] Why *Qq*   211 Scholler,] Scholler *Qq*

were chap-falne, with barking at other mens good fortunes:
'ware how you offend him, he carries oile and fire in his pen,
will scald where it drops: his spirit's like powder, quick, 215
violent: hee'le blow a man vp with a jest: I feare him
worse then a rotten wall do's the cannon, shake an houre
after, at the report. Away, come not neere him.

   S o g. For Gods sake let's be gone, and he be a Scholler,
you know I cannot abide him, I had as leeue see a Cocka- 220
trice, specially as cockatrices goe now.

   C a r. What, you'le stay, signior? this gentleman
S o g l i a r d o, and I, are to visit the knight P v n t a r-
v o l o, and from thence to the citie, wee shall meet there.

   M a c i. I, when I cannot shun you, we will meet.   225
'Tis strange! of all the creatures I haue seene,
I enuie not this B v f f o n, for indeede
Neither his fortunes, nor his parts deserue it:
But I doe hate him, as I hate the deuill,
Or that brasse-visag'd monster *Barbarisme*.   230
O, 'tis an open-throated, black-mouth'd curre,
That bites at all, but eates on those that feed him.
A slaue, that to your face will (serpent-like)
Creepe on the ground, as he would eate the dust;
And to your backe will turne the taile, and sting   235
More deadly then a scorpion: Stay, who's this?
Now for my soule, another minion
Of the old lady *Chance*'s: I'le obserue him.

   I. ii. 213 chap-falne, *F1* : chap-falne *Qq* : chop-falne, *F2* : Chop-fal'n, *F3*   215 drops :] drops, *Qq*   216 jest] iest *Qq 2, 3*   217 houre after,] hower after *Qq*   218 report. Away] report : away *Qq*   219 and] an' *F2*   220 him,] him. *F2*   222 stay,] stay *Qq*   223 Sogliardo, and I,] *Sogliardo* and I *Qq*   Pvntarvolo] *Puntarvolo* Q1   224 *Exeunt Car. and Sog.* add Qq   226 strange!] strange : *Qq*   228 fortunes,] fortunes *Qq, F2*   it :] it ; *Qq*   229 him,] him *Qq*   232 on] not *F3*   him.] him, *Qq 1, 2* : him : *Q3*   235 taile,] taile *Qq*   236 then] than *Qq, F2*   237 soule,] soule *F2*

Act I. Scene III.

SORDIDO, MACILENTE, HINE.

O Rare! good, good, good, good, good! I thanke my Starres, I thanke my Starres for it.
  MACI. Said I not true? doth not his passion speake Out of my diuination? O my senses,
5 Why loose you not your powers, and become Dull'd, if not deadded with this spectacle? I know him, 'tis SORDIDO, the farmer, A Boore, and brother to that swine was here.
  SORD. Excellent, excellent, excellent! as I would wish,
10 as I would wish.
  MACI. See how the strumpet *Fortune* tickles him, And makes him swoune with laughter, ô, ô, ô.
  SORD. Ha, ha, ha, I will not sow my grounds this yeere. Let mee see, what haruest shall we haue? *Iune,*
15 *Iuly, August?*
  MACI. What is't, a Prognostication rap's him so?
  SORD. The xx, xxi, xxij, daies, raine and winde, O good, good! the xxiij, and xxiiij, raine and some winde, good! the xxv, raine, good still! xxvi, xxvij, xxviij, winde and
20 some raine; would it had beene raine and some winde: well 'tis good (when it can be no better) xxix, inclining to raine: inclining to raine? that's not so good now. xxx, and xxxi, winde and no raine: no raine? S'lid stay; this is worse and worse: what saies he of *S. Swithins?* turne
25 back, looke, *S. Swithins*: no raine?
  MACI. O, here's a precious durty damned rogue,

---

1. iii.] *Enter Sordido with a Prognostication.* | SCENA TER. *Qq*   1 O Rare!] *Sord*. O rare, *Qq*   good! I] good, I *Qq*   2 Starres] Christ *Qq*   5 loose] lose *F2, F3*   6 Dull'd, if not deadded] Dead, dull, and blunted *Qq*   7 'tis] it is *G*   8 Boore] Boar *F3*   9 excellent! as] excellent, as *Qq*   14 yeere.] yeere, *Qq 1, 3* : yeare, *Q2*   see,] see *Q3, F2*   15 *Iuly, August?*] Iulie? *Qq 1, 3* : Iuly? *Q2*   16 What is't,] What is't *Qq* : What, is't *G*   17 xx, xxi, xxij,] xx. xxi. xxij. *Qq, and so throughout except* 'xxviij' (19)   daies,] dayes *F2*   18 good!] good ; *Qq 1, 2* : good : *Q3*   19 still!] still ; *Qq 1, 2* : still : *Q3*   26 O,] O *Qq*   here's] there's *Q3*   durty] filthy *Qq*

That fats himselfe with expectation
Of rotten weather, and vnseason'd howers;
And he is rich for it, an elder brother!
His barnes are full! his reekes, and mowes well trod! 30
His garners cracke with store! O, tis well; ha, ha, ha:
A plague consume thee, and thy house.

  S O R D. O here, *S. Swithins*, the xv day, variable
weather, for the most part raine, good; for the most part
raine: Why, it should raine fortie daies after, now, more 35
or lesse, it was a rule held, afore I was able to hold a plough,
and yet here are two daies, no raine; ha? it makes me
muse. Weele see how the next moneth begins, if that bee
better. *September*, first, second, third, and fourth daies,
rainy, and blustering; this is well now: fift, sixt, seuenth, 40
eight, and ninth, rainy, with some thunder; I mary, this
is excellent; the other was false printed sure: the tenth,
and eleuenth, great store of raine; O good, good, good,
good, good! the twelth, thirteenth, and fourteenth daies,
raine; good still; fifteenth, and sixteenth, raine; good 45
still: seuenteenth, and eighteenth, raine, good still; nineteenth, and twentieth, good still, good still, good still,
good still, good still! one and twentieth, some raine;
some raine? well, we must be patient, and attend the
heauens pleasure, would it were more though: the one and 50
twentieth, two and twentieth, three and twentieth, great
tempest of raine, thunder, and lightning.

  O good againe, past expectation good!

---

1. iii. 28 howers] houres *F2*   29 an] and *Q3, F3*   brother!]
brother, *Qq*   30 full!] full, *Qq*   reekes,] reekes *F2*   trod!] trod, *Qq*
31 store!] store. *Qq*   · 32 thee,] thee *Qq*   33 xv] xv. *Qq*   35 Why,]
Why *Qq*   after,] afte- *Qq*   36 held,] held *Qq 1, 2* : helde *Q3*   38
moneth] month *Qq*   39 *September*, first] August : August, first *Qq*
40 fift, sixt] fifth, sixth *F2*   seuenth] seventh *Q1*   41 eight] eighth
F2   rainy] raine *Qc*   42 tenth,] tenth *Qq 1, 2*   44 good!]
good; *Qq 1, 2* : good : *Q3*   twelth *F1* : twelft *Q1* : twelfth *Qq 2, 3,
F2, F3*   45 fifteenth,] fifteenth *Qq*   46 seuenteenth,] seuenteenth
Qq 1, 2   nineteenth,] nineteenth *Qq 1, 2* : ninteenth *Q3*   47
twentieth, good] twentieth, Good *Qq*   48 still! one] still; one
Qq 1, 2 : still: one *Q3*   50 one and twentieth, *om. Q2, G*   51
twentieth] twentith *Qq 1, 2* (*three times*)   52 tempest] tempests *F2,
F3*   53 good!] good: *Qq*

I thanke my blessed angell ; neuer, neuer,
55 Laid I penny better out, then this,
To purchase this deare booke : not deare for price,
And yet of me as dearely priz'd as life,
Since in it, is contain'd the very life,
Bloud, strength, and sinnewes of my happinesse.
60 Blest be the houre, wherein I bought this booke,
His studies happy, that compos'd the booke,
And the man fortunate, that sold the booke.
Sleepe with this charme, and be as true to me,
As I am ioy'd, and confident in thee.

The Hine enters with a paper. MAC I. Ha, ha, ha ? I'not this good ? Is't not pleasing this ?
Ha, ha, ha ! God pardon me ! ha, ha !
Is't possible that such a spacious villaine
Should liue, and not be plagu'd ? or lies he hid
Within the wrinckled bosome of the world,
70 Where heauen cannot see him ? Sbloud (me thinkes)
'Tis rare, and strange, that he should breathe, and walke,
Feede with disgestion, sleepe, enjoy his health,
And (like a boist'rous whale, swallowing the poore)
Still swimme in wealth, and pleasure ! is't not strange ?
75 Vnlesse his house, and skin were thunder-proofe,
I wonder at it ! Me thinkes, now, the hecticke,
Gout, leprosie, or some such loth'd disease
Might light vpon him ; or that fire (from heauen)
Might fall vpon his barnes ; or mice, and rats
80 Eate vp his graine ; or else that it might rot

---

1. iii. 55 out,] out *Qq*   then] than *Qq 1, 2, F2*   58 it,] it *Qq*   59 happinesse.] happinesse : *Qq*   60 houre,] houre *Qq*   61 happy,] happy *Qq 1, 3* : happie *Q2*   62 fortunate,] fortunate *Qq*   booke.] booke : *Qq*   63 me,] me *Qq 1, 2*   64 ioy'd,] joy'd *Q1* : ioy'd *Qq 2, 3*   65 stage-dir. *Enter a Hind to Sordido with a paper.* Qq in text after 64   Hine] Hind Qq : Hinde F2, F3   I'not . . Is't] Is not . . . Is it *Q3*   66 Ha, ha . . . ha, ha !] ha, ha ? Gods ha ? *Q—* add to *l.* 65 (query, Gods precious ha ?)   68 liue,] liue *Qq*   70 Sbloud] why F2, F3   71 rare,] rare *Qq*   strange] admirable *Qq*   breathe,] breath *Qq*   72 enjoy] enioy *Qq 2, 3*   73 whale,] Whale *Qq 1, 2*   74 wealth,] wealth *Qq*   pleasure !] pleasure : *Qq*   is't] is it *Q3*   75 house,] house *Qq*   76 it !] it. *Qq*   thinkes,] thinkes *Qq*   vpon] upon *Q1*   mice,] mice *Qq*

Within the hoary reekes, e'ne as it stands:
Me thinkes this might be well; and after all
The deuill might come and fetch him. I, 'tis true!
Meane time he surfets in prosperitie,
And thou (in enuie of him) gnaw'st thy selfe,   85
Peace, foole, get hence, and tell thy vexed spirit,
" Wealth in this age will scarcely looke on merit.
    S O R D. Who brought this same, sirha?
    H I N E. Mary, sir, one of the Iustices men, he saies 'tis
a precept, and all their hands be at it: 90
    S O R D. I, and the prints of them sticke in my flesh,
Deeper then i' their letters: They haue sent me
Pils wrapt in paper here, that should I take 'hem,
Would poison all the sweetnesse of my booke,
And turne my honey into hemlocke juyce.   95
But I am wiser then to serue their precepts,
Or follow their prescriptions. Here's a deuice,
To charge me bring my graine vnto the markets:
I, much, when I haue neither barne nor garner,
Nor earth to hide it in, I'le bring it; till then,   100
Ech corne I send shall be as big as *Paules*.
O, but (say some) the poore are like to starue.
Why let 'hem starue, what's that to me? are bees
Bound to keepe life in drones, and idle moths? no:
Why such are these (that terme themselues the poore,   105
Only because they would be pittied,
But are indeed a sort of lazie beggers)
Licencious rogues, and sturdie vagabonds,
Bred (by the sloth of a fat plentious yeere)

I. iii. 83 deuill] diuell *Q3*   him.] him: *Qq*   true!] true. *Qq*   85 enuie] envie *Q1*   86 Peace,] Peace *Qq*   87 *italicized, and* 'Exit.' *added in Qq*   88 same,] same *Qq*   89 *(and in the headings to speeches* 114, 116, 124) HINE] Hind Qq   Mary, sir,] Marry sir *Qq 1, 2*: Marrie sir *Q3*   Iustices] justices *Q1*   90 it:] it. *Qq 2, 3*   91 flesh,] flesh *Qq*   92 then] than *Qq 1, 2, F2*   93 paper] a paper *Q3*   95 juyce.]juice: *Q1*: iuice: *Qq 2, 3*   96 then] than *Qq, F2*   to serue] t'observe *W. conj.*   97 prescriptions.] prescriptions: *Qq*   98 vnto] into *Qq 2, 3*   100 till] but till *Qq*   102, 103 starue] sterue *Qq*   104 drones,] Drones *Qq*   106 pittied,] pittied) *Qq*   107 beggers)] Beggers, *Qq*   108 rogues,] Rogues *Qq 1, 2*

456 *Euery Man out of his Humour*

110 Like snakes, in heat of summer, out of dung,
 And this is all that these cheape times are good for :
 Whereas a holsome, and penurious dearth
 Purges the soile of such vile excrements,
 And kils the vipers vp.   H I N E. O, but master,
115 Take heed they heare you not.   S O R D. Why so ?
   H I N E. They will exclaime against you.   S O R D. I,
    their exclaimes
 Moue me as much, as thy breath moues a mountaine !
 Poore wormes, they hisse at me, whilst I at home
 Can be contented to applaud my selfe,
120 To sit and clap my hands, and laugh, and leape,
 Knocking my head against my roofe, with ioy
 To see how plumpe my bags are, and my barnes.
 Sirrah, goe, hie you home, and bid your fellowes,
 Get all their flailes readie, again' I come.   H I N E. I will,
  Sir.
125   S O R D. I'le instantly set all my hines to thrashing
 Of a whole reeke of corne, which I will hide
 Vnder the ground ; and with the straw thereof
 I'le stuffe the out-sides of my other mowes :
 That done, I'le haue 'hem emptie all my garners,
130 And i' the friendly earth bury my store,
 That, when the searchers come, they may suppose
 All's spent, and that my fortunes were belied.
 And, to lend more opinion to my want,
 And stop that many-mouthed vulgar dog,
135 (Which else would still be baying at my dore)
 Each market day, I will be seene to buy
 Part of the purest wheat, as for my houshold :
 Where when it comes, it shall encrease my heapes,

 I. iii. 110 snakes,] snakes *Qq, F2*   summer,] summer *Qq*   112 Whereas] Where as *Qq*   holsome,] holsome *Q1* : holesome *Qq 2, 3* 114 O,] O *Qq, F2*   master] maister *Qq*   117 mountaine !] Mountaine; *Qq*   120 laugh,] laugh *Qq*   121 ioy] joy *Q1*   123 fellowes,] fellowes *Qq*   124 readie, again'] readie againe *Qq*   will,] will *Qq* *Exit Hind.* Qq add to 124.   125 hines] hinds *Qq 1, 2* : Hinds *Q3* 128 out-sides] outsides *Qq*   131 That,] That *Qq*   come,] come *Qq1, 2* 133 And,] And *Qq*   135 baying] bayting *Q3*   138 encrease] increase *F2, F3*

Twill yeeld me treble gaine, at this deare time,
Promisd in this deare booke : I haue cast all.   140
Till then I will not sell an eare, I'le hang first.
O, I shall make my prizes as I list,
My house and I can feed on pease, and barley,
What though a world of wretches starue the while ?
" He that will thriue, must thinke no courses vile.   145

GREX.

COR. Now, Signior, how approue you this ? haue the Humorists exprest themselues truly or no ?

MIT. Yes (if it be well prosecuted) 'tis hitherto happy ynough : but me thinks, MACILENTE went hence too soone, hee might haue beene made to stay, and speake 150 somewhat in reproofe of SORDIDO's wretchednesse, now at the last.

COR. O, no, that had beene extremely improper, besides, he had continued the *Scene* too long with him, as't was, being in no more action.   155

MIT. You may enforce the length, as a necessary reason ; but for propriety, the *Scene* would very well haue borne it, in my iudgement.

COR. O, worst of both : why, you mistake his Humour vtterly then.   160

MIT. How ? doe I mistake it ? is't not enuie ?

COR. Yes, but you must vnderstand, Signior, he enuies him not as he is a villaine, a wolfe i' the common-wealth, but as he is rich, and fortunate ; for the true condition of enuie is, *Dolor alienæ fœlicitatis*, to haue our eyes con- 165

1. iii. 139 gaine,] gaine *Qq*   140 all.] all, *Qq*   142 O,] O *Qq*   143 pease,] Pease *Q1* : Peas *Qq 2, 3*   barley,] barley ; *F2*   144 starue] sterue *Qq*   145 *Exit.* add Qq   146 Now,] Now *Qq*   149 thinks.] thinks *Qq*   150 stay,] stay *Qq 1, 2*   153 O,] O *Qq*   beene] bin *Qq*   improper,] improper ; *F2, F3*   154 besides,] besides *Qq* him,] him *Qq*   156 length,] length *Qq*   157 propriety,] propriety *Qq* would] wold *Qq*   158 iudgement] judgement *Q1*   159 O,] O *Qq* why,] why *Qq*   Humour] Humor *Q1* : humor *Qq 2, 3*   161 is't] is it *Q3*   enuie] Envie *Qq*   162 vnderstand,] vnderstand *Qq*   163 i'] in *Q3*   164 rich,] rich *Qq*   165 enuie] envie, *Q1* : enuy, *Qq 2, 3* is,] is *Qq*   *fœlicitatis*] *felicitatis* Qq

tinually fixt vpon another mans prosperitie, that is, his chiefe happinesse, and to grieue at that. Whereas, if we make his monstrous, and abhord actions our obiect, the griefe (we take then) comes neerer the nature of hate, then 170 enuie, as being bred out of a kinde of contempt and lothing, in our selues.

M I T. So you'le infer it had beene hate, not enuie in him, to reprehend the humour of S O R D I D O ?

C O R D. Right, for what a man truly enuies in another, 175 he could alwaies loue, and cherish in himselfe : but no man truly reprehends in another, what he loues in himselfe ; therefore reprehension is out of his hate. And this distinction hath he himselfe made in a speech there (if you markt it) where he saies, *I enuie not this* B V F F O N, *but I* 180 *hate him.*

M I T. Stay, sir : *I enuie not this* B V F F O N, *but I hate him* : why might he not as well haue hated S O R D I D O, as him ?

C O R. No, sir, there was subiect for his enuie in 185 S O R D I D O ; his wealth : So was there not in the other. He stood possest of no one eminent gift, but a most odious, and fiend-like disposition, that would turne charitie it selfe into hate, much more enuie, for the present.

M I T. You haue satisfied mee, sir ; O, here comes the 190 Foole and the Iester, againe, methinkes.

C O R. 'Twere pitty they should be parted, sir.

M I T. What bright-shining gallant's that with them ? the knight they went to ?

1. iii. 166 is,] is *Qq*   167 Whereas,] Whereas *Qq, F2*   168 monstrous,] monstrous *Qq*   actions] actions, *Qq*   obiect] object *Q1*
169 hate,] Hate *Qq* : hate *F2*   then] than *Qq, F2*   170 lothing,] lothing *Qq*   172 enuie] Envie *Q1*   173 humour] humor *Qq*   175 himselfe :] himselfe ; *Qq 1, 2*   176 another,] another *Qq*   himselfe ;] himselfe, *Qq*   179 markt] marke *Qq 2, 3*   181 Stay,] Stay *Qq*
I enuie] envie L.p. F2 (the *I* not catching the ink)   182 SORDIDO,] Sordido *Qq*   184 No,] No *Qq*   subiect] subject *Q1*   enuie] envie *Q1*   185 other. He] other, he *Qq* (hee *Qq 2, 3*)   186 odious,] odious *Qq*   187 fiend-like] friend-like *Q3*   188 enuie,] Envie *Q1* : Enuie *Qq 2, 3*   After 188 Qq add *Enter Carlo Buffone, Sogliardo, Fastidius Briske, Cinedo.* | ACTVS SECVNDVS, SCENA PRIMA. (ACTUS SECUNDUS, *Q1*)   189 mee, sir ; O,] me sir, O *Qq*   190 Iester, againe,] *Iester* againe *Qq*   191 parted,] parted *Qq 1, 2* : patted *Q3*

Cor. No, sir, this is one Monsieur Fastidius
Briske, otherwise cal'd the fresh Frenchefied courtier. 195
  Mit. A humorist too?
  Cor. As humorous as quick-siluer, doe but obserue
him, the *Scene* is the country still, remember.

Act II.   Scene I.

Fast. Briske, Cinedo, Carlo Bvffone,
Sogliardo.

Cinedo, watch when the knight comes, and giue vs
word.
  Cine. I will, sir.
  Fast. How lik'st thou my boy, Carlo?
  Car. O, well, well. He lookes like a colonell of 5
Pigmies horse, or one of these motions, in a great antique
clock : he would shew well vpon a habberdashers stall, at
a corner shop, rarely.
  Fast. S'heart, what a damn'd witty rogue's this? how
he confounds with his *simile's*?   10
  Carl. Better with *simile's*, then smiles : and whither
were you riding now, Signior?
  Fast. Who, I? what a silly iest's that? whither
should I ride, but to the court?
  Carl. O, pardon me, sir, twentie places more : your 15
hot-house, or your whore-house——
  Fast. By the vertue of my soule, this knight dwels in
Elizium, here.

1. iii. 194 No,] No *Qq*   195 Frenchefied] Frenchfield *Q3*   II. i.]
Act II, Scene I.—*The* Country *before* Puntarvolo's *House.* G   1
Cinedo] *Fast. Cinedo* Qq   3 will,] will *Qq.*   *Exit.* add Qq 1, 2
5 O,] O *Qq*   well. He] wel, he *Qq 1, 3* : wel he *Q2*   a colonell of
the] the colonel of a *Qq 2, 3*   6 motions,] motions *Qq*   antique]
anticke *Q3*   8 shop,] shop *Qq*   9 S'heart, om. F2, F3*   10
simile's] similies Q3   11 *simile's,*] *simile's* Qq 1, 2 : similies *Q3*
then] than *Qq, F2*   whither] whether *Q3, F3*   12 now,] now *Qq*
13 Who,] Who *Qq*   iest's] jest's *Q1*   whither] whether *F3*   14
ride,] ride *Qq*   15 O,] O *Qq*   me,] me *Qq*   16 your whore-
house——] your—— *Qq*   17 soule,] soule *Qq 1, 2*   18 *Elizium,*]
Elizium Qq 1, 2 : *Elisium* Q3

460 *Euery Man out of his Humour*

C A R L. Hee's gone now, I thought he would flie out
20 presently. These be our nimble-spirited *Catso's*, that ha'
their euasions at pleasure, will run ouer a bog like your
wild *Irish*: no sooner started, but they'le leape from
one thing to another, like a squirrell, heigh : dance ! and
doe tricks i' their discourse, from fire to water, from water
25 to aire, from aire to earth, as if their tongues did but e'en
licke the foure elements ouer, and away.

F A S T. Sirrha, C A R L O, thou neuer saw'st my grey-hobbie
yet, didst thou ?

C A R L. No : ha' you such a one ?

30 F A S T. The best in *Europe* (my good villaine) thoul't say,
when thou seest him.

C A R L. But when shall I see him ?

F A S T. There was a noble man i' the court offered me
100. pound for him, by this light : a fine little fiery slaue,
35 he runs like a (oh) excellent, excellent ! with the very sound
of the spurre.

C A R L. How ? the sound of the spurre ?

F A S T. O, it's your only humour now extant, sir : a good
gingle, a good gingle.

40 C A R L. Sbloud, you shall see him turne morris-dancer,
he ha's got him bels, a good sute, and a hobby-horse.

S O G L. Signior, now you talke of a hobby-horse, I know
where one is, will not be giuen for a brace of angels.

F A S T. How is that, Sir ?

45 S O G L. Mary, sir, I am telling this gentleman of a hobby-
horse, it was my fathers indeed, and (though I say it———

C A R L. That should not say it) on, on.

S O G L. He did dance in it, with as good humour, and as

II. i. 20 -spirited *Catso's*,] -sprighted *Catso's* Qq   21 their] there *Q1*
22 *Irish*:] Irish ; *Qq 1, 2*   23 another,] another *Qq*   heigh :
dance !] heigh ; Daunce, *Qq*   24 i'] in *Q3*   25 e'en] eu'n *Q2* : euen
Q3   27 Sirrha,] Sirra *Qq 1, 3* : Sirah *Q2*   28 yet,] yet *F2*
29 No :] No *Q2* : No, *Q3*   34 him,] him *Qq*   slaue] slave *Q1*   35
runs] turnes *Q3*   excellent !] excellent, *Qq*   38 humour] humor
Qq   extant,] extant *Qq*   40 Sbloud, *F1* : Sbloud *Qq 1, 2* : Sbloud
Q3 : om. *F2, F3*   44 that,] that *Qq*   45 Mary, sir,] Mary sir
Qq 1, 2 : Mary sir, *Q3*   46 it———] it *Qq*   48 it,] it *Qq*   humour,
Q3, Ff : humour *Qq 1, 2*. *So Qq spell here and in 51*

good regard, as any man of his degree whatsoeuer, being no
gentleman : I haue danc't in it my selfe too. 50

CARL. Not since the humour of gentilitie was vpon
you? did you?

SOGL. Yes, once; mary, that was but to shew what
a gentleman might doe, in a humour.

CARL. O, very good. 55

GREX.

MIT. Why, this fellowes discourse were nothing, but for
the word Humour.

COR. O, beare with him, and he should lacke matter,
and words too, 'twere pittifull.

SOG. Nay, looke you, sir, there's ne're a gentleman 60
i' the countrey has the like humours, for the hobby-horse,
as I haue ; I haue the method for the threeding of the
needle and all, the———

CAR. How, the method?

SOG. I, the leigeritie for that, and the wigh-hie, and the 65
daggers in the nose, and the trauels of the egge from finger
to finger, all the humours incident to the quality. The
horse hangs at home in my parlor. I'le keepe it for a
monument, as long as I liue, sure.

CAR. Doe so ; and when you die, 'twill be an excellent 70
trophee, to hang ouer your tombe.

SOG. Masse, and I'le haue a tombe (now I thinke on't)
'tis but so much charges.

CAR. Best build it in your life time then, your heires
may hap to forget it else. 75

II. i. 49 regard,] regard *Q1* : gard *Qq* 2, 3   53 Yes,] Yes *Qq*   54
doe,] doe *Qq*   humour] Humor *Qq* (so 57)   55, 58 O,] O *Qq*   56
Why,] Why *Qq*   nothing,] nothing *Qq*   58 and] an' *F2, F3*   matter,]
matter *Qq*   60 Nay,] Nay *Qq*   you,] you *Qq*   61 humours,]
humors *Qq*   -horse,] horse *Qq*   62 haue ;] haue ? *Qq 2, 3*   63
and all *not in Qq*   64 How,] How *Qq*   method ? *F2* : method. *F1* :
Methode. *Qq 1, 2* : Methode ? *Q3*   65 leigeritie] Leigeritie, *Qq 2, 3*
67 humours] humors *Q1* : Humors *Qq 2, 3*   68 parlor.] parlor, *Qq*
69 liue,] liue *Qq*   71 trophee,] Trophee *Qq*   75 may *om. F3*

Sog. Nay, I meane so, Ile not trust to them.

Car. No, for heires, and executors, are growne damnably carelesse, specially, since the ghosts of testators left walking: how like you him, Signior?

80 Fast. 'Fore heauens, his humour arrides me exceedingly.

Car. Arrides you?

Fast. I, pleases me (a pox on't) I am so haunted at the court, and at my lodging, with your refin'd choise spirits, that it makes me cleane of another garbe, another sheafe, I know not how! I cannot frame me to your harsh vulgar phrase, 'tis against my *genius*.

Sog. Signior Carlo.

GREX.

Cor. This is right to that of Horace, *Dum vitant*
90 *stulti vitia, in contraria currunt*: so this gallant, labouring to auoid popularitie, fals into a habit of affectation, ten thousand times hatefuller then the former.

Car. Who, hee? a gull, a foole, no salt in him i' the earth, man: hee looks like a fresh salmon kept in a tub,
95 hee'le be spent shortly. His braine's lighter then his feather already, and his tongue more subiect to lie, then that's to wag: he sleepes with a muske-cat euery night, and walkes all day hang'd in pomander chaines for penance: he ha's his skin tan'd in ciuet, to make his complexion
100 strong, and the sweetnesse of his youth lasting in the sense

---

II. i. 76 Nay,] Nay *Qq*   77 heires,] heirs *Q1* : heires *Q2, F2* : Heires *Q3*   executors,] executors *Qq 1, 2* : Executors, *Q3*   damnably] damnablie *Q2* : damnable *Q3*   78 specially,] specially *Qq 1, 3* : speciallie *Q2*   79 him,] him *Qq*   80 heauens,] heauens *Qq*   humour] Humor *Q1* : humor *Qq 2, 3*   84 court,] court *Q1* : Court *Qq 2, 3*   lodging,] lodging *Qq*   85 sheafe] straine *Qq*   86 how!] how; *Qq 1, 2* : how: *Q3*   88 Carlo] Carla *Qq 2, 3*   90 *vitia,*] *vitia Qq*   currunt] *currant Q3*   gallant,] gallant *Qq*   91 affectation,] Affectation *Qq 1, 2*   92 hatefuller] more hatefull *Qq*   then] than *Qq, F2 (so 95–6)*   93 Who,] Who *Qq*   gull, a foole,] gull? a foole? *Qq*   94 earth,] earth *Qq*   tub,] tub; *Qq 1* : tubbe: *Q2, 3*   95 shortly. His] shortly, his *Qq*   96 subiect] subject *Q1*   99 in *om. Q3*

of his sweet lady. A good emptie puffe, he loues you well, Signior.
  S o g l. There shall be no loue lost, sir, I'le assure you.
  F a s t. Nay, C a r l o, I am not happy i' thy loue, I see : pr'y theè suffer me to enioy thy company a little (sweet *mischiefe*) by this aire, I shall enuy this gentlemans place in thy affections, if you be thus priuate, yfaith. How now? is the knight arriu'd?

C i n e d o.

  C i n e. No, sir, but 'tis guest he will arriue presently, by his fore-runners.
  F a s t. His hounds! by M i n e r v a an excellent figure; a good boy.
  C a r l. You should giue him a french crowne for it: the boy would finde two better figures i' that, and a good figure of your bounty beside.
  F a s t. Tut, the boy wants no crownes.
  C a r l. No crowne: speake i' the singular number, and wee'le beleeue you.
  F a s t. Nay, thou art so capriciously conceited now. Sirra (*damnation*) I haue heard this knight P v n t a r v o l o, reported to bee a gentleman of exceeding good humour; thou know'st him: pr'ythee, how is his disposition? I ne're was so fauour'd of my starres, as to see him yet. Boy, doe you looke to the hobby?
  C i n e. I, sir, the groome has set him vp.
  F a s t. 'Tis well: I rid out of my way of intent to visit him, and take knowledge of his—Nay, good *wickednesse*, his humour, his humour.

  II. i. 101 lady. A] Ladie, A *Qq* 2, 3 : lady: a *F2* well,] well *Qq* 103 lost,] lost *Qq* 104 Nay,] Nay *Qq* CARLO] Carl *Qq* 2, 3 i']
in *Q3* loue,] loue *Qq* 105 see :] see, *Qq* enioy] enjoy *Q1*
106 enuy] envie *Q1* 107 priuate, yfaith. How] priuate I faith : how *Qq* After 108 CINEDO.] *Enter Cinedo.* Qq 109 No,] No *Qq* . guest] gest *Qq* 114 figures] figutes *F2* i'] in *Q3* 117 i'] in *Q3* 119 now.] now: *Q1* : nowe: *Qq* 2, 3 120 PVNTARVOLO] *Puntarvolo* Q1 : *Puntaruallo* Q3 : PVNTARVOIO *F2* 122 humour;] humour : *Qq* him :] him ; *Qq 1, 2* 123 starres,] starres *Qq* 125 I,] I *Qq*
127 his—Nay,] his: Nay *Qq* 128 humour . . . humour] humor . . . humor *Q1*

CARL. Why, he loues dogs, and hawkes, and his wife,
well: he has a good riding face, and he can sit a great horse;
hee will taint a staffe well at tilt: when he is mounted, he
lookes like the signe of the *George*, that's all I know; saue,
that in stead of a dragon, he will brandish against a tree,
and breake his sword as confidently vpon the knottie barke,
as the other did vpon the skales of the beast.

FAST. O, but this is nothing to that's deliuerd of him.
They say he has dialogues, and discourses betweene his
horse, himselfe, and his dogge: and that he will court his
owne lady, as shee were a stranger neuer encounter'd before.

CARL. I, that he will, and make fresh loue to her euery
morning: this gentleman has beene a spectator of it,
Signior Insulso.

Hee leapes from whispring with the boy.

SOGL. I am resolute to keepe a page: say you sir?

CARL. You haue seene *Signior Puntaruolo* accost his
lady?

SOGL. O, I sir.

FAST. And how is the manner of it, pr'ythee, good
Signior?

SOGL. Faith sir, in very good sort, he has his humours
for it, sir: as first, (suppose he were now to come from
riding, or hunting, or so) he has his trumpet to sound, and
then the waiting gentlewoman, shee lookes out, and then
hee speakes, and then shee speakes—very pretty yfaith,
gentlemen.

FAST. Why, but doe you remember no particulars,
Signior?

SOGL. O, yes sir: first, the gentlewoman, shee lookes
out at the window.

II. i. 129 Why,] Why *Qq*   wife,] wife *Qq* : Wife : *F3*   130 well :]
well; *F3*   can] ean *Q3*   132 saue,] saue *Qq*   133 dragon,] Dragon
Qq 1, 2   136 that's deliuerd] that is deliuered *Qq 2, 3*   him. They]
him: they *Qq*   138 dogge :] dogge ; *Q1* : Dogge ; *Q2* : Dogge : *Q3*
139 encounter'd] encountred *Q3*   before.] before, *Qq 1, 2*   143 st.
dir. *not in Qq*   144 *Puntaruolo*] *Puntarvolo Q1*   146 I *om. Q3*
147 it, pr'ythee,] it pr'ythee *Qq*   149 sir,] sir *Qq*   sort,] sort ; *Qq*
humours] humors *Q1*   150 it,] it *Qq*   152 out,] out ; *Qq*   153
shee speakes—] shee speakes : *Qq*   yfaith,] I faith *Qq*   157 gentlewoman,] Gentlewoman *Q1* : gentlewoman *Qq 2, 3*

Euery Man out of his Humour

C a r l. After the trumpet has summon'd a parle? not before? 160

S o g l. No, sir, not before: and then saies he—ha, ha, ha, ha, &c.

C a r l. What saies he? be not rapt so.

S o g l. Saies he—ha, ha, ha, ha, &c.

F a s t. Nay, speake, speake. 165

S o g l. Ha, ha, ha, saies he: God saue you, saies he: ha, ha, &c.

C a r l. Was this the ridiculous motiue to all this passion?

S o g l. Nay, that, that comes after, is—ha, ha, ha, ha, &c.

C a r l. Doubtlesse, he apprehends more then he vtters, 170 this fellow: or else.

S o g l. List, list, they are come from hunting: stand by, close vnder this tarras, and you shall see it done, better then I can shew it. *A cry of hounds within.*

C a r l. So it had need, 'twill scarce poize the obseruation 175 else.

S o g l. Faith I remember all, but the manner of it is quite out of my head.

F a s t. O, with-draw, with-draw, it cannot bee but a most pleasing obiect. 180

Act II. Scene II.

P v n t a r v o l o, H v n t s m a n, G e n t l e-
w o m a n. *To the rest.*

FOrrester, giue winde to thy horne. Inough, by this, the sound hath toucht the eares of the enclosed: Depart, leaue the dogge, and take with thee what thou hast deseru'd, the horne, and thankes.

II. i. 161 No,] No *Qq*   161, 164 he—*F1* : he ; *Qq* : he, *F2*   165, 169 Nay,] Nay *Qq*   166 ha, saies *Qq, corr. F1, F2* : ha, Saies *F1*   you, saies he :] you, *Qq*   169 after,] after *Qq*   is— *F1* : is : *Qq* : is, *F2*   170 Doubtlesse,] Doubtlesse *Qq*   then] then *Qq, F2* (so 174)   173 done,] done *Qq*   179 O, with-draw, with-draw] O withdraw, withdraw *Qq*   180 obiect] object *Q1*   II. ii. *Act* . . . GENTLEWOMAN.] *Enter Puntaruolo, a Huntsman with a greyhound.* (Puntaruolo Q1, Graihound Qq 2, 3) Qq. without change of scene. *To the rest.* add Ff   1 Forrester] *Pun.* Forrester *Qq*   Inough, *F1* : Inough ; *Qq 1, 2* : Inough : *Q3* : Enough ; *F2*   this,] this *Qq*   2 enclosed] inclosed *F2*   3 deseru'd,] deseru'd ; *Qq 1, 2*

5   CARL. I, mary, there's some taste in this.
   FAST. Is't not good?
   SOGL. Ah, peace, now aboue, now aboue!

The gentle-   PVNT. Stay: mine eye hath (on the instant) through
woman
appeares   the bountie of the window, receiu'd the forme of a *Nymph.*
at the win-   I will step forward three pases: of the which, I will barely
dow.
11   retire one; and (after some little flexure of the knee) with
   an erected grace salute her (one, two, and three.) Sweet
   lady, God saue you.
   GENT. No, forsooth: I am but the waiting gentle-
15 woman.
   CARL. He knew that before.
   PVNT. Pardon me: *Humanum est errare.*
   CARL. He learn'd that of his chaplaine.
   PVNT. To the perfection of complement (which is the
20 Diall of the thought, and guided by the Sunne of your
   beauties) are requir'd these three specials: the *gnomon,* the
   puntilio's, and the *superficies*: the *superficies,* is that we
   call, place; the *puntilio's,* circumstance; and the *gnomon,*
   ceremony: in either of which, for a stranger to erre, 'tis
25 easie and facile, and such am I.
   CARL. True, not knowing her *horizon,* he must needes
   erre: which I feare, he knowes too well.
   PVNT. What call you the lord of the castle? sweet face.
   GENT. The lord of the castle is a knight, sir; Signior
30 PVNTARVOLO.
   PVNT. PVNTARVOLO? O.
   CARL. Now must he ruminate.
   FAST. Does the wench know him all this while, then?
   CARL. O, doe you know me, man? why, therein lies

   II. ii. 5 I,] I *Qq*   7 Ah,] Ah *Qq*   aboue! *corr. F1, F2*: aboue. *Qq,*
F1   8 st. dir.] *The waiting Gentlewoman appeares at the window.* (*wayt-
ing Gentlewomen appeare* Q3) Qq in text after 7.   10 pases] paces *Qq,
F2*   12 her (one, two, and three.)] her: 1, 2, and 3. *Qq*   14 No,]
No *Qq*   the] a *Q3*   18 his chaplaine] a Puritane *Qq*   21 specials]
Projects *Q1*: Proiects *Qq* 2, 3   23 call,] call *Qq*   25 facile,] facile ;
Qq   26 horizon] *Horizon* Q1 : *Horison* Qq 2, 3   29 knight,]
knight *Qq*   30 PVNTARVOLO] *Puntarvolo* Q1 (*so* 31)   33 while,]
while *Qq*   34 me,] me *Qq*   why,] why *Qq*   lies] lics *Q1*

the sirrup of the iest; it's a proiect, a designement of his 35
owne, a thing studied, and rehearst as ordinarily at his
comming from hawking, or hunting, as a jigge after a
play.

S o g l. I, e'en like your jigge, sir.

P v n t. 'Tis a most sumptuous and stately edifice! of 40
what yeeres is the knight, faire damsell?

G e n t. Faith, much about your yeeres, sir.

P v n t. What complexion, or what stature beares he?

G e n t. Of your stature, and very neere vpon your
complexion. 45

P v n t. Mine is melancholy:

C a r l. So is the dogges, iust.

P v n t. And doth argue constancie, chiefly in loue.
What are his endowments? Is he courteous?

G e n t. O, the most courteous knight in Christian land, 50
sir.

P v n t. Is he magnanimous?

G e n t. As the skin betweene your browes, sir.

P v n t. Is he bountifull?

C a r l. 'Slud, he takes an inuentory of his owne good 55
parts.

G e n t. Bountifull? I, sir, I would you should know
it; the poore are seru'd at his gate, early, and late, sir.

P v n t. Is he learned?

G e n t. O, I sir, he can speake the *French*, and *Italian*. 60

P v n t. Then he is trauail'd?

G e n t. I, forsooth, he hath beene beyond-sea, once, or
twise.

II. ii. 35 iest] ieast *Q1*   proiect] Project *Q1*   37 hawking,] hawking *Qq 1, 3*   jigge] Iigge *Qq 2, 3*   39 jigge,] jigge *Q1* : Iigge *Qq 2, 3*
40 edifice!] *corr. F1, F2* : edifice ; *Qq 1, 2, F1* ; edifice : *Q3*   of *not in
Qq*   42 Faith,] Faith *Qq*   yeeres,] yeeres *Q1* : yeares *Qq 2, 3*   46
melancholy : *F1* : Melancholly : *Qq 1, 2* : Melancholly. *Q3* : melancholy.
F2   47 iust] just *Q1*   50 O,] O *Qq*   in Christian land,] vpon
Gods earth *Qq*   53 browes,] browes *Qq*   55 'Slud] Sbloud *Qq*
57 I, sir,] I sir *Qq*   58 gate,] gate *Qq 1, 2*   early, and late,] early
and late *Qq*   60 I *om. Q3*   French,] French *Qq*   62 -sea,] -sea
Qq 1, 2 : -seas, *F2, F3*   once,] once *Qq*

H h 2

CARL. As far as *Paris*, to fetch ouer a fashion, and come back againe.

PVNT. Is he religious?

GENT. Religious? I know not what you call religious, but hee goes to church, I am sure.

FAST. S'lid, me thinkes, these answeres should offend him.

CARL. Tut, no; he knowes they are excellent, and to her capacity, that speakes 'hem.

PVNT. Would I might see his face.

CARL. Shee should let down a glasse from the window at that word, and request him to looke in't.

PVNT. Doubtlesse, the gentleman is most exact, and absolutely qualified? doth the castle containe him?

GENT. No, sir, he is from home, but his lady is within.

PVNT. His lady? what, is shee faire? splendidious? and amiable?

GENT. O, Lord, sir!

PVNT. Pr'y thee, deare *Nymph*, intreat her beauties to shine on this side of the building.

Gent. leaues the win- dow.

CARL. That he may erect a new dyall of complement, with his *gnomons*, and his *puntilio's*.

FAST. Nay, thou art such another *Cinique* now, a man had need walke vprightly before thee.

CARL. Heart, can any man walke more vpright then hee does? Looke, looke; as if he went in a frame, or had a sute of wanescot on: and the dogge watching him, lest he should leape out on't.

FAST. O, villaine!

CARL. Well, and e'er I meet him in the city, I'le ha'

II. ii. 64 fashion,] fashion *Qq 1, 2*   68 church,] Church *Qq*   69 S'lid,] S'lid *Qq 1, 2*   thinkes,] thinkes *Qq*   71 Tut,] Tut *Qq*   no;] no: *Q3*   72 capacity,] capacitie *Qq 1, 3* : capacity *Q2*   speakes 'hem] speake them *Q3*   73 see] but see *Q3*   75 in't] in it *Q3*   78 No,] No *Qq*   79 PVNT.] *Pnnt. Q1*   what,] what *Qq*   81 O, Lord,] O Iesu *Qq*   82 Pr'y thee,] Pr'y thee *Qq 1, 2* : Prythee *Q3*   84 st. dir.] *Exit Gent. from the window (Exit. Qq 2, 3)* Qq in text after 83   85 puntilio's] Puntolios *Q3*   86 another] an other *Q3*   Cinique] Cynique F2, F3   88 then *Q3, F1* : than *Qq 1, 2, F2*   90 him,] him *Qq*   lest] least *Qq*   92 O,] O *Qq*   93 e'er] euer *Q3*   ha'] haue *Q3* him ioynted, I'le pawne him in east-cheape, among the butchers else. 95

F A S T. Peace, who be these, C A R L O ?

Act II. Scene III.

SORDIDO, FVNGOSO, LADY. *To the rest.*

YOnder's your god-father; doe your duty to him, sonne.
 S O G. This, sir? a poore elder brother of mine, sir, a yeoman, may dispend some seuen or eight hundred a yeere: that's his son, my nephew, there.

P V N T. You are not ill-come, neighbour S O R D I D O, 5 though I haue not yet said, well-come: what, my god-sonne is growne a great *proficient* by this?

S O R D. I hope he will grow great one day, sir.

F A S T. What does he studie? the law?

S O G L. I sir, he is a gentleman, though his father be 10 but a yeoman.

C A R L. What call you your nephew, signior?

S O G L. Mary, his name is F V N G O S O.

C A R L. F V N G O S O? O, he lookt somwhat like a spunge in that pinckt yellow doublet, me thought: well, 15 make much of him; I see he was neuer borne to ride vpon a moile.

G E N T. My lady will come presently, sir. *Returnd aboue.*
S O G L. O, now, now.

P V N T. Stand by, retire your selues a space: nay, pray *Sordido & Fungoso* you, forget not the vse of your hat; the aire is piercing. *with-draw to the other part of the stage, while the lady is come to the window.*

<small>II. ii. 94 ioynted] joynted *Q1*   east-cheape,] East-cheape *Qq* : East-cheape, *F2*   the butchers] butchers *Qq*   II. iii. *Act* ... LADY] *Enter Sordido, with his sonne Fungoso.* Qq without change of scene. To *the rest.* add Ff.   1 Yonder's] *Sord.* Yonders *Q1* : *Sord.* Yonders *Qq* 2, 3   him,] him *Qq*   2 This,] This *Qq*   mine,] mine *Qq*   4 nephew,] nephew *Qq*   5 ill-come,] ill-come *Q1* : il-come *Qq* 2, 3   6 said,] said *Qq*   well-come] welcòm *Q1* : welcome *Qq* 2, 3   13 Mary,] Mary *Qq*   15 yellow *not in Qq*   doublet,] doublet *Qq*   18 presently,] presently *Qq*   st. dir. *Returnd aboue.*] *Enter Gent. aboue.* add Qq   19 O,] O *Qq*   20 st. dir.] *Sordido and Fungoso withdraw at the other part of the stage, meane time the Ladie is come to the window.* (*time,* ... *Lady* Q3) Qq in text after 21</small>

F A S T. What? will not their presence preuaile against the current of his humour?

C A R L. O, no : it's a meere floud, a torrent, carries all afore it.

P V N T. *What more then heauenly pulchritude is this?*
What magazine, or treasurie of blisse?
Dazle, you organs to my optique sense,
To view a creature of such eminence :
O, I am planet-strooke, and in yond sphere,
A brighter starre then V E N V S *doth appeare!*

F A S T. How? in verse!

C A R L. An extasie, an extasie, man.

L A D Y. Is your desire to speake with me, sir knight?

C A R L. He will tell you that anon ; neither his braine, nor his body, are yet moulded for an answere.

P V N T. Most debonaire, and luculent lady, I decline mee low, as the *basis* of your altitude.

GREX.

C O R D. He makes congies to his wife in geometricall proportions.

M I T. Is't possible there should be any such Humorist?

C O R D. Very easily possible, Sir, you see there is.

P V N T. I haue scarse collected my spirits, but lately scatter'd in the admiration of your forme ; to which (if the bounties of your minde be any way responsible) I doubt not, but my desires shall finde a smooth, and secure passage. I am a poore knight errant (lady) that hunting in the adjacent forrest, was by aduenture in the pursuit of a hart, brought to this place ; which hart (deare Madame) escaped by enchantment : the euening approching (my selfe, and seruant wearied) my suit is, to enter your faire castle, and refresh me.

II. iii. 23 humour] humor Qq   24 O,] O Qq   26, 31 *then*] *than* Qq, F2
28 *you*] *your* Q3   *optique*] *obtique* Q3   30 O,] O Q1   31 *appeare !*]
appeare. Qq   32 verse !] verse ?   Qq   38 low,] as low Qq   45 not,]
not Qq   46 smooth,] smooth Qq   47 knight errant] Knighterrant Qq
48 adjacent] adiacent Qq 2, 3   50 selfe,] selfe Qq   51 enter *om.* F3

LADY. Sir knight, albeit it be not vsuall with me (chiefly in the absence of a husband) to admit any entrance to strangers, yet in the true regard of those innated vertues, 55 and faire parts, which so striue to expresse themselues, in you ; I am resolu'd to entertaine you to the best of my vnworthy power : which I acknowledge to bee nothing, valew'd with what so worthy a person may deserue. Please you but stay, while I descend. 60

PVNT. Most admir'd lady, you astonish me !
CARL. What ? with speaking a speech of your owne penning ?
FAST. Nay, looke ; pr'y thee peace.
CARL. Pox on't : I am impatient of such fopperie.
FAST. O, let's heare the rest.
CARL. What ? a tedious chapter of courtship, after 67 sir LANCELOT, and queene GVENEVER? away. I mar'le in what dull cold nooke he found this lady out ? that (being a woman) shee was blest with no more copie 70 of wit, but to serue his humour thus. 'Slud, I thinke he feeds her with porridge, I: shee could ne're haue such a thick braine else.

SOGL. Why, is porridge so hurtfull, signior ?
CARL. O, nothing vnder heauen more preiudiciall to 75 those ascending subtile powers, or doth sooner abate that which we call, *acumen ingenij*, then your grosse fare : why, I'le make you an instance : your city wiues, but obserue 'hem, you ha' not more perfect true fooles i' the world bred, then they are generally ; and yet you see (by the finenesse 80 and delicacy of their diet, diuing into the fat capons, drinking your rich wines, feeding on larkes, sparrowes,

Shee departs : Puntaruolo falls in with Sordido, and his sonne.

II. iii. 55 innated] inward *Q3*   56 parts,] parts *Qq 1, 3* : partes *Q2*
themselues,] themselues *Qq*   57 entertaine] enterteine *Q1*   58 power :]
power : *Qq 1, 2*   61 st. dir.] *She departs : and Puntaruolo ... sonne.*
(*Puntaruolo Q1*) *Qq* in text after 60   61 me !] me. *Qq*   64 Nay,] Nay
Qq   looke ;] looke, *Q3*   66 O,] O *Qq*   68 GVENEVER] GVEVENER
F1 : *Gueuener Q1*, F3 : *Gueuener Qq 2, 3* : GUEVENER *F2* : Gueuener G
away.] away : *Qq 1, 3* : awaie : *Q2*   71 humour] Humor *Q1*   'Slud]
Sblood *Qq*   72 porridge,] porridge. *F2, F3*   74 Why,] Why *Qq*   75
preiudiciall] prejudiciall *Q1*   77, 80 then] than *Qq, F2*   77 why,] why
Qq   79 i'the] i'rhe *Q2* : in the *Q3*   bred, bred *Qq 1, 2* : bredde, *Q3*

472 *Euery Man out of his Humour*

potato-pies, and such good vnctuous meats) how their wits are refi'd, and rarefi'd ! and sometimes a very *quintessence* of conceit flowes from 'hem, able to drowne a weake apprehension.

F A S T. Peace, here comes the lady.

Lady with her gent. descended, seeing them, turnes in againe.

L A D Y. Gods me, here's company : turne in againe.

F A S T. S'light, our presence has cut off the conuoy of the iest.

C A R L. All the better ; I am glad on't : for the issue was very perspicuous. Come, let's discouer, and salute the knight.

Carlo, and the other two, step forth.

P V N T. Stay : who be these that addresse themselues towards vs ? what, C A R L O ? now, by the sincerity of my soule, welcome ; welcome gentlemen : and how doest thou, thou grand scourge ; or, second *vntrusse* of the time ?

C A R L. Faith, spending my mettall, in this reeling world (here and there) as the sway of my affection carries me, and perhaps stumble vpon a yeoman pheuterer, as I doe now ; or one of *Fortunes* moiles, laden with treasure, and an empty cloke-bagge following him, gaping when a bagge will vntie.

P V N T. Peace, you, ban-dogge, peace : what briske *Nimfadoro* is that in the white virgin boot there ?

C A R L. Mary, sir, one, that I must entreat you take a very particular knowledge of, and with more then ordinary respect : Monsieur F A S T I D I V S.

P V N T. Sir, I could wish that for the time of your vouchsaft abiding here, and more real entertainment, this my house stood on the *Muses* hill ; and these my orchards were those of the *Hesperide's*.

II. iii. 83 potato-pies] Potato pyes Qq   84 refin'd,] refin'd Qq *1, 2* : refinde *Q3*   rarefi'd !] rarefi'd : Qq *1, 2* : ratifide : *Q3*   85 'hem] them *Q3*   85 apprehension.] Apprehension, Q2   88 st. dir.] *Enter Ladie with her Gent. and seeing them, turnes in againe.* (Lady Q3 : turns Q2) Qq in text after 87   90 iest] jest *Q1*   94 st. dir.] *Carlo and the other two, step forth to Punt.* Qq in text after 93   95 what,] what *Qq*   now,] now *Qq*   97 grand . . . time] Grand Scourge ; or, Second Vntrusse of the time Qq (Scourge, or Qq *2, 3*)   98 Faith,] Faith *Qq*   mettall,] mettall *Qq*   101 moiles,] Moyles *Qq*   103 Peace, you; ban-dogge,] Peace you bandogge *Qq* (Bandogge *Q1*)   105 Mary,] Mary *Qq*   take] to take *Q3*   106 then] than *Qq* (so 114, 118)   109 reall] Reall *Qq*

F a s t. I possesse as much in your wish, sir, as if I were made lord of the *Indies* ; and I pray you, beleeue it.

C a r l. I haue a better opinion of his faith, then to thinke it will be so corrupted.

S o g l. Come, brother, I'le bring you acquainted with gentlemen, and good fellowes, such as shall doe you more grace, then———

S o r d. Brother, I hunger not for such acquaintance: Doe you take heede, lest———— *Carlo is cōming toward them.*

S o g l. Husht : my brother, sir, for want of education, sir, somewhat nodding to the boore, the clowne : but I request you in priuate, sir.

F v n g. By heauen, it's a very fine sute of clothes !

GREX.

C o r. Doe you obserue that, signior ? there's another humour has new crackt the shell.

M i t. What ? he is enamour'd of the fashion, is he ?

C o r. O, you forestall the iest.

F v n. I mar'le what it might stand him in !

S o g. Nephew ?

F v n. 'Fore mee, it's an excellent sute, and as neatly becomes him. What said you, vncle ?

S o g. When saw you my neece ?

F v n. Mary, yester-night I supt there. That kinde of boot does very rare too !

S o g. And what newes heare you ?

F v n. The guilt spurre and all ! would I were hang'd, but 'tis exceeding good. Say you, vncle ?

II. iii. 112 wish,] wish *Qq*   113 you,] you *Qq*   116 Come,] Come *Qq*
119 stage dir. *add Qq after 120*   120 lest——] least :—— *Qq*
121 brother,] Brother *Qq*   education,] education *Qq*   122 clowne :]
Clowne ; *Qq*   123 priuate,] priuat *Qq 1, 2*: priuate *Q3*   124
heauen] Iesu *Qq*   it's] it is *Q3*   clothes !] cloathes. *Qq*   126 humour]
humor *Qq 2, 3*   128 O,] O *Qq*   iest] jeast *Q1*   129 mar'le] marl'e
F2   in !] in ? *Qq*   131 mee,] mee *F2* : God *Qq*   it's] it is *Q3*
132 you,] you *Qq*   134 Mary,] Mary *Qq*   135 too !] too. *Qq*   137
all !] all : *Qq*   138 'tis] it is *Q3*   you, vncle ?] you ? *Qq*

474 *Euery Man out of his Humour*

S o g. Your minde is carried away with somewhat else:
140 I aske what newes you heare?

F v n. Troth, we heare none. In good faith, I was neuer so pleas'd with a fashion, daies of my life! O (and I might haue but my wish) I'ld aske no more of god now, but such a suit, such a hat, such a band, such a doublet, such a hose,
145 such a boot, and such a———

S o g. They say, there's a new Motion of the city of *Niniueh*, with I o n a s, and the whale, to be seene at Fleet-bridge? you can tell, cousin?

F v n. Here's such a world of question with him, now:
150 Yes, I thinke there be such a thing, I saw the picture: would he would once be satisfi'd. Let me see, the doublet, say fifty shillings the doublet, and betweene three or foure pound the hose; then bootes, hat, and band: some ten or eleuen pound would doe it all, and suit me *for the heauens*.
155 S o g. I'le see all those deuices, and I come to *London* once.

F v n. Gods s'lid, and I could compasse it, 'twere rare: harke you, vncle.

S o g. What saies my nephew?
160 F v n. Faith vncle, I'ld ha' desir'd you to haue made a motion for me to my father in a thing, that—walke aside and I'le tell you, sir, no more but this: there's a parcell of law-bookes, (some twenty pounds worth) that lie in a place for little more then halfe the money they cost; and
165 I thinke for some twelue pound, or twenty marke, I could goe neere to redeeme 'hem; there's P l o w d e n, D i a r, B r o o k e, and F i t z-H e r b e r t, diuers such, as

---

II. iii. 141 Troth,] Troth *Qq*   none. In] none : in *Qq*   faith,] faith *Qq*   142 fashion,] fashion *Qq*   life !] life ; *Qq*   and] an' *F2, F3*   143 god] God *Qq* : good *F3*   146 say,] say *Qq*   147 Ionas,] *Ionas* Qq   148 tell,] tell *Qq*   149 him,] him *Qq*   151 satisfi'd] satisfied *F2*   153 hat] the Hat *Qq*   154 would] will *F3*   for] 'fore *F2, F3*   155 and] an' *F2, F3*   157 Gods s'lid] Gods S'lid *Q2* : God slid *Q3*   158 you,] you *Qq*   161 that—] that; *Qq 1, 2* : that: *Q3*   162 you, sir *F1* : you sir *Qq* : you; sir *F2*   163 law-bookes] Law books *Q1* : Lawbooks *Q2* : Lawe bookes *Q3* : law---bookes *F1* : law--books *F2*   164 then] than *Qq, F2*   165 pound,] pound *Qq 1, 2* : pounde *Q3*   167 Fitz-Herbert,] *Fitz-Herbert* : Q1 ; *Fitz Herbert* ; Q2 : *Fitz Herbert* : Q3   such,] such *Qq*

I must haue ere long: and you know, I were as good saue fiue or sixe pound as not, vncle. I pray you, moue it for me.

S o g. That I will: when would you haue me doe it? presently?

F v n. O, I, I pray you, good vncle: God send mee good luck; Lord (and't be thy will) prosper it: O, my starres, now, now, if it take now, I am made for euer.

F a s t. Shall I tell you, sir? by this aire, I am the most beholding to that lord, of any gentleman liuing; hee does vse mee the most honorably, and with the greatest respect, more indeed, then can be vtter'd with any opinion of truth.

P v n t. Then, haue you the count G r a t i a t o?

F a s t. As true noble a gentleman too, as any breathes; I am exceedingly endear'd to his loue: by this hand (I protest to you, signior, I speake it not gloriously, nor out of affectation, but) there's hee, and the count F r v g a l e, signior I l l v s t r e, signior L v c v l e n t o, and a sort of 'hem; that (when I am at court) they doe share me amongst 'hem. Happy is he can enioy me most priuate. I doe wish my selfe sometime an vbiquitarie for their loue, in good faith.

C a r l. There's ne're a one of these, but might lie a weeke on the rack, ere they could bring forth his name; and yet he powres them out as familiarly, as if he had seene 'hem stand by the fire i' the presence, or ta'ne tabacco with them, ouer the stage, i' the lords roome.

P v n t. Then you must of necessity know our court-

195 starre there? that planet of wit, MADDONA SAVIO-
LINA?

FAST. O, lord sir! my mistris.

PVNT. Is shee your mistris?

FAST. Faith, here be some slight fauours of hers, sir,
200 that doe speake it, *shee is* : as this scarfe, sir, or this ribband
in mine eare, or so ; this feather grew in her sweet fanne
sometimes, though now it be my poore fortunes to weare
it, as you see, sir : slight, slight, a foolish toy.

PVNT. Well, shee is the lady of a most exalted, and
205 ingenious spirit.

FAST. Did you euer heare any woman speake like her?
or enricht with a more plentifull discourse?

CARL. O, villanous! nothing but sound, sound, a
meere *eccho*; shee speakes as shee goes tir'd, in cob-web
210 lawne, light, thin : good enough to catch flies withall.

PVNT. O, manage your affections.

FAST. Well, if thou beest not plagu'd for this blasphemie, one day—

PVNT. Come, regard not a iester : it is in the power of
215 my purse, to make him speake well, or ill, of me.

FAST. Sir, I affirme it to you (vpon my credit, and
iudgement) shee has the most harmonious, and musicàll
straine of wit, that euer tempted a true eare ; and yet to
see, a rude tongue would profane heauen, if it could.
220 PVNT. I am not ignorant of it, sir.

FAST. Oh, it flowes from her like *nectar*, and shee doth
giue it, that sweet, quick grace, and exornation in the
composure, that (by this good aire, as I am an honest man,

II. iii. 195 SAVIOLINA] *Saviolina* Q1   197 O, lord] O Lord *Qq*
197, 198 mistris] mistresse *Qq*   199 hers,] hers *Qq*   200 *is* :] *is* ; *Qq*
scarfe,] Scarfe *Qq*   202 fortunes] fortune *Qq 2, 3*   203 it,] it *Qq*
see,] see *Qq*   slight, a] slight ; a *Q1*   205 ingenious] ingenous *Qq*
207 enricht] inricht *F2, F3*   208 O,] O *Qq*   209 *eccho* ;] *Eccho*,
Qq 2, 3   cob-web] Cobweb *Qq*   212 blasphemie,] blasphemie *Qq*
213 day—] day :— *Qq 1, 3* : daie : --- *Q 2*   214 iester :] jeaster ; *Q1* :
iester ; *Q2* : Iester : *Q3*   215 purse,] purse *Qq*   well, or ill,] well or
ill *Qq*   216 credit,] Credit *Qq*   217 harmonious,] Harmonious *Qq*
218 true] ttue *Q3*   219 tongue] rogue *Q3*   would] will *Qq*
heauen, if it could.] Heauen. *Qq*   220 it,] it *Qq*   223 (by this good
aire,] (*By this good Heauen*) Qq   223-4 as I am . . . but) *not in Qq*

would I might neuer stirre, sir, but) shee does obserue as pure a phrase, and vse as choise figures in her ordinary conferences, as any be i' the *Arcadia*.

CARL. Or rather in *Greenes* workes, whence she may steale with more security.

SORD. Well, if ten pound will fetch 'hem, you shall haue it, but I'le part with no more.

FVNG. I'le trie what that will doe, if you please.

SORD. Doe so: and when you haue 'hem, studie hard.

FVNG. Yes, sir. And I could studie to get forty shillings more now! well, I will put my selfe into the fashion, as farre as this will goe presently.

SORD. I wonder it raines not! the Almanack saies wee should haue store of raine, to day.

PVNT. Why, sir, to morrow I will associate you to court my selfe; and from thence to the city, about a businesse, a proiect I haue, I will expose it to you, sir: CARLO, I am sure, has heard of it.

CARL. What's that, sir?

PVNT. I doe intend, this yeere of *Iubile*, comming on, to trauaile: and (because I will not altogether goe vpon expence) I am determined to put forth some fiue thousand pound, to be paid me, fiue for one, vpon the returne of my selfe, my wife, and my dog, from the *Turkes* court in *Constantinople*. If all, or either of vs miscarry in the iourney, 'tis gone: if we be successfull, why, there will be fiue and twenty thousand pound, to entertaine time withall. Nay, goe not neighbour SORDIDO, stay to night, and helpe to make our societie the fuller. Gentlemen, frolick: CARLO? what? dull now?

II. iii. 233 Yes, sir.] Yes sir: *Qq*   And] and *Qq*: An' *F2, F3*   234 now!] now: Qq   235 goe] goe, *Q3*   237 raine,] raine *Qq*   238 Why,] Why *Qq*   court] the Court *Qq*   239 a businesse] businesse *Q3*   240 proiect] Project *Q1*   haue,] haue: *Qq*   you,] you *Qq*   240-1 CARLO, ... sure,] *Carlo* ... sure *Qq*   242 that,] that *Qq*   243 intend,] entend *Qq*   243-4 *Iubile*, comming on, to] *Iubile* to *Qq*   244 altogether] altogither *Qq*   246 me,] me *Qq*   249 iourney] journey *Q1*   250 fiue and twenty] xxv. *Qq*   pound,] pound *Qq 1, 2*: pounde *Q3*   251 SORDIDO,] *Sordido* ; *Qq*

CARL. I was thinking on your proiect, sir, and you call
255 it so: is this the dog goes with you?
PVNT. This is the dogge, sir.
CARL. He do' not goe bare-foot, does he?
PVNT. Away, you traitor, away.
CARL. Nay, afore god, I speake simply; he may pricke
260 his foot with a thorne, and be as much as the whole venter
is worth. Besides, for a dog that neuer trauail'd before, it's
a huge iourney to *Constantinople*: I'le tell you now (and
he were mine) I'ld haue some present conference with
a physicion, what antidotes were good to giue him, pre-
265 seruatiues against poison: for (assure you) if once your
money be out, there'll be diuers attempts made against the
life of the poore *animal*.
PVNT. Thou art still dangerous.
FAST. Is signior DELIRO'S wife your kinswoman?
270 SOGL. I, sir, shee is my neece, my brothers daughter
here, and my nephewes sister.
SORD. Doe you know her, sir?
FAST. O, God sir, Signior DELIRO, her husband, is
my marchant.
275 FVNG. I, I haue seene this gentleman there, often.
FAST. I crie you mercy, sir: let me craue your name,
pray you.
FVNG. FVNGOSO, sir.
FAST. Good signior FVNGOSO, I shall request to
280 know you better, sir.
FVNG. I am her brother, sir.
FAST. In faire time, sir.

II. iii. 254 proiect,] Project *Q1* : Proiect *Qq* 2, 3   and] an' *F2, F3*
256 dogge,] Dogge *Qq*   258 Away,] Away *Qq*   traitor] traytour *Q1*
259 Nay,] Nay *Qq*   god] God *Qq*   260 venter] venture *F2, F3*
261 worth] woorth *Qq*   262 iourney] journey *Q1*   and] an' *F2, F3*
264 physicion] Phisician *Q1* : Physician *Q2* : Physitian *Q3*   pre-
seruatiues] and Preseruatiues *Qq*   266 there'll be] theere will be *Q3*
(*corrected to* there will be)   270 I,] I *Qq*   272 her,] her *Qq*   273
O,] O *Qq, F2*   DELIRO,] Deliro *Qq* 1, 3 : *Diliro Q2*   husband,] husband *Qq*   274 marchant] Merchant *Qq, F3*   275 I, I] I, *Q3*
276 mercy,] mercie *Qq* 1, 2 : mercy *Q3*   278 FVNGOSO,] *Fungoso* Qq
280 better,] better *Qq*   281 brother,] brother *Qq*   282 time,]
time *Qq*

P v n t. Come, gentlemen, I will be your conduct.

F a s t. Nay, pray you, sir; we shall meet at signior D e l i r o's often.

S o g l. You shall ha' me at the *Heralds* office, sir, for some weeke or so, at my first comming vp. Come, C a r l o.

GREX.

M i t. Me thinkes, C o r d a t v s, he dwelt somewhat too long on this *Scene* ; it hung i' the hand.

C o r. I see not where he could haue insisted lesse, and t'haue made the humours perspicuous enough.

M i t. True, as his subiect lies: but hee might haue altered the shape of his argument, and explicated 'hem better in single *Scenes*.

C o r. That had beene single indeed: why? be they not the same persons in this, as they would haue beene in those? and is it not an obiect of more state, to behold the *Scene* full, and relieu'd with varietie of speakers to the end, then to see a vast emptie stage, and the actors come in (one by one) as if they were dropt downe with a feather, into the eye of the spectators?

M i t. Nay, you are better traded with these things then I, and therefore I'le subscribe to your iudgement; mary, you shall giue mee leaue to make obiections.

C o r. O, what else? it's the speciall intent of the author, you should doe so: for thereby others (that are present) may as well be satisfied, who happily would obiect the same you doe.

II. iii. 283 Come,] Come *Qq*   284 Nay, . . . you,] Nay . . . you *Qq*
286 *Heralds*] Herals *Q3*   office,] office *Qq*   287 so,] so *F2*   Come,]
Come *Qq*   *Exeunt*. add *Qq*   288 thinkes,] thinks *Qq*   289 hung]
hun'g *Q2*   i'] in *Q3*   291 t'haue] to haue *Q3*   humours] Humors
Qq   292 subiect] Subject *Q1*   293 his *not in Qq*   297 obiect]
object *Q1*   299 then *Q3, F1*: than *Qq 1, 2, F2*   300 feather,]
feather *Qq*   301 spectators] Audience *Qq*   302 then] than *Qq, F2*
303 iudgement] judgement *Q1*   mary,] mary *Qq 1, 2* : marry *Q3*
304 obiections] objections *Q1*   305 O,] O *Qq*   306 author,]
Author *Qq*   307 happily] haply *F3*   obiect] object *Q1*   308 the]
ihe *Q3*

480 *Euery Man out of his Humour*

Mit. So, sir: but when appeares Macilente
310 againe?

Cor. Mary, hee staies but till our silence giue him leaue: here hee comes, and with him signior Deliro, a marchant, at whose house hee is come to sojourne: Make your owne obseruation now, onely transferre your thoughts to
315 the city, with the *Scene*; where, suppose they speake.

Act II.   *Scene* IIII.

Deliro, Macilente, Fido, Fallace.

I'Le tell you by and by, sir.
Welcome (good Macilente) to my house,
To sojourne euen for euer: if my best
4 In cates, and euery sort of good intreaty
Deliro May moue you stay with me.   Maci. I thanke you, sir:
censeth. And yet the muffled *fates* (had it pleas'd them)
His boy Might haue suppli'd me, from their owne full store,
strewes Without this word (I thanke you) to a foole.
flowres.
I see no reason, why that dog (call'd *Chaunce*)
10 Should fawne vpon this fellow, more then me:
I am a man, and I haue limmes, flesh, bloud,
Bones, sinewes, and a soule, as well as he:
My parts are euery way as good as his,
If I said better? why, I did not lie.

II. iii. 309 So, sir:] So sir, *Qq*   After 310] *Enter Macilente, Deliro, Fido, with hearbs and perfumes.* Qq   311 Mary,] Mary *Qq*   312 him] him, *Q3*   Deliro,] *Deliro* Qq   marchant,] merchant *Q1*: Merchant *Qq 2, 3*   313 sojourne] soiourne *Qq 2, 3*   314 now,] now; *Qq 1, 2*: now: *Q3*   315 city,] Cittie *Qq 1, 2* : Citie *Q3*   II. iv. *Act* . . . Fallace.] Scena Tertia. *Qq*: Scene II.—*The City. A Room in* Deliro's *House.* G   1 I'le] *Deliro.* I'le *Qq*   by,] by *Qq*   3 sojourne] soiourne *Qq 2, 3* :   euen] at my house *F2, F3*   euer:] euer; *Qq 1, 2* : euer, *Q3*   4 In cates] Incates *F2, F3*   5 moue] mooue *Q1*   you,] you *Qq*   st. dir. *Deliro . . . flowres.*] *Deliro turnes to his boy, and falls a strowing of flowers.* (*fals* Qq 2, 3) Qq in text after ' me '   7 me, . . . store,] me . . . store *Qq*   8 (I thanke you)] (*I thanke you*) *Qq*   9 reason,] reason *Qq*   10 fellow,] fellow *Qq*   then] than *Qq, F2*   12 soule,] Soule *Qq*   14 why,] why *Qq*   lie,] lie, *Qq 1, 2* : lie ; *Q3*

Euery Man out of his Humour 481

Nath'lesse, his wealth (but nodding on my wants)   15
Must make me bow, and crie : (I thanke you, sir.)
    D E L I. Dispatch, take heed your mistris see you not.
    F I D O. I warrant you, sir. I'le steale by her softly.
    D E L I. Nay, gentle friend, be merry, raise your lookes
Out of your bosome, I protest (by heauen)   20
You are the man most welcome in the world.
    M A C I. (I thanke you, sir,) I know my *cue*, I thinke.
    F I D O. Where wil you haue 'hem burne, sir ?   D E L I. *With more*
    Here, good F I D O :   *perfumes*
                                                                and
What ? shee did not see thee ?   F I D O. No, sir.   D E L I. *herbes.*
    That's well :
Strew, strew, good F I D O, the freshest flowres, so.   25
    M A C I. What meanes this, signior D E L I R O ? all this
censing ?
    D E L I. Cast in more frankincense, yet more, well said.
O, M A C I L E N T E, I haue such a wife !
So passing faire, so passing farre vnkind,
But of such worth, and right to be vnkind,   30
(Since no man can be worthy of her kindnesse.)
    M A C I. What can there not ?   D E L I. No, that is
    sure as death,
No man aliue ! I doe not say, is not,
But cannot possibly be worth her kindnesse !
Nay, it is certaine, let me doe her right.   35
How, said I ? doe her right ? as though I could,
As though this dull grosse tongue of mine could vtter

II. iv. 15 Nath'lesse,] Nath'lesse *Qq*   16 (I thanke you, sir.)] *I thanke you Sir.* Qq (*sir.* Q3)   17 mistris] mistresse *Qq*   18 you,] you *Qq* :   sir. I'le] Sir, I'll *F3*   *Exit Fido.* Qq (after ' sir ')   I'le . . . softly. *not in Qq*   19 Nay, . . . friend,] Nay . . . friend *Qq*   22 (I . . . you, sir,)] *I . . . you Sir*, Qq (*sir*, Q3)   cue,] cue Qq   23 st. dir. *With . . . herbes.*] *Enter Fido with two Censors.* Qq in text after 22   23–5 *F3 divides at* sir ? | DELI. . . . see thee ? | FIDO. No, sir.| DELI. . . . so   23 burne,] burne *Qq*   Here,] Here *Qq*   24 No,] No *Qq*   25 flowres] flowers *Qq*   26 this,] this *Qq*   all this censing ? *not in Qq*   28 O,] O *Qq*   wife !] wife, *Qq*   29 farre vnkind] faire vnkind *Qq* : faire ! unkind *F2, F3* : fair-unkind *W*   30 But] And *Qq*   worth,] worth *Qq*   33 aliue !] aliue : *Qq*   say, is not,] say *is not*, Qq 1, 2 : say *is not* : Q3   34 But] But, *F2* : kindnesse !] kindnesse. *Qq*   35 Nay,] Nay *Qq*   it] that *Qq*   right.] Right : *Qq*   36 How,] How *Qq*

The rare, the true, the pure, the infinite rights,
That sit (as high as I can looke) within her!
40   M A C I. This is such dotage, as was neuer heard.
        D E L I. Well, this must needs be granted.   M A C I.
        Granted, quoth you?
        D E L I. Nay, M A C I L E N T E ; doe not so discredit
The goodnesse of your iudgement to denie it,
For I doe speake the very least of her.
45 And I would craue, and beg no more of heauen,
For all my fortunes here, but to be able
To vtter first in fit termes, what shee is,
And then the true ioyes I conceiue in her.
        M A C I. Is't possible, shee should deserue so well,
50 As you pretend?   D E L I. I, and shee knowes so well
Her owne deserts, that (when I striue t'enioy them)
Shee weighs the things I doe, with what shee merits:
And (seeing my worth out-weigh'd so in her graces)
Shee is so solemne, so precise, so froward,
55 That no obseruance I can doe to her,
Can make her kind to me : if shee find fault,
I mend that fault ; and then shee saies, I faulted,
That I did mend it. Now, good friend, aduise me,
How I may temper this strange splene in her.
60   M A C I. You are too amorous, too obsequious,
And make her too assur'd, shee may command you.
When women doubt most of their husbands loues,
They are most louing. Husbands must take heed
They giue no gluts of kindnesse to their wiues,
65 But vse them like their horses ; whom they feed
Not with a manger-full of meat together,

II. iv. 38 rights,] Rights *Qq*   39 sit] sir *Q3*   her !] her. *Qq*   40 dotage,] dotage *Qq*   41 Granted,] Graunted *Qq 1, 3*: Granted *Q2*   42 Nay,] Nay *Qq*   43 iudgement] judgement *Q1*   45 craue,] craue *Qq*   heauen,] heauen *Qq*   48 ioyes] joies *Q1*   49 possible,] possible *Qq*   well,] well *Qq 1, 3*: wel *Q2*   51 deserts,] deserts *Qq*   enioy] enjoy *Q1*   52 weighs] waies *Qq*   53 out-weigh'd] outwai'd *Qq*   57 fault ;] fault, *Qq*   saies,] saies *Qq*   faulted,] faulted *Qq*   58 Now, . . . friend,] Now . . . Friend *Qq*   me,] me *Qq*   61 her] her, *Qq*   assur'd,] assur'd *Qq*   command] commaund *Q1*   65 horses ;] Horses, *Qq*   66 manger-full *Qq*: manger -- full *F1*: manger --- full *F2*   together] togither *Q3*

Euery Man out of his Humour 483

But halfe a pecke at once : and keepe them so
Still with an appetite to that they giue them.
He that desires to haue a louing wife,
Must bridle all the shew of that desire : 70
Be kind, not amorous ; nor bewraying kindnesse,
As if loue wrought it, but considerate duty.
" Offer no loue-rites, but let wiues still seeke them,
" For when they come vnsought, they seldome like them.
    D E L I. Beleeue me, M A C I L E N T E, this is gospell. 75
O, that a man were his owne man so much,
To rule himselfe thus. I will striue i' faith,
To be more strange and carelesse : yet, I hope
I haue now taken such a perfect course,
To make her kind to me, and liue contented, 80
That I shall find my kindnesse well return'd,
And haue no need to fight with my affections.
Shee (late) hath found much fault with euery roome
Within my house ; one was too big (shee said)
Another was not furnisht to her mind, 85
And so through all : all which, now, I haue alter'd.
Then here, shee hath a place (on my back-side)
Wherein shee loues to walke ; and that (shee said)
Had some ill smels about it. Now, this walke
Haue I (before shee knowes it) thus perfum'd 90
With herbes, and flowres, and laid in diuers places,
(As 'twere on altars, consecrate to her)
Perfumed gloues, and delicate chaines of amber,
To keepe the aire in awe of her sweet nostrils :
This haue I done, and this I thinke will please her. 95
Behold, shee comes.   F A L L. Here's a sweet stinke indeed:

    II. iv. 67 once :] once, *Qq*   71 amorous ;] amorous, *Qq*   72 duty.] Dutie : *Qq 1, 3* : Duty : *Q2*   74 seldome] sildome *Q3*   75 me,] me *Qq*   76 O,] O *Qq*   77 thus.] thus ; *Qq*   i'faith,] i'faith *Q1* : yfaith *Qq 2, 3*   78 yet,] yet *Qq*   80 me,] mee *F2*   86 which, now,] which *Qq*   87 here,] here *Q*   back-side] backeside *Q1* : backside *Qq 2, 3*   88 walke ;] walke, *Qq 2, 3*   89 Now,] Now *Qq*   91 herbes,] herbes *Qq 1, 2* : hearbes *Q3*   flowres] flowers *Qq, F2*   places,] places *Qq*   92 altars,] Altars *Qq*   94 nostrils] nosthrils *Qq 1, 3* : nosthris *Q2*   96 Behold,] Behold *Qq*   *Enter Fallace.* Qq (after ' comes ')

What, shall I euer be thus crost, and plagu'd?
And sicke of husband? O, my head doth ake,
As it would cleaue asunder with these sauours,
100 All my room's alter'd, and but one poore walke
That I delighted in, and that is made
So fulsome with perfumes, that I am fear'd
(My braine doth sweat so) I haue caught the plague.
    D E L I. Why (gentle wife) is now thy walke too sweet?
105 Thou said'st of late, it had sowre aires about it,
And found'st much fault, that I did not correct it.
    F A L L. Why, and I did find fault, sir? D E L I. Nay, deare wife;
I know, thou hast said, thou hast lou'd perfumes,
No woman better. F A L L. I, long since perhaps,
110 But now that sense is alter'd: you would haue me
(Like to a puddle, or a standing poole)
To haue no motion, nor no spirit within me.
No, I am like a pure, and sprightly riuer,
That moues for euer, and yet still the same;
115 Or fire, that burnes much wood, yet still one flame.
    D E L I. But yesterday, I saw thee at our garden,
Smelling on roses, and on purple flowres,
And since, I hope, the humour of thy sense
Is nothing chang'd. F A L L. Why, those were growing flowres,
120 And these, within my walke, are cut and strew'd.
    D E L I. But yet they haue one sent. F A L L. I! haue they so?
In your grosse iudgement. If you make no difference

<hr>

II. iv. 97 crost,] crost *Qq*   98 O,] O *Qq*   ake,] ake *Qq*   99 asunder] asunder, *F2*   these] those *F2, F3*   sauours] sauors *Qq* 1, 2   105 late,] late *Qq*   sowre] sower *Qq*   107 and] an' *F2, F3*   fault,] fault *Qq*   Nay,] Nay *Qq*   108 know, . . . said,] know . . . said *Qq*   111 puddle,] puddle *Qq*   a standing] standing *Q3*   113 pure,] pure *Qq*   sprightly] sprightfull *Q3*   115 fire,] fire *Qq*   116 garden,] garden *Qq*   117 roses,] Roses *Qq*   flowres] flowers *Qq, F2* (so 119, 123)   118 since, I hope,] since I hope *Qq*   humour] Humor *Qq*   119 Why,] Why *Qq*   120 these,] these *Qq*   walke,] walke *Qq*   121 I !] I, *Qq*   122 iudgement. If] judgement: if *Q1* : iudgement : if *Qq* 2, 3

Euery Man out of his Humour 485

Betwixt the sent of growing flowres, and cut ones,
You haue a sense to taste lamp-oile, yfaith.
And with such iudgement haue you chang'd the chambers, 125
Leauing no roome, that I can ioy to be in,
In all your house : and now my walke, and all,
You smoke me from, as if I were a foxe,
And long, belike, to driue me quite away.
Well, walke you there, and I'le walke where I list. 130
    D E L I. What shall I doe ? ô, I shall neuer please her,
    M A C I. Out on thee, dotard ! what starre rul'd his birth ?
That brought him such a starre ? blind *Fortune* still
Bestowes her gifts on such as cannot vse them :
How long shall I liue, ere I be so happy, 135
To haue a wife of this exceeding forme ?
    D E L I. Away, with 'hem, would I had broke a ioynt,
When I deuis'd this, that should so dislike her.
Away, beare all away.   F A L L. I, doe : for feare
Ought that is there should like her. O, this man, 140
How cunningly he can conceale himselfe !
As though he lou'd ? nay, honour'd, and ador'd ?
    D E L I. Why, my sweet heart ?   F A L L. Sweet heart !
    ô ! better still !
And asking, why ? wherefore ? and looking strangely,
As if he were as white as innocence. 145
Alas, you'r simple, you : you cannot change,
Looke pale at pleasure, and then red with wonder :
No, no, not you ! 'tis pitty o' your naturalls.

Fido beares all away.

    II. iv. 124 -oile,] -oyle *F2*   125 iudgement] judgement *Q1*   126 roome,] roome *Qq*   ioy] joy *Q1*   in,] in *Qq*   127 walke,] Walke *Qq*   all,] all *Qq*   129 long, belike,] long belike *Qq*   away,] away : *Qq*   130 Well,] Well *Qq*   131 ô,] oh *Qq*   her,] her. *Qq*   132 thee, dotard !] thee dotard, Qq   137 DELI. *om. Q1*   Away,] Away *Qq*   'hem] them *Q3*   ioynt] joint *Q1*   138 st. dir. *add Qq in text after* ' away ' (l. 139)   st. dir. *beares*] beare *Q3*   this,] this *Qq*   her.] her, *Qq*   139 I,] I *Qq*   140 O, this man,] O this man *Qq*   141 himselfe !] himselfe, *Qq*   142 lou'd ? nay, honour'd,] lou'd ? lou'd ? nay honour'd *Qq*   143 *Two lines in Qq, Ff*   heart ! ô !] heart ? oh, *Qq* still !] still : *Qq*   144 asking,] asking *Qq*   148 you !] you : *Qq* 'tis pitty o' your naturalls. *not in Qq, in which* ' No, no . . . e'en now ' (148–9) *makes one line*

I did but cast an amorous eye, e'en now,
150 Vpon a paire of gloues, that somewhat lik't me,
And straight he noted it, and gaue command,
All should be ta'ne away.   DELI. Be they my bane then.
What, sirra, FIDO, bring in those gloues againe,
You tooke from hence.   FALL. S'body, sir, but doe not,
155 Bring in no gloues, to spite me : if you doe———
    DELI. Ay, me, most wretched; how am I misconstru'd?
    MACI. O, how shee tempts my heart-strings, with her eye,
To knit them to her beauties, or to breake?
What mou'd the heauens, that they could not make
160 Me such a woman? but a man, a beast,
That hath no blisse like to others. Would to heauen
(In wreake of my misfortunes) I were turn'd
To some faire water-*Nymph*, that (set vpon
The deepest whirle-pit of the rau'nous seas,)
165 My adamantine eyes might head-long hale
This iron world to me, and drowne it all.

GREX.

    COR. Behold, behold, the translated gallant.
    MIT. O, he is welcome.

II. iv. 149 amorous eye] amorouseye *F1*   eye,] eye *Q1* : eie *Qq 2, 3*
now,] now *Qq*   150, 155 gloues,] Gloues *Qq*   151 command,] commaund *Qq*   152 then.] then : *Qq*   153 What,] What *Qq*   againe,] againe *Qq*   Enter Fido. add *Qq*   154 S'body,] S'body *Qq* : om. *F2, F3*
sir,] sirra *Qq*   not,] not : *Qq*   155 you] ye *Q3*   156 Ay,] Ay *Qq*
157 -strings,] -strings *Qq*   eye,] eye. *Q1*   160 man,] man ; *Qq*
161 hath] haath *Q3*   heauen] God *Qq*   163 (set] set *Qq*   164 whirle-pit] whirlepit *Qq*   seas,)] Seas, *Qq*   165 adamantine] adamantive *F2, F3*   head-long] headlong *Qq*   After 166 *Enter Fungoso in Briskes Sute.* add *Qq*

Act II.   Scene V.

FVNGOSO.

To the rest.

Saue you brother, and sister, saue you, sir; I haue commendations for you out i' the countrey: (I wonder they take no knowledge of my sute :) mine vncle SOGLIARDO is in towne. Sister, me thinkes, you are melancholy: why are you so sad? I thinke you tooke me for master FASTIDIVS BRISKE (sister) did you not?

FALL. Why should I take you for him?

FVNG. Nay, nothing --I was lately in master FASTIDIVS his company, and, me thinkes, we are very like.

DELI. You haue a faire sute, brother, 'giue you ioy on't.

FVNG. Faith, good ynough to ride in, brother, I made it to ride in.

FALL. O, now I see the cause of his idle demand, was his new suit.

DELI. Pray you good brother, trie, if you can change her mood.

FVNG. I warrant you, let mee alone. I'le put her out of her dumps. Sister, how like you my suit?

FALL. O, you are a gallant in print now, brother.

FVNG. Faith, how like you the fashion? it's the last edition, I assure you.

FALL. I cannot but like it, to the desert.

FVNG. Troth, sister, I was faine to borrow these spurres,

II. v. *Act . . .* FVNGOSO. *not in Qq, which mark no change of scene.* st. dir. *To the rest.* add Ff : 1 Saue . . . saue] *Fung.* God saue . . . God saue *Qq*   you, sir ;] you sir ; *Qq* 1, 2 : you sir : *Q3*   2 (I wonder) I (wonder *Qq* 2, 3   4 towne.] towne ; *Qq* 1, 2 : towne : *Q3*   thinkes,] thinkes *Qq*   5 master] Maister *Q3*   6 not? *Qq* : not. *Ff*   8 Nay, nothing --] Nay nothing, *Qq*   master] Maister *Qq* 1, 3 : maister *Q2* 9 and, me thinkes,] and me thinkes *Qq*   10 sute,] suit *Q1* : sute *Qq* 2, 3 'giue] God giue *Qq*   ioy] joy *Q1*   11 Faith,] Faith *Qq*   in,] in *Qq*   13 demand,] demaund *Qq* 1, 3   15 brother,] Brother ; *Qq* 1, 2 trie,] trie *Qq* 1, 2 : try *Q3*   19 O,] O *Qq*   now,] now *Qq*   20 it's] it is *Q3*   21 edition,] Edition *Qq*   22 it,] it *Qq*   23 Troth,] Troth *Qq*

488 *Euery Man out of his Humour*

I ha' left my gowne in gage for 'hem, pray you lend me an
25 angell.

F A L L. Now, beshrow my heart, then.

F V N G. Good truth, I'le pay you againe at my next exhibition: I had but bare ten pound of my father, and it would not reach to put me wholly into the fashion.

30   F A L L. I care not.

F V N G. I had spurres of mine owne before, but they were not ginglers. Monsieur F A S T I D I V S will be here anon, sister.

F A L L. You iest?

35   F V N G. Neuer lend me penny more (while you liue then) and that I'ld be loth to say, in truth.

F A L L. When did you see him?

F V N G. Yesterday, I came acquainted with him at sir P V N T A R V O L O'S : nay, sweet sister.

40   M A C I. I faine would know of heauen now, why yond foole
Should weare a suit of sattin? he? that rooke?
That painted jay, with such a deale of out-side?
What is his inside trow? ha, ha, ha, ha, ha.
Good heauen, giue me patience, patience, patience.
45 A number of these popenjayes there are,
Whom, if a man conferre, and but examine
Their inward merit, with such men as want ;
Lord, lord, what things they are!

F A L L. Come, when will you pay me againe, now?

50   F V N G. O god, sister!

M A C I. Here comes another.

II. v. 24 'hem] them *Q3*   26 Now,] Now *Qq*   heart,] heart *Qq*
27 truth,] truth *Qq*   32 anon,] anone *Qq* 1, 2 : anon *Q3*   34 iest]
jest *Q1*   39 P V N T A R V O L O'S] *Puntarvolo's* Q1   nay,] nay *Qq*   42
jay,] Iay *Qq 1 2*   out-side] outside *Qq*   43 ha, . . . ha.] ha, ha, ha,
ha. *Q3*   heauen,] Heauen *Qq* 1, 2 : heauen *Q3*   patience, patience,
patience.] patience, *Qq*   46 Whom,] Whom *Qq*   48 lord] Lord *Qq*
49 againe,] againe *Qq*   50 god, sister!] God Sister. *Qq* : good, sister!
F2, F3   After 50] *Enter Fastidius Briske in a new suite.* (*suit.* Q1)
Qq

Euery Man out of his Humour 489

Act II.   Scene VI.

FASTIDIVS BRISKE. ·   *To the rest.*

Aue you, signior DELIRO: how do'st thou, sweet lady?
Let mee kisse thee.
  FVNG. How? a new sute? Ay me.
  DELI. And how do's master FASTIDIVS BRISKE?
  FAST. Faith, liue in court, signior DELIRO; in 5
grace, I thanke god, both of the noble masculine, and
feminine. I must speake with you in priuate, by and by.
  DELI. When you please, sir.
  FALL. Why looke you so pale, brother?
  FVNG. S'lid, all this money is cast away, now.   10
  MACI. I, there's a newer edition come forth.
  FVNG. Tis but my hard fortune! well, I'le haue my
sute chang'd, I'le goe fetch my taylor presently, but first
I'le deuise a letter to my father. Ha' you any pen, and inke,
sister?   15
  FALL. What would you doe withall?
  FVNG. I would vse it. S'light, and it had come but
foure daies sooner, the fashion.
  FAST. There was a countesse gaue me her hand to kisse
to day, i' the presence: did me more good by that light, 20
then—and yesternight sent her coach twise to my lodging,
to intreat mee accompany her, and my sweet mistris, with
some two, or three nameless ladies more: O, I haue beene

II. vi.] *Act* ... BRISKE. *not in Qq, which mark no change of scene.* To
the rest. add Ff   1 Saue you,] *Fast.* Saue you *Qq*   thou,] thou *Qq*
4 master] Maister *Qq*   5 Faith,] Faith *Qq*   court,] court *Q1* :
Court *Qq 2, 3*   DELIRO ;] *Deliro*, Qq   6 grace,] grace *Qq*   god] God
Qq   masculine,] Masculine *Qq*   7 priuate,] priuate *Qq 1, 3* : priuat
Q2   8 please,] please *Qq*   9 pale,] paie *Qq*   10 S'lid,] S'lid
Qq 1, 2 : Slid *Q3*   away,] away *Qq*   12 fortune l] fortune : *Qq*
14 pen, and inke,] pen and inke *Qq*   17 S'light,] S'light *Qq*   and]
an' *F2, F3*   18 sooner,] sooner *Qq*   *Exit.* add Qq   20 day, i']
day i' *Qq 1, 2* : day in *Q3*   did] 'did *Q1* : it did *Qq 2, 3*   by that
light] by Iesu *Qq*   21 then—] then, *Qq* : than— *F2, F3*   22 mistris]
mistresse *Qq*

grac't by 'hem beyond all aime of affection : this's her
garter my dagger hangs in : and they doe so commend, and
approue my apparell, with my iudicious wearing of it, it's
aboue wonder.

F A L L. Indeed sir, 'tis a most excellent sute, and you doe
weare it as extraordinary.

F A S T. Why, I'le tell you now (in good faith) and by
this chaire, which (by the grace of god) I intend presently
to sit in, I had three sutes in one yeere, made three great
ladies in loue with me : I had other three, vn-did three
gentlemen in imitation : and other three, gat three other
gentlemen widdowes of three thousand pound a yeere.

D E L I. Is't possible ?

F A S T. O, beleeue it, sir ; your good face is the witch,
and your apparell the spells, that bring all the pleasures of
the world into their circle.

F A L L. Ah, the sweet grace of a courtier !

M A C I. Well, would my father had left mee but a good
face for my portion yet ; though I had shar'd the vnfortu-
nate wit that goes with it, I had not car'd : I might haue
past for somewhat i' the world then.

F A S T. Why, assure you, signior, rich apparell has
strange vertues : it makes him that hath it without meanes,
esteemed for an excellent wit : he that enioyes it with
means, puts the world in remembrance of his means :
it helps the deformities of nature, and giues lustre to her
beauties ; makes continuall holy-day where it shines ; sets
the wits of ladies at worke, that otherwise would be idle :
furnisheth your two-shilling ordinarie ; takes possession of
your stage at your new play ; and enricheth your oares, as
scorning to goe with your scull.

M A C I. Pray you, sir, adde this ; it giues respect to your

II. vi. 24 'hem] them, *Q3*   this's] this' *Q1* : this is *Qq* 2, 3   25
commend,] commend *Qq*   26 iudicious] judicious *Q1*   30 Why,]
Why *Qq*   31 god] God *Qq*   intend] entend *Qq*   33 vn-did] vndid
Qq   34 three,] three *F2*   35 gentlemen widdowes] Gentlemen,
Widdowes *Qq 1, 2* : Gentlewomen, Widdows *Q3*   37 O,] O *Qq*   it,] it
Qq   44 i'] in *Q3*   45 you,] you *Qq*   47 enioyes] enjoyes *Q1*   50
holy-day] Holiday *Qq*   55 you,] you *Qq*

Euery Man out of his Humour

fooles, makes many theeues, as many strumpets, and no fewer bankrupts.

F a l l. Out, out, vnworthy to speake, where he breatheth.

F a s t. What's he, signior? 60

D e l i. A friend of mine, sir.

F a s t. By heauen, I wonder at you, citizens, what kinde of creatures you are!

D e l i. Why, sir?

F a s t. That you can consort your selues, with such 65 poore seame-rent fellowes.

F a l l. He saies true.

D e l i. Sir, I will assure you (how euer you esteeme of him) he's a man worthy of regard.

F a s t. Why? what ha's he in him, of such vertue to be 70 regarded? ha?

D e l i. Mary, he is a scholler, sir.

F a s t. Nothing else?

D e l i. And he is well trauail'd.

F a s t. He should get him clothes; I would cherish 75 those good parts of trauaile in him, and preferre him to some nobleman of good place.

D e l i. Sir, such a benefit should bind me to you for euer (in my friends right) and, I doubt not, but his desert shall more then answere my praise. 80

F a s t. Why, and he had good clothes, I'ld carry him to court with me to morrow.

D e l i. He shall not want for those, sir, if gold and the whole city will furnish him.

F a s t. You say well, sir: faith, signior D e l i r o, I 85 am come to haue you play the *Alchymist* with me, and

---

II. vi. 57 bankrupts] Bankrups *Q3*   58 speake,] speake *Qq*   62 you,] you *Qq*   63 are!] are? *Qq*   64 Why,] Why *Qq*   65 selues,] selues *Qq*   68 Sir,] Sir *Qq*   70 him,] him *Qq*   72 Mary,] Mary *Q1*: Marry *Qq 2, 3*   scholler,] Scholler *Qq*   75, 81 clothes] cloths *Qq 1, 2*: cloathes *Q3*   76 trauaile] trauell *Qq*   79 and, ... not,] and ... not *Qq*   80 then] than *Qq, F2*   81 and] an' *F2, F3*   82 court] the Court *Qq*   83 those,] those *Qq*   85 well,] well *Q1*: wel *Qq 2, 3*   faith,] faith *Qq*

change the *species* of my land, into that mettall you talke of.

D E L I. With all my heart, sir, what summe will serue you?

90 F A S T. Faith, some three, or foure hundred.

D E L I. Troth, sir, I haue promist to meet a gentleman this morning, in *Paules*, but vpon my returne I'le dispatch you.

F A S T. I'le accompany you thither.

95 D E L I. As you please, sir ; but I goe not thither directly.

F A S T. 'Tis no matter, I haue no other designement in hand, and therefore as good goe along.

D E L I. I were as good haue a quartane feauer follow me now, for I shall ne're bee rid of him : (bring mee a cloke 100 there, one) Still, vpon his grace at court, am I sure to bee visited ; I was a beast to giue him any hope. Well, would I were in, that I am out with him, once, and - - - Come, signior M A C I L E N T E, I must conferre with you, as wee goe. Nay, deare wife, I beseech thee, forsake these moods : 105 looke not like winter thus. Here, take my keyes, open my counting houses, spread all my wealth before thee, choose any obiect that delights thee : If thou wilt eate the spirit of gold, and drinke dissolu'd pearle in wine, 'tis for thee.

F A L L. So, sir.

110 D E L I. Nay, my sweet wife.

F A L L. Good lord ! how you are perfum'd ! in your termes, and al ! pray you leaue vs.

D E L I. Come, gentlemen.

F A S T. Adiew, sweet lady.

115 F A L L. I, I ! Let thy words euer sound in mine eares,

II. vi. 87 change] chaunge *Qq 1, 3*   89 heart,] heart *Qq*   90 Faith,] Faith *Qq*   three,] three *Qq*   foure hundred] fourescore pound *Qq*   91 Troth, sir,] Troth Sir *Qq 1, 2* : Troth sir, *Q3*   92 morning,] morning *Qq*   95 please,] please *Qq*   100 there,] there *Qq*   Still,] Still *Qq*   court,] the Court *Qq*   am I] I am *F2, F3*   102 in,] in *Qq 1, 2* him,] him *Qq*   and - - - Come,] and. - - - Come *Qq*   103 you,] you *Qq* 104 Nay,] Nay *Qq*   thee,] thee *Qq*   105 Here,] Here *Qq 1, 2, F2* : Heere *Q3*   107 obiect] object *Q1*   109 So,] So *Qq*   110 Nay,] Nay *Qq*.   111 lord] Lord *Qq*   perfumed ! in] perfumed in *Qq*   112 termes,] tearmes *Qq*   al !] all : *Qq*   113 Come,] Come *Qq*   114 *Exeunt all but Fallace*. add *Qq*   115 I, I !] I, I, *Qq*

Euery Man out of his Humour 493

and thy graces disperse contentment through all my senses!
O, how happy is that lady aboue other ladies, that enioyes so
absolute a gentleman to her seruant! A countesse giue him
her hand to kisse? ah, foolish countesse! hee's a man
worthy (if a woman may speake of a mans worth) to kisse 120
the lips of an empresse.

F v n g. What's master F a s t i d i v s gone, sister? *Returnd with his taylor.*

F a l l. I, brother (he has a face like a *Cherubin*!)

F v n g. Gods me, what lucke's this? I haue fetcht my
taylor and all: which way went he, sister? can you tell? 125

F a l l. Not I, in good faith (and he has a body like an
angell!)

F v n g. How long is't since he went?

F a l l. Why, but e'en now: did you not meet him?
(and a tongue able to rauish any woman i'the earth!) 130

F v n g. O, for gods sake (I'le please you for your paines:)
but e'en now, say you? Come, good, sir: S'lid, I had forgot
it too: Sister, if any body aske for mine vncle S o g l i-
a r d o, they shall ha' him at the *Heralds* office, yonder by
Paules. 135

F a l l. Well, I will not altogether despaire: I haue
heard of a citizens wife, has beene belou'd of a courtier;
and why not I? heigh, ho: well, I will into my priuate
chamber, locke the dore to mee, and thinke ouer all his
good parts, one after another. 140

II. vi. 116 senses!] sences : *Qq*   117 enioyes] enjoyes *Qq*   119
kisse?] kisse! *Qq*   ah,] ah *Qq*   countesse!] Countesse ; *Qq*   120
worth] woorth *Qq 2, 3*   122 st. dir. *Returnd . . taylor.*] *Enter Fungoso, with his Taylor.* (*Fungoso* Q3) *Qq* in text after 121.   122 master]
Maister *Q3*   123 I, brother [he] I brother : he *Qq*   a *Cherubin*!)]
Cherubin. Qq : Cherubin!) *F2, F3*   125 he,] he *Qq*   126 faith
(and] faith : and *Qq*   127 angell!)] Angell. *Qq*   129 Why,] Why
Qq   (and] and *Qq*   130 i'] in *Q3*   earth!)] earth. *Qq*   131
gods] Gods *Qq*   132 Come, good,] Come good *Qq*   S'lid,] S'lid *Qq,
F2*   133 Sister,] Sister *F2*   134 office,] Office *Qq*   After 135]
Exit, with his Taylor. (*Exit* Q3) Qq   136 altogether] altogither *Qq*
137 wife,] wife *Qq*   belou'd] beloued *Q3*   138 heigh,] heigh *Qq*
well,] well *F2*   priuate] priuat *Qq 1, 2*   140 parts,] parts *Qq 1, 3* :
partes *Q2*   *Exit.* add *Qq*

GREX.

Mit. Well, I doubt, this last *Scene* will endure some grieuous torture.

Cor. How? you feare 'twill be rackt, by some hard construction?

Mit. Doe not you?

Cor. No, in good faith: vnlesse mine eyes could light mee beyond sense. I see no reason, why this should be more liable to the racke, then the rest: you'le say, perhaps, the city will not take it well, that the marchant is made here to dote so perfectly vpon his wife; and shee againe, to bee so *Fastidiously* affected, as shee is?

Mit. You haue vtter'd my thought, sir, indeed.

Cor. Why (by that proportion) the court might as wel take offence at him we call the courtier, and with much more pretext, by how much the place transcends, and goes before in dignitie and vertue: but can you imagine that any noble, or true spirit in court (whose sinowie, and altogether vn-affected graces, very worthily expresse him a courtier) will make any exception at the opening of such an emptie trunke, as this BRISKE is! or thinke his owne worth empeacht, by beholding his motley inside?

Mit. No sir, I doe not.

Cor. No more, assure you, will any graue, wise citizen, or modest matron, take the obiect of this folly in DELIRO, and his wife: but rather apply it as the foile to their owne vertues. For that were to affirme, that a man, writing of

II. vi. 141 doubt,] doubt *Qq*   143 rackt,] rackt *Qq*   146 No,] No *Qq*   147 sense.] *Sence*, *Qq*   reason,] reason *Qq*   racke,] Racke *Qq*
148 then] than *Qq, F2*   say, perhaps,] say perhaps *Qq* (saie *Q2*)   149 marchant *F1*: Merchant *Qq, F3*: merchant *F2*   150 againe,] againe *F2*   152 thought,] thought *Qq*   155 transcends,] transcends *Q1*: transcendes *Qq 2, 3*   157 noble,] Noble *Qq*   court] the Court *Qq*   sinowie,] Sinewie *Qq*: snowie, *F2, F3*   altogether] altogither *Q1*
160 trunke,]·Trunk *Q1*: Trunke *Qq 2, 3*   is!] is? *Qq, F2*   161 empeacht,] empeach *Qq 1, 2*: impeacht *Q3*   163 graue,] graue *Qq, F2*
164 obiect] object *Q1*   DELIRO,] *Deliro* *Qq*   165 wife:] Wife; *Qq*
166 vertues.] vertues: *Qq*   man,] man *Qq*

NERO, should meane all Emperors: or speaking of MACHIAVEL, comprehend all States-men; or in our SORDIDO, all Farmars; and so of the rest: then which, nothing can be vtter'd more malicious, or absurd. Indeed, there are a sort of these narrow-ey'd decypherers, I confesse, that will extort strange, and abstruse meanings out of any subiect, be it neuer so conspicuous and innocently deliuer'd. But to such (where e're they sit conceal'd) let them know, the author defies them, and their writing-tables; and hopes, no sound or safe iudgement will infect it selfe with their contagious comments, who (indeed) come here only to peruert, and poison the sense of what they heare, and for nought else.

MIT. Stay, what new *Mute* is this, that walkes so suspiciously?

COR. O, mary this is one, for whose better illustration; we must desire you to presuppose the stage, the middle isle in *Paules*; and that, the west end of it.

MIT. So, sir: and what followes?

COR. Faith, a whole volume of humour, and worthy the vnclasping.

MIT. As how? what name doe you giue him first?

COR. He hath shift of names, sir: some call him APPLE IOHN, some Signior WHIFFE, mary, his maine standing name is CAVALIER SHIFT: the rest are but as cleane shirts to his natures.

MIT. And what makes he in *Paules*, now?

COR. Troth, as you see, for the aduancement of a *Siquis*, or two; wherein he has so varied himselfe, that if any one

II. vi. 167 Emperors] Emperours: *Qq* 168 MACHIAVEL] *Machiavell* Q1 169 then], than *Qq*, F2 170 malicious, or] malicious and *Qq* Indeed,] Indeed *Qq* 171 decypherers] decypherets F2 172 strange,] straunge *Qq* 173 subiect] Subject Q1 175 author] Authour *Qq* -tables] -table Q3 176 iudgement] judgement Q1 178 peruert,] pervert Q1: peruert *Qq* 2, 3 180 this,] this *Qq* After 181] ACTVS TERTIVS, SCENA PRIMA (ACTUS TERTIUS, Q1: TERTIVS. Q3) | *Enter Caualier Shift, with two Siquisses in his hand.* (Cavalier Q1) *Qq* 182 illustration;] Illustration, Q3 185 So,] So *Qq* 186 Faith,] Faith *Qq* humour] Humor *Qq* 189 names,] names *Qq* 190 mary,] marry *Qq* 191 CAVALIER] *Cavalier* Q1 192 natures] *Natures Qq* 193 *Paules*,] *Paules Qq* 194 Troth,] Troth *Qq* Siquis,] *Siquis* Qq

of 'hem take, he may hull vp and downe i' the humorous world, a little longer.

MIT. It seemes then, he beares a very changing saile?

COR. O, as the wind, sir: here comes more.

Act III.   Scene I.

SHIFT, ORANGE, CLOVE.

This is rare, I haue set vp my bills, without discouery.

ORAN. What? Signior WHIFFE? what fortune has brought you into these west parts?

SHIFT. Troth, signior, nothing but your rheume; I
5 haue beene taking an ounce of tabacco hard by here, with a gentleman, and I am come to spit priuate, in *Paules*. Saue you sir.

ORAN. Adieu, good Signior WHIFFE.

CLOVE. Master APPLE IOHN? you are well met:
10 when shall we sup together, and laugh, and be fat with those good wenches? ha?

SHIFT. Faith, sir, I must now leaue you, vpon a few humours, and occasions: but when you please, sir.

CLOVE. Farewell, sweet APPLE IOHN: I wonder,
15 there are no more store of gallants here!

II. vi. 196 'hem] them *Q3*   i'] in *Q3, F2*   197 world,] world *Qq*   199 wind,] wind *Qq*   III.i. *Act . . .* CLOVE.] Act III. SCENE I.— *The Middle Aisle of St. Paul's.* G: *Enter Orenge.* Qq. (Qq spell *Orenge* throughout the scene.)   1 This] *Shift.* This *Qq*   bills,] bils *Qq*   4 Troth,] Troth *Qq*   5 beene] ben *Q1*   here,] here *Qq 1, 2*: heere *Q3*   6 priuate,] priuate *Qq*: privat *F2*   7 Saue *F1*: 'Save *F2*: God saue *Qq*   8 Adieu,] Adieu *Q1*: Adue *Qq 2, 3*   *Enter Cloue.* add Qq   9 Master] Maister *Qq*   10 laugh,] laugh *Qq*   12 Faith,] Faith *Qq*   13 humours,] Humours *Q1*: Humors *Qq 2, 3*   please,] please *Qq*   *Exit.* add *Qq*   14 Farewell,] Farewell *Qq 1, 3*: Farewel *Q2*   wonder,] wonder *Qq*   15 here!] here? *Qq*

GREX.

MIT. What be these two, signior?
COR. Mary, a couple sir, that are meere strangers to the whole scope of our play; only come to walke a turne or two, i' this *Scene* of *Paules*, by chance.

ORAN. Saue you, good master CLOVE. 20
CLOVE. Sweet master ORANGE.

GREX.

MIT. How? CLOVE, and ORANGE?
COR. I, and they are well met, for 'tis as drie an ORANGE as euer grew: nothing, but *Salutation*; and, *O god, sir*; and, *It pleases you to say so, Sir*; one that can 25 laugh at a iest for company with a most plausible, and extemporall grace; and some houre after, in priuate, aske you what it was: the other, monsieur CLOVE, is a more spic't youth: he will sit you a whole afternoone sometimes, in a booke-sellers shop, reading the *Greeke, Italian*, and 30 *Spanish*; when he vnderstands not a word of either: if he had the tongues, to his sutes, he were an excellent linguist.

CLOVE. Doe you heare this reported, for certainty?
ORAN. O god, sir. 35

III. i. 17 Mary,] Mary *Q1* : Marry *Qq* 2, 3   strangers] straungers *Qq* 1, 2   18 two,] two *Qq*   19 *Paules*,] *Paules* Qq   chance] chaunce *Qq*   St. dir. after 19] *They walke togither.* Qq   20 Saue] 'Save *F2*   24 nothing,] nothing *Qq*   24-5 *Salutation* ; and, *O god, sir* ; and,] *Salutation,* and *O God sir,* and *Qq*   25 so,] so *Qq*   26 iest] jest *Q1*   27 after, in priuate,] after in priuate *Qq*   28 monsieur] mounsieur *F2*   32 tongues,] Tongues *Qq*   34 reported,] reported *Qq*   35 god, sir] good sir *Qq* : god, sir- *F2*

445·3   K k

Act III. Scene II.

PVNTARVOLO, CARLO.

Sirrah, take my cloke: and you sir knaue, follow mee closer. If thou losest my dogge, thou shalt die a dogs death; I will hang thee.

CARL. Tut, feare him not, hee's a good leane slaue, he
5 loues a dog well, I warrant him; I see by his lookes, I: masse hee's somwhat like him. S'lud poison him, make him away with a crooked pinne, or somewhat, man; thou maist haue more security of thy life: and so sir, what? you ha' not put out your whole venter yet? ha' you?

10   PVNT. No, I doe want yet some fifteene, or sixteene hundred pounds: but my lady (my wife) is out of her humour; shee does not now goe.

CARL. No? how then?

PVNT. Mary, I am now enforc't to giue it out, vpon the
15 returne of my selfe, my dogge, and my cat.

CARL. Your cat? where is shee?

PVNT. My squire has her there, in the bag: Sirrah, looke to her: How lik'st thou my change, CARLO?

CARL. Oh, for the better, sir; your cat has nine liues,
20 and your wife ha' but one.

PVNT. Besides, shee will neuer bee sea-sicke, which will saue mee so much in conserues: when saw you signior SOGLIARDO?

CARL. I came from him but now, he is at the *Heralds*
25 office yonder: he requested me to goe afore, and take vp a man or two for him in *Paules*, against his cognisance was ready.

PVNT. What? has he purchast armes, then?

III. ii. *Act* . . . CARLO.] *Enter Puntaruolo, Carlo: two seruingmen following, one leading the Dogge.* (Puntarvolo, Q1: *seruing men* Q1) Qq, without change of scene.   1 Sirrah] *Punt.* Sirrah *Qq*   2 closer. If] closer: if *Qq*   losest] loosest *Qq*   5 well,] well *Qq*   lookes] looke *Q3*   6 S'lud] Sblood *Q1*: Sbloud *Qq* 2, 3   7 somewhat,] somwhat *Q1*: somewhat *Qq* 2, 3   9 venter] Venture *F3*   10 fifteene,] fifteene *Qq*   12 humour] Humor *Qq* 2, 3   17 there,] there *Qq*   19 better,] better *Qq*   20 ha'] has *Qq* 2, 3   25 afore,] afore *Qq* 1, 2   28 What?] What: *F2*   armes,] armes *Qq*

CARL. I, and rare ones too: of as many colours, as e're you saw any fooles coat in your life. I'le goe looke among yond' bills, and I can fit him with legs to his armes——

PVNT. With legs to his armes! Good: I will goe with you, sir.

They goe to looke vpon the bills.

Act III. Scene III.

FASTIDIVS, DELIRO, MACILENTE.

COme, let's walke in *Mediterraneo*: I assure you, sir, I am not the least respected among ladies; but let that passe: doe you know how to goe into the presence, sir?

MACI. Why, on my feet, sir.

FAST. No, on your head, sir: for 'tis that must beare you out, I assure you: as thus, sir. You must first haue an especial care so to weare your hat, that it oppresse not confusedly this your predominant, or fore-top; because (when you come at the presence dore) you may, with once or twice stroking vp your fore-head thus, enter, with your predominant perfect: that is, standing vp stiffe.

MACI. As if one were frighted?

FAST. I, sir.

MACI. Which indeed, a true feare of your mistris should doe, rather then gumme water, or whites of egges: is't not so, sir?

FAST. An ingenious obseruation: giue mee leaue to craue your name, Sir.

DELI. His name is, MACILENTE, sir.

FAST. Good signior MACILENTE: if this gentleman, signior DELIRO, furnish you (as he saies he will) with clothes, I will bring you, to morrow by this time, into

III. ii. 30 saw] say *F2*   31 yond'] yond *Qq 2, 3*   and] an *F2*
armes——] Armes. *Qq*   33 you,] you *Qq*   St. dir. *Qq in text after* 33
III. iii. *Act . . .* MACILENTE.] *Enter Fastidius, Deliro, and Macilente.* Qq, *without change of scene.*   1 Come] *Fast.* Come *Qq   Mediterraneo*] the *Mediterraneum Qq*   you,] you *Qq*   sir,] sir *Qq 1, 2*   3 presence,] Presence *Qq*   sir?] sir. *F2*   4 feet,] feet *Qq*   sir.] sir? *F2*   5 head,] head *Qq*   6 thus, sir.] thus sir: *Qq*   8 predominant,] Predominant *Qq*   9 may,] may *Qq*   10 fore-head] Forehead *Qq*   enter,] enter *Qq*   13 I,] I *Qq*   14 mistris] Mistresse *Qq*   15 then]than *Qq, F2*   16 so,] so *Qq*   18 name,] name *Qq*   19 is,] is *Qq, F2* MACILENTE,] *Macilente* Qq   22 you,] you *Qq*   time,] time *Qq 1, 2*

KK 2

the presence of the most diuine, & acute lady in court :
you shall see sweet silent rhetorique, and dumbe eloquence
25 speaking in her eye ; but when shee speakes her selfe, such
an anatomie of wit, so sinewiz'd and arteriz'd, that 'tis the
goodliest modell of pleasure that euer was, to behold. Oh!
shee strikes the world into admiration of her—(ô, ô, ô) I
cannot expresse 'hem, beleeue me !

30 M A C I. O, your onely admiration is your silence, sir.

P V N T. 'Fore god, C A R L O, this is good ; let's reade
'hem againe.

The first bill. *If there be any lady, or gentlewoman of good carriage,
that is desirous to entertaine (to her priuate vses) a
35 yong, straight, and vpright gentleman, of the age of fiue,
or sixe and twenty at the most : who can serue in the
nature of a gentleman vsher, and hath little legges of
purpose, and a blacke satten sute of his owne, to goe
before her in : which sute (for the more sweetning)
40 now lies in lauander : and can hide his face with her
fanne, if neede require : or sit in the cold at the staire
foot for her, as well as another gentleman : Let her
subscribe her name and place, and diligent respect
shall be giuen.*

45 P V N T. This is aboue measure excellent ! ha?

C A R L. No, this, this ! here's a fine slaue.

The second bill. *If this city, or the suburbs of the same, doe affoord*

III. iii. 23 diuine,] Diuine *Qq*   acute *corr. F1*: *A cute* Qq : *acute* F1 originally, F2   in] of the *Qq*   26 anatomie] Anotomie *Qq 2, 3* 27 was, *Qq, F1* (*but comma faint in some copies*) : was F2   Oh !] Oh, *Qq* 28 her— *corr. F1*: her ; *Qq, F1 originally,* F2   29 'hem,] hem *Qq* me ! *corr. F1*: me. *Qq, F1,* F2   30 admiration *corr. F1, F2* : Admiration, *Qq* : admiration, *F1*   31 god,] God *Qq*   32 againe.] againe : *Qq*   33 margin] The first bill. *corr. F1, F2* : *not in Qq, F1 originally* : *in F3 printed as a heading before* 33   35 yong,] young, Qq 1, 2 : *young* Q3   38 owne,] owne Qq 1, 3 : own Q2   41–2 staire foot] staire-foot F2   42 her,] her Qq   another] an other Qq 45 PVNT. This *corr. F1, F2*: This *Qq, F1 originally* (*see* 66)   excellent !] excellent : *Q1*: excellent ; *Qq 2, 3*   46 No, this, this !] No this, this : *Qq*   47 margin] The second bill. *corr. F1, F2*: *not in Qq, F1 originally* : *in F3 printed as a heading before* 47   *If corr. F1, F2*: PVNT. *If* Qq, F1 *originally*   affoord] affourd Q1 : afford Q2, F2

any young gentleman, *of the first, second, or third head,
more or lesse, whose friends are but lately deceased,
and whose lands are but new come to his hands,* that
(*to bee as exactly qualified as the best of our ordinary
gallants are*) *is affected to entertaine the most gentlemanlike vse of tabacco : as first, to giue it the most
exquisite perfume : then, to know all the delicate
sweet formes for the assumption of it : as also the rare
corollarie, and practice of the* Cuban *ebolition,*
E V R I P V S, *and Whiffe ; which hee shall receiue,
or take in, here at* London, *and euaporate at*
Vxbridge, *or farder, if it please him. If there be any
such generous spirit, that is truly enamour'd of these
good faculties : May it please him, but* (*by a note of
his hand*) *to specifie the place, or ordinarie where hee
vses to eate, and lie ; and most sweet attendance, with
tabacco, and pipes of the best sort, shall be ministred :*
S T E T Q V Æ S O C A N D I D E L E C T O R.

P v n t. Why this is without *paralell*, this !

C a r l. Well, I'le marke this fellow for S o g l i a r d o's
vse presently.

P v n t. Or rather, S o g l i a r d o, for his vse.

C a r l. Faith, either of 'hem will serue, they are both
good properties : I'le designe the other a place too, that we
may see him.

P v n t. No better place, then the Mitre, that wee may
bee spectators with you, C a r l o. Soft, behold, who enters
here : Signior S o g l i a r d o ! saue you.

III. iii. 48 *young* Qq, corr. F1 : *yong* F1 originally, F2   50 *to*] *into*
F2, F3   54 *then*] *then* Q1   *delicate*] *dilicate* Q2   55 *for*] *of* Q3   56
corollarie,] *Corollarie* Q1 : *Corollary* Qq 2, 3   57 *Whiffe* Qq, corr. F1,
F2 : *whiffe* F1 originally.   *receiue,*] *receiue* Qq   58 *in,*] *in* Qq   *euaporate*] *evaporate* Q1   59 *farder*] *farther* F2   63 *eate,*] *eat* Qq   *lie ;*]
Lie, Q1 : *lie,* Qq 2, 3   *attendance,*] *attendance* Qq   64 *sort,*] *sort* Qq
66 P v n t. *not in* Qq, *where Puntarvolo reads the bill*   Why] *why* Qq 1, 2
without] *without,* F2   69 S o g l i a r d o,] *Sogliardo* Qq : S o g l i a r d o F2
70 Faith,] Faith Qq   73 place,] place Qq   then] than Qq, F2   74 you,]
you Qq   75 saue] God saue Qq   *Enter Sog.* add Qq (*Sogliardo.* Q3)

Act III. Scene IIII.

To them. SOGLIARDO.

SAue you, good sir PVNTARVOLO; your dogge's in health, sir, I see: how now, CARLO?

CARL. Wee haue ta'ne simple paines, to choose you out followers here.

5 PVNT. Come hither, signior.

They shew him the bills.

CLOVE. Monsieur ORANGE, yond' gallants obserue vs; pr'y thee let's talke fustian a little, and gull 'hem: make 'hem beleeue we are great schollers.

ORANG. O lord, sir.

10 CLOVE. Nay, pr'y thee let's, beleeue me, you haue an excellent habit in discourse.

ORANG. It pleases you to say so, sir.

CLOVE. By this church, you ha' la: nay, come, begin: ARISTOTLE *in his Dæmonologia, approues* SCALIGER 15 *for the best Nauigator in his time: and in his Hypercritiques, he reports him to be Heautontimorumenos:* you vnderstand the *Greeke*, sir?

ORANG. O god, sir.

MACIL. For societies sake he does. O, here be a couple 20 of fine tame parrats.

CLOVE. Now, sir, whereas the *Ingenuitie* of the time, and the soules *Synderisis* are but *Embrions* in nature, added to the panch of *Esquiline*, and the *Inter-vallum* of the *Zodiack*, besides the *Eclipticke line* being *optike*, and not 25 *mentall*, but by the *contemplatiue & theoricke* part thereof,

III. iv. Act ... SOGLIARDO.] *Qc continue the scene.*   To them add Ff
1 Saue you,] *Sog.* Saue you *Qq*   PVNTARVOLO] *Puntaruolo* Q1   2 health, sir,] health sir *Qq*   now,] now *Qq*   3 paines,] paines *Qq*   5 hither,] hither *Qq*   6 st. dir. *in Qq in text after* 5   Monsieur] Mounsier *F2*
ORANGE] *Orenge* Qq *here and throughout the scene*   obserue] obserues *Qq* 1, 2   7 pr'y thee] pray thee *Q3*   fustian] fustain *F3*   little,] little *Qq*   9 lord,] Lord *Qq*   10 beleeue me,] by Iesu: *Qq*   12 so,] so *Qq*   13 church,] Church *Qq*   nay,] nay *Qq*   14 *Dæmonologia*,] *Dæmonologia* Qq   approues] approoues *Qq*   16 *Heautontimorumenos*] *Hcautontimorumenos* Qq   17 *Greeke*,] *Greeke Qq*   18 god,] God *Q1*: good *Qq* 2, 3   19 O,] O *Qq*   21 Now,] Now *Qq*   whereas] Whereas *Qq*   23 -vallum] -uallum *Qq* 2, 3   24 *Eclipticke line*] *Ecliptickeline* Q3

doth demonstrate to vs the *vegetable circumference*, and the *ventositie* of the *Tropicks*, and whereas our *intellectuall*, or *mincing capreall* (according to the *Metaphisicks*) as you may reade in P L A T O's *Histriomastix* - - - You conceiue me, sir? 30

O R A N G. O lord, sir.

C L O V E. Then comming to the pretty *Animall*, as *Reason long since is fled to animals*, you know, or indeed for the more *modellizing*, or *enamelling*, or rather *diamondizing* of your *subiect*, you shall perceiue the *Hypothesis*, or *Galaxia* 35 (whereof the *Meteors* long since had their *initiall inceptions and notions*) to be meerely *Pythagoricall, Mathematicall*, and *Aristocraticall* - - - For looke you, sir, there is euer a kinde of *concinnitie* and *species* - - - Let vs turne to our former discourse, for they marke vs not. 40

F A S T. Masse, yonder's the knight P V N T A R V O L O.

D E L I. And my cousin S O G L I A R D O, me thinkes.

M A C I. I, and his familiar that haunts him, the deuill with the shining face.

D E L I. Let 'hem alone, obserue 'hem not. 45

S O G L. Nay, I will haue him, I am resolute for that. By this parchment, gentlemen, I haue beene so toil'd among the *Harrots* yonder, you will not beleeue, they doe speake i' the *Sogliardo,* strangest language, and giue a man the hardest termes for *Puntar-* his money, that euer you knew. *uolo, Carlo, walke.*

C A R L. But ha' you armes? ha' you armes?

S O G L. Yfaith, I thanke them, I can write my selfe 52

III. iv. 27 *intellectuall,*] intellectuall Qq 1, 3 : *intellectual* Q2   28 *capreall*] capreall, Q1 : *capreal*, Q2   29 *Histriomastix* - - -] Histriomastix. Qq 1, 2 : Histriomastix : Q3   30 me,] me Qq   31 lord,] Lord Qq   33 *animals,*] Animals Qq   34 *modellizing,*] modellizing Qq 1, 2 : modellizing Q3   35 *Hypothesis,*] Hipothesis Qq   *Galaxia*] Galaxia, Qq   38 *Aristocraticall* - - - For] *Aristocraticall* : for Q1 : *Aristocraticall* : for Q2 : *Astronomicall* : for Q3   you,] you Qq   39 *species* - - -] *Species.* Qq   vs] us Q1   41 PVNTARVOLO] Puntarvolo Q1   42 SOGLIARDO,] Sogliardo Qq   44 the shining] a shining Qq   45 'hem . . .'hem] them . . . them Q3.   After 45 *Sogliardo, Punt. Car. walke.* Qq   46 Nay,] Nay Qq   that. By] that, by Qq   47 parchment,] Parchment Q1 : parchment Qq 2, 3   beene] ben Q1 : been Q2 : bene Q3   48 st. dir. *corr. F1, F2* : *not in Qq   walke*] walkes F2   Harrots corr. F1, F2 : Harrots Qq, F1   i'] in Q3   49 strangest] straungest Q1   52 them, *corr. F1, F2* : God Qq : God, F1

gentleman now, here's my pattent, it cost me thirtie pound, by this breath.

55 P v n t. A very faire coat, well charg'd, and full of armorie.

S o g l. Nay, it has as much varietie of colours in it, as you haue seene a coat haue, how like you the crest, sir?

P v n t. I vnderstand it not well, what is't?

60 S o g l. Mary, sir, it is your Bore without a head *Rampant*.

P v n t. A Boore without a head, that's very rare!

C a r l. I, and rampant too: troth, I commend the *Heralds* wit, hee has decyphered him well: A swine with-
65 out a head, without braine, wit, any thing indeed, ramping to gentilitie. You can blazon the rest, signior? can you not?

S o g l. O, I, I haue it in writing here of purpose, it cost me two shillings the tricking.

70 C a r l. Let's heare, let's heare.

P v n t. It is the most vile, foolish, absurd, palpable, & ridiculous escutcheon, that euer this eye survis'd. Saue you, good monsieur F a s t i d i v s.

C a r l. Silence, good knight: on, on.

75 S o g l. G y r o n y, of eight *peeces*; A z v r e and G v l e s, betweene three *plates*; a C h e v' r o n, *engrailed checkey*, O r, V e r t, and E r m i n e s; on a *cheefe* A r g e n t betweene two A n n' l e t s, *sables*; a Bores head, *Proper*.

80 C a r l. How's that? on a *cheefe* A r g e n t?

They salute as they meet in the walke.

III. iv. 53 gentleman] Gentlemen *Q3*   pound,] pound *Qq*   55 charg'd,] charg'd *Qq 1, 2*: chargde, *Q3*   58 crest,] Crest *Qq*   60 Mary,] Marry *Qq*   Bore *corr.* F1, F2: Bore *Qq*, F1   62 Pvnt. *om.* F2, F3   Boore *corr.* F1: Bore *Qq*, F1 *originally*, F2   rare!] rare. *Qq*   63 troth,] troth *Qq*   64 *Heralds corr.* F1, F2: Heralds *Qq*, F1   swine *corr.* F1, F2: Swine *Qq*, F1   66 rest,] rest *Qq*   68 O,] O *Qq*   72 escutcheon,] Escutcheon *Qq*   survis'd *Q1, Ff*: suruis'd *Q2*: suruisde *Q3*   you,] you *Qq*   73 monsieur] Mounsieur *Q1*   *st. dir. add Qq after* 'Fastidivs'   74 Silence,] Silence *Qq*   75 Gyrony,] GYRONY *Qq*   *peeces*;] peeces, *Q1*: pieces, *Qq 2, 3*   76 *plates*;] plates *Qq*   Chev'ron,] *CHEV'RON Qq*   77 Vert,] *VERT Qq*   78 *sables*;] sables *Qq*   79 head,] head *Qq*   *Proper corr.* F1, F2: Proper F1 *originally*: *PROPER Qq*

Euery Man out of his Humour 505

S O G L. On a *cheefe* A R G E N T, a Bores head *Proper*, betweene two A N N'L E T S *sables*.

C A R L. S'lud, it's a hogs-cheeke, and puddings in a pewter field this.

S O G L. How like you 'hem, signior?

P V N T. Let the word bee, *Not without mustard;* your crest is very rare, sir.

C A R L. A frying pan, to the crest, had had no fellow.

F A S T. Intreat your poore friend to walke off a little, signior, I will salute the knight.

C A R L. Come, lap't vp, lap't vp.

F A S T. You are right well encountred, sir, how do's your faire dog?

P V N T. In reasonable state, sir: what citizen is that you were consorted with? a marchant of any worth?   95

F A S T. 'Tis signior D E L I R O, sir.

P V N T. Is it he? Saue you, sir.   *Salute.*

D E L I. Good sir P V N T A R V O L O.

M A C I. O, what copie of foole would this place minister, to one endew'd with patience, to obserue it?   100

C A R L. Nay, looke you sir, now you are a gentleman, you must carry a more exalted presence, change your mood, and habit, to a more austere forme, be exceeding proud, stand vpon your gentilitie, and scorne euery man. Speake nothing humbly, neuer discourse vnder a nobleman, though 105 you ne're saw him but riding to the *Starre-chamber*, it's all one. Loue no man. Trust no man. Speake ill of no man

Here they shift. Fastidius mixes with Puntaruolo, Carlo, and Sogliardo, Deliro, and Macilente, Cloue and Orange, fou⟨r⟩ couple.

III. iv. 81 head *Proper*, corr. F*1*, F*2* : head, PROPER F*1* originally : head PROPER Qq   82 st. dir. Qq begin at 84 and abbreviate ' *Fast.*' ' *Punt.*' ' *Carl.*' ' *Sogli.*' (' *Car.*' ' *Deli.*' Qq 2, 3)   *Puntaruolo*, corr. F*1*, F*2* : *Puntaruolo* F*1* originally   *foure*] foure Qq, F*2*   83 hogs-cheeke corr. F*1*, F*2* : Hogs-cheeke F*1* originally : Hogs Cheeke Qq   85 'hem,] them Qq   86 word] world Qq 2, 3   mustard ;] mustard, Qq   87 rare,] rare Qq   88 pan, corr. F*1*, F*2* : pan Qq, F*1*   crest Q*3*, corr. F*1*, F*2* : crest F*1* : Crest Qq 1, 2   89 little,] little Qq   92 encountred,] encountred Qq   94 state, sir :] state sir, Qq   95 marchant] merchant Qq, F*2*   96 DELIRO,] *Deliro* Qq   97 you,] you Qq   98 PVNTARVOLO] *Puntarvolo* Q*1*   99 O,] O Qq   minister,] minister Qq   100 patience,] Patience Qq   101 Nay,] Nay Qq, F*2*   102 mood,] mood Qq   103 habit,] habite Qq   106 ne're] neuer Q*3*   107 man. Trust] man, Trust Qq   man. Speake] man, Speake Q*2* : man, speake Q*3*

506 *Euery Man out of his Humour*

to his face: nor well of any man behind his backe. Salute fairely on the front, and wish 'hem hang'd vpon the turne.
110 Spread your selfe vpon his bosome publikely, whose heart you would eate in priuate. These be principles, thinke on 'hem, I'le come to you againe presently.

P v n t. Sirra, keepe close ; yet not so close : thy breath will thaw my ruffe.

115 S o g l. O, good cousin, I am a little busie, how do's my neece ? I am to walke with a knight, here.

Act III. *Scene* V.

To them. F v n g o s o. T a y l o r.

O He is here, looke you sir, that's the gentleman.
T a i l. What, he i' the blush-colour'd sattin ?
F v n g. I, he sir : though his sute blush, hee blushes not, looke you, that's the sute, sir : I would haue mine, such a 5 sute without difference, such stuffe, such a wing, such a sleeue, such a skirt, belly, and all ; therefore, pray you obserue it. Haue you a paire of tables ?

F a s t. Why, doe you see, sir ? they say I am phantasticall : why, true, I know it, and I pursue my humour still, 10 in contempt of this censorious age. S'light, and a man should doe nothing, but what a sort of stale iudgements about this towne will approue in him, he were a sweet asse : I'ld beg him yfaith. I ne're knew any more find fault with a fashion, then they that knew not how to put themselues

---

III. iv. 108 face :] face, *Qq*   111 priuate] priuat *Q1*   112 'hem] them *F3*   After 112 *Exit Car. Sogliardo mixes with Punt. and Fast.* *Qq*   113 close ; ... close :] close, ... close, *Qq*   114 thaw] draw *F3*   115 O,] O *Qq*   116 neece ?] neece, *Qq*   knight,] knight *Qq.* *Enter Fung. with his Tailor.* add *Qq*   III. v. *Act* . . . T a y l o r.] *Qq continue the scene.*   *To them.* add *Ff*   1 O] *Fung.* O *Qq*   2 What,] What *Qq*   3 sir :] sir *Qq*   not,] not : *Qq*   4 sute,] Sute *Q1* : sute *Qq* 2, 3   6 belly,] Belly *Qq* 1, 2 : belly *Q3*   8 Why,] Why *Qq*   see,] see *Qq*   9 why,] why *Qq*   humour] Humor *Qq* still,] stil *Q1* : still *Qq* 2, 3   10 age.] age : *Qq*   S'light,] S'light *Qq, F2*   and] an' *F2*   11 nothing,] nothing *Qq*   12 asse :] Asse, *Qq*   13 yfaith.] yfaith : *Qq*   fault] more fault *F3*   14 then *Qq, F1* : than *F2*

Euery Man out of his Humour

in to't. For mine owne part, so I please mine owne appetite, I am carelesse what the fustie world speakes of me. Puh.

F v n g. Doe you marke, how it hangs at the knee there?

T a i l. I warrant you, sir.

F v n g. For gods sake, doe, note all: doe you see the collar, sir?

T a i l. Feare nothing, it shall not differ in a stitch, sir.

F v n g. Pray heau'n, it doe not, you'le make these linings serue? and helpe me to a chapman for the out-side, will you?

T a i l. I'le doe my best, sir: you'le put it off presently?

F v n g. I, goe with mee to my chamber, you shall haue it - - - but make haste of it, for the loue of a customer, for I'le sit i' my old sute, or else lie a bed, and reade the *Arcadia*, till you haue done.

C a r l. O, if euer you were strucke with a iest, gallants, now, now. I doe vsher the most strange peece of militarie profession, that euer was discouer'd in *Insula Paulina*.

F a s t. Where? where?

P v n t. What is he, for a creature?

C a r l. A pimpe, a pimpe, that I haue obseru'd yonder, the rarest *superficies* of a humour; hee comes euery morning to emptie his lungs in *Paules* here: and offers vp some fiue, or sixe *Hecatomb's* of faces, and sighes, and away againe. Here he comes; nay, walke, walke, be not seene to note him, and we shall haue excellent sport.

III. v. 15 in to't.] into't: *Q1*, *F2* : into it: *Qq* 2, 3   16 me. Puh.] me, puh: *Qq* 1, 2 : me, puh. *Q3*   17 marke,] marke *Qq*   18 you,] you *Qq*   19 gods sake,] Gods sake *Qq*   20 collar,] Coller *Qq*   21 stitch,] stitch *Qq*   22 heau'n,] God *Qq*   23 for] to *Q3*   out-side] outside *Qq*   25 best,] best *Qq*   26 chamber,] chamber *Qq*   27 it - - -] it, *Qq*   a customer] Christ *Qq*   28 bed,] bed *Qq*   After 29] *Exit with tailor.* (*Tailor.* Q3) *Enter Car.* Qq   30 CARL.] Caol. Q3   O,] O *Qq*   iest] jest *Q1*   34 he,] he *Qq*   36 humour] Humor *Q1* : humor *Qq* 2, 3   37 here:] here, *Qq*   fiue,] fiue *Qq*   38 faces,] faces *Qq*   39 nay,] nay *Qq*   40 *Enter Shift:* (*Shift.* Q3) | *Walkes by, and vses action to his Rapier.* add *Qq*

Act III. Scene VI.

To them.   SHIFT.

P v N. S'Lid, hee vented a sigh e'ne now, I thought he would haue blowne vp the church.

C A R. O, you shall haue him giue a number of those false fires ere hee depart.

F A S T. See, now he is expostulating with his rapier! looke, looke.

C A R L. Did you euer, in your daies, obserue better passion ouer a hilt?

P V N T. Except it were in the person of a cutlers boy, or that the fellow were nothing but vapour, I should thinke it impossible.

C A R L. See, againe, he claps his sword o' the head, as who should say, well, goe to.

F A S T. O violence! I wonder the blade can containe it selfe, being so prouokt.

C A R L. *With that, the moody squire thumpt his brest,*
And rear'd his eyen to heauen, for reuenge.

S O G L. Troth, and you be good gentlemen, let's make 'hem friends, and take vp the matter, betweene his rapier, and him.

C A R L. Nay, if you intend that, you must lay downe the matter, for this rapier (it seemes) is in the nature of a hanger on, and the good gentleman would happily be rid of him.

F A S T. By my faith, and 'tis to be suspected, I'le aske him.

M A C I. O, here's rich stuffe, for lifes sake, let vs goe.
A man would wish himselfe a senselesse pillar,
Rather then view these monstrous prodigies:

III. vi. *Act* . . . SHIFT.] *Qq continue the scene*   *To them* add Ff
1 S'lid,] S'lid *Qq*   3 O,] O *Qq*   5 See,] See *Qq*   rapier! looke]
Rapier, Looke *Qq*   7 euer,] euer *Qq*   daies,] daies *Qq 1, 2*: dayes
Q3   14 violence!] violence, *Qq*   17 eyen] Eye F3   heauen,] Heauen
Q1: heauen Qq 2, 3   18 and] an' *F2, F3*   good *not in Qq*   19
matter,] matter *Qq*   rapier,] Rapier *Qq*   20 him] he *Qq*   22
matter,] matter; *F2*   26 O,] O *Qq*   lifes] Christ *Qq*   goe.] goe, *Qq*
28 then] than *Qq, F2*

Nil habet infœlix paupertas durius in se,
Quàm quòd ridiculos homines facit————   30
F A S T. Signior.
S H I F T. At your seruice.
F A S T. Will you sell your rapier?
C A R L. Sbloud, he is turn'd wild vpon the question, hee lookes as hee had seene a serjeant.   35
S H I F T. Sell my rapier? now fate blesse me.
P V N T. *Amen.*
S H I F T. You ask't me, if I would sell my rapier, sir?
F A S T. I did indeed.
S H I F T. Now, lord haue mercy vpon me.   40
P V N T. *Amen,* I say still.
S H I F T. S'lud sir, what should you behold in my face, sir, that should moue you (as they say, sir) to aske me, sir, if I would sell my rapier?
F A S T. Nay (let me pray you, sir) bee not mou'd: I   45
protest, I would rather haue beene silent, then any way offensiue, had I knowne your nature.
S H I F T. Sell my rapier? 'ods lid! Nay, sir (for mine owne part) as I am a man that has seru'd in causes, or so, so I am not apt to injure any gentleman in the degree of falling   50
foule, but (sell my rapier?) I will tell you sir, I haue seru'd with this foolish rapier, where some of vs dare not appeare in haste, I name no man: but let that passe. (Sell my rapier?) death to my lungs. This rapier, sir, has trauail'd by my side, sir, the best part of *France* and the *low Countrey:*   55
I haue seene *Vlishing, Brill,* and the *Haghe,* with this rapier,

<small>III. vi. 29 infœlix] in fœlix Q1   30 Quàm quòd] Quam quod Qq facit——] facit. Qq.   *Exit, with Deliro.* add Qq   34 Sbloud,] Sbloud Q1: S'bloud Qq 2, 3: om. F2   35 serjeant] Serjeant Qq   36 fate] God Qq   37 Amen] Amen Qq   38 rapier,] Rapier Qq   40 Now, lord] Now Lord Qq   41 *Amen,*] Amen Qq 1, 2   42 S'lud,] 'Slid F2   face,] face Qq   43 moue] mooue Qq 2, 3   say,] say Qq   me,] me Qq   45 you,] you Qq   mou'd] moou'd Qq 2, 3   46 protest,] protest Qq   silent,] silent Qq 1, 2   then] than Qq 1, 2. F2   48 'ods lid! Nay,] Gods lid: Nay Qq   50 injure] injurie Q2: iniurie Q3   51 but (sell my rapier?)] but: sell my Rapier? Qq   53 haste,] hast, Qq: haste; F2   passe. (Sell my rapier?) death] passe; Sell my Rapier? Death Qq   54 rapier,] Rapier Qq   trauail'd] trauel'd Q3   55 side,] side Qq   *France*] Fraunce Qq 1, 2   56 Haghe,] Haghe Qq: *Hague,* F3   rapier,] Rapier Qq 1, 2</small>

sir, in my lord of *Leysters* time: and (by gods will) he that should offer to disrapier me now, I would——Looke you sir, you presume to be a gentleman of sort, and so likewise your friends here, if you haue any disposition to trauell, for the sight of seruice, or so, one, two, or all of you, I can lend you letters to diuers officers and commanders in the *low Countries*, that shall for my cause doe you all the good offices, that shall pertaine or belong to gentlemen of your——Please you to shew the bountie of your minde, sir, to impart some ten groates, or halfe a crowne to our vse, till our abilitie be of grow'th to returne it, and we shall thinke our selfe—— Sbloud! sell my rapier?

S o g l. I pray you, what said he, signior, hee's a proper man.

F a s t. Mary, he tells me, if I please to shew the bountie of my mind, to impart some ten groats to his vse, or so.

P v n t. Breake his head, and giue it him.

C a r l. I thought he had beene playing o' the *Iewes* trump, I.

S h i f t. My rapier? no sir: my rapier is my guard, my defence, my reuenew, my honour: (if you cannot impart, be secret, I beseech you) and I will maintaine it, where there is a graine of dust, or a drop of water. (Hard is the choise when the valiant must eat their armes, or clem:) Sell my rapier? no, my deare, I will not bee diuorc't from thee, yet, I haue euer found thee true as steele——and (you cannot impart

---

III. vi. 57 sir, *om*. *Q3*   gods] Gods *Qq*   58 would——] would.—— *Q1*   Looke you] Looke y ou *Qq 2, 3*   59 sort] good sort *Qq*   60 if] If *Qq*   61 seruice,] seruice *Qq*   one] One *Qq*   62 letters] letters, *F2*   commanders] Commaunders *Qq*   63 offices,] offices *Qq*   65 minde,] mind *Qq*   66 groates,] groates *Qq*   67 selfe——] selfe.—— *Qq*.   68 Sbloud!] Sbloud, *Qq 1, 2* : Sbloud *Q3* : What, *F2*   69 you,] you *Qq*   he,] he *Qq*   signior, *Q1, F1* : Signior? *Qq 2, 3* : signior? *F2*   71 Mary,] Mary *Q1* : Marie *Qq 2, 3* : Marry *F2*   if] If *Qq 1, 2*   72 vse,] vse *Qq*   so.] so— *F2*   73 head,] head *F2*   74 beene] been *Q1* : ben *Q2* : bin *Q3*   o'] on *Qq*   75 trump,] Trump *Qq*   77 honour] Honor *Q3*   impart,] impart *Qq 1, 2*   78 secret,] secret *Qq*   and I] andI *Q1*   79 dust,] dust *Qq 1, 2*   water. (Hard] water: (hard *Qq*   80 armes,] Armes *Qq*   81 no,] no *Qq*   diuorc't] deuorc't *Q3* : divorc'd *F2*   thee,] thee *Qq*   yet,] yet; *F2*   82 steele——] Steele: *Qq 1, 2* : steele: *Q3*

Every Man out of his Humour 511

sir ?) Saue you gentlemen: (neuerthelesse if you haue a fancie to it, sir.)

FAST. Pr'y thee away: is Signior DELIRO departed? 85

CAR. Ha'you seene a pimpe out-face his owne wants better?

SOG. I commend him, that can dissemble 'hem so well.

PVNT. True, and hauing no better a cloke for it, then he has neither. 90

FAST. Gods precious, what mischieuous lucke is this! adiew gentlemen.

PVNT. Whither? in such haste, Monsieur FASTI-DIVS!

FAST. After my marchant, signior DELIRO, sir. 95

CARL. O hinder him not, hee may hap lose his tide, a good flounder i'faith.

ORAN. Harke you, signior WHIFFE, a word with you.

CARL. How? signior WHIFFE?

ORAN. What was the difference betweene that gallant that's gone, and you, sir? *Orange and Cloue call Shift aside.*

SHIFT. No difference: he would ha' giu'n mee fiue pound for my rapier, and I refus'd it; that's all.

CLOVE. O, was't no otherwise? wee thought you had beene vpon some termes. 105

SHIFT. No other then you saw, sir.

CLOVE. Adieu, good Master APPLE-IOHN.

CARL. How? WHIFFE, and APPLE-IOHN too?

III. vi. 83 sir ?)] Sir) *Qq 1, 2* : sir) *Q3*   Saue] God saue *Qq*   84 it,] it *Qq*   87 better ?] better. *Qq 1, 2*   88 him,] him *Qq 2, 3* can] he can *Q3*   'hem] them *Qq*   89–90 for it, then he has *F1* : for it, than he has *Q1, F2* (it *Q1*) : than he has for it *Qq 2, 3* : (then *Q3*) 91 this !] this : *Q1* : this ? *Qq 2, 3*   93 FASTIDIVS !] *Fastidius* ? *Qq* 95 marchant] Merchant *Qq 1, 2* : Marchant *Q3* : merchant *F2*   DE-LIRO,] *Deliro Qq*   96 lose] loose *Qq 1, 2*   97 *Exit.* add *Qq* (for 95)   98 ORAN.] *Oren. Qq*, who spell '*Orenge*' up to 101.   you, signior] you Sig. *Qq*   99 st. dir. *in Qq* at 98–9   100 gallant] young gallant *Qq*   101 you,] you *Qq*   sir? *Q3, F2* : sir. *Qq 1, 2, F1*   104 was't] was it *Qq*   105 beene] ben *Qq*   106 then] than *Qq, F2*   saw,] saw *Qq*   107 Adieu,] Adieu *Q1* : Adiew *Qq 2, 3*   APPLE-IOHN] *Apple Iohn Qq*   *Exeūt Oren. & Cloue.* add *Qq (Clou. Q3)*   108 APPLE-IOHN] *Apple Iohn Qq 2, 3* : *Apple Ioan Q1*

Heart, what'll you say if this be the *appendix*, or labell to both yond' indentures?

PVNT. It may be.

CARL. Resolue vs of it, IANVS, thou that look'st euery way: or thou HERCVLES, that hast trauail'd all countries.

PVNT. Nay, CARLO, spend not time in inuocations now, 'tis late.

CARL. Signior, here's a gentleman desirous of your name, sir.

SHIFT. Sir, my name is CAVALIER SHIFT: I am knowne sufficiently in this walke, sir.

CARL. SHIFT? I heard your name varied e'en now, as I take it.

SHIFT. True, sir, it pleases the world (as I am her excellent *Tabbaconist*) to giue me the stile of signior WHIFFE: as I am a poore esquire about the towne here, they call mee Master APPLE-IOHN. Varietie of good names does well, sir.

CARL. I, and good parts, to make those good names: out of which I imagine yond 'bils to be yours.

SHIFT. Sir, if I should denie the manuscripts, I were worthie to be banisht the middle I'le, for euer.

CARL. I take your word, sir: this gentleman has subscrib'd to 'hem, and is most desirous to become your pupill. Mary you must vse expedition. *Signior Insulso Sogliardo*, this is the professor.

SOGL. In good time, sir; nay, good sir, house your head: doe you professe these sleights in tabacco?

III. vi. 109 *appendix*,] *Appendix* Qq 2, 3   111, 112 *one line in Qq*   112 it,] it *Qq*   113 way:] way; *Qq*   115 Nay,] Nay *Qq*   inuocations, now,] Inuocations now; *Q1*: Inuocation now; *Qq 2, 3*   118 name,] name *Qq*   119 Sir, my] My *Qq 2, 3*   120 walke,] walke *Qq*   123 True,] True *Qq*   124 *Tabbaconist*] *Tabbaconist* Qq   126 APPLE-IOHN. Varietie] *Apple Iohn :* varietie *Qq 1, 2* : *Apple Iohn*, varietie *Q3*   127 well,] well *Qq*   130 manuscripts] *Scriptures* Qq   131 I'le,] I'le *Q1*: yle *Qq 2, 3* : ile, *F2*   132 word,] word *Qq*   134 pupill. Mary] Pupill; mary *Qq*   you] yon *Q1*   expedition.] expedition: *Qq*   136 time,] time *Qq*   sir; *corr. F1, F2* : sir, *Qq, F1*   nay, good sir,] nay good sir *Qq*   137 head: *corr. F1, F2* : head, *Qq, F1*   these *Qq, corr. F1, F2* : those *F1*

S H I F T. I, doe more then professe, sir, and (if you please to bee a practitioner) I wil vndertake in one fortnight to bring you, that you shal take it plausibly in any ordinarie, theatre, or the tilt-yard, if need be, i' the most popular assembly that is.

P V N T. But you cannot bring him to the *whiffe*, so soone?

S H I F T. Yes, as soone, sir : hee shall receiue the first, second, and third *whiffe*, if it please him, and (vpon the receit) take his horse, drinke his three cups of *Canarie*, and expose one at *Hounslow*, a second at *Stanes*, and a third at *Bagshot*.

C A R L. Baw-waw!

S O G L. You will not serue mee, sir, will you? I'le giue you more then countenance.

S H I F T. Pardon me, sir, I doe scorne to serue any man.

C A R L. Who? he serue? Sbloud he keepes high men, and low men, he ; he has a faire liuing at *Fullam*.

S H I F T. But in the nature of a fellow, I'le bee your follower, if you please.

S O G L. Sir, you shall stay, and dine with mee, and if wee can agree, weele not part in haste : I am verie bountifull to men of qualitie. Where shall we goe, signior?

P V N T. Your Miter is your best house.

S H I F T. I can make this dogge take as many *whiffes* as I list, and hee shall retaine, or efume them, at my pleasure.

P V N T. By your patience, follow me, fellowes.

S O G L. Sir, P V N T A R V O L O!

III. vi. 138 I, *Ff* : I *Qq* : I, I *Ed. conj.* then *Q3, F1* : than *Qq 1, 2, F2* professe,] professe *Qq* 139 practitioner] practioner *Q1* 141 -yard,] -yard *Qq* be, i'] be ; *Qq 1, 2* : bee ; *Q3* 143 *whiffe*,] *Whiffe Qq* 145 Yes, as soone,] Yes as soone *Qq* sir : *Q3, corr. F1, F2* : sir ; *Q1* : Sir: *Q2* : sir, *F1* 150 -waw !] waw. *Qq* 151 mee,] me *Qq* 152 then] than *Qq, F2* 153 me,] me *Qq 1, 2* ; mee *Q3* 154 Sbloud] he ! *F2* 155 he ;] hee ? *Q2* : he ? *Q3* : he ! *F2* 157 follower,] follower *Qq* 158 Sir,] Sir *Qq 1, 2* stay,] stay *Qq* 160 goe,] go *Q1* : goe *Qq 2, 3* signior ?] Signior. *Q1* 161 Miter] Mitre *Qq 2, 3* 162 *whiffes* corr. F1, F2 : whiffes *Qq, F1* 163 retaine,] retaine *Qq 1, 2* efume] refume *Qq 2, 3* : effume *F2* them,] them *Qq* 164 me,] me *Qq 1, 2* : mee *Q3* 165 Sir, P V N T A R V O L O !] Sir *Puntaruolo*. *Q1* : Sir *Puntaruolo*. *Qq 2, 3*

445·3   L l

P v n t. Pardon mee, my dogge shall not eate in his companie, for a million.

C a r l. Nay, bee not you amaz'd, signior W h i f f e, what e're that stiffeneckt gentleman say's.

170 S o g l. No, for you doe not know the humour of the dogge, as wee doe: where shall we dine, C a r l o? I would faine goe to one of these ordinaries, now I am a gentleman.

C a r l. So you may, were you neuer at any yet?

S o g l. No faith, but they say, there resorts your most 175 choise gallants.

C a r l. True, and the fashion is, when any stranger comes in among'st 'hem, they all stand vp and stare at him, as he were some vnknowne beast, brought out of *Affrick:* but that'll bee help't with a good aduenturous face. You must 180 be impudent ynough, sit downe, and vse no respect; when any thing's propounded aboue your capacitie, smile at it, make two or three faces, and 'tis excellent, they'le thinke you haue trauail'd: though you argue, a whole day, in silence thus, & discourse in nothing but laughter, 'twill 185 passe. Onely (now and then) giue fire, discharge a good full oth, and offer a great wager, 'twill be admirable.

S o g l. I warrant you, I am resolute: come, good signior, there's a poore french crowne, for your ordinarie.

S h i f t. It comes well, for I had not so much as the least 190 portcullice of coine before.

III. vi. 166–7 companie,] companie *Qq 1, 2*: company *Q3, F2*   167 *Exit Puntarvolo with his followers,* add Qq (*Punt.* Qq 2, 3: *fellowes.* Q3) 168 Nay,] Nay *Qq*   amaz'd,] amaz'd *Qq*   170 humour] Humor *Qq* 171 dogge, *corr. F1, F2*: Dogge, *F1*: dog *Q1*: Dog *Qq 2, 3*   dine,] dine *Qq*   172 ordinaries,] Ordinaries *Qq 1, 2*   173 any] none *Qq* 174 say,] say *Qq 1, 2*   176 stranger] straunger *Qq 1, 2*   178 beast,] beast *Qq*   *Affrick*: corr. *F1, F2*: *Affrick, F1*: Affricke, *Qq*   179 aduenturous] adventurous *Q1*   face. You *corr. F1, F2*: face, you *Q1, F1*: face; you *Qq 2, 3*   180 respect;] respect, *Q1*: respect: *Qq 2, 3* 183 trauail'd] trauail'd *Q3*   argue,...day, *corr. F1, F2*: argue...day *Qq, F1*   187 resolute: come,] resolute, come *Qq*   188 crowne,] crowne *Qq*   190 *Exeunt.* add Qq

GREX.

Mit. I trauell with another obiection, signior, which I feare will bee enforc'd against the author, ere I can be deliuer'd of it.

Cor. What's that, sir?

Mit. That the argument of his *Comœdie* might haue beene of some other nature, as of a duke to be in loue with a countesse, and that countesse to bee in loue with the dukes sonne, and the sonne to loue the ladies waiting maid: some such crosse wooing, with a clowne to their seruingman, better then to be thus neere, and familiarly allied to the time.

Cor. You say well, but I would faine heare one of these *autumne*-judgements define once, *Quid sit Comœdia?* if he cannot, let him content himselfe with Ciceros definition (till hee haue strength to propose to himselfe a better) who would haue a *Comœdie* to be *Imitatio vitæ, Speculum consuetudinis, Imago veritatis;* a thing throughout pleasant, and ridiculous, and accommodated to the correction of manners: if the maker haue fail'd in any particle of this, they may worthily taxe him, but if not, why—be you (that are for them) silent, as I will bee for him; and giue way to the actors.

III. vi. 191 obiection,] obiection *Q1* : obiection *Qq* 2, 3   194 that,] that *Qq*   195 *Comœdie*] Comedie *Qq*, *F2* (so 206)   196 beene] ben *Q1* : been *Q2* : bin *Q3*   198 waiting maid] waiting-maid *F2*   200 then] than *Qq*, *F2*   neere,] neere *Qq*   203 -judgements] -iudgements *Qq* 2, 3   *Quid sit*] Quidsit Q3   *Comœdia*] Comedia *F2*   204 Ciceros] Cicero's *F2*   207 *veritatis;*] *veritatis,* Qq   pleasant,] pleasant *Qq*   210 him,] him; *F2*   why—] why; *Qq*

Act III. Scene VII.

SORDIDO, HINE.

With a halter about his necke.

NAy, gods-precious, if the weather and season bee so respectlesse, that beggars shall liue as well as their betters ; and that my hunger, and thirst for riches, shall not make them hunger and thirst with pouertie ; that my sleepes shall be broken, and their hearts not broken ; that my coffers shall bee full, and yet care ; theirs emptie, and yet merry ! Tis time, that a crosse should beare flesh and bloud, since flesh and bloud cannot beare this crosse.

GREX.

MIT. What, will he hang himselfe?

COR. Faith I, it seemes his Prognostication has not kept touch with him, and that makes him despaire.

MIT. Beshrow me, he will be out of his humour then, indeed.

SOR. Tut, these star-monger knaues, who would trust 'hem? one saies, darke and rainy, when 'tis as cleere as christall ; another saies, tempestuous blasts, and stormes, and 'twas as calme as a milke-bowle ; here bee sweet rascals for a man to credit his whole fortunes with : You skie-staring cocks-combs you, you fat braines, out vpon you ; you are good for nothing but to sweat night-caps, and make rug-gownes deare ! You learned men, and haue not a legion of deuils, *a vostre seruice ! a vostre seruice ?* by heauen,

III. vii *Act . . .* HINE.] SCENA SECVNDA. | *Enter Sordido with a halter about his necke.* Qq (SECUNDA. Qq *1, 2*) 1 st. dir. *not in* Qq Nay,] Sord. Nay Qq gods-] Gods- Qq *1, 2* : Gods Q*3* season] the Season Qq 3 hunger,] hunger Qq 6 theirs] their's F*2* 7 merry!] merry: Q*1* : merrie : Qq *2, 3* time,] time Qq 9 What,] What Qq 12 humour then,] Humor then Qq 17 milke-bowle] Milke bowle Qq (Milk Q*3*) 19 cocks-combs you,] Cocks combes you : Qq *1, 2* : Cockscombes you : Q*3* 20 -caps,] caps Qq 21 deare ! You] deare : you Qq 22 seruice !] seruice : Qq seruice ? *by corr.* F*1* : seruice ? By Qq : seruice ! *by* F*1 originally,* F*2* heauen,] heauen Qq

Every Man out of his Humour 517

I thinke I shall die a better scholler then they! but soft, how now, sirra.

HINE. Here's a letter come from your sonne, sir. 25

SORD. From my sonne, sir? what would my sonne, sir? some good newes, no doubt.

Sweet, and deare father (desiring you first to send mee your blessing, which is more worth to me then gold, or siluer) I desire you likewise to be aduertised, that this Shrouetide (contrary to custome) we vse alwaies to haue reuels; which is indeed dancing: and makes an excellent shew, in truth, especially if wee gentlemen bee well attir'd, which our seniors note, and thinke the better of our fathers, the better we are maintain'd, and that they shall know if they come vp, and haue any thing to doe in the law. Therefore, good father, these are (for your owne sake, as well as mine) to re-desire you; that you let me not want, that which is fit for the setting vp of our name, in the honorable volume of gentilitie: that I may say to our calumniators, with TVLLIE, *Ego sum ortus domus meæ, tu occasus tuæ. And thus (not doubting of* 30

The letter.

35

40

III. vii. 23 then] than *Qq 1, 2, F2*   they!] they, *Qq 1, 2* : they: *Q3*   24 now,] now *Qq*   sirra.] sirah. *Qq 1, 2* : sirrah? *Q3*   *Enter a Hind with a letter.* Qq, centred in Q1, appended in Qq 2, 3   25 HINE] Hind Qq   sonne,] Sonne *Qq 1, 2* : sonne *Q3* (so twice in 26)   27 newes,] newes *Qq*   28 margin. The letter.] corr. F1, F2 : not in F1 originally : in *Qq* added as a stage direction to 27 : in F3 printed as a heading to the letter.   *Sweet,* corr. F1 : *Sweet* Qq, F1 originally, F2   *father*] father, Qq 1, 2   29 then] than Qq, F2   30 gold, corr. F1 : Gold Qq 1, 2 : gold Q3, F1 originally, F2   32 *dancing* : corr. F1 : Dauncing, Q1 : Dancing, Q2 : dancing, Q3, F1 originally, F2   33 *shew, in truth,* corr. F1 : shew in truth ; Qq, F1 originally, F2   37 *law. Therefore,* corr. F1 : Law : therefore Q1 : Law : therfore Qq 2, 3 : law : therefore, F1 originally, F2   38 *sake,* Q3, corr. F1 : sake Qq 1, 2, F1 originally, F2   39 *you ; that*] you, that Qq   *want,*] want Qq, F2   40 *name,*] name Qq   *honorable*] honourable Qq 1, 2, F2   41 *gentilitie* : corr. F1 : Gentilitie, Qq 1, 2 : Gentility, Q3 : gentilitie, F1 originally, F2   42 *calumniators,*] Calumnators Q1 : Columniators Qq 2, 3   Ego . . . tuæ] EGO . . . TVÆ Qq   43 occasus] OCCASSUS Q2 : OCCASSVS Q3

your fatherly beneuolence) *I humbly aske you blessing,*
and pray god to blesse you. Yours, *if his owne*.

How's this! *Yours, if his owne?* is he not my sonne, except he be his owne sonne? Belike, this is some new kind of subscription the gallants vse. Wel! wherefore doest thou stay, knaue? Away: goe. Here's a letter indeede! reuels? and beneuolence? is this a weather to send beneuolence? or is this a season to reuell in? Slid the deuil and all takes part to vexe me, I thinke! this letter would neuer haue come now else, now, now, when the sunne shines, and the aire thus cleere. Soule, if this hold, we shall shortly haue an excellent crop of corne spring out of the high waies: the streets, and houses of the towne will be hid with the ranknesse of the fruits, that grow there, in spight of good husbandry. Goe to, I'le preuent the sight of it, come as quickly as it can, I will preuent the sight of it. I haue this remedie, heauen. Stay; I'le trie the paine thus a little, ô, nothing, nothing. Well now! shall my sonne gaine a beneuolence by my death? or any body be the better for my gold, or so forth? No. Aliue, I kept it from 'hem, and (dead) my ghost shall walke about it, and preserue it; my son and daughter shall starue ere they touch it: I haue hid it as deep as hel, from the sight of heauen, and to it I goe now.

Falls off.

III. vii. 44 you] your F3   45 god] God Qq   Yours...owne. *corr.* F1: Yours...owne. Qq, F1 originally, F2: in Q1, in F1 originally, in F2 a separate line   46 this! *corr.* F1, F2: this? Qq, F1   47 sonne?] Sonne. Qq 1, 2   Belike, *corr.* F1: Belike Qq, Ff   kind Qq 1, 2, *corr.* F1, F2: kinde Q3, F1   48 Wel!] *corr.* F1, F2: Well, Qq: Wel, F1   49 stay,] stay, Qq   Exit. Hind. add Qq after 'goe': Qq 2, 3 *begin a new line at* 'Here's'.   indeede! *corr.* F1, F2: indeed; Qq, F1   50 and beneuolence] and benevolence Qq 1, 2   52 me, I thinke!] me I thinke: Q1: mèe I thinke: Qq 2, 3   54 Soule,] Soule Q   55 waies:] waies, Qq   57 fruits,] fruits Qq   there, Q3, *corr.* F1: there Qq 1, 2, F1 originally, F2   58 to,] to Q1   60 remedie, heauen. Stay;] remedie *Heauen*: stay; Qq   61 Well now! *corr.* F1, F2: Well now: Qq 1, 2: Wel, now Q3: Well now, F1 originally, F2   63 gold,] Gold Qq   No. Aliue, Q1, *corr.* F1, F2: No. Aliue Qq 2, 3: No, aliue, F1 originally   64 about it,] about it Qq   preserue it; *corr.* F1: preserue it, Qq, F1 originally, F2   65 starue] sterue Qq   touch it: *corr.* F1: touch it, Qq, F1 originally, F2   66 hel, *corr.* F1: Hell Qq: hell F1 originally, F2   67 st. dir. add Qq 1, 2: *after* 67 *in* Q1

Act III. *Scene* VIII.

RVSTICI.

R v s t. 1.   A Ye me, what pittifull sight is this! help, *To him.*
help, help.

R v s t. 2. How now? what's the matter?

R v s t. 1. O, here's a man has hang'd himselfe, helpe to get him againe.

R v s t. 2. Hang'd himselfe? Slid carry him afore a iustice, 'tis *chance medley,* o' my word.

R v s t. 3. How now, what's here to doe?

R v s t. 4. How comes this?

R v s t. 2. One has executed himselfe, contrary to order of law, and by my consent he shall answer't.

R v s t. 5. Would he were in case, to answere it.

R v s t. 1. Stand by, he recouers, giue him breath.

S o r d. Oh.

R v s t. 5. Masse, 'twas well you went the foot-way, neighbour.

R v s t. 1. I, and I had not cut the halter.

S o r d. How! cut the halter? Aye me, I am vndone, I am vndone.

R v s t. 2. Mary, if you had not beene vndone, you had beene hang'd, I can tell you.

S o r d. You thred-bare horse-bread-eating rascals, if you would needes haue beene meddling, could you not haue vntied it, but you must cut it? and in the midst too! Aye me.

R v s t. 1. Out on me, 'tis the catterpiller S o r d i d o!

III. viii. *Act* . . . Rvstici.] *Enter Rustici,* 5 *or* 6, *one after another.* (5. or 6. Q3) Qq, without change of scene.   1 *To him.* corr. F1: not in Qq, F1 originally.   this!] this? *Qq*   4 O,] O *Qq*   7 medley, o'] medley on *Qq*   10 himselfe,] himselfe *Qq*   order] the order *Qq*   12 case,] case *Qq*   15 foot-way,] footway *Qq* 1, 2: foote-way *Q3*   16 neighbour] neighbor *Q3*   17 and] an' *F2*   18 How!] How? *Qq*   20 Mary,] Marry *Qq* 1, 2: Mary *Q3*   21 hang'd,] hang'd *Qq*   22 thred-bare] thredbare *Qq*   -eating] eating *Qq*   24 too!] too? *Qq*   26 Sordido!] *Sordido* ; *Qq*

how cursed are the poore, that the viper was blest with this
good fortune?

R v s T. 2. Nay, how accurst art thou, that art cause to
30 the curse of the poore?

R v s T. 3. I, and to saue so wretched a caytife?

R v s T. 4. Curst be thy fingers that loos'd him.

R v s T. 2. Some desperate furie possesse thee, that thou
maist hang thy selfe too.

35   R v s T. 5. Neuer maist thou be sau'd, that sau'd so
damn'd a monster.

S o r d i d. What curses breathe these men! how haue
my deeds
Made my lookes differ from another mans,
That they should thus detest, and lothe my life!
40 Out on my wretched humour, it is that
Makes me thus monstrous in true humane eyes.
Pardon me (gentle friends) I'le make faire mends
For my foule errors past, and twenty-fold
Restore to all men, what with wrong I rob'd them:
45 My barnes, and garners shall stand open still
To all the poore that come, and my best graine
Be made almes-bread, to feed halfe-famisht mouthes.
Though hitherto amongst you I haue liu'd,
Like an vnsauourie muck-hill to my selfe,
50 Yet now, my gather'd heapes being spread abroad,
Shall turne to better, and more fruitfull vses.
Blesse then this man, curse him no more for sauing
My life, and soule together. O, how deeply
The bitter curses of the poore doe pierce!
55 I am by wonder chang'd; come in with me
And witnesse my repentance: now I proue,
" No life is blest, that is not grac't with loue.

III. viii. 29 Nay,] Nay *Qq*   31 caytife?] Caytife. *Qq*   37 breathe]
breath *Qq 1, 2*   men!] men? *Qq 1, 2*: men, *Q3*   39 life!] life? *Qq*
40 humour] Humor *Qq*   45 barnes,] Barnes *Qq*   47 -bread,] -bread
Qq 1, 2   48 hitherto] hetherto *Qq 1, 2*   liu'd,] liu'd *Qq*   49
vnsauourie] vnsauorie *Qq*   selfe,] selfe. *Q3*   50 now,] now *Qq*
53 life,] life *Qq*   O,] O *Qq 1, 2*: Oh *Q3*   54 pierce!] *In Q3* ' ! ' *ill-
printed and in some copies resembles* ' l '.   57 *Exit.* add *Qq*

R v s t. 2. O miracle! see when a man ha's grace!

R v s t. 3. Had't not beene pitty, so good a man should haue beene cast away?

R v s t. 2. Well, I'le get our clarke put his conuersion in the *Acts*, and *Monuments*.

R v s t. 4. Doe, for I warrant him hee's a *Martyr*.

R v s t. O god, how he wept, if you mark't it! did you see how the teares trill'd?

R v s t. 5. Yes, beleeue me, like master vicars bowles vpon the greene, for all the world.

3. *or* 4. O neighbour, god's blessing o' your heart, neighbour, 'twas a good gratefull deed.

GREX.

Cor. How now, Mitis? what's that you consider so seriously?

Mit. Troth, that which doth essentially please me, the warping condition of this greene, and soggy multitude: but in good faith, signior, your author hath largely outstript my expectation in this *Scene*, I will liberally confesse it. For, when I saw Sordido so desperately intended, I thought I had had a hand of him, then.

Cor. What? you suppos'd he should haue hung himselfe, indeed?

Mit. I did, and had fram'd my obiection to it ready, which may yet be very fitly vrg'd, and with some necessity:

III viii. 58 grace!] grace. *Qq*   59 pitty,] pitie *Qq*   60 haue beene] haue ben *Qq 1, 2*   61 conuersion] conversion *Q1*   62 *Acts*, and *Monuments*] Chronicle *Qq*   63 *Martyr*] vertuous man *Qq*   64 Rvst.] Rust. 2 *F2*: *the number is accidentally omitted in Qq, F1.*   god,] god *Q1*: God *Qq 2, 3*   wept,] wept *Qq*   it!] it: *Qq*   66 Yes,] Yes *Qq*   me,] mee; *Qq*   master] maister *Q1*: maisters *Q2*: masters *Q3 (corrected to* master)   68 god's] God's *Qq 2, 3*   o' *not in Qq*   heart,] heart *Qq*   neighbour] neighbor *Q3*   69 *Exeunt.* add *Qq*   70 now,] now *Qq*   72 me,] me : *Qq 1, 3* : mee : *Q2*   73 greene,] greene *Qq, F2*   soggy] foggy *W. A. Craigie conj. s. v.* soggy *in N. E. D.* multitude :] multitude, *F2*   74 faith,] faith *Qq 1, 2* : fayth *Q3*   outstript] outstript *Qq 1, 2* : ouer-slipt *Q3*   76 For,] For *Qq*   77 him,] him *Qq*   78 himselfe,] himselfe *Qq, F2*   80 did,] did ; *Qq* obiection] objection *Qq 1, 2*

for though his purpos'd violence lost th'effect, and extended not to death, yet the intent and horror of the obiect, was more then the nature of a *Comœdie* will in any sort admit.

Cor. I? what thinke you of Plavtvs, in his *Comœdie*, called *Cistellaria*, there? where he brings in Alcesimarchvs with a drawne sword ready to kill himselfe, and as hee is e'ne fixing his brest vpon it, to bee restrain'd from his resolu'd outrage, by Silenivm, and the bawd: is not his authoritie of power to giue our *Scene* approbation?

Mit. Sir, I haue this only euasion left me, to say, *I thinke it bee so indeed, your memorie is happier then mine*: but I wonder, what engine hee will vse to bring the rest out of their humours!

Cor. That will appeare anon, neuer preoccupie your imagination withall. Let your mind keepe companie with the *Scene* still, which now remoues it selfe from the countrey, to the court. Here comes Macilente, and signior Briske, freshly suted, lose not your selfe, for now the *Epitasis*, or busie part of our subiect, is in act.

III. viii. 84 obiect,] object, *Qq 1, 3* : object *Q2*   then *Q3*, *F1* : than *Qq 1, 2, F2*   Comœdie] Comedie *Qq*   85 admit] allow *Qq*   86 Plavtvs,] *Plautus* Qq 1, 2   87 *Comœdie*,] Comedie *Qq*   *Cistellaria*,] *Cistellaria* Qq   88 sword] sword, *Qq 2, 3*   90 outrage,] outrage *Qq 1, 2* : out-rage *Q3*   Silenivm,] *Silenium* Qq   93 only] (your only) *Qq*   94 then] than Qq, F2   95 wonder,] wonder *Qq*   96 humours!] Humors? *Qq 1, 2* : Humors. *Q3*   99 countrey,] Countrie *Qq 1, 2* : Countrey *Q3*   100 Macilente,] *Macilente* Qq   101 Briske,] *Briske* Qq   lose] loose *Qq*   102 *Epitasis*,] *Epitasis* Qq   subiect,] Subject *Qq*   act] Action *Qq*

Act III.   Scene IX.

MACILENTE, BRISKE, CINEDO,
SAVIOLINA.

FAST. WEll, now, signior MACILENTE, you are
not onely welcome to the court, but also to my
mistris with-drawing chamber: Boy, get me some tabacco,
I'le but goe in, and shew I am here, and come to you presently, sir.

MACI. What's that he said? by heauen, I markt him
not:
My thoughts, and I, were of another world.
I was admiring mine owne out-side here,
To thinke what priuiledge, and palme it beares
Here, in the court! Be a man ne're so vile
In wit, in judgement, manners, or what else;
If he can purchase but a silken couer,
He shall not only passe, but passe regarded:
Whereas, let him be poore, and meanely clad,
Though ne're so richly parted; you shall haue
A fellow (that knowes nothing but his beefe,
Or how to rince his clammy guts in beere)
Will take him by the shoulders, or the throat,
And kicke him downe the staires. Such is the state
Of vertue, in bad clothes! ha, ha, ha, ha,
That raiment should be in such high request!
How long should I be, ere I should put off

III. ix. *Act . . . SAVIOLINA.*] SCENA TERTIA. |˙ *Enter Macilente, Briske, Cinedo, with Tabacco.* Qq : SCENE III.—*An Apartment at the Court.*| *Enter Macilente,* Fastidious Briske, *both in a new suit, and* Cinedo *with tobacco.* G   MACILENTE,] MACILENTE. F2   1 Well, now,] Well now *Qq*   3 mistris] mistresse *Qq 1, 2*   with-drawing] with drawing *Qq*   Boy,] Boy *Qq*   4 presently, presently *Qq*   5 *Exit.* add *Qq*   6 heauen,] heauen *Qq*   not:] not, *Qq*   7 thoughts,] thoughts *Q3, F2*   I,] I *Qq*   world.] world; *Qq*   8 out-side] outside *Qq*   9 priuiledge,] priuiledge *Qq*   10 Here,] Here *Qq*   court!] court: *Qq*   11 judge-ment] So *Qq, Ff spell here*   manners] in manners *Q3*   14 Whereas,] Whereas *Qq*   poore,] poore *Qq*   16 beefe,] Beefe *Qq*   18 shoulders,] shoulders *Qq*   20 vertue,] vertue *Qq*   clothes!] Cloths, *Qq 1, 2* : clothes, *Q3*   21 request!] request? *Qq*   22 be,] be *Qq*

To the lord *Chancelors* tombe, or the *Shriues* posts?
By heauen (I thinke) a thousand, thousand yeere.
25 His grauitie, his wisedome, and his faith,
To my dread Soueraigne (graces that suruiue him)
These I could well endure to reuerence,
But not his tombe: no more then I'ld commend
The chappell organ, for the guilt without,
30 Or this base violl, for the varnisht face.

FAST. I feare I haue made you stay somewhat long,
sir, but is my tabacco readie, boy?
CINE. I, sir.
FAST. Giue me, my mistris is vpon comming, you shall
35 see her presently, sir, (*Tab.*) you'le say you neuer accosted
a more piercing wit. This tabacco is not dryed, boy, or else
the pipe's defectiue. Oh, your wits of *Italie* are nothing
comparable to her! her braine's a verie quiuer of iests!
and she do's dart them abroad with that sweete loose, and
40 iudiciall aime, that you would—here she comes sir.

She is seene and goes in againe.

MACI. 'Twas time, his inuention had beene bogd else.
SAVI. Giue me my fanne there.
MACI. How now, Monsieur BRISKE?
FAST. A kind of affectionate reuerence strikes mee with
45 a cold shiuering (me thinkes.)
MACI. I like such tempers well, as stand before their
mistresses with feare and trembling, and before their maker,
like impudent mountaines.
FAST. By this hand, I'ld spend twentie pound my

III. ix. 23 To the] To my *Qq*   Shriues] Sheriffs F3   24 thousand,] thousand *Qq*   yeere.] yeare, *Qq 1, 2*   28 tombe:] Tombe, *Qq 1, 2*: tombe, *Q3*   then] than *Qq, F2*   I'ld] Ile *Q1*: Ile *Qq 2, 3*   29 organ,] Organ *Qq*   guilt] gilt *F2*   30 base] bace *Qq 1, 2*   violl,] Violl *Qq*   *Enter Fast.* add *Qq*   31 I feare] In faith *Qq*   long,] long *Qq*   32 sir,] sir; *Q3, F2*   readie,] readie *Qq 1, 2*: ready *Q3*   33 I,] I *Qq*   34 mistris] mistresse *Qq*   35 presently,] presently *Qq*   36 dryed,] dried *Qq*   37 pipe's] pipe is *F2*   38 her!] her, *Qq*   iests!] jests, *Q1*: iests, *Qq 2, 3*   39 sweete] sweet, *F3*   loose,] loose *Qq*   40 iudiciall] judiciall *Qq*   aime,] aime *Qq*   that you *Qq*, corr. *F1, F2*: *not in F1 originally*   41 st. dir. *She ... againe.] Enter Sauiolina, and goes in againe.* *Qq* in text after 40.   43 now,] now *Qq* Monsieur] Mounsieur *Qq 1, 2*   47 maker,] Maker *Qq*   49 this hand] Iesu *Qq*

vauting-horse stood here now, she might see me doe but one 50 tricke?

MACI. Why, do's she loue actiuitie?

CINE. Or if you had but your long stockings on, to be dancing a galliard, as she comes by.

FAST. I eyther. O, these stirring humours make ladies 55 mad with desire: shee comes. My good GENIVS embolden me, boy, the pipe quickly.

MACI. What? will he giue her musicke?

FAST. A second good morrow to my faire mistresse.

SAVI. Faire seruant, I'le thanke you a day hence, when 60 the date of your salutation comes forth.

FAST. How, like you that answere? is't not admirable?

MACI. I were a simple courtier, if I could not admire trifles, sir.

FAST. Troth, sweet ladie, I shall (*Tab.*) be prepar'd to *He talkes,* giue you thanks for those thankes, and (*Tab.*) studie more *and takes* officious, and obsequious regards (*Tab.*) to your faire *tweene.* beauties: (*Tab.*) mend the pipe, boy.

MACI. I ne're knew tabacco taken as a *parenthesis,* before. 70

FAST. Fore god (sweete ladie) beleeue it, I doe honour the meanest rush in this chamber, for your loue.

SAVI. I, you need not tell mee that, sir, I doe thinke, you doe prize a rush, before my loue.

MACI. Is this the wonder of nations? 75

FAST. O, by this ayre, pardon me, I said, for your loue, by this light: but it is the accustomed sharpnesse of your

---

III. ix. 50 vauting-horse] vauting Horse *Qq* : Vaulting-horse *F3* 51 tricke?] trick. *F2* 52 Why,] Why *Qq* 53 on,] on *Qq* 54 dancing] dauncing *Qq 1, 2* 55 O,] O *Qq* humours] humors *Qq* 56 desire:] desire, *Qq 1, 2* 57 boy,] Boy *Qq* Enter Sauiolina. add *Qq* 62 How,] How *Qq* 64 trifles, sir.] trifles sir *Qq 1, 2* : trifles. sir. *Q3,* ending the line at 'trifles.' and adding '(sir.' above on noticing the omission. 65 Troth,] Troth *Qq* ladie,] Ladie *Qq 1, 2* : Lady, *Q3* st. dir. not in *Qq.* 67 officious,] officious *Qq* 68 beauties: *Qq* : beauties. *Ff* pipe,] pipe *Qq* 69 *parenthesis,*] *parenthesis* *Qq* 71 god] God *Qq* 72 chamber,] chamber *Qq* 73 that,] that *Qq* thinke,] think *Qq* 74 rush,] rush *Qq* 76 this ayre,] Iesu *Qq* said,] said *Qq* 77 light:] light; *Qq*

ingenuitie, sweete mistresse, to—— Masse your violl's new
strung, methinkes.

He takes downe the violl, and playes betweene.

M A C I. Ingenuitie. I see his ignorance will not suffer him to slander her, which he had done most notably, if he had said wit, for ingenuitie, as he meant it.

F A S T. By the soule of musicke, ladie (*hum, hum.*)

S A V I. Would we might heare it once.

F A S T. I doe more adore, and admire your (*hum, hum*) predominant perfections, then (*hum, hum*) euer I shall haue power, and facultie to expresse (*hum.*)

S A V I. Vpon the violl *de Gambo*, you meane?

F A S T. It's miserably out of tune, by this hand.

S A V I. Nay, rather by the fingers.

M A C I. It makes good harmonie with her wit.

F A S T. Sweet ladie, tune it. Boy, some tabacco.

M A C I. Tabacco againe? he do's court his mistresse with verie exceeding good changes.

F A S T. Signior M A C I L E N T E, you take none, sir? (*Tab.*)

M A C I. No, vnlesse I had a Mistresse, signior, it were a great indecorum for me to take tabacco.

F A S T. How like you her wit? (*Tab.*)

M A C I. Her ingenuitie is excellent, sir.

F A S T. You see the subiect of her sweet fingers, there? (*Tab.*) Oh, shee tickles it so, that (*Tab.*) shee makes it laugh most diuinely; (*Tab.*) I'le tell you a good iest now, and your selfe shall say it's a good one: I haue wisht my selfe to be that instrument (I thinke) a thousand times, and not so few, by heauen (*Tab.*)

III. ix. 78 ingenuitie,] Ingenuitie *Qq*   mistresse,] Mistresse *Qq*   79 strung,] strung *Qq*   80 st. dir, *He . . . betweene.*] *Takes downe the Violl.* Qq in text after 79.   Ingenuitie.] *Ingenuitie;* Qq: Ingenuitie.! *F2*   81 her,] her ; *Qq*   82 wit,] *Wit* Qq   ingenuitie] *Ingenuitie* Qq   83 musicke,] Musicke *Qq*   85 adore,] adore *Qq*   86 predominant] predominate *Q3*   perfections,] perfections *Qq 1, 2*   then *Ff*: than *Qq*   87 power,] power *Qq*   88 *Gambo,*] *Gambo* Qq   90 Nay,] Nay *Qq 1, 2*   92 ladie,] Ladie *Qq*   Boy,] Boy *Qq 1, 2*   95 none,] none *Qq*   97 Mistresse,] mistresse *Qq*   100 excellent,] excellent *Qq, F1 originally*   101 subiect] subject *Qq*   fingers, *corr. F1, F2*: fingers *Qq, F1 originally*   102 Oh,] Oh *Qq*   103 iest] jeast *Qq 1, 2* : jest *Q3*   106 heauen] Heauens *Qq*

Euery Man out of his Humour 527

M A C I. Not vnlike, sir: but how? to be cas'd vp, and hung by on the wall?

F A S T. O, no, sir, to be in vse I assure you; as your iudicious eyes may testifie. (*Tab.*)

S A V I. Here, seruant, if you will play, come.

F A S T. Instantly, sweet ladie. (*Tab.*) In good faith, here's most diuine tabacco!

S A V I. Nay, I cannot stay to dance after your pipe.

F A S T. Good! nay, deare ladie, stay: by this sweete smoake, I thinke your wit be all fire. (*Tab.*)

M A C I. And, hee's the *Salamander* belongs to it.

S A V I. Is your tabacco perfum'd, seruant? that you sweare by the sweet smoke?

F A S T. Still more excellent! (before heauen, and these bright lights) I thinke (*Tab.*) you are made of ingenuitie, I. (*Tab.*)

M A C I. True, as your discourse is: ô abominable!

F A S T. Will your ladiship take any?

S A V I. O, peace I pray you; I loue not the breath of a woodcockes head.

F A S T. Meaning my head, ladie?

S A V I. Not altogether so, sir; but (as it were fatall to their follies that thinke to grace themselues with taking tabacco, when they want better entertainment) you see your pipe beares the true forme of a woodcockes head.

F A S T. O admirable *simile!*

S A V I. 'Tis best leauing of you in admiration, sir.

III. ix. 107 vnlike,] vnlike *Qq*   vp,] vp *Qq*   109 no,] no *Qq*   110 iudicious] judicious *Qq*   111 Here,] Here *Qq*   112 Instantly,] Instantly *Q1*   ladie. *corr.* F1, F2: Ladie *Qq*, F1   faith,] faith *Qq 1, 2*: fayth *Q3*   113 tabacco!] *Tabacco.* Qq   114 dance] Daunce *Qq*   115 Good! *corr.* F1, F2: Good, *Qq*, F1 *originally*   nay,] nay *Q1*: my *Qq 2, 3*   ladie,] Ladie *Qq*   116 fire. *Qq 2, 3, corr.* F1, F2: fire: *Q1*, F1 *originally*   117 And, *corr.* F1, F2: And *Qq*, F1   belongs to] that liues by *Qq*   118 perfum'd,] perfum'd *Qq*   seruant?] Sir? *Qq 1, 2*: sir, *Q3*   120 excellent!] excellent: *Qq*   (before] before *Qq 2, 3*   heauen] God *Qq*   121 lights)] Heauens) *Qq 1, 2*: Heauens, *Q3*   123 abominable] abhominable *Qq 1, 2*   126 a *om.* F3   128 altogether] altogither *Qq 1, 2*   so,] so *Qq*   132 FAST. *om.* Q3   *simile corr.* F1, F2: *Simile* Qq, F1 *originally*   133 of *not in Qq 2, 3*   Exit *Sauiolina.* Qq in text after 133

528   *Euery Man out of his Humour*

MACI. Are these the admired lady-wits, that hauing so
good a plaine-song, can runne no better diuision vpon it?
S'heart, all her iests are of the stampe, (*March* was fifteene
yeres ago.) Is this the Comet, Monsieur FASTIDIVS,
that your gallants wonder at so?

FAST. Hart of a gentleman, to neglect mee afore
presence thus! Sweet sir, I beseech you be silent in my
disgrace. By the *Muses*, I was neuer in so vile a humour
in my life, and her wit was at the floud too. Report it
not for a million, good sir; let me be so farre endear'd
to your loue.

GREX.

MIT. What followes next, signior CORDATVS?
this gallants humour is almost spent, me thinkes, it ebbes
apace, with this contrarie breath of his mistresse.

COR. O, but it will flow againe for all this, till there
come a generall drought of humour among all our actors,
and then, I feare not but his wil fall as low as any. See,
who presents himselfe here!

MIT. What, i' the old case?

COR. Yfaith, which makes it, the more pittifull, you
vnderstand where the *Scene* is?

III. ix. 134 admired] admirable *Q3*   135 it?] it. *Qq*   136
S'heart, *om. F2, F3*   iests] jests *Qq 1, 3* : jeasts *Q2*   stampe,]
stampe *Qq*   136-7 (*March . . . ago) corr. F1, F2* : *March . . . ago. Qq, F1
originally*   137 Comet, *corr. F1, F2* : *Comet* Qq : comet, *F1 originally*
139 gentleman,] Gentleman *Qq*   140 thus!] thus: *Qq*   141 disgrace.] disgrace, *Q1* : disgrace ; *Qq 2, 3,*   the *Muses*] Iesu *Qq*   was
neuer] neuer was *Qq*   humour] Humor *Qq*   142 too.] too, *Qq 1, 2* :
too : *Q3*   143 million,] million *Qq*   *Exeunt.* add *Qq*   145 next,]
next *Qq*   146 humour] Humor *Qq 1, 3*   spent,] spent *Qq*   149 hu-
mour] Humor *Qq*   150 then,] then *Qq*   See,] See *Qq*   151
here!] here? *Qq*   153 it,] it *Qq*   pittifull,] pittifull ; *Qq 2, 3, F2*

Act IIII. Scene I.

Fallace. Fvngoso.

WHy, are you so melancholy, brother?
    Fvng. I am not melancholy, I thanke you, sister.
  Fall. Why are you not merrie then? there are but two of vs in all the world, and if wee should not bee comforts one to another, god helpe vs.   5
  Fvng. Faith, I cannot tell, sister, but if a man had any true melancholy in him, it would make him melancholy, to see his yeomanly father cut his neighbours throats, to make his sonne a gentleman: and yet when he has cut 'hem, he will see his sonnes throat cut too, ere he make him a true 10 gentleman indeed, before death cut his owne throat. I must bee the first head of our house, and yet he will not giue me the head till I bee made so. Is any man term'd a gentleman that is not always i' the fashion? I would know but that.   15
  Fall. If you bee melancholy for that, brother, I thinke I haue as much cause to bee melancholy, as one: for I'le be sworne, I liue as little in the fashion, as any woman in *London*. By the faith of a Gentlewoman, (beast that I am to say it) I ha' not one friend i' the world besides my 20 husband. When saw you master Fastidivs Briske, brother?
  Fvng. But a while since, sister, I thinke: I know not well in truth. By this hand, I could fight with all my heart, me thinkes.   25

IV. i. *Act . . . Fvngoso.*] Actvs Qvartvs, Scena Prima. | *Enter Fungoso, Fallace following him.* Qq (Actus Quartus *Qq 1, 2*): ACT IV, scene I.—*A Room in Deliro's House.* G   1 Why,] *Fall.* Why *Qq* melancholy,] melancholy *Q1*: Melancholly *Q2*   2 melancholy,] melancholy *Q1*: melancholly *Q2*: melancholy, *Q3*   you,] you *Qq* 4 all *om. Q3*   5 one to] to one *Qq*   ano-|ther, god *corr. F1*: ano-| god *F1 originally*   god] God *Qq, F2*   6 tell,] tell *Qq*   8 throats,] throats *Qq*   9 his] is *some copies of Q3*   13 the head] the head, *Qq*   16 that,] that *Qq 1, 2*   17 one:] one; *Qq*: any one *F3*   18 sworne,] sworne *Qq*   19 By . . . Gentlewoman,] By the Bible of heauen *Qq*   20 ha'] haue *Qq*   21 master] Maister *Q1*   23 since,] since *Qq*   thinke:] thinke, *Qq*   24 By this hand,] By Gods lid *Qq*   heart,] heart *Qq 1, 2*

FALL. Nay, good brother, be not resolute.

FVNG. I sent him a letter, and he writes me no answere neyther.

FALL. Oh, sweete FASTIDIVS BRISKE! ô fine
30 courtier! thou art hee mak'st me sigh, and say, how blessed is that woman that hath a courtier to her husband! and how miserable a dame shee is, that hath neyther husband, nor friend i' the court! O, sweet FASTIDIVS! ô, fine courtier! How comely he bowes him in his court'sie!
35 how full hee hits a woman betweene the lips when hee kisses! how vpright hee sits at the table! how daintily he carues! how sweetly he talkes, and tels newes of this lord, and of that lady! how cleanely he wipes his spoone, at euery spoonfull of any whit-meat he eates, and what a neat case of
40 pick-tooths he carries about him, still! O, sweet FASTIDIVS! ô fine courtier!

Act IIII. Scene II.

DELIRO, MVSICIANS, MACILENTE,
FVNGOSO.

SEe, yonder shee is, gentlemen. Now (as euer you'll beare the name of musicians) touch your instruments sweetly, shee has a delicate eare, I tell you: play not a false note, I beseech you.

5 MVSI. Feare not, signior DELIRO.

IV. i. 26 Nay,] Nay *Qq*   29 Oh,] Oh *Qq*   BRISKE!] *Briske*, Qq
30 courtier!] *Courtier*, Qq   sigh,] sigh *Qq*   31 husband!] husband?
Qq   32 is,] is *Qq*   33 husband,] husband *Qq*   i' *corr. F1, F2* :
in *Qq, F1*   court!] *Court* : Qq 1, 2 : *Court* ? *Q3*   O,] O *Qq*   FASTIDIVS! ô,] *Fastidius*, O *Qq*   34 courtier!] *Courtier*. Qq   court'sie!
corr. F1, F2 : courtesie? *Qq, F1*   35 betweene *corr. F1, F2* : betwixt
Qq, F1   35-8 kisses! . . . table! . . . carues! . . . lady! *corr. F1, F2* :
kisses? . . . table? (Table? *Q1*) . . . carues? . . . Lady? (Ladie? *Q1*) *Qq,
F1*   38 spoone, *corr. F1, F2* : spoon *Qq 1, 2* : spoone *Q3, F1*   40
him, still!] him still? *Qq*   O,] Oh *Q1* : O *Qq 2, 3*   FASTIDIVS!] *Fastidius*, Qq   41 courtier!] *Courtier*! Qq 1, 2 : *Courtier*. *Q3*   IV. ii.
Act . . . FVNGOSO.] *Enter Deliro with Musitians*. (*Musicians*, *Q3*) Qq, without change of scene.   1 See,] *Deli*. See, *Qq* (See *Q1*)   is, gentlemen. Now] is Gentlemen, now *Qq*   you'le *corr. F1, F2* : you'le *Qq, F1
originally*   3 tell you : *corr. F1, F2* : tell you, *Qq, F1 originally*   note,] note *Qq*   5 not,] not *Qq 1, 2*

DELI. O, begin, begin, some sprightly thing: Lord, how my imagination labours with the successe of it. Well said, good yfaith! heauen grant it please her. I'le not be seene, for then shee'le be sure to dislike it.

FALL. Hey---da! this is excellent! I'le lay my life, this is my husbands dotage. I thought so; nay, neuer play peeke-boe with me, I know, you doe nothing but studie how to anger me, sir.

DELI. Anger thee, sweet wife? why didst thou not send for musicians to supper last night, thy selfe?

FALL. To supper, sir? now, come vp to supper, I beseech you: as though there were no difference between supper time, when folkes should be merry, and this time, when they would be melancholy? I would neuer take vpon me to take a wife, if I had no more iudgement to please her.

DELI. Be pleas'd, sweet wife, and they shall ha' done: and would to fate, my life were done, if I can neuer please thee.

MACI. Saue you, lady, where is master DELIRO?

DELI. Here, master MACILENTE: you are welcome from court, sir; no doubt you haue beene grac't exceedingly of master BRISKES Mistris, and the rest of the ladies, for his sake?

MACI. Alas, the poore *phantasticke*! hee's scarce knowne

IV. ii. 6 O,] O *Qq*   thing:] thing; *Qq*   7 it. Well] it: well *Qq*: it! Well *F2*   8 yfaith! *corr. F1, F2*: yfaith, *Qq, F1 originally* grant] graunt *Qq*   her. *corr. F1, F2*; her, *Qq 1, 2, F1 originally*: her: *Q3*   10 Hey---da!] Hey da, *Q1*: Heyda, *Q2*: Hayda, *Q3*   excellent!] excellent, *Qq 1, 2*: excellent: *Q3*   life,] life *Qq*   11 dotage.] dotage, *Qq 1, 2*   so; nay,] so, nay *Qq*   12 peeke-boe] boe-peep *F2, F3*   know,] know *Qq*   13 me,] me *Qq 1, 2*: mee *Q3*   14 why] why, *Qq 2, 3*   15 musicians] Musitians *Qq 1, 2*   night,] night *Qq*   16 supper, sir? now,] Supper sir? now (Sir? *Qq 2, 3*) *Qq*   supper,] Supper *Qq*   18 time, *corr. F1, F2*: time *Qq, F1 originally*   19 would] should *F2, F3*   20 iudgement] indgement *some copies of Q2*   21 pleas'd,] pleas'd *Qq*   done:] done, *F2*   22 fate,] Christ *Qq*   After 23 *Exit Musitians. Enter Macilente. Qq*   24 Saue you, lady,] God saue you Ladie; *Qq*   25 you are] you'r *Qq*   26 court, *corr. F1, F2*: the Court *Qq*: the court, *F1*   doubt] boubt *F2*   27 Mistris *corr. F1*: Mistresse *Qq*: mistris *F1 originally, F2*   ladies,] Ladies *Qq*   29 *phantasticke*!] Phantasticke, *Qq*

30 To any lady there ; and those that know him,
   Know him the simplest man of all they know :
   Deride, and play vpon his amorous humours,
   Though he but apishly doth imitate
   The gallant'st courtiers, kissing ladies pumps,
35 Holding the cloth for them, praising their wits,
   And seruilely obseruing euery one,
   May doe them pleasure : fearefull to be seene
   With any man (though he be ne're so worthy)
   That's not in grace with some, that are the greatest.
40 Thus courtiers doe, and these he counterfeits.
   But sets not such a sightly carriage
   Vpon their vanities, as they themselues ;
   And therefore they despise him : for indeed
   Hee's like the *Zani*, to a tumbler,
45 That tries tricks after him, to make men laugh.

   F A L L. Here's an vnthankfull spitefull wretch ! the good gentleman vouchsaft to make him his companion (because my husband put him into a few rags) and now see, how the vnrude rascall back-bites him !

50   D E L L. Is he no more grac't amongst 'hem, then ? say you ?

   M A C I. Faith, like a pawne, at *Chesse* : fills vp a roome, that's all.

   F A L L. O monster of men ! can the earth beare such
55 an enuious caytiffe ?

   D E L I. Well, I repent me, I e're credited him so much : but (now I see what he is, and that his masking vizor is off) I'le forbeare him no longer. All his lands are morgag'd to

---

iv. ii. 30 there ;] there : *Qq*   32 humours] Humors *Qq*   34 gallant'st] gallans't *Q1* : Gallans't *Qq 2, 3*   36 seruilely] seruily *Q3*
37 fearefull *corr. F1, F2* : Fearefull *Qq, F1 originally*   39 some,] some *Qq, F2*   40 counterfeits. *corr. F1* : counterfeits, *Qq, F1 originally, F2*   44 the] a *Qq*   Zani, *corr. F1, F2* : Zani *Qq, F1 originally*
45 him,] him *Qq 1, 2*   46 wretch !] wretch : *Qq*   48 a few] afew *Q3*
see,] see *Qq*   49 him ! *corr. F1, F2* : him. *Qq, F1 originally*   50
'hem, *corr. F1* : 'hem *Qq, F1 originally, F2*   52 Faith,] Faith *Qq*
pawne,] pawne *Qq, F2*   Chesse : *corr. F1, F2* : Chesse, *Qq, F1 originally*   roome] roume *Qq*   54 O *Qq, corr. F1, F2* : O, *F1 originally*
56 me, *corr. F1* : mee *Q1* : me *Qq 2, 3, F1 originally, F2*   58 longer.
All] longer : all *Q1* : longer. all *Q2* : longer, al *Q3*

me, and forfeited: besides, I haue bonds of his in my hand,
for the receit of now fifty pound, now a hundred, now two 60
hundred: still, as he has had a fan but wagg'd at him, he
would be in a new sute. Well, I'le salute him by a *Sergeant*,
the next time I see him, yfaith, I'le sute him.

MACI. Why, you may soone see him, sir, for hee is to
meet signior PVNTARVOLO at a *Notaries*, by the 65
Exchange, presently: where he meanes to take vp, vpon
returne———

FALL. Now, out vpon thee, IVDAS; canst thou not
be content to back-bite thy friend, but thou must betray
him? wilt thou seeke the vndoing of any man? and of such 70
a man too? and will you, sir, get your liuing by the counsell
of traytors?

DELI. Deare wife, haue patience.

FALL. The house will fall, the ground will open, and
swallow vs: I'le not bide here, for all the gold, and siluer 75
in heauen.

DELI. O, good MACILENTE, let's follow and
appease her, or the peace of my life is at an end.

MACI. Now pease, and not peace, feed that life, whose
head hangs so heauily ouer a womans manger. 80

FALL. Helpe me, brother: 'ods body, and you come *Deliro*
here, I'le doe my selfe a mischiefe. *follow's*
his wife.

DELI. Nay, heare me, sweet wife, vnlesse thou wilt
haue mee goe, I will not goe.

IV. ii. 59 hand, *corr. F1, F2*: hand *Qq, F1 originally* 60 fifty] xx
Qq a hundred] xxx *Qq* two hundred] xxv *Qq* 61 still, *corr. F1,
F2*: still *Qq, F1 originally* 63 see him, *corr. F1, F2*: see him *Qq,
F1 originally* 64 him,] him *Qq* 65 PVNTARVOLO] *Puntarvolo Qq 1,
2*: PUNTARVOLO, *F2* 65–6 *Notaries*, by the *Exchange*, presently:
corr. F1, F2: *Notaries* by the *Exchange* presently, *Qq, F1 originally*
66 vp,] vp *Qq* 67 returne———] returne. *Qq* 68 Now,] Now *Qq*
thee,] thee *Qq* 69 back-bite] backbite *Qq 1, 2* must] wilt *Qq 2, 3*
71 you, sir,] you Sir *Qq 1, 2*: you sir *Q3* 75 here, *corr. F1, F2*: here
Qq, F1 originally gold, *corr. F1*: Gold *Qq 1, 2, F1 originally*: gold
Q3, F2 76 *Exit.* add *Qq* 77 O,] O *Qq* 78 *Exit.* add *Qq* 79
pease] *Pease* Qq peace,] Peace *Qq* 80 *Exit.* add *Qq* st. dir. Deliro . . . *wife. corr.* F1, F2, not in F1 originally: *Enter Fallace running,
at another dore, and claps it too. (doore, . . . to.* Q3) *Qq* in text: SCENE II.
—*Another Room in the same. Enter Fallace and* Fungoso *running, she
claps to the door.* G (cf. 103). 81 me,] me *Qq 1, 2* 'ods body,] Gods
body *Qq* and] an' *F2* 83 me,] me *Qq* 84 *Within.* add *Qq*

534 *Euery Man out of his Humour*

85   FALL. Tut, you shall ne're ha' that vantage of me, to
say, you are vndone by me: I'le not bid you stay, I.
Brother, sweet brother, here's foure angels, I'le giue you
toward your sute: for the loue of gentry, and as euer you
came of christen creature, make haste to the water side (you
90   know where Master FASTIDIVS vses to land) and giue
him warning of my husbands malitious intent; & tel him
of that leane rascals trechery: O heuens! how my flesh
rises at him! nay, sweet brother, make haste: you may say,
I would haue writ to him, but that the necessitie of the time
95   would not permit. He cannot choose but take it extraordinarily from me: and commend me, to him, good
brother, say, I sent you.

FVNG. Let me see, these foure angels, and then, fortie
shillings more I can borrow on my gowne in *Fetter-lane*.
100 Well, I will goe presently, say on my sute, pay as much
money as I haue, and sweare my selfe into credit with my
taylor, for the rest.

Deliro,
and Ma-
cilente,
passe
ouer the
stage.

DELI. O, on my soule you wrong her, MACILENTE,
Though shee be froward, yet I know shee is honest.

MACI. Well, then haue I no iudgement: would any
woman (but one that were wild in her affections) haue broke
107 out into that immodest and violent passion against her
husband? or is't possible——

DELI. If you loue me, forbeare; all the arguments i'
110 the world shall neuer wrest my heart to beleeue it.

IV. ii. 86 say,] say *Qq*   88 sute: *corr. F1, F2* : Sute; *Qq* : sute;
F1 originally   gentry] Iesu *Qq*   89 christen] Christian *F3*   91
malitious *corr. F1, F2* : not in *Qq, F1 originally*   & tel *corr. F1* : and
tell *F1 originally*   92 heuens! *corr. F1* : Iesu, *Qq* : heauens! *F1
originally, F2*   93 him!] him? *Qq*   brother,] brother *Qq*   haste:]
hast; *Qq 1, 2* : haste, *Q3*   say,] say *Qq*   95 permit.] suffer it: *Qq*   96
me,] me *Qq*   him,] him *Qq 2, 3*   97 brother,] brother: *Qq* : brother;
F2   say,] say *Qq*   *Exit.* add *Qq*   98 see,] see; *Qq*   angels,]
Angels: *Qq*   then,] then *Qq, F2*   99 *Fetter-lane.* Well] Fetter-lane:
well *Qq*   100 say] sey *F2*   102 taylor,] Taylor *Qq*   *Exit.* add. *Qq*
103 st. dir. *Deliro . . . stage.*] SCENA SECVNDA. | *Enter Deliro, with Ma-
cilente, speaking as they passe | ouer the Stage.* (SECUNDA. *Qq 1, 2* :
Deliro *Q3*) *Qq* : SCENE III.—*Another Room in the same.* | *Enter* Deliro
and Macilente. G   105 iudgement:] Iudgement; *Q1* : judgement;
Q2 : iudgement; *Q3*   108 husband?] husband: *F2*   110 *Exeunt.*
add *Qq*

GREX.

Cor. How like you the decyphering of his dotage?

Mit. O, strangely! and of the others enuie too, that labours so seriously to set debate betwixt a man, and his wife. Stay, here comes the knight aduenturer.

Cor. I, and his scriuener with him. 115

Act IIII. Scene III.

PVNTARVOLO, NOTARIE, CARLO, SERVANTS.

I Wonder, Monsieur FASTIDIVS comes not! but, NOTARIE, if thou please to draw the indentures the while, I will giue thee thy instructions.

Nota. With all my heart, sir; and I'le fall in hand with 'hem presently. 5

Pvnt. Well then, first, the summe is to be vnderstood.

Nota. Good, sir.

Pvnt. Next, our seuerall appellations, and character of my dog, and cat, must be knowne: shew him the cat, sirrah.

Nota. So, sir. 10

Pvnt. Then, that the intended bound, is the *Turkes* court in *Constantinople*: the time limited for our returne, a yeere: and that if either of vs miscarry, the whole venter is lost. These are generall, conceiu'st thou? or if either of vs turne *Turke*. 15

Nota. I, sir.

Pvnt. Now for particulars: That I may make my

IV. ii. 112 strangely!] strangely; *Qq*   113 labours] labors *Q1* man,] man *Qq, F2*   IV. iii. *Act ... Servants.*] SCENA TERTIA. | *Enter Puntaruolo, Notarie, with Seruingmen.* (Puntarvolo *Qq* 1, 2: Seruingmen. Q1) *Qq*: SCENE IV.—Puntarvolo's *Lodgings.* | *Enter* Puntarvolo, Notary, *and Servants with the dog and cat.* G   1 I wonder,] *Punt.* I wonder *Qq*   Monsieur] Mounsieur *F2*   but,] but *Qq*   3 thy instructions] the *Theorie Qq*   4 heart,] heart *Qq*   5 with'hem *F1* presently] prseently *F2*   6 first,] first ; *Qq*   7 Good,] Good *Q1*   9 dog,] Dog *Qq* 1, 2, *F2* : Dogge *Q3*   cat,] Cat *Qq*   cat,] Cat *Qq* : cat *F2*   10 So,] So *Qq*   11 bound] Point *Qq*   13 venter] Venture *F3*   14 generall,] Generall ; *Qq*   16 I,] I *Qq*

trauails by sea or land, to my best liking: and that (hyring a coach for my selfe) it shall bee lawfull for my dog, or cat, 20 or both, to ride with me in the said coach.

N o t. Very good, sir.

P v n. That I may choose to giue my dogge, or cat fish, for feare of bones : or any other nutriment, that (by the iudgement of the most autenticall physicians, where I 25 trauaile) shall be thought dangerous.

N o t. Well, sir.

P v n. That (after the receit of his monie) he shall neyther in his own person, nor any other, eyther by direct or indirect meanes, as magicke, witchcraft, or other such 30 exoticke artes, attempt, practise, or complot anie thing, to the preiudice of mee, my dogge, or my cat : Neyther shall I vse the helpe of any such sorceries, or enchantments, as vnctions, to make our skinnes impenetrable, or to trauaile inuisible by vertue of a powder, or a ring, or to hang any 35 three-forked charme about my dogges necke, secretly conuey'd into his collar : (vnderstand you ?) but that all be performed, sincerely, without fraud, or imposture.

N o t. So, sir.

P v n. That (for testimonie of the performance) my selfe 40 am to bring thence a *Turkes* mustachio, my dogge a *Græcian* hares lip, and my cat the traine, or taile of a *Thracian* rat.

N o t. 'Tis done, sir.

iv. iii. 18 trauails] travels *F2*   land,] *Land* Qq   to] for *Qq 2, 3*   19–20 dog, or cat, or both,] Dog and Cat *Q1* : Cat and Dog *Qq 2, 3*   21 good,] good *Qq*   22 dogge,] Dog *Q1* : Dogge *Qq 2, 3*   cat *corr. F1, F2* : Cat *Qq* : cat, *F1 originally*   23 bones :] Bones, *Qq 1, 2* : bones, *Q3*   24 iudgement] judgement *Qq 1, 2*   autenticall] authenticall *F2*   physicians, *corr. F1* : *Physicians* Qq 1, 2 : *Phisicians* Q3 : physicians *F1 originally* : physitians, *F2*   25 trauaile] travell *F2*   26 Well,] Well *Qq*   28 nor] or *Q3*   29 meanes, *corr. F1, F2* : meanes ; *Qq, F1 originally*   magicke, *corr. F1, F2*: *Magique*, Qq 1, 2 : *Magicke*, Q3 : magicke *F1 originally*   30 thing,] thing *F2*   31 preiudice] prejudice *Qq 1, 2*   32 sorceries,] Sorceries *Qq* : sorceries *F2*   enchantments, *corr. F1* : Enchantments ; *Qq* : enchantments ; *F1 originally* : inchantments, *F2*   36 (vnderstand you ?) *corr. F1, F2* : vnderstand you ? *Qq, F1 originally*   be *Q1, corr. F1, F2* : bee *Qq 2, 3, F1 originally*   37 fraud, *corr. F1* : fraud *Qq, F1 originally, F2*   38 So,] So *Qq*   41 *Græcian* not in Qq   traine, *corr. F1* : traine *Qq, F1 originally, F2*   42 *Thracian* not in Qq   43 done,] done *Qq*

Euery Man out of his Humour 537

Pvn. 'Tis said, sir, not done, sir: but forward. That vpon my returne, and landing on the Tower-wharfe, with the aforesaid testimonie, I am to receiue fiue for one, according to the proportion of the summes put forth.

Not. Well, sir.

Pvn. Prouided, that if before our departure, or setting forth, either my selfe, or these be visited with sicknesse, or any other casuall euent, so that the whole course of the aduenture bee hindered, thereby; that then, he is to returne, and I am to receiue the prenominated proportion, vpon faire and equall termes.

Not. Verie good, sir, is this all?

Pvn. It is all, sir: and dispatch them, good Notarie.

Not. As fast as is possible, sir.

Pvn. O, Carlo! welcome: saw you Monsieur Briske?

Car. Not I: did he appoint you, to meet here?

Pvn. I, and I muse he should be so tardie: hee is to take an hundred pounds of mee in venter, if he maintaine his promise.

Car. Is his houre past?

Pvn. Not yet, but it comes on apace.

Car. Tut, be not iealous of him: he will sooner breake all the commandements, then his houre, vpon my life, in such a case trust him.

Pvn. Me thinkes, Carlo, you looke verie smooth, ha?

iv. iii. 44 said, sir, *corr. F1, F2* : said Sir, *Qq* : said, sir: *F1 originally* done, sir :] done sir, *Q1* : done sir ; *Qq 2, 3* 45 returne,] returne *Qq* Tower-wharfe,] Tower wharfe *Qq 1, 2* : Towre wharfe, *Q3* 48 Well,] Well *Qq* 49 Pvn.] *Puue. Q1* that *Qq 2, 3, corr. F1, F2* : That *Q1, F1 originally* departure, *corr. F1, F2* : departure *Qq, F1 originally* 52 hindered, *corr. F1* : hindred *Qq* : hindered *F1 originally, F2* 55 good,] good *Qq* sir, *corr. F1, F2* : sir ; *Qq, F1 originally* 56 all,] all *Qq* sir :] Sir ; *Q2* : sir ; *Q3* them,] them *Qq* 57 possible,] possible *Qq* *Exit. Enter Carlo.* add *Qq* 58 O,] O *Qq, F2* Carlo! *corr. F1, F2* : Carlo, *Qq* : Carlo, *F1 originally* Monsieur] Mounsier *Q3* : Mounsier *F2* 60 you,] you *Qq* 62 venter] venture *Q3* : Venture *F3* 66 iealous] iealous *Qq 1, 2* him: *corr. F1, F2* : him; *Qq, F1 originally* 67 the commandements] the ten Commaundements *Q1* : the ten Commaundements *Q2* : the tenne Commandements *Q3* then] than *Qq, F2* houre, *corr. F1* : Houre ; *Qq* : houre ; *F1 originally, F2* life,] life *Qq* 69 thinkes,] thinkes *Qq* smooth ! *corr. F1, F2* : smooth ? *Qq 1, 2, F1 originally* : smoothe : *Q3*

70   C A R. Why, I come but now from a hot-house, I must needes looke smooth.

P v n. From a hot-house!

C A R. I, doo you make a wonder on't? why it's your only physicke. Let a man sweate once a weeke in a hot-
75 house, and be well rub'd, and froted, with a good plumpe juicie wench, and sweet linnen : hee shall ne're ha' the poxe.

P v n t. What, the *French* poxe?

C a r l. The *French* poxe! our poxe. S'bloud we haue 'hem in as good forme as they, man : what?
80   P v n t. Let mee perish, but thou art a salt one! was your new-created gallant there with you? S o g l i a r d o?

C a r l. O, porpuse! hang him, no : hee's a lieger at *Hornes* ordinarie yonder : his villanous G a n i m e d e, and he ha' beene droning a tabacco pipe there, euer sin' yester-
85 day noone.

P v n t. Who? signior T r i p a r t i t e, that would giue my dogge the *Whiffe*?

C a r l. I, hee. They haue hir'd a chamber, and all priuate to practise in, for the making of the *Patoun*, the
90 *Receit reciprocall*, and a number of other mysteries, not yet extant. I brought some dozen, or twentie gallants this morning to view 'hem (as you'ld doe a piece of *Perspectiue*) in at a key-hole : and there wee might see S o g l i a r d o sit in a chaire, holding his snowt vp like a sow vnder an
95 apple-tree, while th' other open'd his nostrils with a poking-sticke, to giue the smoke a more free deliuerie. They had spit some three, or fourescore ounces betweene 'hem, afore we came away.

    iv. iii. 70 Why,] Why *Qq 1, 2, F2*   72 hot-house!] Ho₋ouse? *Qq 1, 2* : Hot-house? *Q3*   75 rub'd,] rubd *Qq*   froted,]   ted *Qq* 76 juicie] iuicie *Q3*   linnen :] linnen, *Q1* : Linnen, *Qq 2,*   ha'] ha *F2*   77 What,] What ? *Qq*   78 our poxe.] our P₋   *Qq* S'bloud *om. F2*   79 they,] they *Qq*   80 salt one !] Villain₋ 81 your] yonr *Q1*   82 O, porpuse !] O *Porpuse*, Qq   83 G₋ mede,] *Ganimede* Qq : Ganimede *F2*   84 beene] been *Q1* : ben bin *Q3*   88 hee. They] hee : they *Qq 1, 2* : he : they *Q3*   chamb₋ *corr. F1, F2* : chamber *Qq, F1 originally*   89 priuate] priuat *Qq 1,* 91 dozen,] dosen *Qq*   93 -hole :] -hole ; *Qq*   97, 99 three,] three *Qq, F2*   98 away. *Qq, corr. F1, F2* : awaie *F1 originally*

Pvnt. How? spit three, or fourescore ounces?

Carl. I, and preseru'd it in porrengers, as a barber does 100 his bloud, when he opens a veine.

Pvnt. Out, *Pagan*: how dost thou open the veine of thy friend?

Carl. Friend? Is there any such foolish thing i'the world? ha? S'lid I ne're rellisht it yet. 105

Pvnt. Thy humour is the more dangerous.

Carl. No, not a whit, Signior: Tut, a man must keepe time in all. I can oyle my tongue when I meet him next, and looke with a good slicke fore-head; 'twill take away all soyle of suspicion, and that's ynough: what Lynceus 110 can see my heart? Pish, the title of a friend, it's a vaine idle thing, only venerable among fooles: you shall not haue one that has any opinion of wit affect it.

Act IIII. Scene IIII.

To them.

Deliro, Macilente.

Saue you, good sir Pvntarvolo.

Pvnt. Signior Deliro! welcome.

Deli. Pray you, sir, did you see Master Fastidius Briske? I heard he was to meet your worship here.

Pvnt. You heard no figment, sir, I doe expect him at 5 euery pulse of my watch.

Deli. In good time, sir.

Carl. There's a fellow now, lookes like one of the *Patricians* of *Sparta*, mary his wit's after tenne i' the hundred.

IV. iii. 99 How? *corr. F1*: How! *Qq, F1, F2* 101 bloud,] Blood *Qq 1, 2* opens] pricks *Qq* 102 Out, *Pagan*:] Out *Pagan*; *Qq* open] pricke *Qq 1, 2* 106 humour] Humor *Qq* dangerous] daungerous *Qq 1, 2* 107 No,] No *Qq* whit,] whit *Qq* 108 all.] all: *Qq* next,] next; *F2* 109 fore-head] forehead *Qq* IV. iv. *Act*. . . . Macilente.] *Enter Deliro, and Macilente.* (*Deliro* Qq 2, 3) *Qq*, without change of scene: Q1 after, Qq 2, 3 add to, iii. 113. *To them.* not in *Qq* 1 Saue you,] *Deli.* Saue you *Qq* Pvntarvolo] Puntaruolo *Qq* 3 you,] you *Qq* 5 Pvnt.] *Puut. Q1* figment,] Figment *Qq* 5–6 at euery . . . watch] euery minute my Watch strikes *Qq* 7 time,] time *Qq* 9 hundred.] hundred : *F2*

10 A good bloud-hound, a close-mouth'd dogge, he followes the sent well, mary he's at a fault now, me thinkes.

PVNT. I should wonder at that creature is free from the danger of thy tongue.

CARL. O, I cannot abide these limmes of sattin, or
15 rather *Sathan* indeed, that'll walke (like the children of darknesse) all day in a melancholy shop, with their pockets full of blankes, readie to swallow vp as manie poore vnthrifts, as come within the verge.

PVNT. So! and what hast thou for him that is with
20 him, now?

CARL. O, (dam' mee) *Immortalitie*! I'le not meddle with him, the pure element of fire, all spirit, extraction.

PVNT. How, CARLO? ha, what is he, man?

CARL. A scholler, MACILENTE, doe you not know
25 him? a lanke raw-bon'd anatomie, he walkes vp and downe like a charg'd musket, no man dares encounter him: that's his rest there.

PVNT. His rest? why has he a forked head?

CARL. Pardon me, that's to be suspended, you are too
30 quicke, too apprehensiue.

DELI. Troth (now I thinke on't) I'le deferre it till some other time.

MACI. Not, by any meanes, signior, you shall not lose this opportunitie, he will be here presently now.

35 DELI. Yes faith, MACILENTE, 'tis best. For looke you, sir, I shall so exceedingly offend my wife in't, that——

MACI. Your wife? now for shame lose these thoughts, and become the master of your owne spirits. Should I (if I had a wife) suffer my selfe to be thus passionately
40 carried (to and fro) with the streame of her humour? and

IV. iv. 10 A] a *F2*   close-mouth'd] close mouth'd *Qq*   11 now,] now *Qq*   13 danger] daunger *Qq 1, 2*   14 O,] O *Qq*   19 So!] So: *Qq*   20 him,] him *Qq*   21 O, (dam'] O (Damne *Qq*   *Immortalitie*!] *Immortalitie*, Qq   23 How,] How *Qq*   he,] he *Qq 1, 2* : hee *Q3*   25 raw-bon'd] rawbon'd *Q1*   33 Not,] Gods-pretious, not *Qq 1, 2* : Gods precious, not *Q3*   meanes,] meanes *Qq*   lose] loose *Qq 1, 2*   35 faith,] faith *Qq*   36 you,] you *Qq*   offend my] offendmy *Q3*   37 lose] loose *Qq*   40 humour] Humor *Qq*

neglect my deepest affaires, to serue her affections ? S'light I would geld my selfe first.

D E L I. O but, signior, had you such a wife as mine is, you would—

M A C I. Such a wife ? Now hate mee, sir, if euer I discern'd any wonder in your wife, yet, with all the speculation I haue : I haue seene some that ha' béene thought fairer then she, in my time ; and I haue seene those, ha' not been altogether so tall, esteem'd properer women ; and I haue seen lesse noses grow vpon sweeter faces, that haue done verie well too, in my iudgement : but in good faith, signior, for all this, the gentlewoman is a good pretie proud hardfauour'd thing, mary not so peerelessely to bee doted vpon, I must confesse : nay, be not angrie.

D E L I. Well, sir, (how euer you please to forget your selfe) I haue not deseru'd to bee thus plai'd vpon, but henceforth, pray you forbeare my house, for I can but faintly endure the sauour of his breath at my table, that shall thus iade me for my courtesies.

M A C I. Nay, then, signior, let me tell you, your wife is no proper woman, and, by my life, I suspect her honestie, that's more, which you may likewise suspect (if you please :) doe you see ? Ile vrge you to nothing, against your appetite, but if you please, you may suspect it.

D E L I. Good, sir.

M A C I. Good sir ? Now horne vpon horne pursue thee, thou blinde egregious dotard.

C A R L. O, you shall heare him speake like enuie. Signior

IV. iv. 41 S'light] Sbloud *Qq*   43 but,] but *Qq*   44 would] wold *Qq*   45 hate mee,] God hate mee *Qq*   46 wife,] wife *Qq*   47 beene] ben *Q2* : bin *Q3*   48 then] than *Qq, F2*   49 properer] proper *Qq*   50 noses] Roses *F3, owing to imperfect printing of the* n *in F2*   51 too,] too *Qq*   iudgement] judgement *Qq 1, 2*   faith, signior,] faith Signior *Qq*   53 peerelessly] peerelesse *Q3*   54 nay,] nay *Qq 1, 2*   55 Well,] Well *Qq*   sir,] sir *Qq 1, 2*   56 vpon,] vpon. *F2 (a misprinted colon ?)* : upon ; *F3*   58 sauour] sauor *Qq* .   59 iade] jade *Qq*   60 Nay, then,] Nay then *Qq*   61 woman, and, by my life,] woman by *Iesu*, and *Qq*   63 nothing,] nothing *Qq*   65 Good,] Good *Qq*   *Exit.* add *Qq*   68 O,] O *Qq*   enuie] ennie *F1*

MACILENTE, you saw monsieur BRISKE lately?
I heard you were with him at court.
   MACI. I, BVFFONE, I was with him.
   CARL. And how is he respected there? (I know youle deale ingenuously with vs) is he made of amongst the sweeter sort of gallants?
   MACI. Faith I, his ciuet and his casting-glasse,
Haue helpt him to a place amongst the rest:
And there, his *Seniors* giue him good sleight lookes,
After their garbe, smile, and salute in *French*
With some new complement.
   CARL. What, is this all?
   MACI. Why say, that they should shew the frothie foole,
Such grace, as they pretend comes from the heart,
He had a mightie wind-fall out of doubt.
Why, all their *Graces* are not to doe grace
To vertue, or desert: but to ride both
With their guilt spurres quite breathlesse, from themselues.
'Tis now esteem'd *Precisianisme* in wit;
And a disease in nature, to be kind
Toward desert, to loue, or seeke good names:
Who feeds with a good name? who thriues with louing?
Who can prouide feast for his owne desires,
With seruing others? ha, ha, ha:
'Tis folly, by our wisest worldlings prou'd,
(If not to gaine by loue) to be belou'd.
   CARL. How like you him? is't not a good spitefull slaue? ha?
   PVNT. Shrewd, shrewd.
   CARL. Dam'me, I could eat his flesh now: diuine sweet villaine!

IV. iv. 69 MACILENTE,] *Macilente* Qq 2, 3   monsieur] Mounsieur *Qq 1, 2*   70 court] the Court *Qq*   71 I,] I *Qq*   73 ingenuously] ingeniously *Qq*: ingenously *F3*   76 rest:] rest, *Qq*   77 there,] there *Qq*   80 What,] What *Qq*   82 grace,] grace *Qq*   84 Why,] Why *Qq*   86 breathlesse,] breathlesse *Qq*   87 wit;] wit, *F2*   88 disease] Diseasure *Qq 2, 3*   nature,] *Nature* Qq   89 names:] names. *F2*   90 louing]. longing *Qq 2, 3*   93 folly,] follie *Qq 1, 2*: folly *Q3*   prou'd,] prou'd *Qq*   98 Dam'me] Damme me *Q1*: Dam me *Q2*: Damne me *Q3*   diuine] Deuine *Qq 1, 2*   99 villaine!] villaine. *Q1*: villain. *Qq 2, 3*

M A C I. Nay, pr'y thee leaue : what's he there? 100

C A R L. Who? this i'the starcht beard? it's the dull stiffe knight P V N T A R V O L O, man ; hee's to trauaile now presently : hee has a good knottie wit, marry he carries little o't out of the land, with him.

M A C I. How then? 105

C A R L. He puts it forth in venter, as hee does his monie ; vpon the returne of a dogge, and cat.

M A C I. Is this he?

C A R L. I, this is hee ; a good tough gentleman : hee lookes like a shield of brawne, at *Shrouetide*, out of date, and 110 readie to take his leaue : or a drie poule of ling vpon *Easter-eue*, that has furnisht the table, all *Lent*, as he has done the citie this last vacation.

M A C I. Come, you'le neuer leaue your stabbing *simile's* : I shall ha' you ayming at me with 'hem by and by, but—— 115

C A R L. O, renounce me then : pure, honest, good *deuill*, I loue thee aboue the loue of women : I could e'en melt in admiration of thee, now ! gods so, looke here, man ; Sir D A G O N E T, and his squire !

Act IIII.   Scene V.

SOGLIARDO, SHIFT. *To them.*

SAue you, my deare *Gallanto's* : nay, come approch, good C A V A L I E R : pr'y thee (sweet knight) know this gentleman, hee's one that it pleases mee to vse as my good friend, and companion ; and therefore doe him good offices : I beseech you, gentles, know him, know him all ouer. 5

IV. iv. 102 PVNTARVOLO] *Puntaruolo* Qq 1, 2 : *Puntaruolo* Q3   104 o't] on't *Qq*   land,] land *Qq*   106 venter] venture, *Q3, F3*   107 dogge,] Dog *Qq*   110 shield] Chine *Qq*   brawne,] Brawne *Qq*   111 vpon] npon *F2*   112 table, *corr. F1* : Table *Qq 1, 2* : table *Q3, F1 originally, F2*   115 'hem] hem *Q2*   118 thee, now !] thee now : *Qq* gods so] Gods so' *Qq*   here,] here *Qq*   119 DAGONET,] *Dagonet* Qq squire !] Squire. *Qq 1, 2* : Esquire. *Q3*   IV. v. *Act . . . SHIFT.*] *Enter Sog. and Shift. Qq add to* iv. 119, *without change of scene.   To them.* add *Ff*   1 Saue you,] *Sog.* Saue you *Qq*   *Gallanto's Qq, corr. F1* : GALLANTO'S *F1 originally, F2*   approch] approach *Qq, F2*   4 friend,] friend *Qq*   5 you,] you *Qq*   gentles] Gentiles *F3*   know him all ouer. *not in Qq*

PVNT. Sir (for signior SOGLIARDO'S sake) let it suffice, I know you.

SOGL. Why (as I am true gentleman) I thanke you, knight, and it shall suffice. Harke you, sir PVNTAR-
10 VOLO, you'ld little thinke it; he's as resolute a peece of flesh, as any is i' the world.

PVNT. Indeed, sir?

SOGL. Vpon my gentilitie, sir: CARLO, a word with you. Doe you see that same fellow, there?

15 CARL. What? CAVALIER SHIFT?

SOGL. O, you know him, crie you mercy: before me, I thinke him the tallest man, liuing within the walls of *Europe*.

CARL. The walls of *Europe*! take heed what you say,
20 signior, *Europe's* a huge thing within the walls.

SOGL. Tut, (and 'twere as huge againe) I'ld iustifie what I speake. S'lid, he swagger'd e'en now in a place, where we were: I neuer saw a man doe it more resolute.

CARL. Nay, indeede swaggering is a good argument of
25 resolution. Doe you heare this, signior?

MACI. I, to my griefe. O, that such muddy flags,
For euery drunken flourish, should atchieue
The name of manhood: whil'st true perfect valour
(Hating to shew it selfe) goes by despis'd!
30 Heart, I doe know now (in a faire iust cause)
I dare doe more then he, a thousand times:
Why should not they take knowledge of this? ha?
And giue my worth allowance before his?

IV. v. 8 (as I am true gentleman) *F1* : (as I am a gentleman) *F2, F3* : by Iesu, *Qq*   8, 9 you,] you *Qq*   9 PVNTARVOLO] *Puntarvolo* Qq 1, 2   11 flesh,] flesh *Qq*   any is *corr. F1*: any's *Qq, F1 originally*: any *F2*   12 Indeed,] Indeed *Qq 1, 2*: Indeede *Q3*   13 gentilitie,] Gentilitie *Qq*   14 you. *corr. F1*: you; *Qq, F1 originally, F2*   fellow,] fellow *Qq*   16 O,] O *Q3*   him, *corr. F1*: him; *Qq, F1 originally, F2*   me] God *Qq*   17 man,] man *Qq*   19 say,] say *Qq*   21 and] an *F2*   iustifie] iustifie *Qq 1, 2*   22 S'lid,] S'lid *Qq 1, 2*   place, *corr. F1*: place *Qq, F1 originally, F2*   24 Nay,] Nay *Qq 1, 2*   26 O,] O *Qq*   flags,] Flags *Qq*   27 flourish] florish *Q1*   28 manhood: *corr. F1*: *Manhood*; *Qq*: manhood; *F1 originally, F2*   29 despis'd !] despis'd. *Qq*   30 Heart] Sbloud *Qq*   iust] just *Qq 1, 2*   31 then] than *Qq 1, 2, F2*   he,] hee; *Qq 1, 2*: hee *Q3*

Because I cannot swagger! Now the poxe
Light on your *Pickt-hatch* prowesse.

SOGL. Why, I tell you, sir, he has beene the only *Bidstand* that euer kept *New-market, Salisbury-plaine, Hockley* i' the hole, *Gads-Hill*; all the high places of any request: he has had his mares and his geldings, he, ha' been worth fortie, threescore, a hundred pound a horse, would ha' sprung you ouer hedge, and ditch, like your grey-hound, he has done fiue hundred robberies in his time, more or lesse, I assure you.

PVNT. What? and scapt?

SOGL. Scapt! yfaith I: he has broken the jayle when he has beene in yrons, and yrons; and beene out, and in againe; and out, and in; fortie times, and not so few, he.

MACI. A fit trumpet, to proclaime such a person.

CARL. But can this be possible?

SHIFT. Why, 'tis nothing, sir, when a man giues his affections to it.

SOGL. Good PYLADES, discourse a robberie, or two, to satisfie these gentlemen of thy worth.

SHIFT. Pardon me, my deare ORESTES: Causes haue their *quiddits*, and 'tis ill iesting with bell-ropes.

CARL. How? PYLADES, and ORESTES?

SOGL. I, he is my PYLADES, and I am his ORESTES: how like you the conceite?

CARL. O, it's an old stale enterlude deuice: No, I'le giue you names my selfe, looke you, he shall be your IVDAS, and you shall bee his Elder tree, to hang on.

MACI. Nay, rather, let him be captaine POD, and this his *Motion*; for he does nothing but shew him.

IV. v. 34 swagger!] swagger. *Qq*   36 Why,] Why *Qq*   you,] you *Qq*   36–7 Bid-stand] Bidstand Qq 2, 3   37 euer] euer was, *Qq*   Salisbury-plaine] Salisburie Plaine *Qq*   39 geldings,] Geldings *Qq*   41 hedge, and ditch,] hedge and ditch *Qq*   grey-hound,] Greyhound: *Qq*: grey-hound; *F2*   45 jayle] iayle *Q3*   47 times,] times *Qq*   48 trumpet,] Trumpet *Qq*   50 Why,] why *Q1*: Why *Q2*   nothing,] nothing *Qq*   52, 56 PYLADES,] *Pylades* Qq   robberie,] Robberie *Qq*   54 me,] me *Qq 1, 3*: mee *Q2*   55 iesting] jesting *Qq 1, 2*   60 selfe,] selfe: *Qq*   61 tree,] tree *Qq*   62 Nay,] Nay *Qq 1, 2*

546 *Euery Man out of his Humour*

CARL. Excellent: or thus, you shall bee HOLDEN,
65 and hee your Camel.

SHIFT. You doe not meane to ride, gentlemen?

PVNT. Faith, let me end it for you, gallants: you shall
be his *Countenance*, and he your *Resolution*.

SOGL. Troth, that's pretty: how say you, *Caualier*,
70 shalt be so?

CARL. I, I, most voices.

SHIFT. Faith, I am easily yeelding to any good impressions.

SOGL. Then giue hands, good *Resolution*.

75 CARL. Masse, he eannot say, good *Countenance*, now
(properly) to him againe.

PVNT. Yes, by an *irony*.

MACI. O, sir, the countenance of *Resolution* should, as
he is, be altogether grim, and vnpleasant.

Act IIII. Scene VI.

To them.   FASTIDIVS BRISKE.

Good houres make musicke with your mirth, gentlemen,
and keepe time to your humours: how now, CARLO?

PVNT. Monsieur BRISKE! many a long looke haue
I extended for you, sir.

5   FAST. Good faith, I must craue pardon; I was inuited
this morning ere I was out of my bed, by a beuie of ladies, to
a banquet: whence it was almost one of HERCVLES
labours for me, to come away, but that the respect of my
promise did so preuaile with me. I know they'le take it very

IV. v. 64 thus,] thus; *Qq*   66 ride,] ride *Qq*   67 Faith,] Faith *Qq*
you,] you *Qq*   69 Troth,] Troth *Qq*   you,] you *Qq*   72 Faith,]
Faith *Qq*   easily] eas'ly *Qq 1, 2*   74 hands,] hands *Qq*   75
Masse,] Masse *Qq*   say,] say *Qq*   Countenance,] Countenance Qq
78 O,] O *Qq*   79 he is, be] hee's *Qq*   altogether] altogither *Q1*   grim,]
grim *Qq*   IV. vi. *Act* . . . BRISKE.] *Enter Briske*. Qq, added to
v. 79 without change of scene.   *To them*. corr. F1, F2: not in Qq, F1
originally   1 Good] *Fast*. Good *Qq*   houres] houres, *F2*   mirth,]
mirth *Qq*   2 time] times *Qq 2, 3*   humours] humors *Qq*   now,] now
Qq   4 you,] you *Qq*   5 faith,] faith *Qq*   8 labours] Labors *Qq 1, 2*
me,] me *Qq 1, 2*: mee *Q3*   9 me.] me: *Qq*

Euery Man out of his Humour 547

ill, especially one, that gaue me this bracelet of her haire 10
but ouer-night, and this pearle another gaue me from her
fore-head, mary, shee———what ? are the writings ready ?

P v n t. I will send my man to know. Sirrah, goe you to
the *Notaries*, and learne if he be readie : leaue the dog, sir.

F a s t. And how does my rare qualified friend, S o g l i- 15
a r d o ? oh, signior M a c i l e n t e ! by these eyes, I saw
you not, I had saluted you sooner else, o' my troth : I hope,
sir, I may presume vpon you, that you will not diuulge my
late checke, or disgrace (indeéd) sir.

M a c i. You may, sir. 20

C a r l. S'heart, he knowes some notorious iest by this
gull, that hee hath him so obsequious.

S o g l. Monsieur F a s t i d i v s, doe you see this
fellow there ? does he not looke like a clowne ? would you
thinke there were any thing in him ? 25

F a s t. Any thing in him ? beshrow me, I : the fellow
hath a good ingenious face.

S o g l. By this element, he is as ingenious a tal man, as
euer swagger'd about *London* : he, and I, call *Countenance*,
and *Resolution*, but his name is C a v a l i e r S h i f t. 30

P v n t. C a v a l i e r, you knew signior C l o g, that
was hang'd for the robbery, at *Harrow* o' the hill ?

S o g l. Knew him, sir ! why, 'twas hee gaue all the
directions for the action.

P v n t. How ? was it your proiect, sir ? 35

S h i f t. Pardon me, *Countenance,* you doe me some

iv. vi. 10 one,] one *Qq* of] off *Q3* 11 ouer-night] ouer night *Qq*
12 fore-head, mary,] forehead, Mary *Qq* the] these *Q3* 14 dog,] Dog
Qq After 14 *Exit Seruingman.* (*Seruing-man.* Q1) *Qq* 15 friend,]
friend *Qq* 16 oh,] oh *Qq* eyes,] eyes *Qq* 17 else, o'] else on *Qq*
17–18 hope, sir,] hope sir *Qq* 18 you,] you *Qq* diuulge] divulge *Qq*
19 disgrace (indeed) *corr. F1, F2* : disgrace indeed (indeede *Q3*) *Qq* : disgrace, indeed, *F1 originally* 20 may,] may *Qq* 21 S'heart,] S'heart
Qq : om. *F2* iest] jest *Qq* 23 Monsieur] Mounsieur *Q2* 25 there
were *corr. F1, F2* : there's *Qq, F1 originally* 26 beshrow] beshrew
Q3 I : *corr. F1, F2* : I ; *Qq, F1 originally* 28 as ingenious a *corr.
F1, F2* : an ingenious *Qq, F1 originally* man,] man *Qq* 29 he,
and I,] hee and I *Qq* Countenance,] *Countenance Qq* 32 robbery,
corr. F1, F2 : robberie *Qq* : robbery *F1 originally* o'] on *Qq* 33
him,] him *Qq* why,] why *Qq* 35 was it *corr. F1, F2* : was't *Qq,
F1 originally* proiect,] Project *Qq* 36 me,] me *Q1* : mee *Qq 2, 3*

N n 2

wrong to make occasions publike, which I imparted to you in priuate.

S o g l. Gods will! here are none but friends, *Resolution*.

40 S h i f t. That's all one; things of consequence must haue their respects: where, how, and to whom. Yes, sir, hee shewed himselfe a true C l o g in the coherence of that affaire, sir: for, if he had manag'd matters as they were corroborated to him, it had beene better for him by a fortie,
45 or fiftie score of pounds, sir, and he himselfe might ha' liu'd (in despight of fates) to haue fed on wood-cocks, with the rest: but it was his heauie fortune to sinke, poore C l o g, and therefore talke no more of him.

P v n t. Why, had he more aiders, then?

50 S o g l. O god, sir! I, there were some present there, that were the nine *Worthies* to him, yfaith.

S h i f t. I, sir, I can satisfie you at more conuenient conference: but (for mine owne part) I haue now reconcil'd my selfe to other courses, and professe a liuing out of my
55 other qualities.

S o g l. Nay, he has left all now (I assure you) and is able to liue like a gentleman, by his quality. By this dogge, hee has the most rare gift in tabacco, that euer you knew.

C a r l. S'heart, hee keepes more adoe with this monster,
60 then euer B a n k e s did with his horse, or the fellow with the elephant.

M a c i. He will hang out his picture shortly, in a cloth, you shall see.

S o g l. O, hee do's manage a quarrell, the best that euer
65 you saw, for termes, and circumstances.

iv. vi. 37 occasions *corr.* F1, F2: that Qq, F1 *originally*.   38 priuate] priuat Qq 1, 2   39 will!] will Qq 2, 3   friends,] friends Qq   41 respects:] respects, Qq   Yes,] Yes Qq   43 affaire,] affaire Qq   for, *corr.* F1, F2: for Qq, F1 *originally*   44 fortie,] fortie Qq   45 pounds,] pounds Qq   46 fates] Fate Qq   wood-cocks,] *Woodcockes* Qq 1, 2: *Woodcocks* Q3   47 fortune] fortunes Qq   sinke,] sinke Qq   49 Why] why Q1   more] no more Q3   aiders,] Agents Qq   50 god, sir!] God sir; Qq   51 him,] him Qq   52 I, sir] I sir Qq   53 reconcil'd] reconci'ld Q3   57 gentleman,] Gentleman Qq   quality] qualities F2   58 tabacco,] *Tabacco* Qq   59 S'heart, *om.* F2   60 then] than Qq, F2   62 shortly,] shortly Qq   cloth] cloath Qq 1, 2   64 quarrell,] quarrell Qq   65 termes,] Termes Qq 1, 2: termes Q3, F2

FAST. Good faith, signior, (now you speake of a quarrell) I'le acquaint you with a difference, that happened betweene a gallant, and my selfe—sir PVNTARVOLO, you know him if I should name him, signior LVCVLENTO.

PVNT. LVCVLENTO! what in-auspicious chance interpos'd it selfe to your two loues?

FAST. Faith, sir, the same that sundred AGAMEMNON, and great THETIS sonne; but let the cause escape, sir: Hee sent mee a challenge (mixt with some few braues) which I restor'd, and in fine we met. Now indeed, sir, (I must tell you) he did offer at first very desperately, but without iudgement: for looke you, sir. I cast my selfe into this figure: now he, comes violently on, and withall aduancing his rapier to strike, I thought to haue tooke his arme (for he had left his whole body to my election, and I was sure he could not recouer his guard) Sir, I mist my purpose in his arme, rasht his doublet sleeue, ran him close by the left cheek, and through his haire. He againe, lights me here (I had on, a gold cable hatband, then new come vp, which I wore about a murrey *French* hat I had) cuts my hatband (and yet it was massie, gold-smithes worke) cuts my brimmes, which by good fortune (being thicke embrodered with gold-twist, and spangles) disappointed the force of the blow: Neuerthelesse, it graz'd on my shoulder, takes me away six purles of an *Italian* cut-worke band I wore (cost me three pound in the exchange, but three daies before.)

---

iv. vi. 66 faith,] faith *Qq*   signior,] Signior *Qq 1, 2*   67 difference,] difference *Qq*   68 gallant,] Gallant *Qq*   selfe—sir] selfe : sir *Qq* : selfe-sir *F1* : selfe ; sir *F2*   PVNTARVOLO] Puntarvolo Qq 1, 2   69 name him,] name him ; *Qq*   70 in-auspicious] inauspicious *Qq*   chance] chaunce *Qq 1, 2*   71 to] betwixt *Qq*   72 Faith,] Faith *Qq*   AGAMEMNON,] *Agamemnon* Qq   73 escape,] escape *Qq*   75 indeed, sir,] indeed Sir *Qq 1, 2* : indeede sir *Q3*   76 desperately] desperatly *Q1, F2*   77 iudgement] judgement *Qq 1, 2*   you,] you *Qq*   sir. I] sir, I *Q3* : sir ; I *F2*   78 aduancing] advancing *Qq 1, 2* : advauncing *Q3*   83 haire.] haire : *Qq*   againe,] again *Q1* : againe *Qq 2, 3*   83-4 here (I had on,] here, I had a *Qq*   84 hatband,] hatband *Qq 1, 2*   which] (which *Qq*   87 embrodered] embroydered *F2*   88 gold-twist] gold twist *Qq*   89 Neuerthelesse,] Neuerthelesse *Qq*   shoulder,] shoulders *Qq 2, 3*   90 wore (cost] wore, cost *Qq*   91 pound] pounds *Qq*   exchange,] exchaunge *Q1* : Exchange *Qq 2, 3*   before.)] before. *Qq*

PVNT. This was a strange encounter!

FAST. Nay, you shall heare, sir: with this wee both fell out, and breath'd. Now (vpon the second signe of his
95 assault) I betooke me to the former manner of my defence; he (on the other side) abandon'd his body to the same danger, as before, and followes me still with blowes: But I (being loth to take the deadly aduantage that lay before mee of his left side) made a kind of *stramazoun,* ranne him vp to the
100 hilts, through the doublet, through the shirt, and yet mist the skin. Hee (making a reuerse blow) falls vpon my emboss'd girdle (I had throwne off the hangers a little before) strikes off a skirt of a thick-lac't sattin doublet I had (lin'd with some foure taffataes) cuts off two panes, em-
105 brodered with pearle, rends through the drawings out of tissew, enters the linings, and skips the flesh.

CARL. I wonder he speakes not of his wrought shirt!

FAST. Here (in the opinion of mutuall dammage) wee paus'd: but (ere I proceed) I must tell you, signior, that
110 (in this last encounter) not hauing leisure to put off my siluer spurres, one of the rowels catcht hold of the ruffle of my boot, and (being *Spanish* leather, and subiect to teare) ouerthrowes me, rends me two paire of silke stockings (that I put on, being somewhat a raw morning, a peach colour and
115 another) and strikes me some halfe inch deepe into the side of the calfe; Hee (seeing the bloud come) presently takes horse, and away. I (hauing bound vp my wound with a peece of my wrought shirt)——

CARL. O! comes it in there?

120 FAST. Rid after him, and (lighting at the court-gate,

IV. vi. 92 strange] straunge *Qq 1, 2*   encounter!] encounter. *Qq*
93 Nay,] Nay *Qq*   heare, sir:] heare sir, *Qq*   94 out,] out *Qq*
breath'd] breath'd: *Qq*   96 danger,] daunger *Qq*   97 blowes:] blowes. *Qq*   98 aduantage] advauntage *Q1*   103 thick-lac't] thick lac't *Qq*: thick---lac't *F1*: thick--lac't *F2*   104 some *om. F2*
off] of *Q1*   panes,] panes *Qq*   embrodered] embroydered *F2*   105 pearle] Pearles *Q3*   rends] rents *Qq*   107 shirt!] Shirt. *Qq 1, 2*:
shirt. *Q3*   109 you,] you *Qq*   112 subiect] subject *Q1*   114 on,] on *Qq*   116 presently] presenly *F2*   117 horse,] horse *Qq 1, 2*
118 shirt)——] Shirt) *Qq 1, 2*: shirt) *Q3*   119 O!] O *Qq*   in *not in Qq*   120 court-gate,] court gate *Q1*: Court gate *Qq 2, 3*

both together) embrac'd, and marcht hand in hand vp into the presence: was not this businesse well carried?

MACI. Well? yes, and by this we can gesse what apparell the gentleman wore.

PVNT. 'Fore valour, it was a designement begun with much resolution, maintain'd with as much prowesse, and ended with more humanitie. How now, what saies the *Notarie?*

SERV. He saies, he is ready, sir, he staies but your worships pleasure.

PVNT. Come, we will goe to him, Monsieur. Gentlemen, shall we entreat you to be witnesses?

SOGL. You shall entreat me, sir: come *Resolution.*

SHIFT. I follow you, good *Countenance.*

CARL. Come, signior, come, come.

MACI. O, that there should be fortune
To clothe these men, so naked in desert!
And that the iust storme of a wretched life,
Beats 'hem not ragged, for their wretched soules,
And, since as fruitless, euen as black as coales!

GREX.

MIT. Why, but signior, how comes it, that FVNGOSO appear'd not with his sisters intelligence, to BRISKE?

COR. Mary, long of the euill angels that she gaue him, who haue indeed tempted the good simple youth, to follow

---

IV. vi. 121 together] togither *Q2* embrac'd,] embrac'd *Qq 1, 2*
122 presence:] Presence. *Qq* was not ... carried? *not in Qq* 123
Well? yes, and by] Well, by *Qq* 125 valour,] God *Qq* 127-8 the
Notarie] he *Qq 1, 2*: hee *Q3* After 128 *His seruingman enters. (Seruingman* Q1) *Qq* 129 He] The *Notarie Qq* saies,] saies *Qq 1, 2*:
sayes *Q3* ready,] readie *Q1*: ready *Qq 2, 3* 131 Come,] Come *Q1*
him,] him *Qq* Monsieur] Mounsieur *Q1* Gentlemen,] Gentlemen *Q1*
132 witnesses?] witnesses. *Qq* 133 me, sir:] mee sir, *Qq 1, 2*: me
sir, *Q3* 134 you,] you *Qq* 135 Come,] Come *Qq* 137 desert!]
desert, *Qq* 139 ragged,] ragged *Qq* 140 And,] And *Qq* coales!]
coales. *Q1*: coles. *Qq 2, 3* After 140 *Exeunt.* Q1: *Qq* 2, 3 add '*Exit.*'
to 140. All three fail to mark any exit at 134 141 Why,] Why *Qq*
it,] it *Qq* 142 intelligence,] intelligence *Qq* BRISKE?] *Briske.*
Qq 143 Mary,] Mary *Q1*: Marrie *Q2*: Marie *Q3* 144 youth,]
youth *Qq*

145 the taile of the fashion, and neglect the imposition of his friends. Behold, here hee comes, very worshipfully attended and with good varietie.

Act IIII. Scene VII.

FVNGOSO, TAYLOR, SHOO-MAKER, HABERDASHER.

Gramercie, good shoo-maker, I'le put to strings my selfe. Now, sir, let me see, what must you haue for this hat?
HABER. Here's the bill, sir.
FVNG. How does't become me? well?
5 TAIL. Excellent, sir, as euer you had any hat in your life.
FVNG. Nay, you'll say so, all.
HABE. In faith, sir, the hat's as good as any man i' this towne can serue you ; and will maintayne fashion as long : ne're trust me for a groat else.
10 FVNG. Do's it apply well to my sute?
TAIL. Exceeding well, sir.
FVNG. How lik'st thou my sute, haberdasher?
HABE. By my troth, sir, 'tis very rarely well made, I neuer saw a sute sit better, I can tell, on.
15 TAIL. Nay, we haue no arte to please our friends, we.
FVNG. Here, haberdasher, tell this same.
HABE. Good faith, sir, it makes you haue an excellent body.

IV. vi. 146 Behold,] Behold Q_I attended] attended, Qq, F_2
IV. vii. Act . . . HABERDASHER.] SCENA QVARTA. | *Enter Fungoso with Taylor, Shoe-maker, and Haberdasher.* (QUARTA. Qq 1, 2: *Fungoso*, Q_3) Qq: SCENE V.—*A Room in Deliro's House.* | *Enter* Fungoso *in a new suit, followed by his Tailor, Shoemaker, and Haberdasher.* G 1 Gramercie,] *Fung.* Gramercie Qq shoo-maker] Shoe-maker Qq put to strings] put too strings Qq 1, 2: put Strings to F_3 *Exit Shoe-maker.* Qq after 'selfe,' beginning a new line at 'Now, sir.'   2 Now,] Now Qq 4 does't] doest Qq 1, 2 me?] me Qq 1, 2 5 Excellent,] Excellent Qq 6 *not in* Qq 7 In faith,] Nay faith Qq 8 you ; and] you. And Qq 1, 2: you, And Q_3 long :] long, Qq 9 trust me for a groat else] trustmefor a groatelse F_2 11 well,] well Qq 12 sute,] suit Q_I : Sute Q_2: sute Q_3 13 troth, sir,] troth sir Qq 14 better,] better Qq tell,] tell Qq 16 Here,] Here Qq haberdasher,] Haberdasher Q_I 17 faith,] faith Qq

Euery Man out of his Humour 553

F v n g. Nay (beleeue me) I thinke I haue as good a body in clothes, as another. 20

T a i l. You lack points, to bring your apparell together, sir.

F v n g. I'le haue points anon: how now? is't right?

H a b e. Faith, sir, 'tis too little, but vpon farther hopes —— Good morrow to you, sir. 25

F v n g. Farewell, good haberdasher. Well, now master S n i p, let mee see your bill.

GREX.

M i t. Me thinkes he discharges his followers too thicke.

C o r. O, therein he saucily imitates some great man. I warrant you, though he turnes off them, he keepes this taylor, in place of a page, to follow him still. 30

F v n g. This bill is very reasonable, in faith (harke you, master S n i p) Troth, sir, I am not altogether so well furnisht at this present, as I could wish I were, but——If you'le doe mee the fauour to take part in hand, you shall haue all I haue, by this hand—— 35

T a i l. Sir——

F v n g. And, but giue mee credit for the rest, till the beginning of the next terme.

T a i l. O lord, sir—— 40

F v n g. 'Fore god, and by this light, I'le pay you to the

---

iv. vii. 20 clothes,] cloths *Q1* : cloaths *Q2* : clothes *Q3* 21 points,] points *Qq* 21–2 together, sir.] together. *Qq 1, 3* : togither. *Q2* 24 Faith, sir,] Faith sir *Qq* hopes——] hopes. *Qq* 25 you,] you *Qq* After 25 *Exit Haberdasher*. Q1 : Qq 2, 3 add to 25 26 Farewell,] Farewell *Qq* haberdasher.] Haberdasher, *Q1* : Haberdasher : *Qq 2, 3* Well,] well *Qq* master] maister *Q1* 27 Snip,] Snip Qq 29 O,] O *Q1* 30 you,] you *Qq* 31 taylor, . . . page,] Taylor . . . Page *Qq* still *om*. *Qq 2, 3* 32 reasonable,] reasonable *Qq* faith (harke you,] faith, harke you *Q1* : faith : hearke you *Q2* : fayth : Hearke you *Q3* 33 master] maister *Q1* Snip)] Snip. Q1 : *Snip*, *Qq 2, 3* Troth, sir,] Troth sir *Qq* altogether] altogither *Q2* 34 were,] were : *Qq* 36 haue,] haue *Qq* this hand—] *Iesu*. Qq 38 And,] And *Qq* 40 lord,] Lord *Qq* 41 god,] God *Qq* light,] light *Qq*

vtmost, and acknowledge my selfe verie deeply engag'd to you, by the courtesie.

TAIL. Why, how much haue you there, sir?

45 FVNG. Mary I haue here foure angels, and fifteene shillings of white monie: it's all I haue, as I hope to be blest.

TAIL. You will not faile me, at the next tearme, with the rest.

50 FVNG. No, and I doe, pray heauen, I be hang'd. Let me neuer breathe againe, vpon this mortall stage, as the philosopher cals it. By this aire, and (as I am a gentleman) I'le hold.

GREX.

CORD. He were an yron-hearted fellow, in my iudge-
55 ment, that would not credite him vpon this volley of othes.

TAIL. Well, sir, I'le not sticke with any gentleman for a trifle: you know what 'tis, remaines?

FVNG. I, sir, and I giue you thankes in good faith. O fate! how happie am I made in this good fortune! Well,
60 now I'le goe seeke out Monsieur BRISKE. 'Ods so, I haue forgot ribband for my shooes, and points. S'lid, what lucke's this! how shall I doe? Master SNIPPE, pray let me reduct some two or three shillings for points, and ribband: as I am an honest man, I haue vtterly disfurnisht my selfe,

---

IV. vii. 42 engag'd] ingag'd *F2* 43 you,] you *Qq* the courtesie] this hand *Qq* 44 Why,] Why *Qq* there,] there *Qq* 46 monie:] money, *Qq* haue,] haue *Qq* I hope] 'hope *Qq* 47 blest] sau'd *Qq* 48 me,] mee *Qq 1, 3* : me *Q2* tearme,] Tearme *Qq 1, 2* : Terme *Q3* 50 No,] No *Qq 1, 2* : No : *Q3* and] an *F2* heauen,] God *Qq* 51 breathe] breath *Qq* againe,] againe *Qq* 54 fellow,] fellow *Qq* iudgement] judgement *Qq 1, 2* 55 this volley of] these monstrous *Qq* : his volley of *F2, F3* 56 Well,] Well *Qq* 57 'tis,] 'tis *Qq* 58 I,] I *Qq* faith.] faith, *Q1* : faith ; *Qq 2, 3* 59 fate !] God *Q1* : God, *Qq 2, 3* fortune !] fortune. *Qq 1, 2* 60 Monsieur] Mounsieur *Q1* 'Ods] Gods *Qq* 61 shooes,] shoes ; *Q1* : shoes, *Q2* S'lid,] S'lid *Qq* 62 this !] this ? *Qq* I] we *Q3* Master] Maister *Q1* 63 points,] points *Q1* : Points *Q2* : poynts *Q3* ribband :] Ribband, *Qq 1, 2* : Rybband *Q3* : Ribbands : *F3* 64 as I ... man,] by Iesu *Qq* selfe,] selfe *Qq*

in the default of memorie, pray' le'me be beholding to you, 65
it shall come home i' the bill, beleeue me.

   T A I L.   Faith, sir, I can hardly depart with ready mony,
but I'le take vp, and send you some by my boy, presently.
What colour'd ribband would you haue?

   F v n G.   What you shall thinke meet i' your iudgement, 70
sir, to my sute.

   T A I L.   Well, I'le send you some presently.

   F v n G.   And points too, sir?

   T A I L.   And points too, sir.

   F v n G.   Good lord! how shall I studie to deserue this 75
kindnesse of you, sir? Pray, let your youth make haste, for
I should haue done a businesse an houre since, that I doubt
I shall come too late. Now, in good faith, I am exceeding
proud of my sute.

GREX

   C o R.   Doe you obserue the plunges, that this poore 80
gallant is put to (signior) to purchase the fashion?

   M I T.   I, and to bee still a fashion behinde with the world,
that's the sport.

   C o R.   Stay: O here they come, from *seal'd, and deliuer'd.*

<small>IV. vii. 65 memorie,] memorie ; *Qq 2, 3*   pray'] pray, *Qq 1, 2* :
pray *Q3* (cf. IV. viii. 84)   66 bill,] bill *Q1* : Bill *Qq 2, 3*   67 Faith,]
Faith *Qq*   ready *not in Qq*   68 vp,] vp *Qq 1, 2*   boy,] boy *Qq*
70 iudgement, sir,] judgement Sir *Qq 1, 2* : iudgement sir *Q3*   73, 74
too,] too *Qq*   After 74 *Exit Taylor.* Q1 : *Qq 2, 3* add to 74   75
lord!] Lord *Q1* : Lord, *Qq 2, 3*   76 of you, sir?] of you sir. *Qq 1,
2* : of you sir? *Q3*   Pray,] Pray *Qq, F2*   77 houre] hower *Q1*
78 Now,] Now *Qq*   faith,] truth *Qq*   exceeding] exceedingly *Qq 2, 3*
After 79 *Exit.* Q1 : Qq add to 78   80 plunges,] plunges *Qq*   81
put to] put too *Qq*   fashion?] Fashion. *Qq, 1 2*   82 with *om. Qq
2, 3*   84 come,] come *Qq*   seal'd,] seal'd Q1 : Seal'd Qq 2, 3</small>

Act IIII. Scene VIII.

PVNTARVOLO, FASTIDIVS BRISKE, SERVANTS, CARLO, SOGLIARDO, MACILENTE, SHIFT.

To them.   FVNGOSO.

WEll, now my whole venter is forth I will resolue to depart shortly.

FAST. Faith, sir PVNTARVOLO, goe to the court, and take leaue of the ladies first.

5 PVNT. I care not, if it be this afternoones labour. Where is CARLO?

FAST. Here he comes.

CARL. Faith, gallants, I am perswading this gentleman to turne courtier. He is a man of faire reuenue, and his 10 estate will beare the charge well. Besides, for his other gifts of the minde, or so, why, they are as nature lent him 'hem, pure, simple, without any artificiall drug or mixture of these two thred-bare beggarly qualities, learning, and knowledge, and therefore the more accommodate, and 15 genuine. Now, for the life it selfe———

FAST. O, the most celestiall, and full of wonder, and delight, that can be imagin'd, signior, beyond all thought, and apprehension of pleasure! A man liues there, in that

---

IV. viii. *Act . . .* FVNGOSO.] SCENA QVINTA. | *Enter Puntaruolo, Fastidius Briske, seruingmen with the Dog.* (QUINTA. *Qq 1, 2: Puntarvolo* Qq 1, 2) Qq : SCENE VI.—Puntarvolo's *Lodgings.* | *Enter* Puntarvolo, Fastidious Briske *in a new suit, and* Servants, *with the dog.* G *To them.* not in Qq, F3 : F3 runs on the names *Shift, Fungoso.*   1 Well,] *Punt.* Well *Qq*   venter] venture Q3, F3   3 Faith,] Faith *Qq* PUNTARVOLO,] *Puntaruolo* Qq 1, 3 : *Puntarvolo* Q2   5 not,] not *Qq* labour.] labor : *Qq 2, 3*   6 Where] where *Qq 2, 3*   After 7 *Enter Carlo, Sogliardo, Shift, and Macilente.* Qq   8 Faith,] Faith *Qq*   9 courtier. He] Courtier, he *Qq*   10 well. Besides,] well, besides *Qq* 12 artificiall] *Artificiall* Qq   13 thred-bare] thredbare *Qq*   beggarly] beggerly *Qq, F2*   learning,] *Learning* Qq   14 knowledge] *Knowledge* Qq   accommodate,] *accomodate* Qq   15 genuine] *Genuine* Qq   Now,] Now *Qq*   16 FAST.] *Fact.* Q3   celestiall] *Celestiall Qq*   wonder,] wonder *Q1* : woonder *Qq 2, 3*   17 delight,] delight *Qq* imagin'd,] imagin'd *Qq*   thought,] thought *Qq*   18 pleasure !] Pleasure. *Qq*   there,] there *Qq*

diuine rapture, that hee will thinke himselfe i' the ninth
heauen for the time, and lose all sense of mortalitie whatsoeuer; when he shall behold such glorious (and almost
immortall) beauties, heare such angelicall and harmonious
voyces, discourse with such flowing and *ambrosian* spirits,
whose wits are as suddaine as lightning, and humorous as
nectar; Oh: it makes a man al *quintessence,* and *flame,* &
lifts him vp (in a moment) to the verie christall crowne of
the skie, where (houering in the strength of his imagination)
he shall behold all the delights of the H E S P E R I D E S, the
Insulæ Fortunatæ, A D O N I S gardens, *Tempe* or what else
(confin'd within the amplest verge of *poesie*) to bee meere
vmbræ, and imperfect figures, conferr'd with the most
essentiall felicitie of your court.

M A C I. Well, this *Encomion* was not extemporall, it
came too perfectly off.

C A R L. Besides, sir, you shall neuer need to goe to a hot-
house, you shall sweat there with courting your mistresse,
or losing your monie at *primero,* as well as in all the stoues
in *Sweden.* Mary this, sir, you must euer be sure to carrie
a good strong perfume about you, that your mistresse dogge
may smell you out amongst the rest; and (in making loue
to her) neuer feare to be out: for you may haue a pipe of
tabacco, or a base violl shall hang o' the wall, of purpose,
will put you in presently. The trickes your *Resolution* has
taught you in tabacco, (the *whiffe,* and those sleights) will
stand you in verie good ornament there.

F A S T. I, to some perhaps: but, and hee should come
to my mistresse with tabacco (this gentleman knowes)

IV. viii. 19 diuine] deuine *Q1*   rapture] *Rapture* Qq   ninth] third
Qq   20 lose] loose *Qq*   whatsoeuer;] whatsoeuer, *F2*   23 *ambrosian*] *Ambrosian* Qq, F2 : *ambrosiam* F1   24 are *not in Qq*
lightning, and] lightningand *Q3*   25 *quintessence,*] *Quintessence* Qq
flame] *Flame* Qq 1, 2 : *Fleame Q3*   26-7 of the] o' the *Qq*   27
imagination] *Imagination* Qq   29 *Tempe*] *Tempe,* Qq   31 *vmbræ,*]
Vmbræ Qq 2, 3   33 Well,] Wel *Q1* : Wel, *Qq* 2, 3   *Encomion*] EN-
COMION *Qq*   35 Besides,] Besides *Qq*   37 losing] loosing *Qq*   38
Sweden] Flaunders *Qq*   this,] this *Qq*   39 mistresse] Mistresses *F3*
42 wall,] wall *Qq*   45 there. *corr. F1, F2 :* there? *Qq, F1 originally.*
46 perhaps] per haps *Qq* 2, 3   and] an' *F2 (so* 56)

558   *Euery Man out of his Humour*

shee'ld reply vpon him, yfaith. O, (by this bright sunne)
shee has the most acute, readie, and facetious wit, that——
50 tut there's no spirit able to stand her. You can report it,
signior, you haue seene her?

P V N T. Then can hee report no lesse, out of his iudgement, I assure him.

M A C I. Troth, I like her well enough, but shee's too selfe-
55 conceited, me thinkes.

F A S T. I indeed, shee's a little too selfe-conceited, and
'twere not for that humour, she were the most-to-be-
admir'd ladie in the world.

P V N T. Indeed, it is a humour that takes from her
60 other excellencies.

M A C I. Why, it may easily be made to forsake her, in my
thought.

F A S T. Easily, sir? then are all impossibilities easie.

M A C I. You conclude too quicke vpon me, signior, what
65 will you say, if I make it so perspicuously appeare now,
that your selfe shall confesse nothing more possible?

F A S T. Mary, I will say, I will both applaud, and admire
you for it.

69   P V N T. And I will second him, in the admiration.

They M A C I. Why, I'le shew you, gentlemen. C A R L O, come
whisper. hither.

S O G L. Good faith, I haue a great humor to the court:
what thinkes my *Resolution?* shall I aduenture?

IV. viii. 48 him,] him *Qq*   O,] Oh, *Q1*: Oh *Qq 2, 3*   49–50 that——
tut] that 8. tut *Q3*   50 there's no] there'sno *Q3*   it,] it *Qq*   52
lesse,] lesse *Qq*   iudgement] judgement *Qq 1, 2*   54 Troth,] Troth *Qq*
55 -conceited,] -conceited *Qq*   57, 59 humour] Humor *Qq*   57 most-
to-be-admir'd] most to be admir'd *Qq*   59 Indeed,] Indeed *Qq*   61
Why,] Why *Q1*: why *Qq 2, 3*   her,] her *Qq*   63 Easily,] Easily *Qq*
64 me,] me *Qq*   signior,] signior; *F2*   65 say,] say *Qq*   per-
spicuously] conspicuously *Qq 2, 3*   66 possible?] possible. *Qq*   67
Mary,] Marry *Q1*: Mary *Qq 2, 3*   I will... for it. *italicized in Qq*
applaud] *applaud you* Qq   69 him,] him. *Qq*   in the admiration. *not
in Qq*   70 Why,] Why *Qq*   you,] you *Qq*   gentlemen.] Gentlemen,
Q1: Gentlemen; *Qq 2, 3*   CARLO,] *Carlo* Q1   71 hither] hether *Q1*
They whisper.] *Macilente, Carlo, Puntavolo, and Briske, whisper.* Qq *in
text after* 71   72 faith,] faith *Qq*   humor] Humour *F2*   court:]
Court, *Qq*   73 Resolution?] Resolution, Qq 2, 3

SHIFT. Troth, *Countenance*, as you please ; the place is a place of good reputation, and capacitie. 75

SOGL. O, my trickes in tabacco (as CARLO sayes) will shew excellent there.

SHIFT. Why, you may goe with these gentlemen now, and see fashions : and after, as you shall see correspondence.

SOGL. You say true. You will goe with me, *Resolution* ? 80

SHIFT. I will meet you, *Countenance*, about three or foure of clocke, but, to say to goe with you I cannot, for (as I am APPLE-IOHN) I am to goe before the *Cocatrice* you saw this morning, and therefore pray', present mee excus'd, good *Countenance*. 85

SOGL. Farewell, good *Resolution*, but faile not to meet.

SHIFT. As I liue.

PVNT. Admirably excellent !

MACI. If you can but perswade SOGLIARDO to court, there's all now. 90

CARL. O let me alone, that's my taske.

FAST. Now, by wit, MACILENTE, it's aboue measure excellent : 'twill be the onely court-exploit that euer prou'd courtier ingenious.

PVNT. Vpon my soule, it puts the ladie quite out of her 95 humour, and we shall laugh with iudgement.

CARL. Come, the gentleman was of himselfe resolu'd to goe with you, afore I mou'd it.

MACI. Why then, gallants, you two, and CARLO, goe afore to prepare the iest : SOGLIARDO, and I will come 100 some while after you.

iv. viii. 74 Troth,] Troth *Qq*   75 reputation,] *Reputation* Qq   76 O,] O *Qq* 2, 3   78 Why,] Why *Qq*   79 fashions :] fashions ; *Qq* 80 me,] me *Qq*   81 you,] you *Qq*   82 of clocke,] aclock ; *F2*   cannot,] cannot ; *Qq* 2, 3   83 APPLE-IOHN] *Apple Iohn* Qq   84 pray', *Ff* : pray, *Qq*   85 excus'd,] excus'd *Qq*   86 Farewell,] Farewell *Qq* 87 *Exit Shift.* add *Q1*   After 87 *They breake silence*: Q1 : *They breake silence. Exit Shift.* Qq 2, 3   88 Admirably] Admiraby *F1*   excellent !] excellent. *Qq*   90 court] the Court *Qq*   92 Now, by wit,] Now by Iesu *Qq*   93 court-exploit] Courtly exploit *Qq*   94 prou'd] proou'd *Q2*   95 soule,] soule *Qq*   the ladie] my Lady *Q3*   96 humour] Humor *Qq*   iudgement] judgement *Qq* 1, 2   98 mou'd] moou'd *Q2*   99 then,] then *Qq*   two,] two *Qq*   CARLO,] *Carlo* Qq 100 iest] jeast *Q1* : jest *Q2*   SOGLIARDO,] *Sogliardo* Qq

CARL. Pardon me, I am not for the court.

PVNT. That's true: CARLO comes not at court, indeed. Well, you shall leaue it to the facultie of monsieur BRISKE, and my selfe, vpon our liues wee will manage it happily. CARLO shall bespeake supper, at the Mitre, against we come backe : where we will meet, and dimple our cheekes with laughter at the successe.

CARL. I, but will you all promise to come?

PVNT. My selfe shall vndertake for them : he that failes, let his reputation lye vnder the lash of thy tongue.

CARL. Gods so', looke who comes here!

SOGL. What, nephew!

FVNG. Vncle, god saue you ; did you see a gentleman, one Monsieur BRISKE? a courtier, he goes in such a sute as I doe.

SOGL. Here is the gentleman, nephew, but not in such a sute.

He swounes.

FVNG. Another sute!

SOGL. How now, nephew?

FAST. Would you speake to me, sir?

CARL. I, when he has recouered himselfe, poore poll.

PVNT. Some *Rosa-solis*.

MACI. How now, signior?

FVNG. I am not well, sir.

MACI. Why, this it is, to dogge the fashion.

CARL. Nay, come gentlemen, remember your affaires; his disease is nothing but the *fluxe* of apparell.

IV. viii. 102 the court *corr. F1, F2* : the Court *Qq* : court *F1 originally* 103 court, *corr. F1, F2* : the Court *Qq* : court *F1 originally* 104 indeed.] indeed: *Qq 2, 3* Well] well *Qq* facultie] *facultie Qq* monsieur] Mounsieur *Q1* 105 selfe,] selfe ; *Qq, F2* 106 supper,] supper *Q1* : Supper *Qq 2, 3* Mitre, *corr. F1, F2* : Miter *Q1* : Mitre *Qq 2, 3* : Miter, *F1 originally*. 109 come?] come. *Qq* 110 vndertake *corr. F1, F2* : manfrede it *Qq, F1 originally*. 112 so'] so *F2* here!] here. *Q1* : here? *Qq 2, 3* After 112 *Enter Fungoso. Qq* 113 nephew!] Nephew? *Qq* 114 god] God *Qq, F2* 115 courtier *corr. F1, F2* : Courtier *Qq, F1 originally*. 117 gentleman,] Gentleman *Qq* 119 st. dir. *swounes*] Swonnes *Q3* 120 now,] now *Qq* 121 me,] mee *Q1* : me *Qq 2, 3* 122 recouered] recouer'd *Qq 2, 3* : recouerd *F2* himselfe, *corr. F1, F2* : himselfe : *Qq, F1 originally*. 124 now,] now *Qq* 125 well,] well *Qq* 126 Why,] Why *Qq* dogge] dodg *F3* 127 Nay,] Nay *Qq*

Euery Man out of his Humour

P v n t. Sirs, returne to the lodging, keepe the cat safe: I'le be the dogs *Guardian* my selfe.

S o g l. Nephew, will you goe to court with vs? these gentlemen, and I are for the court: nay, be not so melancholy.

F v n g. By gods lid, I thinke no man in christendome has that rascally fortune that I haue.

M a c i. Faith, your sute is well enough, signior.

F v n g. Nay, not for that, I protest, but I had an errand to Monsieur F a s t i d i v s, and I haue forgot it.

M a c i. Why, goe along to court with vs, and remember it, come. Gentlemen, you three take one boat, and S o- g l i a r d o and I will take another: we shall be there instantly.

F a s t. Content: good sir, vouchsafe vs your pleasance.

P v n t. Farewell, C a r l o; remember.

C a r l, I warrant you: would I had one of *Kemps* shooes to throw after you.

P v n t. Good *Fortune* will close the eyes of our iest, feare not: and we shall frollicke.

GREX.

M i t. This M a c i l e n t e, signior, begins to bee more sociable on a suddaine, mee thinkes, then hee was before: there's some portent in't, I beleeue.

C o r. O, hee's a fellow of a strange nature. Now do's hee (in this calme of his humour) plot, and store vp a world of malicious thoughts in his braine, till hee is so full with 'hem,

---

iv. viii. 129 safe: *corr. F1, F2*: safe; *Qq, F1 originally*. 130 *Exeunt Seruingmen.* add *Qq* 131 court] the Court *Qq* vs?] vs; *Qq* 132 gentlemen,] Gentlemen *Qq* nay,] nay *Qq* 134 gods lid,] Gods lid *Qq* 136 Faith,] Faith *Qq* enough,] enough *Qq* 137 that,] that *Qq* protest, *corr. F1, F2*: protest; *Qq, F1 originally*. 139 Why,] Why *Qq* court] the Court *Qq* 140 come. Gentlemen] come Gentlemen *F3* 143 sir,] Sir *Qq* 144 Farewell,] Farewell *Qq* 147 iest] jest *Qq* 148 *Exeunt.* add *Qq* 149 MACILENTE,] Macilente *Qq* signior,] Signior *Q1* 150 suddaine,] suddaine *Qq* then] than *Qq*, *F2* before:] before, *Qq* 152 O,] O *Qq* strange] straunge *Qq 2, 3* 153 humour) plot,] Humor) plot *Qq* 154 with 'hem] with'him *Q3*

445·3   O O

155 that you shall see the very torrent of his enuie breake forth like a land-floud: and, against the course of all their affections oppose it selfe so violently, that you will almost haue wonder to thinke, how 'tis possible the current of their dispositions shall receiue so quick, and strong an alteration.

160 MIT. I mary, sir, this is that, on which my expectation has dwelt al this while: for I must tel you, signior (though I was loth to interrupt the *Scene*) yet I made it a question in mine owne priuate discourse, how he should properly call it, *Euery man out of his Humour*, when I saw all his actors so 165 strongly pursue, and continue their humours?

COR. Why, therein his art appeares most full of lustre, and approcheth neerest the life: especially, when in the flame, and height of their humours, they are laid flat, it fils the eye better, and with more contentment. How tedious 170 a sight were it to behold a proud exalted tree lopt, and cut downe by degrees, when it might bee feld in a moment? and to set the axe to it before it came to that pride, and fulnesse, were, as not to haue it grow.

MIT. Well, I shall long till I see this fall, you talke of.
175 COR. To helpe your longing, signior, let your imagination be swifter then a paire of oares: and by this, suppose PVNTARVOLO, BRISKE, FVNGOSO, and the dogge arriu'd at the court gate, and going vp to the great chamber. MACILENTE, and SOGLIARDO, wee'le leaue them 180 on the water, till possibilitie and naturall meanes may land 'hem. Here come the gallants, now prepare your expectation.

IV. viii. 155 enuie] Envie *Q1*   forth] forth, *Qq*   156 like a land-floud: *not in Qq*   and,] and *Qq*   158 wonder] woonder *Qq 2, 3* thinke,] thinke *Qq*   159 quick,] quicke *Q1*: quick *Qq 2, 3, F2*   160 mary,] marry *Qq*   that,] that *Qq*   161 you,] you *Qq*   163 priuate] priuat *Q2*   164 *Humour*] *Humor Qq*   165 pursue,] pursue *Qq* humours] Humors *Qq 1, 2*: humors *Q3*   166 Why,] Why *Qq*   167 life:] life, *Qq*   especially,] especially *Qq*   168 flame,] flame *Qq* humours,] Humors *Qq*   170 lopt,] lopt *Qq*   172 to it] to it, *Qq* pride,] pride *Qq, F2*   173 were,] were *Qq*   174 Well,] Well *Qq 1, 2* fall,] fall *Qq*   176 then] than *Qq 1, 2, F2*   oares:] Oares, *Qq* 177 PVNTARVOLO] *Puntaruolo* Qq 1, 2   dogge] Dog, *Qq*   178 great] gteat *Q3*   179 MACILENTE,] *Macilente Qq*   180 water,] water *Qq* till] tilll *Q3*   181 the *om. Q3*   expectation] Epectation *Q3*

Act v. Scene 1.

Pvntarvolo, Fastidivs Briske, Fvngoso, Groome, Macilente, Sogliardo.

Come, gentles. Signior, you are sufficiently instructed.
Fast. Who, I, sir?
Pvnt. No, this gentleman. But stay, I take thought how to bestow my dogge, he is no competent attendant for the presence.

Fast. Masse, that's true indeed, knight, you must not carrie him into the presence.

Pvnt. I know it, and I (like a dull beast) forgot to bring one of my cormorants to attend me.

Fast. Why, you were best leaue him at the porters lodge.

Pvnt. Not so: his worth is too well knowne amongst them, to bee forth-comming.

Fast. Slight, how'll you doe then?

Pvnt. I must leaue him with one, that is ignorant of his qualitie, if I wil haue him to be safe. And see! Here comes one that will carrie coales, *ergo*, will hold my dogge. My honest friend, may I commit the tuition of this dogge to thy prudent care?

Groo. You may, if you please, sir.

Pvnt. Pray thee, let me find thee here at my returne:

---

v. i. *Act* . . . Sogliardo.] Actvs Qvintvs, Scena Prima. | *Enter Puntarvolo, Fastidius Briske, Fungoso, and the Dog.* (Actus Quintus, *Qq 1, 2*) Qq : ACT V. | Scene i.—*The Palace Stairs.* | *Enter* Puntarvolo, *with his dog, followed by* Fastidious Brisk *and* Fungoso. G   1 Come,] *Punt.* Come *Qq*   gentles.] Lordings. *Qq* : Gentile, *F3*   Signior,] Signior *Qq*   2 Who, I,] Who I *Qq 1, 2* : Who, I *Q3*   6 Masse,] Masse *Qq* indeed,] in deed *Q1* : indeed *Qq 2, 3*   10 Why,] Why *Qq*   you were *corr. F1* : you're *Qq, F1 originally, F2*   15 one,] one *Qq*   16 see!] see ; *Qq 1, 2* : see : *Q3*   Here] Heres *Q2*   17 that] thac *Q2*   After 19 *Enter a Groome with a basket. Qq*   20 may,] may *Qq*   please,] please *Qq*   21–93 *Q3 transposes Niij verso* (21 ' *Punt.* Pray thee '—57 ' her Fanne, when ') *and Niv* (57 ' she laughs '—93 ' make it appeare '). *See above*, p. 409.   21 Pray thee, *corr. F1* : Pray thee *Qq, F1 originally, F2*

it shall not bee long, till I will ease thee of thy imployment, and please thee. Forth, gentles.

FAST. Why, but will you leaue him with so slight command, and infuse no more charge, vpon the fellow?

PVNT. Charge? no, there were no policie in that: that were to let him know the value of the gemme he holds, and so, to tempt fraile nature against her disposition. No, pray thee let thy honestie be sweet, as it shall be short.

GROO. Yes, sir.

PVNT. But harke you gallants, and chiefely Monsieur BRISKE. When we come in eye-shot, or presence of this ladie, let not other matters carrie vs from our proiect: but (if wee can) single her forth to some place——

FAST. I warrant you.

PVNT. And bee not too suddaine, but let the deuice induce it selfe with good circumstance. On.

FVNG. Is this the way? good truth, here be fine hangings.

GROO. Honestie sweet, and short? mary it shall, sir, doubt you not: for euen at this instant if one would giue mee twentie pounds, I would not deliuer him; there's for the sweet: but now, if any man come offer me but two pence, he shall haue him; there's for the short, now. Slid, what a mad humorous gentleman is this to leaue his dogge with me? I could run away with him now, and hee were worth any thing.

MACI. Come on, signior, now prepare to court this all-witted ladie, most naturally, and like your selfe.

v. i. 22 ease] Ease *Qq*   imployment] emploiment *Qq*   23 please] Please *Qq*   Forth,] Forth *Qq*   gentles] Gentiles *F3*   25 charge,] charge *Qq*   26 no, *Qq*, corr. *F1*: no; *F1 originally, F2*   that :] that ; *Qq*   28 tempt] temp *Q1*   29 sweet, as it shall be short] sweet and short *Qq*   30 Yes,] Yes *Qq 1, 2* : yes *Q3*   32 BRISKE.] Brisk : Q1 (an ill-printed colon ?) : Briske, Q2 : Briske Q3   -shot,] -shot *Qq*   33 other] others *Qq 2, 3*   proiect] Project *Qq 1, 2*   34 place——] place. *Qq*   37 circumstance. On] Circumstance: on *Qq*   38 truth,] truth *Qq*   After 38 *Exeunt Puntaruolo, Briske, Fungoso. Qq*   39 Honestie sweet,] Honestie, Sweet *Qq*   shall,] shall *Qq*   42 sweet : *corr. F1* : Sweet: *Qq* : sweet ; *F1 originally, F2*   42–3 two pence] two-pence *Qq*   43 short, *corr. F1*: Short *Qq* ; short *F1 originally, F2*   Slid] S'bloud *Qq*   45 me?] me : *Qq 1, 2*   now,] now *Qq*   and] an' *F2* (so 49)   46 thing.] thing : well, I pray God send him quickly againe. | *Enter Macilente and Sogliardo*. *Qq*   47 on,] on *Qq*   48 naturally,] Naturally *Qq*

S o g l. Faith, and you say the word, I'le begin to her in tabacco.

M a c i. O, fie on't : no. You shall begin with, *How does my sweet ladie?* or, *Why are you so melancholy, Madame?* though shee bee verie merrie, it's all one : be sure to kisse your hand often inough ; pray for her health, and tell her, how *more then most faire* she is. Screw your face at' one side thus, and protest ; let her fleere, and looke a skaunce, and hide her teeth with her fanne, when she laughs a fit, to bring her into more matter, that's nothing : you must talke forward (though it be without sense, so it be without blushing) 'tis most court-like, and well.

S o g l. But shall I not vse tabacco at all ?

M a c i. O, by no meanes, 'twill but make your breath suspected, and that you vse it onely to confound the rankenesse of that.

S o g l. Nay, I'le be aduis'd, sir, by my friends.

M a c i. Gods my life, see, where sir P v n t a r s dog is.

G r o o. I would the gentleman would returne for his follower here, I'le leaue him to his fortunes else.

M a c i. S'heart, 'twere the onely true iest in the world to poison him now : ha? by this hand, I'le doe it, if I could but get him of the fellow. Signior S o g l i a r d o, walke aside, and thinke vpon some deuice, to entertaine the ladie with.

S o g l. So I doe, sir.

M a c i. How now, mine honest friend? whose dog-keeper art thou?

G r o o. Dogge-keeper, sir? I hope I scorne that yfaith.

v. i. 49 Faith,] Faith *Qq*   51 on't :] on't. *Q1* : on't, *Q2* : on't *Q3* no. You *corr. F1* : no : you *Qq, F1 originally, F2*   52 ladie?] Ladie ; *Qq*   you so] youso *Q2*   melancholy,] melancholly *Qq*   54 inough] enough *Qq*   55 how *Qq, corr. F1* : how, *F1 originally, F2*   then] than *Qq, F2*   is.] is : *Qq*   at' one] a t' one *Qq*   56 fleere,] fleere *Qq* a skaunce] a scew *F2, F3*   58 matter,] matter ; *Qq*   60 court-like,] Courtlike *Qq*   63 suspected,] suspected ; *Qq*   that you] that that you *Q3*   65 aduis'd, sir,] aduis'd sir *Qq*   66 see,] see *Qq*   69 S'heart, *om. F2*   iest] jest *Qq 1, 2*   70 this hand,] Gods will *Qq*   72 deuice,] deuise *Qq*   74 doe,] doe *Qq 1, 2* : do *Q3*   *Sog. walkes off, meditating.* add *Qq*   75 now,] now *Qq*   77 -keeper.] keeper *Qq*

Hee
thr wes
off the
dogge.

78   MACI. Why? do'st thou not keepe a dogge?
        GROO. Sir, now I doe, and now I doe not : I thinke this
be sweet and short. Make me his dogge-keeper?
        MACI. This is excellent, aboue expectation : nay stay,
sir, you'ld bee trauailing ; but I'le giue you a dramme shall
shorten your voyage : here. So sir, I'le be bold to take my
leaue of you. Now to the *Turkes* court in the deuils name,
85 for you shall neuer goe o' gods name. SOGLIARDO,
come.
        SOGL. I ha' 't yfaith now, will sting it.
        MACI. Take heed you leese it not, signior, ere you come
there : preserue it.

GREX.

90   CORD. How like you this first exploit of his?
        MITIS. O, a piece of true enuie : but I expect the
issue of the other deuice.
        CORD. Here they come, will make it appeare.

Act v.   Scene 11.

SAVIOLINA, PVNTARVOLO, FASTIDIVS
BRISKE, FVNGOSO,
To them.   MACILENTE, SOGLIARDO.

WHy, I thought, sir PVNTARVOLO, you had bin
gone your voyage?
        PVNT. Deare, and most amiable ladie, your diuine

v. i. 79 st. dir. *Hee . . . dogge.*] *Throwes off the Dogge, & Exit.* (*Throwe
. . . Dog, . . . exit.* Q3) Qq in text after 80   80 short. Make] Short :
make *Qq*   81 excellent,] excellent *Qq 1, 2* : cxcellent *Q3*   stay,] stay
Qq   82 trauailing] trauelling *Q3* : travelling *F3*   83 here. So]
here : so *Qq*   84 you. Now] you : now *Qq*   deuils] Deuils *Qq 1, 2* :
diuels *Q3*   85 o' gods] on Gods *Qq*   After ' name '.] [*Kicks him out.*]
Qq (*Kickes* Q3)   88 not,] not *Qq*   89 *Exeunt.* add Qq   91 en-
uie :] Enuie, *Qq*   v. ii. *Act . . .* SOGLIARDO.] SCENA SECVNDA. | *Enter
Puntarvolo, Sauiolina, Fastidius Briske, Fungoso.* (SECUNDA. *Qq 1, 2* :
Sauiolina Q3 : *Factidius* Q3) Qq : SCENE II.—*An Apartment in the
Palace.* | *Enter* Saviolina, Puntarvolo, Fastidious Brisk, *and* Fungoso. G
To them add Ff ; in F1 ranged with the name of Sogliardo, who enters
with Macilente at l. 62 : in F2 incorrectly ranged with the first line of
names   1 Why,] *Saui.* Why (Wy *Q1*) *Qq*   thought,] thought *Qq.*
PVNTARVOLO] *Puntarvolo* Qq   bin] been *Qq* : beene *F2*

beauties doe bind me to those offices, that I cannot depart
when I would. 5
    S A V I. 'Tis most court-like spoken, sir : but how might
we do to haue a sight of your dogge, and cat ?
    F A S T. His dogge is in the court, ladie.
    S A V I. And not your cat ? how dare you trust her be-
hind you, sir ? 10
    P V N T. Troth, madame, shee hath sore eyes, and shee
doth keepe her chamber : mary I haue left her vnder sufficient guard, there are two of my followers to attend her.
    S A V I. I'le giue you some water for her eyes : when doe
you goe, sir ? 15
    P V N T. Certes, sweet ladie, I know not.
    F A S T. He doth stay the rather, madame, to present
your acute iudgement with so courtly, and wel-parted a
gentleman, as yet your lady-ship hath neuer seene.
    S A V I. What's hee, gentle Monsieur B R I S K E ? not 20
that gentleman ?
    F A S T. No ladie, this is a kinsman to iustice *Silence*.
    P V N T. Pray' sir, giue me leaue to report him : he's a
gentleman (ladie) of that rare and admirable facultie, as
(I protest) I know not his like in *Europe* : hee is exceedingly 25
valiant, an excellent scholler, and so exactly trauail'd, that
hee is able in discourse, to deliuer you a modell of any
princes court in the world : 'speakes the languages with
that puritie of phrase, and facilitie of accent, that it
breeds astonishment : his wit, the most exuberant, and 30
(aboue wonder) pleasant, of all that euer entred the con-
caue of this eare.

---

    v. i. 6 court-like spoken, sir :] Courtlike spoken sir ; *Qq*   7 dogge,]
Dog *Qq*   8 FAST.] *Fact.* Q3   dogge is] Dogge's *Qq*   9 hcw dare]
howdare *F2*   10 you,] you *Qq*   11 Troth, madame,] Troth Madame
Qq   12 doth] dooth *Qq* 1, 2, 3   13 guard,] guard : *Qq*   followers]
Hinds *Qq*   15 goe,] goe *Qq* 1, 2 : go *Q3*   16 Certes,] Certes *Qq*   17
FAST.] *Fact.* Q3   rather,] rather *Qq*   18 acute] *Acute* Qq   iudge-
ment] judgement *Qq* 1, 2   19 lady-ship] Ladiship *Qq*   20 Monsieur]
Mounsieur *Qq* 2, 3   22 to] of *Qq*   23 sir,] sir : *Q3*   he's *corr.* F1,
F2 : hee's *Qq* : h'is *F1* originally.   24 facultie] *facultie* Qq   26 an]
and *F3*   trauail'd] travel'd *F3*   29 phrase] *Phrase* Qq 1, 2 : Phrase
Q3   accent] *Accent* Qq

FAST. 'Tis most true, ladie: mary, he is no such excellent proper man.

35   PVNT. His trauailes haue chang'd his complexion, madame.

SAVI. O, sir PVNTARVOLO, you must thinke, euery man was not borne to haue my seruant BRISKES feature.

40   PVNT. But that which transcends all, ladie; hee doth so peerelessely imitate any manner of person for gesture, action, passion, or whateuer——

FAST. I, especially a rusticke, or a clowne, madame, that it is not possible for the sharpest-sighted wit (in the 45 world) to discerne any sparkes of the gentleman in him, when he does it.

SAVI. O, Monsieur BRISKE, be not so tyrannous to confine all wits within the compasse of your owne: not find the sparkes of a gentleman in him, if he be a gentleman?

50   FVNG. No in truth (sweet ladie) I beleeue you cannot.

SAVI. Doe you beleeue so? why, I can find sparkes of a gentleman in you, sir.

PVNT. I, he is a gentleman, madame, and a reueller.

FVNG. Indeed, I thinke I haue seene your ladiship at 55 our reuels.

SAVI. Like enough, sir: but would I might see this wonder you talke of: may one haue a sight of him, for any reasonable summe?

PVNT. Yes, madame, he will arriue presently.

60   SAVI. What, and shall we see him clowne it?

FAST. I faith (sweet ladie) that you shall: see, here he comes.

v. ii. 33 true, ladie: mary,] true Ladie; mary *Qq*   35 trauailes] Travels *F3*   37 O,] O *Qq*   PVNTARVOLO] *Puntarvolo* Qq   thinke,] thinke *Qq*   40 doth] dooth *Q2*   42 whateuer] what euer *Qq*   43 rusticke, ... clowne,] Rusticke ... Clowne *Qq*   44 wit] with *Q3*   47 Monsieur] Mounsieur *Qq 2, 3*   51 why,] why *Qq*   52 you,] you *Qq*   53 gentleman,] Gentleman *Qq*   54 Indeed,] Indeed *Qq*   56 Like] Lik *Q3*   enough,] enough *Q1* : inough *Qq 2, 3*   57 him,] him *Qq*   59 Yes,] Yes *Qq*   61 see,] see *Qq*   After 62 *Enter Macilente with Sogliardo.* Qq

Euery Man out of his Humour 569

P v n t. This is he! pray obserue him, ladie.

S a v i. Beshrew me, he clownes it properly indeed.

P v n t. Nay, marke his courtship.

S o g l. How does my sweet ladie? hote, and moyst? beautifull and lustie? ha?

S a v i. Beautifull, and it please you, sir, but not lustie.

S o g l. O ho, ladie; it pleases you to say so in truth: and how does my sweet ladie? in health? *Bona roba, quæso, que nouelles? que nouelles?* sweet creature.

S a v i. O excellent: why gallants, is this hee that cannot bee decipher'd? they were verie bleare-witted, yfaith, that could not discerne the gentleman in him.

P v n t. But, doe you, in earnest, ladie?

S a v i. Doe I, sir? why, if you had any true court-iudgement in the carriage of his eye, and that inward power that formes his countenance, you might perceiue his counterfeiting as cleere, as the noone-day: Alas——Nay, if you would haue tryed my wit, indeed, you should neuer haue told me he was a gentleman, but presented him for a true clowne indeede; and then haue seene if I could haue decipher'd him.

F a s t. 'Fore god, her ladiship sayes true (knight:) but does he not affect the clowne most naturally, mistresse?

P v n t. O, shee cannot but affirme that, out of the bountie of her iudgement.

S a v i. Nay, out of doubt hee does well, for a gentleman, to imitate; but I warrant you, he becomes his natural carriage of the gentleman, much better then his clownerie.

---

v. ii. 63 he!] hee; *Q1*: he; *Qq 2, 3*   him,] him *Qq*   66 ladie?] Ladie; *Qq 1, 2*: Lady; *Q3*   hote ... lustie? *italicized in Qq*   hote *Qq*: hot *F2*   68 Beautifull,] *Beautifull* Qq   and] an' *F2*   you,] you *Q*   lustie] *lustie* Qq   69 ho,] ho *Qq*   70 ladie?] Ladie; *Qq 1, 2*: Lady; *Q3*   quæso,] quæso? Qq   71 nouelles? ... nouelles?] *Novelles? ... Novelles?* Qq   73-4 -witted, yfaith,] -witted yfaith *Qq*   75 But,] But *Qq*   you,] you; *Q2*   earnest,] earnest *Qq*   76 I,] I *Qq*   why,] why *Qq*   77 -iudgement] judgement *Qq 1, 2.*   79 counterfeiting] counterfaiting *Qq 1, 2*   cleere,] cleere *Qq*   noone-day] noone day *Qq*   Alas——Nay,] Alas; Nay *Qq*   80 wit,] Wit *Qq*   84 god] God *Qq*   (knight:)] (knight) *F2*   88 Nay,] Nay *Qq*   gentleman,] Gentleman *Qq*   90 then] than *Qq, F2*

F a s t. 'Tis strange, in truth, her ladiship should see so farre into him!

P v n t. I, is't not?

S a v i. Faith, as easily as may be: not decipher him, quoth you?

F v n g. Good sadnesse, I wonder at it!

M a c i. Why, has she decipher'd him, gentlemen?

P v n t. O, most miraculously, and beyond admiration!

M a c i. Is't possible?

F a s t. Shee hath gather'd most infallible signes of the gentleman in him, that's certaine.

S a v i. Why, gallants, let mee laugh at you, a little: was this your deuice, to trie my iudgement in a gentleman?

M a c i. Nay, ladie, doe not scorne vs, though you haue this gift of perspicacie aboue others: What if hee should bee no gentleman now, but a clowne indeed, ladie?

P v n t. How thinke you of that? would not your ladiship bee out of your humour?

F a s t. O, but shee knowes it is not so.

S a v i. What if he were not a man, yee may as well say? nay, if your worships could gull me so, indeed, you were wiser then you are taken for.

M a c i. In good faith, ladie, hee is a verie perfect clowne, both by father, and mother: that I'le assure you.

S a v i. O, sir, you are verie pleasurable.

M a c i. Nay, doe but looke on his hand, and that shall resolue you: looke you, ladie, what a palme here is.

S o g l. Tut, that was with holding the plough.

M a c i. The plough! did you discerne any such thing in him, madame?

---

v. ii. 91 strange,] straunge *Qq 1, 2*: strange *Q3*   92 him!] him. *Qq*   93 not?] not. *Qq*   94 Faith,] Faith *Qq*   96 it!] it. *Qq*   97 has] hath *Q3*   98 O,] O *Qq*   admiration!] Admiration. *Qq*   100 gather'd] giuen *Qq*   102 Why,] Why *Qq 1, 2, F2*   you,] you *Qq*   103 iudgement] judgement *Qq 1, 2*   104 Nay,] Nay *Qq*   105 perspicacie] Perspicacie *Qq*   106 indeed,] indeed *Qq*   108 humour] Humor *Qq 2, 3*   111 nay,] nay *Qq*   so,] so *Qq*   112 then] than *Qq, F2*   are] were *Q3*   113 faith,] faith *Qq*   114 father,] Father *Qq*   115 O,] O *Qq*   117 you,] you *Qq*   120 him,] him *Qq 1, 2*

Fast. Faith no, she saw the gentleman as bright, as at noon-day, she: shee decipher'd him at first.

Maci. Troth, I am sorrie your ladiships sight should be so suddainly strooke.

Savi. O, you're goodly beagles! 125

Fast. What, is she gone?

Sogl. Nay, stay, sweet ladie, *que nouelles? que nouelles?*

Savi. Out, you foole, you.

Fvng. Shee's out of her humour yfaith. 130

Fast. Nay, let's follow it while 'tis hot, gentlemen.

Pvnt. Come, on mine honour wee shall make her blush in the presence: my splene is great with laughter.

Maci. Your laughter wil be a child of a feeble life, I beleeue, sir. Come, signior, your lookes are too deiected, 135 mee thinkes: why mixe you not mirth with the rest?

Fvng. By gods will, this sute frets me at the soule. I'le haue it alter'd to morrow, sure.

Act v. Scene iii.

Shift.

Fastidivs, Pvntarvolo, Sogliardo, *To him.*
Fvngoso, Macilente.

I Am come to the court, to meet with my *Countenance* Sogliardo: poore men must be glad of such countenance, when they can get no better. *Wel.* Need may insult vpon a man, but it shal neuer make him despaire of

---

v. ii. 121 the] ths *Q3*   bright,] bright *Qq*   122 -day,] -day *Qq*
shee] he *Qq*   123 Troth,] Troth *Qq*   124 strooke] struck *F2*   125
goodly] good *Q3*   127 Nay, stay,] Nay stay *Qq*   ladie,] Ladie ; *Qq*
1, 2 : Lady ; *Q3*   nouelles?] Novelles, *Qq*   nouelles?] Novelles. *Qq*
1, 2 : Novelles? *Q3*   129 foole,] foole *Qq*   *Exit Saui.* add *Qq*
130 humour] Humor *Qq*   131 hot,] hot *Qq* 1, 2 : hote *Q3*   132 wee
shall] wee'le *Qq* 1, 2 : wee le *Q3*   134 life,] life *Qq*   135 beleeue,]
beleeue *Qq*   Come,] Come *Qq*   deiected,] dejected *Qq* 1, 2 : deiected
Q3   137 gods will,] Gods will *Qq*   138 morrow,] morrow *Qq*   *Exeunt.*
add *Qq*   v. iii. *Act* . . . Macilente.] *Enter Shift.* Qq, without change
of scene : Scene iii.—*The Palace Stairs.* | *Enter* Shift. G   *To him.*
add Ff   1 I] *Shift.* I *Qq*   court,] Court *Qq*   3 Wel.] Wel, *Qq*

consequence. The world wil say, tis base : tush, base ! 'tis base to liue vnder the earth, not base to liue aboue it, by any meanes.

FAST. The poore ladie is most miserably out of her humour, yfaith.

PVNT. There was neuer so wittie a iest broken, at the tilt of all the court-wits christen'd.

MACI. O, this applause taints it, fouly.

SOGL. I thinke, I did my part in courting. O! *Resolution!*

PVNT. Aye me, my dogge.

MACI. Where is hee?

He sends away Fungoso. FAST. Gods precious, goe seeke for the fellow, good signior.

PVNT. Here, here I left him.

MACI. Why, none was here when we came in now, but CAVALIER SHIFT, enquire of him.

FAST. Did you see sir PVNTARVOLO's dogge here, *Caualier*, since you came?

SHIFT. His dog sir? he may looke his dog, sir, I saw none of his dog, sir.

MACI. Vpon my life, he hath stol'ne your dogge, sir, and beene hir'd to it by some that haue ventur'd with you : you may gesse by his peremptorie answeres.

PVNT. Not vnlike; for he hath beene a notorious thiefe by his owne confession. Sirrah, where is my dogge?

SHIFT. Charge mee with your dogge, sir? I ha' none of your dog, sir.

---

v. iii. 5 consequence.] Consequence: *Qq* 1, 2   base :] base ; *Qq* 1, 2 : base, *Q3*   After 7 *Enter Puntarvolo, Fastidius, Sogliardo, Fungoso, Macilente. Qq*   8 FAST.] *Fost. Q3*   9 humour,] Humour *Qq*   10 iest] jeast *Q1* : jest *Q2*   broken,] broken *Qq*   11 tilt] Tilt, *Qq*   12 it,] it *Qq*   fouly] fowly *Qq*   13 thinke,] thinke *Qq*   O !] O *Qq*   17 st. dir. *He . . . Fungoso.*] *Sends away Fungoso.* (*sends Q3*) *Qq* in text after 18.   precious] pretious *Qq*   20 Why,] Why *Qq*   22 PVNTARVOLO'S] *Puntarvolos Qq*   here,] here *Qq*   23 *Cauallier*] *Cavalier Qq*   24 dog, sir, I] Dog sir ; I *Qq*   saw] see *Qq*   25 dog,] Dog *Qq*   26 life,] life *Qq*   hath] has *F2*   dogge,] Dog *Qq*   27 beene hir'd] ben hir'd *Q2* : benhir,d *Q3*   you :] you ; *Qq*   30 where is] where's *Qq*   31 dogge,] Dog *Qq*   ha' none] ha'non *Q3*   32 dog, sir] Dog Sir *Q1* : dog sir *Q2* : dogsir *Q3*

Euery Man out of his Humour 573

Pvnt. Villaine, thou lyest.

Shift. Lie, sir? S'bloud, y' are but a man, sir.

Pvnt. Rogue, and thiefe, restore him. 35

Sogl. Take heed, sir Pvntarvolo, what you doe: heele beare no coales, I can tell you (o' my word.)

Maci. This is rare.

Sogl. It's mar'le hee stabs you not: by this light, he hath stab'd forty, for forty times lesse matter, I can tell you, 40 of my knowledge.

Pvnt. I wil make thee stoope, thou abiect.

Sogl. Make him stoop, sir! gentlemen, pacifie him or hee'le be kill'd.

Maci. Is he so tall a man? 45

Sogl. Tall a man? if you loue his life, stand betwixt 'hem: make him stoope!

Pvnt. My dogge, villaine, or I will hang thee: thou hast confest robberies, and other fellonious acts, to this gentleman thy *Countenance*—— 50

Sogl. I'le beare no witnesse.

Pvnt. And, without my dogge, I will hang thee, for them.

Sogl. What? kneele to thine enemies? *Shift kneeles.*

Shift. Pardon me, good sir; god is my witnesse, I neuer did robberie in all my life. 55

Fvng. O, sir Pvntarvolo, your dogge lies *Fungoso* giuing vp the ghost in the wood-yard. *return'd.*

Maci. Heart! is he not dead, yet?

Pvnt. O, my dog, born to disastrous fortune! pray you conduct me, sir. 60

v. iii. 34 Lie,] Lie *Qq*   S'bloud,] S'blood *Qq* : *om. F2*   man,] man *Qq*   35 Rogue,] Rogue *Qq*   36 heed,] heed *Qq*   Pvntarvolo,] Puntarvolo *Qq*   doe:] doe; *Qq*   37 coales,] coales *Qq*   o'] of *Qq* word.)] word. *Q3*   40 forty,] fortie *Qq*   42 abiect] Abject *Qq 1, 2* 43 stoop,] stoupe *Qq*   gentlemen,] Gentlemen *Qq*   him] him, *Qq* 46 life,] life *Qq*   48 dogge,] Dog *Q1* : dog *Qq 2, 3*   49 acts,] acts *Qq* 50 *Countenance*—] *Countenance*. *Q1* : *Countenance Qq 2, 3*   52 And... dogge,] And...Dog *Qq*   53 st. dir. *Qq in text after* 52   enemies] enemie *Qq*   54 me,] me *Q1* : mee *Qq 2, 3*   god] God *Qq*   witnesse,] Iudge *Qq*   56 st. dir. *Fungoso return'd.*] Fungo return'd. *F3* : *Enter Fungoso.* add *Qq* at 55   O,] O *Qq*   Pvntarvolo] Puntarvolo *Qq* 58 Heart!] S'bloud *Q1* : S'bloud *Qq 2, 3*   dead,] dead *Qq*   59 dog,] Dogge *Qq*   60 me,] me *Qq*   *Exit Punt. with Fung.* add *Qq*

So GL. How? did you neuer doe any robberie, in your life?
MACI. O, this is good : so he swore, sir.
So GL. I, I heard him. And did you sweare true, sir?
SHIFT. I, (as I hope to be forgiuen, sir) I ne're rob'd any man, I neuer stood by the high-way-side, sir, but only said so, because I would get my selfe a name, and be counted a tall man.

So GL. Now out, base *viliaco:* Thou my *Resolution?* I thy *Countenance?* By this light, gentlemen, he hath confest to mee the most inexorable companie of robberies, and damn'd himselfe that he did 'hem; you neuer heard the like: out skoundrell, out, follow me no more, I commaund thee: out of my sight, goe, hence, speake not : I wil not heare thee: away *camouccio.*

MACI. O, how I doe feed vpon this now, and fat my selfe! here were a couple vnexpectedly dishumour'd : well, by this time, I hope, sir PVNTARVOLO and his dog are both out of humour to trauaile. Nay, gentlemen, why doe you not seeke out the knight, and comfort him ? our supper at the Mitre must of necessitie hold to night, if you loue your reputations.

FAST. 'Fore god, I am so melancholy for his dogs disaster, but I'le goe.

So GL. Faith, and I may goe too, but I know, I shall be so melancholy.

MACI. Tush, melancholy? you must forget that now, and remember you lie at the mercy of a *furie:* CARLO will racke your sinewes asunder, and raile you to dust, if you come not.

v. iii. 61 robberie,] robberie *Qq 1, 2* : robbery *Q3*   62 O,] O *Qq*   swore,] swore *Qq*   63 I, I] I *Q3*   true,] true *Qq*   64 I hope to be forgiuen,] God shall haue part of my soule *Qq*   65 man, I] man I ; *Qq*   high-way-side,] high way side *Q1* : high-way side *Qq 2, 3*   66 name,] name *Qq 1, 2*   68 out,] out *Qq*   69 light,] light *Qq*   72 skoundrell,] skoundrell *Qq*   more,] more *Qq*   commaund] command *Q3, F2*   thee :] thee ; *Q3*   73 thee :] thee ; *Qq*   76 selfe !] self ? *Q1* : selfe ? *Qq 2, 3*   dishumour'd] dishumor'd *Qq*   77 time, I hope,] time I hope *Qq*   PVNTARVOLO] *Puntarvolo* Qq   78 humour] Humor *Qq*   trauaile.] trauaile : *Qq* : travel. *F3*   Nay,] nay *Qq 1, 2* : nay, *Q3*   82 god,] God *Qq*   84 Faith,] Faith *Qq*   know,] know *Qq*   88 dust,] dust *Qq*   *Exeunt.* add Qq

GREX.

Mit. O, then their feare of Carlo, belike, makes them hold their meeting.

Cor. I, here he comes: conceiue him but to be enter'd the Mitre, and 'tis enough.

Act V.   Scene IIII.

Carlo, Drawer, George.

HOlla: where be these shot-sharkes?
   Draw. By and by: you're welcome, good master Bvffone.
   Carl. Where's George? cal me George hither, quickly.
   Draw. What wine please you haue, sir? I'le draw you that's neat, master Bvffone.
   Carl. Away Neophite, do as I bid thee, bring my deare George to me: Masse, here he comes.
   Geor. Welcome, master Carlo.
   Carl. What! is supper ready, George?
   Geor. I, sir, almost: will you haue the cloth laid, master Carlo?
   Carl. O, what else? are none of the gallants come, yet?
   Geor. None yet, sir.
   Carl. Stay, take mee with you, George: let mee haue a good fat loyne of porke laid to the fire, presently.
   Geor. It shall, sir.
   Carl. And withall, heare you? draw me the biggest

---

v. iii. 90 O,] O *Qq*   Carlo,] *Carlo* Qq   93 and 'tis enough. *om. Q3*
v. iv. Act ... George.] Scena Tertia. | *Enter Carlo.* Qq: Scene iv.—
A Room at the Mitre. | *Enter* Carlo. *G*   1 Holla] *Carl.* Holla *Qq*
shot-sharkes] Shot-sharkes *Q1*: Shotmarkes *Q2*: Shotmakers *Q3*
Enter Drawer. add Qq (*Drawer* Q3)   2 you're] you are *Q3*   welcome,]
welcome *Qq*   4 hither,] hither *Qq*   6 haue,] haue *Qq*   7 neat,]
neat *Qq*   master *om. Q3*   8 bid thee,] bid ;   9 Masse,] Masse
Qq   *Enter George.* add Qq   10 Welcome,] Welcome *Qq*   master]
Maister *Q3* (*so* 13)   11 What! is] What's *Qq*   12 I,] I *Qq*   cloth]
cloath *Q1*   14 else?] else : *Qq*   come,] come *Qq*   15 yet,] yet *Qq*
16 you,] you *Qq*   17 fire,] fire *Qq*   18 shall,] shall *Qq*

20 shaft you haue, out of the butt you wot of : away, you know my meaning, GEORGE, quicke.

GEOR. Done, sir.

CARL. I neuer hungred so much for thing in my life, as I doe to know our gallants successe at court : now is that leane
25 bald-rib MACILENTE, that salt villaine, plotting some mischieuous deuice, and lyes a soking in their frothy humours like a drie crust, till he has drunke 'hem all vp : could the pummise but hold vp his eyes at other mens happiness, in any reasonable proportion : S'lid, the slaue
30 were to be lou'd next heauen, aboue honour, wealth, rich fare, apparell, wenches, all the delights of the belly, and the groine, whateuer.

GEOR. Here, master CARLO.

CARL. Is't right, Boy?

35 GEOR. I, sir, I assure you 'tis right.

He puts forth the drawers, and shuts the dore.

CARL. Well said, my deare GEORGE, depart : Come, my small gymblet, you in the false scabberd, away, so. Now to you, sir *Burgomaster*, let's taste of your bountie.

GREX.

MIT. What, will he deale vpon such quantities of wine,
40 alone?

COR. You will perceiue that, sir.

CARL. I mary, sir, here's puritie : O, GEORGE, I could bite off his nose for this, now : Sweet rogue, he has drawne *Nectar*, the very soule of the grape ! I'le wash my

v. iv. 20 haue,] haue *Qq*   21 meaning,] meaning *Qq*   22 Done,] Done *Qq*   Exit. add Qq   23 I] S'bloud, I *Qq*   24 court] the Court *Qq*   25 bald-rib] Blad-rib *Q3*   26 soking] soaking *Q1*   27 humours] Humors *Qq 1, 3*   28 pummise] Kecks *Qq*   vp his] vp's *Qq*   29 happiness,] happinesse *Qq*   proportion :] proportion, *Qq*   S'lid,] S'lid *Qq* : 'Slid, *F2*   30 lou'd] loued *Qq*   32 Enter Geor. add *Q1* : om. Qq 2, 3.   33 Here,] Here *Q1*   master] maister *Q3*   35 I,] I *Qq*   36 st. dir. He puts] Puts Qq   drawers,] Drawer Qq   dore.] dore Q3   said,] said *Q1*   37 away, so.] away ; so. : *Qq*   38 you,] you *Qq*   39 What] what *Qq 2, 3*   wine,] Wine *Q1* : wine *Qq*   41 will] shall *Qq*   that,] that *Qq*   He drinkes. add Qq   42 mary,] marry *Q1* : mary *Qq 2, 3*   O,] O *Qq*   43 his] thy *Qq*   this,] this *Qq*   44 grape !] Grape : *Qq*

temples with some on't presently, and drinke some halfe a score draughts; 'twill heat the braine, kindle my imagination, I shall talke nothing but crackers, and fire-worke, to night. So, sir! please you to be here, sir, and I here: So.

GREX.

Cor. This is worth the obseruation, signior.

Carl. 1. *Cup.* Now, sir; here's to you; and I present you with so much of my loue.

2. *Cup.* I take it kindly from you, sir, and will returne you the like proportion: but withall, sir, remembring the merry night wee had at the countesses, you know where, sir.

1. By heauen, you put me in minde now of a very necessarie office, which I will propose in your pledge, sir: the health of that honorable countesse, and the sweet lady that sate by her, sir.

2. I doe vaile to it with reuerence. And now, signior, with these ladies, I'le be bold to mixe the health of your diuine Mistris.

1. Doe you know her, sir?

2. O lord, sir, I: and in the respectfull memorie and mention of her, I could wish this wine were the most precious drugge in the world.

1. Good faith, sir, you doe honour me in't exceedingly.

Hee sets the two cups asunder, and first drinkes with the one, and pledges with the other.

GREX.

Mit. Whom should he personate in this, signior?
Cor. Faith, I know not, sir, obserue, obserue him.

v. iv. 47 crackers,] Crackers *Qq*   -worke,] -worke *Qq*   48 So, sir!] So sir; *Qq*   here,] here *Qq*   foll. st. dir. *in text in Qq*   50 1. *Cup.*] 1 *cup.* Qq 1, 2: 1 *cap.* Q3   Now, sir;] Now sir, *Qq*   52 you, sir, and] you Sir. (*Drinks*). And *Q1* : you sir. (*Drinkes.*) And *Qq* 2, 3.   53 withall,] withall *Qq*   54 countesses,] Countesses; *Qq*   where,] where *Qq*   55 heauen,] Iesu *Qq*   put] doe put *Qq*   56 pledge,] pledge *Qq*   58 her,] her *Qq*   59–65 *Qq print as one paragraph*   59 reuerence. And] reuerence. (*Drinks.*) 2. And *Qq*   now,] now *Qq*   61 Mistris] Mistresse *Qq*   62 her,] her *Qq*   63 lord, sir, I :] Lord sir, I, *Qq*   64 precious] pretious *Qq*   66 faith,] faith *Qq*   sir,] sir *Q3*   honour] honor *Qq*   (*Drinks.*) add *Qq*   68 Faith,] Faith *Qq*   not,] not *Qq* sir,] sir ; *F2*

2. If it were the basest filth, or mud that runnes in the channell, I am bound to pledge it, respectiuely, sir. And now, sir, here is a replenisht bowle, which I will reciprocally turne vpon you, to the health of the count F R V G A L E.

1. The count F R V G A L E s health, sir? I'le pledge it on my knees, by this light.

2. Will you, sir? I'le drinke it on my knee, then, by the light.

GREX.

M I T. Why, this is strange!

C O R. Ha' you heard a better drunken dialogue?

2. Nay, doe me right, sir.
1. So I doe, in good faith.
2. Good faith you doe not; mine was fuller.
1. Why, beleeue me, it was not.
2. Beleeue me, it was: and you doe lie.
1. Lie, sir?
2. I, sir.
1. S'wounds!
2. O, come, stab if you haue a mind to it.
1. Stab? dost thou thinke I dare not?

C A R L. Nay, I beseech you, gentlemen, what meanes this? nay, looke, for shame respect your reputations.

Speakes in his owne person, and ouerturnes wine, pot, cups, and all.

v. iv. 69–76 *Qq print as one paragraph* 69 filth,] filth *Qq* 70 it, respectiuely, sir.] it by God sir. (*Drinks.*) Qq 71 now,] now *Qq* is] is againe *Qq* bowle,] bowle sir, *Qq* 71–2 reciprocally turne] *reciprocally returne Qq* 72 you,] you *Qq* 73 health,] health *Qq* 74 knees,] knees *Qq* by this light.] by Iesu *Qq* 75 you,] you *Qq* knee,] knees *Qq* by the light.] by the Lord. (*Drinkes.*) Qq 77 Why,] Why *Qq* strange!] strange. *Q1*: straunge. *Qq* 2, 3 78 heard] hard *Q3* 79–90 *Qq print as one paragraph* 79 right,] right *Qq* 80 doe,] doe *Qq 1, 2*: do *Q3* 82 Why, beleeue me,] Why by Iesu *Qq* 83 Beleeue me,] By Iesu *Qq* was:] was, *Qq* 84 Lie, sir?] Lie sir. *Qq* 85 I,] I *Qq* 86 S'wounds!] S'wounds you Rascall. *Qq* (rascall. *Q3*): 'Swounds! *F2* 88–9 not? CARL.] not? [*In his owne person.*] *Q1*: not? (*In his owne person*) *Qq* 2, 3 89 foll. st. dir. *not in Qq* you,] you *Qq* 90 this?] this; *Qq* nay,] nay *Qq* Ouerturnes Wine, Pot, Cuppes, and all. (Ouerturnes *Q1*: wine, pot *Q3*: Cups, *Q2*, cups, *Q3*) *Qq in text after* 90

Act v.   *Scene* v.

MACILENTE, CARLO, GEORGE.

WHy, how now CARLO! what humour's this?
  CARL. O, my good *Mischiefe!* art thou come? where are the rest? where are the rest?
  MACI. Faith, three of our ordinance are burst.
  CARL. Burst? how comes that?   5
  MACI. Faith, ouer-charg'd, ouer-charg'd.
  CARL. But did not the traine hold?
  MACI. O, yes, and the poore lady is irrecouerably blowne vp.
  CARL. Why, but which of the munition is miscarried? 10 ha?
  MACI. *Inprimis*, sir PVNTARVOLO: next, the COVNTENANCE, and RESOLVTION.
  CARL. How? how for the loue of wit?
  MACI. Troth, the *Resolution* is prou'd recreant; the 15 *Countenance* hath chang'd his copie: and the passionate knight is shedding funerall teares ouer his departed dogge.
  CARL. What's his dogge dead?
  MACI. Poison'd, 'tis thought: mary, how, or by whom, that's left for some cunning woman here o' the *Banke-side* 20 to resolue. For my part, I know nothing, more then that wee are like to haue an exceeding melancholy supper of it.
  CARL. S'life, and I had purpos'd to be extraordinarily merry, I had drunke off a good preparatiue of old sacke here: but will they come, will they come?   25
  MACI. They will assuredly come: mary, CARLO (as

---

v. v. *Act* . . . GEORGE.] *Enter Macilente.* Qq, without change of scene
1 Why,] *Mac.* Why *Qq* (*Mae.* Q1)   CARLO!] *Carlo*; Q1: *Carlo*, Qq
2, 3   humour's] Humor's *Qq*   2 O,] O *Qq*   *Mischiefe!*] *Mischiefe*,
Qq 1, 2: *Mischief*, *Q3*   4 Faith,] Faith *Qq*   6 Faith,] Faith *Qq 1, 2*
8 O,] O *Qq*   12 PVNTARVOLO] *Puntarvolo* Qq   14 wit] God *Qq*
15 Troth,] Troth *Qq*   prou'd] proou'd *Qq*   16 copie:] Coppie ; *Qq*
17 knight] Knight, *Qq*   19 Poison'd,] Poison'd *Qq*   mary,] mary
Q1: marry *Qq 2, 3*   21 resolue.] resolue : *Qq*   then] than *Qq*, *F2*
24 merry,] merry : *Qq 1, 3* : merrie : *Q2*   26 mary,] marry *Q1* :
mary *Qq 2, 3*

thou lou'st me) run ouer 'hem all freely to night, and especially the knight; spare no sulphurous iest that may come out of that sweatie forge of thine: but ply 'hem with all manner of shot, minion, saker, culverine, or any thing what thou wilt.

CARL. I warrant thee, my deare case of petronels, so I stand not in dread of thee, but that thou'lt second me.

MACI. Why, my good *Germane* tapster, I will.

He danceth.

CARL. What, GEORGE. *Lomtero, Lomtero, &c.*

GEOR. Did you call, master CARLO?

CARL. More *nectar*, GEORGE: *Lomtero, &c.*

GEOR. Your meat's ready, sir, and your company were come.

CARL. Is the loyne of porke enough?

GEOR. I, sir, it is enough.

MACI. Porke? heart, what dost thou with such a greasie dish? I thinke thou dost varnish thy face with the fat on't, it lookes so like a glew-pot.

CARL. True, my raw-bon'd-rogue, and if thou would'st farce thy leane ribs with it too, they would not (like ragged lathes) rub out so many doublets as they doe: but thou know'st not a good dish, thou. O, it's the only nourishing meat in the world. No maruaile though that saucie, stubborne generation, the *Iewes*, were forbidden it: for what would they ha' done, well pamper'd with fat porke, that durst murmure at their maker out of garlicke, and onions. S'light, fed with it, the whorson strummell-patcht,

v. v. 28 sulphurous] *Sulphurious* Qq 2, 3 iest] jest *Q1* : jeast *Qq 2, 3* 29 thine :] thine *Qq* 30 minion, saker, culverine] Minion, Saker, Culverine Qq 32 thee,] thee *Qq* case of petronels] Case of *Petronels* Qq 1, 2 : Cale of *Petrione* Q3 33 I stand] stand I *Q3* 34 Why,] Why *Qq* 35 What,] What *Qq* st. dir. *He danceth.*] Daunceth. add Qq 38 ready,] readie Qq 1, 2 : ready *Q3* sir,] sir *Q1* and] an *F2* 40 of] a *Q1* 41 I,] I *Qq* 42 heart,] S heart Qq 1, 2 : S heart *Q3* dost] doest Qq 2, 3 43 dish ?] Dish ; *Qq 1, 2* : Dish : *Q3* 45 raw-bon'd-rogue,] Raw-bond Rogue : *Qq* 47 doublets] Dublets *Qq 1, 2* : Dubletes *Q3* 49 world.] world : *Qq* saucie,] saucie *Qq* 50 generation,] Generation *Qq* 52 garlicke,] Garlicke *Qq* : garlicke *F2* 53 S'light,] Sblood *Qq* strummell-patcht] strummell patcht *Qq 1, 2* : strummell patch *Q3* : strummell, patcht *Ff* : strummel-patched *G*

goggle-ey'd Grumbledories, would ha' *Gigantomachiz'd.*
Well said, my sweet G E O R G E, fill, fill. 55

GREX.

M I T. This sauours too much of prophanation.

C O R. O, *seruetur ad imum, qualis ab incepto processerit, & sibi constet.* The necessitie of his vaine compels a toleration : for, barre this, and dash him out of humour, before his time.

C A R L. 'Tis an *Axiome* in naturall philosophie, *What* 60 *comes neerest the nature of that it feeds, conuerts quicker to nourishment, and doth sooner essentiate.* Now nothing in flesh, and entrailes, assimulates or resembles man more, then a hog, or swine———

M A C I. True ; and hee (to requite their courtesie) often- 65 times d'offeth his owne nature, and puts on theirs ; as when hee becomes as churlish as a hog, or as drunke as a sow : but to your conclusion.

C A R L. Mary, I say, nothing resembling man more then a swine, it followes, nothing can be more nourishing : for 70 indeed (but that it abhorres from our nice nature) if we fed one vpon another, we should shoot vp a great deale faster, and thriue much better : I referre mee to your vsurous *Cannibals*, or such like : but since it is so contrary, porke, porke, is your only feed. 75

M A C I. I take it, your deuill be of the same diet ; he would ne're ha' desir'd to beene incorporated into swine else. O, here comes the melancholy messe : vpon 'hem C A R L O, charge, charge.

v. v. 54 Grumbledories] Grumbledoryes *Q1*   55 said,] said *Qq*   57 O,] *O* Qq : *O*, Ff   *seruetur*] servetur Qq   *incepto*] *incœpto* F2   59 for,] for *F2*   humour,] Humor *Qq*   62 doth] dooth Q2   63 flesh,] Flesh *Qq*   assimulates] assimilates *F2*   64, 69 then] than *Qq*, F2   64 hog,] Hog *Qq*   swine———] Swine. (*Drinkes.*) Qq   66 d'offeth] d'offeth off *Qq*   67 drunke as] a drunke ar *Q3*   68 (*Drinkes.*) add Qq 1, 2 : (*Drinkes*) add Q3   69 Mary,] Marry *Q1* : Mary *Qq* 2, 3   73 vsurous] Long-lane *Qq*   74 it is] 'tis *Qq*   76 it,] it *Qq*   deuill] Deuill *Qq*   77 to beene] to have been *W*   78 O,] *O Qq*   melancholy] Malancholly *Q3*   After 79 *Enter Puntaruolo, Fastidius, Sogliardo, Fungoso.* Qq

80   CARL. 'Fore god, sir PVNTARVOLO, I am sorry
for your heauinesse: body a me, a shrewd mischance!
why, had you no vnicornes horne, nor bezoars stone about
you? ha?

Act V.   Scene VI.

PVNTARVOLO, CARLO, MACILENTE,
FAST. BRISKE, SOGLIARDO,
FVNGOSO.

SIr, I would request you, be silent.
    MACI. Nay, to him againe.
    CARL. Take comfort, good knight, if your cat ha'
recouered her catarrhe, feare nothing; your dogges mis-
5 chance may be holpen.
    FAST. Say how (sweet CARLO) for so god mend mee,
the poore knights mones draw mee into fellowship of his misfortunes. But be not discourag'd, good sir PVNTARVOLO,
I am content your aduenture shall be perform'd vpon your
10 cat.
    MACI. I beleeue you, muske-cod, I beleeue you, for
rather then thou would'st make present repayment, thou
would'st take it vpon his owne bare returne from *Calice*.
    CARL. Nay, 'ds life, hee'ld bee content (so hee were well
15 rid out of his company) to pay him fiue for one, at his next
meeting him in *Paules*. But for your dogge, sir PVNTAR,
if hee bee not out-right dead, there is a friend of mine, a
quack-saluer, shall put life in him againe, that's certaine.
    FVNG. O, no, that comes too late.

v. v. 80 god,] God *Qq*   PVNTARVOLO] *Puntarvolo Qq*   81 heauinesse:] heauinesse; *Qq 1, 2*: heauines. *Q3*   81–2 mischance! why,]
mischaunce: why *Qq*   82 horne] hornes *Q3*   bezoars] *Bezars Qq*
v. vi. Act . . . FVNGOSO. *not in Qq, which continue the scene*   1 Sir]
Punt. Sir *Qq*   you,] you *Qq*   3 comfort,] comfort *Qq*   4 catarrhe]
Cataract *Qq*   mischance] mischaunce *Q1*   5 may] my *F2*   6
god] God *Qq, F2*   8 discourag'd,] discouraged *Qq*   PVNTARVOLO]
Puntarvolo Qq   11 you, muske-cod,] you Muske-cod, *Qq*   12 then]
than *Qq, F2*   13 vpon] vp on *Q3*   14 Nay, 'ds] Nay Gods *Qq*
15 one,] one *Qq*   16 PVNTAR,] PVNTAR. *F2*   17 mine,] mine *Qq*
18 *quack-saluer*] *Quack-sauer Q3*   19 O,] O *Qq*

Every Man out of his Humour

M A C I. Gods precious, knight, will you suffer this? 20
P V N T. Drawer, get me a candle, and hard waxe, presently.
S O G L. I, and bring vp supper; for I am so melancholy.
C A R L. O, signior, where's your *Resolution* ?
S O G L. *Resolution!* hang him rascall: O, C A R L O, if 25 you loue me, doe not mention him.
C A R L. Why, how so? how so?
S O G L. O, the arrant'st crocodile that euer Christian was acquainted with. By my gentrie, I shall thinke the worse of tabacco while I liue, for his sake: I did thinke him to be as 30 tall a man——
M A C I. Nay, B V F F O N E, the knight, the knight.
C A R L. S'lud, hee lookes like an image carued out of boxe, full of knots: his face is (for all the world) like a *dutch* purse, with the mouth downeward; his beard the tassels: and hee 35 walkes (let mee see) as melancholy as one o' the Masters side in the *Counter*. Doe you heare, sir P V N T A R ?
P V N T. Sir, I doe entreat you no more, but enioyne you to silence, as you affect your peace.
C A R L. Nay, but deare knight, vnderstand (here are 40 none but friends, and such as wish you well) I would ha' you doe this now; Flea me your dogge presently (but in any case keepe the head) and stuffe his skin well with straw, as you see these dead monsters at *Bartholmew* faire——
P V N T. I shall be suddaine, I tell you. 45
C A R L. Or if you like not that, sir, get me somewhat a lesse dog, and clap into the skin; here's a slaue about the towne here, a *Iew*, one Y O H A N; or a fellow that makes

---

v. vi. 20 precious,] pretious *Qq 1, 2* : precious *Q3*   21 Drawer,] Drawer ; *Qq*   candle,] Candle *Qq*   waxe,] waxe *Qq*   24 O,] Ah *Qq*   25 O,] O *Qq*   26 me,] me *Q1*   28 O,] O *Qq*   29 my gentrie] Iesu *Qq*   30 liue,] liue *Qq*   32 Nay,] Nay *Qq*   33 S'lud] Sblood *Qq*   34 *dutch*] Dutch *Qq*   purse,] purse *Qq*   35 downeward ;] downward *F2*   beard] beard's *Qq*   37 heare,] heare *Qq*   38 more,] more., *Q3*   enioyne] enjoyne *Qq 1, 2*   40 Nay,] Nay *Qq*   knight,] Knight *Qq*   42 Flea] Fleay *Q3*   44 you] ye *Q3*   Bartholmew] Bartholomew *F3*   faire——] faire. *Qq, F2* 45 suddaine,] suddaine *Qq 1, 2* : sodaine *Q3*   46 that,] that   get] giue *Qq 2, 3*   47 dog,] dog *Qq*

perrukes, will glew it on artificially, it shall ne're be dis-
50 cern'd, besides, 'twill be so much the warmer for the hound
to trauaile in, you know.

MACI. Sir PVNTARVOLO, 'death, can you be so
patient?

CARL. Or thus, sir: you may haue (as you come
55 through *Germany*) a familiar, for little or nothing, shall turne
it selfe into the shape of your dogge, or any thing (what you
will) for certaine houres——'ods my life, knight, what doe
you meane? youle offer no violence, will you? hold, hold.

The knight beates him.

PVNT. 'Sdeath, you slaue, you bandog, you.

60 CARL. As you loue wit, stay the enraged knight,
gentlemen.

PVNT. By my knighthood, he that stirres in his rescue,
dies. Drawer, be gone.

CARL. Murder, murder, murder.

65 PVNT. I, are you howling, you wolfe? Gentlemen, as
you tender your liues, suffer no man to enter, till my
reuenge be perfect. Sirha, BVFFONE, lie downe; make
no exclamations, but downe: downe, you curre, or I will
make thy bloud flow on my rapier hilts.

70 CARL. Sweet knight, hold in thy furie, and 'fore heauen,
I'le honour thee more, then the *Turke* do's MAHOMET.

PVNT. Downe (I say.) Who's there?

Within.

CONS. Here's the Constable, open the dores.

CARL. Good MACILENTE——

75 PVNT. Open no dore, if the ADALANTADO of
Spaine were here, he should not enter. One helpe me

v. vi. 49 perrukes,] Periwigs *Qq 1, 2*: periwigs *Q3*   discern'd,] discern'd; *Qq 1, 2*; discern'd: *Q3*   51 trauaile] travell *Q1, F3*: trauell *Qq 2, 3*   in,] in *Qq*   52 PVNTARVOLO, 'death,] *Puntaruolo*, Sdeath *Qq*   54 thus,] thus *Qq*   55 familiar,] Familiar *Qq*: familiar *F2*   little] a litle *Q3*   nothing,] nothing *Qq 1, 2*   57 houres——*corr. F1*: howers *Qq*: houres: *F1 originally*: houres:—*F2*   st. dir. *not in Qq*   'ods] Gods *Qq*   life,] life *Qq*   59 'Sdeath,] Sbloud *Qq*   bandog,] Bandog *Qq*   60 wit] God *Qq*   63 Drawer,] Drawer *Qq*   65 howling,] houling *Qq*   67 Sirha,] Sirha *Qq*   68 downe: downe,] downe; downe *Qq*   69 hilts.] hilts: *Qq*   70 knight,] knight *Qq*   heauen,] God *Qq*   71 more,] more *Qq*   then] than *Qq, F2*   72 Who's] Whose *Qq*   74 MACILENTE——] *Macilente.* Qq   76 enter. One *corr. F1*: enter: On, *Qq, F1 originally*: enter: One *F2*

Every Man out of his Humour

with the light, gentlemen: you knocke in vaine, sir officer.

CARL. *Et tu Brute!*

PVNT. Sirha, close your lips, or I will drop it in thine eyes, by heauen.

CARL. O, O.

CONS. Open the dore, or I will breake it open.

He seales vp his lips.

MACI. Nay, good Constable, haue patience a little, you shall come in presently, we haue almost done.

PVNT. So; now, are you out of your humour, sir? Shift, gentlemen.

They all draw, and disperse.

Act V. Scene VII.

CONSTABLE, OFFICERS, DRAWERS.

To them.

Ay hold vpon this gallant, and pursue the rest.

FAST. Lay hold on me, sir! for what?

CONS. Mary, for your riot here, sir, with the rest of your companions.

FAST. My riot! master Constable, take heed what you doe. CARLO, did I offer any violence?

CONS. O, sir, you see he is not in case to answer you, and that makes you so paramptorie.

FAST. Peremptorie, s'life I appeale to the drawers, if I did him any hard measure.

GEOR. They are all gone, there's none of them will bee laid any hold on.

v. vi. 77 vaine,] vaine *Qq*   79 Brute *!*] Brute. *Qq*   80 Sirha,] Sirha *Qq*   81 eyes, *corr.* F1: eyes *Qq*, F1 *originally*, F2   82 st. dir. *He seales*] *They seale* Qq   84 Nay,] Nay *Qq*   Constable,] Constable *Qq*   86 humour, sir?] humor sir. *Q1*: humour sir. *Qq 2, 3*   87 Shift,] Shift *Qq*   st. dir. *disperse*] *Exeunt.* Qq   v. vii. *Act . . . DRAWERS.*] *Enter Constable with Officers, and stay Briske.* Qq, *without change of Scene*   *To them.*] so F2: in F1 at l. 1: not in Qq   1 Lay] *Const.* Lay *Qq 1, 2*: *Const.* Lady *Q3*   2 me, sir!] me sir! *Qq 1, 2*: me! *Q3*   3 Mary,] Mary *Qq*   here,] here *Qq*   5 master Constable] God's my judge *Qq* (iudge *Q3*)   6 doe.] doe; *Qq*   CARLO,] *Carlo*, Q1: *Carlo* Q2: *Carlo.* Q3 (as the heading of a speech, the word beginning a new line)   7 O,] O *Qq*   8 paramptorie *Qq 1, 2*, F1: peramptorie *Q3*: peremptorie *F2*   10 *Enter George.* add Qq   11 there's none] there'snone *Q3*   12 on.] on, *Q3*

586 *Euery Man out of his Humour*

    C o n s. Well, sir, you are like to answere till the rest can be found out.

15   F a s t. Slid, I appeale to G e o r g e, here.

    C o n s. Tut, G e o r g e was not here: away with him to the *Counter*, sirs. Come, sir, you were best get your selfe drest somewhere.

    G e o r. Good lord, that master C a r l o could not take 20 heed, and knowing what a gentleman the knight is, if hee bee angrie.

    D r a w. A poxe on 'hem, they haue left all the meate on our hands, would they were choakt with it for me.

Macilente comes backe.
    M a c i. What, are they gone, sirs?

    G e o r. O, here's master M a c i l e n t e.

26   M a c i. Sirha, G e o r g e, doe you see that concealement there? that napkin vnder the table?

    G e o r. Gods so', signior F v n g o s o!

    M a c i. Hee's good pawne for the reckoning; bee sure 30 you keepe him here, and let him not goe away till I come againe, though hee offer to discharge all: Ile returne presently.

    G e o r. Sirrah, we haue a pawne for the reckoning.

    D r a w. What? of M a c i l e n t e?

35   G e o r. No, looke vnder the table.

    F v n g. I hope, all be quiet now: if I can get but forth of this street, I care not, masters, I pray you tell me, is the Constable gone?

Lookes out vnder the table.

    G e o r. What? master F v n g o s o?

40   F v n g. Was't not a good deuice this same of me, sirs?

---

    v. vii. 13 Well,] Well *Qq*   15 Slid,] Sbloud *Qq*   appeale *Qq*, *F2* : appeare *F1*   GEORGE,] George *Qq*   16 Tut,] Tut *Qq*   17 *Counter*,] *Counter* Qq 1, 2 : *counter* Q3   Come,] Come *Qq*   sir,] sir *Q1*   After 18 *Exeunt. Manent two Drawers.* Qq   19 lord,] Lord *Q1* : Lord, *Qq* 2, 3   master] maister *Q1*   20 is,] is *Qq* 1, 2   24 st. dir. *Macilente comes backe.] Enter Macilente.* Qq in text after 23   24 What,] What *Q1*   gone,] gone *Qq*   sirs?] sirs. *Q1*   25 O,] O *Qq*   master] maister *Q1*   26 Sirha,] Sirha *Q1* : Sirrah *Qq* 2, 3   GEORGE,] George Q1   29 Hee's *F2* : Hee's a *Qq* 1, 2 : Here's a *Q3* : Hei's *F1*   31 all :] all ; *Qq*   33 Sirrah,] Sirrah *Qq* 2, 3   35 No,] No ; *Qq*   36 hope,] hope *Qq*   now :] now ; *Qq*   37 not, masters] not. Masters *Qq* : not ; masters, *F2*   38 st. dir. *Qq* add to 38 ; *in F1* at 39–40   Lookes] He looks F3   40 this] the *Qq*   me,] me *Qq*   sirs?] sirs. *F2*

Euery Man out of his Humour 587

GEOR. Yes faith ; ha' you beene here all this while ?

FVNG. O god, I: good sir, looke, and the coast be cleere, I'ld faine be going.

GEOR. Al's cleere, sir, but the reckoning ; and that you must cleare, and pay before you goe, I assure you. 45

FVNG. I pay ? Slight, I eate not a bit since I came into the house, yet.

DRAW. Why, you may when you please, sir, 'tis all readie below, that was bespoken.

FVNG. Bespoken ? not by me, I hope ? 50

GEOR. By you, sir ? I know not that : but 'twas for you, and your companie, I am sure.

FVNG. My companie ? S'lid, I was an inuited guest, so I was.

DRAW. Faith, we haue no thing to doe with that, sir, 55 they're all gone but you, and we must be answer'd ; that's the short and the long on't.

FVNG. Nay, if you will grow to extremities, my masters, then would this pot, cup, and all were in my belly, if I haue a crosse about me. 60

GEOR. What, and haue such apparell ? doe not say so, signior, that mightily discredits your clothes.

FVNG. As I am an honest man, my taylor had all my monie this morning, and yet I must be faine to alter my sute too : good sirs, let me goe, 'tis friday night, and in good 65 truth I haue no stomacke in the world, to eate anie thing.

DRAW. That's no matter, so you pay, sir.

FVNG. Pay ? gods light, with what conscience can you aske me to pay that I neuer dranke for ?

GEOR. Yes, sir, I did see you drinke once. 70

v. vii. 42 god,] God *Qq*   sir,] sirs *Qq*   looke,] looke *Qq, F2*   and] an' *F2*   44 cleere,] cleere *Q1* : cleare *Qq 2, 3*   45 cleare,] cleare *Qq*   47 house,] house *Qq*   48 Why,] Why *Qq 1, 2*   please,] please *Qq*   sir, *om. F3*   49 below,] below *Qq*   51 By you,] By you *Qq*   for you,] for you *Qq*   53 S'lid,] S'lid *Qq*   55 Faith,] Faith *Qq, F2*   no thing] nothing *Qq*   that,] that *Qq*   57 the long] they long *Q3*   59 then] than *F2*   63 As I am an honest man, my] By Iesu the *Qq*   65 night,] night ; *Qq*   66 world,] world *Qq*   67 matter,] matter *Qq*   pay,] pay *Qq*   68 Pay ? *om. F3*   gods] Gods *Qq*   70 Yes,] Yes *Qq*

Fvng. By this cup, (which is siluer) but you did not, you doe mee infinite wrong, I look't in the pot once, indeed, but I did not drinke.

Draw. Well sir, if you can satisfie our master, it shall bee all one to vs. (by and by.)

GREX.

Cord. Lose not your selfe now signior.

Act v. Scene viii.

Macilente, Deliro, Fallace.

TVt, sir, you did beare too hard a conceit of me in that, but I will now make my loue to you most transparent, in spight of any dust of suspition, that may bee raysed to cloud it: and henceforth, since I see it is so against your humour, I will neuer labour to perswade you.

Deli. Why, I thanke you, signior, but what's that you tell mee may concerne my peace so much?

Maci. Faith, sir, 'tis thus. Your wiues brother, signior Fvngoso, being at supper to night at a tauerne, with a sort of gallants, there happened some diuision amongst 'hem, and he is left in pawne for the reckoning: now, if euer you looke that time shall present you with a happie occasion to doe your wife some gracious and acceptable seruice, take hold of this opportunitie, and presently goe, and redeeme him; for, being her brother, and his credit so amply engag'd as now it is, when she shal heare (as hee cannot him selfe,

v. vii. 72 once,] once *Qq*   74 our] my *Qq*   master] Maister *Qq 1, 3* 75 (by and by.)] By and by.   *One calls George within.* | *Exeunt.* Qq (cals Q1)   76 Lose] Loose *Qq*   your] you *F3*   v. viii. *Act*... Fallace.] *Enter Macilente and Deliro.* Qq, without change of scene: Scene V.—*A Room in* Deliro's *House.* | *Enter* Macilente *and* Deliro. G 1 Tut,] Maci. Tut *Qq*   3 cloud] dimme *Qq*   4 henceforth,] henceforth *Qq*   since] since. Q3   humour] Humor *Qq*   6 Why,) Why *Qq* you,] you *Qq*   8 Faith,] Faith *Qq*   sir,] sir *Q1*   brother,] brother *Qq*: brothet, *F2*   signior] seignior *F2*   9–10 tauerne, ... gallants,] Tauerne ... Gallants: *Qq*   11 now,] now *Qq*   12 a] an *F3*   14 goe,] go *Qq*   15 for,] for *Qq*   engag'd] engaged *Qq*

but hee must out of extremitie report it) that you came, and offered your selfe so kindly, and with that respect of his reputation, why, the benefit cannot but make her dote, and grow madde of your affections.

DELI. Now, by heauen, MACILENTE, I acknowledge my selfe exceedingly indebted to you, by this kinde tender of your loue; and I am sorrie to remember that I was euer so rude, to neglect a friend of your importance: bring mee shooes, and a cloke there, I was going to bed, if you had not come, what tauerne is it?

MACI. The Mitre, sir.

DELI. O, why FIDO, my shooes. Good faith it cannot but please her exceedingly.

FALL. Come, I mar'le what peece of nightwork you haue in hand now, that you call for your cloke, and your shooes! what, is this your Pandar?

DELI. O, sweet wife, speake lower, I would not he should heare thee for a world———

FALL. Hang him rascall, I cannot abide him for his trecherie, with his wilde quick-set beard there. Whither goe you now with him?

DELI. No whither with him, deare wife, I goe alone to a place, from whence I will returne instantly. Good MACILENTE, acquaint not her with it by any meanes, it may come so much the more accepted, frame some other answere. I'le come backe immediately.

FALL. Nay, and I be not worthie to know whither you goe, stay, till I take knowledge of your comming backe.

MACI. Heare you, mistresse DELIRO.

v. viii. 17 out of] of *Qq 2, 3*   came,] came *Qq*   19 why,] Slud *Qq*
21 Now, . . . heauen,] Now . . . heauen *Qq*   24 rude,] rude *Qq*   importance :] worth, *Qq*   25 shooes,] shoes *Qq*   bed,] bed *Qq*   26 come,] come ; *F2*   27 Mitre,] Miter *Q1* : Mitre *Qq 2, 3*   28 O,] O ; *Qq*   29 *Enter Fallace*. add Qq   30 mar'le] marl'e *Qq 2, 3*   31 your cloke,] your cloke *Q1* : your cloake *Qq 2, 3* : a Cloke *F3*   32 shooes !] shoes : *Qq*   Pandar] Pandor *Qq*   33 O,] O *Qq*   wife,] wife *Qq*
36 Whither] Whether *Q1*   38 whither] whether *Q1*   him,] him *Qq*   39 MACILENTE,] *Macilente* Qq   40 not] nor *F2*   41 answere.] answere, *Qq*   42 *Exit Deliro*. add Qq   43 and *retained here in F2, F3*   whither] whether *Q1*   44 stay,] stay *Qq*   45 you,] you *Qq*

F A L L. So sir, and what say you?

M A C I. Faith ladie, my intents will not deserue this slight respect, when you shall know 'hem.

F A L L. Your intents? why, what may your intents bee, 50 for gods sake?

M A C I. Troth, the time allowes no circumstance, ladie, therefore know, this was but a deuice to remoue your husband hence, and bestow him securely, whilest (with more conueniencie) I might report to you a misfortune that hath 55 happened to Monsieur B R I S K E——nay comfort, sweet ladie. This night (being at supper) a sort of young gallants committed a riot, for the which he (onely) is apprehended and carried to the *Counter*, where if your husband, and other creditours should but haue knowledge of him, the poore 60 gentleman were vndone for euer.

F A L L. Aye me! that he were.

M A C I. Now therefore, if you can thinke vpon any present meanes for his deliuerie, doe not forslow it. A bribe to the officer that committed him, will doe it.

65 F A L L. O god, sir, he shall not want for a bribe: pray you, will you commend me to him, and say I'le visit him presently?

M A C I. No, ladie, I shall doe you better seruice, in protracting your husbands returne, that you may goe with 70 more safetie.

F A L L. Good truth, so you may: farewell, good sir. Lord, how a woman may be mistaken in a man? I would haue sworne vpon all the testaments in the world, he had not lou'd master B R I S K E. Bring me my keyes

v. viii. 49 intents bee,] intents be *Q1* : intent be *Qq 2, 3*   50 gods] Gods *Qq, F2*   51 Troth,] Troth *Qq*   circumstance,] circumstance *Qq*   52 remoue] remooue *Q2*   53 whilest] whil'st *Qq 2, 3*   55 Monsieur] Mounsieur *Q1*   BRISKE——] *Briske* ; Qq   comfort,] comfort *Qq*   56 supper)] *Qq, F2* : supper *F1*   58 husband,] Husband *Qq 1, 2* : husband *Q3*   59 creditours] Creditors *Qq*   61 me!] me, *Qq*   63 forslow] foreslow *Q3, F2*   65 god,] God *Qq*   bribe:] bribe; *Q3, F2*   67 presently?] presently *Qq, F2*   68 No,] No *Qq*   seruice,] seruice *Qq*   70 safetie.] safetie? *Qq 1, 2*   After 70 *Exit.* *Qq*   71 truth,] truth *Qq*   may: farewell,] may ; farewell *Qq*   72 Lord,] Lord *Qq*   73 testaments] Testaments *Qq*   world,] world *Qq*   74 master] maister *Q1*

Every Man out of his Humour

there, maide. Alasse, good gentleman, if all I haue i' this 75
earthly world will pleasure him, it shall be at his seruice.

GREX.

MIT. How MACILENTE sweates i' this busines, if
you marke him.
COR. I, you shall see the true picture of spight anon:
here comes the pawne, and his redeemer. 80

Act V.   Scene IX.

DELIRO, FVNGOSO, DRAWERS,
MACILENTE.   ⟨*To them.*⟩

COme, brother, be not discourag'd for this, man, what?
FVNG. No truly, I am not discourag'd, but I protest
to you, brother, I haue done imitating any more gallants
either in purse or apparell, but as shall become a gentleman,
for good carriage, or so. 5
DELI. You say well. This is all, i' the bill here? is't
not?
GEOR. I, sir.
DELI. There's your monie, tell it: and brother, I am
glad I met with so good occasion to shew my loue to you. 10
FVNG. I will studie to deserue it in good truth, and I
liue.
DELI. What, is't right?
GEOR. I, sir, and I thanke you.
FVNG. Let me haue a capons legge sau'd, now the 15
reckoning is paid.

v. viii. 75 there, maide. Alasse,] there maid : Alasse *Qq* (mayd *Q3*)
76 *Exit.* add *Qq*   78 him.] him? *Qq 1, 2* : him *Q3*   79 anon:]
anone, *Q1* : anon, *Qq 2, 3*   80 pawne,] Pawne *Qq*   v. ix. *Act* ... MACI-
LENTE.] *Enter Deliro, Fungoso, Drawer following them.* Qq, without
change of scene : SCENE VI.—*A Room at the* Mitre. | *Enter* Deliro,
Fungoso, *and* George. *G*   DELIRO ... MACILENTE *one line in F2* :
the arrangement in F1 suggests the marginal note ' *To them.*' *as in* IV. viii,
v. ii.   1 Come,] Deli. Come *Qq*   this,] this *Qq*   man,] man ; *F2*
2 FVNG.] *Drawer.* Qq 1, 2 : *Draw.* Q3   3 you, brother,] you Brother
Qq 1, 2   4 gentleman,] Gentleman *Qq*   5 carriage,] carriage *Qq*
6 all,] all *Qq*   8 I,] I *Qq*   11 and] an' *F2*   13 What,] What
Qq   14 I,] I *Qq*

GEOR. You shall, sir.
MACI. Where's signior DELIRO?
DELI. Here, MACILENTE.
20 MACI. Harke you, sir, ha' you dispatcht this same?
DELI. I marie haue I.
MACI. Well then, I can tell you newes, BRISKE is i' the *Counter*.
DELI. I' the *Counter*?
25 MACI. 'Tis true, sir, committed for the stirre here to night. Now would I haue you send your brother home afore, with the report of this your kindnesse done him, to his sister, which will so pleasingly possesse her, and out of his mouth too, that i' the meane time you may clap your action on
30 BRISKE, and your wife (being in so happie a moode) cannot entertaine it ill, by any meanes.
DELI. 'Tis verie true, she cannot indeed, I thinke.
MACI. Thinke? why 'tis past thought, you shall neuer meet the like opportunitie, I assure you.
35 DELI. I will doe it. Brother, pray you goe home afore, this gentleman, and I haue some priuate businesse; and tell my sweet wife, I'le come presently.
FVNG. I will, brother.
MACI. And, signior, acquaint your sister, how liberally
40 and out of his bountie, your brother has vs'd you. (Doe you see?) made you a man of good reckoning; redeem'd that you neuer were possest of, credit; gaue you as gentlemanlike termes as might be; found no fault with your comming behind the fashion; nor nothing.
45 FVNG. Nay, I am out of those humours now.
MACI. Well, if you be out, keepe your distance, and be not made a shot-clog any more. Come, signior, let's make haste.

v. ix. 17 shall,] shall *Qq*   sir.] Sir : *Q1*   *Exit. Enter Macilente.* add *Qq* (*Maci.* Qq 2, 3)   19 Here,] Here *Qq*   20 you,] you *Qq* 25 true,] true *Qq*   27 him,] him *Qq*   31 ill,] ill *Qq*   33 why 'tis] why 'ts *Qq*   35 Brother,] Brother *Qq*   afore, this] (afore this *F2, an error for* 'afore (this'   36 gentleman,] Gent. *Qq*   businesse;] businesse) *F2*   38 will,] will *Qq*   39 And,] And *Qq*   liberally] liberally, *F2*   42 gentleman-like] Gentlemanlike *Qq*   45 Nay,] Nay *Qq*   humours] Humors *Qq*   47 any] no *Qq*   Come, signior,] Come Sig. *Qq*   *Exeunt.* add *Qq*

Act v. Scene x.

FALLACE, FAST. BRISKE.

O Master FASTIDIVS, what pitty is't to see so sweet a man as you are, in so sowre a place?

GREX.

COR. As vpon her lips, do's shee meane?
MIT. O, this is to be imagin'd the *Counter*, belike?

FAST. Troth, faire lady, 'tis first the pleasure of the *Fates*, and next of the Constable, to haue it so: but, I am patient, and indeed comforted the more in your kind visitation.

FALL. Nay, you shall bee comforted in mee, more then this, if you please, sir. I sent you word by my brother, sir, that my husband laid to rest you this morning, I know not whether you receiu'd it, or no.

FAST. No, beleeue it, sweet creature, your brother gaue me no such intelligence.

FALL. O, the lord!

FAST. But has your husband any such purpose?

FALL. O sweet master BRISKE, yes: and therefore be presently discharg'd, for if he come with his actions vpon you (lord deliuer you) you are in for one halfe a score yeere; he kept a poore man in *Ludgate* once, twelue yeere, for sixteene shillings. Where's your keeper? for loues sake call

---

v. x. Act ... BRISKE.] *Enter Briske and Fallace.* Qq, without change of scene : SCENE VII.—*The Counter.* | *Enter* Fallace *and* Fastidious Briske. G   1 O Master] *Fallace.* O maister *Qq*   2 are,] are *Qq* 2, 3   sowre *F1, corr.* F2 : soure *Qq* : sower *F2 originally.   and kisses him.* (*kisse* Q3) Qq (after 2 in Q1, added in Qq 2, 3)   3 lips,] lips *Qq*   4 *Counter,*] *Counter* Qq   5 Troth,] Troth *Qq*   6 Constable,] Constable *Qq*   so :] so, *Qq*   but,] but *F2*   8 visitation] visit *F2*   9 mee,] me *Qq*   then] than *Qq, F2*   10 please,] please *Qq*   brother,] Brother *Qq 1, 2* : brother *Q3*   12 no.] no ? *Qq*   13 No,] No *Qq*   15 O,] O *Qq*   lord] Lord *Qq*   17 sweet master] God Maister *Qq*   18 discharg'd,] discharg'd ; *Qq*   19 lord] Lord *Qq*   20 yeere ;] year *Qq*   21 keeper ?] keeper, *Qq*   loues sake] Gods loue *Qq*

him, let him take a bribe, and dispatch you. Lord, how my heart trembles! here are no spies? are there?

FAST. No, sweet mistris, why are you in this passion?

25 FALL. O lord, Master FASTIDIVS, if you knew how I tooke vp my husband to day, when hee said hee would arrest you; and how I rail'd at him that perswaded him to't, the scholer there, (who on my conscience loues you now) and what care I tooke to send you intelligence by my 30 brother; and how I gaue him foure soueraignes for his paines; and now, how I came running out hither without man or boy with me, so soone as I heard on't; youl'd say, I were in a passion indeed: your keeper, for gods sake. O, Master BRISKE (as 'tis in EVPHVES) *Hard is the choise,* 35 *when one is compelled either by silence to die with griefe, or by speaking to liue with shame.*

FAST. Faire lady, I conceiue you, and may this kisse assure you, that where aduersitie hath (as it were) contracted, prosperitie shall not——gods me! your husband.

40 FALL. O, me!

Act V.   Scene XI.

DELIRO, MACILENTE, FALLACE, FAST. BRISKE.

I? is't thus!

MACI. Why, how now, signior DELIRO? has the wolfe seene you? ha? hath GORGONS head made marble of you?

5 DELI. Some *Planet* strike me dead.

MACI. Why, looke you, sir, I told you, you might haue

---

v. ix. 22 you. Lord,] you, Lord *Qq*   24 No,] No *Qq*   mistris] mistresse *Qq*   passion?] passion. *Qq* 2, 3   25 lord, Master] Christ Maister *Qq*   31 hither *corr.* F1, F2: hether *Qq*, F1   33 keeper,] keeper *Qq*   gods] Gods *Qq*   O,] O *Qq*   34 Master] Maister *Q1*   35 *one*] *on* Q3   *either by* Qq, corr. F1, F2: *by* F1 originally   37 lady,] Ladie *Qq*   39 gods me!] Gods light *Qq*   40 O,] O *Qq*, F2
v. xi *Act* . . . BRISKE.] *Enter Deliro, Macilente.* (*Deliro.* Qq 2, 3) Qq, without change of scene   1 I?] *Deli.* I? *Qq*   2 Why,] Why *Qq* now,] now *Qq*   4 of] on *Qq*   6 Why,] Why *Qq*   you, sir] you sir *Qq*

suspected this long afore, had you pleas'd; and ha' sau'd this labour of admiration now, and passion, and such extremities as this fraile lumpe of flesh is subiect vnto. Nay, why doe you not dote now, signior? Mee thinkes you should say it were some enchantment, *deceptio visus*, or so, ha? if you could perswade your selfe it were a dreame now, 'twere excellent: faith, trie what you can do, signior; it may be your imagination will be brought to it in time, there's nothing impossible.

FALL. Sweet husband:

DELI. Out lasciuious strumpet.

MACI. What? did you see, how ill that stale vaine became him afore, of sweet wife, and deare heart? and are you falne iust into the same now? with sweet husband. Away, follow him, goe, keepe state, what? Remember you are a woman, turne impudent: gi' him not the head, though you gi' him the hornes. Away. And yet mee thinkes you should take your leaue of *Enfans-perdus* here, your forlorne hope. How now, Monsieur BRISKE? what? friday night? and in affliction too? and yet your *Pulpamenta*? your delicate morcels? I perceiue the affection of ladies, and gentlewomen, pursues you wheresoeuer you goe, Monsieur.

FAST. Now, in good faith (and as I am gentle) there could not haue come a thing, i' this world, to haue distracted me more, then the wrinckled fortunes of this poore spinster.

v. xi. 8 labour] labor *Qq 1, 2*   passion,] Passion; *Q3*   10 now,] now *Qq*   11 enchantment] Enchauntment *Q3*   12 if you] if you, *F2 (probably this comma was intended for 'faith' in l. 13, and was inserted in the proof-reading: 'you' and 'faith' end two successive lines in Ff)*   13 faith, *F1*: faith *Qq, F2*   do,] doe *Qq*   16 husband: *F1 (marking an interrupted speech)*: Husband? *Qq*: husband. 2   17 *Exit Deliro.* add Qq   18 see,] see *Qq*   20 iust] just *Qq 1, 2*   21 state,] state; *F2*   22 woman,] woman: *Qq*   23 hornes.] horns, *Q1*: hornes, *Qq 2, 3*   *Exit Fallace.* 'Qq, after 'Away', beginning a new line at 'And yet'   24 *Enfans-*] *Infans-* Qq   25 now, Monsieur BRISKE?] now Mounsieur *Brisk*: Qq   26 night] at night *Qq*   affliction] affection *Q3*   *Pulpamenta*] *Pulpamemta* F2   27 morcels?] Morsels: *Qq 1, 2*: morsels: *Q3*   perceiue] perceiue, *F2*   Ladies,] Ladies *Qq*   28-9 goe, Monsieur] goe Mounsieur *Qq* (go *Q3*)   30 Now,] Now *Qq*   gentle] gentile *F3*   31 thing, ... world,] thing ... world *Qq*   32 more,] more *Qq*   then] than *Qq, F2*   spinster] Dame *Qq*

MACI. O, yes, sir: I can tell you a thing will distract you much better, beleeue it. Signior DELIRO has entred three actions against you, three actions, Monsieur; mary, one of them (I'le put you in comfort) is but three thousand, and the other two, some fiue thousand a peece, trifles, trifles.

FAST. O, I am vndone.

MACI. Nay, not altogether so, sir, the knight must haue his hundred pound repai'd, that'll helpe too, and then sixe-score pound for a diamond, you know where. These be things will weigh, Monsieur, they will weigh.

FAST. O, heauen!

MACI. What, doe you sigh? this it is to kisse the hand of a countesse, to haue her coach sent for you, to hang poinards in ladies garters, to weare bracelets of their haire, and for euery one of these great fauours to giue some slight iewell of fiue hundred crownes, or so, why 'tis nothing. Now, Monsieur, you see the plague that treads o' the heeles of your fopperie: well, goe your waies in, remoue your selfe to the two-penny ward quickly, to saue charges, and there set vp your rest to spend sir PVNTARs hundred pound for him. Away, good pomander, goe.

Why, here's a change! Now is my soule at peace.
I am as emptie of all enuie now,
As they of merit to be enuied at.
My humour (like a flame) no longer lasts
Then it hath stuffe to feed it, and their folly,

v. xi. 33 O, yes,] O yes *Qq*   35 actions, Monsieur;] Actions Mounsieur: *Qq*   mary,] mary *Q1*: marry *Qq* 2, 3   36 thousand] thousand mark *Qq*   37 two,] two *Qq*   a peece] pound together *Qq*   38 O] O God *Qq*   39 Nay,] Nay *Qq*   so,] so *Qq*   sir,] sir; *F2*   40–1 sixe-score pound] sixescore pound *Qq 1, 2*: sixscore pound *Q3*: Six-score Pounds *F3*   41 diamond,] Diamond: *Qq*   where.] where? *Qq*   42 weigh, Monsieur,] weigh Mounsieur; *Qq*   43 O, heauen] O Iesu *Qq*   44 What,] What *Qq*   45 her] hir *Qq*   46 poinards] Poniards *Q3*   49 Now, Monsieur] Now Mounsieur *Qq*   50 fopperie:] fopperie, *Qq*   in,] in; *Qq*   51 quickly,] quickly *Qq*   53 Away,] Away *Qq*   pomander] *Pomardo Q3*   *Exit Briske.* *Qq* (in *Q1* after 'Away': in *Qq* 2, 3 after 53)   54 Why,] Why *Qq*   change!] change: *Qq*   peace.] peace, *Qq*   55 enuie] Envie *Q1*   56 of] *om. Q3*   enuied] envied *Qq 1, 2*   at.] at, *Qq 1, 2*   57 humour] Humor *Qq*   8 Then] Than *Qq, F2*   it,] it; *F2*   folly] vertue *Qq*

Being now rak't vp in their repentant ashes,
Affords no ampler subiect to my spleene. 60
I am so farre from malicing their states,
That I begin to pitty 'hem. It grieues me
To thinke they haue a being. I could wish
They might turne wise vpon it, and be sau'd now,
So heauen were pleas'd : but let them vanish, vapors. 65
Gentlemen, how like you it ? has't not beene tedious ?

GREX.

C o r. Nay, we ha' done censuring, now.
M i t. Yes, faith.
M a c. How so ?
C o r. Mary, because wee'le imitate your actors, and be 70
out of our Humours. Besides, here are those (round about
you) of more abilitie in censure then wee, whose iudgements
can giue it a more satisfying allowance: wee'le refer you to
them.
     M a c. I ? is't e'en so ? Wel, gentlemen, I should haue 75
gone in, and return'd to you, as I was A s p e r at the first :
but (by reason the shift would haue beene somewhat long,
and we are loth to draw your patience farder) wee'le intreat
you to imagine it. And now (that you may see I will be
out of humour for companie) I stand wholly to your kind 80
approbation, and (indeed) am nothing so peremptorie as I
was in the beginning : Mary, I will not doe as P l a v t v s,

---

   v. xi. 59 their repentant ashes] embers of their Follie *Qq* (Folly *Q3*)
60 Affords no] Affordsno *Q3*   subiect] Subject *Qq 1, 2*   spleene.]
Spirit ; *Qq*: speene. *F2*   62 'hem. It] 'hem : it *Q1* : them : it *Qq 2, 3*
grieues] greeues *Qq*   63 being.] *being* ; *Qq*   65 vanish,] vanish *Qq*
66–87 *are Jonson's final recension, the third state of the text. The play
originally ended with an address to Queen Elizabeth, most of which is
preserved on pp. 599–600, and with the final criticism of the Grex, ll. 66–87
above. This was cancelled, and a verse address to the audience, continuing
Asper's speech (ll. 54–65), concluded the play. These alternative endings
of Qq are printed in Appendix X.*   66 Gentlemen,] *Maci.* How now
sirs ? *Qq* (Sirs ? *Q1*)   beene] ben *Qq 1, 2* : bene *Q3*   67 censuring,] censuring *Q3*   68 Yes,] Yes *Qq*   70 Mary,] Mary *Qq*   71
Humours] *Humors Qq* 1, 2 : Humors *Q3*   72 then *Q3*, *F1* : than
Qq 1, 2, *F2*   75 Wel,] Wel ; *Q1*   76 you,] you *Qq*   78 farder]
any farder *Qq*   80 humour] *Humor Qq* : my Humor *Q3*   82
Mary,] Mary *Q1* : Marie *Qq 2, 3*   Plavtvs,] *Plautus Qq*

in his *Amphytrio*, for all this (*Summi Iouis causa, Plaudite* :) begge a *Plaudite*, for gods sake ; but if you (out of the
85 bountie of your good liking) will bestow it ; why, you may (in time) make leane M A C I L E N T E as fat, as Sir I O H N F A L-S T A F F E.

THE END.

v. xi. 83 *Amphytrio,*] *Amphytrio* Qq   84 *Plaudite,*] *Plaudite* Qq
gods] Gods *Qq, F2*   86 fat,] fat *Qq*   87 FAL-STAFFE] *Fallstaffe*
Qq 1, 2 : *Fall-staffe* Q3 : FAL-STAFFE *F2*   After 87 *Exeunt.* | *Non ego ventosæ plebis suffragia venor.* Qq   THE END. *add Ff*

Additional notes.

II. iv. 161 *Q3 reads* Would to Cod
III. i. 33 Lingnist *Q3 originally*
v. ii. 75 doe you *Qq, F1* : you doe *F2*
v. xi. 27 perceiue, *corr. F1, F2* : perceiue *Qq, F1 originally*
    ladies *corr. F1, F2* : Ladies, *Qq* : ladies, *F1 originally*

Which, in the presentation before

Queene E. was thus varyed,

By Macilente.

Neuer till now did obiect greet mine eyes
    With any light content : but in her graces,
All my malicious powers haue lost their stings.
Enuie is fled my soule, at sight of her,
And shee hath chac'd all black thoughts from my bosome,   5
Like as the sunne doth darkenesse from the world.
My streame of humour is runne out of me.
And as our cities torrent (bent t' infect
The hallow'd bowels of the siluer *Thames*)
Is checkt by strength, and clearnesse of the riuer,   10
Till it hath spent it selfe e'ene at the shore ;
So, in the ample, and vnmeasur'd floud
Of her perfections, are my passions drown'd :
And I haue now a spirit as sweet, and cleere,
As the most rarefi'd and subtile aire.   15
With which, and with a heart as pure as fire,
(Yet humble as the earth) doe I implore,
O heauen, that shee (whose presence hath effected
This change in me) may suffer most late change
In her admir'd and happie gouernement :   20
May still this *Iland* be call'd *fortunate*,
And rugged treason tremble at the sound
When *Fame* shall speake it with an *emphasis*.

Which . . . varyed,] not in Qq : The Epilogue at the presentation
before Queene Elizabeth F2   By Macilente. not in Qq   1
obiect] Obiect Qq   2 graces,] Graces Qq   3 malicious] malitious Qq
stings.] stings : Qq   4 soule,] Soule Qq   7 humour] Humor Qq
me.] me : Qq   8 as om. Q3   10 strength,] strength Qq   riuer]
Riuers Q3   11 shore ;] shore ? Q3   12 So,] So Qq   ample,]
ample Qq, F2   14 sweet,] sweet Qq, F2   15 aire.] Aire ; Qq   17
He kneeles. add Qq   18 heauen,] Heauen : Qq   presence] Figure Qq
19 suffer most late] neuer suffer Qq

600   *Euery Man out of his Humour*

  Let forraine politie be dull as lead,
25 And pale inuasion come with halfe a heart,
  When he but lookes vpon her blessed soile.
  The throat of warre be stopt within her land,
  And turtle-footed peace dance *fayrie* rings
  About her court : where, neuer may there come
30 Suspect, or danger, but all trust, and safetie :
  Let flatterie be dumbe, and enuie blind
  In her dread presence : death himselfe admire her :
  And may her vertues make him to forget
  The vse of his ineuitable hand.
35 Flie from her age ; Sleepe time before her throne,
  Our strongest wall falls downe, when shee is gone.

  24 politie] *Pollicie* Qq   25 heart,] heart *Qq*   26 soile.] Soile : *Qq*
28 dance] daunce *Qq*   29 court : where,] Court ; where *Qq*   30
Suspect,] *Suspect* Qq   danger] *Daunger* Qq   trust,] *Trust* Qq   32
death] *Death* Qq : Death *F2*   35 age] *Age* Qq : Age *F2*   Sleepe]
sleep *F2*   time] *Time* Qq : Time *F2*   36 downe,] downe *Qq*   After
36 *Here the Trumpets sound a flourish in which time Macilente conuerts himselfe to them that supply the place of GREX, and speakes.* (*florish,* Q1) Qq, continuing with ll. 66–87 on pp. 597–8.

This Comicall Satyre was first
acted in the yeere
1599.

By the then Lord Chamberlaine
his Seruants.

The principall Comœdians were,

RIC. BVRBADGE.⎫ ⎧IOH. HEMINGS.
AVG. PHILIPS.   ⎬ ⎨HEN. CONDEL.
WIL. SLY.   ⎭ ⎩THO. POPE.

With the allowance of the Master of REVELS.

This page was added in F1. In F2 the statements about the date, the company, and the Master of the Revels were omitted, and the list of 'The principall Comœdians' *was transferred to the back of the half-title, where it followed* 'The Names of the Actors'.

APPENDIX X

1. THE ORIGINAL CONCLUSION IN THE QUARTOS

The original conclusion was printed in the Quartos with the following preface :—

IT had another *Catastrophe* or Conclusion, at the first Playing: which (διὰ τὴν Βασίλισσαν προσωποποιεῖσθ) many seem'd not to rellish it ; and therefore 'twas since alter'd : yet that a right-ei'd and solide *Reader* may
5 perceiue it was not so great a part of the Heauen awry, as they would make it ; we request him but to looke downe vpon these following Reasons.

  1 *There hath been* President *of the like Presentation in diuers Playes : and is yeerely in our Cittie* Pageants *or shewes of*
10   Triumph.

  2 *It is to be conceiu'd, that* Macilente *being so strongly possest with* Enuie, *(as the* Poet *heere makes him) it must bee no sleight or common* Obiect, *that should effect so suddaine and straunge a cure vpon him, as the putting him cleane* Out of
15   his Humor.

  3 *If his* Imagination *had discours't the whole world ouer for an* Obiect, *it could not haue met with a more Proper, Eminent, or worthie* Figure, *than that of her Maiesties : which his* Election *(though boldly, yet respectiuely) vs'd to a* Morall
20   and Mysterious *end.*

  4 *His greedinesse to catch at any* Occasion, *that might expresse his affection to his* Soueraigne, *may worthily plead for him.*

  5 *There was nothing (in his examin'd* Opinion) *that could more neare or truly exemplifie the power and strength of*
25   *her Inualuable* Vertues, *than the working of so perfect a*

2 διὰ . . . προσωποποιεῖσθ] *Qq* 1, 2 : DIA TO TEN BASILISSAN PROSO-POPOESTHAI *Q3*   4 alter'd] altered *Q3*   -eid'] -eyd *Q3*   *Reader*] Reader *Q3*   13, 17 Obiect *Q3* : Object *Qq* 1, 2   13 *suddaine*] sodaine *Q3*   14 *straunge*] strange *Q3*   Out of his Humor] out of his Humour *Q3*   16 *discours't*] discourst *Q3*   21 Occasion] occasion *Q3*   23 Opinion] opinion *Q3*   25 *Inualuable*] inualuable *Q3*   than] then *Q3*

Miracle *on so oppos'd a* Spirit, *who not only persisted in his* Humor, *but was now come to the* Court *with a purpos'd resolution* (*his Soule as it were new drest in* Enuie) *to maligne at any thing that should front him* ; *when sodainly* (*against expectation, and all steele of his* Malice) *the verie wonder of her* Presence *strikes him to the earth dumbe, and astonisht. From whence rising and recouering heart, his* Passion *thus vtters it selfe.*   30

Maci. Blessed, Diuine, Vnblemisht, Sacred, Pure,
Glorious, Immortall, and indeed *Immense* ;   35
O that I had a world of Attributes,
To lend or adde to this high *Maiestie* :
Neuer till now did *Obiect* greet mine eyes ...

   26 Miracle] *Miracle* Q3   Spirit] *Spirit* Q3   27 Court] Court, Q3   28 new] now Q3   29 him ;] him : Q3   31 Presence] *Presence* Q3   34 Blessed] Blesse *Q3*   35 Glorious, Immortall *Q1* : Glorious immortall *Qq* 2, 3   38 *Followed by the rest of the address to Elizabeth* (pp. 599–600, ll. 1–36) *and by* ll. 66–87 *of the Folio text* (pp. 597–8).

2. THE REVISED CONCLUSION IN THE QUARTOS

  After cancelling the address to Queen Elizabeth, Jonson concluded the play as follows after 'but let them vanish, vapors' (p. 597, l. 65) :—

And now with *Aspers* tongue (though not his shape)
Kind *Patrons* of our sports (you that can iudge,
And with discerning thoughts measure the pace
Of our strange Muse in this her *Maze* of Humor,
You, whose true Notions doe confine the formes   5
And nature of sweet *Poesie*) to you
I tender solemne and most duteous thankes,
For your stretcht patience and attentiue grace.
We know (and we are pleas'd to know so much)

   2 iudge *Q3* : judge *Qq 1, 2*   3 pace *Qq 1, 2* : space *Q3*   4 strange *Q1* : straunge *Qq 2, 3*   7 duteous *Qq 1, 2* : durious *Q3*   8 stretcht *Qq 1, 2* : stretch *Q3*

10 The Cates that you haue tasted were not season'd
For euery vulgar Pallat, but prepar'd
To banket pure and apprehensiue eares :
Let then their Voices speake for our desert ;
Be their *Applause* the Trumpet to proclaime
15 Defiance to rebelling Ignorance,
And the greene spirits of some tainted Few,
That (spight of pietie) betray themselues
To Scorne and Laughter ; and like guiltie Children,
Publish their *infamie* before their time,
20 By their owne fond exception. Such as these
We pawne 'hem to your *censure*, till Time, Wit,
Or Obseruation, set some stronger seale
Of *iudgement* on their iudgements ; and intreat
The happier spirits in this faire-fild Globe,
25 (So many as haue sweet minds in their breasts,
And are too wise to thinke themselues are taxt
In any generall Figure, or too vertuous
To need that wisdomes imputation :)
That with their bounteous *Hands* they would confirme
30 This, as their pleasures *Pattent* : which so sign'd,
Our leane and spent Endeauours shall renue
Their Beauties with the *Spring* to smile on you.

FINIS.

17 pietie W. W. Greg conj. : pitie *Q1* : pittie *Qq 2, 3*   betray] do betray *G conj.*   19 *infamie* P. Simpson conj. : *infancie* Qq   20 exception. *Q1* : exception : *Qq, 2, 3*   21 till *Qq 1, 2* : tell *Q3*   23 intreat *Q1* : entreat *Qq 2, 3*   27 too *Qq, 1, 2* : to *Q3*   31 leane and *Qq 1, 2* : leaue nnd *Q3 (hence G conj.* leaven'd)

CORRECTIONS TO VOLUMES I & II

i. p. 26, l. 13. *For* Whitehall *read* Hampton Court.
    l. 26. *For* Nathaniel Field *read* Nathan Field.
i. p. 29, n. l. 8. For *Shippinge* read *Snippinge*.
i. p. 30, n. 2. The inscription should run : ' The Testemony of my Affection, & Obseruance to my noble Freind S^r. Robert Townseehend wch I desire may remayne wth him, & last beyond Marble.'
i. p. 45, l. 27. '*Alchemist.*^{2}' Transfer the note to *Epicoene*, l. 20.
i. p. 53. Delete ll. 18–22 ' " Charis " was . . . in 1608 ' : the part of Charis in the masque would be played by a boy.
i. p. 61, ll. 30–1. *For* ' Mime ' (cxv) *read* ' Mime ' (cxxix).
    For Honest Man ' (cxxix) *read* Honest Man ' (cxv).
i. p. 64, ll. 5–6. *For* This edition *read* The two opening sections consisting of the *Plays* and the *Epigrams*.
i. p. 67, l. 32. *For* Duplessis and Mornay *read* d'Aubigné and Duplessis-Mornay (F. C. Danchin in *Les Langues Modernes*, March 1926, p. 176 n.).
i. p. 70. l. 21. Transfer the note-number to l. 17.
i. p. 77, l. 16. *For* Poetry *read* Poesy.
i. p. 83, l. 5. *For* Charles *read* Henry.
i. p. 85, ll. 16–17. *For* the Triple Tun *read* the Three Tuns. (So also p. 112, l. 7.)
i. p. 90, ll. 5–8. *Delete the sentence*: ' His momentary arrest, a few months later . . . .' *The date of this is October 1628.*
i. p. 99, l. 7. *For* unfinished *read* unprinted.
i. p. 107, ll. 17–18. Saint-Amant's quotation is from his *Albion* in 1644, written on his second visit to London.
i. p. 110, l. 32. *For* 1663 *read* 1632.
i. p. 135. *Conv.* 108. *For* Martia *read* Martialls.
i. p. 139. *Conv.* 232. *For* earle *read* now earle.
i. p. 146. *Conv.* 504 cr. note. *For* Laing *read* F. Cunningham.
i. p. 160. *Conv.* 164 n. *For* Nathaniel Field *read* Nathan Field.
i. p. 167. *Conv.* note on 361, l. 1. *For* March 7, 1617 *read* January 4, 1618.
i. p. 168. *Conv.* note on 393, l. 1. *For* five *read* four.
    ib., l. 3. Delete ' *The Case is Altered*, 1598 '.
i. p. 169. *Conv.* note on 411, l. 5. *For* eight *read* seven. Delete ' *Nigromansir* '.
    ib., note on 418, l. 5. *For* Granville *read* Grenville.
i. p. 194, l. 18. *Delete* who was the authority to license plays.
i. p. 203, ll. 7–11. A more exact text of the warrant is in British Museum Additional MS. 11402, fol. 108. It is probably from this that the transcript quoted in the text was taken.

i. p. 237, l. 11. *For* Mo *read* My.
i. p. 241 (fourth line from bottom). *For* neuer *read* newer.
i. p. 242, l. 2. *For* 1629 *read* 1628.
i. p. 260, l. 37. *Delete* Mabbe's *Celestina*.
i. p. 263. English Works, l. 8. *For* MS. 3 D *read* MS. 3 D 1387.
i. p. 275, l. 5. *For* Blackfriars *read* the Cockpit.
i. p. 333, l. 19. *For* It contains no work *read* The two opening sections of the *Plays* and the *Epigrams* contain no work.
i. p. 350, l. 20. *For* humanists *read* humorists.
i. p. 389, l. 24. *For* cure *read* cue.
i. p. 393, l. 22. *For* early in 1600 *read* in the winter of 1599.
ii. p. 31, l. 16. *For* 1604 *read* 1605.
ii. p. 32, l. 15. *For* Palgrave *read* Palsgrave.
ii. p. 49, n. 1, l. 14. *For* Quarto *read* Folio.
ii. p. 60, l. 3. *For* Eumolpius *read* Encolpius.
ii. p. 69, l. 4. *For* that year *read* 1610.
ii. p. 75, l. 17. *For* exhaustibly *read* inexhaustibly.
ii. p. 95, n. 2, l. 2. *For* 1591 *read* 1602.
ii. p. 96, n. 1, l. 2. *For* N. Tomkis's *read* T. Tomkis's.
  ib., l. 3. *For* 1614 *read* 1615.
ii. p. 170, l. 14. *Delete* and Fletcher.
ii. p. 191, l. 7. 'A *second* stroke of paralysis.' Delete 'second'. Jonson was 'strucken with the Palsey in the Yeare 1628' (i. p. 213), evidently after the Attorney-General's examination of him on October 26; at that date he went to 'Sr Robert Cottons house as he often doth' (ib., p. 242).
ii. p. 231, l. 28. *For* Centaur *read* Cyclops.
ii. p. 255, l. 23. *For* Henry's *read* Arthur's.
ii. p. 264. Delete the note: the scandal about Lady Ann (not Dorothy) Cornwallis arose later.
ii. p. 267, marginal note. *For* 1605 *read* 1606.
ii. p. 276, marginal note. *For* Harington's *read* Haddington's.
ii. p. 304, l. 14. *For* stories *read* stores.
ii. p. 317, l. 21. *For* materializing *read* neutralizing.
ii. p. 324, n. 2. *For* Stevens *read* Steevens.
ii. p. 325, l. 28. For '*A Game of Chess*' read '*A Game at Chess*'.
ii. p. 332, l. 21. *For* worthy *read* unworthy.
ii. p. 389, l. 8. *For* French *read* Latin.
ii. p. 419, l. 16. *For* '*A Consolation*' *read* ' John Brinsley's *A Consolation* '.
  ib., l. 18. *For* John Webb *read* Joseph Webb.

ADDITIONAL NOTES TO VOLUMES I & II

An important article on *The Riddle of Jonson's Chronology*, by Dr. W. W. Greg, appeared in *The Library*, vol. vi, No. 4, March 1926, pp. 340–7. It is the first systematic attempt to grapple with the problem as a whole, and it discusses the disputable dates in the Folio of 1616. The conclusion is that ' about 1620 Jonson abandoned his former habit of using Calendar dates ' (i. e. beginning the year on January 1) ' and adopted the Legal reckoning ' (i. e. beginning the year on Lady Day). No solution of the problem is free from difficulty. Dr. Greg himself admits that ' Completely consistent Jonson's practice certainly was not ', and his theory requires us to believe that Jonson disturbed the chronological arrangement of the masques in the 1616 Folio, placing *Mercury Vindicated* before *The Golden Age Restored* for purely literary effect, the last ¹ supplying an appropriate ending for the collection '. We shall discuss the question later in reference to the 1616 Folio.

One puzzling date in the 1640–1 Folio seems to have been cleared up. We hesitated over the date of *Pan's Anniversary*.[1] Mr. W. J. Lawrence points to Thomas Cooke's bill of January 1620 [2] as decisive on the point. A Prince's masque was given at Court on January 17, 1619–20, and repeated on the following Shrove Tuesday (*Calendar of Venetian State Papers*, 1620, pp. 138, 190). ' If this was not *Pan's Anniversary*,' Mr. Lawrence asks, ' what other masque of Jonson's could it have been ? '[3]

i. 129. Laing's paper announcing his discovery of the Sibbald transcript of the *Conversations with William Drummond* was dated January 9, 1832. Dr. R. F. Patterson points out that the first notice of the manuscript is found in Scott's *Kenilworth* in the 1831 edition of the *Waverley Novels*, vol. xxii, p. x, where Scott, quoting Ashmole about the poisoning of the Earl of Leicester, has this foot-note :

' Ashmole's Antiquities of Berkshire, vol. i, p. 149. The tradition as to Leicester's death was thus communicated by Ben Jonson to Drummond of Hawthornden : " The Earl of Leicester gave a bottle of liquor to his Lady, which he willed her to use in any faintness, which she, after his returne from court, not knowing it was poison, gave him, and so he died." BEN JONSON's *Information to* DRUMMOND *of Hawthornden, MS.*—SIR ROBERT SIBBALD'S *Copy*.'

i. 140. The vision of Jonson's son, immediately after his death of the plague, appearing to him ' of a Manlie shape & of yt Grouth that he thinks he shall be at the resurrection ', should have been illustrated from Saint Augustine's discussion in the *De Civitate Dei*, xxii, ch. 14, of the question ' An infantes in ea sint resurrecturi habitudine corporis

---

[1] Vol. ii p. 324.   [2] Appendix III, ix (i, p. 235).
[3] *The Irish Statesman*, August 15, 1925.

quam habituri erant aetatis accessu ? ' He decides that children will rise again with their bodies fully developed.

Jonson's Increased Pension (i. 245).

The term 'original warrant' is incorrect. The Rawlinson MS., which is reproduced, is the first draft called the Attorney-General's Bill, submitted to the King for signature ; after he had signed it, it was renamed the King's Bill (Anson, *Law and Custom of the Constitution*, 1892, ii. 45 n.).

Memorandums of the Immortal Ben (i. 188–9).

Sir E. K. Chambers suggests [1] that the document is an eighteenth-century fake. It ' does not contain anything which could not be conveyed or perverted from obvious sources, and the distribution of emphasis between Jonson's exploits as a poet and as a toper respectively can hardly have proceeded from his own mind '. The document is of slight importance, but it seems to echo traditional gossip and even to convey some scraps of Jonson's talk crudely reported in the first person. The reference to ' honest Ralf ', the drawer at the Swan tavern (otherwise known only from Aubrey's manuscript [2] and from G. Powell's *The Treacherous Brothers*, 1690, sig. A 2 verso), seems genuine. The account which follows of Ben drinking bad wine at the Devil has some point, as if Ralf's death put an end to ' lyric feasts ' at the Swan.

[1] *The Library*, vol. vi, no. 2, September 1925.
[2] See vol. i, p. 180.

PRINTED IN GREAT BRITAIN
AT THE UNIVERSITY PRESS, OXFORD
BY CHARLES BATEY, PRINTER TO THE UNIVERSITY